PRINTMAKING in the Age of Rembrandt

3
Hendrik Goltzius
Nox (Goddess of Night), designed about
1588–89
Chiaroscuro woodcut
Museum of Fine Arts, Boston

4
Hendrik Goltzius
A Sea Goddess, designed about 1588–89
Chiaroscuro woodcut
Museum of Fine Arts, Boston

35 (enlargement)
Claes Jansz. Visscher
Table of Contents with Lighthouse at Zandvoort, about 1611–12
Etching
Museum of Fine Arts, Boston

PRINTMAKING
in the Age of Rembrandt

Clifford S. Ackley

Museum of Fine Arts

Boston

New York Graphic Society

Boston

14 (actual size)
Hendrik Goltzius
Landscape with a Seated Couple,
designed about 1596–1598
Woodcut on blue paper heightened with
white
vi   Museum of Fine Arts, Boston

15 (actual size)
Hendrik Goltzius
Landscape with a Seated Couple,
designed about 1596–1598
Chiaroscuro woodcut
Museum of Fine Arts, Boston

Copyright © 1981 by the Museum of Fine Arts, Boston, Massachusetts

Library of Congress Catalog Card no. 80-84002

ISBN 0-87846-196-5

Typeset by Typographic House, Inc., Boston

Printed by The Meriden Gravure Company, Meriden, Connecticut

Designed by Carl Zahn

Dates of the Exhibition:

Museum of Fine Arts, Boston, October 28, 1980 – January 4, 1981

The Saint Louis Art Museum, February 19 – April 12, 1981

Contents

28
Attributed to Esaias van de Velde
Arcadian Landscape
Chiaroscuro woodcut
Museum of Fine Arts, Boston

x

30 (actual size)
Hercules Segers
*Rocky Landscape, a Church Tower
in the Distance*
Etching and drypoint
Museum of Fine Arts, Boston

Lenders to the Exhibition

ALLEN MEMORIAL ART MUSEUM,
OBERLIN COLLEGE
Oberlin, Ohio

THE ART INSTITUTE OF CHICAGO
Chicago, Illinois

BRITISH MUSEUM
London

CINCINNATI ART MUSEUM
Cincinnati, Ohio

CLEVELAND MUSEUM OF ART
Cleveland, Ohio

DAVISON ART CENTER,
WESLEYAN UNIVERSITY
Middletown, Connecticut

FOGG ART MUSEUM, HARVARD UNIVERSITY
Cambridge, Massachusetts

GEMEENTEARCHIEF
Haarlem

GRAPHISCHE SAMMLUNG ALBERTINA
Vienna

THE HOUGHTON LIBRARY,
HARVARD UNIVERSITY
Cambridge, Massachusetts

THE METROPOLITAN MUSEUM OF ART
New York

MUSÉE DU PETIT PALAIS
Paris

MUSEUM BOYMANS-VAN BEUNINGEN
Rotterdam

MUSEUM OF FINE ARTS
Boston, Massachusetts

NATIONAL GALLERY OF ART
Washington, D.C.

THE NEW YORK PUBLIC LIBRARY
New York

THE PIERPONT MORGAN LIBRARY
New York

RIJKSMUSEUM
Amsterdam

RIJKSMUSEUM
MEERMANNO-WESTREENIANUM
The Hague

THE SAINT LOUIS ART MUSEUM
St. Louis, Missouri

TEYLERS MUSEUM
Haarlem

MR. AND MRS. ARTHUR E. VERSHBOW

WORCESTER ART MUSEUM
Worcester, Massachusetts

YALE CENTER FOR BRITISH ART
New Haven, Connecticut

YALE UNIVERSITY ART GALLERY
New Haven, Connecticut

PRIVATE COLLECTIONS
in Amsterdam, Boston, Des Moines, and New York

Preface

The painter, poet, and art historian Karel van Mander closes his book on the lives of the Dutch artists, *Het Schilder-Boeck (The Painter's Book)*, published in 1604, with the apologetic statement that he had intended to write about the "glass painters, engravers, and Netherlandish women who exercised the brush" but finds that his book has become too fat and that he is impatient to return to the easel.[1] I hope that the present initial exploratory survey of Dutch printmaking from the late sixteenth century to the end of the seventeenth century will help to rectify some of the omissions of Van Mander and of later writers on Dutch art, at least so far as printmaking is concerned.

When one considers the subject of seventeenth-century Dutch painting, it is not only the great masters who come to mind — Rembrandt, Vermeer, Hals, and Steen — but also a host of brilliant minor masters. The situation in printmaking is similar, but the reputation of Rembrandt, the greatest etcher of all time, has overshadowed all but a few of the Dutch printmakers contemporary with him. Many of these are artists well known for their paintings and drawings. The exhibition presents for the first time Rembrandt the etcher in the context of the printmakers who immediately preceded him and of those who were his contemporaries.

My own curiosity about seventeenth-century Dutch printmakers other than Rembrandt was first stimulated in 1960, when, at the end of my Fulbright year in the Netherlands, I had the opportunity to study the Rijksprentenkabinet's incomparable collection of the prints of Hercules Segers. A longer period of residence in the Netherlands, from 1964 to 1966, enabled me to become acquainted with the collections of two of the greatest repositories of Dutch printmaking, the Rijksprentenkabinet of the Rijksmuseum, Amsterdam, and the Print Room of the British Museum, London. Without this experience I could not have attempted the present survey. Furthermore, I would not have considered such an undertaking if the collection of Dutch prints in the Museum of Fine Arts were not unusually strong, the product of the collecting efforts of several generations of curators, including the late Henry P. Rossiter, with his profound love for the little Dutch masters, and Eleanor A. Sayre, the present curator. The ambitious scale of this exhibition is consistent with Miss Sayre's policy of advocating the organization of major old master print shows accompanied by a comprehensive catalogue that gives the exhibition lasting value; "Rembrandt: Experimental Etcher" (1969), "Albrecht Dürer: Master Printmaker" (1971), and "The Changing Image: Prints by Francisco Goya" (1974) have been part of this series.

"Printmaking in the Age of Rembrandt" seeks to demonstrate through impressions of the highest quality available the great range and diversity of theme and of use of the media in Dutch printmaking at this time. The limited edition was an invention of the late nineteenth century. Many of the plates of seventeenth-century Dutch printmakers passed from publisher to publisher, sometimes being printed as late as the nineteenth century. In this exhibition early impressions of the highest quality have been brought together to better illuminate the artist's original intentions. In recent years late sixteenth-century and

33 (actual size)
Hercules Segers
The Enclosed Valley
Etching and drypoint
xiv   The National Gallery of Art

34 (actual size)
Hercules Segers
The Enclosed Valley
Etching and drypoint
Rijksmuseum, Amsterdam

seventeenth-century Dutch prints have often been reproduced in publications on Dutch painting for their usefulness as keys to emblematic or iconographical interpretation rather than for their merits as independent works of art. The present selection emphasizes original prints, that is, prints designed by the artists who executed them. Nevertheless, a number of expressive reproductive prints after others' designs have been included, the most artistically significant being the engravings of Hendrik Goudt after the paintings of Adam Elsheimer. A selection of books illustrated with prints reflects a vital, if sometimes neglected, facet of seventeenth-century Dutch printmaking.

The exhibition and catalogue are arranged in a chronological sequence according to decade. Within a decade liberties have often been taken with strict chronological sequence so that the treatment of subject and use of the media in the work of different artists can be better compared or contrasted.

Such a sweeping survey cannot be all-inclusive. The work of a single artist must often stand for that of other artists who worked in the same style or treated similar themes; Paulus Potter's horses, for example, must stand for those etched by Dirk Stoop. Some artists of consequence have been omitted because they apparently produced no original prints (Jan van Goyen or Pieter Lastman, for example) or because those they produced were judged to be less successful as works of art than those shown here.

William Robinson's essay "This Passion for Prints," which grew out of our mutual discussions, explores for the first time the attitude toward prints in northern Europe in the seventeenth century: the manner in which they were collected and the beginnings of their appreciation as works of art. One important topic must remain a subject for future research. Our knowledge of the market for Dutch prints in the seventeenth century— how they were commissioned, printed, published, and sold — is still too slight to allow us to draw many conclusions. We are left with such tantalizing clues as Willem Buytewech's notation on his drawing of the element of *Air* (etched and engraved by Jan van de Velde) that he "hopes that these will sell better than the preceding ones."[2]

1. Van Mander/Floerke, 1906, vol. 2, pp. 378–379.
2. Rotterdam/Paris, 1975, no. 22, p. 24. I would like to thank A.W.F.M. Meij for calling this to my attention.

Acknowledgments

I would like to thank Jan Fontein, director of the Museum of Fine Arts, and Eleanor A. Sayre, curator of the Department of Prints, Drawings, and Photographs for allowing me the time to realize the project "Printmaking in the Age of Rembrandt." Study, travel, and planning were supported by a research grant from the American Philosophical Society and an exhibition planning grant from the National Endowment for the Arts, a Federal agency. The exhibition and catalogue are supported in part by a grant from the National Endowment for the Arts, a Federal agency, Washington, D.C.

In order to arrive at the selection of prints for the exhibition the collections of a number of print rooms in Europe and the United States were studied closely: Amsterdam; Rotterdam; the Teylers Museum and the Atlas of the Gemeentearchief, Haarlem;

London; the Fondation Custodia (Lugt Collection), the Dutuit Collection of the Petit Palais, and the Cabinet des Réserves of the Bibliothèque Nationale, Paris; Vienna; Hamburg; Berlin; Munich; Coburg; Braunschweig; Washington, D.C.; the Rosenwald Collection; Chicago; Cleveland; Cincinnati; Oberlin; Wesleyan University; Harvard University; Yale University; The Metropolitan Museum of Art, The New York Public Library, and The Pierpont Morgan Library, New York. Many of these institutions were generous lenders to the exhibition. I would like to express my gratitude to the directors, curators, and curatorial staffs of all the print rooms for their kind attention to my requests during my visits. I would like to thank in particular: in Amsterdam, at the Rijksprentenkabinet, K.G. Boon, J.W. Niemeijer, D. de Hoop Scheffer, J.P. Filedt Kok, Peter Schatborn, and Irene de Groot; in Rotterdam, at the Museum Boymans-van Beuningen, B.L.D. Ihle, whose series of print catalogues has proved so useful, Robin Adèr, A.W.F.M. Meij, Juriaan Poot, and Jeroen Giltay; in Haarlem, at the Teylers Museum, J.H. van Borssum Buisman, and at the Gemeentearchief, J.J. Temminck and Frans Tames; in the Hague, at the Rijksmuseum Meermanno-Westreenianum, R.E.O. Ekkart; in London, at the British Museum, John Gere, Antony Griffiths, and John Rowlands; in Paris, at the Fondation Custodia (Lugt Collection), Carlos van Hasselt and Maria van Berge, and at the Dutuit Collection of the Petit Palais, Adeline Cacan de Bissy and Marie-Christine Boucher; in Vienna, at the Albertina, Dr. Walter Koschatsky and Veronika Birke; in Hamburg, Eckhard Schaar; in Berlin, Hans Mielke; in Munich, Konrad Renger; in Washington at the National Gallery, Andrew Robison; in Jenkintown at the Rosenwald Collection, Ruth Fine; in Chicago at the Art Institute, Harold Joachim; at the Cleveland Museum of Art, Louise Richards; at the Cincinnati Art Museum, Kristin Spangenberg; at Oberlin University, Richard Spear; at Wesleyan University, Connecticut, Richard Field and Ellen d'Oench; at the Fogg Art Museum of Harvard University, Henri Zerner; at the Yale University Art Gallery, James Burke and Richard Field; in New York, at The Metropolitan Museum of Art, Colta Ives, Suzanne Boorsch, and David Kiehl, at the New York Public Library, Elizabeth Roth, and at the Pierpont Morgan Library, Felice Stampfle and Cara Denison.

During the course of my research many scholars in the Dutch field patiently answered my inquiries: in the Netherlands, J.G. van Gelder and Mrs. I. van Gelder-Jost, Albert Blankert, E. de Jongh, George S. Keyes, J.R. ter Molen, S.A.C. Dudok van Heel, Theo Laurentius, and the staff of the Rijksbureau voor Kunsthistorische Documentatie in the Hague, especially An Zwollo. In this country I am grateful for discussions with Seymour Slive, Richard Judson, William S. Heckscher, Nancy Bialler, Alison Kettering, Peter Sutton, Anne-Marie Logan, Franklin Robinson and, in the Paintings Department of the Museum of Fine Arts, Boston, with John Walsh, Jr., Cynthia Schneider, and Lawrence Nichols. Egbert Haverkamp-Begemann and William W. Robinson were particularly patient in discussing various questions that arose during the writing of the catalogue. Konrad Oberhuber's exhibitions in the "Kunst der Graphik" series at the Albertina made me realize how valuable such a broad survey could be.

The preparation of the catalogue required the assistance of many dedicated individuals. Jane M. Boyle worked for a year under a planning grant from the National Endowment for the Arts doing initial research on the prints drawn from the Museum of Fine Arts collection.

In the Department of Prints, Drawings, and Photographs, Sue Welsh Reed, despite the pressure of other projects, steadfastly and efficiently assisted in coordinating every aspect of the exhibition, both catalogue and installation, from the inception of the project to its completion. In addition, she prepared the headings for the catalogue entries, catalogued the illustrated books, and supervised the preparation of the bibliography. Barbara Stern Shapiro helped with research on the Rembrandt biography and entries. Both were dedicated checkers and readers of galley proof. Jane Larsen took on the herculean task of loan correspondence and manuscript typing. Another volunteer, Edith Schmidt, assisted with checking, as did Margaret Lampert and Richard Berman. Karin Peltz assisted with Dutch translation and typing. I was aided in library research by Ann Adams, Karl Johns, and Uta Low. Assistance with Latin translation was provided by H. Chr. Albertsz and by Daan MacGillavry and Kitty MacGillavry.

I would like to thank Nancy Allen and the staff of the library of the Museum of Fine Arts for their generous assistance during a difficult period and the staff of the library of the Fogg Art Museum, especially Richard Simpson, for supplying essential literature. Wendy Greenhouse of the Museum of Fine Arts library compiled the bibliography. I would also like to thank Carl Zahn, director of publications, for the handsome design of a very complex catalogue; Christine Gebhard, assistant designer, for her careful handling of the production, and, above all, Margaret Jupe, editor, for her patience with the author's stylistic excesses and grammatical lapses. Geraldine Stevens, freelance editor, read proofs with meticulous attention.

Roy Perkinson, conservator of works on paper, skillfully restored a number of the works included in the exhibition. Elizabeth Lunning, assistant conservator, did original research on watermarks. David Ross, assisted by Judith Tiernan, matted and framed many of the prints for the exhibition.

Judith Downes and Tom Wong provided the ingenious and elegant design of the installation. Polaroid Corporation and photographers Victoria Lyons Ruzdic and Denise Dunn-Ryan prepared the splendid magnifications of prints for the technical display. Rhoda Rosenberg of the Museum School executed the demonstration plates for the technical display.

For assistance with grants, I would like to thank Lisa Simon, Diane Bruno, William Bodine, and George Peabody Gardner III of the museum's Development Office.

At the Saint Louis Art Museum, which is sharing the exhibition, I would like to thank James Wood, the former director; James Burke, the present director; and Judith Weiss of the Print Department.

Last but not least, I would like to thank my "Dutch family," the MacGillavrys, for their unfailing kindness and hospitality from my first visit to the Netherlands in 1959 to the present day.

Printmaking in the Age of Rembrandt: The Quest for Printed Tone

Dutch printmaking in the seventeenth century is characterized by great diversity of style and use of the printmaking media, but one unifying theme is the printmaker's quest for tone rather than line and, above all, for dark tonalities.[1] Many of the issues touched upon in this essay are explored at greater length and in greater detail in the catalogue entries.

Mannerist Engraving

Two directions can be discerned in Dutch Mannerist engraving: one that emphasizes sculptural values and one that emphasizes coloristic suggestion. The human figure, its grace of gesture and ornamental beauty, was the central preoccupation of Mannerist art. It is therefore hardly surprising that some of the finest engravings of the late Renaissance printmaker Hendrik Goltzius have a closer affinity to sculpture than to painting (see the *Apollo,* cat. no. 2). Goltzius's highly systematized engraving vocabulary lent itself superbly to the forceful rendering of sculptural volumes in the *Farnese Hercules* (cat. no. 6, see detail) as well as in the portrait of his teacher, Coornhert, in which the concentric lines that powerfully model Coornhert's cheek, eye socket, and eyeball serve to intensify his penetrating glance (cat. no. 5, see detail). The initial attraction of the chiaroscuro woodcut for Goltzius (see his series of gods and goddesses designed about 1588–89) was undoubtedly the medium's ability to render the sculptural volumes of the human figure rather than the decorative appeal of the colors that could be used for printing these woodcuts.

The second direction in Dutch Mannerist engraving — the interest in painterly suggestion of color, texture, and the play of light in engraving — was to have more profound implications for the future. It is impossible to conceive of the circle of Dutch and Flemish engravers who so brilliantly reproduced Rubens's paintings in the early seventeenth century without this Mannerist prologue. Joachim von Sandrart, in his *Teutsche Academie* of 1675, refers to one of those engravers, Lucas Vorsterman, as the "painter with the graver," ("Maler mit dem Grabstichel"), alluding to his ability to suggest the painterly play of light and shadow in black and white engraving.[2] Cornelis Visscher, who worked for Pieter Soutman (a printmaker of the Rubens School who was probably Visscher's teacher), epitomizes the vivid colorism of which these engravers were capable in his 1656 engraving of the ruddy-faced and silken-bearded preacher Gellius de Bouma (cat. no. 136). This colorism, essentially a revival of the power of coloristic suggestion Albrecht Dürer had achieved in his "Master Engravings" *Knight, Death, and the Devil* (B. 98, dated 1513), *St. Jerome in His Study* (B. 60, dated 1514), and *Melencolia* (B. 74, dated 1514), is first seen in Dutch Mannerist engraving in Goltzius's 1587 engraving of the standard bearer (cat. no. 1), whose elaborate costume and crackling banner stress textural variety.

The same interest in colorism characterizes the engraving style of two of Goltzius's principal followers: Jacques de Gheyn II (see the *Vanitas,* cat. no. 11) and Jan Saenredam (see the *Stranded Whale,* cat. no. 24). It also characterizes a number of Goltzius's later engravings such as the *Frederick de Vries* (cat. no. 13). Goltzius's later woodcuts, such as

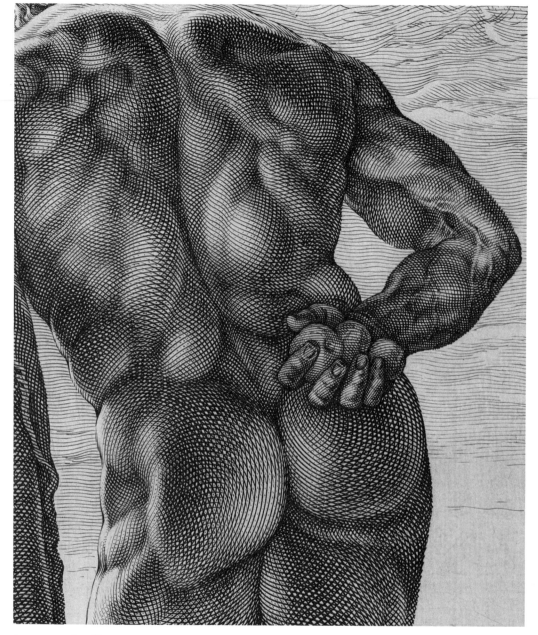

(cat. no. 6, detail)

(cat. no. 5, detail)

the four small landscapes designed about 1596–1598 (see cat. nos. 14, 15) are also touched by the painterly approach to printmaking. The final development in this growth of painterliness in Dutch Mannerist engraving is a logical if rather startling one: around 1600 both Hendrik Goltzius and Jacques de Gheyn abandoned printmaking for painting!

The booming Mannerist print industry of the late sixteenth century undoubtedly lent impetus to the printmaking activities of the seventeenth century. It is hardly coincidental that some of the most creative printmakers of the second decade — Esaias van de Velde, Jan van de Velde II, and Willem Buytewech — were active in Haarlem, the center of Goltzius's activity (Jan van de Velde II studied there with Goltzius's stepson, Jacob Matham).

Etching, the Painter's Print Medium

The early seventeenth century saw the rise of the painter's print medium: etching. While the demanding craft of engraving, the professional printmaker's medium, required years of apprenticeship to learn, drawing with the etching needle in the waxy etching ground covering the copper plate was comparable to drawing with pen or paper and was therefore easily accessible to the painter or draftsman who wished to express himself in printmaking. Several seventeenth-century and early eighteenth-century writers on art commented on this. Constantijn Huygens observed in the fragment of his autobiography (about 1629–1631): "the art consists of drawing with a point on little plates covered with wax, just as if with the pen" ("de kunst is, om met de stift te teekenen op met was bestreken plaetjes en, evenals de uitdrukking aan de pen").[3] The French etcher Abraham Bosse advocated in his handbook on etching (published in Paris, 1645) a style of etching based on the style of Jacques Callot, which imitated the neat, swelling and tapering calligraphic line of engraving; nevertheless he was forced to acknowledge grudgingly that there was another kind of etching, one characterized not by neatness but rather by a sketch-like freedom. Etchings of the latter type Bosse dubbed *l'eau-forte croquée* (the sketchy etching).[4] Sandrart in his *Teutsche Academie* of 1675 commented that etching enables an artist to express his ideas directly on the copper and thus avoid entrusting their expression to the possibly less reliable hand of an engraver.[5] In his life of the Italian painter and etcher Pietro Testa, Sandrart observed that, as Testa was not able to master the technique of engraving, he took up etching.[6] Rembrandt's pupil Samuel van Hoogstraten, in his *Introduction to the Noble School of Painting* of 1678, commented thát etching is much more draftsmanly than engraving ("maer het etsen is veel teykenachtiger").[7] In his *Great Painter's Book* (first published in 1707) Gerard de Lairesse compared engraving and etching; he stressed not only that etching was easily accessible to the artist and provided him with the opportunity to express himself directly but also that it made for greater speed of execution.[8]

Although Gerrit Pietersz., the first important painter-etcher in the period under discussion (see cat. nos. 9, 10), essentially based the linear vocabulary of his etchings on the systematic vocabulary of contemporary engraving, other painters soon introduced a new inventiveness in the tonal use of line, substituting stipples, flicks, and short, broken hatchings for conventional contour drawing. Some of these innovative etchers were Flemish-

(cat. no. 37, detail)

(cat. no. 153, detail)

(cat. no. 30, detail)

(cat. no. 68, detail)

xxii

(cat. no. 97, detail)

born painters, such as Jacob Savery (see cat. no. 16) and David Vinckboons (see cat. nos. 21, 22), who brought the stipple-and-dash graphic vocabulary of Pieter Bruegel with them when they emigrated north in the late sixteenth century. Bruegel had used this graphic vocabulary to better describe effects of atmosphere in landscape. In the early seventeenth century, particularly in the second decade in Haarlem, painters who etched used line in a tonal, "non-linear" fashion to evoke more vividly the fleeting effects of light and atmosphere in landscape; see, for example, the highly original use of stipple to describe a tremulous sunset sky in Willem Buytewech's etching of the *Ruins of the Huys te Kleef* (cat. no. 37, see detail).[9] Later landscape etchers used masses of etched lines, skeins and tangles of line, in a tonal fashion to realize their painterly or draftsmanly vision of landscape; see, for example, Claes Beresteyn's *Landscape with a Clump of Oaks* (cat. no. 153, detail).

The painter Hercules Segers, the most experimental of seventeenth-century Dutch etchers, was inventive not only in his use of color – printing in color on paper or cloth prepared in color – but also in his use of a great variety of means of creating tone on a plate. In a number of his prints, such as the *Rocky Landscape* (cat. no. 30), bundles of fine drypoint lines with burr produce a continuous tone that resembles a passage of dark wash (see detail). In other instances Segers reversed the usual graphic relationship of dark marks on a light ground and created a flat continuous tone by etching the exposed areas around areas masked with acid-resistant wax or varnish, as in *The Large Tree* (cat. no. 68, see detail). In *The Large Tree* and other etchings Segers also produced areas of tone by etching a fine crisscrossing mesh of lines into the plate (see the sky in the detail of *The Large Tree*).

In certain rare instances Segers made controlled use of a fine, granular bitten tone in his etchings. Rembrandt in his portrait of Sylvius (cat. no. 97) also used a fine, granular bitten tone in a highly calculated manner to describe the subtle play of light and shadow over the preacher's sensitive features (see detail). To the naked eye this granular bitten tone resembles a delicate wash of ink. In a similar fashion the goldsmith Jan Lutma the Younger used various goldsmith's punches to achieve subtle tonal gradations resembling a wash (see cat. no. 195).

The Quest for Dark Tonalities

Rembrandt is known for his expressive use of darkness in both his paintings and his prints. In his etchings he achieved effects of profound darkness either by biting, scratching, and engraving them into the plate, as in the *Annunciation to the Shepherds* of 1634 (cat. no. 80) and the *St. Jerome in a Dark Chamber* of 1642 (cat. no. 99) or by leaving a dark film of translucent printer's ink on the plate before printing, as in the impression of *The Entombment* of about 1654 shown here (cat. no. 167). Hercules Segers often left streaks of excess ink on the surface of the printing plate that enrich the painterly character of his prints, but he did not manipulate this film of extra ink in the controlled manner of Rembrandt. What is less well known is that the desire to achieve profoundly dark tonalities in printmaking characterizes Dutch printmaking from Jan Muller's engraving of the *Adoration of the Magi* of 1598 (cat. no. 8, see detail) to the mezzotints of the later seventeenth century and sets it apart from other European schools of printmaking in that cen-

(cat. no. 8, detail)

(cat. no. 45, detail)

(cat. no. 99, detail)

Ludwig von Siegen
Amelia of Hesse
Mezzotint, 1642
Museum of Fine Arts, Boston

(cat. no. 194, detail)

tury. This unique aspect of seventeenth-century Dutch printmaking was recognized by contemporary collectors and writers. (See the essay on collecting by William Robinson in this catalogue.) The collection of the English amateur of prints Richard Maitland, fourth Earl of Lauderdale, for example, included the "black prints" of Hendrik Goudt (see cat. nos. 44, 45) and Jan van de Velde II (see cat. no. 61). In 1699 the French writer on art Florent Le Comte described the ideal print collection; one of the many volumes composing the collection featured the "representations of night scenes" and "black pieces" of "different masters of all nations," but the only masters mentioned were Dutch: Goudt, Jan van de Velde, Uyttenbroeck, Rembrandt, Van Vliet, and "others."

Hendrik Goudt was the pivotal figure in the development of dark tonalities in seventeenth-century Dutch printmaking. Six of his seven engravings reproducing the paintings of Adam Elsheimer, the German painter known for his poetic effects of illumination, are nocturnal scenes; see Goudt's *The Mocking of Ceres* (cat. no. 45, detail). These had a profound effect on the nocturnal engravings of Jan van de Velde in the 1620s (*The Pancake Woman,* cat. no. 61) as well as on Rembrandt's dark prints such as the *Annunciation to the Shepherds* (cat. no. 80) of 1634 and the *St. Jerome in a Dark Chamber* of 1642 (cat. no. 99, detail). Rembrandt's deep chiaroscuro was achieved, however, by means of an unsystematic mesh of etched, scratched, and gouged lines rather than by means of the regularized, systemized grid of engraved lines of Goudt and Van de Velde. Like the early states of Jan Lievens's *St. Jerome* of about 1630 (cat. no. 81), Rembrandt's etchings have the deep velvety textures that were to characterize the medium of mezzotint.

The first primitive mezzotint was made in Amsterdam in 1642 (the same year as Rembrandt's *St. Jerome in a Dark Chamber*) by an amateur, a military man attached to the court at Cassel, Ludwig von Siegen (see his *Amelia of Hesse*). Von Siegen's method was an additive one, in which areas of the plate were selectively roughened with a roulette, a spiked wheel on a handle. The subtractive method, or true mezzotint, was perfected by another military man, Prince Ruprecht von der Pfalz, assisted by a professional draftsman and painter, Wallerant Vaillant (see cat. nos. 190, 191). In Prince Ruprecht's process the entire plate was first roughened with a "rocker," or "hatcher" (a serrated blade with a handle), and the lights were then created by scraping and burnishing them from this dark field; see for example, Allart van Everdingen's *Nocturnal Landscape* (cat. no. 185). At last a printmaking process was available in which the printmaker need not depend on line in order to produce a finely graded continuous tone (see Michiel van Musscher's 1685 *Self-Portrait,* cat. no. 194, detail).[10] The mezzotint process tended to dictate the use of darker tonalities, as may be seen by comparing Dirck Maas's equestrian etching and mezzotint from the same period (cat. nos. 199, 200). The etching has the fashionable light tonality of international classicizing etching, while the mezzotint is characterized by a rich spectrum of dark tones.

1. My ideas concerning printed tone in Dutch printmaking were greatly stimulated by Egbert Haverkamp-Begemann's discussion of Hercules Segers's use of printed tone; Haverkamp-Begemann, 1973.

2. Sandrart/Peltzer, 1925, pp. 243–244.

3. Worp, 1891, p. 112.

4. Bosse, 1645, p. 3.

5. Sandrart/Peltzer, 1925, p. 245.

6. Ibid., p. 293.

7. Hoogstraten, 1678, pp. 195–196 (on printmaking).

8. Lairesse/Davaco, 1740/1969, vol. 2, p. 375.

9. Constantijn Huygens, in his autobiographical fragment, observed that his drawing teacher, the rather old-fashioned engraver Hendrik Hondius, was better at rendering inanimate things such as columns and marble than "loose and mobile things such as grass, leaves and bushes" or "the charm…that gray and formless ruins can have"; Worp, 1891, p. 109.

10. Hoogstraten, 1678, pp. 195–196 (on printmaking) characterized mezzotint as "printing without drawn lines" ("om als zonder trekken te drukken").

"This Passion for Prints": Collecting and Connoisseurship in Northern Europe during the Seventeenth Century

By William W. Robinson

This Passion for Prints, which is one of the hall-marks of the finest minds, could not be held in greater esteem.

FLORENT LE COMTE

This testimony to a universal regard for prints appeared in Florent Le Comte's *Cabinet des Singularitez* of 1699.[1] The passion he describes had only recently infected legions of French amateurs. Forty years earlier the Abbé de Marolles wrote that there were fewer than a dozen serious collectors in the kingdom.[2] That small brotherhood of connoisseurs burgeoned into a zealous multitude by the close of the century, when Le Comte declared that engravings "delight both the scholar and the plebeian," and "the love and knowledge of prints appeals to the taste of all great men."[3]

The statements of Marolles and Le Comte attest to an important development in the culture of their time. During the seventeenth century, printed images came to play an increasingly vital role in the education of the eye and in the dissemination of knowledge in virtually every field.

The Uses of Prints

Before the invention of photography, prints were the primary means of communicating visual information.[4] The passion for prints reported by Florent Le Comte resulted in part from a new consciousness of the didactic value of engravings, etchings, and woodcuts. His contemporaries recognized that the thousands of prints in circulation constituted a comprehensive encyclopedia of the visible world. In 1699 Roger de Piles observed that printmakers had illustrated "all the visible Productions of Art and Nature."[5] Their works had become "the Depositories of all that is Fine and Curious in the World."[6] It followed, De Piles reasoned, that anyone, whatever his profession or social rank, could profit from the study of prints.[7]

Seventeenth-century amateurs believed that engravings should delight as well as instruct. Desire for aesthetic pleasure contributed no less than the thirst for knowledge to their passion for prints. We learn from a decree of Louis XIV, promulgated in May 1660, that informed Frenchmen regarded engravings as works of fine art, created to please the senses as well as edify the mind. An attempt to demote printmaking to a craft provoked a vigorous defense of its free status from the king. It was in the interest of the glory of France, the document stated, to encourage the liberal arts. Such were etching and engraving, "which depend upon the imagination of their authors and cannot be subject to any laws other than those of their genius; this art has nothing in common with the crafts and manufactures; none of its products being among the necessities which serve the subsistence of civil society, but only among those which minister to delight, or pleasure, and to curiosity."[8] The law also recognized the engraver's artistic individuality; it prohibited the subordination of printmaking to the homogenizing standards of a craft guild, because "the style of each engraver is different from that of another."[9]

The invention of printmaking, Roger de Piles declared in 1699, was "one of the

Aegidius Sadeler
The Great Hall of the Castle at Prague (detail)
Engraving, 1607
Rijksmuseum, Amsterdam

Customers inspect the wares at a printseller's stall.
Engravings by Hendrik Goltzius and artists in his
circle probably figured among the prints sold here.

happiest Productions of latter Ages."[10] De Piles went on to cite some of the blessings bestowed by this discovery. His list offers a valuable insight into the basic motives for collecting prints in his time.

Engravings, he wrote, facilitated the recollection of matters that have escaped our memories. Being small and manageable, they permitted easy comparison of one thing with another. Moreover, the frequent study of prints cultivated good judgment and taste, and contributed to our understanding of the history of the fine arts.[11] The most fundamental benefit listed by De Piles was that engravings represented "absent and distant Things, as if they were before our Eyes."[12] Men and women of the seventeenth century relied on prints, as we depend on photographs, for information about history, art, nature, and foreign cultures. Artists and connoisseurs, for example, required prints to keep abreast of the latest developments throughout Europe. Painters, sculptors, and designers called upon engravers to broadcast their inventions to an international audience. Since the early sixteenth century, many printmakers had specialized in reproducing the works of other artists. Samuel van Hoogstraten vividly characterized the contribution of reproductive engravers in his *Introduction to the Noble School of Painting* of 1678: "Surely, engravers have been the heralds and trumpeters of the greatest painters, and prints the spokesmen and ambassadors who proclaim to us the contents of ingenious works of art which are distant or out of fashion."[13]

As ambassadors and spokesmen for an artist's achievements, prints could spread his fame to all corners of Europe and beyond. The Dutch engraver Hendrik Goltzius commanded such a reputation that, in order to protect his privacy, he traveled incognito when he visited Italy in 1590.[14] Goltzius's works reached the frontiers of the known world during his lifetime. A Dutch ship trading in Southeast Asia in 1602 carried more than five thousand Netherlandish prints in its cargo, among them engravings by Goltzius and his pupil Jacob de Gheyn II.[15]

The etchings of Rembrandt were known from the Baltic coast to Sicily before his death.[16] When the Bolognese artist Guercino received the commission to paint a pendant to Rembrandt's *Aristotle Contemplating the Bust of Homer,* he could claim familiarity with the Dutchman's style through "various works of his in prints which have come to our region." On the basis of the "good taste" and "fine manner" of Rembrandt's etchings, Guercino assumed "that his work in color is likewise of complete exquisiteness and perfection."[17]

Many artists collected prints. A few, notably Rembrandt and Pieter Lely, ranked among the most discerning and ambitious amateurs of their time. Painters, sculptors, printmakers, and architects studied engravings to absorb and occasionally to borrow from the works of their predecessors and contemporaries.

Artists also used prints to teach their pupils to draw. In the Netherlands copying engravings was a basic exercise in an apprentice's training. The painter Caspar Netscher kept a portfolio of 327 prints and sketches "of little value, serving for the students to draw from."[18] Netscher handed on to his pupils a habit he must have acquired from his own teacher, Gerard ter Borch. A collection of copies by Gerard and members of his family has

Jacob van der Ulft
View of the Dam Square, Amsterdam (detail)
Etching
Rijksmuseum, Amsterdam

This mid-seventeenth century view shows the shops of the book and print sellers clustered together on the left side of the square and at the beginning of the Kalverstraat. On the shop sign on the first house at left is the symbolic dog *(hond)* of the publishing family Hondius.

come down to us in an album assembled by his stepsister. It includes drawings after prints by Holbein, Goltzius, Carracci, Bloemaert, and Rembrandt.[19]

Collectors acquired prints from a variety of sources. Booksellers sold them in their shops. Vendors hawked them on the street.[20] In Holland prints figured in public auctions throughout the century.[21] They first appeared in London auctions, particularly in library sales, during the 1680s and 1690s.[22] Print publishers operated shops that offered impressions from the engraved plates in their stock. Artists who published their own prints often traded directly with the public.[23]

Prints were mounted in albums, stacked in drawers or chests, and hung on the wall. In the last case, they might be displayed in gilt or ebony frames or simply suspended between two wooden rods, called *rollen* in Dutch inventories.[24] Samuel Pepys, who decorated his study with maps and engravings, had the prints mounted on boards and varnished before he set them into frames.[25]

Serious amateurs, including Samuel Pepys, preserved most of their prints in albums, often covered elegantly in leather or horn. The following survey of seventeenth-century collecting deals primarily with such volumes, which constituted the backbone of every collection or "cabinet" formed during that period. An examination of the contents and arrangement of the albums, will, it is hoped, illuminate the evolving ideas and attitudes of print connoisseurs from the late sixteenth to the early eighteenth century.

Print Collecting, 1565 – about 1650

This survey begins with the earliest known proposal for an ideal print collection, which was set forth in Samuel van Quicchelberg's *Inscriptiones vel tituli theatri amplissimi,* published in 1565.[26]

Quicchelberg's book is a treatise on the encyclopedic *Kunstkammer,* or *Kunst- und Wunderkammer,* the type of omnibus private museum established by men of means in the sixteenth and seventeenth centuries. In theory the *Kunstkammer* embodied a microcosm of the visible world in a rich selection of natural and man-made objects. The proprietor of a *Kunstkammer* endeavored to lead a virtuous life through the pursuit of universal knowledge; hence the terms *virtuoso* and *curieux,* often applied to collectors of the period. Because an educational purpose took precedence over aesthetic pleasure, masterpieces of painting, sculpture, and the graphic arts shared the limelight with natural and ethnographic rarities. Moreover, the didactic basis of the *Kunstkammer* collections often led to the classification of paintings or prints according to their subject matter, rather than by artist or national school.[27]

Quicchelberg formulated an ideal *Kunstkammer,* or "universal theater," divided into five general classes. Each class consisted of several separate but related collections. In the "Fifth Class" – which also encompassed oil paintings, watercolors, textiles, furnishings, portraits, and material illustrating heraldry and geneaology – the author prescribed the establishment of a repository of the graphic arts. He styled the collection "Images Printed from Copper" but admitted drawings and woodcuts as well as etchings and engravings.[28]

Quicchelberg classified the prints by subject. He stipulated that complete sets be

Flemish School
Connoisseurs in a Cabinet of Rarities (full view and detail)
Oil on panel, about 1620
National Gallery, London

The painting depicts the interior of a *Kunstkammer*. On the table at the left, amid coins, medals, and scientific instruments, is an album with engravings by Albrecht Dürer and Lucas van Leyden. An impression of Hendrik Goudt's *Mocking of Ceres* after Elsheimer (1610, cat. no. 45) lies beside it.

bound and loose sheets organized into albums. Each volume should bear a title identifying its contents. Quicchelberg compiled a list of thirty-two thematic headings under which the collector could assemble his prints. They range from the Bible, Christianity, and classical mythology to natural history, portraits, geography, modern customs, architecture, and ornament. He also designed a plan for the installation of the albums on three shelves. Most subjects assigned to the same shelf are loosely related.[29]

The principle of classification by subject governed the organization of one of the largest print collections formed in the sixteenth century. The collection was part of the dazzling *Kunstkammer* created in the 1570s by Archduke Ferdinand II (1529–1595) at Schloss Ambras in Tirol. Eighteen cabinets placed back-to-back on the main axis of the room constituted the focal point of the *Kunstkammer*. Each cabinet housed precious objects arranged according to the raw materials from which they were fashioned: gold in one, silver in another, and so on. One case displayed only items made of feathers.[30] In accordance with this system, the prints were shelved in a cabinet with other fine works on paper and parchment. Besides printed images, it contained all kinds of illustrated manuscripts. An inventory of the *Kunstkammer,* compiled in 1596, lists nearly 200 books and illuminated rolls in the cabinet.[31]

Ferdinand had most of his prints mounted in albums covered with leather or parchment. Some complete sets, such as Dürer's *Apocalypse,* were bound separately. The collection comprised a minimum of thirty albums and probably included as many as forty or more. Nearly thirty have come down to us, and the inventory designates another dozen or so, very probably composed of prints, which have not survived. The volumes and sets still preserved – roughly three-quarters of the original number – contain some 6,500 impressions.[32]

Virtually all the books were compiled by subject. Illustrations of biblical and Christian themes filled several volumes, including one limited to "crucified figures," another devoted to the Virgin, and two composed of representations of saints. Architecture, ornamental designs, and prints reproducing goldsmith's work each occupied one or more albums. Other books contained portraits of learned men, depictions of the pagan gods, and engravings documenting the geneaology of the House of Austria. A topographical volume incorporated "city ruins, maps, together with landscapes."[33]

Classification by subject implies that Quicchelberg and Archduke Ferdinand regarded prints primarily as illustrations and attached little or no aesthetic value to them. Not all early collectors subscribed to this method of organization. Even at Schloss Ambras, a volume housing 224 prints and 8 drawings was consecrated to the work of a single master: Albrecht Dürer.[34] By the first quarter of the seventeenth century, other connoisseurs were arranging their choicest albums by artist. This approach attests to a respect for the creative powers of individual printmakers and to an esteem for their prints as remarkable works of art.

A collection belonging to several generations of the Ayrer family of Nuremberg featured albums devoted to outstanding German and Netherlandish engravers from the late fifteenth to the mid-sixteenth century. A partial inventory has come down to us in

Joachim von Sandrart's *Teutsche Academie*. Melchior Ayrer (1520–1570) laid the foundations of the collection between 1550 and 1570. The system of classification, which Sandrart commended to other connoisseurs, was introduced during the first quarter of the seventeenth century by Melchior's grandson, Johann Aegidius Ayrer.[35]

Johann Aegidius compiled his albums by artist. They contained the work of twelve engravers, ranging from the fifteenth-century pioneers Martin Schongauer and Israel van Meckenem through Dürer and Lucas van Leyden to the Nuremberg "Little Masters" Barthel Beham, Hans Sebald Beham, and Georg Pencz.[36] It is no surprise that prints by the leading protagonists of the northern Renaissance constituted the showpieces of the Ayrer cabinet and other early collections organized by artist. We know from Karel van Mander's *Schilder-Boeck* and other sources that the engravings of northern masters active at the outset of the sixteenth century aroused tremendous admiration among critics, artists, and collectors during the years around 1600.[37] Most significantly, Ayrer shelved his albums in chronological order. The chronological arrangement indicates that he envisioned the volumes as a survey of the origins and development of German and Netherlandish engraving of the Renaissance. His collection ranks among the earliest examples of the use of prints to illustrate the history of art.[38] The Ayrer albums did not belong to an encyclopedic *Kunstkammer*. As far as we know, the collection included only paintings, drawings, prints, and a fine library. Sandrart referred to it as a "Kunststube" and a "Kunstcabinet."[39]

Volumes of prints classified by artist occasionally figured in *Kunstkammer* collections as well. The painter and art dealer Jan Basse the Elder (1571–1636) installed a magnificent *Kunstkammer* in his house on Amsterdam's Prinsengracht. It featured paintings, sculpture, porcelain, sea shells, jewels, and minerals, in addition to such rarities as a trumpet made from an elephant's tusk. "Nine various sea monsters," a crocodile, and a mermaid's rib were suspended from the ceiling.[40]

Basse displayed many of his precious objects in two oak cabinets. One of them housed the bulk of his prints, which he divided into two groups. One group consisted of twenty-two packets, or small piles, of prints. Some of these he organized by subject, others by artist.[41] This group may have belonged to his dealer's stock. The finest prints were mounted in twelve albums. All volumes but one were compiled by artist, and each book was inscribed with the monogram of the master(s) whose work it contained. Here, too, works by German and Netherlandish painter-engravers of the fifteenth and sixteenth centuries constituted the acme of the collection.[42]

A few of these albums fetched considerable sums at the auction of Basse's estate in March 1637. The engravings by Lucas van Leyden attracted the highest price by far (637 guilders), followed by the volume devoted to Israel van Meckenem and Martin Schongauer (280 guilders), the Dürer woodcuts (265 guilders), and the Dürer engravings (200 guilders).[43] The sale attracted international attention,[44] but the most conspicuous bidder was a local artist. Rembrandt acquired a few sea shells and some forty lots of prints.[45] His purchases were destined for his own *Kunstkammer*, which resembled Basse's collection in many ways. Not long ago, biographers portrayed Rembrandt as an unsophisticated bohemian. It certainly requires an adjustment of this image to picture him as an aspirant to the brotherhood of gentlemen-*virtuosi,* cultivating universal knowledge in an encyclopedic *Kunstkammer.* Nonetheless, the collection he assembled conformed to this type in structure and content.[46]

The well-known inventory of 1656 describes Rembrandt's extensive holdings in the graphic arts under the rubric *Kunst boecken* ("Art Books"). They amounted to thirty-four albums of prints, intershelved with thirty-two volumes of drawings and three containing some of each. Rembrandt organized most of his books of prints by artist, although several were compiled by subject. The latter included albums of portraits, landscapes, erotica, statues, architecture, costume, and Turkish buildings and customs.[47]

The artists represented attest to the breadth of Rembrandt's curiosity and taste. Particularly striking are the numerous volumes of prints by and after Italian painters, such as the "kostelijcke boeck" ("precious book") of Andrea Mantegna;[48] three albums of engravings after Raphael;[49] a volume devoted to the Carracci, Guido Reni, and Ribera; and "a very large book with nearly all the works [after] Titian."[50] Albums dedicated to Netherlandish artists featured engravings and woodcuts by Lucas van Leyden, prints after Pieter Bruegel and Maarten van Heemskerck, proof impressions after Rubens and Jacob Jordaens, and the graphic works of Jan Lievens and Ferdinand Bol. In one book Rembrandt mounted a complete set of his own prints.

In the ideal *Kunstkammer* imagined by Quicchelberg, and in the real ones established by Archduke Ferdinand, Jan Basse, and Rembrandt, prints made up only one element in vast schemes that aimed to encapsulate the entire visible world. Robert Burton, a habitué of *Kunstkammer* collections, has left us a vivid image of the variety, exoticism, and genial clutter that constituted their appeal. In his *Anatomy of Melancholy,* published in 1621, Burton asked: "Whom will it not affect…in some princes cabinet…or noblemen's houses, to see such varieties of attires, faces, so many, so rare, and such exquisite pieces, of men, birds, beasts, etc., to see those excellent landskips, Dutch works, and curious cuts of Sadeler of Prague, Durer, Goltzius, Vrintes [Frans Floris], etc., such pleasant pieces of perspective, Indian pictures made of feathers, China works, frames, thaumaturgical notions, exotic toys, etc.?"[51] The "curious cuts" of Sadeler, Dürer, and Goltzius are only one ingredient in an enchanting miscellany that delights by virtue of its sheer diversity.

Print Collecting about 1650 – about 1720

During the second half of the seventeenth century the concept of a print collection underwent a profound transformation. Collectors and critics, aware that prints could furnish information about every conceivable subject, formulated the notion of a visual encyclopedia composed exclusively of engravings, etchings, and woodcuts. Prints outgrew the circumscribed role of rarities in a *Kunstkammer.* After 1650 ambitious collectors assembled all-inclusive museums of paper art, designed to foster the pursuit of universal knowledge.[52] Appropriately, these collections often constituted a subdivision of a comprehensive library.[53]

The formation of encyclopedic collections was predicated upon the diversification of the subject matter of prints and the steady growth of print production during the sixteenth and seventeenth centuries. In 1699 Roger de Piles wrote that over the previous two hundred years engravers "had published an infinite number of Prints on all sorts of subjects, as well as Histories, Fables, Emblems, Devises, Medals, Animals, Landskips, Flowers, Fruits, as in general all the visible Productions of Art and Nature."[54] Collectors realized that judicious organization would transform this amorphous universe of images into a powerful instrument of knowledge. As far as we know, the first amateur to appreciate the educational possibilities of an encyclopedic print collection was Michel de Marolles, Abbé de Villeloin (1600–1681). Not only did he establish the first such cabinet, but he also publicized the idea in his *Mémoires* of 1656–57 and in a 182-page catalogue of his holdings, which appeared in 1666.[55] Marolles boldly defined the potential of a print collection as an aid to learning: "Prints, well selected and well ordered, will conveniently supply information, not only about all the sciences and all the fine arts, but about everything imaginable."[56]

The English diarist and print collector John Evelyn, who read the description of Marolles's collection in the *Mémoires,* was also fired by the didactic value of Marolles's visual encyclopedia. In his treatise on engraving, published in 1662, Evelyn advocated the use of prints in the education of children and adolescents. The latter, he wrote, "might receive incredible advantages… by an Universal and choice Collection of *prints* and *cuts* well design'd, engraven and dispos'd, much after the manner and method of the above nam'd [Marolles], which should contain, as it were, a kind of *Encyclopaedia* of all intelligible, and memorable things that either are, or have ever been, *in rerum Natura*."[57]

The most complete definition of a universal print collection appeared in Florent Le Comte's *Cabinet des Singularitez…* of 1699. Like Samuel van Quicchelberg, Le Comte designed an imaginary collection, which he entitled "Idea of a Fine Library of Prints."[58] In its rigorous organization and encyclopedic compass, Le Comte's "Idea" is a product of the rational and systematizing spirit of the latter half of the seventeenth century. Its hypothetical contents were selected and arranged with the aim of extending the mind's reach over the entire universe of nature, history, morality, and art.

The "Idea of a Fine Library of Prints" consists of 151 albums divided into 4 sections. The first category, composed of eighty-seven volumes, recapitulates the course of Western history from the Book of Genesis to the reign of Louis XIV. Le Comte presented the titles in a chronological sequence. For each country and each epoch, the albums would display the appropriate maps; portraits of rulers and renowned citizens; illustrations of costumes, ceremonies, buildings, and artifacts; and depictions of important events, such as battles and triumphal entries.

The second section is an anthology of painting, sculpture, and engraving in fifty volumes. Here, too, the titles follow a historical scheme, beginning with the origins of art in hieroglyphs and primitive reliefs and concluding with French painters of the late seventeenth century. The great majority of the albums represent the period from about 1475 to 1690 in Italy, France, Germany, and the Netherlands. Le Comte organized most of these by artist, usually assigning two or more masters to a volume. The chronological arrangement would permit the collector to compare the growth of the arts in antiquity with their decadence in the Middle Ages and reestablishment, since 1500, "to the strength and splendor in which we see them today."[59]

Five volumes of moral subjects make up the third section of Le Comte's "Idea." These would contain prints of the virtues and vices, emblems, heraldic devices, and illustrations of fables and other stories that teach proper conduct. Finally, he prescribed a section of "Miscellaneous Subjects." Seven of the nine titles in this category feature famous or infamous women. They range from heroines of the Bible and female rulers to "violent and debauched women, ancient and modern."

The idea of a consummate print collection had undergone a fundamental transformation between Samuel van Quicchelberg's project of 1565 and Florent Le Comte's plan of 1699. For the sixteenth-century theorist, "Images Printed from Copper" made up only one of some fifty-five separate collections in his universal theater. By the end of the following century, albums of prints constituted an independent, comprehensive "library." Quicchelberg arranged his entire selection by subject, with no provision for segregating the work of an outstanding artist or for representing the history of art. Following the practice of collectors like Johann Aegidius Ayrer, Le Comte introduced a section devoted to reviewing the development of painting, sculpture, and engraving. Perhaps the most significant difference between the two schemes lies in their respective systems of classification. Le Comte's encyclopedic compendium of 151 titles dwarfs the list of 32 subjects drawn up by Quicchelberg. The latter's arrangement of the albums on three shelves is not a random one; but it looks casual compared with Le Comte's encompassing historical program, which encapsulates the evolution of Western art and civilization in a coherent, chronological system.

Le Comte's dream of a perfect library of prints had no exact equivalent in reality. However, his project was modeled in part after the awesome collection of the Abbé de Marolles. Between 1644 and 1666 Marolles assembled the most comprehensive cabinet of the century. His albums became the nucleus of the greatest repository of prints in existence today, the Cabinet des Estampes in the Bibliothèque Nationale, Paris. The quantity of prints he amassed is staggering: 123,400 impressions mounted in 400 large albums and some 120 small ones.[60]

Marolles composed about one-half of the volumes by subject; more than seventy different categories were represented.[61] He shelved these albums in a random manner, without following any definite system of classification.[62] Approximately one-third of the volumes were organized by artist; these were ordered according to quality, beginning with the masters "whose works are esteemed above all others."[63] Reproductive prints after Raphael, Michelangelo, Titian, the Carracci, and Rubens figured in this class, together with a collection of 500 chiaroscuro woodcuts and original works by Dürer, Lucas van Leyden, Parmigianino, and Callot.

Marolles delighted in registering the number of impressions preserved in each album. The statistics underscored the quality and scope of his cabinet. His portfolios, we learn, housed 740 prints after Raphael, 402 by Lucas van Leyden, 601 by and after

Nicolaes Verkolje after Arnold Houbraken
Portrait of the Collector Jacob Moelaert
Mezzotint before letters
Rijksmuseum, Amsterdam

In 1721 Arnold Houbraken wrote of Moelaert that "his favorite diversion was to assemble the prints of all the famous masters." This mezzotint of around 1700 shows Moelaert examining an album of prints. "Each album," Houbraken wrote, "was a pleasure garden for him, blooming with the best Italian, French and Netherlandish art."

Parmigianino, and 1468 by Callot. Contemporary Dutch printmakers were well represented: the Abbé owned 224 works by Rembrandt, 36 by Adriaen van Ostade, 73 by Cornelis Visscher, and 4 by Hercules Segers, among hundreds of others.[64]

In addition to sections arranged by subject and by artist, Marolles devised a third category to illustrate the history of printmaking from its origins to the early seventeenth century. He organized this division into "Old Masters" and "Little Masters."[65] Under the former rubric, he classified the earliest prints in his collection, many of them rare works by anonymous fifteenth-century artists. It is noteworthy, in a period notorious for its classical taste, that Marolles, Florent Le Comte, and Joachim von Sandrart exhibited a special interest in late Gothic prints.[66] The "Little Masters" – so called because of their exquisite works on a small scale – were engravers of the sixteenth and seventeenth centuries, such as Heinrich Aldegrever and members of the Wierix family.

Louis XIV purchased Marolles's collection *en bloc* in 1667. The Abbé was invited to help install his treasures in the Royal Library. The prints were remounted, following his original system of classification, in 234 new albums. Within a few years, the indefatigable Marolles had amassed a second collection, comparable in size and quality to the first. He described its contents – 111,424 sheets in 237 volumes – in a catalogue published in 1672.[67]

The organization of encyclopedic collections varied according to the interests and outlook of the proprietor. Michel de Marolles had no need for a rigorously structured system, such as the one that governed Florent Le Comte's "Idea." Some collectors, on the other hand, followed orderly historical or geopolitical schemes, which prefigured the plan devised by Le Comte in 1699. As an example of these, we may refer to the method of classification employed by Georg Augustin von Stubenberg (1628–1691). His cabinet at Regensburg was established by 1679, when Sandrart described it in his *Teutsche Academie*.[68]

Von Stubenberg mounted his prints in thirty-two albums. More than half were organized according to a historical system. In the seven volumes devoted to religious themes, the order of the prints followed the chapter and verse of the Bible, beginning with Genesis. Ten albums featured secular subjects, including histories, allegories, and landscapes. Prints depicting historical events appeared in chronological sequence, "according to the year, from the earliest down to our present times."[69]

In the classification of the remaining fifteen albums, Von Stubenberg observed different principles. Portraits filled ten books; here, the order was determined by the sitter's social rank, rather than by chronology. Four volumes dedicated to topography were arranged by city, each city being represented by prints of its most notable sights. Finally, one large book housed a collection of mezzotints, most of them portraits, by Dutch artists. At that time, mezzotint was still a novelty. Other connoisseurs also set aside one or more albums to display works in the recently invented medium.[70]

Sandrart's thorough and enthusiastic account leaves no doubt about his admiration for the orderly installation of Von Stubenberg's collection. He was equally impressed by its magnitude. Sandrart counted 81,777 prints by some 550 masters of the fifteenth, sixteenth, and seventeenth centuries.[71]

Not all collectors during the second half of the seventeenth century built encyclopedic cabinets similar to those established by G.A. von Stubenberg and the Abbé de Marolles. Some specialized, concentrating on images related to a specific subject;[72] others acquired prints primarily for their beauty as works of art. Most amateurs of the period shared a passionate interest in portraits. A few, like Nicolas Clément, collected nothing else. Clément (1656–1712), who served as curator of prints in the library of Louis XIV, owned 18,000 portraits, which he bequeathed to the king.[73] Portraits also made up a substantial part of the extraordinary ensemble of prints and drawings amassed by the Parisian François-Roger de Gaignières (1642–1715). Gaignières organized his collection to illustrate the history and civilization of the principal nations of Europe. The breadth of his holdings and his method of classification earned encomiums from several contemporaries, including Roger de Piles. His portraits alone filled no fewer than 100 albums.[74]

It is not difficult to explain the affection for portraits displayed by seventeenth-century amateurs. Renaissance humanism encouraged the emulation of virtuous men; hence the preservation and study of their likenesses. In addition, collectors perused the effigies of illustrious persons as a means of organizing and understanding the past.

John Evelyn vividly rehearsed the reasons for acquiring portraits in a letter to Samuel Pepys dated August 12, 1689. Pepys was planning to decorate his library with paintings of eminent men, and Evelyn advised him to invest instead in a collection of printed portraits: "I am sure you would be infinitely delighted with the assembly, and some are so very well don to the life, that they may stand in competition with the best paintings. This were a cheape and so much more useful curiosity, as they seldome are without their names and elogies of the persons whose portraits they represent: I say you will be exceedingly pleas'd to contemplate the effigies of those who have made such a noise & bustle in the world, either by their madnesse & folly, or a more conspicuous figure by their wit and learning."[75] Pepys followed his friend's counsel. His print collection, still preserved with the rest of his library at Magdalene College, Cambridge, features some 2,800 portraits.[76]

In Jan Pietersz. Zomer (1641–1724), an Amsterdam art appraiser, dealer, and auctioneer, we encounter an altogether different species of collector.[77] Zomer's values were those of the print connoisseur. It was the beauty of the work of art that motivated him, not a thirst for universal knowledge. Zomer aspired to assemble the complete works of outstanding artists in the finest impressions. He pursued their rare plates and proof impressions and endeavored to secure all the states of every print.

Zomer built up his collection over a period of fifty years, from about 1670 to 1720. Our knowledge of his holdings derives from a catalogue of 96 pages he published in the early 1720s. It describes his rare books and 139 portfolios of drawings, as well as 93 albums of prints by Italian, French, Dutch, Flemish, and German masters.[78] The great majority of the albums were arranged by artist. The connoisseur's approach colors nearly every page of the catalogue. A typical entry reads: "The entire work, complete, of [Federico Barocci], beautiful, the etchings as well as the engravings, various proof impressions, with the changes in state."[79] Zomer took particular pride in his magnificent collection of 428 prints by Rembrandt. He acclaimed the collection, gathered and refined during the half-century after Rembrandt's death, as "complete, including every state, excellent impressions, and such that neither he [Zomer], nor anyone else could collect their likes, with the same expense and all the pains he took during 50 years."[80]

As Zomer published the catalogue to advertise the sale of his cabinet, such warm appraisals may reflect his commercial motive as much as his connoisseur's judgment. Nevertheless, the laudatory terms that crop up consistently – "extra beautiful impressions," "complete works," "rare," "proof impressions" – leave no doubt as to the criteria that governed his selection of the prints in the first place. Zomer was by no means the first amateur to subscribe to these principles. Collectors born a generation earlier, such as Rembrandt and Michel de Marolles, also appreciated the value of a fine impression, a complete oeuvre, and a great rarity. That Zomer should invoke such terms in an appeal to potential buyers implies that by 1720 the criteria he observed had gained general acceptance. On the other hand, Zomer certainly ranks among the first amateurs whose entire approach to collecting was based upon the values of print connoisseurship. Concentrating on the quality and rarity of the individual impression, he strove to establish a choice collection, not a universal one.

Print Connoisseurship in the Seventeenth Century

Zomer's sophisticated approach to collecting raises the question of the beginnings of print connoisseurship. To be sure, we cannot pinpoint the exact moment when collectors began to discriminate between a good and an excellent impression, to seek out trial proofs, or to pursue the rare sheet that would perfect their oeuvre of Dürer or Lucas van Leyden. However, we can affirm that most criteria applied today to the evaluation of old master prints were well established by 1700.

The problem of authenticity has never preoccupied connoisseurs of engravings to the degree that it has exercised collectors of paintings or drawings. Seventeenth-century amateurs recognized two kinds of spurious prints: copies intended to pass as originals and impressions from exhausted, reengraved plates. Copies of works by Lucas van Leyden, Albrecht Dürer, and other popular masters had circulated since the sixteenth century.[81] In his *Sculptura* of 1662, John Evelyn listed some of the "skillfully accurate" counterfeits, "for their sakes, who are collectors of these curiosities, and may not happily be yet arriv'd to the judgment of being able to discerne them from the Originals."[82]

In 1649 the etcher Abraham Bosse published his *Sentiments sur la Distinction des diverses Manières de Peinture, Dessein & Gravure, & des Originaux d'avec leurs Copies,* a handbook for connoisseurs of painting, drawing, and engraving. Bosse filled four pages with pointers for distinguishing a copy from an original print. Copyists lacked the inventiveness and facility characteristic of more gifted masters, he asserted. Their lines and hatchings were labored and failed to capture the delicate half-tones; they were "hard, dry and very often blacker than the originals."[83]

Bosse, Evelyn, and Roger North addressed the problem of reengraved plates. North, as executor of Pieter Lely's estate, arranged the first sale of the painter's fabulous collection of prints and drawings in 1688. It was North who stamped the collector's mark "PL" on some 10,000 sheets prior to their dispersal.[84] In his manuscript autobiography, North recorded some of the fine points of connoisseurship he had imbibed during the Lely sale. After noting the existence of copies, he mentioned the practice of strengthening an exhausted plate: "Another disguise prints have, which they call touched up, is when a plate with many stamps is worn and its delicacy taken off, some graver will pass his tool lightly over all the strokes, and give them a little briskness or sharpening. This is harder to discern, but I found that the printmongers soon discovered it."[85] Bosse advised his readers that an image from a reengraved plate, even if printed well, looks pale and gray next to an early impression from the unretouched plate.[86]

The quality of the impression and the condition of the paper were carefully appraised by seventeenth-century collectors. As early as 1609 these factors influenced the market value of Dürer prints. In his *Splendor of the German Nation,* published in that year, Matthias Quadt von Kinckelbach wrote that a complete album of Dürer engravings consisted of 100 prints, plus 4 or 5 others, "very difficult to find," which the master had left uncompleted. Such an album usually sold for 100 "Goldgulden," provided that the engravings were "distinctly and well printed." However, he went on, one could find them priced at more than 150 gulden and at less than 60, according to whether they were "fresh or poor in the paper and printing."[87]

In 1649 Bosse affirmed that avid connoisseurs acquired only fine and well-preserved impressions: "Those who are most curious of prints insist on the earliest impressions, when the lines and hatchings print black and very distinctly, and that the paper itself be very white."[88] Florent Le Comte divided print collectors into three categories, depending upon their capacity to select and procure outstanding impressions. The collector in the first category, "le grand Curieux,...can have the best without worrying about the price, and will not experience many difficulties in the search for beautiful proofs, true originals, and the finest impressions."[89] Collectors in the second category sacrificed quality for the sake of economy or expediency. They truly desired good prints but balked at the trouble and expense of finding excellent impressions in good condition. As for the third group, quality did not concern them at all. They required prints only for the decoration of their apartments.[90]

The "grand Curieux" of the seventeenth century, like his descendants in our time, placed a premium on proof impressions. A bemused Roger North observed the ardor for proofs and other early impressions among the connoisseurs at the Lely sale in 1688: "The matter of prints is very nice, for such as come off the same plate shall be decuple the value of others. For this is by the earliness of the stamp before the plate is worn, for with often printing the delicacy of the graver will wear off...but above all a proof print is most esteemed, which is an impression before the plate is finished, done for the satisfaction of the graver, who perhaps while he is at work will often roll off a sheet to see how the draught proves, that he may mend or alter it if he sees cause. And these proof prints are known by some unfinished part that appears."[91] An advertisement for the Lely auction carried by the *London Gazette* in February 1688, referred explicitly to the proofs that were among the highlights of the collection.[92] Other connoisseurs shared Lely's predilection for such prints. J.P. Zomer, as mentioned, repeatedly vaunted the proofs in his cabinet.[93] Rembrandt assembled an entire album of *proefdrukken* (proof impressions) of engravings after Rubens and Jacob Jordaens.[94]

The allure of a rare plate and the satisfaction of owning the complete works of a favorite master provoked lively competition and extraordinary expenditures for certain prints. Fine engravings by Lucas van Leyden were notoriously difficult to come by.[95] Sandrart described the rivalry among connoisseurs who vied for "more and better impressions" of them on the Amsterdam market. At one auction Rembrandt bid 1,400 guilders – nearly the amount he received for painting the *Night Watch* – for fourteen engravings by Lucas.[96]

Sandrart, a keen and well-informed connoisseur, knew only one impression of Lucas's so-called *Uilenspiegel* (B. 159). The celebrated rarity belonged to Peter Spiering, a Swedish agent at the Hague. In order to complete his album of the "most perfect impressions" of all Lucas's engravings and etchings, Spiering laid out 400 guilders for the *Uilenspiegel* and 500 for the large *Expulsion of Hagar* (B. 17), another rare plate.[97] An *Uilenspiegel* also graced Rembrandt's album of etchings and engravings by Lucas. "This love for paper art has gone so far in our time," wrote Rembrandt's pupil Samuel van Hoogstraten, that Rembrandt paid some 200 guilders for that print alone.[98] Veneration for Lucas was not confined to his native Holland. Michel de Marolles proudly claimed the unique complete album of Lucas's works in his country, "including the *Uilenspiegel*, the only one in France, the other one having been sold for 16 Louis d'or."[99]

The infatuation with rarities and the complete oeuvre inspired La Bruyère's immortal caricature of a print connoisseur. In his classic *The Characters, or the Customs of this Century*, published in 1688, La Bruyère created the monomaniacal collector Démocède.

"You wish to see my prints," says Démocède, and he forthwith brings them out and sets them before you. You see one which is neither black nor neat nor well designed.... He admits that it is engraved badly and designed worse, but hastens to inform you that it is the work of an Italian artist who produced very little, and that the plate had hardly any printing; that, moreover, it is the only one of its kind in France; that he paid much for it, and would not exchange it for something far better. 'I am,' he adds, 'in such serious trouble that it will prevent any further collecting. I have all of Callot but one print, which is not one of his best, but actually one of his worst; nevertheless, it would complete my Callot. I have been looking for it for twenty years, and, despairing of success, I find life very hard, indeed."[100]

Connoisseurs bent on assembling Rembrandt's complete works were undeterred by his practice of issuing some prints in multiple states. Arnold Houbraken, who published a biography of Rembrandt in his *Great Theater of Netherlandish Painters and Painteresses* of 1718, testified that even during the master's lifetime, collectors could not rest until they owned all the states of every print: "the passion was so great at that time, that people would not be taken for true connoisseurs who did not have the Juno with and without the crown, the Joseph with the white face and the brown face and other such things."[101] J.P. Zomer, as we have seen, hailed his collection of Rembrandt's etchings as "complete, including every state."[102] In 1689 the English connoisseur and bibliophile Richard

Maitland, fourth Earl of Lauderdale (1653–1695), sold at auction "Rembrandt's Complete Work, 420 figures."[103] Like Zomer, whose albums contained 428 prints, Maitland had probably tried to secure every available state.[104]

Collectors of Rembrandt's etchings knew that the Dutch master endeavored to create exquisite nuances of tone by printing some impressions on delicate and absorbent oriental papers. The rarity and beauty of these impressions ensured the demand for them. In 1699 Roger de Piles wrote, "Rembrandt had a number of his proofs taken on half tint paper, especially China paper…impressions of which are sought by connoisseurs."[105]

Criticism: "the best resemblance of Painting"

Seventeenth-century collectors applied the criteria of print connoisseurship in evaluating an individual impression. Critics, however, invoked a different set of principles in their appraisals of a printmaker's style. A thorough consideration of their ideas would require a separate essay, but for the purpose of this essay, discussion will be limited to one theme that is particularly pertinent to the contemporary appreciation of Dutch prints.

Although critics enjoyed the neatness and finish typical of engravings by Dürer or Lucas,[106] they reserved their warmest praise for printmakers who created effects of light and tone that simulated the fluidity and coloristic richness of a painting or wash drawing. Gifted reproductive engravers, such as Cornelis Bloemaert and Lucas Vorsterman, as well as innovative etchers like Rembrandt and Hercules Segers, were applauded for the pictorial qualities of their prints.

Seventeenth-century writers did not regard reproductive engraving as a mindless, mechanical operation. To be sure, a printmaker was expected to represent accurately the appearance of the original; nevertheless, each engraver had his personal style. Every plate resulted from an act of interpretation that demanded judgment, skill, and imagination.[107]

Several authors maintained that the most successful reproductive prints conveyed a clear idea of the tonal harmony and coloration of the original painting.[108] John Evelyn attributed the aesthetic appeal of engravings to the agreeable sensation communicated by modulations of tone. He likened the ineffable charm of tonal nuance to musical harmony. Through the union of delicately graduated shades of black and gray, the printmaker could approximate the colorism of the painter's art. Colorism in engraving, Evelyn wrote, was a "certain admirable effect," achieved "where the shades of the Hatches intend, and remit to the best resemblance of *Painting,* the Commissures of the light and dark parts, imperceptably united, or at least so sweetly conducted as that the alteration could no more certainly be defin'd, than the *Semitons* and *Harmoge* in *musick*… yet it is so gentle, and so agreeable, as even ravishes our senses, by a secret kind of charme not to be expressed in words, or discerned by the ignorant."[109] The challenge confronting the reproductive engraver, Evelyn went on, lay in the difficulty of realizing this undefinable harmony. To translate the subtle brushwork of a great artist into an equivalent system of lines and cross hatchings required a thorough knowledge of painting and drawing, and "more than the ordinary talent of *Gravers*."[110]

A capacity to describe pictorial qualities in black and white was indispensable to an engraver working after the supreme colorist, Peter Paul Rubens. Lucas Vorsterman (1595–1675), the most gifted printmaker in Rubens's circle, was celebrated for his handling of light and tone. According to Sandrart, Vorsterman's virtuosity earned him an appropriate nickname: "the Painter with the Burin."[111]

Sandrart recounted Vorsterman's development of a naturalistic and pictorial style appropriate to the task of reproducing the paintings of Rubens. Vorsterman's earliest prints, with their swelling and tapering *tailles* and "beautiful elegance of the burin," aped the graceful manner of Hendrik Goltzius. On the advice of Rubens, however, Vorsterman abandoned the laborious and decorative technique of his youth. Instead, "he observed completely and exclusively the thing itself which he intended to depict, namely, in addition to correct proportion in everything, the areas of daylight, juxtaposed with the half and full areas of shadows and reflections; wherein he became so astonishingly skillful that everything appeared rounded, discrete, and in relief as strongly as he wished."[112] Vorsterman's new style so effectively reproduced the appearance of a painting, Sandrart added, that "it could not be done better with a brush in black and white."[113]

The appreciation of pictorial qualities in prints was not limited to engravings after paintings. Samuel van Hoogstraten praised Hercules Segers's efforts to introduce color into his etchings. Hoogstraten aptly characterized the images Segers printed on tinted cloths and papers. Segers, he wrote, "printed painting."[114] He likened the results of the artist's innovations to the effect of a chiaroscuro woodcut. The latter process, Hoogstraten noted, gave painterly ("schilderachtige") prints: "But *Herkules Zegers* first covered papers and canvasses with soft grounds of color, for skies, backgrounds, and foregrounds, and then printed on them, very artfull and painterly."[115]

Rembrandt's etchings also appealed to the taste for pictorial effects. In a treatise on etching and engraving, published in 1686, Filippo Baldinucci applauded Rembrandt's expressive chiaroscuro and his ability to suggest color through the manipulation of light and shade. The Dutch artist's unique and "most bizarre" technique, Baldinucci wrote, consisted of "certain scribbles and little scratches and irregular, isolated strokes, the result of the whole, however, being a deep and powerful chiaroscuro, and a thoroughly pictorial sensibility; covering the plate in some places with an intense black, and leaving in others the white of the paper; and according to the coloration he wished to give to the costumes of his figures, either in the foregrounds or in the backgrounds, using sometimes the lightest shading and sometimes a simple stroke, nothing more."[116]

The climax of Rembrandt's search for pictorial effects roughly coincided with the invention of mezzotint, the most painterly of engraving techniques. Critics did not fail to recognize the similarity between his manner of etching and the tonal qualities of the new medium. Arnold Houbraken wrote of Rembrandt's portrait of *Jan Cornelisz. Sylvius* (cat. no. 97) that "the tender, sparkling shadows were…as well and as delicately handled as mezzotint work."[117]

In a few seventeenth-century collections, Dutch prints distinguished by their chiaroscuro and painterly style were organized into distinct albums. Florent Le Comte included a volume of "Nuits et pièces noires" by Rembrandt, Hendrik Goudt, J.G. van Vliet, Jan van de Velde, and others in the art-historical division of his ideal cabinet.[118] Prints by Van de Velde, Goudt, and Van Vliet figured in an album entitled "Various Nocturnes" in the collection of the Abbé de Marolles.[119] Next to his book of "Nocturnes," Marolles shelved another volume containing Dutch prints notable for their pictorial qualities. It housed an especially beautiful group of Goudt's engravings after Adam Elsheimer, 224 works by Rembrandt, and 36 etchings by Adriaen van Ostade.[120]

Richard Maitland, fourth Earl of Lauderdale, was especially attracted to Dutch masters who strove for coloristic effects in their prints. In addition to the "Complete Work of Rembrandt," Maitland owned "Eight Landskips in Colours by *Herc. Segers*," "A Small *Oeuvre* of Ostade, forty prints," "Ten Black Prints by [Jan] *van de Velde*," and Goudt's engravings after Elsheimer. The last, most of them night scenes, were also described as "black prints" in the earl's auction catalogue of 1689.[121]

NOTES

I am especially grateful to Clifford S. Ackley, who invited me to write this essay and who, in frequent and lengthy conversations, contributed significantly to its form and content. For assistance in the preparation of the essay I would also like to thank David Becker; S.A.C. Dudok van Heel, Gemeentearchief, Amsterdam; Egbert Haverkamp-Begemann, Institute of Fine Arts, New York University; Margaret Jupe, Museum of Fine Arts, Boston; Thomas Kaufman, Princeton University; Robert Nikirk, the Grolier Club; Konrad Oberhuber, Fogg Art Museum, Harvard University; Peter Parshall, Reed College; Sue Welsh Reed, Museum of Fine Arts, Boston; Elizabeth Roth, The New York Public Library; Richard Simpson, Fine Arts Library, Harvard University.

1. Le Comte, 1699, vol. 1, pp. 158–159.

2. Marolles, 1755, p. 296.

3. Le Comte, 1699, vol. 1, p. 158.

4. The role of prints in the dissemination of visual information is the subject of Ivins, 1953.

5. De Piles, 1699, p. 77; English translation, De Piles, 1706, p. 56 (the English edition is referred to hereafter as De Piles, 1706).

6. De Piles, 1699, p. 75; De Piles, 1706, p. 54.

7. De Piles, 1699, pp. 77–78; De Piles, 1706, p. 56.

8. "L'Arrêt de St. Jean-de-Luze," 26 May 1660; quoted by Bouvy, 1924, pp. 31–32.

9. Bouvy, 1924, p. 32.

10. De Piles, 1699, p. 75; De Piles, 1706, p. 54.

11. De Piles, 1699, p. 85.

12. Ibid.; De Piles, 1706, p. 63.

13. Hoogstraten, 1678, p. 196.

14. Van Mander/Davaco, 1969, fol. 282–283; Reznicek, 1961, pp. 3–6.

15. Ijzerman, 1926, discusses the prints traded on the Malay peninsula in 1602. A Dutch expedition seeking a northern route to the Far East in 1596 also carried quantities of prints by Goltzius, De Gheyn, and others; see cat. no. 1 in this volume. See also Vos, 1978, pp. 52–53.

16. Slive, 1953, pp. 30, 32–33, 63.

17. Ibid., pp. 59–62; Rosenberg, 1944, p. 130.

18. A portfolio listed in the inventory of Netscher's widow contained "327 soo prenten als teyckeningen van weijnigh waarde, dienende voor discipelen om na te teyckenen"; Bredius, 1887, p. 273.

19. The album is in the Rijksprentenkabinet, Amsterdam; Münster, 1974, cat. no. 115, pp. 238–241. The print collection of the Ter Borch family has also survived; Münster, 1974, pp. 207–208. Amateurs, too, learned to draw by copying prints. In November, 1666, Samuel Pepys bought prints from William Faithorne "for my wife to draw by this winter."; Levis, 1915, p. 65.

20. Karpinski, 1963, p. 211.

21. Prints were sold in Amsterdam estate auctions at least as early as 1612; Bredius, *Künstler-Inventare*, vol. 2, pp. 396–397; vol. 7, pp. 1746–1748. One hundred and fifty advertisements for later Amsterdam art auctions, many of them including prints, were published by Dudok van Heel, 1975.

22. One of the earliest London library auctions to include prints was the sale of Arthur, Earl of Anglesey, Oct. 25, 1686. Eighteen lots of prints were offered; Lawler, 1898, p. 154.

23. Abraham Bosse published and sold his own prints; Karpinski, 1963, p. 213. So did the English engraver William Faithorne. During the 1660s Samuel Pepys paid several visits to Faithorne's shop, where he purchased many of the artist's portrait engravings; Levis, 1915, pp. 65–68, 72.

24. Pepys put Faithorne's portrait of *Lady Castlemaine*, one of his favorite prints, into a gilt frame; Levis, 1915, p. 68. Eleven etchings and sixty-four mezzotints in gilt frames are listed in the inventory of Cornelis Dusart's estate, 1702; Bredius, *Künstler-Inventare*, vol. 1, pp. 36, 189, 190. "A print by Goltzius in an ebony frame" hung in the house of the Haarlem painter Bartolomeus Molenaer in 1650; Bredius, *Künstler-Inventare*, vol. 6, p. 2047. The inventory of the portraitist David Beckx,

1656, included "13 small prints in frames, round as well as rectangular," and ten prints on "rolletgens." Prints and maps on *rollen* appear in the paintings of Nicolaes Maes, for example, in his *Lacemaker,* National Gallery of Canada. Some prints were sold already framed. A London bookseller's advertisement of 1688 offered "all sorts of Curious Prints, *English, French,* and *Dutch,* either in Frames or in Sheets, very ornamental for Closets and other Rooms"; Levis, 1915, p. 30. In 1695 Queen Mary decorated her "closet" in the new building at Hampton Court with framed prints; Huygens, *Journalen*, p. 551.

25. Levis, 1915, pp. 72–73.

26. The following discussion of Quicchelberg's *Inscriptiones…* and of the role of prints in his theoretical collection is based upon Hajós, 1958, and Berliner, 1928, pp. 329–331.

27. Scheller, 1969, is an excellent introduction to *Kunstkammer* collections and their place in the culture of the sixteenth and seventeenth centuries.

28. Hajós, 1958, pp. 151–152.

29. Hajós, 1958, p. 153, lists the thirty-two subject headings, following Quicchelberg's arrangement of the volumes on three shelves.

30. For Ferdinand's *Kunstkammer* at Schloss Ambras, see Lhotsky, 1941–1945, pp. 179–202; and Innsbruck, 1977, "Introduction."

31. Ambras, Schloss, Inventory, 1596, pp. CCLXXXVIII–CCXC.

32. I am indebted to Dr. Peter Parshall, who is preparing a study of the print collection from Schloss Ambras, for his help in identifying the albums in the inventory that contained prints and for his estimate of the number of impressions in the surviving albums. The latter are preserved in the Kunsthistorisches Museum, Vienna, Sammlung für Plastik und Kunstgewerbe; Innsbruck, 1977, cat. no. 197. Another important sixteenth-century collection, containing some 7,000 prints, has survived intact. It is in the library of the Palace of El Escorial; El Escorial, cat., 1963–1966.

33. Ambras, Schloss, Inventory, 1596, pp. CCLXXXVIII–CCXC.

34. Dr. Peter Parshall called my attention to the Dürer album, which does not appear in the inventory of 1596.

35. Sandrart, 1679, pp. 316–318. Sandrart gave a muddled account of the collection's history. It was founded by Melchior Ayrer, a physician, between 1550 and 1570. Sandrart wrongly maintained that the founder was a Dr. Johann Aegidius Ayrer, who lived in Dürer's time; Heller, 1831, p. 63. According to Heller, Melchior bequeathed his collection of paintings, drawings, prints, and books to his son, Julius. Julius Ayrer built up the holdings of engravings and woodcuts, which amounted to 20,000 sheets when inherited by his son, Johann Aegidius; Heller, 1831, pp. 63–64.

36. The twelve artists appeared in the following order in the Ayrer albums: Israel van Meckenem, Martin Schongauer, Albrecht Dürer, Lucas van Leyden, Master MZ (Matthaeus Za[i]singer), Heinrich Aldegrever, Hans Brosamer, Jacob Binck, Albrecht Altdorfer, Barthel

Beham, Hans Sebald Beham, Georg Pencz; see Sandrart, 1679, pp. 316–318.Another Nuremberger, Paul Behaim III (1592–1637), also established an extensive and important collection. His northern prints of the fifteenth and sixteenth centuries included 71 engravings by Dürer, 69 by Lucas van Leyden, 39 by Schongauer, all the works of Master MZ, and nearly all the prints of Pencz. Behaim organized his collection by artist but not chronologically. A manuscript catalogue, compiled by Behaim himself, has come down to us; Wessely, 1883. As early as 1565, Quicchelberg called attention to the rich print collections formed by Nurembergers; Hajós, 1958, p. 154, n. 22.

37. For the "Dürer Renaissance" of about 1600, see cat. no. 7. See also Reznicek, 1961, p. 54, n. 15; Wessely, 1877, p. 22. Ample evidence of the appreciation of Dürer and Lucas van Leyden in the Netherlands can be found in Van Mander/Davaco, 1969, particularly in his lives of the two masters and in his biography of Hendrik Goltzius, folio 284–285. The earliest history of printmaking in Germany and the Netherlands, which appeared in Quadt von Kinckelbach, 1609, focused largely on the achievements of Dürer, Lucas, and Dürer's followers; Kutter, 1926–27, p. 230; Pelka, 1934, pp. 190–191; Fuhse, 1895, p. 74.

38. Sandrart certainly understood the Ayrer albums as a survey of the history of printmaking. At the beginning of his partial inventory of the collection, Sandrart noted the chronological arrangement and referred the reader to his own account of the origins and development of engraving, etching, and woodcut; Sandrart, 1679, p. 316. Later authors, such as Roger de Piles and Florent Le Comte, recommended the study of prints as a means of cultivating good taste and understanding the history of the fine arts; De Piles, 1699, pp. 82–83; Le Comte, 1699, vol. 1, "Differens Catalogues," p. 3. An important precedent for the use of works on paper to illustrate the history of art is Giorgio Vasari's "Libro dei disegni." Vasari arranged his collection of drawings to document the development of Italian art from the fourteenth to the sixteenth century; Degenhart and Schmitt, 1968.

39. Sandrart, 1679, p. 316.

40. The inventory of Basse's estate was published by Bredius, *Künstler-Inventare*, vol. 1, pp. 127–147.

41. Bredius, *Künstler-Inventare*, vol. 1, pp. 136–137, nos. 40–62.

42. Ibid., nos. 63–76. This page of the manuscript of the inventory, including a list of the printmakers' monograms, is reproduced by Strauss/Van der Meulen, 1979, p. 142.

43. Bredius, *Künstler-Inventare*, vol. 1, pp. 137–138, and Supplement, pp. 10, 12.

44. The Earl of Arundel must have communicated an interest in the sale to his agent in the Netherlands, Daniel Mytens. Mytens wrote to the earl's secretary on 12 March 1637: "Concerning the Auxion or outcry of John Basse at Amsterdam, is past and begon the 9th of this presente, and there was great store of printes and drawings. Mr. Everard solde by smale parcells, but verie fewe pictures, not for my Lordes turne"; Hervey, 1921, p. 405.

45. Strauss/Van der Meulen, 1979, pp. 140–143. The album of prints by Lucas van Leyden was bought by Rembrandt's pupil Leendert Cornelisz. van Beyeren. Bredius, *Künstler-Inventare,* vol. 1, pp. 127–128, assumed that Van Beyeren was acting on Rembrandt's behalf and that the album entered Rembrandt's collection. However, as Dudok van Heel pointed out, an album of prints by Lucas was listed in the inventory of Van Beyeren's estate. For a summary of this issue, see Strauss/Van der Meulen, 1979, pp. 143, 576.

46. Scheller, 1969, established that Rembrandt's collection belonged to the *Kunstkammer* type. Bredius, *Künstler-Inventare,* vol. 1, p. 128, called attention to the similarity between Rembrandt's collection and the collection of Jan Basse.

47. The inventory of Rembrandt's *Kunstboecken* is published in Strauss/Van der Meulen, 1979, pp. 367–379.

48. Strauss/Van der Meulen, p. 369, no. 200. The "kostelijcke boeck" of Mantegna presumably housed mainly prints but may also have contained Mantegna's drawing *The Calumny of Apelles,* which Rembrandt copied around the time the inventory was compiled. For Rembrandt's drawing see Benesch, 1973, no. 1207.

49. Strauss/Van der Meulen, p. 369, no. 205; p. 369, no. 206 ("very precious"); p. 371, no. 214 ("very beautiful impressions").

50. Ibid., p. 371, no. 216.

51. Quoted by Scheller, 1969, p. 130.

52. A fine introduction to print collecting in this period is Koschatzky, 1963.

53. The print collection assembled by Louis XIV was a division of the Royal Library. For print collections that were associated with private libraries, see Turner (Samuel Pepys); Maitland, cat., 1688; Maitland, cat., 1689; Beeresteyn, cat., 1695; Boucot, cat., 1699.

54. De Piles, 1699, p. 77; De Piles, 1706, p. 56.

55. Marolles, 1755, pp. 288–297. Marolles, 1666, is the earliest published catalogue of a collection of prints. Excerpts from Marolles's preface to the catalogue are quoted by Thibaudeau, 1857, pp. XXX–XLIV. For Marolles and his collections, see also Lugt, p. 339, no. 1855; Koschatzky, 1963, pp. 9–11.

56. Marolles, 1666, "Discours en forme de Preface," quoted by Thibaudeau, 1857, p. XXXIX.

57. Evelyn, 1662, p. 141. Evelyn's discussion of the usefulness of prints in education appears on pages 138–145. In his treatise on engraving, John Evelyn translated into English much of the section on print collecting in Marolles's *Mémoires;* Evelyn, 1662, pp. 134–137. Marolles, 1672, p. 68, also supported the use of prints in the education of young people, "to cultivate their memories and to mould their judgment."

58. The "Idée d'une belle bibliothèque d'Estampes" appears in Le Comte, 1699, vol. 1, "Differens Catalogues," pp. 2–28.

59. Le Comte, 1699, vol. 1, "Differens Catalogues," p. 3.

60. Marolles, 1666, p. 15.

61. A list of the subjects covered in Marolles's collection is published in Marolles, 1755, pp. 289–290. The list was translated into English by Evelyn, 1662, p. 136.

62. Marolles, 1666, album nos. LXXXV–CCLXXVI.

63. Ibid., p. 19.

64. Ibid., album nos.: I (Raphael); XXIX (Lucas van Leyden); XV (Parmigianino); XX (Callot); LXIV (Rembrandt and Ostade); LXIII (Cornelis Visscher).

65. Ibid., album nos. CCLXXVII–CCXCV ("Vieux Maistres"); and CCCLVI–CDXI ("Petits Maistres").

66. For Marolles's collection of fifteenth-century and early sixteenth-century prints, see his albums of "Vieux Maistres," n. 65. Sandrart wrote an interesting account of the origins of printmaking. He rightly claimed that engraving, woodcut, and chiaroscuro woodcut were invented in Germany, correcting Vasari's statements about the early history of prints; Sandrart/Peltzer, 1675, pp. 59–61. Here, and elsewhere in his *Teutche Academie,* Sandrart displays an unexpected knowledge of and interest in early northern prints; see also Sandrart, 1679, pp. 316–318. For Le Comte's discussion of Gothic prints, see Le Comte, 1699, vol. 1, pp. 160–187.

67. Marolles, 1672.

68. See Sandrart, 1679, pp. 314–315, for Von Stubenberg's collection. On Von Stubenberg's life see Loserth, 1911, pp. 256–259.

69. Sandrart, 1679, p. 315.

70. For other collectors who organized distinct albums or groups of albums containing mezzotints, see Sandrart, 1679, pp. 315–316 (Carl Welser, Nuremberg); Van Dyk, 1790, no. 39 (Michiel Tymensz. Hinloopen, 1619–1708); Beeresteyn, cat., 1695, "Nederlantsche Printen," nos. 97–107; Maitland, cat., 1688, no. 64; Boucot, cat., 1699, no. 123, and "Portraits," no. 8. In the latter entry, mezzotint is called "la maniere d'Angleterre."

71. For other encyclopedic print collections, see Koschatzky, 1963, p. 11 (J.W. Valvasor, collection complete in 1691); Turner, pp. 12–13 (Samuel Pepys); Van Dyk, 1790; Boon, 1964; and Dudok Van Heel, 1969 (Michiel Tymensz. Hinloopen, 1619–1708); Maitland, cat., 1688; Maitland, cat., 1689 (Richard Maitland, fourth Earl of Lauderdale, 1653–1695); Boucot, cat., 1699 (Nicolas Boucot, died 1699).

72. For example, the Dutch collector François Halma (1653–1722) established a cabinet devoted exclusively to the geography and topography of the Netherlands; Lugt, p. 33, no. 195.

73. On Clément, see Lugt, p. 106, no. 588, with earlier literature.

74. Gaignières's prints were arranged by country. For each nation, he divided the prints into three groups. A topographical category began with general maps of the country, followed by detailed maps of its provinces, plans of the cities, and views of the environs and principal buildings of each city. Another group consisted of prints relating to the history of the country, including illustrations of festivals, processions, ceremonies, fashions, and other customs. The third division was devoted to the illustri-

ous men and women who played a role in the nation's history. It began with portraits of the rulers and nobility, followed by high officials of the state, the church, and the army, distinguished representatives of the professions, and so on. On Gaignières and his collection, see De Piles, 1699, pp. 86–87; Lugt, p. 200, no. 135. Forerunners of Gaignières's historical collection are the "paper museum" of Cassiano dal Pozzo, which, like Gaignières's albums, contained both prints and drawings; and the albums of drawings assembled by Jacopo da Strada (1515–1588). Both collections were devoted to the civilization of antiquity. On Cassiano dal Pozzo, see Haskell, 1963, pp. 100–102. On Jacopo da Strada, see Lhotsky, 1941–1945, pp. 160–163. I owe the latter reference to Konrad Oberhuber.

75. Levis, 1915, p. 82.

76. Charrington, 1936; Turner, pp. 12–13.

77. Zomer's career as auctioneer and appraiser is studied by Dudok van Heel, 1977. His activity as a collector of prints and drawings is summarized by Lugt, pp. 276–277, no. 1511.

78. Zomer, cat. Both Lugt, p. 227, and Dudok van Heel, 1977, p. 105, date Zomer's catalogue between 1720 and his death in 1724.

79. Zomer, cat., portfolio 3.P.

80. Zomer sold his Rembrandt etchings to A.M. Zanetti in 1720, before he published the catalogue of the rest of his collection. The appraisal quoted here appeared in one of the albums sold to Zanetti; Lugt, p. 277.

81. For some copies after Dürer, see Boston, 1971, nos. 65, 89, 196, 200.

82. Evelyn, 1662, p. 71. Evelyn further discusses copies after Dürer and Lucas on p. 63, and on p. 129, "How to detect a copy of a *Print* from an original Print." According to Evelyn, almost everything engraved by Dürer and Lucas had been copied; Evelyn, 1662, p. 64. The Abbé de Marolles compiled an entire album of "Copies de Lucas et d'Albert"; Marolles, 1666, album no. CCLXVIII.

83. Bosse, 1649, p. 83. Bosse's discussion of copies appears on pp. 82–85.

84. Lugt, pp. 387–389, gives a thorough account of the Lely sales and of North's role in them.

85. Jessopp, 1887, p. 204.

86. Bosse, 1649, p. 85.

87. Fuhse, 1895, p. 74.

88. Bosse, 1649, p. 85.

89. Le Comte, 1699, vol. 1, p. 160.

90. Ibid.

91. Jessopp, 1887, p. 202.

92. *London Gazette*, 13–16 Feb. 1688: "The Prints are all the Works of Mark Antoine after Raphael, and other the best Italian Masters, and of the best Impressions, and Proof Prints, in Good Condition, and Curiously preserved"; quoted by Lugt, pp. 388–389.

93. Zomer, cat., portfolio 23. P, portfolio 3.P, and title page.

94. Strauss/Van der Meulen, 1979, p. 375, no. 245. References to proof impressions also appear in the advertisements for art auctions published by Dudok van Heel, 1975, p. 154, no. 2; p. 162, no. 70.

95. Sandrart, 1679, p. 317, noted the scarcity of good impressions of Lucas's works in Germany. The engravings, he wrote, were, "fast alle sehre rar zu bekommen und von den besten Abtrucken in Teutschland selten zu finden."

96. Sandrart/Peltzer, 1925, p. 86.

97. Ibid., p. 86. The subject of the so-called *Uilenspiegel* was not identified until 1976; Silver, 1976.

98. According to Hoogstraten, Rembrandt paid 80 Rijksdaalders for his *Uilenspiegel;* Hoogstraten, 1678, p. 212; Slive, 1953, p. 97, n. 2. One Rijksdaalder was equal to 2.5 guilders. Another collector of Lucas's prints was the publisher-bookseller Johannes Blaeuw. Evelyn, 1662, p. 63, reported that Blaeuw paid the equivalent of 100 pounds sterling for a complete oeuvre of engravings by Lucas. Johannes Wtenbogaert, the Receiver General portrayed in Rembrandt's etching B. 281, also formed an important collection of prints by Lucas. His Lucas album now belongs to the Rijksprentenkabinet, Amsterdam; Dudok van Heel, 1978, pp. 152–153.

99. Marolles, 1666, album no. XXIX. References to complete oeuvres of various masters also appear in the auction advertisements published by Dudok van Heel, 1975, p. 159, no. 42; p. 162, no. 70.

100. Metcalfe, 1912, p. 340.

101. Houbraken, 1718–1721, vol. 1, p. 271. Slive, 1953, p. 190, n. 4, identified the prints referred to by Houbraken as *Medea*, B. 112, and *Joseph Telling His Dreams*, B. 37.

102. Lugt, p. 277.

103. Maitland, cat., 1689, p. 1, no. 14: "Renbrantii Opera integra, four hundred and twenty figures." See also below, note 121.

104. An album in the sale of Cornelis Dusart's estate, 1704, might have housed all the states of the etchings by Dusart's teacher, Adriaen van Ostade. The catalogue of the auction described the contents of the volume as follows: "All the works of Adr. van Ostade, and the impressions of them complete"; Bredius, *Künstler-Inventare,* vol. 1, p. 69, no. 58.

105. De Piles, 1699, p. 434. Florent Le Comte also mentioned impressions of Rembrandt's etchings on oriental papers; Le Comte, 1699, vol. 1, p. 126. For a discussion of these references, see Slive, 1953, p. 137.

106. For the appreciation of neatness and finish in engraving, see Van Mander/Floerke, 1906, vol. 1, p. 82, 84 (on Dürer), 108 (on Lucas); Bosse, 1649, p. 75 (Dürer).

107. In his biography of Aegidius Sadeler, Sandrart wrote that many engravers turned out mere "projections of the originals," failing to capture their "essence." Sadeler's judicious burin, on the other hand, conveyed the "total meaning" of his model. Indeed, his engravings often seemed to improve the original; Sandrart/Peltzer, 1925, p. 241. On the creative imagination required of reproductive engravers, see also the "Maximes de Robert Nanteuil sur la gravure," Loriquet, 1886, pp. 78–79, nos. I, III, and VIII; "Arrêt de St. Jean-de-Luze," Bouvy, 1924, p. 32.

108. The ability of the best engravings to convey a sense of the color and tonal harmony of a painting is discussed by Evelyn, 1662, p. 127; Bosse, 1649, pp. 80–81; De Bie, 1661, pp. 476, 485; Le Comte, 1699, vol. 1, p. 155.

109. Evelyn, 1662, pp. 127–128.

110. Ibid., p. 128.

111. Sandrart/Peltzer, 1925, p. 244.

112. Ibid., p. 243.

113. Ibid., pp. 243–244.

114. Hoogstraten, 1678, p. 312. See Haverkamp-Begemann, 1973, p. 48.

115. Hoogstraten, 1678, p. 196. See also Haverkamp-Begemann, 1973, p. 48, 50.

116. Baldinucci, 1686, p. 80.

117. Houbraken, 1718–1721, vol. 1, p. 271. Rembrandt etched two portraits of Sylvius, B. 266 and B. 280. It is not clear which one Houbraken is referring to; Slive, 1953, p. 190, n. 1. De Piles, 1699, p. 434, and Le Comte, 1699, vol. 1, p. 126, also likened Rembrandt's etchings to mezzotint. See cat. no. 99 in this volume.

118. Le Comte, 1699, vol. 1, p. 21; Slive, 1953, p. 139.

119. Marolles, 1666, album no. LXIII.

120. Ibid., album no. LXIV.

121. Maitland, cat., 1689, p. 2, nos. 46, 59, 60, 63. Lugt, 1938, vol. 1, confused Richard Maitland, fourth Earl of Lauderdale, with his brother John, first Duke of Lauderdale, who died in 1682. For the correct identification, see Lawler, 1898, pp. 170–171. Following Lugt, K.G. Boon incorrectly assigned the collection of eight Hercules Segers etchings sold in 1689 to John Maitland; see Boon's "Introduction," in Haverkamp-Begemann, 1973, pp. 4–5. The Segers etchings belonged to Richard Maitland (1653–1695).

Use of the Catalogue

The catalogue is arranged in chronological order. Within a given decade liberties have often been taken with strict chronological sequence in order to bring into closer juxtaposition prints related in theme, style, or use of the media.

The artist's biography precedes the first entry on the artist's prints. As a result of the chronological ordering, an artist's works frequently do not occur together. See the index for a listing of catalogue numbers for each artist.

Catalogue entries

The dimensions of plate, block, or (if trimmed) sheet are given in millimeters: height precedes width. For abbreviations of frequently cited print catalogues, see the Bibliography (e.g., B. is the abbreviation for Bartsch, Holl. for Hollstein). Watermarks have not been cited unless clearly visible. Collectors' marks are cited according to Lugt numbers (see Bibliography). Unless the identification of the subject has changed, the titles of the prints used here are generally based on the titles of previous cataloguers. Dates assigned to undated prints in the headings are discussed in the text of the catalogue entry.

Illustrations are reduced unless indicated as "actual size." In text and footnotes the names of cities (e.g., Amsterdam, Rotterdam, Vienna) refer to the principal print rooms of those cities (e.g., Rijksmuseum, Boymans-van Beuningen, Albertina). Short bibliographical references have been used throughout. For the full reference see the Bibliography.

Latin terms engraved on prints

in., inv., inventor, invenit: invented or designed [it]
fe., fec., fecit, faciebat: made [it] (often used to indicate that the artist both designed and executed the print)
sc., sculp., sculpsit: engraved [it]
ex., exc., excudit, excudebat: published [it]
For other Latin terms on prints and their abbreviations, see Mayor, 1971, Appendix.

Hendrik Goltzius
1558–1617

Hendrik Goltzius was regarded by his contemporaries and by later generations as one of the most brilliant engravers of all time. Between his first dated engravings of 1576–1578 and his last dated print, a drypoint of 1605, Goltzius produced some 350 engravings, about 20 woodcuts, a series of 12 etchings, and 3 drypoints.[1] He published his own work and encouraged the sale of his prints abroad.[2] In addition, about five hundred of his designs were engraved by his followers. Through his activities and through the prints of his pupils Jacob Matham, Jacques de Gheyn II, and Jan Saenredam, Goltzius was responsible for a wave of late Renaissance printmaking in the North Netherlands so strongly stamped with his personality that one author has dubbed it the "Goltzius style."[3]

Goltzius's friend and biographer, the painter Karel van Mander, the "Dutch Vasari," records that Goltzius was born in 1558 at Mühlbracht near Venlo, in the Rhine country near the Dutch border.[4] After his family moved to Duisburg, Goltzius studied with his father, Jan Goltz, a glass painter. In spite of a childhood accident in which the "fat, wild and lively" child fell into a fire and permanently crippled his right hand, Goltzius was apprenticed about 1575 to Dirck Volckertsz. Coornhert to study the meticulous and demanding craft of engraving (see Glossary). Coornhert, a citizen of Haarlem, was then in Xanten and Cleves undergoing one of his not infrequent political exiles, for, in addition to being an engraver, he was a controversial humanist writer and politician whose outspoken liberal opinions on society and religion frequently embroiled him with the authorities. Coornhert, who often reproduced in his engravings the designs of the Italian-influenced Haarlem painter Maarten van Heemskerck, introduced the young Goltzius to the thriving Netherlandish print industry. Goltzius's first published prints were issued by the Antwerp engraver and publisher Phillips Galle, a pupil of Coornhert and successor to Hieronymus Cock, the mid-sixteenth-century publisher of prints after Bruegel,[5] as the leading print publisher of the Netherlands.

About 1576–77 Goltzius returned with Coornhert to settle in Haarlem, and in 1579 he married the widow Matham, whose eight-year-old stepson, Jacob Matham, became his pupil and engraved in his manner. In 1582 Goltzius began to publish his own prints. The fall of Antwerp to the Spanish in 1583 discouraged future collaboration with South Netherlandish publishers such as Galle.

The Spanish occupation of the South Netherlands resulted in a massive infusion of cultural vitality for the northern provinces as artists and craftsmen streamed north, impelled by the threat to their Protestant faith or by the disruption of artistic and economic life. These emigrants contributed greatly to the flourishing of the print publishing industry in Haarlem and Amsterdam in Goltzius's time.

Among the emigrant artists who settled in Haarlem was Karel van Mander. He had visited Italy, and he introduced Goltzius and other Haarlem artists, such as Cornelis Cornelisz., to the latest international developments in art and theory. He showed Goltzius drawings by Bartholomeus Spranger, the cosmopolitan Antwerp artist who was to become the court painter of the Holy Roman Emperor, Rudolph II, in Prague. Until this time Goltzius had engraved after and been influenced by the art of more conservative Italianizing Netherlandish artists, followers of Maarten van Heemskerck and Frans Floris. In 1585 he published his first engravings after Spranger or in Spranger's style, thus becoming one of the leading exponents of a highly sophisticated international style, which stressed a stylized elegance in the proportions and gestures of the human figure and placed the highest value on the artist's imagination or inventiveness. This international style, known to modern scholars as Mannerism, had its origins in the work of Italian artists such as Michelangelo and Parmigianino and can be viewed both as an extension and refinement of the works of the Italian artists of the "High Renaissance" of the early sixteenth century and as a conscious, often capricious, reaction against them.

Spurred on by a desire to see and study the works of ancient and modern masters and hoping to alleviate the effects of his consumptive condition, Goltzius departed for Italy in 1590, returning the following year. He never again engraved from the works of Spranger or the Mannerist artists of Haarlem but produced engravings after the works of Italian artists such as Raphael and Polidoro da Caravaggio or after the sculpture of classical antiquity. He began to produce his own virtuoso inventions in the styles of various sixteenth-century Italian painters and, above all, in the styles of the two great early sixteenth-century engravers of the Northern Renaissance, Albrecht Dürer and Lucas van Leyden. There was now a relaxation of the complex Mannerist torsions and tensions that had once characterized his figural compositions.

About 1600 Goltzius turned from printmaking to painting and was seldom active as a printmaker after that date. Van Mander suggests that he took up the brush because of the

---

1. These three late fantasy portrait busts, often wrongly described as etchings, are executed on round plates that have concentric marks, possibly resulting from turning on a lathe.

2. Hirschmann, 1919, p. 12. Karel van Mander reports that Goltzius saw his prints for sale in Rome. Goltzius also made arrangements for the sale of his prints in Paris and London.

3. Oberhuber, Vienna, 1967–68, pp. 196–203.

4. Possibly the village now called Bracht. See Rotterdam, 1972, pp. 3–4. For Goltzius's biography see Van Mander/Floerke, 1906, vol. 2, pp. 222–261.

5. For a discussion of Cock and the Netherlandish print industry of the sixteenth century see Riggs, 1971.

overwhelming, sensuous impression that Italian, especially Venetian, painting had made on him during his Italian journey.[6]

Throughout his life he was a many-faceted draftsman, particularly celebrated among his contemporaries for his "pen works" *(penwercken)*, elaborate, finished pen drawings on vellum or prepared canvas that imitated the calligraphic vocabulary of his engravings and sometimes rivaled paintings in their scale.

Goltzius died on New Year's Day, 1617, and was buried in Haarlem's great church of St. Bavo. His personal motto, a punning play on his own name that typifies the Haarlem Mannerists' love of literary conceits, was "Eer Boven Golt" (honor, glory above gold or wealth).

6. Van Mander/Floerke, 1906, vol. 2, pp. 250–251. Reznicek, 1960, mentions Goltzius's poor health and failing eyesight, the higher position occupied by painting in contemporary art theory, and the stimulus provided by the influx of painters from the South Netherlands as other probable reasons for Goltzius's turning from printmaking to painting.

1

HENDRIK GOLTZIUS
The Standard Bearer, 1587

Engraving
B. 125, Hirschmann 255, Holl. 255, Strauss 253
Lower center: *A° 1587. HGoltzius fe.*
287 x 192 mm. (sheet)
Rijksmuseum, Amsterdam. OB4639

The depiction of standard bearers was part of a tradition among German and Dutch engravers that reached back to the early sixteenth century, to Albrecht Dürer (B. 87) and to Lucas van Leyden (B. 140). Goltzius's *Standard Bearer* of 1587, however, is the boldest solution of all, surpassing even his own previous treatments of the subject (Hirschmann 251, 252) in originality of conception. Beginning with Dürer's engraving of about 1502–03, the standard bearer was usually represented as a static frontal figure with only the banner in motion. In Lucas's ver-

Signifer ingentes animos, et corda ministro,
Me stat stante phalanx, me fugiente fugit.

1

3

sion and in Goltzius's 1585 engraving (Hirschmann 252) the banner whips round behind the standard bearer, setting off his figure.

In the 1587 *Standard Bearer* the rippling, crackling banner billows out like a sail and has grown so large that it can no longer be contained within the frame. It is, indeed, the banner's floating folds that contribute the strongest sense of movement to the standard bearer's figure. The standard bearer combines foppishness and manly vigor as he strides forward, simultaneously turning with an elegant Mannerist torsion to encourage the following troops. The Latin verses engraved below the image state that when the standard bearer advances, the troops advance; when he flees, they flee.

The extreme refinement of the standard bearer's costume and its elegant, if bizarre, transformation of the human figure parallel the inventive transformations of Mannerist art. The slashed peascod (peapod) belly doublet with its surprising bird-breast silhouette may have restricted certain movements but, with a liberal use of stuffing, did succeed in defeating expectations about the shape of the human figure.[1] It is hardly surprising that Hirschmann suggested the possibility that the print represented a satire on the extravagances of contemporary fashion,[2] but it should also be remembered that it was part of the function of the standard bearer to be readily visible to the troops and through the splendor of his dress to embody the pride of his company.[3] The same dandified extravagance of costume is to be seen in the standard bearers or ensigns in the painted group portraits of Dutch militia com-

1. Larry Salmon, curator of the Department of Textiles, Museum of Fine Arts, kindly provided information on this extraordinary garment.

2. Hirschmann, 1919, pp. 99–100.

3. Egbert Haverkamp-Begemann pointed out in conversation that it was a great honor to be a standard bearer, that they were usually drawn from the upper classes and were traditionally bachelors because of the danger of their exposed position in combat.

panies of the late sixteenth and early seventeeth century.[4]

The *Standard Bearer* is one of a pair of military figures; the other, a pikeman (Hirschmann 254), is of similar dimensions and has a corresponding Latin inscription relating to military valor. One might assume that they were part of an incomplete series,[5] such as the series of military figures published by Goltzius in the same year and engraved by his pupil Jacques de Gheyn II after Goltzius's designs (Holl. 353–364), were it not for the fact that Jacques de Gheyn II published a very similar pair of prints (Holl. 144, 145) from his own designs in 1589. The Dutch Mannerist engravers' emphasis on military subjects, which climaxed in the publication in 1607 of the *Wapenhandelinghe*, a practical manual on the exercise of arms illustrated with engravings designed by De Gheyn (Holl. 146–262), reflects the ongoing military conflicts in the years after the Union of Utrecht of 1579 in which the provinces of the North banded together in a loose confederation of independent provinces that was to become the Dutch Republic.

The *Standard Bearer* is a bravura example of the use of engraving to suggest color and texture, a trend that was to be increasingly dominant in Dutch Mannerist engraving in the next two decades and that was to result in a softening of sculptural values. Without these developments it would be difficult to imagine the existence of the group of "coloristic" engravers who worked after the Flemish painter Peter Paul Rubens in the early seventeeth century.

Although the pose of the standard bearer calls to mind the bronzes of Giovanni da Bologna, the South Netherlandish Mannerist sculptor working in Florence, Goltzius has deemphasized sculptural values by superimposing texture upon texture: the satiny sheen of the doublet against the silken texture of the

4. See, for example, Frans Hals's *Banquet of the Officers of the St. George Civic Guard Company*, of 1616, Haarlem, Frans Hals Museum; Slive, 1970, vol. 2, pls. 15, 18, 19.

5. Strauss, 1977, vol. 2, p. 432, suggests that they are part of a series begun in 1582, but the differences in dimension and conception are too great.

banner. Each material has its own vocabulary of strokes, from the dotted texture of the hose to the rippling, parallel strokes of the banner.

The success of Goltzius's prints in his own time is demonstrated by the number of unauthorized copies that were made. Nine years after the publication of this print, Dutch explorers seeking to reach the Far East by ship via the North Pole were forced to halt their journey at the island of Nova Zembla off Siberia. In modern times the remnants of their winter camp have been excavated from the snow and ice, and among their cargo were found quantities of Haarlem Mannerist engravings, including several impressions of a reverse copy of the Goltzius *Standard Bearer* of 1587.[6] Only the year before the expedition, in 1595, Goltzius had been granted an imperial privilege or copyright that sought to protect his work from such copyists for six years after publication throughout the Holy Roman Empire; copyists risked seizure of goods and fines.[7]

6. Vos, 1978, pp. 52–53, and J.P. Filedt Kok in conversation.

7. Hirschmann, 1919, p. 12.

2

HENDRIK GOLTZIUS
Apollo, 1588

Engraving
B. 141, Hirschmann 131, Holl. 131, Strauss 263
Lower center: *HG. fe. / A° 88.*
352 x 265 mm. (oval)
Rijksmuseum, Amsterdam. 43:378

The sun god Apollo strides across the clouds, baton uplifted; his lyre, symbol of his musical gifts and leadership of the Muses, lies at his feet. A trellis-like rainbow arcs behind him; in the distance he is seen again, driving the chariot of the sun through a tunnel of clouds. The gestures of legs, torso, and right arm echo those of the *Standard Bearer* of 1587 (cat. no. 1), pointing up the fondness of Dutch Mannerist artists of this period for conventionalized poses, particularly those which display the unclothed human body with ornamental or balletic grace.[1] In contrast to the strong coloristic suggestion in the *Standard Bearer,* the *Apollo* is primarily conceived as sculptural form, as statuary. It is also a series of virtuoso variations on the themes of oval, circle, and arc, a rhythmic curvilinear play interrupted only by the angular forms of the floating drapery.

The 1588 *Apollo* is wholly in the style of the works after Spranger's designs that Goltzius executed in 1587, particularly the large engraving of the *Wedding Feast of Cupid and Psyche* printed from three plates (Hirschmann 322), which is wreathed in the same visceral cloud forms that enframe the *Apollo.*

The sculptural impact of the *Apollo* is largely the product of Goltzius's superbly controlled net of engraved modeling lines that follow, as in a topographical relief map, the projections of the forms they describe. At a slight distance these lines meld together into masses of tone; close to, as in so many Dutch Mannerist engravings, they form a wonderfully precise and highly ornamental pattern of swelling and tapering calligraphic lines. It is not surprising that the great calligrapher Jan van de Velde should have dedicated a page of his 1605 writing manual (see cat. no. 26) to Hendrik Goltzius.

An example of Goltzius's own inventiveness as a calligrapher is seen in the Latin inscription that forms a halo around the sun god's fiery locks. The text of this inscription informs us that the ruddy sun has dispelled the shadows with his radiant shock of hair and flickering brilliance and thereby illuminated the globe. As the flowing letters of the script swell and diminish in size, they contribute subtly to the

1. Oberhuber, Vienna, 1967–68, p. 208, noted the similarity. For another Mannerist *Apollo* comparable in pose, see Jan Muller's engraving (B. 81) after a sculptural design by Adriaen de Vries, a Netherlandish follower of Giovanni da Bologna. An early state of the engraving is reproduced in Reznicek, 1956, p. 70.

sense of light emanating from Apollo's head.[2]

The theme of radiance is continued in the light that shimmers and plays over the figure of the sun god, particularly in the reflected lights that penetrate the shadows and further intensify the sculptural modeling of the figure.

2. I am grateful to Carl Zahn, director of publications, for this observation.

3

HENDRIK GOLTZIUS
Nox (Goddess of Night), designed about 1588–89

Chiaroscuro woodcut with two tone blocks in shades of gray
B. 237, Hirschmann 372[II], Holl. 372[II], Strauss 420
Lower center: *HG. f.*
346 x 261 mm. (oval)
Wm.: Eagle (Briquet 1460)
Museum of Fine Arts, Boston, Horatio Greenough Curtis Fund. 53.7

Drawn by bats and seen as if from below, the wagon of the Goddess of Night careens across the night sky. Seated beside an owl, creature of darkness, Night holds a torch to light the way. On the back wall of the wicker canopy behind the goddess we see the sun beaming down on the orb of the earth, which casts a deep shadow. A procession of rats clambers over the canopy, while at its top a crowing rooster anticipates the dawn. In the rear of the wagon sits the personification of Sleep, crowned with a chaplet of poppy pods.[1] In the sky behind this sleeping figure appears a circle of signs of the Zodiac, a reference to the cycle of the months and to the passage of time. The image conforms to some of the attributes of Night listed by Karel van Mander in his short introduction for artists and poets to the antique gods and to hieroglyphs, the *Wtbeeldinge der Figueren (Representation of Figures)* of 1604: Night is a black woman; her garment glimmers with the "ornaments of the heavens," the stars; she is

1. The opium poppy is sometimes referred to in Dutch as a *Slaapbol* (sleep-bulb). See *Woordenboek N.T.,* p. 1462.

followed by Sleep; she has a wagon with four wheels which signify the four divisions of the night.[2]

Night is one of a series of six oval-format chiaroscuro woodcuts of male and female deities, which are often described as pairs, Night being paired with Helios (Hirschmann 371), the sun god, representative of Day. The other pairs are Pluto and Persephone (Hirschmann 369 and 370) and Neptune and his consort (Hirschmann 367 and 368). These couples might be considered as representative of, respectively: the heavens, the earth, and the waters of the earth. Some of the pairs complement each other visually better than others; Neptune and his consort are quite convincing as a pair, while Night and Helios are rather ill-matched with respect to figural scale and overall conception. A seventh woodcut of similar format (Hirschmann 374) has been identified by recent scholars as the *Creator of the World in the Cave of Eternity.*[3] The last, creator of the gods, would logically be the first in the series.

Vasari, in his discussion of chiaroscuro woodcuts (see Glossary), refers to them as having the effect of a wash drawing heightened with white.[4] As Vasari ascribed their invention to an Italian, Ugo da Carpi, these woodcuts are designated by an Italian term, meaning light-dark. The earliest dated chiaroscuros were in fact made in Germany in the first decade of the sixteenth century, followed by dated Italian works in the second decade of the sixteenth century. In the classic German chiaroscuro the image is virtually complete in the line block and is given greater sculptural force by the addition of the tone blocks. In Italian chiaroscuros in their most radical form, the image is primarily created by the broadly conceived

2. Van Mander/Davaco, 1969, p. 124 verso: "sy was oock swart/dan haer cleedt is wat blinckende/en so beschildert/datmer de vercierselen des Hemels in siet/de Sterren haer dochteren volghen haer nae/soo doen den Slaep/ende Droomen. Sy heef eenen waghen met vier raders/welcke de vier deelen der Nacht aenwijsen."

3. See Mielke's discussion of this iconographic interpretation in Berlin, 1979, pp. 57–58.

4. Vasari/Milanesi, 1878–1885, vol. 5, pp. 420–421.

masses of the tone blocks, and the line block is often reduced to a few accents. These ideal distinctions and definitions are, however, those of modern art historians and not those of the artists of the sixteenth century, who freely combined both traditions. Goltzius's Italian contemporary Andrea Andreani (active 1584–1610), who also republished or pirated many early sixteenth-century chiaroscuros, combines the two approaches.

In the light of Vasari's description of chiaroscuro woodcuts it is interesting to note that Goltzius as a draftsman frequently drew on toned or colored grounds and often highlighted his drawings with opaque white watercolor. Karel van Mander in his instructional poem for young artists recommends this method of drawing as a means of learning the rendering of three-dimensional form and recommends to the same end that the student artist copy chiaroscuro prints, particularly mentioning those after the designs of Parmigianino.[5]

In Goltzius's earliest and only dated chiaroscuro woodcut, the *Hercules and Cacus* of 1588, the image is essentially complete in the line block. The tone blocks, including the one in which Goltzius signed the design "HGoltzius Inve.," are supplementary, further modeling and dramatically lighting the complex design. The *Cave of Eternity* (Hirschmann 374), close in style, execution, and, very probably, date to the *Hercules and Cacus,* shows more dependence on the line block to convey the meaning of the image than do the six gods and goddesses. Impressions of the *Hercules and Cacus* design exist in line block only, but neither the *Cave of Eternity* nor the six gods and goddesses are known in line-block-only impressions.

The linear vocabulary of the line block in the *Nox* is closely related to the linear systems of Goltzius's engravings such as the *Apollo* (cat. no. 2). If the line block were printed without the two tone blocks, however, we would lose not only certain key elements of the print's imagery (the stars in Night's shining mantle,

5. Van Mander/Hoecker, 1916, pp. 58–59.

the sun and the earth's orb, the circle of the Zodiac) but also the torchlight or moonlight that establishes the nocturnal setting and defines many of the forms (the wheels, the clouds, the interior modeling of Night's nude figure). A sense of torchlight or moonlight illumination is as important to the essential meaning of the woodcut as is the play of sunlight to the engraved *Apollo*. A particularly bold effect is the shadow cast across Night's right thigh.

No preparatory drawings for the six gods and goddesses are known, but a comparison with other surviving drawings and, above all, with the *Apollo* engraving of 1588 strongly suggests a date of about 1588–89. In the 1589 series of the "Days of Creation," engraved by Jan Muller after designs by Goltzius, Apollo and the Goddess of Night in the *Separation of Light from Darkness* (B. 39) are very similar in style and conception to Apollo in Goltzius's 1588 engraving and Night in the woodcut.[6]

In the fifteenth and sixteenth centuries woodcuts were generally executed by professional cutters rather than by the artists who designed them. In the case of *Hercules and Cacus* the inscription "inve[nit]" suggests that it was executed by a professional cutter. The inscription "f." or "fe." (fecit) in the line blocks of *Night* and of four of the other five deities led Hirschmann to propose that Goltzius cut the blocks himself.[7] Although this is an attractive idea, given the inventive use of tone blocks in the six woodcuts and the vigor of the cutting, it is unfortunately difficult to document.

The tradition of the division of labor in the woodcut medium and the possible involvement of publishers complicate the dating of all Goltzius's woodcuts. Impressions of the *Hercules and Cacus* and of other Goltzius woodcuts occur with the address of the famous Amsterdam book and map publisher Willem Janssen (or Jansz.) Blaeu, active about 1599–1638, who published around the second decade of the seventeenth century chiaroscuro versions

6. Reproduced in Berlin, 1979, pl. 80.
7. Hirschmann, 1919, pp. 134–135.

of Albrecht Dürer's woodcuts the *Rhinoceros* of 1515 (B. 136) and *Ulrich Varnbüler* of 1522 (B. 155).[8] Although the design of the six deities clearly dates from the period 1588–89, it does not immediately follow that the execution of the blocks or the various printings date from the same time.[9]

Like Goltzius's other chiaroscuro prints, *Night* occurs in various combinations of colors: grays; greens; yellow and green; ocher yellow and brown.[10] Judging from the superior condition of the line block, gray impressions such as the one shown here seem to be earlier.

In assessing quality in Goltzius's chiaroscuro woodcuts, it is important to keep in mind not so much the decorative appeal of color as the registration of the blocks and the value relationships between the various blocks, both factors that affect the sculptural impact of the design; for the object of late Renaissance chiaroscuro woodcuts is, surely, to give a strong sense of sculptural masses in space. The yellow and brown impressions of this group, for example, are often appealing in their boldness, but the value transitions between the various blocks are often abrupt and destructive of modeling and spatial coherence. The gray impressions are not always carefully printed; when they are well printed, as is the present impression, in which the color is so well suited to the subject, they are among the most expressive impressions of Goltzius's chiaroscuro woodcuts.[11]

8. I would like to thank Egbert Haverkamp-Begemann for calling my attention to the problems posed by Blaeu's involvement.

9. Strauss, 1977, makes some suggestions regarding watermarks and dating of impressions, but an examination of the woodcuts in the collection of the Museum of Fine Arts, Boston, indicates that further research is needed. The papers show, in transmitted light, either a very irregular formation or very little contrast between the watermark and the surrounding area, and these factors, in conjunction with the continuous and often dark tones of the printing ink, make the watermarks unusually difficult to read, sometimes even to see.

10. Hirschmann, 1921, p. 162.

11. I am indebted to Nancy Bialler, who is writing a dissertation on Goltzius's woodcuts, for the observation about the priority of gray impressions.

4

HENDRIK GOLTZIUS
A Sea Goddess, designed about 1588–89

Chiaroscuro woodcut with two tone blocks in yellow ocher and olive green
B. 235, Hirschmann 368[II], Holl. 368[II], Strauss 422
Lower right: *HG. fe.*
350 x 265 mm. (oval)
Wm.: Three crowns with illegible name below (of the type shown in Briquet 5097)
Museum of Fine Arts, Boston, Purchase 1905. M20382

The bizarre, sea-borne shell chariot that Goltzius conceived for the sea goddess, consort of Neptune, is no less brilliantly imagined than the high-wheeled wagon of Night. Crowned with shells, the goddess is seated astride a saddle of ridged shell, her foot resting on a footstool of slippery, wriggling sea creatures. From an urn-like shell at her side, a ribbon of water spills back into the waves. In the distance, seen as if through a veil of mist, tritons and nereids sport and frolic.

The convoluted forms of the shell chariot are a splendid example of the grotesque biomorphic style so popular with Dutch silversmiths in the first half of the seventeenth century and known to scholars today as the auricular, lobate (ear, earlobe), or cartilage style. The Adam van Vianen model book of etched designs for silversmiths (cat. no. 138) and the dish on the table beside the great silversmith Jan Lutma in Rembrandt's portrait etching (cat. no. 137) are examples of this highly imaginative style.

Though identified by Bartsch and Hirschmann as Galatea, the sea goddess of Goltzius's woodcut has, as more recent authors have noted, no connection with the tale of the sea nymph Galatea who fled the embraces of the one-eyed giant, Polyphemus. The identifications of Amphitrite and Venus Marina have also been proposed.[1] Amphitrite, who became the bride of Neptune after he sent his dolphins

1. The identification of Amphitrite was proposed by Ames, 1949, p. 432, and that of Venus Marina by Strauss, 1977, vol. 2, p. 750.

to plead his cause, seems the most plausible of the suggested identifications. In this context it is interesting to note that Karel van Mander identifies the wife *(huysvrou)* of Neptune as the nymph Salacia.[2]

The *Sea Goddess* is the only one of the six deities for which working proofs or variant blocks are known.[3] There are a number of impressions of this woodcut in which only the darker of the two tone blocks has been printed.[4] In addition, there is in the Veste Coburg print collection a variant impression in gray in which the lighter of the two tone blocks, the one responsible for most of the highlights, is markedly different from that used to print the impressions normally seen. The highlights in the Coburg impression create a more agitated, flickering effect that tends to confuse rather than to clarify the overall design and the modeling of forms.[5]

Like the choice of gray for the *Nox* (cat. no. 3), the combination of light yellow ocher and olive green for the *Sea Goddess* is peculiarly appropriate to the subject, evoking a slightly murky marine atmosphere. Hirschmann remarks that these color combinations are particularly subtle in impressions of the six chiaroscuro deities.[6]

2. Van Mander/Davaco, 1969, p. 126 recto.

3. George Keyes informed me by letter as the catalogue was in preparation that he had recently seen in the Budapest collection proof impressions in gray of the *Nox* (Hirschmann 372) and the *Cave of Eternity* (Hirschmann 374), in which certain details of the image had not yet been cut into the tone blocks (*Nox* before light area on the rim of the right front wheel and *Cave of Eternity* before comet). He also observed in the Munich collection an impression in gray of the *Cave of Eternity* before the comet.

4. See the impression in dark yellow ocher, Museum of Fine Arts, Boston, W.G. Russell Allen Bequest, 63.607. The impression seems to be earlier than most impressions with two tone blocks, as the large break in the upper borderline has not yet occurred.

5. Inv. VII, 31, 178. Nancy Bialler also noticed this variant and plans to discuss it in her forthcoming dissertation on the woodcuts of Goltzius.

6. Hirschmann, 1919, p. 134.

Both the *Nox* and the *Sea Goddess* are delightful examples of the Northern European gift for invention in the realm of the fantastic and the grotesque that Goltzius brought to international Mannerism.

5
HENDRIK GOLTZIUS
Dirck Volckertsz. Coornhert, about 1591–92

Engraving
B. 164, Hirschmann 180[III], Holl. 180[III], Strauss 287[III]
Around the frame: THEODORUS CORNHERTIUS, AD VIVVUM DEPICTUS ET AERI INCISVS AB H. GOLTZIO.
420 x 320 mm. (oval platemark)
Wm.: Shield with fleur-de-lis and letters WR(?)
Coll.: F. Rechberger (L. 2133); H.F. Sewall (L. 1309)
Museum of Fine Arts, Boston, Harvey D. Parker Collection. P7209

A short time before Goltzius's departure for Italy late in the year 1590, Dirck Volckertsz. Coornhert (1522–1590) died in Gouda, where he had sought refuge after being driven from his last place of residence, Delft, because of his liberal convictions.

Outside of the Netherlands one might assume, as did Bartsch, that this portrait, the most ambitious of Goltzius's engraved portraits, was motivated primarily by the artist's desire to do honor to the man who taught him engraving.[1] Coornhert was indeed one of the best of the reproductive engravers active in the mid-sixteenth century, but his work as an engraver seems to have been primarily a means of supporting himself after he had alienated his wealthy Amsterdam cloth-merchant family by an early and unpopular marriage.

An able musician and fencer as well as an engraver, Coornhert was first of all a Christian humanist writer and thinker whose rational and humane ideas regarding religion and society were explosively controversial in his own time but were one of the principal inspirations for the religious toleration and progressive

1. Bartsch, vol. 3, p. 50.

THEODORVS CORNHERTIVS, AD VIVVM DEPICTVS ET ÆRI INCISVS AB H. GOLTZIO.

NATVS AMSTELREDAMI Aº CIƆ IƆ XC.

DENATVS GOVDÆ Aº CIƆ IƆ XXII.

charitable and correctional institutions that characterized seventeenth-century Dutch society and set Holland apart from the rest of Europe.[2] Coornhert remained a Catholic, but his writing and his outspokenness in public debate on the subjects of freedom of conscience and religious toleration offended authoritarians both Protestant and Catholic. Some of his convictions, such as his belief in the essential goodness and perfectibility of mankind and that ignorance was the primary source of evil, irritated Calvin to the point that he referred to Coornhert as a "mortal plague" and a "savage beast."[3] Because of his erudition, largely self-acquired, and his philosophical interests, he was unique among reproductive engravers in being able to suggest literary programs on didactic moral and ethical themes to the designer of the prints, the Haarlem painter Maarten van Heemskerck.[4]

Although the Latin inscription on the print indicates that Coornhert has been "depicted from life," no drawing for the print survives. The conception of the portrait compares closely with that of the bust-length drawings of artists, such as that of the Florentine sculptor Giovanni da Bologna, which Goltzius made during his Italian journey.[5] The engraving was probably executed shortly after Goltzius's return in the period 1591–92.

It has been observed that it was in his portraits that Goltzius first expressed his individuality as an engraver. Indeed, the *Coornhert* is in many respects a much magnified and intensified version of Goltzius's numerous smaller medallion portraits of a circular or oval format. Some of these were literally medallions, portraits engraved on silver plates and only incidentally occurring as printed impressions.[6] If

2. See Amsterdam, 1965–66, for the influence of Coornhert's ideas on social and charitable institutions.

3. Bonger, 1941, p. 29.

4. Karel van Mander's statement to this effect has recently been demonstrated in Veldman, 1977, pp. 55ff.

5. Observed by Oberhuber, Vienna, 1967–68, p. 213. For the drawing see Reznicek, 1961, no. 263.

6. The letters of the engraved inscriptions in such impressions are generally reversed.

we go back to one of Goltzius's earliest dated portrait engravings, the 1578 portrait of his father, Jan Goltz (Hirschmann 171), we see a conception surprisingly similar to that of the *Coornhert,* a strongly lighted portrait bust viewed through a frame and casting a shadow on a concave niche. Like Coornhert, Goltzius's father looks directly at us with a concentrated gaze.

The *Coornhert* portrait is, however, unprecedentedly large in scale, contributing to the vivid sensation of an eye-to-eye encounter with a highly individual and volatile personality. The strength of characterization is enhanced by the intensity of the illumination and by the almost tangible sculptural presence of the sitter. The curving, concentric modeling lines that follow the projections of the form, as in the 1588 *Apollo,* build to a climax in the penetrating gaze of Coornhert's left eye. Goltzius provides us with a highly detailed and sculpturally heightened map of the furrows of Coornhert's brow and of the lines of experience about his eyes. The sense of an indwelling intelligence and a critical spirit is vividly communicated. This "warts-and-all" portrait of a plain-spoken man, conveying a sense of the continuing presence of one deceased, looks forward to such portraits as Rembrandt's posthumous etching of the preacher Sylvius (cat. no. 97). The space of the *Coornhert* portrait, however, is not the illusionistic one of the *Sylvius,* in which the preacher freely leans out of the frame. The space of the *Coornhert* portrait, for all the sculptural power of head and shoulders, is a more ambiguously Mannerist one, in which Coornhert's body is trapped in a shallow space between oval frame and concave oval niche.

The size and format of the portrait were to have a direct effect on seventeenth-century Dutch portrait engravers. Among them was Willem Jacobsz. Delff (1580–1638), whose engravings of the monarchs and courtiers of northern Europe after painters such as his father-in-law Mierevelt, enjoyed considerable

success in the first half of the seventeenth century.[7]

Impressions of the portrait also occur in which a rectangular frame adorned at the four corners with implements symbolic of Coornhert's activities as scholar, engraver, musician, and fencer have been printed from a second plate. Although this second plate, usually credited to Goltzius's hand, is skillfully executed, its silvery tonality and relatively unsculptural, busy, small-scale conception suggest that someone in the Goltzius circle like the talented Jan Saenredam may be responsible for both design and execution.

7. Hirschmann, 1919, p. 109.

6
HENDRIK GOLTZIUS
The Farnese Hercules, about 1592–93

Engraving
B. 143, Hirschmann 145[II], Holl. 145[II], Strauss 312[II]
Lower left: *HGoltzius Sculp…/ Herman Adolfz excud. Haerlemen….* Lower margin: *…opus posthumum HGoltzy, iam primum divulgat. An°. M.D.C.X.VII.*
410 x 292 mm. (plate)
Wm.: Shield with fleur-de-lis and letters WR (close to Briquet 7165)
Coll.: H.F. Sewall (L. 1309)
Museum of Fine Arts, Boston, Harvey D. Parker Collection. P7206

During much of his Italian journey Goltzius, whose prints signed with his monogram had made his name known throughout Europe, traveled incognito, calling himself Hendrik van Bracht (Hendrik from Mühlbracht). Protected by this anonymity, he was enabled during his nearly half-year stay in Rome to draw without interruption the famous works of antiquity and of modern times that filled the city and that were such a magnet for northern artists. Van Mander described the thirty-three-year-old Goltzius working with the intensity of a dedicated art student, undeterred by the dead and dying, victims of the plague that raged in Rome at that period.

Around the time of Goltzius's visit a number of guidebooks were published directing the visitor to the wonders of Rome, including the antique sculptures drawn by Goltzius. From Roman publishers such as Lafreri he could also have purchased engravings, some rather crudely executed, of many of the sculptures.[1] Some forty-three of Goltzius's drawings of Roman sculpture survive and are preserved in the collection of the Teyler's Museum, Haarlem. As Reznicek points out, these drawings differ from the drawings of Roman ruins and antiquities made by Maarten van Heemskerck in the 1530s.[2] Heemskerck's drawings were part of a sketchbook, whereas those by Goltzius were apparently intended as models for an extended series of engravings, of which only three were engraved by Goltzius.

Goltzius's drawings convey with unprecedented vividness an objective sense of the physical reality of the sculptures, of their being made of durable, resistant marble. The drawings exist in two versions: a looser sketch in black chalk on blue paper, which gives a sense of execution on the spot, and a more highly finished drawing in red chalk on white paper. After his return to Holland, probably about 1592–93, Goltzius executed three engravings from the finished drawings. The corresponding red chalk drawings show signs of indentation with a stylus for transfer of the design.[3] The *Hercules* is the liveliest of the three engravings; the others, the *Apollo Belvedere* (Hirschmann 147) and the *Emperor Commodus as Hercules* (Hirschmann 146), are almost neoclassical in their cool sobriety.

According to the Latin inscription in the center of the lower margin of the *Hercules,* these three plates were first published after Goltzius's death in 1617 by the Haarlem pub-

1. Reznicek, 1961, p. 90.
2. Heemskerck's sketchbooks were owned by Goltzius's friend the Haarlem Mannerist painter Cornelis Cornelisz.; Reznicek, 1961, p. 92 and n. 16.
3. For Goltzius's working methods and the relationship between the two types of drawings and the prints, see Miedema, 1969.

lisher Herman Adolfsz., whose name appears below Goltzius's imperial copyright in the lower left corner of the image. The date of the posthumous publication has led to considerable confusion about the date of execution of these prints. Reznicek's comparison with the engraving style of the *Nine Muses* (Hirschmann 148-156) of 1592 is very persuasive.[4] A further comparison with the 1593 *Pygmalion* (Hirschmann 158) encourages one to extend the range of possible dates of execution to 1592-93.

Goltzius had already begun to turn away from the extremes of Sprangerism before the Italian journey, as is readily visible in his large engraving of the *Judgment of Midas* of 1590 (Hirschmann 132). The *Hercules* retains, however, the Haarlem Mannerists' love of surprising viewpoints. Even though Goltzius has drawn a more conventional front view (Reznicek, no. 225, pl. 176), he rejected it in favor of the more novel back view as he had done in earlier figures, such as the *Pluto* from the set of six oval woodcut deities designed about 1588-89.

As the Latin inscription in the center of the lower margin indicates, the sculpture was part of the collection of Cardinal Farnese in the Farnese Palace when Goltzius drew it. It was apparently set up under the vaults of the arcade surrounding the central courtyard.[5] Goltzius has omitted all traces of the palace architecture and made the hero of antiquity more heroic by silhouetting his colossal bulk against the open sky, framing his figure with clouds that echo the muscles of the demi-god's back. According to the inscription on the base of the sculpture and the verses by the Latinist schoolmaster and historian Theodoor Schrevelius (1572-1591),[6] the victorious Hercules, "terror of the Globe," is resting from his labors. He clutches in his right hand the golden apples he had stolen from the dragon-protected garden of

4. Reznicek, vol. 1, p. 419.

5. Reznicek, vol. 1, pp. 336-367.

6. *N. N. Biografisch Woordenboek,* vol. 5, p. 703.

the Hesperides, the "daughters of the evening," situated at the edge of the world.

The sculpture, a signed copy by Glycon of an original by Lyssipos, was found in the Baths of Caracalla about 1540 and quickly acquired by the Farnese family. A somewhat grotesque exaggeration of Lysippos's original, the sculpture was without head and lower legs when discovered and was restored by Michelangelo's follower Guglielmo della Porta. In 1560 the missing parts came to light but were not restored to the sculpture until the Farnese antiquities were inherited by the rulers of Naples in the eighteenth century. Michelangelo is reported to have said, not surprisingly, that the modern additions were too beautiful to replace.[7]

Although the engraving is justifiably admired as one of the most brilliant examples of Goltzius's systematic linear web of engraved lines and the vibrant decorative patterns it could produce, the artist seems to have been concerned above all to convey as vividly as possible the experience of being in the presence of the sculpture. Our sense of viewing the sculpture from below is heightened by the admiring upward gaze of the two spectators on the far side of the sculpture.[8]

These two portrait-like heads, as yet unidentified, also lead us in our imagination around the sculpture, encouraging us to imagine the front view. Since a drawing of the front view exists, it is tempting to speculate whether Goltzius intended to include both views in his larger series. The notion that sculpture was to be viewed in the round was one of the central

7. Reznicek, no. 227, p. 337.

8. There is in the Fodor Collection housed in the Amsterdam Historical Museum a separate study, a small metal-point drawing in reverse, of the two spectators. See Amsterdam, 1979, no. 38; also Reznicek, 1961, no. 388. Goltzius included a portrait-like draftsman in the engraving of the Apollo Belvedere, and a number of the drawings from the antique on blue paper include sketchy indications of spectators. Some of the prints after antique sculptures being published in Rome at this time included draftsmen or spectators as, for example, the engraving issued by Lafreri of the river god known as the "Marfuori." See Rotterdam, 1969, no. 53, illus.

preoccupations of Mannerist sculptors such as Giovanni da Bologna[9] and Adriaen de Vries. About the same time Jan Muller engraved two sets of three prints (one set is dated 1593) in which sculptural designs by Adriaen de Vries are viewed from three different vantage points.

Another way in which Goltzius has made the experience more immediate for us is in his elaborate detailing of the play of reflected lights over the hero's back. One imagines the strong southern sunlight bouncing off the paving and back wall of the cortile, highlighting every muscle.

9. See Andrea Andreani's chiaroscuro woodcuts of 1584 (B. vol. 12, pp. 93-94, nos. 1-3) that present Giovanni da Bologna's sculpture of the *Rape of the Sabines* from three different vantage points.

7

HENDRIK GOLTZIUS
Pietà (The Sorrowing Virgin with the Dead Christ in Her Lap), 1596

Engraving
B. 41, Weig. 41[II], Hirschmann 50[II], Holl. 50[II], Strauss 331[II]
Lower center: *HG*; at right: *A° 96*
187 x 127 mm. (platemark)
Wm.: Foolscap (fragment)
Coll.: R. Balmanno (L. 213); H. F. Sewall (L. 1309)
Museum of Fine Arts, Boston, Harvey D. Parker Collection. P7233

When Van Mander discusses Goltzius's prints he devotes most of his attention to those in which Goltzius imitated the styles of earlier and modern masters, particularly the graphic styles of the two great early sixteenth-century printmakers, Albrecht Dürer and Lucas van Leyden. Van Mander first describes the series of six engravings of scenes from the Life of the Virgin, known to later generations as the "masterpieces," in which each plate was executed in the manner of a modern Italian painter (Bassano or Barocci, for example) or in the graphic manner of Dürer or Lucas (Hirschmann 9-14, dated 1593-94). He relates how

Goltzius worked with great speed to complete the prints in time for the Frankfurt fair and explains that the dedication of the set to the Duke of Bavaria resulted in the presentation to the artist of a golden chain and medal with the duke's portrait, the kind of distinction that was much coveted by Renaissance artists. Van Mander then describes with great relish how Goltzius proceeded to "age" an impression of the *Circumcision* in the style of Dürer, burning out the monogram and darkening the paper, and consequently deceiving both connoisseurs and fellow engravers, who believed the print to be a lost work of the great German master. Also mentioned by Van Mander are the Passion engravings in the manner of Lucas, published in 1597, and the *Pietà* in the manner of Dürer discussed here.[1] Van Mander calls Goltzius a Proteus or Vertumnus of art, comparing the artist's ability to change his style to the ability of these figures from classical mythology to change their shape.[2] Goltzius's protean stylistic diversity is also very evident in his later drawings.

Van Mander's admiration for Goltzius's dazzling sleight-of-hand may seem excessive, but there can be little doubt that Van Mander believed that in these works Goltzius had out-stripped the Old Masters. When Goltzius is mentioned as a printmaker by other writers on art in his own time or in the later seventeenth century, it is generally these virtuoso productions that are alluded to. In a manuscript treatise on the "Art of Limning," datable about 1598–1602, the great English miniature painter Nicholas Hilliard writes, for example, "Hendrick Goltzius approched Albertus very neer, most admirably imitating him and Lucas of Leyden also in their severall handling the graver, which he hath done in sertaine peces to showe what he could doe if he list, but he afecteth another maner of line, which is

1. Van Mander reports that the printing plate for the *Pietà* was in the collection of a Haarlem art lover named Berensteyn. He omits only one of the Dürer or Lucas imitations from his survey, the little engraved oval *Madonna and Child in the Crescent Moon* (Hirschmann 20).

2. Van Mander/Floerke, 1906, vol. 2, pp. 242–247.

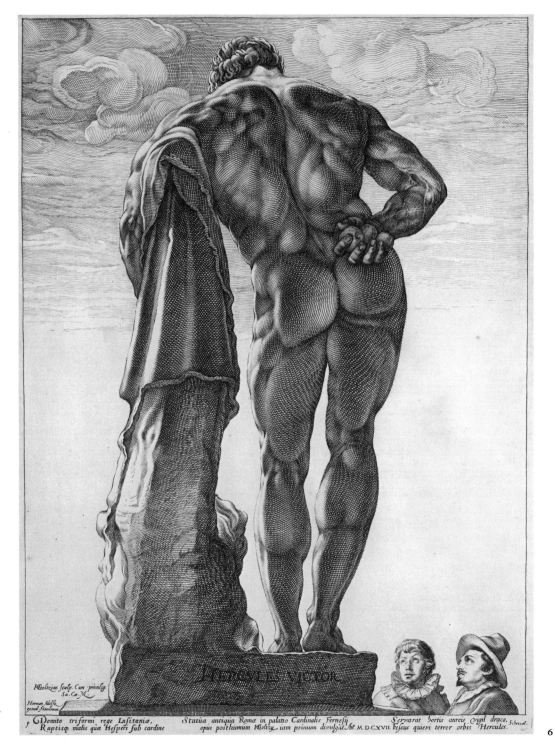

swifter acording to his spirit, and doubtles very excellent and most folowed."[3]

The *Pietà* is a far more deceptive image than the *Circumcision* and closer in scale to Dürer's engravings. Were it not monogrammed and dated, this engraving might easily be taken for an unfamiliar Dürer by the viewer not well acquainted with Dürer's work.[4] Goltzius takes the motif of Michelangelo's *Pietà*, places it in a landscape setting, and presents it to us in the style of Dürer's 1520 engraved *Madonna with Swaddled Infant* (B. 38), in which corpse-like sleeping child and somber sky anticipate Christ's sacrifice.[5] Goltzius undoubtedly also saw Michelangelo's *Pietà* during his Roman sojourn, but he might also have known Agostino Carracci's engraving of 1579 (B. 104, Bohlin 9),[6] which places the Michelangelo sculpture in a vague landscape setting and also surrounds Christ's head with a Trinitarian halo.

When one compares the Dürer engraving with the Goltzius engraving, the latter seems rather flashy, glittering with a metallic brilliance.[7] The individual lines do not fuse as readily into masses of dark tone as they do in the Dürer. This is especially evident in the rays of light from the halos. It is possible that Goltzius wished to produce a genuinely moving devotional image, but the melodrama of the great, glassy tears of the Virgin and the

3. Norman, 1911–12, pp. 19–20. I would like to thank William Robinson for reminding me of this passage. See also Samuel Ampzing's description of Haarlem of 1628 (cat. no. 62), which includes in the discussion of Goltzius a pair of verses: "If when Dürer or Lucas made something beautiful, didn't Goltzius surpass it with his burin?" ("Heeft Durer wel iets fraeijs of Lukas oyt gemaekt/ Dat door dijn ijser niet noch beter is geraekt?")

4. Early engraved copies of Goltzius's *Pietà* significantly either omit his monogram and the date or substitute Dürer's monogram instead; see Hirschmann, 1921, no. 50, under "Copies."

5. Strauss, 1977, vol. 2, p. 608, notes that the legs of Goltzius's Christ are inspired by those of Christ in Dürer's *Holy Trinity* woodcut (B. 122).

6. Reproduced in Bohlin, 1979, p. 83. I would like to thank Scott Schaefer for calling my attention to this comparison.

7. Reproduced side by side in Berlin, 1979, pls. 71, 72.

brilliance of the performance make it difficult to experience the image in this way. The emphasis on the drapery folds in Goltzius's engraving is interesting in the light of Karel van Mander's recommendation to young artists, in his instructional poem about painting, that they take the drapery of Dürer and Lucas as models. [8]

Goltzius was not alone in his admiration for and rivalry with Dürer and Lucas. The period around 1600 was the occasion of an extensive Dürer and Lucas revival in Germany and the Netherlands. The Emperor Rudolph II in Prague was actively collecting their works, and in 1602 Goltzius and his Haarlem friends foiled an attempt by the emperor, with the Amsterdam engraver Jan Muller acting as intermediary, to purchase Lucas van Leyden's great Last Judgment altarpiece from the city fathers of Leyden. [9] Goltzius's imitations of these masters also signal the beginning of the notion that there are masters of printmaking as well as of painting. Inventories of the collections of artists from the first half of the century with their separate portfolios and albums of the work or "all the work" of Dürer and Lucas further testify to the reverence in which these printmakers were held.

8. Van Mander/Hoecker, 1916, pp. 246–247.

9. See Reznicek, 1956, pp. 75–76. The painting is now in the collection of the Lakenhal, Leyden.

Jan Muller
1571–1628

The Amsterdam engraver and draftsman Jan Harmensz. Muller, born in 1571, was the third generation of a family of professional book printers, engravers, and art dealers. It is probable that he studied with his father, the engraver and print publisher Harmen Jansz. Muller. He never married and resided throughout his life at his father's house and shop at the sign of the "Vergulde Passer" (Gilded Compass) in the Warmoesstraat. With his sister Marritgen he carried on the printing and publishing concern and the art shop after their father's death in 1617.

Muller was perhaps more of a rival than a follower of Goltzius. He is often described as having studied with Goltzius because of the stylistic parallels between their work, but his only direct connection with Goltzius is the series of engravings after Goltzius's designs, the "Days of Creation," of 1589 (B. 35–41), and there is no record of his having resided in Haarlem. Active throughout his life as a reproductive engraver, he frequently engraved the designs of artists associated with the court of Rudolph II at Prague, especially the painter Bartholomeus Spranger, and also the sculptor Adriaen de Vries and the painter Hans van Aachen. Unlike Goltzius, who after 1587 no longer reproduced the work of Spranger and whose Italian journey resulted in a clear break with Spranger's style, Muller continued to reproduce Spranger's work into the early seventeenth century. His handsome 1615 portraits of Archduke Albert and Archduchess Isabella, the rulers of the Southern Netherlands, are among the earliest engravings after the paintings of Rubens.

Although Muller was obviously successful as a reproductive engraver, among his some hundred prints there are a number from his own drawings, both religious compositions and portraits, that reveal a genuine originality, particularly in the exploration of dramatic lighting effects and an innovative use of the engraver's burin to create dark tonal passages.

Muller died in Amsterdam in 1628. The presence in his estate of a drawing of Naples and two large unframed paintings of a "Nativity" and an "Expulsion of the Moneychangers," said to have been made in Italy, provides possible evidence for an Italian journey as well as for his activity as a painter. About his activity as a draftsman we are better informed. Reznicek's provisional catalogue lists some forty drawings in a variety of techniques. [1]

1. For the biography and the drawings see Reznicek, 1956. Reznicek, 1975, n. 33, p. 113, pl. 16, attributes the painting of *Joseph and His Family before Pharaoh* in the Dunkirk Museum, which has previously been attributed to Karel van Mander, to Jan Muller. This attribution seems very plausible in the light of the engraved *Adoration of the Magi* exhibited here (cat. no. 8).

8

JAN MULLER
The Adoration of the Magi, 1598

Engraving
B. 2, Weig. 2 II, Wurz. 2, Holl. 14 II
Upper left: *Joan Muller inventor et sculpsit*. In lower
margin at right: *Harman Muller excude*. (date:
1598, trimmed away)
346 x 436 mm. (sheet)
Wm.: Strasburg bend crowned with lily and
letters WR
Private Collection

Jan Muller, who seems to have remained a
Catholic throughout his life, designed and
executed a number of images of pious or
devotional subjects, often with an emphasis
on expressive, dramatic illumination. Such
an emphasis was unusual in the medium of
engraving in 1598, the year *The Adoration of the
Magi* was published, and was to have important consequences for the later quest for darker
tonalities in printmaking that can be charted in
the work of Hendrik Goudt (cat. nos. 44, 45)
and Rembrandt (cat. nos. 99, 167, 170).

Netherlandish art had a strong tradition of
the realistic representation of nocturnal effects
and nocturnal illumination that can be traced
back to the Nativity scenes of the late fifteenth-
century painters such as Geertgen tot Sint Jans
and that may be found in the scenes of balls
and banquets of late sixteenth-century South
Netherlandish painters such as Joost van
Winghe. In printmaking Goltzius anticipated
the showiest of Jan Muller's engraved night
scenes, *Belshazzar's Feast* (B. 1), with his engraving of a nocturnal banquet from the *Lucretia*
series of about 1580 (Hirschmann 171).

Jan Muller's large engraving of *The
Adoration of the Magi* is a pious pageant, a spectacle dominated by broadly conceived effects of
mystic illumination. The richly garbed Magi
and their entourages advance like foreign
ambassadors to pay homage to the infant
Christ, the "God clothed in human flesh" of
the Latin verses.[1] He sits enthroned on his

mother's lap under the light of the star that
guided the Magi to the stable. This blazing star
is the apex from which the whole composition
radiates.

Muller exploits here a favorite device of
Mannerist artists, that of placing the focal
point of interest and meaning in the far distance. The pearl-like smallness of the Christ
Child clasped in the great hands of the kneeling
king emphasizes by contrast the spiritual magnitude of the event. Although Muller's tonal
use of engraving is surprisingly forward-
looking, the proportions of the tapering
figures and their faceted, angular drapery
are thoroughly Mannerist, Muller's personal
adaptation of Bartholomeus Spranger's style.

In *The Adoration of the Magi* and the
Belshazzar engravings Jan Muller was closer
than Goltzius in his *Pietà* (cat. no. 7) to the
tonal manner of Dürer's later engraved works.
Close to, we are conscious of the "watered silk"
patterns formed by Muller's engraved lines, but
from a slight distance the closely laid, parallel
lines fuse together, and we experience areas of
tone rather than linear calligraphy. Although in
certain works Muller magnified the Dutch
Mannerist engravers' systematic grid of calligraphic lines to a greater degree than any
Dutch engraver of his time, turning it into
eye-dazzling optical patterns (see the engraving of the philosopher *Chilon*, B. 13), in *The
Adoration of the Magi* and *Belshazzar's Feast*
he subordinated it to his desire for broad
tonal effects.

A surprising aspect of Jan Muller's engraved
work is the large number of unfinished working proofs that survive, some with drawn cor-
rections or additions. In his will made in 1624,
Muller bequeathed a book containing all his
engravings, "van deneersten druck" (from the
first or earliest printing), to his nephew; that
album may have been the original source of the
proofs.[2] The majority of the proofs are now
preserved in the collection of the Rijksmuseum,
Amsterdam. The Amsterdam and Rotterdam
print rooms each have an unfinished working

proof of the *Adoration*. In both instances the
figures and foreground are essentially complete
save for a few textile patterns, while the background stable, ruins, and star are as yet only
sketchily indicated with drypoint. Engravers
traditionally worked this way, completing
entire areas of the plate before moving on to
the next.

When one encounters Rembrandt's large-
scale religious prints such as *The Three Crosses*
(cat. nos. 169, 170), with their expressive use
of masses of light and darkness, one wonders
whether there was any precedent for such
breadth of conception of illumination in the
works of earlier Dutch printmakers. Muller's
Adoration of the Magi seems to offer one.[3]

3. Oberhuber, Vienna, 1967–68, p. 228, suggests such a
comparison.

1. See Berlin, 1979, for a complete German translation of
these unsigned verses.

2. Boon, 1953, pp. 31–33.

En, Deus humaná vestitus carne, pudicæ   O quám præclarum diuini pignus amoris,   Aurum, thus, myrrham, Regiq́, Deoq́, hominiq́,
In gremio Matris conspiciendus adest.   Quo nullum toto certius Orbe fuit!   Mystica pro modulo munera quisq. paret.

8

Gerrit Pietersz.
1566 – before 1616

Regarded by Burchard, in his book on the Dutch etchers before Rembrandt, as the first significant figure in a continuous tradition of etching by Dutch painters,[1] Gerrit Pietersz. was first of all a painter and draftsman, whose work in these media is gradually being rediscovered by twentieth-century scholars.[2] Like many of the painters in the exhibition, Pietersz. produced only a few etchings during a brief period in his career. Five of his six etchings, all of which are on religious themes, are dated 1593 and were probably executed in Haarlem.

Born in Amsterdam in 1566, the son of an organist and brother of the famous composer for the organ Jan Pietersz. Sweelinck, Gerrit first studied about 1588/89 with the Amsterdam glass painter Jacob Lenartz., with whom he may have learned etching on glass. He then studied for a year or so with the Haarlem Mannerist painter, Cornelis Cornelisz., whose style was to determine the course of his art. He remained in Haarlem for a few years as an independent artist, drawing, as Van Mander records, the nude figure from life. After a residence in Antwerp about 1594/95, he spent several years in Rome, returning to settle in Amsterdam. Van Mander complains that Gerrit Pietersz. was so successful with his portraits and "small things" that he had little time to devote to the ambitious large-scale histories he ought to have been painting. The Latin verses on his portrait in Hendrik Hondius's series of prints of famous painters, datable no later than 1616, speak of him in the past tense.

1. Burchard, 1917, pp. 19–28, and biographical documentation, pp. 99–102.

2. See Bauch, 1938, and Van Thiel, 1963.

9

GERRIT PIETERSZ.
Mary Magdalene at the Foot of the Cross, 1593

Etching
Bur. 6, Holl. 6
Lower left: *1593*
315 x 210 mm. (platemark)
Graphische Sammlung Albertina, Vienna.
HB. 50(2), p. 11.

Mary Magdalene, the most popular of the repentant sinners of the Christian tradition, kneels in adoration before the crucified Christ. Her left hand rests on the emblem by which she is known, the jar of ointment, which refers both to her anointing of Christ's feet before the events of the Passion unfold and the anointing of his body for burial. Against the base of the cross rests the skull of Adam, a reminder of Christ's redemption of mankind from original sin. The image, although set on Calvary with Jerusalem in the distance, is, like the *Pietà* of Goltzius, a devotional image rather than a narrative one.

An aspect of Dutch Mannerism in painting as well as in graphic art is a "soft" style, in which inanimate forms heave and undulate as if alive and the human figure has a plant-like flexibility. This sense of form is characteristic not only of the work of Gerrit Pietersz. but also of the early work of the Utrecht painter Abraham Bloemaert.[1] In German this style is sometimes referred to as *Teigstil* ("doughy" style).

The minimal resistance of the etching ground (see Glossary) to the needle enabled Gerrit Pietersz. to achieve in his etchings a flowing, undulant line like a pen line that would be difficult, if not impossible, to achieve in engraving. In 1593, the year in which Gerrit Pietersz. made this etching, Goltzius began to make pen drawings with undulant forms and sweeping parallel lines. Reznicek suggests that Goltzius's drawings in this style were inspired by the woodcuts of Titian and the Venetian

1. See, for example, the 1593 *Annunciation* engraving by Jacques de Gheyn II after Bloemaert (Holl. 329).

School of the first half of the sixteenth century.[2]

The etched lines of Gerrit Pietersz.'s prints do not rhythmically swell and taper like an engraved line or a quill pen line but tend to be blunt-ended and unvaried in thickness throughout their length. The crosshatching used to create the darkest tones is still part of the vocabulary of contemporary engraving and is not to be found in the pen and wash drawings firmly attributed to Gerrit Pietersz. The linear patterns of the etching, however, are much simpler, less rigidly systematic, than those in a contemporary engraving by a professional engraver such as Hendrik Goltzius (see the *Farnese Hercules*, cat. no. 6).

In this, Gerrit Pietersz.'s most ambitious, most expressive etching, there is a concern with dramatic or mystic illumination that parallels that of Jan Muller in the *Adoration of the Magi* (cat. no. 8). Light breaks through beneath the overhanging clouds, singling out the figure of the Magdalene and her fluttering, agitated draperies and dramatically highlights the suspended body of the crucified Christ. The tragic significance of Christ's sacrifice is emphasized by the dark clouds massed behind the cross. In a surprising passage of illusionism the arm of the cross juts out over the borderline.

2. See Reznicek, 1961, nos. 71, 437, 438.

10

GERRIT PIETERSZ.
Saint Cecilia, 1593

Etching
Bur. 5¹, Holl. 5¹
Lower right: *1593*
205 x 143 mm. (platemark)
Rijksmuseum, Amsterdam. OB4640

A Christian martyr of second- or third-century Rome, Cecilia, according to the sacred legend, was such a gifted musician that her hymns of praise brought the angels down from heaven to listen. Although she played all instruments expertly, she invented the organ to be able to express more fully the divine harmony that filled her soul. We see her, apparently seated among the clouds, playing the organ,¹ while turning to look ecstatically toward heaven. Behind her, two small angels consult a hymn-book. It is amusing that Gerrit Pietersz., with his love of soft forms and undulating lines should choose to surround Cecilia with clouds, as Cecilia is rarely represented in such a setting when not in the company of other saints. It is also singularly appropriate that the son and brother of organists should portray the saint who is purported to have invented the organ.

   The wide blank margin at the bottom of the print was undoubtedly intended to receive engraved Latin verses, as in Gerrit Pietersz.'s four other etchings not exhibited here, but the verses were never engraved.

   In early impressions of Gerrit's prints the polishing scratches resulting from the manufacture or preparation of the smooth copper plates print quite strongly (here they run vertically) and read as a light continuous tone. In a few instances Gerrit burnished these fine scratches away from an unworked area of the plate in order to create a brighter area, as here in the oval highlight that models Cecilia's thigh or in his etching of the *Rest on the Flight* (Bur. 4), in which he burnished the area around the sun to suggest its radiance.

1. A portable organ of the positive type. I would like to thank Barbara Lambert, keeper of the Musical Instruments Collection at the Museum of Fine Arts, for the information.

.1593.

Jacques de Gheyn II
1565 – 1629

Like Hendrik Goltzius, Jacques (or Jacob)
de Gheyn II was the son of a glass painter.
De Gheyn's parents were from Utrecht but at
the time of his birth in 1565 were resident in
Antwerp. Karel van Mander records that he
studied glass painting and miniature painting
with his father, who encouraged his first efforts
in engraving. About 1585 De Gheyn began to
work as an engraver under Hendrik Goltzius
in Haarlem and, according to Van Mander,
remained with Goltzius for two years.[1] In 1591
De Gheyn settled in Amsterdam and in 1595
married a woman from a wealthy patrician
family in the Hague. After a period of residence in Leyden they settled in the Hague,
where De Gheyn was enrolled in the artists'
guild of St. Luke in 1598 as painter and
engraver. He continued to reside and work in
the Hague for the rest of his life, enjoying
many close connections with the courts of
the stadholders, Prince Maurits and Prince
Frederik Hendrik, and serving as an adviser
on art and architecture. He died in the Hague
in 1629.[2]

After the Haarlem years De Gheyn usually
seems to have functioned as his own publisher.
He received important and well-paid commissions from the Estates General in the Hague
for prints commemorating critical battles in
the conflict with the Spanish and for his
visual manual of the exercise of arms
(*Wapenhandelinghe*). He reproduced many
designs of other Mannerist artists, such as
Abraham Bloemaert and Karel van Mander,
but was no longer active as a reproductive
engraver after 1596. The last known engraving
from his own design is dated 1603. His principal pupils in the art of engraving were Jan
Saenredam and Zacharias Dolendo.

1. Life of De Gheyn in Van Mander/Floerke, 1906,
vol. 2, pp. 319 – 329.

2. See biography, Van Regteren Altena, 1936, pp. 1 – 22.

10

Hollstein's catalogue credits over four hundred engravings and a few etchings to De Gheyn, but when one scrutinizes these works carefully, taking as a point of departure works in which De Gheyn's name is followed by "sculpsit" or "fecit" (see "Use of Catalogue"), one comes to the conclusion that a rather large number of the prints may have been executed after De Gheyn's designs by skilled engravers in his shop. A better-defined image of the styles of the engravers in De Gheyn's circle is required, however, before this can be persuasively demonstrated.

In his unpublished autobiography the many-faceted Constantijn Huygens, writer, politician, and gifted draftsman, wondered at his friend and neighbor De Gheyn's versatility and command of many media. Like Goltzius, De Gheyn around 1600 turned from printmaking to painting. Van Mander reports that he complained of wasted time and turned to painting because it provided the most accurate means of reproducing all aspects of the natural world. Although De Gheyn painted mythological and literary subjects, his most important contribution as a painter was in the category of still life. His flower pieces and *Vanitas* still lifes are among the earliest and most expressive examples of these genres.

De Gheyn is best known today for his drawings, with their spontaneity of execution, lively combination of direct observation, and often grotesque fantasy.[3] They are often regarded as one of Rembrandt's sources of inspiration for his drawing style.

3. For the drawings see Judson, 1973.

II

JACQUES DE GHEYN II
Vanitas, 1595 – 96

Engraving
Le Bl. 109, Pass. 73, Wurz. 73, Holl. 104
Lower left: *IDGheÿn. fe. et ex*
279 x 186 mm. (platemark)
Wm.: Bear (similar to Briquet 1059)
Rijksmuseum, Amsterdam. 42:113

"Vanity of vanities; all is vanity." This despairing cry from the Old Testament book of Ecclesiastes (1:2) is engraved in Latin on the torturously writhing banderole held by a rather melancholy Amor perching on the windowsill of a room in which a richly clad woman preens as she admires her reflection in a hand mirror. The engraving is virtually a catalogue of images emblematic of the transience of earthly things and attachments. These seductive images are no more substantial than the fleeting reflections in the mirror or the smoke vanishing upward from the urn on the sill beside Amor. The ornate table is strewn with the vain toys of this world: toilet articles, jewelry, coins, goldsmiths' work, playing cards, and a backgammon board with dice.

The image emphasizes the folly of earthly love or physical passion. The chained ape that leers up at the woman's snarling lap dog traditionally signifies the base sensuous desires that bind us to the material world.[1] Behind the figure of the woman in love with her reflected image there hangs in a dark alcove a half-concealed tapestry with a motif of coupling lovers.

Even the fortified castle on a distant hilltop is part of this complicated web of literary reference. The Latin inscription on another *Vanitas* print of the period, engraved by Jan Saenredam after a design by Abraham Bloemaert (B. 30), proclaims that no fortress is safe from the dominion of Death.[2]

De Gheyn's personal device appears to have been a winged hourglass on which the sun's

1. Janson, 1952, chap. 5, "The Fettered Ape," pp. 145ff.
2. See the German translation and reproduction in Berlin, 1979, no. 87.

rays beam down, an allusion to the passing of time and an admonition to the artist not to waste it.[3] In the last will and testament drawn up by De Gheyn and his wife, Eva Stalpaert, in 1599 appears the statement that human life is as transient as a shadow and that nothing is more certain than death.[4]

The Dutch Mannerist engravers enjoyed erudite and complicated literary allegories. De Gheyn himself engraved or produced designs for two other engravings on the *Vanitas* theme (Holl. 98 and Holl. 103), but neither suggests as strongly as does the present one a genre scene, a peep into an upper-class interior.

The vividly rendered table-top still life reminds us that De Gheyn's painting of 1603 in the Metropolitan Museum, New York, is the earliest known example of the *Vanitas* still-life paintings so popular in Holland after 1620.[5]

In an exceptionally brilliant impression like one exhibited here, it is easy to grasp how much De Gheyn's engraving style contributes to the meaning of the image. It could be said that De Gheyn as an engraver takes his point of departure from Goltzius's 1587 *Standard Bearer* (cat. no. 1), for in the engravings from his own designs that can be securely attributed to him he places specific description of surface textures and coloristic suggestion before sculptural values. Here De Gheyn's descriptive skill with the burin lends a glittering surface allure to worldly things (see the woman's silk or satin skirt) that gives the moral more edge.

The punning Latin verses[6] with the signature of the scholarly prodigy Hugo de Groot, latinized as Grotius (1583 – 1645), give the author's age as twelve, which fact, supported by the style of the engraving, would date the print about 1595 or 1596. Grotius, whose

3. In De Gheyn's portrait in the series of portrait engravings of artists published by Hendrik Hondius, reproduced as frontispiece in Van Regteren Altena, 1936.

4. Cited in Bergström, 1970, p. 150.

5. Bergström, 1970, and Walsh, 1974, pp. 341 – 342. For the *Vanitas* still life see also Bergström, 1956, chap. 4, and Leyden, 1970.

Remonstrant religious beliefs caused him to spend a good deal of his career in exile, was not only a precocious Latinist but also, in his maturity, a jurist whose writings were to make a lasting contribution to our conception of law.[7] During his early years Grotius wrote Latin verses for a number of De Gheyn's prints. In 1599 De Gheyn engraved for Grotius's edition of the works of the antique writer Martianus Capella a medallion-format portrait in which the fifteen-year-old scholar proudly displays the chain and medallion awarded him by King Henri IV of France (Holl. 314).

6. I would like to thank Mr. A. C. Eijffinger of the Grotius Instituut of the Koninklijke Nederlandse Akademie van Wetenschappen for providing me with a Dutch translation of these verses. He points out that the engraver made a mistake in the first word of the second line, which should read "Quae." My own literal translation of Mr. Eijffinger's Dutch follows: "O senseless senses of mankind, full of meaninglessness, which only finds an end, when, miserable ones, we find our miserable end."

7. For Grotius's career see Amsterdam, 1975, p. 75.

12

JACQUES DE GHEYN II
The Prodigal Son (Allegory of Idleness and Luxury), 1596

Engraving after Karel van Mander
Pass. 190, Valentiner 78, Holl. 410[1]
Left center: *KvMandere inuen, Iacobus de geÿn sculptor et excu;* at left: *Anno S. M D XC VI*
425 x 670 mm. (platemark; printed from two plates; sheets trimmed and joined at center)
Wm.: fleur-de-lis
Museum of Fine Arts, Boston, Gift of the Print and Drawing Club. 1979.123

There is a tradition in sixteenth-century Netherlandish painting in which the passage in Christ's parable of the prodigal son that recounts how the prodigal "wasted his substance with riotous living" in a far country (Luke 15:13) is illustrated by scenes of high life or by tavern or bordello scenes. In De Gheyn's large engraving of 1596 after a design by Karel van Mander,[1] the prodigal is a very young man dressed in a fashionable peascod doublet. He bows and doffs his hat to his dancing partner, a young woman whose shimmering gown is reminiscent of that of the woman who personifies vanity in De Gheyn's *Vanitas* (cat. no. 11). Musicians accompany the dance, while at the right an extravagantly dressed company carries on flirtations around a Fountain of Love. In the right foreground a woman whose costume emphasizes her voluptuousness, drinks deep and lolls back in a man's lap. Under the table behind them a dog peers out, responding to the licentious behavior with a baleful look, while at left a group of jesters or fools laughingly point out the follies of idleness and luxury. In the left background a young man, his funds presumably exhausted, is driven by women from an inn or bordello, which has as its sign the orb of the world. Below this admonitory episode, in a ravine beyond which

crumbling Roman ruins are visible, a bent old man, apparently burnt out by worldly pleasures, hobbles away with the aid of crutches.

The engraving is dedicated to Georg Eberhard, Count of Solms and Lord of Müntzenberg (1566–1602), a leader of the Dutch military forces in the struggle with Spain.[2] The heavily moralizing Latin verses by the physician and poet Pieter Hogerbeets (1542–1599),[3] a friend of Karel van Mander, warn the sinner of the wiles concealed by the seduction of love and observe how repentance accompanies pleasure. The poet implores him who has strayed from the straight path not to fear the anger of a Father who is quick to forgive the one who has truly repented.

An ambiguity that confronts one when viewing and "reading" late sixteenth- and early seventeenth-century pictorial moralities on the theme of worldly pleasures is that the sensual appeal and visual extravagance of the image constantly threaten to overwhelm the moral message.

Karel van Mander in his instructional poem for young artists and his lives of the artists frequently gives examples of the ways in which riotous living can endanger the artist's work and career. Appropriately enough in this context he relates, in his life of De Gheyn, how the attractions of youthful company distracted the artist from his work before he married and settled down.[4]

De Gheyn made more engravings after Van Mander than after any other artist. Engravings by De Gheyn and other engravers after Van Mander's designs have been extremely useful to modern scholars in their continuing attempt to reconstruct Van Mander's works in painting and drawing. This represents a latter-day confirmation of Samuel van Hoogstraten's statement in his *Hooge Schoole der Schilderkonst* of 1678 that such prints are the "booden en tolken" (ambassadors and spokesmen) that

proclaim the artist's fame to the world.[5] De Gheyn's engraving of *The Prodigal Son* continued to proclaim Van Mander's fame right through the seventeenth century. The plates of the *Prodigal*, like those of many Dutch Mannerist engravings, passed from hand to hand, and the last publisher's address to appear on the print is that of Gerard Valck, a late seventeenth-century publisher (about 1651/2–1726).

Large-scale engravings printed from more than one plate and teeming with detail are one of the characteristic products of the Dutch Mannerist engravers of the late sixteenth century. The *Prodigal* was printed from two plates and lost a few millimeters from the center of the image when it was trimmed and pasted together by a previous owner. Fine, early, well-preserved impressions of these engravings that have the scale of paintings are rare. Many of them were probably lost when the prints were mounted on boards and framed unglazed like paintings or mounted on cloth between rollers like maps, the "prentbordekens" and "prenten op rollekens" listed in seventeenth-century estate inventories.[6]

It is interesting to note that, although this engraving after Van Mander is not lacking in brilliant passages of textural description, De Gheyn devotes less attention to description of surfaces and textures than he did in the contemporary engraving from his own design, the *Vanitas* (cat. no. 11).

5. Hoogstraten, 1678, p. 196.
6. De Roever, 1885, p. 268.

1. See the discussion of the imagery of the print in Valentiner, 1930, pp. 51–52. The print was preceded by a series of prints on the subject of the Prodigal Son after designs by Karel van Mander engraved by Jacob Matham and dated 1592 (Valentiner 74–77). Valentiner lists a total of 158 prints after Van Mander's designs.

2. Ter Laan, 1939.
3. See biography in Rotterdam, 1974, p. 21.
4. Van Mander/Floerke, 1906, vol. 2, pp. 320–321.

Mandere inuen, Iacobus de geyn sculptor et excu.

Disce voluptati comes est metanaea, merasq́   Libertas abeat quo tam speciosa benigni   Dilapsum suic retulisse pedem ne culpa pudoris   Tardus vzk irasci, sic est ignoscere promptus
Sub blando Meretrix nectua amore tricas;   Quae patris excuso quaeritur Imperio: Terreat, aut tanti quae subit ira Patris: Quos rudet admisi poenituisse mali.   Plegeli.

12

24

13

HENDRIK GOLTZIUS
Frederick de Vries, 1597

Engraving
B. 190, Dut. 190[II], Hirschmann 218[II], Holl. 218[II],
Strauss 344[II]
Lower left: *Anno 1597/HG*
357 x 264 mm. (platemark)
Wm.: Crowned shield (close to Briquet 1476)
Coll.: C. Schniewind (see L. 638)
The Art Institute of Chicago, The Stanley Field
Fund. 1959.217

Frederick de Vries, the boy who smiles out
at us, was apprenticed to Goltzius. During
Goltzius's stay in Venice, some six years before
this engraving was made, he had visited the
boy's father, the still-life painter Dirk de Vries,
and drawn his portrait.

   In the Latin inscription in the cartouche at
bottom center, Goltzius dedicates the engraving to Dirk de Vries in Venice as a token of
friendship and as a means of showing him how
well his absent son is faring.[1] Frederick is
shown holding a dove aloft in one hand while
throwing his leg over a large hunting dog,[2] as
if about to take a ride on him (note the reins).

   The somewhat additive character of the
design and the rather awkward pose of the
child may be partly due to the emblematic
character of the image. Latin verses in the
lower margin by the poet and publisher Petrus
Scriverius (1576–1660),[3] inform us that simplicity seeks out and loves faithfulness; the simple, guileless boy is drawn to the faithful dog.[4]
The dog seems to have been part of Goltzius's
household, for he made a number of drawings
of it. A portrait-like, painterly study of the
dog's head in colored chalks (Reznicek, 1961,
no. 415) relates closely to the print.

   Goltzius's dog stands in for the artist here,
representing his function as faithful guardian
and teacher of the boy. As Reznicek noted, in

1. German translation in Berlin, 1979, p. 40.

2. A *Drentse patrijshond* (literally, partridge dog from
Drente).

3. See biography, Rotterdam, 1974, pp. 37–38.

4. German translation in Berlin, 1979, p. 40.

the hieroglyphics section of Karel van Mander's *Wtbeeldinge der Figueren (Representation of Figures)*, the first meaning of the figure of a dog is "the upright teacher" who fearlessly keeps watch over the souls of men and punishes their sins.[5] The dove held by the boy may signify his simplicity or innocence. Van Mander in his *Wtbeeldinge der Figueren* lists simplicity as one of the possible meanings of the figure of a dove.[6] Frederick de Vries died relatively young and in his will testified to his warm feelings for his teacher.[7]

This highly original friendship portrait makes private relationships public by perpetuating them in an engraving. Ambitious engraved portraits of children or adolescents were by no means common at this time, particularly outside aristocratic circles. Even more original is the genre-like conception of an allegorical or emblematic image. This sense of everyday reality is heightened by Goltzius's renewed desire to achieve a painterly suggestion of color and texture in engraving (see the *Standard Bearer,* cat. no. 1), an interest most clearly expressed in the coat of the dog. Goltzius was, in fact, on the point of abandoning engraving for painting.

The outdoor setting reflects Goltzius's increasing involvement with landscape, both in drawings and in prints during these years and, appropriately enough, is Goltzius's personal adaptation of the Venetian landscape style of Titian and his circle. A comparable "Venetian" landscape background already appears in the 1593 *Holy Family with St. John* (Hirschmann 14) in the series of "master engravings."

5. Reznicek, 1961, no. 415, pp. 439–440.

6. Van Mander/Davaco, 1969, p. 131 verso.

7. Hirschmann, 1919, p. 112.

14

HENDRIK GOLTZIUS
Landscape with a Seated Couple, designed about 1596–1598

Woodcut on blue paper heightened with opaque white watercolor
B. 243, Hirschmann 379[I], Holl. 379[I], Strauss 409[I]
Lower center: *HG*
113 x 144 mm. (block)
Museum of Fine Arts, Boston, Gift of the Children of Dr. James B. Ayer. M28768

15

HENDRIK GOLTZIUS
Landscape with a Seated Couple, designed about 1596–1598

Chiaroscuro woodcut with two tone blocks in shades of green
B. 243, Hirschmann 379[II], Holl. 379[II], Strauss 409[II]
Lower center: *HG*
114 x 147 mm. (block)
Wm.: Caduceus above a shield (see Briquet 5513)
Coll.: J. Hofmann (L. 1264)
Museum of Fine Arts, Boston, Bequest of W.G. Russell Allen. 63.617

A number of the woodcuts that bear Goltzius's monogram or that have been traditionally associated with his woodcut production (see cat. nos. 27, 28) occur both in impressions from the line block on coarse-fibered grayish blue paper of a kind known traditionally as "Venetian" blue paper and in chiaroscuro versions with tone blocks printed in color on white paper. Among these are the series of four small landscapes to which the *Landscape with the Seated Couple* belongs (Hirschmann 378–381).

Impressions of these landscapes on blue paper are frequently highlighted with freely applied touches of opaque white watercolor that relate in their general pattern to but are by no means identical with the highlights cut into the tone blocks of the chiaroscuro versions. In the impression exhibited here, for example, the white highlights actually cover or cancel out some of the printed lines on the little hillock in the right foreground.

The impressions on blue paper with their lively hand-applied white highlights call to mind Van Mander's recommendation to young artists learning to draw that gray or blue papers provide a useful middle tone from which to develop darks or lights.[1]

Impressions from the line block only, especially those heightened with white, are quite complete in effect without the addition of tone blocks. The tone blocks in the chiaroscuro versions are, in fact, less integral to the effect of the print than are the tone blocks in the set of the six deities designed about 1588–89, which appear never to have been printed without tone blocks (see cat. nos. 3, 4.)

The tone blocks in the chiaroscuro versions of the landscapes do contribute highlights and, in the frequently encountered impressions in combinations of greens, a suggestion of the natural colors of the landscape.

Strauss notes that the condition of the line blocks is generally less good (see the breaks in the border lines) in the chiaroscuro impressions than in the majority of the blue paper ones and suggests that they were printed later.[2] The issue is complicated, however, by the existence of a few impressions on blue paper in which the line block has most of the breaks and losses associated with the chiaroscuro versions.[3] It is not known how rapidly the line blocks deteriorated in the interval before printing or during the process of printing, but damage is so common that on encountering a "perfect" impression, one immediately looks to see if the damage has been filled in with pen and black ink. Further compilation of watermark information should be helpful in determining the date of the chiaroscuro versions but is complicated by the fact that little is known about the blue paper, its manufacture, and the dating of its scarce watermarks.[4]

1. Van Mander/Hoecker, 1916, p. 58.

2. Strauss, 1977, vol. 2, p. 718.

3. I have seen such impressions in the collection of the Berlin print room.

4. Of the four images in this series (Hirschmann 378–381) the Museum of Fine Arts, Boston, has nine impressions, each represented once on blue paper with only the

14 (actual size)

As in the case of the woodcuts of the six deities, it is not known how these woodcuts were produced or who cut them. I cannot agree with Strauss, who discovers the name "Matham" concealed in the shading of all four line blocks and therefore concludes that they were cut by Goltzius's stepson, Jacob Matham.[5]

The four small landscapes are radically different in style and execution from the set of six deities designed about 1588–89 (cat. nos. 3, 4), testifying to the new directions Goltzius's art took after his Italian journey. In the eighth chapter of his instructional poem, the section devoted to landscape, Van Mander recommends as models for the young artist the woodcuts of Titian and the prints of Alpine views of Bruegel.[6] These prints after designs of

line block and once in the chiaroscuro version on white paper; of the *Landscape with Farmhouse* (Hirschmann 380) there is an additional impression on blue. All nine impressions, as well as other Goltzius woodcuts in the collection, were examined for watermarks, and beta-radiographs were made of the papers by Elizabeth Lunning, assistant conservator in the Department of Prints, Drawings, and Photographs. Two of the landscapes printed on white paper, the *Landscape with Seated Couple* (Hirschmann 379) and the *Rock on the Seacoast* (Hirschmann 381), bear marks related to Briquet 5515, a coat of arms surmounted by a caduceus, which Briquet dates from 1591 to 1600. The remaining two on white paper, *Landscape with a Waterfall* (Hirschmann 378) and *Landscape with Farmhouse* (Hirschmann 380), bear the mark of a fleur-de-lis with the letter R appended. Apart from the R, these marks are similar to Briquet 6970 in size and configuration and are dated by him from 1561 to 1620. It is interesting to note that the marks on Hirschmann 378 and 380, though not precisely the same, are so close to each other that they were almost certainly produced at the same time on a pair of molds. Furthermore, a mark identical to that on *Landscape with a Waterfall* was found on *Mary Magdalene* (Hirschmann 363), and on *Seascape with Two Sailing Vessels* (Hirschmann 383), and a mark identical to that on *Landscape with Farmhouse,* was found on the *Monk Fed by Ravens* (Hirschmann 363a).

The five impressions on blue paper were radiographed, and none have watermarks. An impression of the line block of the *Mary Magdalene* on blue paper was also radiographed, however, and revealed a large and well-formed, uncrowned, double-headed eagle of a type related to Briquet 234 and dated by him from 1560 to 1564.

5. Strauss, 1977, vol. 2, p. 718.

6. Van Mander/Hoecker, 1916, pp. 206–207.

the Venetian and Netherlandish masters were sources of inspiration for the landscape drawings in pen that Goltzius made from about 1593–94 to about 1597–98.

These drawings are very helpful in localizing the date of the design of the set of four little woodcut landscapes. When one considers the 1596 Besançon *Landscape with Mercury* (Reznicek, 1961, no. 393) and the three landscapes on gray or brown paper, all heightened with white, which Reznicek dates in the years 1597–1599 (Reznicek, 1961, nos. 398, 401, 406), as well as the landscape background of the 1597 Frederick de Vries engraving, which so closely resembles these woodcut landscapes in style and motif, it seems plausible to suggest the period 1596–1598 for the design of the woodcuts.

The cursive parallel shading lines and the luxuriance of the foliage call to mind the woodcuts after Titian and his circle, especially those after designs of Domenico Campagnola (see, for example, Boldrini after Campagnola, *Landscape with St. John the Baptist*).[7] As in his drawings that are Venetian in inspiration Goltzius tends to emphasize much more than would the Venetians the rhythmic undulation of the landscape forms. All four landscapes are seen from above and at a certain remove, as in the prints after Bruegel's Alpine landscape inventions. The Goltzius landscapes are of course much smaller, more miniaturistic in scale than most of the woodcuts of the Titian school or the engravings after Bruegel. The landscape with the waterfall (Hirschmann 378) and the rocky coastal view (Hirschmann 381) are full of a wilder fantasy that is part of a sixteenth-century Netherlandish tradition going back to the rocky landscapes of Patinier, but the landscape shown here and, above all, that with the farmhouse (Hirschmann 380) prepare the way for the gentler, less dramatic landscapes that characterize the new developments in landscape in the early seventeenth century.

7. Reproduced in Washington, 1976–77, p. 161.

15 (actual size)

Jacob Savery
about 1565-70 – about 1602/03

Jacob Savery was one of the links in an artistic chain whereby the graphic vocabulary of the South Netherlandish artist Pieter Bruegel (about 1525-1569) was transmitted to seventeenth-century Holland. Born in Courtrai (Kortrijk) about 1565-1570, Savery was a pupil of Hans Bol, a follower of Pieter Bruegel. Painter, miniature painter, and draftsman, Savery, like a number of other artists working in the Bruegel tradition (see in this exhibition Vinckboons cat. nos. 21, 22), fled the disruptions caused by war in the south and settled in the north, being recorded as a citizen of Amsterdam in 1591. He died of the plague in Amsterdam about 1602-03.[1] The painter Roelant Savery (cat. no. 19) was his younger brother.

We know eight landscape etchings from Savery's hand: a pair of related large hunting scenes (Bur. 7 and 8) and a series of six small wooded landscapes (Bur. 1-6).[2] All appeared first as pure etchings and then were reworked with the burin and republished by Hendrik Hondius, who added his republication dates, 1602 and 1639 respectively, to the two groups, thereby creating confusion as to the date of execution of the etchings.

1. According to Van Mander in his life of Hans Bol (van Mander/Floerke, 1906, vol. 2, p. 60), Savery died in 1602, but the Fondation Custodia (Lugt Coll.), Paris, has in its collection a pen drawing dated 1603 (Paris, 1968-69, no. 136).

2. There is also an engraved title page with a view of the center of the Hague signed "I Saverij Fe" for Paullo Merula, *Synopsis Praxeos Civilis,* Amsterdam, 1592. M.D. Henkel in Thieme-Becker, vol. 29, p. 504, gives further attributions of unsigned prints.

16 (actual size)

16

JACOB SAVERY
Landscape, about 1595-1600

Etching
LeBl. 7, no. 4, Bur. 4[1]
Lower left: 4
121 x 92 mm. (platemark)
Coll.: H.F. Sewall (L. 1309)
Museum of Fine Arts, Boston, Harvey D. Parker Collection. P8403

The simplest in motif and the most atmospheric of Savery's six small etched landscapes,[1] this marshy woodland derives its vocabulary from Bruegel's only etching, the *Rabbit Hunt* of 1560 (Van Bastelaer 1). Short hatches, dots, and flicks have replaced continuous contour lines, emphasizing the softness of the masses of foliage and of the grassy mounds and suggesting a painterly indistinctness, a melding of the landscape forms with the surrounding atmosphere. Savery's vocabulary of strokes, as in the etchings of his teacher Hans Bol, is more regular, more decorative in effect than Bruegel's lively, unpatterned, less predictable vocabulary of strokes.[2]

Savery's Bruegel-like use of broken strokes and stipples to suggest a painterly dissolution of forms in atmosphere was to be significant for Dutch etchers of the second decade of the seventeenth century such as Claes Jansz. Visscher and Willem Buytewech.

1. An Zwollo proposed in conversation dating the series in the period 1595-1600.

2. Jacques de Gheyn II's 1598 etching after a Bruegel drawing of 1561 (Holl. 338) is another example of emulation of Bruegel's graphic style contemporary with the Savery etchings.

Paulus van Vianen
about 1570–1613/14

If Paulus van Vianen had not worked on a small scale and in precious metals, he would probably be more widely recognized today for his achievement as a sculptor. Born about 1570, he was one of a family of distinguished Utrecht gold and silversmiths that included his father Willem Eerstensz. van Vianen, his brother Adam, and his nephew Christiaen. After a period of apprenticeship with the Utrecht silversmiths Bruno and Cornelis Ellardsz. van Leydenberch, he traveled abroad and by 1599 had been in France, Italy, and Germany. From 1596 to 1601 he was active at the court of the Dukes of Bavaria and then spent two years in the service of Bishop Wolf Dietrich von Raitenau in Salzburg. From 1603 until his death in 1613 or 1614, he served as official goldsmith *(kammergoldschmied)* to the Holy Roman Emperor Rudolph II at Prague.[1]

Although he produced cups and vessels in silver and gold, Paulus van Vianen is best known for his small, highly refined relief plaquettes that place mythological subjects in a northern forest setting.[2] His delicate, atmospheric pen and wash drawings of woodlands in the Alps and around Prague are some of the freshest, most sensitive landscape drawings of the early seventeenth century.[3]

The punch engraving exhibited here is the only print attributed to him.

1. See biography by J.R. ter Molen, pp. 367–368, in Amsterdam/Toledo/Boston, 1980. Mr. ter Molen is preparing a dissertation on the Van Vianen family.

2. For Paulus van Vianen's work in silver and gold see Frederiks, 1952, vol. I, pp. 111–161.

3. For Paulus van Vianen's drawings see Berlin, 1975, p. 178.

17
Attributed to PAULUS VAN VIANEN
Landscape with Tancred and Herminia

Punch engraving
100 x 107 mm. (platemark)
Wm.: fragment of coat of arms
Rijksmuseum, Amsterdam. A12028

This delicate punch engraving illustrates a popular episode from the Italian poet Torquato Tasso's epic romance on the theme of the First Crusade, *Gerusalemma Liberata* (Jerusalem Delivered), which enjoyed an immediate international success after first being published in its entirety in 1581.[1] Herminia and Tancred's squire, Vafrin, have just discovered Herminia's beloved Tancred, wounded in the combat in which he had slain his Saracen opponent Argantes, whose body is here half-visible in the vale below. Herminia, watering Tancred with her tears, restores him to consciousness and nurses him back to life, cutting off her long tresses to bind his wounds. The episode was chosen for one of the illustrations in the first illustrated edition of the poem issued in Genoa in 1590[2] and was featured in most of the many subsequent illustrated editions.

The engraving, although catalogued in the Rijksmuseum collection under Paulus van Vianen's name, is published here for the first time. The attribution to Paulus van Vianen is supported by the similarity of the engraving to the artist's drawings and relief plaquettes of the Prague period as well as by the unusual technique in which the print is executed. The northern forest landscape, with its feathery trees, cascading stream, and log dams, provides a magical if incongruous setting for the events of Tasso's poem and closely parallels the pen and wash studies from nature made by Paulus in the mountain forests around Salzburg and Prague about 1603–04.[3] The delicate drawing

1. The subject is identified in a Dutch inscription on the verso: "Verlost Jerusalem 19ᵈᵉ Zang" "Tancred door Herminie en Vafri verpleegd-"

2. Mortimer, 1974, vol. 2, pp. 681–683, illus. p. 682.

3. For a discussion of the sketchbook drawings in Budapest and Berlin, some of which are dated 1603, see Teréz

of a mountain woodland gorge with log dams, cascades, and a ruined temple in the Rijksmuseum collection (Amsterdam, cat. drawings, 1978, no. 465) is quite similar in motif and mood to the engraving. Between 1606 and 1613 Paulus van Vianen produced subtle sculptural reliefs in an oblong format, some of which are close in scale to the print and place history subjects, mostly mythological, in such a woodland setting.[4] There is even one remarkable plaquette that is a pure landscape (Rijksmuseum, Amsterdam, Frederiks, no. 77). Paulus's reputation is in part founded on his ability to translate into sculptural terms a painterly conception involving highly sophisticated late Mannerist figures set in an atmospheric, directly observed landscape.

The fact that the print was executed entirely in punchwork provides additional confirmation that it was made by a goldsmith. Beginning about 1580, as Jessen informs us in his book on the ornament print,[5] German goldsmiths began to publish, as models for other goldsmiths, ornament prints in which the lines were executed entirely in dots made with goldsmith's punches. (See, for example, Hans Kellerthaler's series of the *Elements* of 1589, Holl., German, 1–4.)[6] Paulus van Vianen's print, unlike the majority of these late sixteenth-century punch prints, consists not merely of neat dotted outlines but also of irregular masses of dots or stipples, which suggest either the blended tones of a wash or the sharper accents made by the touch of a pen.

In the early seventeenth century other members of the Kellerthaler family produced plates with elaborate shading effects achieved with punchwork, but impressions from these decorative plates produce a negative image with the values reversed, indicating that the plates were

Gerszi, in Budapest, cat. drawings, 1971, vol. I, p. 98. For a further discussion of this group of drawings, see Carlos van Hasselt in Paris, 1968–69, vol. I, p. 164, and K.G. Boon in Amsterdam, cat. drawings, 1978, vol. I, pp. 170–172.

4. Frederiks, 1952, vol. I, pp. 130ff.

5. Jessen, 1920, pp. 115ff.

6. Reproduced in Holl., German, vol. 16, p. 46.

17

not originally intended for printing. (See
Daniel Kellerthaler, Holl., German, vol. 16, pp.
42–44.) In Paulus van Vianen's print, thus far
known in only one impression, the value relationships are not reversed, and the lower margin has been left blank as if prepared to receive
an engraved inscription or verses, as one would
expect of a print with a literary subject at this
time.

Abraham Bloemaert
1564–1651

The painter Abraham Bloemaert, who was born in Gorinchem in 1564 and died in Utrecht in 1651, enjoyed one of the longest and most successful artistic careers of his time, bridging the generations from the "Spranger" period to Rembrandt's artistic maturity. Karel van Mander at the beginning and end of his life of Bloemaert cannot resist making rhetorical plays on the painter's name (Bloem-aert is the equivalent of "flower-like").[1] According to Van Mander, Bloemaert, while still young, moved with his family to Utrecht. He first studied drawing with his father, Cornelis Bloemaert, a sculptor, architect, and engineer, copying works of Frans Floris. He was then placed by his father with one inadequate teacher after another, the most successful of whom was Joos de Beer, in whose house he had the opportunity to study and copy works by the Italianizing artists Anthonie Blocklandt and Dirk Barendsz.

At age fifteen or sixteen Bloemaert was sent to Paris, where he studied with three masters in succession, among them the Flemish artist Hieronymus Francken. He returned to Utrecht about 1583 but moved with his father to Amsterdam in 1591, where he found roomy studio space in a church building. Here he began to paint mythological subjects under the influence of Spranger. After marrying in 1592, he again returned to Utrecht. A second marriage around 1600 produced six children. Four of the sons, Adriaen, Cornelis, Hendrik, and Frederik, studied with their father and became artists. Jan Both was probably his pupil, and other significant painters such as Cornelis Poelenburg, Hendrik Terbrugghen, Gerard Honthorst, and Jan Baptist Weenix are said to have studied with him. We hear of him still painting at age eighty-one.

Bloemaert's paintings seem to have brought substantial sums in his lifetime, and he owned several houses in Utrecht. In our own time his paintings are slowly being rediscovered, but his drawings are more widely appreciated. Van Mander, who discusses at length Bloemaert's landscape paintings, also singles out for praise his landscape drawings in pen, noting that they are often washed with color.

Bloemaert seems to have executed only one print himself, the *Juno* exhibited here, but over six hundred engravings, etchings, and woodcuts were produced after his designs by other artists. When engravers worked after Bloemaert, they customarily altered their touch to accord with Bloemaert's style, adopting a more delicate calligraphic line and a silvery tonality. Van Mander in his life of Bloemaert also discusses engravings after designs prepared by Bloemaert, mentioning those by Jan Muller and in particular Jan Saenredam. Van Mander notes Saenredam's feeling for Bloemaert's drawings and how he did his utmost to reproduce their qualities. In the light of the oil studies, often monochrome or grisaille, produced by Rubens and Van Dyck at a later date, as a guide to engravers reproducing their work, it is interesting that Van Mander describes Bloemaert as making pen drawings that he then worked up with black and white oil pigments to serve as models for the engravers.[2]

Given the fluidity of Bloemaert's pen line, the plant-like pliability of his figures, and the undulant contours of his landscape forms, it is not surprising that many of the prints after his designs are etchings. The landscapes with picturesque farmhouses etched by printmakers such as Boetius A. Bolswert and Claes Jansz. Visscher after Bloemaert's drawings play an important role in the development of the etched landscape in the early seventeenth century.

Chiaroscuro woodcuts were also used to reproduce Bloemaert's designs. Those by his son Frederik usually combined an etched line plate and woodcut tone blocks in the manner of the Italian chiaroscuro print after Parmigianino (B. vol. 12, p. 78, no. 27) or the sixteenth-century Netherlandish chiaroscuros by Crispin van den Broeck. Frederik Bloemaert's chiaroscuros form part of a drawing book, a compilation of models for draftsmen after Bloemaert, which first appeared about 1650 and was published in a deluxe edition in 1740.[3] Ludolf Büsinck, the German woodcut artist working in Paris, made a chiaroscuro *Holy Family* after Bloemaert (Strauss, 1973, no. 72).[4] Another group is composed of the chiaroscuro woodcuts with an interlaced monogram formed from the letters A, B, L, and O.[5]

1. Van Mander/Floerke, 1906, vol. 2, pp. 350–361.

2. Ibid., pp. 360–361.

3. Bolten, 1979, pp. 26–37.

4. For Büsinck's chiaroscuro woodcuts see Stechow, 1938, pp. 393–419.

5. First, three small chiaroscuro woodcuts: the *Virgin and Child,* bust length, Strauss, 1973, no. 147; a half-length *Holy Family,* Holl., Bloemaert, 7, both tentatively attributed by Stechow, Vassar, 1970, no. 27a, to Bloemaert himself, and a half-length bust of Joseph or St. Jerome, Holl., Bloemaert, 9. All of the foregoing are attributed by Pieter van Thiel, 1978, p. 12, to Ludolph Büsinck. Secondly, two prints in which etching is used for line and woodcut for tone, a kneeling *Magdalene,* Holl., Bloemaert, 10, and the *Three Maries,* Holl., Bloemaert, 8. The last two both relate to another seated *Magdalene* in the same combination of techniques signed by Boetius A. Bolswert, Holl., Bolswert, 95.

18

ABRAHAM BLOEMAERT
Juno

Etching
LeBl. 17, Wurz. 2[1], Holl. 4[1]
Lower center: *ABloem: fe.*
144 x 114 mm. (platemark)
The Metropolitan Museum of Art, Harris Brisbane
Dick Fund. 33.52.4

The only print that can with some confidence
be regarded as executed by Bloemaert's own
hand is this etching of Juno, consort of Jupiter,
accompanied by her symbol the peacock. The
etching, with its abbreviated inscription of
"fe." for "fecit" was subsequently published by
Boetius A. Bolswert, who added his name as
publisher to the plate in the next state and
issued it as the third in a series together with
his engravings after Bloemaert's drawings of
Athena and Venus (Holl. 284, 285). The three
goddesses were the participants in the beauty
contest in which the Trojan nobleman Paris
awarded the prize of the golden apple to
Venus, who had promised him the most beautiful woman in the world. Paris's abduction of
his prize, Helen, wife of Menelaus, unleashed
the events that led to the Trojan war. In the set
of three prints the victorious Venus occupies
the central position.[1]

These engravings after Bloemaert were considered by Burchard to be among the earliest
efforts in that medium by Bolswert, who, like
his brother, Schelte A. Bolswert, later became
one of the leading engravers reproducing the
work of Rubens in Antwerp. Burchard dates
the engravings and Bloemaert's etching about
1610.[2]

Bloemaert's preparatory drawing in reverse
for the *Venus* engraving is executed in pen and
wash highlighted with opaque white watercolor; it is in the collection of the Albertina,

1. Van Mander in his life of Bloemaert mentions a series
of large painted roundels of the heads of the three goddesses in the collection of Jacques Razet of Amsterdam;
see Van Mander/Floerke, 1906, vol. 2, pp. 358–359.

2. Burchard, 1917, pp. 26–27.

18 (actual size)

Vienna.[3] The preparatory drawing in reverse for the *Athena* engraving, executed in the same technique as the Albertina drawing, is in the Düsseldorf museum.[4]

Bloemaert's etching of *Juno,* with its simplicity and freedom of execution, is a continuation of Gerrit Pietersz.'s approach to the handling of the medium in his etchings of 1593 (cat. nos. 9, 10). Bloemaert's sketch-like fluency of line is especially evident in comparison with the somewhat labored engraved line of Bolswert.

In relation to the coloristic developments noted in North Netherlandish engraving of the late sixteenth century, it is interesting to observe that in Bolswert's engravings more attention is devoted to the shimmer of light on glossy fabrics than in Bloemaert's etching.

3. Albertina, cat. drawings, 1928, no. 430, illus.

4. Düsseldorf, 1968, no. 7, pl. 22. The catalogue dates it in the 1590s. A Bloemaert drawing of *Juno* related in style and conception to the set of three prints was in 1966 in a German private collection; see Bremen, 1966, no. 118, pl. 144.

Roelant Savery
about 1576 – 1639

Roelant Savery was a pupil of his brother, Jacob, and, like him, based his art on pictorial traditions initiated by Pieter Bruegel the Elder, particularly Bruegel's Alpine views. Born in Courtrai about 1576, Roelant Savery moved north with his family, probably settling in Amsterdam at the same time as his brother, about 1591. There he was strongly influenced by the forest landscapes of another southern emigrant, Gillis van Coninxloo. By 1605 he was in Prague in the service of Emperor Rudolph II, who commissioned him to spend two years drawing landscapes in the Tyrolean Alps. After the death of Rudolph in 1612, he briefly returned to Amsterdam but was recalled to Vienna to serve Rudolph's successor, Emperor Mathias. In 1619 Roelant Savery settled permanently in Utrecht, joining the artists' guild there in that year. He died in Utrecht in 1639. His pupils included Gilles d'Hondecoeter, Willem van Nieuwlandt, and Allart van Everdingen.

Roelant Savery is known for his paintings and drawings that capture the chaotic wildness of Alpine landscapes and for his encyclopedic animal paintings on themes such as the Garden of Eden or Orpheus and the Animals inspired by Rudolph's private menagerie in Prague.

Two landscape etchings can be given with certainty to his hand (Wurz. 1 and 2), and a third etching, unsigned and apparently unique, in Hamburg (inv. no. 4694), can be tentatively attributed to him on the basis of style (see illus.).[1] The last, a small (117 x 42 mm. plate) etching of a wanderer or pilgrim leaning against the gnarled base of a tree is simpler in execution and more delicate in the etched line than the two larger etchings but virtually identical in style of drawing. The tall, narrow format is very unusual for the time.

1. Erasmus, 1908, pp. 184–185, observed the close stylistic relationship but felt there was not enough comparative material to confirm the attribution.

Numerous etchings and engravings after Roelant's designs[2] by contemporary printmakers such as Aegidius and Jan Sadeler widely advertised his landscape style.

2. Including the *Stag-hunt* (Wurz. 3) and the *Fox-hunt* (Wurz. 4), which Wurzbach attributed to Roelant's hand.

19

ROELANT SAVERY
Gnarled Trees in a Swamp

Etching
Nag. 1[1], And. 1[1], Wurz. 1[1]
124 x 144 mm. (platemark)
Davison Art Center, Wesleyan University, Middletown, Connecticut, Gift of George W. Davison, B.A., 1892. 43. DI. 293

Roelant Savery's experiences in the Tyrolean Alps seem to have impressed upon him a vision of the tangled density of untamed woodlands and the drama of the growth and death of trees in their struggle for existence.

Here a screen of intricately interwoven vegetation almost denies us a view of the deeper recesses of the landscape. The distant travelers seem puny compared with the titanic limbs of the foreground trees. These stuggling tree forms have a sense of anthropomorphic life about them comparable to that of the tree in Goltzius's *Frederick de Vries* engraving (cat. no. 13), but here it is intensified by the snaky fluidity and freedom of the etched line.

An undated preparatory drawing in reverse of the etching and indented for transfer is in the collection of the Rijksprentenkabinet, Amsterdam.[1] A group of chalk drawings of more expansive Alpine forest landscapes with streams and marshes, some dated 1608 and 1609 and engraved by Aegidius Sadeler (Wurz. 107, 1–5), compare quite closely in style and motif, suggesting a possible dating for the landscape etchings from Savery's own hand.[2]

1. Rijksmuseum, Amsterdam, *Bulletin,* 23, 1975, no. 4, p. 238, pl. 10.

2. See the *Wooded Landscape with Hunters,* dated 1609, Fondation Custodia, Institut Néerlandais, inv. 2436, Paris, 1968–69, no. 138, pl. 1, and the *Mountainous and Wooded Landscape* in the Louvre, dated 1608, inv. 20.439, Paris, cat. drawings, 1931, vol. 2, no. 712.

Attributed to Roelant Savery
Resting Wanderer
Etching
Kunsthalle, Hamburg

19 (actual size)

Jan Pynas
about 1583/84 – 1631

Only one etching, and that an experimental or trial effort, is attributed with any certainty to the painter of biblical and literary subjects, Jan Symonsz. Pynas.[1] He is one of a number of Dutch painters who made the Italian journey, who were strongly influenced by the art of Adam Elsheimer, a German painter working in Rome, and who returned to settle in Amsterdam. The central figure of this group was Pieter Lastman. The young Rembrandt studied briefly with Lastman and perhaps with Jan Pynas's brother, the painter Jacob Pynas. These Amsterdam "history" painters painted biblical and mythological subjects, frequently placing them in a landscape setting. Jan Pynas's sister married another member of this circle, the painter Jan Tengnagel.

Jan Pynas, son of a merchant, was born in Amsterdam about 1583–84. His teachers are not known, but in 1605 he made his first Italian journey and is recorded as being in Amsterdam again in 1607. Apart from a stay in Leyden in 1610, Pynas continued to reside in Amsterdam, purchasing a house there in 1611 and leasing it to his father. He was apparently hot-headed, for documents of 1613 record his involvement in a number of quarrels and brawls. He seems occasionally to have been employed in his merchant father's business. In 1615 he traveled again to Rome. In 1630, aged forty-six, he married a widow. He died in Amsterdam the following year.[2]

1. Two small etchings monogrammed "I.P.," *Jacob's Dream* and the *Annunciation,* are catalogued in the print collection of the Metropolitan Museum, New York, under the traditional attribution "Porcellis" (inv. nos. 17.50.15-180 and 17.50.15-291). The etchings, relatively free in execution, do not have the feel of prints after another artist's design and are consistent in style with the work of Jan Pynas. Burchard, 1917, p. 27, n. 1, knew of the *Jacob's Dream* but had not seen it.

2. Sacramento, 1974, biography of Jan Pynas, n. 24, p. 148.

20
JAN PYNAS
Jacob's Dream

Etching
Bur., p. 27; Holl. vol. 17, p. 116
Lower right: 16 – – [last two digits unclear]
154 x 207 mm. (platemark)
Lent by the Trustees of the British Museum (Dutch and Flemish Schools, Select Prints D.7–163)

In this episode from the Old Testament book of Genesis (28:10-22) Jacob, who had tricked his father, Isaac, into blessing him instead of his elder brother, Esau, was encouraged by his mother, Rebekah, to flee his brother's anger and go into the land of Haran. One night on his journey Jacob lay down to rest, taking a stone for a pillow. He dreamed and saw a ladder reaching to heaven with the angels of the Lord ascending and descending. The Lord appeared and granted to Jacob and to his myriad descendants the land on which he rested. In the morning Jacob arose, set up the stone on which he slept as a pillar, and anointed it, founding a temple for the worship of the Lord and naming the place Bethel.

Jacob, conceived here as a kind of modern pilgrim, slumbers, holding his walking stick and cushioning his head on his broad-brimmed hat. His traveling pack with its lock and carrying strap and his gourd water bottle lie at his feet. At the left, in the middle distance, an angel negotiates a very narrow and literally conceived ladder, while another waits at the bottom.

Jan Pynas's etching is unsigned, but the drawing style is certainly his.[1] The print is apparently a first experiment in etching, and the plate is underbitten, the lines printing as a light gray. The Amsterdam impression was

1. The pen drawing, in the Dresden print room (140 x 210 mm.), is in reverse of the print and may have been a study for the print, but it is so heavily watercolored, possibly after use, that it is difficult to be certain whether it is the original working drawing or a copy thereof. I would like to thank Peter Schatborn, who showed me a photograph of the drawing and who had recently studied the original, for this information.

thought to be unique until its publication in Hollstein brought to light the London impression exhibited here. The date, which has been published as 1600 or 1602 is, in fact, nearly impossible to decipher.[2] Pynas, inexperienced with the reversal that customarily occurs in printmaking, apparently had difficulty getting the last two digits to read correctly and reworked them, making them virtually illegible. Since the composition is pervaded by Elsheimer's style, or by Pieter Lastman's interpretation of that style, it is difficult to imagine that the print would have been executed before Pynas's Italian journey in 1605. Lastman's Italian journey took place about 1603–04, and both Lastman and Pynas are recorded as being back in Amsterdam in 1607.[3] The earliest securely dated print by a Dutch artist that reveals an Elsheimer-like organization of this kind, with the principal figures in the immediate foreground and masses of "cauliflower" trees seen across an intervening body of water, is Hendrik Goudt's first engraving after Elsheimer, the small *Tobias and the Angel* (Holl. 1), published in Rome in 1608 (for Goudt see biography and cat. nos. 44, 45). The surprising draftsmanly freedom of execution of the Pynas etching is closer to the *Tobias and the Angel* etching attributed to Elsheimer himself than to the Goudt engraving, with its controlled, systematic net of fine engraved lines.[4]

The rendering of figures and drapery folds in Pynas's etching agrees well with that in his painting of the *Raising of Lazarus,* in the Johnson Collection of the Philadelphia Museum of Art, which Keith Andrews dates about 1605–

2. If allowance is made for the phenomenon of reversal, the date can be read alternatively as 1600, 1601, 1602, 1608, 1620, or 1621.

3. Bauch, 1960, p. 126, expresses uncertainty about the reading of the date but states that the etching must have been done in Rome in Elsheimer's circle.

4. Both the Goudt engraving and the etching attributed to Elsheimer are reproduced in Andrews, 1977, pls. 74 and 75.

1608.[5] This would seem to be the earliest conceivable range of dates for the etching, which anticipates in its remarkable directness and freedom of drawing the earliest etchings of Lievens and Rembrandt of about 1625–26. One would not be surprised to discover that it dated from the second or third decade of the century rather than the first.

5. See Andrews, 1977, pl. 129 and caption. The painting has usually been published as being dated "1615," but Keith Andrews informs me that there is no visible date on the painting.

20

David Vinckboons
1576 – about 1632

David Vinckboons, like the Savery brothers Jacob and Roelant, was yet another emigrant driven from the South Netherlands by political and religious troubles who settled in Amsterdam and whose art was an extension and elaboration of that of Pieter Bruegel the Elder.

Born in Mechelen (Malines) in 1576, Vinckboons moved with his Protestant family to Antwerp in 1579 and then in 1586 to the North Netherlands, settling in Amsterdam by 1591.[1] Vinckboons first studied with his father, Philip, a watercolor painter. According to Van Mander, David was self-taught in the other media he practiced, such as oil painting, glass painting, etching, and engraving.[2] He married in 1602 and was the father of ten children. Vinckboons continued to work in Amsterdam and died there about 1632.

Vinckboons executed a small number of etchings and engravings from his own designs. In addition to being a painter and printmaker, he was a prolific draftsman, and many of his drawings were reproduced in engraving by other printmakers. Burchard observes that Vinckboons was more frequently reproduced in engraving than any other early seventeenth-century artist of the North Netherlands.[3] In this respect, too, Vinckboons was faithful to the Bruegel tradition, for many of Bruegel's drawings were made to be engraved by the printmakers employed by his Antwerp publisher Hieronymus Cock. Engravings after Vinckboons often show a new lightness of touch, particularly the many large-scale landscapes animated with vignettes from contemporary life or with biblical and mythological subjects. Van Mander singled out Nicolaes de Bruyn as one of the engravers after Vinckboons who developed an excellent manner of engraving landscape; indeed, the large

1. Biography in Goossens, 1977, pp. 2–5.
2. Van Mander/Floerke, 1906, vol. 2, pp. 370–373.
3. Burchard, 1917, p. 40.

engraved landscapes of Nicolaes de Bruyn and Jan van Londerseel after Vinckboons reveal a new openness and freedom of execution that accords well with the lightness of touch and atmospheric qualities of Vinckboons's pen and wash drawings. Prominent among the several engravers of Vinckboons's work is Claes Jansz. Visscher (cat. nos. 35, 36), whose earliest engravings and etchings are either after Vinckboons or in his style.

21
DAVID VINCKBOONS
Bagpiper and Child under a Tree, 1606

Etching and drypoint
Wurz. 7
Lower center: *DvB.f. 1606*
81 x 55 mm. (borderline)
Coll.: Albert von Saxe-Teschen (see L. 324, 345)
Graphische Sammlung Albertina, Vienna. H. III (4), p. 24

The *Bagpiper,* known only in this impression, is the one print unanimously accepted as having been executed by Vinckboons himself.[1] The attribution is supported not only by the abbreviated "fecit" inscription but also by the extraordinary sketch-like freedom of execution. The print transmits to the seventeenth century the spirit of Bruegel's painterly freedom and unconventional, unsystematic use of etching as seen in his unique venture into this medium, the *Rabbit Hunt* of 1560. One has only to compare the execution of the landscape in the *Bagpiper* with Jacob Savery's little landscape (cat. no. 16) to see how much less codified or ornamental is Vinckboons's free, draftsmanly use of the etching needle. In the *Bagpiper* the lines are much more varied in thickness and length, more unpredictable than those that delineate Roelant Savery's gnarled trees in a swamp (cat. no. 19). Vinckboons's print conveys a sense of a more vibrant, active light and atmosphere.

Another likely reason that scholars have focused on the *Bagpiper* as the one authentic print by Vinckboons is that it is an etching, a

1. See Burchard, 1917, p. 41, and Goossens, 1970, p. 80.

medium more accessible to a painter who dabbles in printmaking than the demanding craft of engraving. However, Van Mander in his lives of the painters, published in 1604, tells us that Vinckboons had tried both etching and engraving. Apart from the *Annunciation to the Shepherds* (cat. no. 22), with its lively combination of those media, there is one other print, close in motif and conception to the *Bagpiper and Child,* that can be attributed with some assurance to Vinckboons's hand and that is executed primarily in engraving reinforced by drypoint (see Glossary), the *Beggarwoman with Two Children,* monogrammed and dated 1604 (Wurz. 1).[2] There the burin is handled in an extremely free and unconventional manner that compares closely with the loose linear vocabulary and short cursive strokes that model forms in the 1606 *Bagpiper.*

About this time Vinckboons painted a number of street musicians. As in the etching a child seems to be imploring the bagpiper to play, so in a painting attributed to Vinckboons, which Goossens dates about 1608, the bagpiper is surrounded by flocks of enthusiastic village children.[3]

2. Also accepted by Oberhuber, Vienna, 1967–68, no. 367, p. 246.
3. Goossens, 1970, pp. 106–107, pl. 57.

39

21 (actual size)

22

DAVID VINCKBOONS
Annunciation to the Shepherds (1604)

Etching, drypoint, and engraving
Lower left: *DvB*
157 x 117 mm. (sheet)
Wm.: two-handled pot with letters DB, sur-
mounted by crescent (see Briquet 12876 for type)
Rijksmuseum, Amsterdam. OB4629

The *Annunciation to the Shepherds* is one of
three prints that scholars in recent years have
persuasively attributed to Vinckboons's own
hand.[1] Held based his attribution on the only
other known impression, that in the collection
of the Metropolitan Museum of Art, New
York. Goossens, in the revised edition of his
Vinckboons monograph, first related the print
to the preparatory pen and wash drawing in
reverse, indented for transfer and dated 1604,

1. Held, 1951, pp. 241–242. The print bears the same
interlaced DvB monogram as the two prints discussed in
the preceding entry (cat. no. 21).

22 (actual size)

in the collection of the Rijksmuseum (inv. no. 1935:22).[2]

A freely drawn combination of etching supplemented with engraving and drypoint, Vinckboons's print anticipates Rembrandt's 1634 etching (cat. no. 80) of the annunciation of Christ's birth to the shepherds "keeping watch over their flocks by night" in its strong emphasis on the shepherds and their herds. Beginning in the late sixteenth century, this New Testament subject became increasingly popular with Dutch painters, particularly those who painted pastoral or herder subjects, seemingly as much for the opportunity it gave to depict the homely life of the shepherds and their flocks as for its religious meaning. Jan Saenredam's large 1599 engraving after a design by Abraham Bloemaert (B. 24; see illus.) is a fine example of the early stages of this development. In the Saenredam engraving attention is equally divided between the sky, opening with a burst of light as the heavenly messenger descends, and the shepherds and their encampment. In Vinckboons's smaller, more intimate print, light from above bathes the scene, but the heavenly apparition is simpler, consisting only of the angelic messenger holding a blank banderole, which represents the "tidings of great joy." Proportionately greater attention is paid to the reaction of the shepherds, who are less idealized, more bumpkin-like, than in Bloemaert's design; see, for example, the awkward, adoring stance and grotesque foreshortening of the upturned head of the farthest shepherd. There is a note of touching comedy in the reaction of the wonderstruck shepherds and the baying sheepdog.

The short hatchings, flicks, and stipples that compose Vinckboons's etching vocabulary here effectively evoke the leafy, grassy clearing, the rather shaggy shepherds, the wooly coats of the sheep and the angel's tousled head and soft wing feathers.

2. Goossens, 1977, p. 155, n. 63.

Jan Saenredam after Abraham Bloemaert
Annunciation to the Shepherds
Engraving, 1599 (B. 24)
Museum of Fine Arts, Boston

23

23
After (?) Jacques de Gheyn II
Witches Preparing for the Sabbath

Engraving
Pass. 56, Wurz. 56, Holl. 96
Lower left: *Jaques de Gheÿn Inventor.;* lower right:
Nicolaes de Clerck Excudebat.
438 x 659 mm. (sheet)
Wm.: Crowned shield flanked by lions
Museum Boymans-van Beuningen, Rotterdam.
BdeH 22771

During the first decade of the seventeenth century Jacques de Gheyn made a number of vividly imagined drawings of witches preparing to celebrate their unholy sabbaths, brewing noxious potions and ointments in their hellish kitchens. (See, for example, the Oxford and Berlin drawings of witches' kitchens, reproduced in Judson, 1973, pls. 96 and 101.) One of the largest of these drawings is the preparatory drawing in reverse for the engraving shown here, rediscovered in recent years in the collection of the Stuttgart Museum (inv. no. 1095) by Professor J. G. van Gelder. [1]

This exceptionally large engraving is executed in a calligraphic manner that quite faithfully reproduces De Gheyn's drawing style of the middle of the first decade of the seventeenth century. It shows witches preparing the ointments that they will smear on their bodies to enable them to fly off to the sabbath or to change their shape. [2] In the center foreground three witches consult their recipe book, while corpses and bones strewn about the site hint at the loathsome ingredients. Cats, frogs, lizards, and compound monsters, the familiars of the witches, inhabit the scene below, while a witch, straddling her broomstick, rises on the current of roiling vapors from a cauldron, assisted by a demon who tugs at her hair. At

the upper left another witch lolls back among the intestinal-looking clouds to receive the attentions of a demon. Other witches astride demonic mounts clutch fiery bolts, a reference to the power of witches to raise storms of hail and lightning, blighting the crops. [3]

The most surprising detail in this tableau, teeming with grotesque details, is the Amor, or Eros, at left crowned with laurel (victorious?); he tugs at a rein attached to a ring in the snout of the winged monster he is riding and appears to be plunging one of his arrows into the monster. In the foreground are a lizard, which has received an arrow in the shoulder, and a toad, transfixed through the belly, whose bowels appear to have ejected a heap of coins. [4] Whether this Amor, or Eros, represents a pure form of love struggling to overcome the perverse, demonic loves of the witches or an anarchic, vicious form of love perfectly attuned to the witches' amours is difficult to determine. [5]

One of the reasons De Gheyn's grandly theatrical peep into the witches' pursuits is so effective is that many of the details are founded on direct observation, as may be seen in his drawings of this time: natural history studies of frogs, lizards, rats, and other small creatures, anatomical drawings from cadavers, and a series of tree studies from nature. Whether De Gheyn believed in the reality of witches and their pursuits, as did so many of his European contemporaries, we cannot know, but in De Gheyn's time the boundaries between what we accept as objective scientific description and what we would regard as pseudo-science or superstition were often unclear. Hendrik Goltzius, for example, is said to have occupied his declining years with alchemy. [6]

The drawings related in style to this undated print all seem to date from about 1600 or later, the period when De Gheyn was less active as a printmaker. His last dated print was the portrait of Gorlaeus of 1603. [7] The preparatory drawing in Stuttgart does not appear to be dated, but analogies with the spatial configurations of the print, in which smoke and clouds play such a central role, are to be found in three ambitious drawn compositions by De Gheyn of the first decade of the seventeenth century: the 1603 *Devil Sowing Tares* in Berlin (Judson, pl. 1a), the 1605 *Orpheus in the Underworld* in Braunschweig (Judson, pl. 10), and the 1609 *Landscape with Robbers* in the Victoria and Albert Museum (Judson, pl. 40).

The engraving shown here is one of a group that includes *The Fortune Teller* (Holl. 105), *The Cross Bowman* (Holl. 108), and the *Landscapes* (Holl. 287–292), all of which are undated, signed either "Inventor" or "in." rather than "fecit," and published by Nicolaes de Clerck. [8] These prints, among the most inventive in imagery of those associated with De Gheyn, are all executed in a calligraphic manner. This calligraphic quality frequently characterizes De Gheyn's pen drawings, but it is in marked contrast to the fine, miniaturistic technique, with shorter and more varied burin strokes, and emphasis on the rendering of specific textures and play of light on surfaces, that characterizes De Gheyn's engravings after his own designs signed "fecit." I would like to suggest that this group of prints, which includes the *Witches Preparing for the Sabbath,* is either after De Gheyn by one of the gifted engravers of the Goltzius school or represents a wholly new, and late, stylistic development for De Gheyn the engraver. [9]

1. The drawing is cited in the entry on the print in the catalogue of the exhibition on the theme of witchcraft, Paris, Bibliothèque, 1973, no. 41, p. 31.

2. Ibid. See also Robbins, 1959, pp. 364ff., "Ointment, Flying"; pp. 511ff., "Transvection"; pp. 414ff., "Sabbat."

3. See Robbins, 1959, p. 487, "Storm-raising." See also Albrecht Dürer's engraving (B. 67) in which a witch rides a goat backwards and is accompanied by a blast of hail.

4. See the bewitched frog on the heap of coins in the Berlin drawing, reproduced in Judson, 1973, pl. 61, and Berlin, 1979, no. 34.

5. I would like to thank William S. Heckscher and J. Richard Judson for their conversation and correspondence with me on this thorny bit of iconography.

6. See Reznicek, 1961, pp. 118–119.

7. Holl. 313, incorrectly recorded as 1601.

8. Wurzbach, vol. 1, p. 288, states that De Clerck was active in the Hague and in Delft in the period 1614–1625, but the style of the prints suggests that he was active at an earlier date. According to Waller, 1938, p. 63, he was active in Delft 1599–1621.

9. Another engraving that relates in style to this calligraphic group is the *Vanitas,* Holl. 103, published by Hendrik Hondius.

Jan Saenredam
1565–1607

Jan Pietersz. Saenredam was, after Jacques de Gheyn, the most gifted engraver in Hendrik Goltzius's immediate circle. Born in Saerdam (Zaandam) in 1565, we first hear of him at age nine as an orphan living with an uncle in Assendelft. In 1589 he studied briefly with Goltzius and then spent two years in Amsterdam, possibly with Jacques de Gheyn, who, according to Van Mander, was his teacher. In the period 1593 to 1597, while Goltzius's stepson and assistant, Jacob Matham, was in Italy, Saenredam was actively employed by Goltzius to reproduce the latter's designs. He returned to Assendelft, where he married, making a will together with his wife in 1595. He died there in 1607.[1] His son was the great painter of church interiors, Pieter Saenredam (see cat. no. 62).

There are a few drawings by Saenredam,[2] but he is otherwise known exclusively as an engraver. Saenredam produced over 115 engravings, of which only a small number are original prints from his own design. His brilliance as a reproductive engraver has overshadowed this small but significant contribution as an original printmaker. A series such as his *Wise and Foolish Virgins* (B. 2–6) of 1605–06 introduced to the medium of engraving a lighter, more delicate, silvery tonality and very subtle effects of artificial illumination.

1. Biography by Wolfgang Stechow in Thieme-Becker, vol. 29, pp. 20–21.
2. For the drawings see Reznicek, 1961, pp. 175–176.

24
JAN SAENREDAM
Stranded Whale near Beverwyck, 1602

Engraving
B. 11¹, F.M. 1160, Wurz. 11¹
At left (on the artist's drawing): *Johannes Saenredam inue./et Sculptor Anᵒ./1602*
405 x 595 mm. (platemark)
Rijksmuseum, Amsterdam. OB4635

Jan Saenredam's large 1602 engraving of the sperm whale cast ashore at Beverwyck on January 13, 1601, is the most ambitious of the numerous engravings and etchings of stranded whales made in Holland in the late sixteenth and early seventeenth centuries. Saenredam's engraving surpasses all other prints of stranded whales in its sense of spectacle; see, for example, the great marching throngs of the curious, dappled by cloud shadows, who swarm over the beach that extends far into the distance. The high panoramic viewpoint and the location of the monster's body in relation to the spectators and the dune-lined coastal landscape are reminiscent of Jacob Matham's 1598 engraving after a drawing by Goltzius of a sperm whale stranded on the beach at Katwyck (Holl. 317).

Saenredam went to considerable lengths to assure the viewer of the strict veracity of his reporting. The Latin inscription in the shell-form cartouche, which rises from a mound of sand at the lower center, gives the date and place of the event, provides the vital statistics of the whale's measurements, and ends with a statement that the artist has drawn the proportions of the whale and all its parts with geometrical exactitude. In the left foreground we see the artist himself, his drawing board resting on a cask, in the act of drawing the whale. A friend spreads out the artist's cloak to serve as a protective screen to keep the drawing from being blown away by the strong beach winds. This drawing provides Saenredam with a witty means of signing and dating the print. At the exact center of the composition stands the whale's most distinguished visitor, Count

Ernest Casimir of Nassau-Dietz (1573–1632), the noble patron to whom the print is dedicated at top center.[1] The count, a military leader of the day, is dressed in his fur-lined coat, holding to his nose a large handkerchief, which is probably scented to combat the stench of the whale. Although the count is shown from the back, Saenredam has engraved an inscription at the count's feet that assures us this is a true likeness.

As in the contemporary engraving of a witches' kitchen designed by Jacques de Gheyn (cat. no. 23), the central scene is surrounded with an elaborate ornamental enframement. Here, however, the frame is a literal one, resembling a proscenium arch. Saenredam's profoundly ornamental conception of the scene is revealed in the way in which the line of foreground spectators echoes the rise and fall of the great curve of the whale's body.

In the sixteenth and early seventeenth centuries, not only was a stranded whale an object of great curiosity, wondrous evidence of God's boundless creativity, but also its death out of its natural element was frequently regarded as evidence of divine anger and as a dark portent of impending disasters or military reversals.[2] The verses by the Latinist and historian Theodoor Schrevelius[3] combine with the elaborate visual allegory of the frame to make explicit the theme of the stranded monster as portent of disaster. These extensive Latin verses narrate the whale's stranding and death struggle, including the breaking in two of its body through its own weight, allude to eclipse of sun and moon and to earthquake, as well as to the military reverses that followed upon the

1. See P.J. Blok in *N.N. Biografisch Woordenboek,* vol. 1, p. 833.
2. For stranded whales as portents of disaster, see Van de Waal, 1952, vol. 1, pp. 19–20, and vol. 2, p. 8, n. 4 (Dutch translation of Latin verses); Timm, 1961, pp. 76–93.
3. See biography in *N.N. Biografisch Woordenboek,* vol. 5, p. 703.

24

stranding of the Katwyck whale of 1598.[4] The "winged rumor" of the verses that carried the news of the wonder to the Dutch cities is personified by the winged, trumpet-blowing figure flying over the dunes to the right. At the upper left Father Time, armed with scythe and hour glass, watches expectantly the course of events.

In the next state of the print yet another grim detail was added by the engraver in the sky at left: a skeletal figure of death appears in the clouds, preparing to launch its burning darts at the winged figure of the maid of Amsterdam who recoils, tumbling backward. It seems as if Saenredam could not resist filling this "empty" space in the already richly decorated sheet.

4. The breaking up of the whale's body, the eclipse of sun and moon, and the earthquake are all illustrated in the frame at top, the earthquake or "moving earth" being represented in the pendent cartouche as a land mass on wheels.

25

JACQUES DE GHEYN II
Carolus Clusius, 1600 – 01

Engraving
Pass. I, F.M. 1063, Wurz. I, Holl. 306
Lower center: *IDGheÿn fecit*
220 x 183 mm. (platemark)
Wm.: arms of Basle (Tschudin 301)
Museum Boymans-van Beuningen, Rotterdam.
BdeH 8056

When first confronted with Jacques de Gheyn's engraved portrait of Carolus Clusius (Charles de l'Écluse, 1526 – 1609), one might understandably feel that the miniature-like portrait bust of the seventy-five-year-old sitter is overwhelmed by the delightfully overexuberant frame. With its specific symbolic references to the great botanist's career and accomplishments, the frame is, however, an integral part of the portrait and extends our understanding of the subject of the portrait. A frame of this kind, intricate both decoratively and intellectually, is characteristic of late Mannerist portrait engraving.

Before being hired by Leyden University in 1593 to create its botanical garden, Clusius had created a scientific herb garden for the emperor in Vienna. He introduced many varieties of plants and flowers into Holland for the first time, especially bulb-grown varieties, his most famous importation being the tulip.[1] Tulips and other bulb-grown flowers are prominently featured in the two precariously balanced vases at the top of the print. These pots of flowers also remind us that the artist, De Gheyn, was one of the central figures in the early stages of the development of the painted flower piece in the North Netherlands.

The meticulously described accumulation of natural history specimens from land and sea strewn across the ledge at the bottom of the frame, which includes pine cones, peanuts,

1. For Clusius and the celebrated botanical garden, see the catalogue of the exhibition celebrating the four hundredth anniversary of Leyden University, Amsterdam, 1974, pp. 167 – 169, and Clusius's biography in Rotterdam, 1974, pp. 12 – 13.

goose barnacles, and fan coral, calls to mind De Gheyn's marvellously exact, "scientific" natural history drawings and watercolors. Judson suggests that these natural history studies may, in fact, have been stimulated by contact with Clusius during De Gheyn's 1597 – 98 period of residence in Leyden.[2] Here, the specimens, which suggest the natural history section of one of the encyclopedic collections of rarities so characteristic of the period, challenge De Gheyn's ability to evoke specific qualities of color and texture with the engraver's burin.

The whimsical caryatids, who balance stacks of sea urchins on their heads, evoke with their wings, their girdles of vegetation, and their fishy tails the elements of air, earth, and water so essential to the gardener. The print appeared as the author's portrait in the first volume of Clusius's collected writings on rare plants, *Rariorum plantarum historia,* published in Antwerp in 1601.

2. Judson, 1973, pp. 14-15.

EFFIGIES·A·NATO·CHRISTO CIƆIƆC·CAROLI·CLVSI·ATREBATIS·LXXV·AETATIS·ANNVM·AGENTIS·

VIRTVTE·ET·GENIO non nitimur; at mage CHRISTO
Qui nobis istæc donat, et Ingenium.

IShcyn fecit

Jan van de Velde I
1569 – 1623

During the first half of the seventeenth century the art of calligraphy flourished in the North Netherlands. The majority of the leading practitioners of this art, which Van Mander dubbed the "tenth muse," were, like Jan van de Velde I, emigrants who had moved north after the fall of Antwerp in 1585. They were generally schoolmasters connected with "French" schools, where one could study not only French, the language of international trade and commerce, but also the various hands or scripts appropriate for writing business correspondence in the different European languages.[1] Jan van de Velde I, whose French motto was "La voix se perd, l'écriture demeure" (The voice is lost, handwriting remains) was awarded third place in a calligraphy competition in Rotterdam in 1590 and became, partly through the publication of his several model books, the most internationally famous of Dutch calligraphers or *schoonscrijvers* (literally: "beautiful writers").

Son of a nailmaker, Hans van de Velde, Jan was born in Antwerp in 1569. By 1588 he had probably settled in Delft along with other French schoolmasters and calligraphers. In 1592 he married in Rotterdam Mayke van Bracht, who was related by marriage to the foremost bookprinting family of Rotterdam, the Van Waesberghes.[2] In the same year he was named writing master of the Rotterdam Latin school and opened a French school in his own house. About 1620 he moved to Haarlem, where he

1. For the cultural significance of calligraphy in this period and the reputation of Jan van de Velde I, see Croiset van Uchelen in The Hague, 1978; Croiset van Uchelen, 1976, with a catalogue of Van de Velde's principal writing manuals on p. 336; and Broos, 1970. The association of calligraphic skills with business schools had a long life, for my grandfather attended a business school in Portland, Oregon, around 1900, where his revered writing teacher was a calligrapher who produced pen pictures.

2. See Van Gelder, 1933, pp. 1–3.

taught at the Latin school until his death in 1623. His son was the etcher Jan van de Velde (cat. nos. 42, 43).

26

SIMON FRISIUS after
JAN VAN DE VELDE I
*Characteres Latini…*in Jan van de Velde, *Spieghel der Schrijfkonste.* Rotterdam, Jan van de Velde, 1605.

Etching
(folio 40)
212 x 320 mm. (platemark); 214 x 328 mm. (page size); stamped vellum
Bonacini 1931, Marzoli 67
Coll.: Harvard College Library by 1720
Houghton Library, Harvard University. 47-1432F

The *Spieghel der Schrijfkonste (Mirror of the Art of Writing)* of 1605 is the most celebrated of Dutch calligraphy model books. It was available in French and Latin versions and went through many reprintings. The original edition was published by Van de Velde's wife's brother-in-law, Jan van Waesberghe. The title page was designed by Karel van Mander and engraved by Goltzius's stepson, Jacob Maltham, who also engraved Jan van de Velde's portrait, not included in this copy.

The original drawings on vellum for the *Spieghel* are preserved in the Rijksprentenkabinet, Amsterdam. The etchings that reproduce them in facsimile are by Simon Frisius, himself a calligrapher, who, during a period of residence in Paris in the late sixteenth century, produced the prints for the model books of various French calligraphers. He published his own calligraphy model book in 1610.[1] (For Frisius see biography and cat. no. 46.) The French printmaker Abraham Bosse, who believed that etching should imitate the precise calligraphic systems of engraving, singled out Frisius in his 1645 treatise as the first of the etchers whose work inspired him to pursue this approach.[2] Bosse certainly would have been

1. Croiset van Uchelen, 1978, pp. 20–21.

2. Bosse, 1645, p. 2.

impressed by the precision with which Frisius employed etching to emulate engraving in the *Spieghel.* Etching was, of course, a more flexible and rapid medium for reproducing calligraphic writing. Frisius signed his work with a clever conceit, in which the hand that illustrates how to hold the pen at the beginning of the first section writes Frisius's name on the page.

Many of the pages are dedicated by Van de Velde to an individual or group with whom he was acquainted or whom he particularly admired. One page is dedicated to Hendrik Goltzius, whose own inventiveness in calligraphy has been noted (*Apollo,* cat. no. 2), and one to Hendrik Goudt, whose beautiful calligraphic inscriptions on his prints after Elsheimer reveal a profound interest in the art (see cat. nos. 44, 45).

The page reproduced here is from the second of the three sections of the manual and is one of the more pictorially elaborate, being decorated with flourishes and a hippocamp, or sea horse. The Latin text is written in an Italic hand and is intended for the instruction of pupils in Latin schools. Adriaan Smouts, to whom the page was dedicated, was a teacher at the Latin school in Rotterdam, a fiery and intolerant preacher, and the author of many controversial pamphlets on theological matters.[3]

Calligraphy books are rare because they received so much use. The present copy, which has been in the Harvard library since the early eighteenth century,[4] still has its original stamped vellum binding, but the pages show signs of vigorous use and embellishment by Harvard students of earlier generations. An inscription accompanied by trial flourishes on the back of the last plate reads: "If I had Time & Capacity I would Learn some of these Flourishes."

3. Haverkorn van Rijsewijk, 1904, pp. 18–19.

4. One of the pages of this copy is inscribed "Collegii Harvardini Liber/1720."

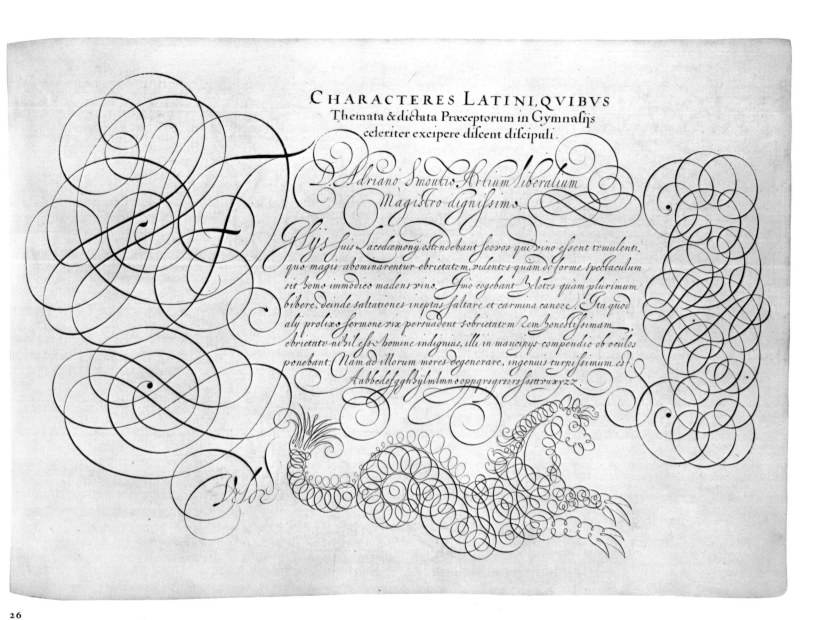

CHARACTERES LATINI, QVIBVS

Themata & dictata Præceptorum in Gymnasijs

celeriter excipere discent discipuli.

D. Adriano Smoutio, Artium liberalium

Magistro dignissimo.

Illys suis Lacedæmonij ostendebant servos qui vino essent temulenti,

quo magis abominarentur ebrietatem, videntes quam deforme spectaculum

sit homo immodice madens vino. Imo cogebant Helotes quam plurimum

bibere, deinde saltationes ineptas saltare et carmina canere. Ita quod

alij prolixo sermone vix persuadent sobrietatem rem honestissimam

ebrietatu nihil est homine indignius, illi in mancipijs compendio ob oculos

ponebant. Nam ad illorum mores degenerare, ingenuis turpissimum est.

Aabbedefgghijklmnoppqrsqrsrssttvuxyzz.

Esaias van de Velde
about 1590/91 – 1630

Although the paintings, drawings, and etchings of Esaias van de Velde are generally quite modest in scale, he was, particularly during his Haarlem years, one of the most innovative landscape artists of the early seventeenth century. Born in Amsterdam about 1590/91, Esaias was the son of a painter, Anthony van de Velde, and the nephew of the calligrapher Jan van de Velde I (see biography and cat. no. 26). We do not know who his teachers were, but his early work suggests contact with two South Netherlandish painters who had settled in Amsterdam: Gillis van Coninxloo, known for his mountain and woodland views, and David Vinckboons (cat. nos. 21, 22), whose compositions of elegant outdoor parties influenced Esaias's paintings of such subjects. Esaias was in Haarlem by 1610. He was married there in 1611, and in 1612 he became a member of the Haarlem artists' guild of St. Luke. In 1618 he moved to the Hague, where he died in 1630.

The majority of Esaias's some forty to fifty etchings[1] seem to have been executed in Haarlem in the period between about 1612 and 1617.[2] Except for the etched broadsheet that describes the bringing to justice of the murderer of the jeweler Jan Wely in 1616, which was designed by Willem Buytewech, all are original etchings of Esaias's own design. Their popularity is attested to by their frequent republication in the seventeenth century and the many contemporary copies. Woodcuts have not previously been attributed to him.

27
Attributed to ESAIAS VAN DE VELDE
Arcadian Landscape

Woodcut on blue paper
As Goltzius: B. 241, Hirschmann 377, Holl. 377, Strauss 407[1]
180 x 250 mm. (block)
Coll.: Friedrich August II (L. 971)
Prints Division, The New York Public Library, Astor, Lenox and Tilden Foundations. 78509

28
Attributed to ESAIAS VAN DE VELDE
Arcadian Landscape

Chiaroscuro woodcut with two tone blocks in shades of green
As Goltzius: B. 241, Hirschmann 377[II], Holl. 377[II], Strauss 407[III]
180 x 248 mm. (line block); 182 x 253 mm. (image)
Wm.: coat of arms with two lions surmounted by sword (variant of Briquet 1976)
Coll.: W.G. Russell Allen
Museum of Fine Arts, Boston, Bequest of W.G. Russell Allen. 63.614

This imaginative woodcut landscape, with a shepherd guarding his flock, rocky mountain slopes cut through with cascades, round antique temple, and winding road that leads to a distant city, has traditionally been attributed to Hendrik Goltzius. Although the print is unsigned, the fact that, like Goltzius's four small signed woodcut landscapes (see cat. nos. 14, 15), it occurs both in line-block impressions on blue paper and chiaroscuro impressions is sufficiently unusual to have reinforced the Goltzius attribution until recently. The *Arcadian Landscape* relates closely in style, particularly in the motif and the drawing of the sinuous framing tree with its hanging vines, to a second unsigned woodcut associated with Goltzius, the *Monk Fed by Ravens* (Hirschmann 363a; see illus.), which also occurs both in line-block impressions on blue paper and in chiaroscuro impressions. The notion that woodcuts associated with Goltzius or his workshop were designed by another Haarlem contemporary is not a new one, as two marine woodcuts (Hirschmann 382, 383), the first of them monogrammed "CW," have long been considered to have been executed from designs supplied by a friend of Goltzius, the marine painter Cornelis Claesz. van Wieringen (about 1580-1633). These woodcuts also occur in line-block impressions on blue paper and in chiaroscuro versions.

Various scholars have remarked that the *Arcadian Landscape* and the *Monk Fed by Ravens* are remarkably advanced in conception for a printmaker who seems rarely to have made or designed prints after 1600. The landscape of the *Arcadian Landscape,* with rocky mountainside and round antique temple and figure and tree placed in the immediate foreground, is a type that was popular in the Netherlands in the first three decades of the seventeenth century. These landscapes were inspired by the work of two artists working in Rome in the early seventeenth century, the South Netherlandish painter Paulus Bril and the German painter Adam Elsheimer. The landscape backgrounds in the early work of Pieter Lastman, Rembrandt's teacher, and the landscapes of Jan and Jacob Pynas, the latter possibly another of Rembrandt's teachers, are good examples of such "Pre-Rembrandtist" landscapes.[1] All three artists visited Rome just after 1600.

The *Monk* woodcut is very compatible in conception with drawings and prints by artists

---

1. Although the first numbered plate in the series of sixteen small landscapes (Bur. 18-33) as published by Claes Jansz. Visscher bears a banderole with Esaias's name followed by "fecit," I find the series too disparate in style and conception to be from the same hand. Bur. 18-24 and 27 seem to me to be authentic etchings by Esaias. It has been suggested (see Van Gelder, 1933, p. 38) that Bur. 25-33 are early works of Esaias, but I believe that two other hands are involved, one responsible for Bur. 25, 26, 28-31 and another, closely resembling the drawing style of Cornelis Claesz. van Wieringen, for Bur. 32 and 33. George S. Keyes, who is preparing a monograph on Esaias van de Velde, has agreed in recent correspondence with the attribution of Bur. 18-24 to Esaias and suggests the possibility of an attribution of Bur. 27 to Jan van de Velde II. He also rejects Bur. 25, 26, and 28-31 as by Esaias but is equally unable to suggest an author for this group. For Bur. 32 and 33 he tentatively suggests an attribution to Cornelis Bol.

2. A clear exception is the etching of a dike break of 1624 (Bur. 4).

1. For a landscape of this type in Lastman's work see the background of the 1608 painting of the *Flight into Egypt* in the Museum Boymans-van Beuningen, Rotterdam (inv. 1442) or the *Landscape with Tobias and the Angel,* etched by Simon Frisius after Lastman (Holl. Frisius, 192). For the landscapes of the Pynas brothers see Sacramento, 1974.

Attributed to Esaias van de Velde
Monk Fed by Ravens
Chiaroscuro woodcut
Museum of Fine Arts, Boston

active in Haarlem in the second decade of the seventeenth century such as Willem Buytewech (*The Cannoneer,* cat. no. 57) and Esaias van de Velde (*The Hunter,* cat. no. 58).

In a recent article on the Dutch woodcut in the first quarter of the seventeenth century, Pieter van Thiel tentatively suggested the possibility of an attribution of the *Arcadian Landscape* and the *Monk* to Moses van Uyttenbroeck (about 1600 – about 1646/47), an artist working in the Hague in the period 1515-1520,[2] or to someone artistically akin to him. The comparison with Uyttenbroeck's woodcut style is difficult to accept because there is little of Uyttenbroeck's engraving-like woodcut style with its systematic crosshatching in these woodcuts. They are instead characterized by a sketchy freedom more akin to etching.

2. Van Thiel, 1978, pp. 31-32.

A comparison with etchings by Esaias van de Velde dating from about 1614-1616, the *Hunter* (cat. no. 58) and the *Landscape with Round Building and Cascades* (cat. no. 29), suggests another solution to the question of who designed the *Arcadian Landscape* and the *Monk.* The etched landscape, which was unknown to Burchard when he catalogued Esaias's prints, is fully signed with the early "VAN DEN" form of Esaias's signature used by the artist during the period 1614-1616.[3] The rock forms of the woodcut landscape have a scalloped rhythm, which is different from the smoother, undulant rhythms of the rock forms in Goltzius's prints and drawings but extremely close in contour drawing and systems of shading to the rocks in Esaias's etching. The rather abrupt, almost right-angle cascades are characteristic of both woodcut and etching, as are the sinuous, framing tree forms and elliptical clouds. The cloud forms and the sunbeams or rain streaks seen in the unique first state of the woodcut are quite comparable to those that appear in the sky in the background of the *Hunter* etching (cat. no. 58). If Esaias was indeed the designer of the two "Goltzius" woodcuts, it is still not known whether they were executed in Goltzius's workshop or somewhere else. It is, however, quite likely that Esaias, who was so active as a printmaker during his Haarlem period, had been attracted to that city by the printmaking activity in Goltzius's circle. Esaias's cousin Jan van de Velde II (see biography and cat. nos. 42, 43) studied with Jacob Matham, Goltzius's stepson.

The Arcadian landscape woodcut is known today in three states. The unique first state exhibited here, first published by Strauss,[4] is an unusually strong impression on blue paper that is extremely well preserved in color. In the next state the rayed lines in the sky and most of the clouds were cut away, and the line block was again printed on blue paper. The sky in this sec-

3. Stechow, 1947, p. 84.

4. Strauss, 1972.

ond state is blank and rather lifeless. It is not until the next state and the addition of both dark and light clouds in the tone blocks that the sky once again comes to life.

In the unique first state the sky does not seem wholly successful. The rayed lines are ambiguous and are abruptly terminated at the upper center. The sky seems to crowd the space of the print; the landscape does not have as much depth as in the chiaroscuro version. The banding of the landscape with alternating zones of light and dark suggestive of cloud shadows also gives a great deal of animation to the chiaroscuro version.

Judging from the condition of the line block, less time elapsed between the printings of the blue paper and chiaroscuro versions than in the case of the four woodcut landscapes signed by Goltzius (see cat. nos. 14, 15).[5] The great differences in condition that are usually found between the line-block impressions and chiaroscuro impressions of Goltzius's four small woodcut landscapes do not appear here; there are a few additional breaks and wormholes, but the differences are not radical ones. The same holds true for the line-block impressions on blue paper and the chiaroscuro printings of the *Monk* woodcut.

The majority of the chiaroscuro impressions of the *Arcadian Landscape* are printed in combinations of green as here, but an impression in the collection of the Museum Boymans, Rotterdam (L. 1958/36), in light gray-green and darker gray-blue provides an interesting footnote to the use of blue paper because it suggests an impression on blue paper heightened with opaque white watercolor.

5. Strauss, 1977, vol. 2, p. 712, sees greater differences in the condition of the line block between the blue paper and chiaroscuro versions of the *Arcadian Landscape* woodcut and consequently dates the blue paper impressions earlier than the *Hercules and Cacus* woodcut of 1588.

27

28

29

ESAIAS VAN DE VELDE
*Landscape with Round Building and
Cascades,* about 1614-1616

Etching
Upper left: ·E·VANDEN·VELDE·; lower right
(engraved): *II*
103 x 139mm. (sheet)
Wm.: Shield with letter M (of the type shown in
Heawood 3030–3031)
Coll.: K.F.F. von Nagler (L. 2529); Berlin
Kupferstich Sammlung duplicate (L. 2482, 1606)
Museum Boymans-van Beuningen, Rotterdam.
L. 1954/1

Burchard apparently did not know this fully
signed print and did not include it in his catalogue of Esaias's etchings. He nevertheless realized, as have later writers, that there coexisted
in Esaias's landscape works, during his
Haarlem period and later, a tendency to a direct
and simple naturalism focused on the native
Dutch landscape and a tendency to the decorative and the ornamental, involving invention
from the imagination.[1]

As Esaias is increasingly viewed as one of the
principal figures in the development of Dutch
landscape realism, his more decorative side has
sometimes been undervalued. Writers conscious of the triumph of realism in French
Barbizon and impressionist art of the nineteenth century have been inclined to assign a
positive value to all that advanced the cause of
realism in seventeenth-century Dutch art and
to assign a negative value to all that looked
back to the "artificial" beauty of Mannerist art.
The advance of realism also became an issue
tinged with chauvinism: the inherent realism
native to the Dutch temperament pitted
against the "foreign" or imported art of
Mannerism. In printmaking it is difficult to
deny the vitality of Mannerism and the ornamental grace and rhythmic beauty it contributed to the art of the Haarlem printmakers of
the second decade of the seventeenth century.
It is the unique blend of direct, fresh observa-

1. Burchard, 1917, p. 63.

54

29 (actual size)

tion of the native landscape with ornamental
linear rhythms that characterizes the graphic
art of Esaias van de Velde, Willem Buytewech,
and Jan van de Velde.

The *Landscape with Round Building and
Cascades* is one of the most fanciful of Esaias's
etched landscapes, the kind of invented image
usually considered more characteristic of his
cousin Jan (see cat. no. 43). Its linear vocabulary is extremely close to that of one of the
more ornamental of Esaias's ten small landscapes (Bur. 8–17) dated by Stechow about
1615–16, the *Brewery* (Bur. 17). The handling
of the sky compares quite closely with that in
his *Stranded Whale of Noordwijk* of about
1614–15 (Bur. 3). I would date it about
1614–1616.

It would be easy to assume from the landscape's invented character that it must be an

unusually early work, if one did not know that,
as a painter, Esaias created as many or more of
these imaginary landscapes in the Hague during the 1620s. The rocky landscape with bridge
and cascades of 1625, now in the Smith College
Art Museum, is a particularly fine example.[2]

2. Reproduced in Bol, 1969, pl. 122, p. 137. The date is
usually read as 1623 but Betsy Jones, associate director of
the Smith College Museum of Art, informed us in correspondence that the date should be read as 1625.

Hercules Segers
about 1589/90 – about 1638

The most experimental of seventeenth-century Dutch printmakers, Hercules Segers demonstrated in his prints, as did Rembrandt, the ability of a great painter to stretch the limits of a medium to make it fit his expressive requirements. Not even Rembrandt employed such a wide-ranging variety of techniques to realize his painterly ideas in printmaking. As Haverkamp-Begemann points out in his explication of the techniques used by Segers, most of them had been employed by printmakers prior to Segers,[1] but it is equally important to stress that he used them in new and surprising combinations and to new expressive ends.[2]

Documentary evidence of the artist's life is tantalizingly scarce. Samuel van Hoogstraten in his *Inleyding tot de Hooge Schoole der Schilderkonst (Introduction to the Noble School of Painting)* of 1678 (cat. no. 192) recounts a melodramatic and legendary-sounding tale of the artist's despair at his lack of success and of how he sought consolation in drink and died from a fall downstairs while intoxicated.[3] In Hoogstraten's chapter on the artist and the power of fortune, he uses Segers's career as an example of the artist's work being discovered only after his death.

Hercules Pietersz. Segers was born in Haarlem about 1589/90, the son of a cloth merchant who had fled the South Netherlands. By 1596 the family had moved to Amsterdam, where Segers was one of the last pupils of another Flemish emigrant, the landscape painter Gillis van Coninxloo, who died in 1607. Segers returned to Haarlem and joined the artists' guild there, most likely in 1612, the year that Esaias van de Velde and Willem Buytewech became members of the guild. By late in the year 1614 Segers was again in Amsterdam, for

we hear of his making a settlement with the mother of his illegitimate daughter and promising to take the child and raise her. Shortly thereafter he married a woman several years older than he. In 1619 he acquired a large and fairly expensive house, but the source of the money that paid for it is not known. Beginning with the year 1625 Segers began to incur serious debts and was at last forced to sell his house in 1631. In the same year he was in Utrecht, where, like many other seventeenth-century Dutch painters who required a second profession to support themselves, he dealt in paintings. In 1633 he was in the Hague and still dealing in paintings on a large scale. The date of his death is uncertain, but a Cornelia de Witte (not Anneken van der Brugghen, his first wife) is mentioned in 1638 in the Hague as the widow of a Hercules Pietersz., who may be Segers.[4]

Segers's paintings are rare, and only two authentic drawings are known.[5] Haverkamp-Begemann, in his meticulous catalogue of the prints, lists fifty-four etchings and, more significant, 183 impressions,[6] for Segers tended to treat each impression as a unique and individual work of art. The plates seem never to have been in the hands of professional print publishers or subjected to a standardized edition. As Hoogstraten says, Segers "drukte… Schildery" ("printed… painting").[7]

Although we are grateful to be able to show such a large selection of Segers's rare prints, certain important themes or motifs are absent here, such as the scarce marine views and still lifes and the panoramic Dutch landscapes that were to be so important for later painters and printmakers such as Rembrandt and Philips Koninck.

1. Haverkamp-Begemann, 1973, pp. 52–53.

2. See my review of Haverkamp-Begemann, Ackley, 1974.

3. Hoogstraten, 1678, p. 312.

4. See critical biography in Haverkamp-Begemann, 1973, pp. 17–22.

5. For these drawings see Amsterdam, 1967, no. T1, pl. 63, and no. T2, pl. 64. The latter, a gouache, is more a painting on paper than a drawing.

6. Haverkamp-Begemann, 1973, pp. 63ff.

7. Hoogstraten, 1678, p. 312. Haverkamp-Begemann, 1973, p. 49, points out that Hoogstraten's phrase can be interpreted alternatively as "printed paintings," "printed colors," or "printed with painterly means."

As the chronology of Segers's prints is extremely difficult to establish,[8] I have taken the liberty of introducing the prints into the chronological sequence of the catalogue at the point at which they provide the best comparisons with the works of Segers's contemporaries.

8. Haverkamp-Begemann, pp. 53–55.

30
HERCULES SEGERS
Rocky Landscape, a Church Tower in the Distance

Etching and drypoint printed in blue on paper prepared with a pink ground, with olive-green wash
Springer 14b, Haverkamp-Begemann 7[II]b
133 x 187 mm. (sheet)
Coll.: Friedrich August II (L. 971); Felix Somary; unidentified mark
Museum of Fine Arts, Boston, Kate D. Griswold, Ernest Longfellow, Jessie Wilkinson, Katherine Eliot Bullard in memory of Francis Bullard, and M. and M. Karolik Funds. 1973.208

Segers's numerous etchings of mountain ranges and valleys are central to our conception of his work as a printmaker. These haunted spaces are among his most profoundly personal expressions, but they are also firmly rooted in a long Netherlandish tradition of dramatic Alpine views that had its origins in the Alpine drawings of Bruegel and the prints etched and engraved after those drawings.

Pieter Bruegel's vision of mountain terrain was founded on his direct experience of the Alps, but there is no evidence that Segers visited that region. Artists who depicted Alpine views in the Bruegel tradition and whose works would have been known to Segers were the Antwerp painter Joos de Momper II, Roelant Savery, and Segers's own teacher Gillis van Coninxloo. When Hoogstraten described Segers as being "pregnant with whole provinces" and giving birth to their immeasurable spaces, he was apparently remembering Karel van Mander's striking, earthy image of Pieter Bruegel swallowing the Alps and spewing them out again on his canvases and panels in his studio.[1]

The present landscape is one of the more fantastic of Segers's etched mountain views, the fantasy consisting not only in the forms themselves and the highly individual way in which they are drawn but also in the choice of color. The etching was printed in blue on a sheet of paper prepared in pink and then washed over with olive green pigment after printing. Although Segers often preferred to print a color on a ground that was a variation of the same color (green on green, for example), he used this surprising combination of pink and blue for ten impressions, including the only other impression of this state of the *Rocky Landscape* (Leningrad, Hermitage, Haverkamp-Begemann 7[II]c, with facsimile reproduction).

Segers customarily used rather thick papers for printing his etchings, probably because they supported the coating of pigment better than the thinner papers normally used for printing etchings in Holland in the seventeenth century. Although Segers's papers are frequently warm toned, as here, he did not use manufactured colored papers such as the blue Venetian paper chosen by Goltzius to print some impressions of his woodcuts (cat. no. 14) or the gray-brown *cardoes* (cartridge paper) Rembrandt used a few times for etchings (cat. no. 166).

Segers usually coated the paper roughly, leaving strongly textured traces of the brush and allowing the color of the paper to show through. The very free, almost careless overpainting of the lines with a wash of color after printing seen in this impression occurred on a number of occasions. One wonders whether this was only a stage in the development of the image and whether Segers intended to later add highlights and additional detail by hand, as he did in other comparable impressions.

These washes and overpaintings applied after printing often make it extremely difficult to determine or describe the original color of the printed lines. Here it is only the foul biting in the sky that indicates the color with which the plate was originally inked. The translucent overlays of color in which the color of the support itself plays a part are one of the factors that make many impressions of Segers's prints so difficult to reproduce and often cause them to be viewed more as unique paintings than as etchings in the conventional sense.

Aside from drawings on colored grounds and rare instances of colored grounds and highlighting or coloring by hand in the work of earlier printmakers, one of the most immediate sources of inspiration for Segers's printed images in color were the chiaroscuro woodcuts by or associated with Hendrik Goltzius (see cat. nos. 3, 4, 15, and 28, the last here attributed to Esaias van de Velde). Segers's color, however, was printed from a single plate inked in one color rather than from the multiple blocks of the chiaroscuro woodcuts.[2] All additional color resulted from the coloring of the support or of the impression.

Segers's mountain ranges and valleys are not richly forested like those of his teacher Coninxloo. An occasional shattered stump or mossy branch only heightens the wasteland feeling. Here the discovery of a solitary figure or the church tower and houses of a settlement within the maze of wandering lines increases by poignant contrast our sense of the vast geological forces of this rather inhospitable landscape.

In the *Rocky Landscape* Segers's manner of drawing with the etching needle is so individual that one would be forgiven for assuming that there is something technically unusual about the etched lines. The whole fabric of the world seems here to be made up of nervously wriggling lines or fragments of lines, which come together to form knots and tangles that read as dark fissures in the rocks. These lines convey a vivid sense of geological processes, of the life of the earth's crust.

The fact that the lines and dark tangles vary little in weight from foreground to background makes the space of the print appear surprisingly shallow. Some definition of space, however, is contributed by the tonal patches composed of extremely fine parallel drypoint lines with burr that read like passages of wash. Drypoint (see Glossary), particularly without burr, was frequently used by seventeenth-century Dutch etchers for supplementary detail or for the very fine lines needed to suggest distance or clouds, but Segers's use of drypoint for tonal effects was highly original. Only Rembrandt made as original or as expressive use of this medium in the Netherlands in the seventeenth century.

Haverkamp-Begemann makes it clear that one of Segers's primary goals was to achieve tone that could be printed from the copper plate. This is demonstrated by the etchings in which Segers made various additions and subtractions to the image on the copper plate relating to tone. The first state of the *Rocky Landscape,* known only in a rather ghostly impression in grayish blue-green on white paper in the Rijksmuseum (Haverkamp-Begemann 7[1]a), consists only of the etched lines before the tonal drypoint additions of the second state.

Another tonal effect that may have been accidental in origin but that Segers retained and used is the granular foul biting visible here in the sky. The foul biting must have resulted from the use of a soft and porous etching ground. Segers, in other prints not exhibited here,[3] and Rembrandt, in the portrait of *Sylvius* (cat. no. 97) and the *Landscape with the Three Trees* (cat. no. 133), appear to have used porous grounds in a planned or controlled way to achieve passages of granular tone.

Another factor that makes most impressions of Segers's prints unique was his habit of

1. Hoogstraten, 1678, p. 312; Van Mander/Floerke, pp. 254–257.

2. In one instance (Amsterdam, Haverkamp-Begemann 16) Segers inked a landscape plate in two colors, green and bluish gray. The bluish gray represents an atmospheric haze over the distant mountains.

3. See, in particular, the granular tone that shades the waterfall in *River Valley with a Waterfall: Version II,* Haverkamp-Begemann 22.

30 (actual size)

recomposing the image by cropping. We know from a comparison with the Leningrad and Amsterdam impressions that a few millimeters of rocky landscape have been clipped from the right-hand side of the Boston impression. Complete platemarks on impressions of Segers's prints are rare, and his sketchy, free-hand borderlines are often very irregular, as can be seen here at the left. The composition often dwindles off at the edge rather than being sharply defined, as may be seen here at the bottom of the design. In the impression of the first state at Amsterdam this indefinite area has simply been clipped away.

31

HERCULES SEGERS
Plateau in Rocky Mountains

Etching and drypoint printed in dark blue-green on paper prepared with a gray-green ground, with colored washes
Haverkamp-Begemann 10IIf (see Springer 17)
105 x 138 mm. (sheet)
Coll.: Earl of Pembroke
The Metropolitan Museum of Art, Harris Brisbane Dick Fund. 1923. 23.57.3

The *Plateau in Rocky Mountains* belongs to the same group of mountain landscapes as the *Rocky Landscape* (cat. no. 30), but in this impression of the *Plateau* the colors are closer to our conventional conception of the colors of the real world. As is frequently the case in Segers's prints, ground and printed line are variations of the same color, resulting in a harmonious and painterly blending of colors and, in this instance, a more naturalistic effect than that of the blue on pink of the *Rocky Landscape*. The ground has been freely applied, leaving clearly visible vertical striations, and the warm yellowish paper glows through the slightly murky gray-green ground, suggesting the sun behind mist.

The addition of watercolor washes here clarifies and articulates the space of the landscape. This is one of the instances in which the artist added detail by hand, as in the fore-

31 (actual size)

ground rocks at right and at center. Whereas in the *Rocky Landscape* the houses of the distant settlement can barely be untangled from the mesh of wandering lines, here reddish touches of watercolor identify the tile roofs of the houses and bring the astonishing scale of the landscape into focus.

The suggestion of the puniness of human habitations among the infinite spaces of wild nature is even more surprising when we learn that this impression of the second state of the *Plateau* is one of Segers's more radically cropped impressions. The inhabited plateau is brought more clearly into focus: a new landscape is discovered within the larger landscape.

Like the *Rocky Landscape,* the *Plateau* exists in two stages, or states, related to Segers's desire to create tonal passages in the printing plate. In the first state the tone was created by

bundles of fine parallel drypoint lines with burr.[1] As these wore away or were reduced by scraping, Segers replaced them with etched stipples, often triangular in section, which were probably produced by puncturing the etching ground with the faceted steel shaft of an engraver's burin.[2] The irregular stippling not only shades forms but also contributes textures that suggest crumbling rock or scrubby vegetation. The faint drypoint lines are still visible here, particularly in the sky beside the rocky prominences to the right.

1. See, for example, the British Museum's impression (Haverkamp-Begemann 10Ib, facsimile reproduction in Haverkamp-Begemann, 1973), in which the drypoint is particularly strong. A comparison with that impression also makes it clear how radically the Metropolitan impression is cropped.

2. Haverkamp-Begemann, 1973, p. 43.

32

HERCULES SEGERS
The Enclosed Valley

Etching printed in black on buff cloth with washes
in brown, gray, blue-gray, and blue-green
Springer 12e, Haverkamp-Begemann 13¹f
108 x 192 mm. (sheet)
Coll.: Jacob Houbraken; Augustus III, Elector of
Saxony; Dresden (see Lugt 1645); F. Lugt (L. 1028)
Allen Memorial Art Museum, Oberlin College,
R.T. Miller, Jr., and Mrs. F.F. Prentiss Funds. 58.152

33

HERCULES SEGERS
The Enclosed Valley

Etching and drypoint printed in dark brown on
thin gray-tan paper
Haverkamp-Begemann 13ᴵᴵᴵu (see Springer 12)
107 x 186 mm. (sheet)
Coll.: L.J. Rosenwald (L. 760b)
The National Gallery of Art, Rosenwald
Collection, 1943. B-10,043

34

HERCULES SEGERS
The Enclosed Valley

Etching and drypoint printed in blue on paper prepared with an off-white ground and washes in
browns and grays
Springer 12c, Haverkamp-Begemann 13ᴵᴵᴵq
110 x 185 mm. (sheet)
Coll.: C.C.J. de Ridder
Rijksmuseum, Amsterdam. OB 814

The *Enclosed Valley* has survived in more
impressions than any other Segers etching.
Haverkamp-Begemann in his catalogue lists
twenty-one impressions and one counterproof.[1]
Three impressions are shown here to illustrate
the strikingly different moods and atmospheres
Segers could evoke from the same plate.

The *Enclosed Valley* belongs to the same
group of mountain landscape views as the two
preceding prints (cat. nos. 30, 31). Once again
an area of human habitation, including in this
instance fenced-off fields, is surrounded by
formidable barren cliffs and peaks.

The Oberlin impression of the first state

1. Haverkamp-Begemann, 1973, pp. 71–73.

32

33

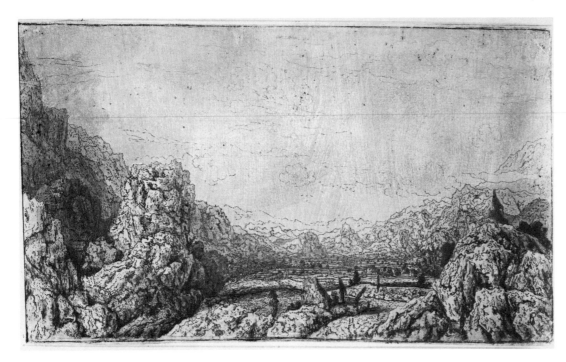

34

(cat. no. 32), which consists of etching only and has yet no areas of drypoint tone or etched stippled tone, is printed on a fine-textured cloth. Samuel van Hoogstraten was aware that Segers printed on cloth as well as paper. In his highly colored account of Segers's life he tells how the artist used up all the household linen for his prints and paintings to the despair of his wife.[2]

As Haverkamp-Begemann notes, all ten impressions of the first state of the *Enclosed Valley* are printed on a fine-textured cloth, and all were overpainted after printing. It might seem logical that a painter should conceive the notion of printing on cloth, but it was certainly not standard procedure for the printing of etchings in Europe in the seventeenth century. Segers usually preferred to print his etchings on a strongly textured ground, for when he applied a colored ground to a sheet of paper (see cat. nos. 30, 31), he usually applied it roughly, leaving the traces of the brush. The strongly textured relief of the surface of

Segers's prints is one of the principal painterly characteristics of his etchings.

In the Oberlin impression the cloth was dyed or stained a buff color, and the delicate etched lines printed in black. The impression was then colored with watercolor, with zones of color from brown to blue-green representing recession into depth in the rather schematic manner of contemporary painters of mountain landscapes such as Joos de Momper II. Many of the areas here shaded with wash become areas of drypoint tone worked into the plate in the second state. The distant mountain peaks have been extended beyond their etched contours with the brush.

In the third state from the Rosenwald Collection of the National Gallery (cat. no. 33), the extensive passages of drypoint shading added to the plate in the second state were reduced by scraping and polishing, and a few new passages of drypoint were added. In the fourth state (not shown here) etched stipples comparable to those in the *Plateau* (cat. no. 31) replace the drypoint.

The Rosenwald impression of the third state is printed in dark brown on thin grayish tan paper and has not been worked up by hand with color after printing.[3] The landscape has a rather bleak, arid aspect to which a random film of ink left on the plate before printing contributes a suggestion of smoky atmosphere. Segers's expressive use of a film of ink left on the plate was to be developed much further by Rembrandt (see cat. no. 169). The inky imprint at top center is probably Segers's fingerprint. At left a cloth texture was accidentally off-printed onto the surface of the print. Segers was surprisingly casual about such "imperfections"; he apparently was more concerned with the total expressive effect than with niceties that would have concerned a professional printmaker or printer at the time.

In Segers's total etched work there is an enormous range of degrees of coarseness or delicacy in his etched lines. He must have used etching needles of greatly varying breadth or sharpness. Here the lines are extremely delicate, and from a short distance the fine contour lines dissolve away optically, leaving the tonal patches of drypoint and the dark accents formed by clusters and tangles of line as the principal elements that define the landscape.

If the Rosenwald impression of the third state is characterized by a desert-like aridity, the Amsterdam impression of this state (cat. no. 34) is pervaded by misty atmosphere. Printed in blue on paper prepared with a roughly applied off-white ground,[3] it has been so thoroughly retouched after printing that it resembles a small painting. The sky and most distant mountains are veiled by a layer of rather opaque grayish white, but the warm tone of the paper is still visible through the various overlays.

2. Hoogstraten, 1678, p. 312.

3. According to Haverkamp-Begemann, 1973, p. 72, the paper is not prepared. The authors of the Segers exhibition catalogue, Amsterdam, 1967, no. 22, p. 21, maintain that the paper is prepared but characterize the color of the ground as gray-blue. These differing descriptions are the inevitable result of the originality of Segers's procedures and the translucency of the overlays of color of which his images are frequently composed.

Claes Jansz. Visscher
1587 – 1652

Claes Jansz. Visscher, born in Amsterdam in 1587, the son of a ship's carpenter, was one of the most important publishers of prints, maps, and topographical views of the first half of the seventeenth century. After his death in Amsterdam in 1652, his son Nicolaes (1618–1709) took over the firm. Visscher published or republished prints by some of the most important printmakers of the second decade of the seventeenth century, Esaias and Jan van de Velde and Willem Buytewech. He himself etched over two hundred plates, including a significant number from his own design.

His teachers are not known, but his early engravings and etchings from the first decade of the seventeenth century are often after David Vinckboons (see cat. nos. 21, 22) or influenced by the art of Vinckboons and the Bruegel tradition.[1] Constantijn Huygens mentioned in his autobiography that Jacques de Gheyn II taught Visscher to etch,[2] and, indeed, De Gheyn's 1598 etching after a Bruegel landscape drawing (Holl. 338) or his etched view and plan of Schiedam (Holl. 296) would have provided useful models for Visscher's neat, precise style of etching.

Visscher's fresh, simple pen landscape sketches made directly from nature in the vicinity of Haarlem and Amsterdam between about 1606 and 1608 are increasingly seen as milestones in the development of the seventeenth-century conception of the Dutch landscape.[3]

1. Simon, 1958.
2. Burchard, 1917, p. 42.
3. Stechow, 1966, pp. 18–19.

35

CLAES JANSZ. VISSCHER
Table of Contents with Lighthouse at Zandvoort, about 1611–12

No. 2 from "Pleasant Places around Haarlem"
Etching
Wurz. 23
In center: *t'Amsterdam, Gedrukt by Klaes Iansz Visscher...*; lower right: *2*
100 x 144 mm. (platemark)
Museum of Fine Arts, Boston, Stephen Bullard Memorial Fund. 69.1239

36

CLAES JANSZ. VISSCHER
Ruins of the Huys te Kleef, about 1611–12

No. 12 from "Pleasant Places around Haarlem"
Etching
Wurz. 23
Lower right: *12*
102 x 156 mm. (platemark)
Wm.: Crozier (Heawood 1189)
Museum of Fine Arts, Boston, Stephen Bullard Memorial Fund. 69.1249

Claes Jansz. Visscher's series of eleven small etched landscapes with title page, published about 1611–12,[1] was the first of a number of etched landscape series published in the period 1611–1616 in which a new, native vision of the Dutch landscape, its modest pleasures and characteristic spaces, was formulated. Similar series were produced by artists such as Esaias van de Velde, Willem Buytewech, and Jan van de Velde. Visscher's series presents, according to the Dutch inscription on the title page, "Pleasant places...situated outside the delightful city Haarlem or thereabouts" for "nature lovers who have no time to travel far" and advises them "to buy without pondering too long over it."[2]

As the list engraved on the *Table of Contents* (cat. no. 35) confirms, Visscher's is also the first

1. Simon, 1958, p.55.
2. "Plaisante Plaetsen hier, meught ghij aenschouwen radt. / Liefhebbers die geen tijt en hebt om veer te reijsen, / Ghelegen buijten de ghenoechelijke Stadt, / Haerlem of daer ontrent, koopt sonder lāg te peijsē." Reproduced in De Groot, 1979, no. 23.

seventeenth-century landscape print series in which the views, however anonymous or unassuming in appearance, are identified as specific places. A number of the etched views relate in motif to a group of freely executed pen sketches by Visscher, with titles identifying the places represented, that date from 1607. These drawings encouraged an earlier dating of the etchings until Maria Simon pointed out that Visscher did not move to the Amsterdam Kalverstraat address engraved on the *Table of Contents* until 1611.[3] The house address is given here as "inde Visscher," and the figure of the fisherman *(visser)* etched below the address not only is a play on Visscher's name but also possibly represents his shop sign. In this context it is amusing to note that the landscape Visscher chose for this page is the beach at Zandvoort, with the lighthouse and fishermen hauling in their catch.

One reason to date Visscher's etched landscapes in the period 1611–12 is their stylistic affinity to the etched copies he published in 1612 of the series of etched "little landscapes" of rural scenes with farmhouses and village streets published by Hieronymous Cock in 1561 (Van Bastelaer 34–63). The design of the original series, which Visscher's title page significantly credited to Pieter Bruegel, has recently been attributed to Joos van Lier.[4] Two such series were published by Cock. The title page of the first (Van Bastelaer 19–32), published in 1559, informs us that these rural scenes are situated "around Antwerp," just as Visscher's are announced as being around Haarlem. Visscher's copies of these quiet landscapes, so important for the evolution of landscape ideas in early seventeenth-century Holland, are free interpretations in which the sixteenth-century landscapes acquire the ornamental skies and curving calligraphic rhythms that characterize Visscher's etchings "around Haarlem."

3. Simon, 1958, p. 55.
4. By Egbert Haverkamp-Begemann, see Berlin, *Bruegel,* pp. 17ff.

NAMEN DER VOLGEN
2. Vierbake t'Sandtvoordt.
3. Sandtvoordt.
4. Paters herbergh.
5. Potjes herbergh.
6. Aende Wegh na Leyden.
7. Onder wegen Heemstee.
8. Blekeryen door den Houdt.
9. Lasery van Haerlem.
10. Plaisante plaets aëde duy hät.
11. Blekeryë aëde durnë gelegen.

t'Amsterdam, Gedrukt, by
Klaes Iansfi Visscher wonëde inde
Kalverstraet inde Visscher

DE LANDTSCHAPIENS
12. t'Huys te Kleef.

35 (actual size)

The *Table of Contents* etching may be seen as a kind of emblem of the Dutch landscape print in the first half of the seventeenth century. It is a window opening into nature, and on the window ledge are disposed the landscape artist's tools. The printmaker's implements occupy a central position: a copper plate resting on an engraver's cushion, bottles of acid, burins, and etching needles. The printmaker's paraphernalia is flanked on the left by the draftsman's sketchbooks and pens and ink and on the right by the painter's palette, brushes, and maulstick. A half-unrolled map under the maulstick may allude to the documentary, topographical function of the landscape artist.

The ruins of the Huys te Kleef, the manor house destroyed by the Spanish during the siege of Haarlem in 1573, is the last plate in Visscher's series (cat. no. 36). It was probably not accidental that this, the only ruin in the series, a symbol of transience and of past glory, was placed at the end of the topographical series as a moralizing note. The animated life of the landscape provides a sharp contrast with the still ruins: the traveler with his pack, the begging woman seated by the side of the road, the birds lighting on the fence, and the horse capering off to the left. The idea of the landscape animated with varied incidents of human and animal life is an aspect of the Bruegel tradition.

For all the freshness and originality of the conception of the series, the graphic vocabulary, with its distinct overtones of the regular, systematic patterns of engraving and closed contour drawing, does not attempt a fresh rendering of light and atmosphere. The spatial structuring of the landscape is pleasantly decorative but somewhat jumpy and schematic, as may be observed in the characteristic dark strip of foreground, which suggests depth in the manner of stage flats rather than continuously flowing space. One should not be too hasty about assigning a negative value to these qualities just because they are not "advanced." At the same time, in another part of Europe, the great printmaker Jacques Callot was developing a highly decorative style of etching that was also schematic, stage-like in organization, and far more imitative of engraving.

36 (actual size)

Willem Pietersz. Buytewech
about 1591/92 – 1624

During his short life Willem Pietersz. Buytewech, known in his time as "Geestige [ingenious, inventive] Willem," produced a varied and lively group of works that encompass landscape (cat. nos. 37, 38), vignettes from daily life (cat. no. 57), reportage (cat. no. 56), political allegory (cat. no. 53), and biblical and historical subjects (cat. no. 48). A small number of his paintings of fashionable youth flirting and carousing survives, but it is above all for his drawings and etchings that he is appreciated. Buytewech's some thirty-five etchings are among the most original and expressive made in the Netherlands in the seventeenth century and epitomize the appealing blend of fresh, direct observation of nature and lively sense of the ornamental value of line that so frequently characterizes printmakers active in Haarlem in the second decade of the century.

Although Buytewech is identified with the school of Haarlem, he was born in Rotterdam about 1591/92, the son of a shoemaker, Pieter Jacobsz. His teacher or teachers are unknown. About 1611 he settled in Haarlem, where in 1612 he became a member of the artists' guild of St. Luke. In 1613 he married Aaltje Jacobs van Amerongen. Of their five children, one, Willem, became a painter. In 1617 he was back in Rotterdam, where he died in 1624 at the age of thirty-three. After returning to Rotterdam he continued to have connections with Haarlem, for Haarlem printmakers such as Jan van de Velde and Gillis van Scheyndel continued to reproduce his drawings.

37
WILLEM BUYTEWECH
Ruins of the Huys te Kleef near Haarlem, about 1616

No. 3 from "Various Landscapes"
Etching
V.d.K. 30 II, Van Gelder 23 II, Holl. 37 II, Haverkamp-Begemann 23 II
Lower left: *WB;* lower right: *3*
87 x 124 mm. (platemark)
Coll.: Waldburg Wolfegg (L. 2542)
Museum of Fine Arts, Boston, Helen and Alice Colburn Fund. 34.18

38
WILLEM BUYTEWECH
Landscape with Bare Trees and a Man Gathering Wood, about 1616

No. 9 from "Various Landscapes"
Etching
V.d.K. 36 II, Van Gelder 29 II, Holl. 43 II, Haverkamp-Begemann 29 II
Lower left: *WB;* lower right: *9*
87 x 123 mm. (platemark)
Wm.: Church (Heawood 3774)
Coll.: Waldburg Wolfegg (L. 2542)
Museum of Fine Arts, Boston, Helen and Alice Colburn Fund. 34.20

Willem Buytwewech's "Various Landscapes" is another series of small-scale etched landscapes from the second decade of the seventeenth century that introduced in an intimate format radically new conceptions of Dutch landscape. The edition exhibited here is that published by Claes Jansz. Visscher in Amsterdam in 1621. The rare first edition without the numbers and the artist's monograms on the plates was published by Broer Jansen in the Hague and is not dated. J.G. van Gelder has demonstrated, on the basis of comparison with Buytewech's datable etched works and by means of a Jan van de Velde copy after one of the prints in this series, published in 1616 (Fr. – v.d.K. 296 after no. 2 in Buytewech's series, *Ruins of Brederode*), that Buytewech's "Various Landscapes" should be dated 1616.[1] The title page of the series refers to the land and its produce;[2] the shield that bears the title and publisher's address is wreathed in fruits and flowers and flanked by a peasant man and woman seated amidst farm produce. Behind them the rays of a great glowing sun fill the entire background.

Buytewech's vision of the ruins of the Huys te Kleef is simpler and more dramatic than Visscher's animated view in the "Pleasant Places" series (cat. no. 36). The horizon line is low, on the viewer's eye level, and we enter directly into a continuously flowing landscape space that extends to the distant dunes. The dramatic silhouetting of the ruins against the sky, with its subtle suggestion of a sunset atmosphere, is intensified by the low horizon line. Buytewech has chosen to see the ruins from another angle than Visscher, emphasizing their desolation by isolating them and reducing the living human presence to a single, small, anonymous figure at the lower left, a peasant with his burden trudging homeward. This figure is so well integrated into the fabric of the landscape as to be almost invisible on first viewing. One of the most quietly radical aspects of Buytewech's series is that the landscapes are either totally devoid of human figures or, more frequently, populated by only a single small peasant figure so unified with the landscape as to seem part of it.

Three of the prints in Buytewech's series, including the *Ruins of the Huys te Kleef,* have as their central motif ruins of Dutch medieval structures (see V. d. K. 29, ruins of Brederode Castle near Haarlem; and V. d. K. 37, the ruins of the abandoned Catholic chapel at Eykenduynen near the Hague). The representation of the ruins of Roman antiquity in prints already had a long tradition going back to Hieronymus Cock's series of etched Roman ruins of 1551 (Holl. 22–47), but medieval ruins became popular as a subject for Dutch printmakers in the second decade of the seventeenth century.

1. Van Gelder, 1931, p. 60.

2. Haverkamp-Begemann, 1959, p. 18.

37 (actual size)

38 (actual size)

For Samuel Ampzing's book of 1628 describing and eulogizing the city of Haarlem (cat. no. 62) Jan van de Velde made two large etchings of the ruins of Brederode Castle and the Huys te Kleef after Pieter Saenredam's drawings. In the verses composed by Ampzing for inscription beneath the two plates, two themes emerge: the brevity and transience of man's works and a patriotic concern with Holland's glorious past and the events of the struggle for independence of the northern provinces.

The theme of the impermanence of man's works is intensified in Buytewech's etching of the Huys te Kleef by the highly original graphic vocabulary. There are few continuous contours; forms are delineated by short hatches, curving or straight, and by dots and stipples. Buytewech's graphic vocabulary may possibly be inspired by the Bruegel tradition of draftsmanship but is not in any way imitative of it (for comparison, see Jacob Savery's etched *Landscape,* cat. no. 16, which is). The use of fine dots and stipples is particularly effective in suggesting the shimmer of light and atmosphere and the insubstantiality of clouds in the sky with its sunset mood. One has only to compare the sky of Buytewech's etching with the conventionalized sky of Visscher's Huys te Kleef print to see how fresh a conception this is. The ruins are also rendered largely in dots and stipples, which suggest courses of brickwork but also give the crumbling structure an openness and transparency, a visual affinity with the trembling, evanescent sky, thus heightening the sense of the fragility of human works, of nature's ongoing cycle of growth and decay.

The theme of the cycle of nature is nowhere so clearly stated in Buytewech's series as in the etching with the line of bare trees and the woodcutter (cat. no. 38). The sinuous trees quiver with a life that suggests the rising sap. In front of these living trees can be seen the stumps of trees that have been cut down and the small stooping figure of a man gathering wood, scarcely distinguishable from the logs

65

and branches that he is collecting and stacking up behind him. Through the screen of living trees we glimpse a building that appears to be another of the medieval ruined brick structures that recur in the series.

The undulant silhouettes of the trees illustrate how creatively this generation of artists could use the rhythms that are associated with an earlier generation of "Mannerist" landscapists such as Goltzius (see cat. nos. 14, 15) or Roelant Savery (see cat. no. 19). Buytewech's vocabulary of loosely associated short strokes is particularly effective in rendering the clusters of smaller branches or budding growth on the crowns of the trees.

The remarkable suggestive power of which Buytewech's fine etching needles were capable is seen in the few strokes that suggest ducks floating on the surface of the water without fully delineating their contours. The parallel rows of open stipples in the sky are so fine that they dissolve optically into a continuous tone that suggests the gradation from darker to lighter blue and the open, aerial qualities of a cloudless sky.

39

ESAIAS VAN DE VELDE
Fishermen before the Fortifications, about 1615–16

No. 8 from a series of ten landscapes
Etching and engraving
Bur. 15^{II}
Upper left: *E. V. VELDE fecit. / I. P. Beerendrecht excud.;* upper center: *8*
89 x 181 mm. (platemark)
Museum of Fine Arts, Boston, Katherine E. Bullard Fund in memory of Francis Bullard. 61.747

40

ESAIAS VAN DE VELDE
Landscape with the Gallows, about 1615–16

No. 9 from a series of ten landscapes
Etching and engraving
Bur. 16
Upper left: *E. V. VELDE fecit. / I. P. Beerendrecht excud.;* upper center: *9*
88 x 173 mm. (platemark)
Museum of Fine Arts, Boston, Katherine E. Bullard Fund in memory of Francis Bullard. 61.748

The various series of landscape etchings that were published in the second decade of the seventeenth century played an important role in the evolution of the kind of landscape paintings, drawings, and prints that have come to be identified with the Dutch seventeenth century. These landscapes represent the Dutch countryside and its characteristic spaces and atmospheres in a pictorial language that suggests direct observation, a sense of being there, even if the artist has synthesized the landscape in his studio.

Esaias van de Velde's series of ten oblong landscapes (Bur. 8–17), which is usually dated about 1615–16,[1] is perhaps the most significant of these series. It does, however, pose a number of problems having to do with what is represented in the series. Burchard referred to the series as "the ten smaller landscapes from the

vicinity of Haarlem" ("Die zehn kleineren Landschaften aus der Umgebung von Haarlem"). When originally published by Esaias's Haarlem publisher Jan Pietersz. Berendrecht, the series had no title, and the places represented were not identified.

In 1645, after Esaias's death, the publisher Hendrik Hondius reissued the reworked plates as a series of twelve prints (Bur. 38 a–m), adding two prints from another of Esaias's series (Bur. 34c and 34d). The first print in Berendrecht's series now received the engraved title: "12 Lantschappen nae t' leven geteckent" ("12 Landscapes drawn from nature"), and all the other etchings were given an engraved title identifying the place represented. Burchard used these posthumous titles in cataloguing the prints. Some of the sites in the posthumous titles are indeed in the vicinity of Haarlem, but others, such as the fortifications on the river Schelde (Bur. 15; cat. no. 39 here) and on the island of Tholen (Bur. 13) are far to the south in Zeeland.

It is ironic that the first print in the series, the one that bears the "drawn from life" title of the posthumous edition, represents a round Roman temple similar to that in the woodcut here attributed to Esaias van de Velde (cat. no. 27),[2] set in a rather anonymous landscape. It is also conceivable that this plate was not originally the first in the series, for Burchard's catalogue of the Berendrecht edition mentions a number of instances of changes of numbering. The earliest impressions of the *Road to Lisse* (Bur. 12), an etching that, with its road winding its way into a characteristically Dutch landscape, would have been an appropriate print to begin the series, are numbered "1" rather than "5."[3]

2. Irene de Groot noted the similarity; De Groot, 1979, no. 54.

3. I would like to thank George S. Keyes for calling this to my attention.

1. Stechow, 1947, p. 84.

39 (actual size)

40 (actual size)

The history of the etchings in the hands of the enterprising print and book publishers of the day has made it more difficult to determine the original intent and topographical content of the series, but when one is confronted, as here, with fine early impressions taken before the reworking of the plates with the burin, it is easy to comprehend the quietly radical influence of the series.

In the etching of the fishermen unloading their catch (cat. no. 39), it is less important to determine that the fortifications in the background are indeed those on the river Schelde than to recognize how sensitively Esaias has evoked the space and atmosphere of a characteristic kind of Dutch landscape in which water dominates over land. The etched lines are extraordinarily fine, and there is much use of short broken hatches and stipples to suggest different textures of the landscape or to render reflections in water. At left, sky and water seem almost continuous, and the faint strip of land on the horizon nearly melts away. A very light random film of ink left on the plate before printing adds to the painterly feel of the etching. In the right foreground, engraving has been discreetly integrated with the finer etched lines to provide stronger shadows and modeling for the fish baskets, river banks, and the boat pointed toward the viewer. The landscape is animated, as in Visscher's *Huys te Kleef* print (cat. no. 36), but here the figures of men and animals are more completely immersed in the space that flows in a great arc toward the distant horizon.

One is nowhere so conscious of the oblong panoramic format of the series as in the *Landscape with the Gallows* (cat. no. 40).[4] The landscape of most of the Netherlands is notoriously flat, relieved only by the high dunes lining the coast. In such a level terrain the sense of the landscape's lateral extension is intensified, and the sky, with its rapidly moving clouds, becomes more prominent. Esaias's series of ten

4. It is interesting to note that the earliest dated landscape etching, Albrecht Dürer's *Landscape with the Cannon* of 1518 (B. 99), had a similar panoramic format.

prints, like the etchings of his cousin Jan (cat. nos. 42, 43), are among the first to acknowledge these characteristics of the Dutch landscape in the format chosen.[5]

The *Landscape with the Gallows,* with its gently rolling sand hills, is one of the most mundane landscapes of the series and is the more strikingly so when one acknowledges the more fanciful tendencies of which Esaias was capable (see cat. nos. 29 and 41). Even the potential melodrama of the place of execution is reduced by its placement off to the side with the cows placidly grazing before it. Although they seem particularly lugubrious to us, these places of execution, where the bodies of criminals were exposed outside the city walls, were everyday sights in Esaias's time.[6]

It is difficult to deny, on the other hand, that this motif in combination with the relative barrenness of the landscape lends it a melancholy air. It is conceivable that the place of execution and the wayfarers on the road below are intended as a commentary on the cycle of human life, but the important fact is still the relatively undramatic way in which Esaias presents it.

The open panoramic character of the landscape is enhanced by the highly original treatment of the sky, which is perfectly blank except for the long thin curving clouds with their ragged profiles that have the feeling of clouds illuminated by a sunset glow. Such use of blank paper to represent atmosphere anticipates the blank skies of Rembrandt's landscapes (see cat. nos. 158, 163).

The etched lines of the *Landscape with the Gallows* are more heavily bitten than those of the *Fishermen,* giving the landscape a solid, earthbound character that contrasts with the

5. These landscape etchings were anticipated, not only in their wide format but also in their low horizons, in their sense of being on eye level with the landscape, by the panoramic profile views of Dutch cities engraved by Pieter Bast around 1600; see Amsterdam/Toronto, 1977, no. 28, *Profile of Franeker,* 1598.

6. See the place of execution in Pieter Bast's 1599 *View of Amsterdam from the North,* Holl., vol. 1, p. 168.

aerial, watery atmosphere of the latter. As in the *Fishermen,* a faint tone of extra ink left on the plate contributes to the sense of atmosphere.

41
ESAIAS VAN DE VELDE
Wooded Landscape with Travelers (The Square Landscape)

Etching and engraving
Bur. 5 (before Burchard's first state)
Upper left: *ESAIAS VANDEN VELDE Fecit./I. P. Beerendrecht. excudit.*
173 x 176 mm. (platemark)
Museum of Fine Arts, Boston, Katherine E. Bullard Fund in memory of Francis Bullard. 61.739

Esaias van de Velde's *Wooded Landscape* is concerned less with evoking open space and atmosphere than with filling the inherently decorative square format with graceful arabesques of branches and greenery.[1] The sinuous tree trunk that frames the landscape at the right stretches from edge to edge, just touching the borderline at the top, thereby calling attention to the format. The carefully considered placement of the leaf-like birds and even of the artist's and publisher's names enhance this decorative scheme. The sky is blank but does not so much suggest open space and atmosphere as act as a foil for the decorative silhouettes of the landscape forms. The silhouetting of the trees and the cauliflower-like masses of foliage suggest the influence of the landscapes of Adam Elsheimer or engravings after them (see Goudt after Elsheimer, cat. no. 44).

The decorative character of the landscape does not mean that it does not communicate a sense of living growth. Esaias has made extremely sensitive use of clusters of stipples and short strokes to convey the softness of the foliage and to suggest the variety of color and texture of the landscape's vegetation.

Three states of the print in the Berendrecht edition can now be described owing to George

1. Esaias's cousin Jan van de Velde II also etched a landscape with a square format, the motif being a ruined round Roman temple (Fr.-v. d. K. 413).

ESAIAS VANDEN VELDE Fecit.
I.P. Beerendrecht. excudit.

41 (actual size)

S. Keyes's recent recognition of the first state in the Municipal Archives, Haarlem.[2] The first state consists of pure etching before the numerous engraved additions that model the foreground or differentiate the tree trunks, cottage roofs, and masses of foliage of the background. The second state, seen here, has these additions; in the third state, the place of publication, "Haerlemensis" is added to the publisher's name.[3] This third state is Burchard's first state.

The *Wooded Landscape* is difficult to date. It employs the "VAN DEN" form of Esaias's signature, which Stechow associated with works datable between 1614 and 1616.[4] J.G. van Gelder dates it as late as 1620-1624.[5] George S. Keyes, in recent correspondence, suggests on the basis of comparison with dated paintings a date of 1618-19, shortly after Esaias's move to the Hague. The presence of the address of the Haarlem publisher J.P. Berendrecht inclines one to place the print in Esaias's Haarlem period, but one must remember that it was not unusual for an artist's prints to be issued by a publisher residing in another city.

2. Communicated in conversation. I subsequently examined this first state.

3. Jane M. Boyle, assistant in this project, recognized that the publisher's line in the Boston impression was at variance with Burchard's description.

4. Stechow, 1947, p. 84.

5. Van Gelder, 1959, no. 46, p. 46.

Jan van de Velde II
1593 – 1641

Son of the famous calligrapher (see biography and cat. no. 26), Jan van de Velde II was born in Rotterdam in 1593. In 1613 he was in Haarlem, where he was apprenticed to Goltzius's stepson, Jacob Matham. In a letter to his son the elder Van de Velde indicates that he had hoped that the son would study with Simon Frisius, the calligrapher and etcher who etched the plates of his *Mirror of the Art of Writing*.[1]

In 1614 the younger Van de Velde became a member of the Haarlem artists' guild of St. Luke, two years after his cousin Esaias van de Velde had been admitted. His first print series from his own designs appeared in 1615 and 1616, published by Amsterdam publishers such as Claes Jansz. Visscher. In 1617 he may have made a brief trip to Italy. He married Christina Non in Enkhuizen in 1618 but soon settled again in Haarlem. After his marriage he rarely worked from his own designs but primarily reproduced the work of others such as Willem Buytewech, Pieter Molijn, and Frans Hals, probably motivated by economic need, for there is increasing evidence of debts. In 1636 he moved to Enkhuizen, where he died in 1641. It is quite likely that the printmakers Willem Akersloot and Cornelis van Kittensteyn were his pupils.[2] The still-life painter Jan van de Velde III was his son.

Jan van de Velde II etched and engraved nearly five hundred prints, of which the numerous landscapes, many from his own design, are his most significant contribution. His paintings are rare, but more and more drawings have come to light, a number closely related to his prints.

As a printmaker Van de Velde's contribution has sometimes been underrated because, unlike Esaias van de Velde and Willem Buytewech,

1. Van Gelder, 1933, p. 5.

2. Ibid., pp. 71-72.

who influenced him, he was more of a professional craftsman than a painter-etcher who translated painterly values into etching. One suspects that his penchant for the landscape of fantasy has sometimes been viewed as a handicap by modern art historians who see realism in landscape as the progressive tendency of Van de Velde's time.

42

JAN VAN DE VELDE II
Wide Landscape with Haarlem in the Distance, about 1618

From a series of eight landscapes
Etching and engraving
Fr.-v.d.K. 335[1]
Lower right: 5
145 x 411 mm. (platemark)
Wm.: fragment of crown
Museum Boymans-van Beuningen, Rotterdam.
L. 1959/48

Jan van de Velde II etched two series of landscapes from his own design that are unusually panoramic in format: a series of eighteen published by Claes Jansz. Visscher in 1615 (Fr.-v.d.K. 217-234; see cat. no. 43), which are the earliest dated prints by Jan van de Velde; and the series of eight published by another Amsterdam publisher, Robert de Baudous, from which the present etching comes (Fr.-v.d.K. 331-338) and which J.G. van Gelder dates about 1617.[1] The latter series, which is of unusually large format, is missing from many collections and is rarely complete. Perhaps these large landscapes with their painting-like scale were destroyed by being mounted on boards to be hung on the wall.

The most surprising landscape of the series is the present one in which the principal motif, carefully framed and bracketed by the trees at each side, is open space, the view toward the distant city of Haarlem, identified by the characteristic profile of the great church of St. Bavo. Jan van de Velde's bold panoramic etching

1. Van Gelder, 1933, pp. 54-55.

42

43

anticipates in its wide format and open vista Rembrandt's panoramic etching of 1651 of a view toward Haarlem, traditionally known as *The Goldweigher's Field* (cat. no. 158).

Jan van de Velde, however, does not share Rembrandt's interest in using line sparingly to suggest or evoke in shorthand fashion the unifying atmosphere of the landscape. He glories in the ornamental, pattern-making possibilities of the etched line. Rembrandt leaves his sky blank, whereas Van de Velde fills the center of the sky with a dark wedge of ruled clouds. In the Rembrandt the edges of forms shimmer and dissolve, but Van de Velde's stylized landscape forms, with their toy-like charm, are quite clearly defined. Jan van de Velde's penchant for ornament and pattern-making is particularly apparent when the trees of his *Wide Landscape* are compared with those of Esaias's *Square Landscape* (cat. no. 41); Jan's trees are much more literally suggestive of knobbly masses of cauliflower than are Esaias's softer masses of foliage.

43
JAN VAN DE VELDE II
Ruins with Hexagonal Tower, 1615

No. 6 from "Some most pleasant landscapes..."
Etching
Fr.-v.d.K. 222
Lower right: 6
121 x 319 mm. (platemark)
Museum of Fine Arts, Boston, George Peabody Gardner Fund. 58.466

Jan van de Velde's 1615 series of panoramic etchings (Fr.-v.d.K. 217–234) "Some most pleasant landscapes and ruins of ancient monuments" is his earliest dated series of prints.[1] Ruins are prominent in the majority of the plates, and the tone is set by the rather fanciful ancient buildings of the title page (Fr.-v.d.K. 217), including a polygonal brick structure at center on which the Latin title is inscribed. A large number of Jan van de Velde's etched land-

1. "Amoenissimae aliquot Regiunculae, et/antiquorum monumentorùm ruinae."

scapes are devoted to ruins, whether medieval, Roman, or hybrid inventions. The Latin title of another series of landscape etchings (Fr.-v.d.K. 255–270) of 1616 speaks of ancient ruins and some very charming landscapes "to please the eye." One has the sense that ruins, with their irregular crumbling forms and surprising maze-like vistas, represented for Jan van de Velde not only national history or the brevity of human works (see Buytewech no. 37) but also sheer visual delight.

The ruins in the present etching suggest the ruined brick structures of medieval Netherlandish monuments such as Brederode Castle near Haarlem, but they have not been identified with a particular site, and they create the impression of being rather too vast to be the ruins of a Dutch castle or manor house. The sense of deep perspective recession, of the extension of the ruins, is heightened by the tiny figures glimpsed through the distant archway at center. Jan van de Velde's feeling for the undulant calligraphy that characterizes the landscapes of Goltzius and of Claes Jansz. Visscher, publisher of this series, is seen in the dark trees, whose melodramatic writhings frame the ruins, and in the dark clouds that rise like a column of smoke from the piles of masonry on the right. The systematic crosshatching and long regular parallels used for shading allude to the vocabulary of engraving, but they are loosely adapted, not literally imitated as in the etchings of Jan van de Velde's French contemporary Jacques Callot.

Van de Velde makes extensive use of variation in strength of the biting of the lines with acid in order to dramatize the ruins with sharply contrasting zones of light and dark. The melancholy theatrics of the ruins are played off against the gentle pastoral vista opening to the right.

Hendrik Goudt
1580-85 – 1648

Only seven prints by Hendrik Goudt are known, and all are engravings after the paintings of a German painter who worked in Rome, Adam Elsheimer (1578-1610); nevertheless Goudt was one of the most influential printmakers of the Dutch seventeenth century. Although virtually nothing is known about his early years or his education as an artist, he is the pivotal figure in the quest for dark tonalities in seventeenth-century Dutch printmaking, a quest that was to culminate in the 1640s in the first dark-manner prints of Rembrandt (cat. no. 99) and in the beginnings of mezzotint (see introductory essay).

Goudt, a member of the lesser nobility, was born about 1580-85, most likely in the Hague.[1] He was the son of Arnout Goudt, steward *(hofmeester)* of Louise de Coligny, who was the widow of the father of the Dutch republic, William of Orange.[2] It is not known from whom he received instruction in art, but two artists resident in the Hague, Jacques de Gheyn II and Simon Frisius, have been proposed as possible teachers. The inscriptions on his prints reveal his skill as a calligrapher, and the dedication of a page of Jan van de Velde I's 1605 *Spieghel der Schrijfkonste* (etched by Frisius) to Goudt has led to the suggestion that Van de Velde was Goudt's calligraphy instructor.[3]

About 1604 Goudt went to Rome; known as "Henrico pittore" (Hendrik the painter), he lived in Elsheimer's house until he moved to another house nearby in 1610.[4] Goudt may have been Elsheimer's pupil; according to the German painter and art historian Sandrart, he was Elsheimer's patron, purchasing all the work Elsheimer could produce.[5] But the painter, who worked slowly, contracted debts

1. Möhle, 1966, Chronology, p. 107.
2. Weizsäcker, 1928, p. 111.
3. Van Gelder, 1933, p. 4.
4. Andrews, 1977, p. 38.
5. Sandrart/Peltzer, 1925, pp. 162, 180.

and was thrown into debtors' prison. Goudt, who apparently did nothing to prevent this, is said to have had a falling out with the German artist, but they were supposedly reconciled before Elsheimer's death in 1610 after his release from prison. Goudt's first two engravings after Elsheimer (dated 1608 and 1610; see cat. no. 45) were done while he was still in Rome.

In 1611 Goudt settled in Utrecht, where he was enrolled in the artists' guild as "nobleman" and "engraver." In 1612 he acquired valuable real estate property in Utrecht, the primary evidence we have of his wealth. In 1625–26 Sandrart visited him several times and found Goudt to be feeble-minded, supposedly owing to a love potion administered to him by a woman then living in the house who wished to gain control of his property. There are indeed documentary references to Goudt as feeble-minded or "simple" in 1625 and 1628.[6] He died in Utrecht in 1648.

Although Goudt is mentioned in Rome as a painter, no securely attributed paintings have come to light. Modern scholars have given a growing number of drawings to him, many of them previously attributed to Elsheimer. These drawings often anticipate Rembrandt's draftsmanship in their spontaneity of execution.

6. Weizsäcker, 1928, pp. 113–114.

44

HENDRIK GOUDT
The Flight into Egypt, 1613

Engraving and etching after a painting by Adam Elsheimer
Dut. 3, Wurz. 3, Reitlinger 3, Holl. 3
Lower center: *HGoudt Palat. Comes, et Aur. Mil. Eques. 1613*
362 x 413 mm. (platemark)
Wm.: Strasbur bend and lily (Heawood 141)
Museum of Fine Arts, Boston, Katherine E. Bullard Fund in memory of Francis Bullard. 63.526

When Joachim Sandrart visited Hendrik Goudt in Utrecht, Goudt showed him Elsheimer's original painting on copper of *The Flight into Egypt,* which Goudt reproduced in reverse in his print. Sandrart describes in detail the varied light sources of the painting: the shepherds' fire; the moon and its reflection in water; the stars, especially the Milky Way; and the torch that Joseph carries. It was precisely this highly original combination of vividly described poetic effects of natural and artificial illumination that made the small panels of Elsheimer so significant for seventeenth-century Dutch artists. Many of them probably knew Elsheimer's rare works only through Goudt's interpretation of them. Sandrart concedes that Goudt's engraving after *The Flight into Egypt* surpasses other engravings, yet it is put to shame by the original painting. Using an image of darkness and of light, Sandrart demonstrates the degree to which painting surpasses print: "it overshadows it as does the full light of the sun earthly [i.e., artificial] light."[1]

In the *Flight into Egypt,* the largest and most ambitious of Goudt's seven engravings, the image area is only slightly smaller than the best version of the painting, which is in the Alte Pinakothek, Munich.[2] It is one of three engrav-

1. Sandrart/Peltzer, 1925, p. 162: "ja es werden solche also davon verfinsteret, gleichwie das irdische Licht von der klaren Sonnen verfinsteret und beschämet wird."
2. Inv. 216, dated on the back 1609; see Andrews, 1977, no. 26.

ings dated 1613, the last year in which Goudt is known to have produced prints. The engravings Goudt made after Elsheimer in Italy credit Elsheimer as the designer, but the *Flight into Egypt,* like all the other engravings after Elsheimer that Goudt made in Holland after the painter's death, does not.

The unsigned Latin verses play metaphorically on Elsheimer's dramatic departure of placing the *Flight into Egypt* in a nocturnal setting: they speak of the "Light of the World" fleeing into the darkness. Goudt also proudly includes in the calligraphic inscription, as he did in all the prints he published in Holland, his title of papal count or knight, which had been conferred upon him while in Italy, perhaps as a reward for conversion to the Catholic faith.[3] Goudt's settling in Utrecht upon his return to the Netherlands may be related not only to that city's reputation as a center for Italianizing artists but also to the fact that it was a center of the Catholic faith in the Netherlands. The beautiful calligraphic inscriptions of Goudt's prints, which were often cut off by later owners, are very much part of the total aesthetic effect of his engravings.

The *Flight into Egypt* is the most difficult of Goudt's prints to find in early well-preserved impressions. It may be another of those prints which, because they had the scale of a painting, were damaged or destroyed by mounting and framing. The impression exhibited here, although it has suffered small losses at upper right and lower left, is one of the scarce, unusually rich impressions in which the individual lines virtually disappear in masses of dark velvety tone comparable to those in a mezzotint.

This large plate is usually described as an engraving, but in this single instance Goudt seems to have made extensive use of etching. The dark masses of the trees are defined by a dense web of systematically crisscrossing etched lines. The rough character of the bitten line gives a more matte, velvety texture to the massed foliage than would engraved lines. Much of the sky consists of closely laid parallel

3. See Weizsäcker, 1928, pp. 115–116.

73

Profugit in tenebris Lux mundi, et conditor orbis   *Rebus in aduersis exemplum sine sumite Christi;*
Exul apud Pharios latitat res mira Tyrannos.   *Quem semper tristi fortuna exercuit ira.*

Houdt Palat. Comes, et Aur. Mil. Eques. 1613

etched lines whose blunt ends are quite visible where they stop to define the stars of the Milky Way. Wherever illumination – whether moonlight, torchlight, or firelight – occurs, the precise lines of the engraver's burin have been used to give the lights a crystalline sharpness. This is particularly evident in the foreground group of the Holy Family. Short flicks or stipples made with the burin define the glassy globe of the moon and its watery reflection. These regularized webs of crisscrossing lines that give the effect of a continuous tone and the small areas of bright white paper glimpsed through deeply etched areas of intense black were to be very important for certain of Hercules Segers's prints (see cat. no. 67).

Night pieces, or "black" prints, by Goudt and the printmakers influenced by him were featured in one of the 151 volumes that compose the ideal print collection as described by Florent Le Comte in 1699.[4]

4. Le Comte, 1699, vol. 1, p. 21, the 22nd volume of prints: "je voudrois le remplir de representations de nuits & pieces noires de differens Maîtres de toutes nations, comme de *L. Gouth, J. Velde, Vuittembrouck, Renbrant, Vanvliet & autres* [all those mentioned are Dutch]." See also William Robinson's essay in this catalogue on collecting and connoisseurship of prints in seventeenth-century Europe.

44 (detail)

Dum frugum genitrix, tædas accendit in Ætna,
Et toti natam quærit in orbe suam.
Picta siti conspexit anum. Limb lianquæ cogenit,
Deanti Limbram rustica dulce dedit.
AElsheimer pinxit.

Scipioni Burghesio
S. R. E.
Cardinali amplissimo in devoti animi testimonium

Dum bibit acceptum, risit puer improbus illam,
Nec satis hoc, auidam dixerat ille Dïam,
Ridentem Liquida fertur sparsisse polenta,
fugisset, sed iam Stellis factus erat.
H Goudt sculpsit et dicauit Romæ. 1610

Janus Rutgeri.

45

HENDRIK GOUDT
The Mocking of Ceres, 1610

Engraving after a painting by Adam Elsheimer
Dut. 6, Wurz. 5, Reitlinger 6, Holl. 5
Below: *AEhlsheimerpinxit….HGoudt sculpsit et dicauit Romae. 1610.*
321 x 248 mm. (platemark)
St. Louis Art Museum, Purchase 79:32

The *Mocking of Ceres* of 1610, Goudt's second engraving (the first was the *Tobias and the Angel* of 1608), was executed while he was in Rome. It is dedicated to Cardinal Scipione Borghese, a leading art collector who was very favorably disposed toward the Dutch and German artists working in Rome.[1] The Latin verses, by the poet and diplomat Janus Rutgers,[2] paraphrase the account of the mocking of Ceres in the fifth book of Ovid's *Metamorphoses.* When Proserpina, the daughter of Ceres, goddess of the earth and of fertility, was abducted by Pluto, lord of the underworld, Ceres set out to look for her. As the verses relate, Ceres, bearing a torch lit from the fires of Mount Aetna, sought her daughter until, overcome by thirst, she asked an old peasant woman for a drink and was given water with grains of barley in it. When a young boy made fun of the greedy fashion in which she drank, Ceres flung the barley at him in anger, transforming him into a spotted lizard. In Elsheimer's design the boy's limp posture and naked belly seem to anticipate the transformation.

The original painting of this subject by Elsheimer is apparently lost, the best surviving version being that in the Prado, Madrid.[3] In this, Goudt's earliest nocturnal scene after Elsheimer, there is the same diversity of sources of illumination as in the *Flight into Egypt* (cat. no. 44): the light from the open doorway, the candle, the fire, the torch, the moon, and stars. The light from the torch ripples like ascending flames on Ceres' garments, lending a sense of

1. Weizsäcker, 1928, p. 115.
2. *Biographisch Woordenboek,* 1852–1878, p. 179.
3. Inv. 2181; Andrews, 1977, no. 23.

latent power to the goddess's figure. The dense web of fine crosshatching and closely laid parallel lines that evoke the deep tones of the night here consist exclusively of engraving. The regular, systematic nature of this engraved tonal grid is sharply pointed up when compared with the boldly scribbled etched version of the subject attributed to Elsheimer himself.[4]

The *Mocking of Ceres* inspired at least two other nocturnal versions of the subject by Dutch printmakers: Willem Akersloot's engraving after a design by Jan van de Velde (Holl. 10), in which the boy is already transformed into a lizard, and Karel van Mander III's etching (Holl. 2), which represents the same moment in the story as Goudt's engraving.

Goudt's engravings after Elsheimer's night scenes inspired not only Dutch artists but Italian and French printmakers as well. The Italian etcher of Caravaggist night scenes Bernardino Capitelli etched a boldly simplified reverse copy of the print in 1633 (B. 25), copying both the verses and Rutger's signature. It is quite likely that Jacques Callot's etched night scenes of the 1620s, the *Holy Family at Table* (Lieure 595) and the *Card Game* (Lieure 596), in which a dense regularized web of lines evokes darkness, are at least in part inspired by Goudt's example.

4. Hamburg, Kunsthalle (inv. 12870); see Andrews, 1977, pl. 85.

Simon Frisius
about 1580–1629

Although Simon Wynhoutsz. Frisius (or de Vries) was a prolific printmaker (Hollstein lists over 230 prints and book illustration projects), he was at the same time a prominent merchant who traveled abroad in the company of Dutch ambassadors and served as agent or representative in Holland of foreign rulers such as the Duke of Saxe Weimar.[1] The majority of his prints, whether after his own design or designs provided by other artists, are etchings.

Frisius was born in Harlingen in Friesland about 1580. Nothing is known of his artistic training or where it took place, but Amsterdam is a likely possibility in the light of his later association with the publishers in that city and the topographical views he made around Amsterdam early in his career. About 1598 he settled in Paris, where his abilities as a calligrapher and his skill in imitating in engraving and etching the rhythmically swelling lines formed by a quill pen led to his executing the illustrations in books by leading French calligraphers.[2] Before 1605 he was back in the Netherlands, and in 1611 he was in the Hague, enrolling in the chapter of the Guild of St. Luke there in 1614. Frisius was apparently quite prosperous and had substantial holdings in real estate in the Hague. He died there in 1629.

Frisius's work as an etcher includes diverse subjects such as portraits, topographical views, and landscapes. His book illustrations are often concerned with Northern European history. A painting by him is listed in his wife's estate, and Welcker published a large-scale pen drawing on prepared linen executed by Frisius in the style of engraving, a "pen work" in the Goltzius tradition.

1. Welcker, 1936, pp. 219ff.
2. Van de Waal, 1940.

46

SIMON FRISIUS
Christ Presented to the People (Ecce Homo), about 1615

Etching
Holl. 2
250 x 136 mm. (sheet)
Graphische Sammlung Albertina, Vienna. H.B. 57 (2), p. 45, no. 76

More a devotional image than a depiction of an incident from the narrative of Christ's trial and condemnation to death, Frisius's rare etching combines elements of the soldier's mocking of Christ as King of the Jews and Pilate's presentation of Christ to the people for their judgment.[1] The setting is indeterminate. At right a soldier, with a marvelously contorted gesture typical of Frisius's figures, places the robe around Christ's shoulders. At left a figure with turban-like headdress and long robe, holding Christ's mock scepter, a reed, fixes us with a penetrating gaze and points to Christ as if commanding our attention. The treatment of the subject is close to that of Goltzius's Berlin *Ecce Homo* drawing of 1607, which Reznicek suggests may have been a preparatory compositional study for a lost painting on copper panel.[2] In Frisius's etching Christ with eyes cast down is flanked by a soldier and by Pilate, who wears an Eastern turban and robe and holds the reed scepter. Reznicek notes that in Karel van Mander's supplement to his 1604 lives of the Netherlandish painters, the *Wtbeeldinge der Figueren,* the reed signifies human weakness or irresolution. Pilate, who transferred responsibility for the judgment and execution of Christ to the mob, fixes us with a probing look as if to suggest that we are the mob that condemns Christ to suffer for our sins.

1. John 19.2–3, King James version: "And the soldiers platted a crown of thorns, and put it on his head, and they put on him a purple robe, and said, Hail, King of the Jews!" John 19.5: "Then came Jesus forth, wearing the crown of thorns and the purple robe. And Pilate saith unto them, Behold the man!"
2. Reznicek, 1961, no. 45.

When Van de Waal first attributed the etching to Frisius,[3] the print was filed in the Albertina collection under Jan Lutma, an interesting categorization, considering the closeness of Frisius's conception of human anatomy to the grotesque biomorphic inventions in the lobate, or cartilage, style of Lutma and other Dutch silversmiths active in the first half of the seventeenth century (see cat. no. 138). Frisius's prints as a whole, even those after others' designs, are pervaded by a compulsively wavy calligraphic rhythm that is virtually his signature.

In the second decade of the seventeenth century, as seen in Goudt's *Mocking of Ceres* (cat. no. 45), light itself becomes one of the most active protagonists in prints that deal with literary or dramatic themes (see also Van den Valckert's *Venus* (cat. no. 47) and Buytewech's *Bathsheba* (cat. no. 48). In Frisius's *Christ Presented* the bold configuration of light and shadow makes Pilate's searching expression more dramatic. The play of reflected lights that intensifies the modeling of the musculature of Goltzius's *Apollo* and *Hercules* (cat. nos. 2, 6) is here further exaggerated in the fluid highlights on Christ's body and on the soldier's legs. These softly interpenetrating lights and shadows are largely rendered by masses of fine dots, which also suggest the texture of flesh.

The print is undated, but the figures of Mars and Mercury from the title page of Frisius's 1615 series "De Nassausche Oorloghen" ("The Nassau Wars") are very similar in drawing as well as in illumination and modeling: use of strong reflected lights in shadows and modeling of the flesh with dots.[4]

The *Christ Presented,* like many of the prints on biblical and mythological themes produced by Dutch artists in the second decade of the seventeenth century, is a lively combination of stylized, ornamental use of line that may be seen as an extension of Late Renais-

3. Van de Waal, 1940, pp. 136–137.
4. Reproduced in Welcker, 1936, p. 242.

sance or Mannerist sense of form[5] and a new, bold use of light and shadow for dramatic purposes.

5. Frisius's close association with Renaissance traditions is best demonstrated by the etchings of his friend the Frisian artist Pieter Feddes van Harlingen (1586–about 1634), some of which look as if they might have been produced by Frans Floris in the mid-sixteenth century.

Werner van den Valckert
about 1585 – about 1627/28

The painter Werner van den Valckert executed some of the most interesting etchings on literary themes in the second decade of the seventeenth century. With the exception of a single self-portrait, his some fifteen etchings depict biblical and mythological subjects or moralizing allegories. All seem to fall between 1612 and 1618, the years of his earliest and latest dated etchings. Valckert also designed four woodcuts (see cat. no. 50). His paintings on literary themes tend to be strikingly original in conception, but his painted portraits are more consistent in quality. Few drawings have been identified.

Documentable facts concerning Van den Valckert's life are few. He was probably born about 1585, possibly in the Hague.[1] According to Houbraken, his teacher was Hendrik Goltzius,[2] and, indeed, given the direction Valckert took in his art, a period of apprenticeship with one of the Dutch Mannerists such as Goltzius or Jacques de Gheyn II would have been a logical background. In 1612 he was resident in the Hague, where he took on an apprentice, and in 1614 he settled in Amsterdam.[3] He married, and a daughter was baptized in Amsterdam in 1619.[4] The style of his portraits and the identity of the sitters, as well as an inscription on a painting of 1623, suggest that he was primarily active in Amsterdam.[5] He died about 1627–28, probably in Amsterdam.

1. Van Thiel, 1978, pp. 20–21.
2. Houbraken, 1718, vol. 1, pp. 215–216.
3. Van Thiel, 1978, p. 21.
4. Hudig, 1937, p. 55.
5. De Jonge, 1942, p. 140.

47
Werner van den Valckert
Sleeping Venus Surprised by Satyrs, 1612

Etching
Bur. 2
Lower left: *wer v valckert In fe / 1612*
293 x 371 mm. (platemark)
Coll.: Waldburg Wolfegg (L. 2542); Leonard Baskin Museum of Fine Arts, Boston, Gift of Mr. and Mrs. Moses Alpers and Stephen Bullard Memorial Fund. 1979.17

The motif, the fullness of the forms, and the use of stipple to model flesh have all been seen as reasons for relating the *Venus and Satyrs* to the works of the Bolognese painters the Carracci, particularly the etchings of Annibale Carracci from the 1590s.[1] The swooping curvilinear rhythms and the stark dramatic lighting that transform the three-dimensional forms of figures and drapery into bold two-dimensional patterns, however, are very much Valckert's contribution.

A satyr unveiling a sleeping Venus is the motif of Annibale Carracci's *Venus and Satyr* etching of 1592 (B. 17),[2] but a similar motif was described by Karel van Mander as that of a 1604 painting (now lost) by Jacques de Gheyn II.[3] Valckert's satyr signals us to keep quiet, making us part of the conspiracy. The almost biomorphic forms of the drapery wrapped around the tree to fashion a canopy seem more excited and aroused than the satyrs themselves.

As Burchard pointed out, Valckert frequently made expressive use of variations in biting.[4] Some of the etched lines here are

1. Hudig, 1937, pp. 54ff.
2. Bohlin, 1979, pp. 450–451, illus. The amorous escapades of satyrs were also favorite themes of Annibale's older brother, the painter and engraver Agostino Carracci.
3. Van Mander/Floerke, 1906, vol. 2, pp. 326–327: "de slapende Venus,...waer by light eenen slapenden Cupido: aen haer voeten comen twee Satyren, waer van den eenen al schroemende bestaet op te lichten een dunne doeck, dat harē schoot oft schaemte bedeckt" ("the Sleeping Venus,...by whom lies a sleeping Cupid: at her feet approach two satyrs, one of which is already engaged in warily lifting a thin cloth that covers her lap or privy parts").
4. Burchard, 1917, p. 37.

47

extremely delicate, hair fine, while other passages such as the bolder shadows are very heavily bitten. Fine stippling gives a softness to the modeling of both the flesh and the draperies that frame the scene like a stage curtain.

The second state of the *Venus and Satyrs,* exhibited here, reveals a highly original and experimental use of tonal etching.[5] Apparently acid was brushed through a porous etching ground or a corrosive paste was spread on the plate, resulting in a delicate, grainy tone that prints like a light gray wash. Bubbles resulting from the etching of this tone are visible at the lower center. The granular tone is very similar in character to that employed by Rembrandt in his etched portrait of the preacher Sylvius (see cat. no. 97 for further discussion of etched granular tone) and other etchings of the 1640s.[6] Valckert scraped or burnished this tone on Venus's belly and forearm to create highlights, just as later in mezzotint the lights would be subtracted or scraped.

5. Noted by Burchard, 1917, pp. 37–38.

6. Accidental or intentional, this bitten continuous tone seems too coarse and grainy to be the result of direct application of the acid to the exposed copper plate.

Isolated instances of direct application of acid to create a permanent tone on an etching plate are the background in Samuel van Hoogstraten's small etching of a *Bust of an Oriental with Turban* (Holl. 18) and, more significantly, there Christ's halo was reserved by painting on an acid-resistant substance, and the background was then washed over with acid, resulting when printed in a burst of white light against a gray-toned ground. The most extensive seventeenth-century use of direct application of a wash of acid to produce a continuous bitten tone was in certain etchings of the Italian etcher Stefano della Bella dating from the 1650s.

48
WILLEM BUYTEWECH
Bathsheba Reading David's Letter, about 1615/16

Etching and drypoint
V.d.K. 3, Van Gelder 35, Holl. 4[1],
Haverkamp-Begemann 35[1]
Below: *WB fec.* [monogram] *CIV exc.*
162 x 151 mm. (platemark)
Wm.: fragment of pendant letter W
Coll.: J. Camberlyn (L. 514)
Gemeentearchief, Haarlem. V.S. 46

The Old Testament story of King David's sin and repentance (2 Samuel 11–12) begins when David spies from his palace the beautiful Bathsheba, wife of Uriah the Hittite, at her evening bath and conceives a sudden passion for her. David arranges to have Uriah placed in "the forefront of the hottest battle," where he is killed. Jehovah in retribution causes David and Bathsheba's first child to sicken and die. David repents his sin, and their second child, Solomon, finds favor in the eyes of the Lord.

No paintings by Buytewech on biblical themes survive, but Buytewech made three etchings on the theme of Bathsheba at her bath. In the first two (V.d.K. 1 and 2), both dated 1615, Bathsheba is nude, for Bathsheba bathing, like the story of Susannah and the Elders, gave artists of the late sixteenth and early seventeenth century a splendid opportunity to portray the glories of the female nude within a safely moralizing context. The smaller of the two 1615 *Bathshebas* (V.d.K. 1) is less involved with dramatic narrative. Bathsheba combs her hair, while David studies her from a distant rooftop. In the other 1615 *Bathsheba* etching, nearly identical in scale and format to the one exhibited here, the crone-like messenger has arrived, but Bathsheba has not yet received David's letter. In the present *Bathsheba,* dated by Haverkamp-Begemann about 1615–16,[1] the leering old crone, a kind of procuress figure, has just delivered the letter to an agitated Bathsheba, while David, a small,

1. Haverkamp-Begemann, 1959, pp. 178–179.

sketchy figure, looks on from a distant window. The letter is faintly inscribed with the first letters of the Dutch form of Bathsheba's name: "Beth[sabee]."

Buytewech's treatment of the theme, like Rembrandt's great tragic nude in the Louvre, the 1654 painting of Bathsheba musing over the contents of David's letter,[2] acknowledges the human suffering often linked with beauty and sensuous pleasure. At the right, behind Bathsheba, the rim of the basin is inscribed: "*Vanitas.*" The withered age and procuress-like character of the messenger add to the moralizing tone.[3]

Although Bathsheba is clothed, the tumbled satiny folds of her gown, the rich vessels, and lush vegetation layered one upon another create an overwhelmingly sensuous impression. The bold, flickering pattern of lights and shadows fuses all these elements together in a pinwheeling baroque design. The shadow that makes it difficult for us to read the expression on Bathsheba's face and the restless lights that play over her limbs and draperies vividly convey Bathsheba's inner agitation and indecision.

2. Louvre, Paris, Bredius/Gerson, 1965, no. 521.

3. Rotterdam/Paris, 1975, no. 113.

48 (actual size)

Jacques de Gheyn III
about 1596–1641

Born about 1596 in Leyden or the Hague, Jacques de Gheyn III was the pupil of his father, Jacques de Gheyn II. Like his father, he was closely associated with the literary and humanistic circle around Constantijn Huygens, poet and secretary to the stadholders at the court in the Hague. Huygens's son Maurits and Jacques de Gheyn III were good friends and were painted by the young Rembrandt in a pair of matching portraits.[1] As the younger De Gheyn's will reveals, he was one of the first to purchase Rembrandt's paintings.[2]

In 1615 De Gheyn was enrolled in the Hague Guild of St. Luke as a painter, and in 1618 he was traveling in England with Maurits Huygens. In 1620 he escorted some of his father's works that were to be shown to the Swedish king. In the elder Huygens's autobiography, written about 1629–31, he complains that prosperity has caused the younger De Gheyn to neglect his earlier promise.[3] About 1633 De Gheyn moved to Utrecht, where in 1634 he became a canon of the Church of St. Mary's. From his will made in the year of his death, 1641, it is evident that he was very well-to-do.

The majority of De Gheyn's etchings are dated between 1614 and 1619; over twenty were produced from his own designs. His first four etchings were part of a series of nine prints after designs by Antonio Tempesta (Bur. 1) of 1614.[4] In recent decades a number of drawings by DeGheyn III have been separated from the work of his father, but there is still much confusion of the two hands.[5] Few

1. Hamburg, Kunsthalle, and Dulwich College Picture Gallery, Bredius/Gerson, 1969, pp. 161–162.
2. Van Regteren Altena, 1936, pp. 102–106 and Appendix VI.
3. Worp, 1891, p. 115.
4. He also probably etched his father's design *The Peaceable Couple (Vreedsamich Paer,* Holl., De Gheyn II, 97).
5. For the drawings see Möhle, 1963, pp. 3–12.

paintings have been attributed to him in spite of references to his activity as a painter. One of the eulogies at the time of his death refers to his talents as a sculptor.[6]

6. Van Regteren Altena, 1936, p. 22.

49
JACQUES DE GHEYN III
Sleep (1616)

Etching
Bur. 9,[1] Holl. 24[1]
Lower right: [monogram] *IDGI*
226 x 168 mm. (platemark)
Wm.: coat of arms (probably Heawood 136)
Rijksmuseum, Amsterdam, A. 928

The figure of Sleep sits slumped forward; wrapped in a heavy cloak, his hood decorated with poppy pods, he slumbers on.[1] Before him are two horns, at left a light-toned one like an elephant's tusk and at right a darker, mottled horn; from the latter billows a column of smoke in which float delicate bubbles. The smoke casts its shadow on the sleeper. The French verses below the image tell of the comfort that sleep brings to all classes of humanity, "cowherd and king, the happy and the miserable," providing a "sweet release" from our troubles.

Van Mander in his *Wtbeeldinge der Figueren (Representation of Figures;* i.e., personifications or allegorical figures), published as a supplement to the *Schilder-Boeck* in 1604, describes Sleep as we see him here: he is youthful because he is for mortals the pleasantest of gods. The sentiment parallels that of the French verses of De Gheyn's print. Van Mander also informs us that Sleep is accompanied by two horns, a translucent one, from which true dreams issue, and one of elephant ivory, from which come mendacious or false dreams.[2]

1. Compare De Gheyn III's drawing of *Iris Appearing to the God of Sleep,* reproduced in Möhle, 1963, pl. 1. In the drawing Sleep wears a chaplet of poppy pods.
2. Van Mander/Davaco, 1969, p. 124 verso.

In his other supplement to the *Schilder-Boeck,* the *Wtlegghingh op den Metamorphosis* (Explanation of or commentary on the *Metamorphoses* of Ovid), Van Mander speaks of Sleep as the seer or foreteller of things to come for mortal man. Van Mander warns that overindulgence can fill the body with evil vapors, which cloud the soul so that it cannot distinguish true from false dreams.[3] In De Gheyn's print the true dreams or prophecies billow forth from the translucent horn, while nothing issues from the opaque horn of ivory.

In his etchings the younger De Gheyn was drawn to literary or learned subjects, which he realized with great visual immediacy: the symbolic smoke casts a real shadow. The choice of French for the verses is part of the literary atmosphere of his circle; one hears, for example, of his inquiring after a Hebrew inscription appropriate to a painting of King David.[4]

De Gheyn's etched figures are frequently lacking in animation: they often have the hunched or slumped-over posture of the figure of Sleep. These drooping postures are emphasized by the long, flowing folds of the heavy cloaks that envelop their figures. The heavy draperies with their rhythmic folds are like a fantastic carapace whose form is often relatively independent of the body beneath.[5] The leathery forms of these heavy cloaks are not unlike the garments worn by the prophets, scholars, and apostles painted by the young Rembrandt;[6] see, for example, the painting of two scholars disputing, which was in De Gheyn's collection and is now in Melbourne.[7] It is quite possible that such early paintings reflect Rembrandt's study of the dramatically illumined drapery forms in the younger De Gheyn's etchings, which preceded Rembrandt's paintings by a decade.

3. Ibid., pp. 97–98.
4. Van Regteren Altena, 1936, p. 17.
5. See the headless, limbless standing draperies in the drawing by the younger De Gheyn in the Lugt collection, New York/Paris, 1977–78, no. 47.
6. Van Regteren Altena, 1936, pp. 103–105.
7. Bredius/Gerson, 1969, no. 423.

Le sommeil dont l'apast égale charitable,
Le boüuier & le Roy, l'heureux le miserable
Et nous faizant gouster l'alme prezent des nuits,
Procure un doux relasche à noz tristes ennuys.

Burchard observed that the younger De Gheyn's style of etching is very much indebted to that of Frisius and of Valckert.[8] All three have in common a stress on stylized, curvilinear rhythms, great delicacy in the etched lines, the use of stipple, and highly dramatic illumination.

Sleep is very close in style to De Gheyn's series of seven etchings with title page representing the sages of ancient Greece dated 1616 (Bur. 2) and should probably be assigned the same date.

8. Burchard, 1917, p. 71.

49

50

WERNER VAN DEN VALCKERT
Saint Jerome, 1613

Woodcut
Upper right, on tablet: *W.VA/IF;* at left, on book:
1613
121 x 80 mm. (sheet)
Private Collection, Amsterdam

Many will have no difficulty in associating the medium of etching with seventeenth-century Dutch art, but woodcut as a means of artistic expression in seventeenth-century Holland still has an unfamiliar ring. Woodcuts of genuine artistic interest occur sporadically throughout the century. Woodcut continued to be used by the book illustration industry, as it was in the fifteenth and sixteenth centuries, but it was now overshadowed by the use of etching and engraving when illustrations of the highest artistic quality were desired.

Werner van den Valckert's small woodcut of St. Jerome was long considered to be designed by Titian or by a North Italian painter under the influence of the woodcuts of the Titian school. When the present impression recently came to light, it became evident that the correct reading of the date on the print was 1613 and that the date on the only previously known impression (Bibliothèque Nationale, Paris) had been accidentally or intentionally altered so as to read 1513.[1] The inscription on the tablet or text held by the figure behind St. Jerome, more legible here than in the Paris impression, was found to read "W.VA/IF" (the abbreviation for "Werner van den Valckert Invenit et Fecit"). It is hardly surprising that Valckert's very Italianate conception of St. Jerome as a heroic nude figure should have been taken for a genuine Italian work. Valckert, who seems to have been quite conscious of the graphic work of Agostino and Annibale Carracci, could easily have found a prototype for his conception of St. Jerome in their work.[2] Van Mander's rec-

ommendation of the woodcuts of Titian as a model has already been discussed in relation to Goltzius's landscape woodcuts (cat. nos. 14, 15).

St. Jerome, who lived in the fourth and fifth centuries, was responsible for the standard Latin translation of the Bible, the Vulgate. Having spent a period of penance and study in the desert of Palestine, Jerome was often shown working on his translation in a rocky desert setting accompanied by his faithful companion and symbol, the lion. Here he dips his pen in the inkwell, while turning his head as if to receive divine inspiration, perhaps from the tablet held by the angel-like figure behind him.

Valckert's woodcut, like the copper plate of his *Susanna* etching (Bur. 12), is quite irregular in shape. The linear vocabulary is based on the systems of engraving, but the lines are so broad and the cutting is so vigorous and choppy that there is never any doubt that we are looking at a woodcut. The "Fecit" inscription, and perhaps the very free cutting as well, led Van Thiel to suggest that Valckert cut the block himself. The lighting in the woodcut has some of the boldness of the lighting in Valckert's etched *Venus and Satyrs* (cat. no. 47).

Until Van Thiel's article on the woodcuts of Werner van den Valckert and Moses van Uyttenbroeck appeared, there was a good deal of confusion between the works in woodcut of these two artists; Uyttenbroeck's *Nativity* woodcut, for example, had been given to Valckert.[3] In addition, certain woodcuts that Van Thiel has persuasively demonstrated to be by Uyttenbroeck had been associated with an anonymous monogrammist of the Titian school.[4] The linear vocabulary of Uyttenbroeck's woodcuts (dated by Van Thiel about 1615) like that of Valckert's *St. Jerome,* is closely related to the linear systems of copper-plate engraving.

3. As in Van de Waal, *Halcyon,* 1940, p. 7.
4. Monogrammist MB, Nagler, *Mon.* vol. 4, no. 1648.

1. Van der Tweel, 1977, pp. 567–568; Van Thiel, 1978, pp. 20–22.
2. For example, Agostino's engraving of about 1602, B. 75, Bohlin, 1979, pp. 346–349.

50 (actual size)

Christoffel van Sichem I
about 1546 – 1624

Christoffel van Sichem I is the first and most artistically significant of four Christoffel van Sichems who were all professional cutters of woodblocks, and used an identical monogram; the last of the four, Christoffel IV, grandson of Christoffel I, died in the 1690s. Their overlapping careers and identical monograms have frequently made precise attributions difficult.

Born about 1546 in Amsterdam, Christoffel I was the son of a bookseller, Cornelis Karelsz., originally from the village of Sichem in Brabant. He studied with another Amsterdam bookseller and professional cutter of woodblocks, Jan Ewoutsz. Van Sichem worked for the book trade from 1569 to 1597 in Basle, where, in 1570, he married the daughter of a Calvinist cloth merchant from Antwerp. In 1598 he was back in Amsterdam, and he died there in 1624.[1]

Much of the family's production consists of routine, uninspired work for the book trade of the day, but the few works that Christoffel I produced after designs by Goltzius and Matham are among the most attractive of seventeenth-century Dutch woodcuts. He was also active as an engraver.

1. See biographical discussions by M.D. Henkel in Thieme-Becker, vol. 30, pp. 585–586; Wijnman, 1929; Lehmann-Haupt, 1977, pp. 39–48.

51
CHRISTOFFEL VAN SICHEM I
Young Man with a Turban, 1613

Woodcut after Jacob Matham
Nag. 23, Wurz. 21, Holl. vol. 11, p. 251, no. 16
Upper left: *1613.*; lower left: *I Matham.*
In./[monogram]*CVSichem. Scalps.*
320 x 220 mm. (block)
Wm.: fleur-de-lis with letter R (see Briquet 6970)
Museum of Fine Arts, Boston, Stephen Bullard Memorial Fund. 1977.116

About 1593 Hendrik Goltzius began to make fantasy portrait drawings. These bust-length figures in vaguely Renaissance dress, often referring in style and motif to Albrecht Dürer and Lucas van Leyden, were in many cases executed in Goltzius's calligraphic pen manner, which imitated the vocabulary of engraving. After returning from Italy about 1600, Jacob Matham, Goltzius's stepson and disciple (1571–1631), also began to produce fantasy portrait busts of a similar type, pen drawings in the style of his engravings or etchings.[1]

Christoffel van Sichem's woodcut of a young man in an elaborate turban is a skillful facsimile of such a pen drawing and is cut with a professional precision and neatness greatly at variance with the free-hand cutting of Valckert's small *St. Jerome* (cat. no. 50). Reproducing engraving-like crosshatching is very laborious in woodcut because the process is the reverse of engraving a line in a copper plate. In the woodcut the blank spaces that print as white must be cut away or hollowed out, leaving the lines that will print as black standing up in relief.

The costume of the young man holding the scroll is somewhat Near Eastern in character. The combination of youthful androgynous beauty (resembling that of a Bacchus by Goltzius) and the elaborately imagined headdress suggest the fantasy portrait drawings of Michelangelo rather than graphic works by Dürer and Lucas. The brilliant highlights, however, give the modeling of the figure the

1. See the 1612 drawing by Matham from the Witt collection, reproduced in Reznicek, 1961, vol. I, pl. 36.

metallic gleam associated with a Goltzius engraving.

The *Young Man with a Turban,* after Matham, and two woodcuts after Goltzius, *Portrait of a Man with Plumed Hat, Holding a Glove* (Wurz. 19, dated 1607) and *Young Man Accompanying Four Singers* (Wurz. 20, not dated)[2] are similar in size, style of execution, and use of a double borderline. They vary, however, in the relationship of the scale of the figures to the format. It is quite likely that all three woodcuts were executed at the same time, about 1613.

Fantasy portraits of this type by Goltzius and Matham must have been one of the sources of inspiration for the fantasy portraits, character heads, busts of Orientals and "types" portrayed in all media by Lievens and by Rembrandt and his circle.

2. Reproduced in Lehmann-Haupt, 1977, pp. 43, 47.

1613.

J. Matham. In.
Sichem. sculps.

Paulus Moreelse
1571 – 1638

The Utrecht painter Paulus Moreelse designed two chiaroscuro woodcuts. Their subjects, a tale of ancient Roman virtue and a moralizing allegory, may be somewhat surprising to those who know Moreelse primarily as a successful portrait painter, but, like his teacher the Delft portrait painter Michiel van Mierevelt, he also painted biblical and mythological subjects.

Born in Utrecht in 1571, Moreelse was enrolled as an artist in the Utrecht saddlers' guild in 1596. Later, in 1611, he was one of the founding members of a separate guild for artists, the Guild of St. Luke. After a period of two years' study with Mierevelt, Moreelse traveled in Italy. In 1602 he was in Utrecht, where he married. From time to time he resided in Amsterdam to fulfill portrait commissions, but he remained a citizen of Utrecht, where he was active not only in the Guild of St. Luke but also in the city government, filling various posts including that of architect, designing one of the city gates. His prosperity is evident from his various real estate investments. In spite of his active public life, he continued to paint until the year of his death, 1638.[1]

1. De Jonge, 1938, pp.1–7.

Aligerum trahit hic puerum lasciua Iuventas,
Sed quem non firmæ concomitantur opes:
Luxus & ad tenebras effrons hos ducit opacæ
Noctis, vt æternæ vinciat ira necis.

Morelse
1612

52

88

52

PAULUS MOREELSE
Two Young Women Dancing with Cupid,
1612

Chiaroscuro woodcut with one gray tone block
Nag. 2, Wurz. 1, De Jonge 17, Holl. 2, Strauss,
1973, 153.
Lower left: *PMorelse/ 1612*
237 x 292 mm. (line block)
Wm.: small coat of arms and countermark PP
Museum of Fine Arts, Boston, Gift of the Children
of Dr. James B. Ayer. M28795

In this chiaroscuro woodcut designed by
Paulus Moreelse, two frivolous young women
in fluttering, billowing draperies lead Cupid a
merry dance.

The Latin verses printed in dark gray type on
the enframing tablet above them indicate the
consequences of their shameless, wanton
behavior: it will lead them to the deep shadows
of night, where eternal death will hold them in
its chains. The details of the central cartouche
and foreground reinforce this grim message.
The cartouche is composed of a goat's head,
symbol of lust; a bat, creature of darkness; and
the apes who reach for their chains, symbol of
enslavement to the sensual and the material. In
the foreground strewn roses indicate fleeting
pleasures, while at left Cupid's quiver and bow
are paired with moneybags, signifying mercenary love.

Moreelse's delicate, fluid draftsmanship,
shimmering highlights, and almost rococo
lightness of touch combined with heavy moralizing evoke Jan Saenredam's engraved series
"Wise and Foolish Virgins" of 1606 (B. 2–6).
Moreelse's relaxed figural style parallels the
later, post-Mannerist phase of that central figure of the Utrecht School, Abraham Bloemaert
(see cat. no. 18). Closely related in style to this
woodcut, with the same curling, tendril-like
lines for hair and draperies, is Moreelse's chalk
drawing of Aristotle and Phyllis dated 1618 in

Gottfridt Müller's album (1616–1618) of drawings by various artists.[1]

Both the *Young Women Dancing with Cupid*
and the other chiaroscuro designed by
Moreelse, the *Death of Lucretia* (Holl. 1),
apparently occur in two states. In the first the
tone block is printed in light ocherish brown,
and the type of the text in dark gray. In the second state the tone block is printed in light gray,
and the type in black. The first state of the
Lucretia bears the signature of the cutter, a cursive monogram, above a little knife. This monogram has been interpreted by Nagler as an
"H" and identified with the publisher and
printmaker Hendrik Hondius.[2] The anonymous cutter, whose monogram consists of
more than a simple "H" and who undoubtedly
also cut the blocks of the *Young Women Dancing,* has yet to be identified. In the second state
of the *Lucretia* the background receives vertical
shading, and the cutter's monogram is
obscured, suggesting that the blocks had fallen
into the hands of another publisher.

1. The album was given by Friedrich von Nagler to the
Print Room in Berlin. Moreelse's drawing is reproduced
in Oertel, 1936, pl. 4.
2. Nagler, *Mon.* vol. 3, no. 554.

53

WILLEM BUYTEWECH
*Allegory on the Deceitfulness of Spain and the
Liberty and Prosperity of the Dutch Republic,*
about 1615

Etching, engraving, and drypoint
V.d.K. 8, F.M. 1304, Van Gelder 17[1],
Holl. 15[1], Haverkamp-Begemann 17[1]
Lower left: *WB*
138 x 178 mm. (platemark)
Wm.: fragment of pot with letter M
Private Collection, New York

Prints that reported on or commented on current events were produced in quantity in the
Dutch seventeenth century, but they are rarely
as lively, as vividly imagined as Buytewech's
political allegory on the flourishing state of the
United Provinces of the Netherlands during
the twelve-year truce in the conflict with Spain
(1609–1621). The print served as title page for
a twenty-page pamphlet, published anony-
mously in 1615, in which the Dutch Maid
("Batavia" or "Hollandia") engages in a dialogue with a "friend of the fatherland."[1] The
theme of the dialogue is inscribed across the
top of the print and may be translated as follows: "Notice the renowned wisdom of Dutch
housekeeping and perceive the nature of the
leopard who is not to be trusted."[2]

Buytewech's illustration is a quite literal rendering of the dialogue, many parts of the image
being carefully labeled. The victorious Dutch
Maid is seen enthroned on the Chair of Liberty
in a niche of the facade of her house, the
"Batavian," or Dutch, dominion. The "friend
of the fatherland" stands, bowing slightly, to
the left. Above them, in the Late Renaissance
gable with its strapwork ornament, the coats of
arms of the United Provinces surround the
coat of arms of the House of Nassau. The copper plate arches at the top center to accommodate the high gable. The Dutch Maid describes

1. Haverkamp-Begemann, 1959, pp. 14, 170–171.
2. Based on the English translation in Haverkamp-
Begemann, 1962, p. 72.

53 (actual size)

the flourishing state of the land under the farmer, the city man, and the sea man, who are seen on the right as the "united community," while the soldier (behind them) "sits and rests."[3] Hollandia then describes her garden, which is enclosed by a willow fence named "Loyalty," its gate guarded by a many-eyed lion. Within the garden is the severed trunk of an orange tree, from which emerges new growth, an allusion to the House of Orange, to the assassination in 1584 of William (the Silent) of Orange and to his sons, especially the brilliant general of the Dutch forces, Prince Maurits, to whose personal motto the image is related. Two gardeners, "Might" and "Reason," keep the garden free of such weeds as *Dood-kruyt* (death herb) and *Pijn-appel* (pain apple).

The "friend of the fatherland" warns the Maid of Holland of the two-faced figure outside the gate of the garden, showing a sweet woman's face before and, behind, a fierce warrior's face turned to the soldiers that follow. The seductress holds out a sweet-smelling but poisonous flower, "monk's hood," which will put the maid to sleep, a reference to the Catholic religion. This ambiguous figure, whose aim is to lead Hollandia "up the garden path," is accompanied by a wily, blood-thirsty leopard.[4]

The image of the garden of Holland has a long tradition, but Buytewech has conceived of it in wonderfully literal terms, treating it as a real place with its own light and atmosphere. The wedge of peaceful Dutch landscape visible at left provides the maximum contrast with the wedge of landscape at right, which is almost obscured by thronging soldiers.

3. For the truce and the pictorial theme of the Sleeping Mars, see Erik de Jong in Utrecht, 1980.

4. Haverkamp-Begemann, 1959, pp. 170–171.

54

CLAES JANSZ. VISSCHER

"Tis misselijck waer een geck zijn gelt aen leijt" ("It's sickening what a fool will spend his money on") and *"Een dwaes en zijn gelt zijn haest ghescheijden"* ("A fool and his money are soon parted") in Roemer Visscher, *Sinnepoppen*. Amsterdam, Willem Jansz. [Blaeu], 1614.

Etchings
(pages 4 and 5)
95 x 60 mm. (platemark); 145 x 185 mm. (page size); vellum
De Vries 53; Praz, 1975, p. 532; Landwehr, 1962, 250a
Coll.: Edward Huydecoper van Nigtevecht; L.G. Visscher 1820
The Houghton Library, Harvard University.
54-1437

The emblem book, a singular marriage of word and image, was very popular in seventeenth-century Holland. Dutch emblem books of this period are often distinguished by an emphasis on imagery drawn from daily reality, from direct observation of the world around us. Roemer Visscher's *Sinnepoppen,* with its etchings by Claes Jansz. Visscher, was the first significant example of such a characteristically Dutch emblem book. Dutch emblem books were frequently heavily moralizing, offering positive and negative examples for the moral conduct of the individual.

An emblem consists of a motto, an image, and text or commentary on the image.[1] As Roemer Visscher explains in his preface, the title of his book gives literal expression to the literary-visual amalgam that is an emblem (*sinne:* "sense" or "meaning;" *pop:* "doll," "figure," or "image"). Visscher, who contributed greatly to the development of Dutch as a literary language,[2] also expresses his satisfaction

1. For the emblem book and the seventeenth-century Dutch emblem book in particular, see De Jongh, 1967, pp. 8–22.

2. Roemer Visscher (1547–1620) was not only an innovator in the use of Dutch as a literary language but also a

that the term or title is expressed in "our pure mother tongue." He also indicates in his preface that he had the images made first and then narrated the commentary to a friend, friends and printer subsequently begging him to publish it. The images were probably pen and wash drawings rather than prints.[3] A small number of preparatory drawings for the *Sinnepoppen* still exist. The priority of the images is interesting because Roemer Visscher subsequently states in his preface addressed to the reader that he has kept the texts brief because he wants to delight our eyes with the images rather than burden us with too much reading.

The etched plates are not signed, and Claes Jansz. Visscher is never mentioned by name, but the style of the preparatory drawings and of the etchings confirms the attribution to Claes Jansz. Visscher.[4] The printmakers and designers of Dutch book illustrations in the seventeenth century were often anonymous, and as a result, many of the most expressive book illustrations of that period have yet to be properly attributed. The long narrow format of the *Sinnepoppen* is also characteristic of the seventeenth century and was used for many of the songbooks or ballad books so popular at this time.

Roemer Visscher states in his preface that the emblems should not be immediately accessible to "Jan alleman" (Jan Everyman); on the other hand, they should not be too obscure. The emblems chosen here for exhibition are certainly not in the least obscure. Their mottos are proverbial (IV: "It's sickening what a fool will spend his money on"; V: "A fool

prosperous Amsterdam merchant whose wealth was based on the shipping of grain and the insurance of ships and cargo. His house was a salon for artists, poets, and writers, and his two gifted daughters, Anna Roemer and Maria Tesselschade, were "Renaissance women" of many accomplishments, who, thanks to their father's beliefs, received an unusually liberal education. For Roemer Visscher see the introduction to the facsimile edition of the *Sinnepoppen,* Brummel, 1949.

3. "Dit werck had ick doen conterfeyten of malen in sekere pampieren bladen."

4. See Simon, 1958, pp. 231–236.

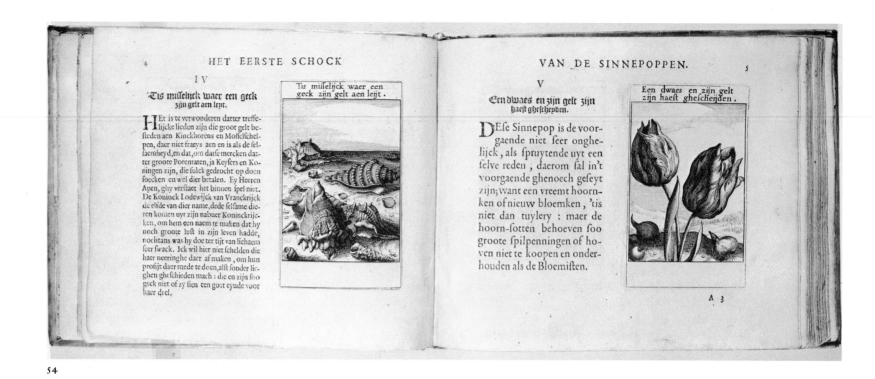

and his money are soon parted") and sharply critical of two forms of collecting very fashionable at the time. Although Roemer Visscher sometimes used Latin mottos in the *Sinnepoppen,* here the entire text is in the "pure mother tongue."

Roemer Visscher has taken advantage of the format with its facing pages to launch a double-barreled assault on contemporary follies.[5] Shell collecting, the folly under attack in *Sinnepop* IV, was a fashionable pursuit associated with the encyclopedic collections of the day – the cabinet of rarities, both natural and artistic, assembled by princes and members of the leisured classes. Rembrandt, who made an etching of a cone shell (B. 159), had shells and other natural history rarities in his collection,[6]

5. Roemer Visscher's text for the fifth *Sinnepop* (tulips) begins: "This emblem is not unlike the foregoing."

6. For Rembrandt and the encyclopedic collections, see Scheller, 1969, pp. 81ff.

and shells, minerals, and other natural history objects were prominently featured in Jacques de Gheyn III's will.[7] Roemer Visscher accuses the shell collectors of loving rarity more than beauty and of aping the habits of kings and emperors. The accompanying etching shows a variety of types of shells strewn across a beach.[8]

The etching for the fifth *Sinnepop* is reminiscent of Crispijn van de Passe's *Hortus Floridus* (cat. no. 55) in that it shows flowers and bulbs in a landscape context. Tulips were imported into Holland in 1593 by the botanist Clusius. The curiosity aroused by the exotic blooms

7. The will is printed in full in Van Regteren Altena, 1936, pp. 128ff. (Appendix VI): "alsmede alle sijne coquilien ofte zeeschelpen, soe rare suyvere als ruwe onsuyvere, mit oock alle sijne mineralia, steene ende zeegewassen." (p. 129).

8. The shells include large conchs or whelks as well as, at left, a small cone shell, the type etched by Rembrandt. I would like to thank John H. Welsh and Kenneth Boss for an exchange of information about shells and shell-collecting.

eventually resulted in a wild speculation in rare varieties, the so-called "tulpomania," which reached a peak of intensity in 1636 and collapsed in the spring of 1637, bringing financial ruin to many speculators.[9] Roemer Visscher's emblem is a relatively early criticism of the folly of too passionate an attachment to tulips: "for an exotic shell or new flower is none other than gambling."

9. For the "tulpomania" see Zumthor, 1959, pp. 67–70; 1963, pp. 49–52.

IV

'Tis misselijck waer een geck zijn gelt aen leijt.

HEt is te verwonderen datter treffe-
lijcke lieden zijn die groot gelt be-
steden aen Kinckhorens en Mosselschel-
pen, daer niet fraeys aen en is als de sel-
saemheyd, en dat, om datse mercken datter groote Potentaten, ja Keysers en Ko-
ningen zijn, die sulck gedrocht op doen
soecken en wel dier betalen. Ey Heeren
Apen, ghy verstaet het binnen spel niet.
De Koninck Lodewijck van Vranckrijck
de elfde van dier name, dede selsame die-
ren komen uyt zijn nabuer Koninckrijc-
ken, om hem een naem te maken dat hy
noch groote lust in zijn leven hadde,
nochtans was hy doe ter tijt van lichaem
seer swack. Ick wil hier niet schelden die
haer neeringhe daer af maken , om hun
profijt daer mede te doen, alst sonder lie-
ghen gheschieden mach : die en zijn soo
geck niet of zy sien een goet eynde voor
haer deel.

Tis misselijck waer een geck zijn gelt aen leijt.

Crispijn van de Passe II
about 1597 – about 1670

Crispijn van de Passe II was perhaps the most gifted member of a family of engravers. His father, Crispijn van de Passe the elder (about 1565-1637), who was born in Zeeland, was probably a pupil of Hendrik Goltzius's teacher, Dirck Volckertsz. Coornhert.[1] The elder Crispijn was first active in Antwerp, where he joined the artists' guild in 1585 and engraved for the famous book publishing house of Plantijn. He next moved via Aachen to Cologne, where he remained from about 1594 until his move to Utrecht about 1612 because of his Mennonite (Baptist) faith. His four children, who all became engravers, were born in Cologne: Simon (1595-1647), Crispijn II (about 1597-about 1670), Willem (about 1598-about 1637), and Magdalena (1600-before 1640).

Crispijn II, like his brothers and sister, was apparently a pupil of his father. He worked with his father until the period 1617-1630, during which he was mostly in Paris, teaching drawing at the Riding School, Pluvinel's school for young aristocrats and court pages, and engraving for book illustration. In the period 1630-1639 he was again in Utrecht, employed in his father's workshop. His father died in 1637, and in 1640 the younger Crispijn settled in Amsterdam, establishing his own printing and publishing firm. After 1645 his production declined, and there is evidence that he suffered from mental illness. He died about 1670.

Crispijn the younger's long period of activity in Paris was not unusual. The Van de Passe family, like most professional engravers, had strong international connections. Crispijn the elder had already established contact with England while in Cologne, and two of his sons, Simon and Willem, were active there.

1. Biographies by M.D. Henkel in Thieme-Becker, vol. 26, pp. 280-282; in Hollstein, vols. 15 and 16; in Rotterdam, 1972, pp. 29-31.

Willem died there; Simon went on to work for the Danish court and died in Copenhagen.

The family's collective production was enormous, amounting to nearly 1,400 items exclusive of individual book illustrations. All of the family members were active in portrait engraving, which, together with book illustration, accounted for much of the international demand for their services.

55
CRISPIJN VAN DE PASSE II
Cyclamen (Cyclaminus folio hederae)
Plate 14 of the third part, *Autumnus,* in Crispijn van de Passe, *Hortus Floridus.* Arnhem, Jan Jansson, 1614.

Engraving
134 x 204 mm. (platemark); 180 x 268 mm. (page size); vellum
Franken 1346, Nissen 1494
Mr. and Mrs. Arthur E. Vershbow

The *Hortus Floridus* (Dutch title: *Bloemhof),* or *Flower Garden,* was Crispijn the younger's first significant work to appear under his own name. First issued in 1614, the book was published in a number of editions in Dutch, Latin, French, and English between 1614 and 1617. Considering that it is one of the most beautiful flower books of all time, it is rather surprising to find that both drawings and engravings were made by a young man around seventeen years of age.

According to the Latin title page, the flowers were drawn from life with the utmost accuracy and reveal the most incredible labor and diligence. The Latin title page, which is adorned with the portraits of the botanists Carolus Clusius (see cat. no. 25) and Rembertus Dodonaeus,[1] also informs us that the work is divided according to the four sea-

1. An international figure like Clusius, Rembertus Dodonaeus (1517-1585) was born and educated in the South Netherlands, employed by the Hapsburg emperors and ended his career in Leyden. He was a highly literate doctor of medicine who published on botany. See *Biographisch Woordenboek,* vol. 4, pp. 202-207.

sons of the year, and, indeed, each section is prefaced by an engraving of a garden divided into parterres and surrounded by galleries or covered passageways in the form of arbors (see illus.). The book is a *florilegium,* a collection of depicted flowers with little text, a type of printed book that reflects the growth and popularity of the flower garden. In the Dutch edition Crispijn van de Passe included a list of the amateurs of herbs and flowers in whose gardens in Utrecht, Amsterdam, Haarlem, and Leyden he had drawn the flowers.

The sense of the flowers' having been drawn from life is heightened by the fact that many of the plates show the flowers growing in the soil and that the scene is enlivened by characteristic insect or animal life. Here, in the plate of the ivy-leafed cyclamen from the Autumn Garden, we see a dragonfly and a centipede. Crispijn van de Passe's close-up vision puts us right down among the plants on eye level with the horizon.

The tradition established in sixteenth-century botanical books was to show the whole plant out of the soil on a blank background to allow study of the root system. Crispijn van de Passe often includes uprooted or unburied bulbs resting on the soil in his plates so as to provide information about the entire plant. In the case of the *Cyclamen* he engraved the roots separately on a blank background on another plate (no. 26 in the *Autumnus* section). In the upper right corner of each plate Van de Passe engraved the name of the plant in several languages. The facing page provides a typeset Latin description of the plant.

Contributing further to the vivid sense of study from life is the strong suggestion of color and texture in the black and white engraving. See, for example, the mottled color of the cyclamen's leaves in this plate. It is therefore rather surprising to discover that the book is prefaced by a section in which the artist provides detailed instructions for coloring the plates according to the true colors of the flowers, including the mixing of the pigments.

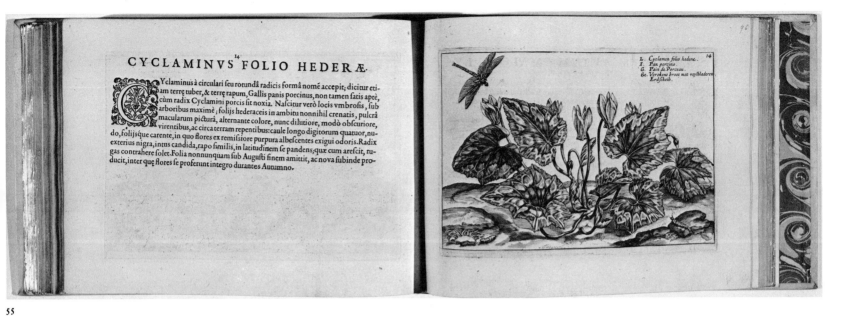

This masterpiece of coloristic suggestion in engraving is a coloring book! The meticulous directions for the coloring of the plates, however, present yet another aspect of the artist's desire to convey the most immediate sense of the true appearance of the flowers in their natural setting.

Meridies

Oriens

Occidens

Septentrio

55

56

WILLEM BUYTEWECH
Whale Stranded between Scheveningen and Katwijk, 1617

Etching
V.d.K. 7, Van Gelder 34 [II], Holl. 13 [II], Haverkamp-Begemann 34 [II]
Lower left (on barrel): *WB*; below: *tot broer Jans in Schraven haege*
222 x 325 mm. (sheet)
Coll.: K.E. von Liphart (L. 1687)
Gemeentearchief, Haarlem. V.S. 60

Jan Saenredam, in his ambitious, large-scale engraving of 1602 of a stranded whale, went to great lengths to *tell* the viewer that the artist had been present. In Willem Buytewech's more modestly scaled etching of 1617 the overall visual impression is so immediate, so reportorial in nature, that we are persuaded that the event was directly observed by the artist. A free, impressionistic pen and wash sketch of this scene, apparently made on the spot, in which the basic elements of the etching's structure are already present, is preserved in the Berlin print room.[1]

At the time that Buytewech's print was published, the public was very likely still prone to regard stranded whales as ominous portents. One of the reasons for the popularity of such prints in the Netherlands in the first quarter of the seventeenth century was the fear and anxiety attendant on these events.[2] Buytewech's shorthand etching was capable of being rushed to completion for immediate publication, whereas Saenredam's elaborate engraved plate probably took months to complete. Broer Jansz., the Hague bookseller and publisher who issued the print, was also the publisher of a newspaper and probably treated the etching as a kind of broadsheet.[3]

1. Haverkamp-Begemann, 1959, p. 29; Rotterdam/Paris, 1975, no. 36.
2. Haverkamp-Begemann, 1959, pp. 29–30.
3. Rotterdam/Paris, 1975, no. 124.

Defen vis is geftant tuffchen fcheveling ēn katwijck den 21 Jannewarij A° i d i 7

tot broer Jans

lanck fijnde 5 2 voet ēn 3 ð dick
lanck ēn 5 voet de ftaert breet

in fchraven haege

Buytewech's spontaneous etching, however, is totally free of the elaborate allegorical imagery and lengthy verses concerning portents of disaster that characterize Saenredam's glorious piece of rhetorical overstatement. Buytewech enframes the scene simply, with a lobate-style shell cartouche at bottom center and an equally appropriate and witty border of delicately etched garlands of sea creatures and seaweed. The only text is the objective description of the event and the creature's dimensions: "This fish was stranded between Scheveningen and Katwijk on January 21, 1617; it is 52 feet long and 36 thick, the tail being 5 feet wide."[4]

The whale is seen not from above, as in Saenredam's print, but at eye level; and the viewer is much closer to the whale, instead of being provided with a sweeping coastal panorama. Buytewech made a few changes between drawing and print, reducing the scale of the spectators so as to emphasize the bulk of the whale. He also added the elegantly dressed aristocratic couple in the left foreground to provide the maximum social contrast with the simple fisherfolk. Buytewech gloried in the extravagance of the fashions of his time, as is evident in his paintings of merry companies and his etched costume series of seven noblemen (V.d.K.14–21).

Print series of both upper-class and peasant costume were very popular in this period. Buytewech himself designed two series of peasant women's costumes to be etched and engraved by other artists such as Gillis van Scheyndel.[5]

Buytewech's vocabulary of shorthand etching strokes that suggest rather than fully delineate add greatly to the animation, immediacy, and atmospheric feeling of the print; see, for example, the short, flickering strokes and dots that define the sand dunes of the background and the animated figures that scurry over them. In Saenredam's engraved spectacle each of the myriad spectators, no matter how distant, was fully delineated. Perhaps no one before the

4. Translation from Haverkamp-Begemann, 1962, p. 77.
5. Rotterdam/Paris, 1975, nos. 144–149, 153–160.

mature Rembrandt knew better than Buytewech how to use blank paper in an etching to suggest light and atmosphere. Here the vocabulary of the etched lines ranges from areas of rather conventional crosshatching to areas of open stipple, as in the light-streaked sky, to bold areas of blank paper that suggest both brilliant light and color, as on the whale's body.

57
WILLEM BUYTEWECH
The Cannoneer and the Provisioner, about 1616

Etching
V.D.K. 9[I], Van Gelder 32[I], Holl. 16[I], Haverkamp-Begemann 32[I]
Lower right: *WB*
142 x 93mm. (platemark)
Coll.: D. Franken (L. 964)
Rijksmuseum, Amsterdam. A20580

57

One of Buytewech's most delightful prints, *The Cannoneer and the Provisioner* poses problems of interpretation because, as in Rembrandt's drypoint of the *Young Couple and Death* of 1639 (B. 109), the couple is dressed in period costume. The young gunner (or guard), wearing the uniform of a German mercenary, or *Landsknecht,* of the first half of the sixteenth century, turns his head to look at a provisioner, who demurely lowers her eyes. The young woman is barefoot and carries on her belt not only her shoes but also the gunner's steel helmet and a supply of food, including a whole rooster. Behind her, leaning against the wickerwork fortifications, is a smoldering torch to light the cannon, which is trained on the distant city. Smoke rises from the city, which is presumably under siege.

The drawing of the young soldier in this print is very similar to that of the single figures (some in period costume) in a group of Buytewech's drawings that are somewhat satirical or humorous in flavor; see, for example, his pen and wash drawing of a man in sixteenth-century costume with a dog, in the collection of the Louvre, Paris (inv. 7512 bis).[1]

Haverkamp-Begemann, who dates the etching about 1616, compared it with a print by Gillis van Breen after Karel van Mander (Holl. 78), which shows a soldier and provisioner on the march with a battle scene in the background. The inscription on Van Breen's print indicates that war is sweet for those who have little experience of it.[2] The soldier of Buytewech's print does seem young and rather callow. Soldier and provisioner appear to be more engaged in a private battle of the sexes than in the actual siege. The smoking torch behind them may well allude to the smoldering fires of love. The dog looks toward the viewer with a mistrustful expression, which seems to express some doubt about the outcome of the encounter.

1. Rotterdam/Paris, 1975, no. 65.
2. Haverkamp-Begemann, 1959, p. 31.

58

Attributed to ESAIAS VAN DE VELDE
The Hunter and Two Dogs, about 1612/13

Etching and drypoint
V.d.K., p. 122, Bur. 35[1], Haverkamp-Begemann,
1959, p. 182, no. 16
128 x 77 mm. (platemark)
Coll.: Friedrich August II (L. 971)
The Metropolitan Museum of Art, New York,
Harris Brisbane Dick Fund, 1933. 33.52.48

The man who looks alertly out at us, leaning
on his staff and accompanied by two tensely
poised dogs, has traditionally been described as
a shepherd, but he more likely represents a
hunter.[1] His staff is not a shepherd's crook; he
has a game bag attached to his belt, and his
swift, greyhound-like dogs seem more appropriate for hunting than for herding.

Van der Kellen was the first to suggest that
this unsigned print was by Esaias van de
Velde.[2] His suggestion was supported by
Burchard and by Haverkamp-Begemann, who
both dated it about 1612–13.[3] It was published
by Claes Jansz. Visscher as part of a series of
eight small prints of vertical format mostly
representing only one figure.[4] The first print in
the series as published is by Moses van
Uyttenbroeck and is dated 1615. The series,
apparently not conceived originally as a unit
but assembled later by the enterprising publisher, perhaps to provide models for figures
with which artists could animate their compositions, includes, in addition to *The Hunter,*
two Uyttenbroecks, three Buytewechs, and
two etchings quite plausibly attributed by
Van der Kellen and Haverkamp-Begemann to
Visscher himself.

Esaias's earliest works reflect his contact
with David Vinckboons. The vertical format of
the print, the figure from daily life who looks

1. I would like to thank Alison Kettering for this
suggestion.

2. V.d.K., pp. 122–123.

3. Burchard, 1917, pp. 66–67; Haverkamp-Begemann,
1959, p. 182, no. 16.

4. Burchard, 1917, pp. 147–150, nos. 1–8.

58

out at the viewer, and the framing tree all recall
Vinckboons's *Bagpiper* (cat. no. 21), even
though the linear vocabulary is totally different. Figures related in drawing and in proportions, as well as such an ornamental framing
tree with pendent vines or tendrils, may be
seen in one of Esaias's earliest dated paintings
of a garden party in the Mauritshuis.[5] The
drawing of the drapery folds compares closely
with that in Gillis van Breen's engraving after a
lost early composition by Esaias representing
mercenary love (Holl. 72). The character and
rhythm of the etched line are reminiscent of
some of the early small etched landscapes by
Esaias included in the series of sixteen landscapes published by Claes Jansz. Visscher
(Bur. 18–24, 27; see the biography of Esaias
van de Velde in this catalogue, note 1).

5. The Hague, cat. paintings, 1977, no. 199.

59

ESAIAS VAN DE VELDE
A Garden Party, about 1615

Etching
Bur. 7[II]
Lower right: *EV VELDE fe*
104 x 112 mm. (platemark)
Coll.: Friedrich August II (L. 971)
Museum of Fine Arts, Boston, Special Print Fund.
33.564

A number of Esaias van de Velde's earliest
dated paintings represent garden parties with
elegant young couples eating, drinking, and
flirting. These paintings show the influence of
similar subjects by David Vinckboons, who
was possibly Esaias's teacher, but they are surprisingly restrained and decorous beside
Vinckboons's rowdy picnics. Esaias's rare etching of a garden party, represented in many collections only by an early reverse copy, is like an
intimate close-up or detail of one of the early
garden party paintings, such as that dated 1615
in the collection of the Rijksmuseum, Amsterdam (inv. A 1765).[1]

The composition of the etching is unusual
when compared with the paintings, not only in
that the figures are seen close up and dominate
the composition, but also in the off-center
placement, in which the left border slices
through one of the figures, the pheasant pie,
and the wine cooler. The more modest print
format apparently encouraged Esaias to try out
an idea he would have been unlikely to attempt
in painting. Surely only a printmaker, accustomed to cutting down the copper plate to
adjust its dimensions, would have arrived at
such an unorthodox solution.

Although the figures are slightly wooden
and doll-like, as in the 1615 painting, we are
unusually conscious of their expressions and
gestures. The principal figure's face is hidden;
he looks down at the wine cup, probably a
Venetian glass *tazza,* which he holds by the
base. Two of the figures at the table study his
face with sympathetic concern, and a third
casts her eyes down. There is a delicate melan-

1. Bol. 1969, pl. 120.

59 (actual size)

choly about the scene, a wistfulness, as if youth
had just discovered the brevity and transience
of the pleasures of this world. This extremely
understated moralizing tone contrasts sharply
with that of the scene of outdoor carousing in
De Gheyn II's *Prodigal Son* after Van Mander
(cat. no. 12), with its explicit pointing fools
and hobbling cripple. Representations of the
Prodigal Son squandering his fortune nevertheless formed the tradition from which compositions such as Esaias's *Garden Party* evolved.

Light strikes across the scene, heightening
subtly the underplayed drama of the moment
and casting the young servant in the background into shadow. Only a peep is afforded
into the landscape or park, where a couple
strolls toward a round greenery-covered structure that closes the vista. The etched line is
finer and is handled more sketchily than in the
Standing Hunter (cat. no. 58); there is also
greater exploitation of stippling and short
hatchings to lend a painterly variety and color
to the scene.

Joost Cornelisz. Droochsloo
1586 – 1666

The Utrecht painter of scenes of village and
peasant life, Joost Cornelisz. Droochsloot produced only two etchings, which were executed
quite early in his career. Born in 1586, probably
in Utrecht, he entered the artists' Guild of
Saint Luke in 1616 and continued to be a very
active member of the organization. We do not
know the name of his teacher. He married in
1618 and in 1620 purchased a house in
Utrecht. In 1628 he donated a painting to
Utrecht's St. Job's Hospital, on whose board of
regents he served in 1638. He began as a
painter of biblical or literary subjects, but from
the 1630s until his death in 1666 he produced
primarily village scenes and peasant kermises
in a rather conservative style related to the
work of late Bruegel followers such as
David Vinckboons and Adriaen van de Venne.
His most important pupil was Jacob Duck
(see cat. no. 83).[1]

1. Biography based on Karel Lilienfeld in Thieme-Becker,
vol. 9, pp.574–575, and information assembled by
Cynthia Schneider, intern, Department of Paintings.

60
JOOST CORNELISZ. DROOCHSLOOT
Company of Beggars Carousing, 1610

Etching and drypoint
Wurz. 1[1], Holl. 1[1]
Lower left: *1610*
128 x 172 mm. (platemark)
Wm.: unidentified fragment
Rijksmuseum, Amsterdam. B.I. 7156

The *Company of Beggars Carousing* is unsigned
in this, the first, state. In the following state,
issued by the Haarlem publisher Berendrecht,
the date "1610" is removed, and the plate is
signed with Droochsloot's name followed by
the abbreviation "fe." for "fecit." Droochsloot's
only other known etching (Holl. 2), very similar in style to the *Beggars,* represents a prostitute and her cohorts fleecing a peasant. This

60

undated, unsigned print was issued by the Hague publisher Broer Jansz.

The great numbers of beggars and vagabonds were a serious social problem for the North Netherlands in the seventeenth century. A short time after Droochsloot made his print, in 1613, the city of Amsterdam forbade all begging. Beggars were often sent to workhouses, where they could make themselves useful to society.[1]

Droochsloot shows beggars and vagabonds relaxing, indulging in simple pleasures, a scene cut through with the irony of those in rags enjoying themselves or cripples dancing. At the right an impressive-looking figure with a rather haunted expression turns his head toward us and holds out an empty bowl. The partly obliterated beginning of an inscription

in Dutch below the image is not complete enough to be comprehensible. Perhaps its theme would have been an ironic or cynical one, like that of the inscription under Droochsloot's etching of peasant and prostitute, in which the prostitute testifies that she's happy to make love to the peasant as long as he has money in his purse.

Below Pieter Serwouters's engraving (Wurz. 6) after a drawing of 1608 by David Vinckboons, showing beggars carousing outside an inn named "De Laserus Clep" ("The Leper's Clapper"), is the inscription "Soo gewonnen – Soo geronnen" ("Spent as soon as it's earned"). It represents a savage attack on the deceptions practiced by beggars in order to dupe people into giving them money and the speed with which they are healed of their pretended afflictions once they reach an inn,

where they promptly proceed to fritter away their dishonest earnings.[2] In Droochsloot's print the church tower sketched in drypoint at the center of the view through the window may be intended as a moral reminder, an intentional contrast with the beggars' behavior.

The simple etching style of the *Beggars,* with its curving parallel shading lines, is related to that of Gerrit Pietersz. (see cat. no. 10). The combination of rather stylized decorative drawing and low-life subject suggests the later etchings of carousing peasants of the Utrecht artist Andries Both, the vagabond or gypsy etchings of Gerrit A. de Heer, and the etchings of beggars designed by Pieter Quast.[3]

1. On begging and workhouses see Amsterdam, 1965–66.

2. Goossens, 1977, pp. 70, 101.

3. Hollstein, vol. 3, pp. 151ff.; vol. 9, pp. 1ff.; vol. 17, pp. 241ff. De Heer's prints were sometimes printed on vellum.

Surgito. iam vendit pueris ientacula pistor
Cristatæq. sonant undique lucis aues. Marti. lib. xiv.

J. Velde fec. et excud.

61
(actual size)

61

JAN VAN DE VELDE II
The Pancake Woman, about 1626

Engraving
Fr.-v.d.K. 109[1]
Lower margin: *J. Velde fec. et excud.*
186 x 129 mm. (platemark)
Wm.: undecipherable fragment
Coll.: W.G. Russell Allen
Museum of Fine Arts, Boston, Gift of Lydia Evans
Tunnard in memory of W.G. Russell Allen.
63.2880

From about 1622 Jan van de Velde began to
employ his own adaptation of Hendrik
Goudt's tonal system of engraving to render
more vividly effects of night or twilight. *The
Pancake Woman,* one of the most successful
prints in this manner, is close in style to another
of his prints with dramatic nocturnal illumination, *The Witch* of 1626 (Fr.-v.d.K.114), and
probably should also be dated about 1626, as
Haverkamp-Begemann suggests.[1] I do not
agree with Haverkamp-Begemann, on the
other hand, that the design of the *Pancake
Woman,* signed "fec." (abbreviation for "fecit"),
need necessarily be credited to a lost drawing
by Pieter Molijn. Pieter Molijn designed two
prints that Jan van de Velde engraved in his
nocturnal manner, *The Star of the Kings* (Fr.-
v.d.K. 110) and the *Mardi Gras Dancers* (Fr.-
v.d.K. 111), and both of these bear Molijn's
name as designer. However, an etched frontispiece by Jan van de Velde (Fr.-v.d.K. 283) to
the second part of a series (the third part is
dated 1616) shows a figure of an old market
woman seated in profile (facing left) that is
nearly identical with the figure of the old pancake woman in this engraving (see illus.).

This subject from everyday life is embellished with a quotation in Latin from the
Roman writer Martial, which summons us to
rise, for the baker has already begun to sell his
bread to the children, and everywhere the
cocks are crowing. The quotation seems less to
explicate the meaning of the print than to lend
a literary tone to the "low" subject matter that

may have made it more appealing to the taste of the educated classes. The inscription is executed in a calligraphy that is reminiscent of Hendrik Goudt's inscriptions (see cat. nos. 44, 45).

The illumination gives a slightly sinister character to the old crone with her knife. She appears to be about to slice up an apple to make apple pancakes, while in the background a child holds up a coin to purchase a cake. The deep shadows of the interior rendered by a dense web of regular crosshatching and flicks reflect Goudt's engraving style as seen in his 1612 print after Elsheimer of a lamp-lit interior. Goudt's print, which shows Mercury and Jupiter visiting Philemon and Baucis (Holl. 6), looks forward to Rembrandt's 1642 etched and engraved *St. Jerome in a Dark Chamber* (cat. no. 99). The motif of Jan van de Velde's print was one of the sources of inspiration for Rembrandt's lively *Pancake Woman* etching of 1635 (cat. no.72).

1. Haverkamp-Begemann, 1959, p. 108.

Jan van de Velde
Market Scene (Frontispiece)
Etching
Museum of Fine Arts, Boston

62

62

JAN VAN DE VELDE after PIETER
SAENREDAM
*The Interior of the Church of St. Bavo,
Haarlem* in Samuel Ampzing,
*Beschryvinge ende Lof der Stad Haerlem in
Holland.* Haarlem, Adriaen Rooman, 1628.

Engraving and etching
(following page 502)
Fr.-v.d.K. 486
Lower right: *P. Zaenredam Invent./I.V. Velde.
Sculp.*
158 x 224 mm. (platemark); 190 x 140 mm. (page
size); vellum, gold stamped with arms of Haarlem
Fr.v.d.K. 477–488; Wurzbach 6
The Houghton Library, Harvard University.
Neth 3401.1

The preacher and historian Samuel Ampzing's
Description and Eulogy of the City of Haarlem of
1628 is the most pictorially vivid of the several
illustrated descriptions of Dutch cities
published in the seventeenth century. Other
examples include Orler's description of Leyden
of 1614 (first edition) and 1641 and Balen's
description of Dordrecht of 1677. Ampzing's
book was a collaborative effort that includes
plates designed by the Haarlem painter Jan
Bouckhorst (allegorical and heraldic designs)
and engraved by Theodor Matham and Willem
Akersloot. The majority of the plates, however,
were designed by Pieter Saenredam, son of the
brilliant engraver of the Goltzius circle, Jan
Saenredam, and were etched and engraved by
Jan van de Velde II. Two small plates of manor
houses in the book (Assumburg, Wurz. 3, and

Berkenrode, Wurz. 2) were etched by Saenredam, who was just beginning his career as a
painter of church architecture.[1]

The text of Ampzing's book, written in
rhyme (in an age when every person of some
education seems to have been capable of turning out doggerel verse by the yard), concerns
the history of Haarlem, its famous citizens and
buildings, with special attention to the Spanish
siege of the city in the 1570s. Two illustrations
are devoted to bird's-eye views of Haarlem during and after the siege. A supplement to
Ampzing's text is formed by Petrus Scriverius,
*Laurel Wreath for Laurens Coster of Haarlem,
First inventor of book printing.* Coster was
Haarlem's candidate for the first inventor of
printing with movable type. The supplement is
also illustrated with prints designed by Saenredam and etched by Jan van de Velde.

The copy of Ampzing's book exhibited here
is bound in plain vellum, both covers stamped
in gilt with the coat of arms of Haarlem. The
illustration chosen for exhibition shows the
spacious interior of Haarlem's Grote Kerk
(Great Church), St. Bavo's, completed about
1400. This medieval church interior, like so
many others in the North Netherlands, was
stripped of its devotional sculpture, white-
washed, and adapted to Protestant preaching.
Entering this space today, one has the feeling
of stepping into the seventeenth century. This
is one of Saenredam's earliest views of a church
interior; his first dated painting of a church
interior was made in the same year.[2] One sees
already in Jan van de Velde's lucid translation
of Saenredam's design, the architectural
painter's concern to record not only the charac-

1. Pieter Jansz. Saenredam was born in Assendelft in
1597. His father, the engraver, died when Pieter was ten.
In 1608 he moved with his mother to Haarlem, where he
was placed in the studio of the painter Frans de Grebber
in 1612 and remained until 1622. In 1623 he became a
member of the Guild of St. Luke. He died in Haarlem in
1665. See Wolfgang Stechow in Thieme-Becker, vol. 29,
pp. 306–307. One other etching by Saenredam is known,
a portrait of Laurens Coster dated 1630 (Wurz. 1).

2. A pen and wash drawing for the etching dated 1627 is
reproduced in Utrecht, 1961, no. 30, pl. 31.

teristic space of a building but also the play of light within that space. The manner in which the double-page illustration is folded into the book heightens the deep perspective of the church interior. This interior view of St. Bavo's is in an appendix to the main text and is preceded by a ground plan of the building. In the main body of the text is included a profile view by Saenredam and Van de Velde of the church's exterior, with a long structure housing shops (still to be seen today) and a passing funeral procession.[3]

Ampzing's verses beneath the view of the interior praise its beauty but remind the reader that its true significance is as a space where God is worshipped.[4] We see the congregation at center huddled around the raised pulpit with its sounding-board canopy. Ampzing himself was a preacher at St. Bavo's, and today's visitor can read his name on a painted board with a chronological list of preachers of the church that hangs inside.

3. Reproduced in Amsterdam/Toronto, 1977, no. 40.
4. Translated in Utrecht, 1961, p. 76.

63 (actual size)

63

WILLEM VAN DE PASSE
after ADRIAEN VAN DE VENNE
The Melancholy Poet Regarding His Reflection

Illustration to the poem by Adriaen van de Venne, *Zeeusche Mey-Clacht. ofte Schyn-Kycker,* in *Zeeusche Nachtegael ende des selfs dryderley gesang.* Middleburgh, Jan Pietersz. van de Venne, 1623.

Engraving
(page 55)
Franken 1359
Upper right: *W: Pass fecit*
102 x 138 mm. (platemark); 232 x 180 mm. (page size); stamped vellum
Praz (1975) p. 540, Frederiks (1896), Landwehr (1962) 167a
Mr. and Mrs. Arthur E. Vershbow

The poet and painter Adriaen Pietersz. van de Venne (Delft, 1589 – The Hague, 1662) was one of the most prolific designers for book illustration. No other seventeenth-century Dutch painter or illustrator recorded in such detail the daily life of all classes of Dutch society. His many illustrations for the moralizing texts of the popular, best-selling author and politician Jacob Cats (known affectionately in Holland as "Father" Cats) are inseparable from the texts.[1]

Adriaen van de Venne's father moved to Middelburg in Zeeland in 1605, and his older brother, Jan Pietersz. van de Venne, the publisher of the book *Zeeusche Nachtegael (Zeeland Nightingale)* established a printing, publishing,

1. For Adriaen van de Venne's life and career, see Bol, 1958. For Adriaen van de Venne as illustrator, see De la Fontaine Verwey, 1967, pp. 66–69. For the *Zeeusche Nachtegael* see Meertens, 1943, pp. 217ff.

and art-dealing firm there. His shop dealt in art, decorative arts, literature, optical and nautical instruments, and musical instruments. In 1614 Adriaen married and settled down in Middelburg, in a house adjoining his brother's shop and printing concern.

The *Zeeland Nightingale* is a poetic anthology affirming Zeeland's right to its own literary and poetic culture. Also included are a number of poems eulogizing Roemer Visscher's daughter, the poetess Anna Roemer Visscher, who had recently paid a visit to Zeeland. In popular usage the phrase "Zeeland nightingale" refers to a frog, a creature that thrived in this watery province. The *Zeeusche Nachtegael* turns the tables by giving this jeering epithet a positive meaning: it alludes to Zeeland's poetic muse.

The *Nightingale* is divided into three "songs," or sections. Adiaen van de Venne's poem, the *Zeeusche Mey-Clacht. (Zeeland May-Plaint),* for which Willem van de Passe engraved the illustration, is in the first section, the *Minne-Sang* (love song). The following sections are the *Seden-Sang* (song of manners or morals) and the *Hemel-Sang* (heavenly song).

The *Mey-Clacht* is a kind of personal artistic credo of the Zeeland painter-poet. The poem opens just before dawn on May Day with the melancholy poet wandering in the Zeeland landscape. Narcissus-like, he looks into a pool and discovers his reflection, every movement perfectly mimicked on the still surface of the water. The poet takes up his lute to raise his spirits and rouses first Echo and then the Zeeland nightingale. The true nightingale's melodious voice is contrasted with the coarse utterance of that other "Zeeland nightingale," the frog.

The bulk of the poem is devoted to an investigation of the nature of painting and its relation to poetry. Much attention is devoted to painting's ability to capture the whole of the visible world. The poem ends with a description of Zeeland.

The engraved illustration designed by Adriaen van de Venne shows the poet-Narcissus regarding his features in a still pool, his lute beside him. In the water, at the lower left, a frog studies the poet. The city in the distance is undoubtedly Middelburg. In this fine impression of Willem van de Passe's engraving one fully experiences the subtle evocation of the early morning light.

The image of the illustration, the poet-painter wondering at the perfect reflection of his features, is apparently an allusion to the power of painting to capture or reflect the appearance of the visible world in all its details, as Van de Venne did in his own paintings. The subtitle of the poem is *Schyn-kycker,* the Looker-at-Appearances.

Despite his patriotic feelings for Zeeland, Adriaen van de Venne moved in 1625 to the Hague, where he worked for the rest of his life.

Pieter Molijn
1595 – 1661

The Haarlem painter of landscapes and genre scenes Pieter Molijn executed and published under his own name a single set of four landscape etchings, animated with rural figures and picturesque dilapidated structures.[1]

Born in London of Flemish parents in 1595, Molijn joined the Haarlem chapter of the artists' Guild of St. Luke in 1616. Nothing is known of his early training or his teachers. He continued to be active in the affairs of the guild and was a resident of Haarlem until his death in 1661.[2]

1. Another set of four landscapes (Holl. 5–8) designed by Molijn (inscribed "inve.") are very close in motif and technique, but the etcher is not known. They were certainly designed about the time of Molijn's 1626 series and are probably also contemporary in execution.

2. See biography by T.H. Fokker, in Thieme-Becker, vol. 25, pp. 49–50.

64
PIETER MOLIJN
Landscape with Travelers, 1626

From an untitled series of four prints
Etching and drypoint
B. 2, Holl. 2[II]
Lower right: 4
155 x 189 mm. (sheet)
The Cleveland Museum of Art, The Mr. and Mrs. Lewis B. Williams Collection. 43.590

Pieter Molijn's four etchings do not reflect to the same degree as his paintings the brief moment in the 1620s when he was one of the most inventive landscape artists of the time. Molijn's painted landscapes often portray sandy roads with travelers along the high dunes that line the coast near Haarlem. These are most likely the "hills" that appear in the fourth of Molijn's 1626 etchings, shown here. The etchings were published at a time when the emphasis in Molijn's painting was turning from subjects in which the actions of the figures are dominant to startlingly simple landscapes in which space, light, and atmosphere are the principal motifs,[1] as they are in Esaias van de Velde's radically stark etching *Landscape with the Gallows* (cat. no. 40). The *Landscape with Travelers* reveals more concern than the other three etchings with the opening up of the landscape space.

The etched contours of the four prints are continuous, not sketchy or broken, and they set up an undulant rhythm that combines with the tumbledown fences, dilapidated rural dwellings, and ragged peasant types to suggest strongly the series of picturesque farmhouses etched by Boetius A. Bolswert and Claes Jansz. Visscher after designs of Abraham Bloemaert a few years earlier (1614 and 1620 respectively). Molijn's etchings, however, are more earth-bound, less sinuous and decorative in their rhythms than the etchings after Bloemaert, and there is greater variety in the use of line, particularly in the highly original use of drypoint. Drypoint without burr is employed throughout in fine parallel lines to create subtle passages of shadow that enliven both earth and sky.[2]

1. Stechow, 1966, p. 23.

2. The black chalk and wash drawing on light brown paper in Rotterdam (inv. no. H 44), presumed to be a preparatory drawing for this print, is in the same direction as the print. Although free in execution, it is perhaps too late in style and could conceivably have been made after the print.

64

65

Gillis van Scheyndel
active 1622 – 1654

Although Gillis van Scheyndel made over one hundred etchings after his own designs and the designs of others, little is known of his life. He was apparently active primarily in Haarlem, and his signed and dated works range from 1622 to 1654. Many of his prints were published by the Haarlem publisher who issued some of Esaias van de Velde's finest prints, J.P. Berendrecht. Van Scheyndel etched two costume series after Willem Buytewech and a garden party after Esaias van de Velde. His own designs for etched landscapes and series of figures drawn from everyday life, somewhat hybrid in style, reflect the influence of those printmakers as well as that of Jan van de Velde and Jacques Callot. Van Scheyndel also made etchings for book illustration.

65
GILLIS VAN SCHEYNDEL
The Towing Barge

Etching
77 x 130 mm. (platemark)
Wm.: crowned shield with fleur-de-lis (type of Heawood 1663–1667)
Museum Boymans-van Beuningen, Rotterdam.
BdH 19921

Like the majority of Gillis van Scheyndel's prints of his own design, *The Towing Barge* is quite small in scale, almost miniaturistic in feeling. It should probably be dated in the 1620s and perpetuates and elaborates landscape conceptions formulated by Willem Buytewech (cat. no. 38), Esaias van de Velde (cat. no. 41) and Jan van de Velde II in Haarlem in the previous decade. Everything is aligned parallel to the picture plane, the line of trees profiled in decorative silhouette against the sky in the manner of Dutch landscapes inspired by Adam Elsheimer. Each kind of vegetation is executed with a different vocabulary of strokes. The landscape forms are all rendered in a nonlinear fashion, in soft clusters of fine short strokes or

107

stipples; only the figures and the boat are described in continuous line work, the boat defined and modeled by precise tapering lines that resemble engraved lines – a debt to the etching style of Jacques Callot. In some of Van Scheyndel's small pieces, his fondness for describing each separate element with a different linear vocabulary leads to confusion; here he achieves within a small compass an astonishing variety of texture.

Travel by towing barge was eminently practical in the Netherlands, with its many inland waterways and level terrain.

66

HERCULES SEGERS
A Road Bordered by Trees, a City in the Distance

Etching, printed in black on white paper
Springer 5a, Haverkamp-Begemann 26a
139 x 104 mm. (platemark)
Wm.: coat of arms (Heawood 606, Churchill 154)
Coll.: P.C. Baron van Leyden
Rijksmuseum, Amsterdam. OB 801

A Road Bordered by Trees is a highly original synthesis of the dense, moss-hung northern forest view and the profile view of the Dutch city, usually an open panorama.[1] This kind of image of the northern forest evokes the landscapes by early sixteenth-century German painters of the Danube school such as Albrecht Altdorfer. Altdorfer's landscape etchings, together with Dürer's *Cannon* (B. 99), are the earliest known landscape etchings and could well have served as a source of inspiration for Segers in this etching and in his etching of *The Mossy Tree* (HB 32). Segers could also have studied Alpine woodlands dripping with moss in the paintings of Roelant Savery and other late Bruegel followers. The Dutch followers of Elsheimer, too, were fond of the motif of trees with pendent moss or creepers (see Esaias van

66 (actual size)

1. Haverkamp-Begemann, 1973, p. 36. For the panoramic profile city view and the influence of Pieter Bast's engravings of about 1600, see in this catalogue Esaias van de Velde, cat no. 40.

67

de Velde, cat. nos. 27, 28, 58, and Van Scheyndel, cat. no. 65).

A Road Bordered by Trees is one of a number of prints by Segers in which one is unusually conscious of the separate existence of each individual mark or stroke; the stroke is broad and emphatic like that of a thick pen or a brush. Etchings in this style are usually printed on white paper rather than on colored grounds, and they are often, as here, printed in black.[2] There is a surprising lack of transitional tones between these emphatic marks, resulting in a strong sense of two-dimensional pattern that is very appealing to the sensibility of our own time but unusual in the context of seventeenth-century Dutch conception of space in landscape. These loosely associated clusters of

2. Although Segers is usually identified with printing in color, about one-third of the surviving impressions are printed in black; Haverkamp-Begemann, 1973, p. 48.

stipples, patches, and short strokes can be seen as an exaggeration of the more delicate atmospheric stipples and short broken strokes that characterize the series of small etched landscapes by Willem Buytewech of about 1616 (cat. nos. 37, 38).

A number of the prints in this style appear to employ a technique new to the history of printmaking, a technique that only Segers seems to have used in the seventeenth century, that of "lift-ground" etching.[3] In this process the artist uses ink mixed with a water-soluble substance such as sugar and draws with a pen or brush on a copper plate the lines to be etched. The plate is then covered with a ground and exposed to

3. For Segers's use of lift ground, see Haverkamp-Begemann, 1973, pp. 43–44. Although most scholars who make a close study of Segers's prints would concede that he used the lift-ground process, it may be a long while before there is a consensus on which prints he employed it in; see the review of Haverkamp-Begemann, 1973, in Ackley, 1974, p. 92 and n. 10.

warm water. The ink mixture dissolves, and the ground lifts away, exposing the copper that will be bitten with acid to create the lines that will hold the ink. This was a convenient way for Segers to etch lines or marks of greater breadth. Some passages of *A Road Bordered by Trees* may have been created in this fashion, such as, for example, the large dots or scallops. Other lines and marks were more likely produced by an unusually prolonged or powerful biting of the plate. The embossed white patch at the upper right may have resulted from a hole produced by acid biting through the plate.

The present impression in black on white paper stresses the vibrant patterns formed by the etched marks, but in two of the other five known impressions, both in the Rijksmuseum collection (HB 26b and 26c), Segers printed the plate in gray-green or pale gray on white paper, producing a more atmospheric, painterly feeling.

67

HERCULES SEGERS
Ruins of the Abbey of Rijnsburg: Large Version

Etching printed in yellowish white on paper prepared with brownish black; penned borderline
Springer 54c, Haverkamp-Begemann 46c
201 x 317 mm. (sheet)
Coll.: S. Woodburn (see L. 2584)
Lent by the Trustees of the British Museum. 1854-6-28-73

Hercules Segers etched a number of ruin views, the largest of which is the large version of the *Abbey of Rijnsburg* exhibited here. He made two or three etchings of Roman ruins, borrowing the motifs from prints, but the majority of the ruin views are of medieval Dutch structures, which Segers could have recorded directly from nature. These views are rarely reportorial in nature and are more concerned with the evocation of mood;[1] the large version of the *Abbey of Rijnsburg* is the most hallucinatory of all.

The abbey had a distinguished history.[2] It was founded in the thirteenth century by a Count of Holland as a cloister for young noblewomen and served as a burial place for many Counts and Countesses of Holland.[3] In 1573-74 it was destroyed by the Spanish during the siege of Leyden. Segers etched two versions of the ruins, a larger and a smaller. They are identical not only in viewpoint but also in the figures included and their placement: man, dog, and sheep. The smaller version (HB 47) makes a more conventional use of line and of value relationships. It is always printed in a darker tone on a lighter ground. All six recorded impressions of the large *Abbey,* on the other hand, are printed in yellowish white on a darker ground, usually brownish black as here. This surprising reversal of values lends the

1. For Segers ruin subjects see Haverkamp-Begemann, 1973, pp. 37-39.
2. For a history of the Abbey of Rijnsburg and its ruins, see Haverkamp-Begemann, 1973, no. 46, p. 90.
3. See inscriptions to plates LXXVII and LXXVIII in Rademaker, 1725/1966.

scene an eerie, phosphorescent glow, a spectral, moonlit feeling.[4] Segers printed only a few times in white or pale colors on a dark ground. This expressive use of printing may also be seen in his two unique etchings of ships tossed about in storms at sea (HB 48, Amsterdam, printed in yellow on brown, and HB 49, Vienna, printed in yellowish green on black); the ships are almost swallowed up by the darkness.

In the large *Abbey of Rijnsburg* Segers chose to deemphasize conventional contour drawing, describing each individual unit of the landscape – each blade of grass, leaf, brick, patch of mortar – in terms of its own linear vocabulary so as to be able to convey more intensely its characteristic texture. The ruin and the landscape that surrounds and creeps over it are an accretion of individual strokes: comma-like ones for leaves, hairy ones for grasses, spidery ones for bricks and mortar.

The visitors, human and animal, are subordinated to the ruin and its vegetation; enmeshed in the riot of patterns, they shift in and out of focus.

4. In one impression in the Rijksmuseum (HB. 46a), printed in yellow on black, Segers colored the print by hand (blue sky, red bricks), producing a more naturalistic effect. Discoloration of the varnish applied to the print now creates a more bizarre impression than originally intended (the sky appears green rather than blue).

68

HERCULES SEGERS
The Large Tree

Etching printed in black ink on white paper; upper corners rubbed with black chalk at a later date
Springer 39a, Haverkamp-Begemann 34a
218 x 277 mm. (sheet)
Wm.: indecipherable fragment
Coll.: P.C. Baron van Leyden
Rijksmuseum, Amsterdam. OB 849

In certain of his prints, such as the large version of the *Abbey of Rijnsburg* (cat. no. 67) and *The Large Tree,* Segers revealed an ability to think not only in terms of dark marks on a light ground but also in terms of light on dark. In

the large *Abbey of Rijnsburg* he had inked the lines in a light pigment and printed on a dark prepared ground. In *The Large Tree* he combined both ways of visualizing – dark on light and light on dark – but made the relationships permanent by biting them into the plate.

Segers's *Large Tree* represents one of the most important stages in the development of the single tree or clump of trees as a dominant motif in the Dutch landscape print, a development that culminates in the landscape prints of the 1640s. Here the tree, probably a venerable oak, is the central axis of the design. Its dominance is increased by the arch of crosshatched sky that enframes it, the upper left and right corners of the plate having been masked out with an acid-resistant varnish or wax.[1]

The tree with its rounded cluster of "cauliflower" foliage grows according to the pattern established by Adam Elsheimer, as do the trees of Esaias van de Velde's *Square Landscape* (cat. no. 41) and Nicolaes Moeyaert's *Landscape with Mercury and Argus* (cat. no. 69). The landscape with its miscellaneous assortment of rather haunted-looking buildings and solid-looking sea dotted with sails is reminiscent of Segers's painting *The Valley,* in Rotterdam, in which a similar round building occurs.[2] There is the same emphasis on defining each separate leaf, blade of grass, or brick as in the large version of the *Abbey of Rijnsburg.*

The method of execution of the *Large Tree,* however, is quite different from that of the *Abbey of Rijnsburg.* Haverkamp-Begemann has provided a quite persuasive analysis of the painstaking buildup of this complex plate.[3]

1. These irregular, blank, masked-out areas are less obvious than they might have been because someone, apparently disturbed by their blankness, rubbed black chalk into them, probably at a later date. Segers masked out areas of sky in this rather puzzling fashion in a number of his landscapes. In some hand-colored examples these areas have been painted over and are no longer obtrusive.
2. Comparison cited by Haverkamp-Begemann, 1973, p. 85. Reproduced in Rowlands, 1979, pl. 41.
3. Haverkamp-Begemann, 1973, p. 85.

68

The plate was bitten in two stages, and the separation between the different tonal areas is as crisp and distinct as in a chiaroscuro woodcut printed with tone blocks. The darkest passages were created by means of the lift-ground process in one bite. In another biting of the plate the negative "white" areas were reserved, or stopped out, with a wax or varnish as in the batik process of textile decoration. After each blade of grass or comma-like leaf had been painted onto the plate, the plate was exposed to acid, resulting in a bitten gray tone surrounding a reserved blank area in which the white of the paper shows through. The manner of working, the value relationships, and the style are those of Segers's drawing *Farm Building near a Country Road,* in Amsterdam, in which accents of yellow and black were brushed onto a gray ground.[4] The reserved white areas of paper also suggest the light highlights that Segers applied by hand to some impressions of his etchings printed on a dark prepared ground.

The sky of *The Large Tree* is toned by a fine mesh of regular crosshatching, which consists of two layers: a layer of "positive" lines drawn into the etching ground with a very fine needle and a layer of fine "negative" crosshatching painted on with resist. Segers used a fine mesh of regular crosshatching as a tone or texture in a number of prints, including the sky of the large *Abbey of Rijnsburg.* Although this crosshatching suggests the texture of the fine woven cloth that Segers sometimes used for his prints, it is more likely inspired by the mesh of regular crisscrossing lines employed by Hendrik Goudt to achieve dark tones in engravings after Elsheimer such as the *Flight into Egypt* (cat. no. 44). It is conceivable that Segers's procedure of painting on small areas of resist to create crisp accents of white paper within an area of tone was also encouraged or inspired by Goudt's *Flight into Egypt,* where the sharply defined areas of white paper in the midst of deeply engraved and etched lines represent points of light shining in the darkness.

4. Ibid.

Claes Cornelisz. Moeyaert
about 1590/91 – 1655

The Amsterdam painter of biblical and mythological subjects, Claes Cornelisz. Moeyaert, executed some twenty-five etchings.[1] A number of book illustrations are also attributed to him. Tümpel believes that Moeyaert may have begun his career primarily as an etcher and places many of his etchings prior to the first dated paintings of 1624.[2]

Moeyaert was probably born about 1590–91, but it is not known where; in 1605 he was in Amsterdam. His teachers are not known. A trip to Italy is presumed on the basis of the Italian journeys made by the other Amsterdam painters of literary subjects with whom he was associated, Pieter Lastman and the Pynas brothers, but cannot be documented. He married in 1617. In the following year a eulogistic poem was written about his work. Moeyaert was of Catholic background and received many Catholic commissions, both portraits and altarpieces. In the period 1639 – 1641 he was involved in the Amsterdam Theater, both as a member of the board of directors and as scenic designer. He seems to have been relatively well-to-do and moved in literary circles. Among his pupils were Salomon Koninck, Nicolaes Berchem, and Jan Baptist Weenix. He died in Amsterdam in 1655.[3]

1. Holl. 28 is not by Moeyaert but probably by the German seventeenth-century etcher Johann Wilhelm Baur. The four London landscapes Holl., Moeyaert, 29–32 relate as much to Moses van Uyttenbroeck as to Moeyaert.

2. Sacramento, 1974, p. 36.

3. Biographies in Tümpel, pp. 8–34, and Sacramento, 1974. p. 79.

69
CLAES CORNELISZ. MOEYAERT
Landscape with Mercury and Argus,
about 1620

Etching
V.d.K. 24, Wurz. 24, Holl. 25[1]
Lower right: *Claes Moeyaert fe*
110 x 190 mm. (platemark)
Wm.: foolscap
Museum of Fine Arts, Boston, Katherine E. Bullard Fund in memory of Francis Bullard. 1972.24

The story of Mercury and Argus, related in the first book of Ovid's *Metamorphoses,* is an episode from one of Jupiter's extramarital entanglements that roused the anger of his consort, Juno. Jupiter fell in love with the nymph Io and embraced her in the guise of a dark cloud. He was discovered by Juno, however, and he changed Io into a white heifer to protect her. Juno, pretending ignorance, begged the heifer as a gift and confided her to the care of the hundred-eyed herdsman, Argus. Mercury, the trickster, commissioned by Jupiter to rescue Io, first lulled Argus's hundred eyes to sleep with his storytelling and piping and then cut off Argus's head. Juno used Argus's hundred eyes to bejewel the tails of her peacocks. Here the subject is virtually subordinated to the pastoral landscape with its rounded masses of Elsheimer-like foliage and ancient ruins. Mercury piping to the drowsy many-eyed Argus at the far right is echoed by the herdsman with his bagpipe who leans against the tree at the far left.

Moeyaert, like many seventeenth-century Dutch artists who favored pastoral subjects with herdsmen and cattle, often chose mythological as well as Old Testament subjects that lent themselves to such a treatment, whether Old Testament patriarchs with their nomadic herds, the Annunciation to the Shepherds, episodes from Ovid such as the present one, or the nearly identical motif of Mercury and Battus, which Moeyaert treated in an etching (Holl. 26) very similar in style and format.

69

The *Mercury and Argus* certainly belongs to the group of prints, drawings and paintings that Tümpel dates earlier than the first dated works of 1624, such as the *Allegory of Spring* painting in Nuremberg.[1] The etching relates to the latter in motif, but in organization it is more casual, less stable, and resembles the earlier undated painting of the *Prodigal as Shepherd* in the Bredius Museum in the Hague.[2] A drawing in Berlin that appears to be a compositional study for the *Spring* painting of 1624 is closely related in style to the present etching.[3] It bears the surprising date of 1615, but the signature and date are apparently so disturbed or traced over that the date is not to be trusted. A provisional date for the *Mercury and Argus* etching would be about 1620.

The etched line of the *Mercury and Argus* is closely related to the pen lines of Moeyaert's drawings; compare, for example, the vocabulary of pen strokes in the Hamburg study for an etching[4] in Moeyaert's early Tobit series (Holl. 17-20). Moeyaert's etched line is here precise, sharp, and wiry. The more heavily bitten passages have the definition and tapering profile of engraved strokes. Moeyaert must have used a fairly hard etching ground to achieve such definition in the line. There is little reference, however, to the regularized systems of hatching and crosshatching of contemporary engraving. A new draftsmanlike, scribbling energy is being introduced into the linear vocabulary of etching.

4. Reproduced in Stubbe, 1967, pl. 66.

1. Reproduced in Tümpel, p. 77.
2. Reproduced in Tümpel, p. 72.
3. Reproduced in Tümpel, p. 11.

Jan Lievens
1607 – 1674

Rembrandt's friend and close artistic associate during his Leyden years, the painter Jan Lievens, is one of the most significant and productive painter-printmakers of the Dutch seventeenth century. No artist's reputation has suffered more than Lievens's, however, from proximity to and comparison with Rembrandt. There are undoubtedly still many who think of Lievens as Rembrandt's pupil in spite of all the evidence to the contrary. The fact that much of his work after 1631 was inspired by Flemish art, by Van Dyck, and Adriaen Brouwer, has not helped his reputation among historians who choose to emphasize the aspects of seventeenth-century Dutch art that are a unique expression of the culture of the independent Northern provinces.

Lievens's work as a printmaker still needs to be studied more closely to ascertain which of the works attributed to him are truly from his hand.[1] The task is complicated by the many versions that exist of Lievens's character heads, or "types," and by our still insufficient knowledge of the other etchers around Rembrandt. Lievens probably made some sixty to sixty-five etchings,[2] and he designed eight to ten woodcuts, the latter being among his most original accomplishments in a period when the woodcut as a medium of expression for painters was in relative eclipse.

Jan Lievens (or Lievensz.) was born in Leyden in 1607, the son of an embroiderer, Lieven Hendricx, who had emigrated from Ghent in Flanders. He was a year younger than his Leyden contemporary Rembrandt. Lievens's training differed from his friend Rembrandt's, however; he was apprenticed by his father in 1615 at the tender age of eight to a

1. Schneider's catalogue of the prints, which includes traditional attributions that he rejects, is a useful point of departure. See Schneider/Ekkart, 1932/1973, pp. 261–273, 397–398.
2. Hollstein's catalogue, which apparently attempts to assemble all previous attributions, lists 98.

local Leyden painter, Joris van Schooten, whereas Rembrandt attended Latin School and, for a brief time, Leyden University before beginning his artistic training. About 1619–1621 Lievens studied for two years in Amsterdam with Pieter Lastman, with whom Rembrandt also studied a few years later. After leaving Lastman, he returned to Leyden and continued to work independently until the period of his close association with Rembrandt, 1625–1631.

Constantijn Huygens, secretary to the stadholder Frederik Hendrik in the Hague and a great dilettante of the arts, describes in his unfinished autobiography (about 1629–1631) his impressions of the work of Lievens and Rembrandt, who were probably sharing studio space at the time. Huygens, whose portrait was painted by Lievens in 1629, is fervent in his praise of the hard work and dedication of the two young artists but distressed that they will not take the time to make the Italian journey he considers so essential for the final perfecting of their art. Although Huygens's praise of Rembrandt is more profound, focusing on that artist's gift for the expression of emotion in a literary subject, he writes at greater length about Lievens. The picture that emerges is of a young artist who is immensely productive and ambitious, concerned with breadth and grandeur of effect in his inventions but who is a little too self-confident, not receptive to criticism. The account of Lievens's persistence in his pursuit of the execution of Huygens's portrait makes the artist's ambition amusingly clear.[3]

Lievens's close association with Rembrandt ended in 1631, when the latter moved to Amsterdam. From 1632 to 1635 Lievens was apparently in England, executing portrait commissions for the court of Charles I. There he had his first contact with the great master of the aristocratic portrait, Anthonis van Dyck,

whose art was to have such a transforming effect on Lievens's manner of painting portraits and literary subjects or "histories." In 1635 he was enrolled as a member of the Guild of St. Luke in Antwerp, where he resided until he moved to Amsterdam in 1644.

In Antwerp his artistic associates besides Van Dyck were Adriaen Brouwer, the painter of low-life subjects, whose landscape style profoundly affected Lievens's way of painting landscapes; the still-life painter Jan Davidsz. de Heem, whom he had known in Leyden; the engravers who worked after Rubens, Lucas Vorsterman and Paulus Pontius; and the printmaker who was to publish or republish so many of Lievens's prints, Frans van den Wyngaerde. In 1638 Lievens married the well-to-do daughter of the sculptor Andries Colyns de Nole. Their first son died young, but their second son, Jan Andrea, baptized in 1644, became an artist and a collaborator of his father. In 1639 Lievens was in Leyden to discuss a commission for a mantelpiece picture for the town hall. The end of his residence in Antwerp was marked by financial difficulty and seizure of his property. In early 1644 Lievens was in Amsterdam, which remained his principal place of residence although he spent periods of time in the Hague and Leyden. Immediately after his return to Amsterdam, he shared rooms or studio space with the painter of low-life subjects Jan Miensz. Molenaer. We do not know the date of his first wife's death, but in 1648 he married Cornelia de Bray. During the following years he received a number of official commissions for ambitious paintings on literary or allegorical themes, including paintings for the new town hall of Amsterdam.

Lievens also executed commissions for the Great Elector of Brandenburg in Berlin, where he is mentioned in 1655. During the Amsterdam years he painted, drew, and etched the portraits of many figures distinguished in literary and intellectual circles such as the great Dutch poet and playwright Vondel. His final years were troubled, marked by financial difficulties, the misconduct of his son Jan Andrea, and the death of his second wife in 1668.

Lievens died in Amsterdam in 1674.[4]

In recent decades Lievens's work as a painter has been undergoing reevaluation, and a concerted effort has been made by scholars to separate his early work from that of Rembrandt. His landscape paintings, his chalk portrait drawings in the Van Dyck manner, and his pen landscapes, often drawn on the Japanese papers Rembrandt used for prints, are today among the most accessible and readily appreciated of his works.

4. For Lievens's biography see Schneider/Ekkart, 1932/1973, pp. 1–10, and the chronology in Braunschweig, 1979, pp. 36–38.

70

JAN LIEVENS
Mercury and Argus, about 1625–26

Etching
B. 10, Dut. 10[1], Rov. 10[1], Holl. 18[1]
195 x 165 mm. (platemark)
Coll.: Robert-Dumesnil (L. 2200), Dutuit
(L. 708)
Musée du Petit Palais, Paris. Dut. 5717

Lievens's etching of Mercury and Argus illustrates the same episode from Ovid's *Metamorphoses* as Moeyaert's etching (cat. no. 69), but here the human figure and the narrative take precedence over the landscape and the pastoral life of herders and their animals. The same moment has been chosen in both etchings: Argus nods off to sleep as Mercury pipes, but here Argus is shown with the normal complement of eyes rather than as many-eyed. Io, in the guise of the white heifer, is an active participant; wearing a fillet on her brow, she watchfully follows the course of events.

The *Mercury and Argus* is identical in style and execution to two other early etchings by Lievens generally dated about 1625–26, *John the Evangelist* (Rov. 4) and *Jacob Anointing the Stone on which He Slept* (Rov. 9).[1] These early Lievens prints parallel in their scribbling freedom of execution Rembrandt's forceful and expressive, but cruder and less polished, etch-

3. See Slive, 1953, pp. 9–18; Haak, 1969, pp. 42–43. For a complete translation of the Latin text of Huygens's autobiography, see the Dutch translation of Worp, 1891, and the German translation in Braunschweig, 1979, pp. 33–34.

1. Braunschweig, 1979, nos. 99, 100.

ings of about 1626, *The Circumcision* (White/Boon S 398) and the *Rest on the Flight* (B. 59). Lievens's *St. John* etching and Rembrandt's *Circumcision* were published or republished by the same Haarlem publisher, Jan Pietersz. Berendrecht, who published a number of Esaias van de Velde's prints in the foregoing decade.[2]

Lievens's figures have the slightly inflated look that characterizes many of his figures of the Leyden period. The rather complicated play of light on the figures, with light reflected into the shadows, and the use of stipple to model and texture flesh are reminiscent of Frisius's *Christ Presented to the People* (cat. no. 46). This use of stipple also recalls the etchings of Willem Buytewech, which Lievens is said to have copied as a young art student.[3] The nude figures of Pieter Lastman, Lievens's teacher, often have a similarly strong illumination and glassy, polished look.

The bold, scribbling freedom of Lievens's etched line and his total lack of interest in creating decorative patterns with lines or dots set this etching apart from the etched work of Frisius and Buytewech and other earlier print-makers. Only Jan Pynas's etching of *Jacob's Dream* (cat. no. 20) shows a comparable freedom and spontaneity of drawing. It is therefore a little surprising to find that the pen drawing in the reverse direction in Dresden, which is preparatory to the etching, is so close to the final etching in linear character and structure.[4] This suggests that Lievens's spontaneity was very carefully "mapped out" in advance.

The impression exhibited here is an unusually early impression, with a bit of random plate tone and inky plate edges, printed before the addition of Lievens's monogram and the address of the Antwerp publisher, Frans van den Wyngaerde.

70

2. See the chapter "Rembrandt und Lievens," pp. 88–95, in Burchard, 1917.

3. In the biography of Lievens in Jan Orlers's 1641 description of Leyden; German translation in Braunschweig, 1979, p. 35. See also Haverkamp-Begemann, 1959, pp. 46–47.

4. Schneider/Ekkart, 1932/1973, Z.26 and pl. 38.

Rembrandt van Rijn
1606 – 1669

The painter of portraits and biblical subjects Rembrandt Harmensz. van Rijn made about three hundred etchings and drypoints. His activity as a printmaker ranges from about 1626 to about 1665, with dated works from 1628 to 1661. No other Dutch painter of the time produced so large a body of work in printmaking or one so varied in scale, subject matter, and style. Only Hercules Segers was more experimental in the use of materials. Rembrandt's use of a variety of printing surfaces – oriental papers in different weights and hues, *cardoes* (cartridge or oatmeal paper), and vellum – is not to be found in the same degree in the work of any other European printmaker of the time. No other contemporary Dutch printmaker, not even Segers, made such radical revisions in the image on the copper plate as Rembrandt. His use of painterly inking in his later prints was to have a great influence on the course of nineteenth-century printmaking. Rembrandt, in fact, became for the nineteenth century the very definition of etching. Whereas many Dutch painters confined their printmaking to one phase of their career or only dabbled in it and then abandoned it, Rembrandt's production spanned nearly his entire career as an artist. (His first dated painting was executed in 1625, and his last was left unfinished on his easel at his death in 1669.) Rembrandt's prints only rarely reproduce his own work in painting and often treat themes or motifs not to be found in his paintings; the development of his work in prints parallels but does not duplicate that of his work in painting and drawing.

Rembrandt was born in Leyden in 1606, the second youngest in a large family. His father, Harmen Gerritsz., was a miller. Rembrandt attended the Latin School for seven years and then in 1620, at age fourteen, was briefly enrolled at Leyden University. His first instructor in art seems to have been the Leyden painter of hell scenes, Jacob van Swanenburgh, with whom he studied for three years, from about 1621 to 1623. In 1624 he studied for six months in Amsterdam with Pieter Lastman; it was during this period that he was introduced to the modern manner of painting "histories" – compositions with biblical, mythological, and literary themes. The Leyden teacher of Jan Lievens, Joris van Schooten, has also been mentioned as a possible teacher of Rembrandt. It has further been suggested that he studied briefly in Amsterdam with Jacob Pynas, either before or after study with Lastman.

About 1625 Rembrandt began to work as an independent artist but in close association with his friend Jan Lievens, with whom he probably shared a studio. About 1629 the two young artists were visited by Constantijn Huygens, the learned secretary to the stadholder in the Hague and a sensitive connoisseur of art who had wished to become an artist himself. Huygens berated both artists for not making the Italian journey necessary in his eyes to the education of any artist of substance, but they replied that they were too busy to travel and could see sufficient Italian works of quality outside of Italy. Huygens perceptively singled out for special praise Rembrandt's mastery of the expression of emotion in "histories," citing his *Judas Returning the Pieces of Silver*.[1]

Rembrandt's first pupil was Gerrit Dou, who studied with him for about three years, beginning in 1628. Later, in Amsterdam, Rembrandt had a large number of apprentices in his studio; he was thereby assured of a considerable income, both from the apprentices' fees and from the sale of their work.

By July 1632 he had moved to Amsterdam, where he resided for the rest of his life. In Amsterdam he first lived in the house of an acquaintance, the art dealer Hendrik van Uylenburgh (or Ulenborch), where he had a studio. There he met Van Uylenburgh's niece Saskia, the orphaned daughter of a prominent and prosperous Frisian family, whom he married in 1634. Beginning in 1632 Rembrandt enjoyed great success as a fashionable

portraitist in Amsterdam, 1632 and 1633 being the peak years of his production of commissioned portraits. He continued to produce portraits throughout his career but never again enjoyed the same degree of modish and lucrative success as he had in the 1630s. During this decade he also painted a series of paintings of the Passion of Christ for the stadholder Frederik Hendrik. He added two more paintings to this prestigious series in 1646. His monumental group portrait of a militia company, the "Night Watch," was completed in 1642.

A son, Rumbartus, was born to Rembrandt and Saskia in 1635, and two daughters, both named Cornelia, in 1638 and 1640, but these children died soon after birth. In 1641 their son Titus was born, their only child to survive to maturity. In the 1630s Rembrandt made many purchases for his collection of rarities of art, nature, and ethnography. In 1638 Saskia's family complained that the young couple were squandering Saskia's inheritance. In 1639 Rembrandt bought a fine house in the Breestraat, two doors away from Saskia's uncle. This purchase, which Rembrandt could not really afford, marked the beginning of his financial troubles. In 1642 Saskia died, possibly after years of illness. In her will she left half of her estate to Rembrandt and half to Titus, allowing Rembrandt the use of the income until Titus's maturity. If Rembrandt remarried, however, Titus's share would revert to her relatives.

Rembrandt hired as Titus's nurse Geertje Dircx, who became Rembrandt's mistress. In 1648 she made a will in Titus's favor, but she was soon replaced in Rembrandt's affections by Hendrickje Stoffels, the housekeeper and companion of his later years. In 1649 Geertje Dircx sued Rembrandt for breach of promise, but the artist failed to appear in court. In 1650 he had Geertje Dircx confined to an institution, apparently in order to escape his obligations to her. In 1654 Hendrickje was called before the church council and condemned for living in sin with Rembrandt. A daughter, Cornelia, was born to them, and Hendrickje conceded to the

---

1. Worp, 1891, pp. 123–131.

demands of the church authorities that the child be baptized.

Rembrandt's financial situation gradually worsened. In 1656 he signed his house over to Titus; all his possessions were inventoried, and the first sale took place. In 1657 the contents of the house were sold at auction. These disastrous events in Rembrandt's life have, ironically, benefited historians, who might otherwise have had no record of his extensive and varied collections of art, natural history specimens, and exotic curios. The house in the Breestraat was sold, but Rembrandt continued to live there for two years. In 1659 Titus was given power of attorney, and the following year he and Hendrickje formed a company to deal in Rembrandt's art since, according to guild regulations, a bankrupt artist was not allowed to sell his own art. In the same year the family moved to a less fashionable address on the Rozengracht. In 1662 the painting commissioned from Rembrandt for Amsterdam's grand new town hall, the *Oath of Claudius Civilis,* was installed but then returned to the artist. Again ironically, the town hall was chiefly decorated with the paintings of Rembrandt's pupils such as Ferdinand Bol and the friend of his youth, Jan Lievens. In 1663 Hendrickje died. One of a number of indications that Rembrandt was not totally neglected in his last years was the visit of Duke Cosimo de' Medici to his studio in 1667. In 1668 Titus married but died a few months later. A daughter, Titia, was born after his death. In 1669 Rembrandt died and was buried in Amsterdam's Westerkerk. The unfinished painting on the easel in his studio represented the aged Simeon holding the Christ Child (Bredius 600).[2]

2. See biographies and chronologies in MacLaren, 1960, pp. 302–304; White, 1966; Filedt Kok, 1972, p. 16; Schwartz, 1977, pp. 8–12. For the documents see Hofstede de Groot, 1906; Strauss/Van der Meulen, 1979.

71
REMBRANDT VAN RIJN
Beggar Warming His Hands, about 1630

Etching
G. 167, B. 173, Hind 8, Münz 112, BB. 30–1, W.-B. 173[II]
77 x 46 mm. (platemark)
Coll.: A.J. Godby (L. suppl. 1119b)
Museum of Fine Arts, Boston, Katharine E. Bullard Fund in memory of Francis Bullard. 1970.316

During Rembrandt's last Leyden years, from about 1628 to 1631, he made a number of drawings and etchings of beggars and street people.[1] Although the majority of the etchings are small, they vary a good deal in scale and format. There is no evidence that a series was intended. Most of the early beggar etchings have the immediacy and spontaneity of a rapid notation on a sketchbook page. The *Beggar Warming His Hands* over a pot of coals, datable about 1630,[2] reveals, as do most of these plates, the artist's delight in the irregular, tattered shapes of the beggar's garb. The illumination is harsh, the transition from lights to shadows abrupt.

It is generally acknowledged that Jacques Callot's etched series of beggars (Lieure 479–503), published in Nancy in the 1620s, stimulated Rembrandt's interest in beggars as subjects for etchings. The influence of Callot's etchings, with their emulation of the crisp, stylized calligraphy of engraving, is most evident in some of Rembrandt's early drawings of beggar subjects. In the *Beggar Warming His Hands* Rembrandt may well have taken the handwarming motif from Callot, but the fine, scratchy, etched lines and the unsystematic tangles that define patches of shading in no way resemble Callot's precise, rather thick contour lines and systematically disposed clusters of neat, tapering parallel lines that shade forms. Frequently, as here, Rembrandt included a sug-

1. For Rembrandt's beggars see Bauch, 1960, pp. 152–168; Filedt Kok, 1972, under B. 163, pp. 108–109.
2. Compare B. 164, *Beggar Man and Beggar Woman,* dated 1630.

71 (actual size)

gestion of background or handled shadows in such a way as to suggest a setting. Rembrandt's beggars do not resemble Callot's beggars, which, with their blank backgrounds and crisply defined contours, have the appearance of cut-out patterns or archtypes.

Rembrandt's visual fascination with beggars and street types is clear from his twenty or more early etchings, but we cannot know what degree of empathy or fellow feeling he had for them. That beggars were frequently regarded with suspicion and mistrust in the seventeenth century has been noted in the discussion of Droochsloot's 1610 etching of carousing beggars (cat. no. 60). Jan Joris van Vliet, an etcher active in Leyden about 1630–1635, who made a number of etchings that reproduce early works of Rembrandt and Lievens, published in 1632 a series of etchings of beggars and street people (rat-poison sellers, etc.) entitled "By t geeve/ Bestaet Ons Leeve" ("Giving is our Living", B. 73–82); though inspired by Rembrandt's etchings, they are more obviously caricatural in nature. The question of

Rembrandt's empathy or lack of it must remain unresolved, but there is the extraordinary instance of his 1630 etching (B. 174) in which a seated beggar, holding out his hand and crying out, has Rembrandt's own features. Is one to regard this as a good joke or as identification with the beggar's lot?

72

REMBRANDT VAN RIJN
The Pancake Woman, 1635

Etching and drypoint
G. 120, B. 124, Hind 141, Münz 257, BB. 35–I, W.-B. 124[II]
Lower center margin: *Rembrandt f. 1635*
108 x 78 mm. (platemark)
Coll.: W. Esdaile (L. 2617); H.F. Sewall (L. 1309)
Museum of Fine Arts, Boston, Harvey D. Parker Collection. P518

Like the *Beggar Warming His Hands* (cat. no. 71), the *Pancake Woman* has much of the freedom and immediacy of a pen sketch from life. This is particularly true in impressions of the rare first state, in which the composition exists only in outline, and the heavier passages of shading that give weight and solidity to the impassive figure of the old pancake baker have not yet been added to the plate.[1]

This vivid slice of street-corner life is closely related to a group of contemporary drawings of life on the doorstep, which record without sentimentality the maternal chores of women and the robust vitality of young children.[2] The mood of Rembrandt's street scene is rowdier and more rambunctious than that of Jan van de Velde's rather eerie firelit interior (cat. no. 61). Jan van de Velde's engraving is one likely source of inspiration for Rembrandt's etching, but the artist most closely identified with the development of the pancake woman as subject is the Flemish painter of low life and landscape

72 (actual size)

Adriaen Brouwer, who was in the north during the 1620s and studied with Frans Hals in Haarlem.[3] The 1656 inventory of Rembrandt's possessions lists several works by Brouwer, among them a small painting of a "koekebacker" (cake baker).[4]

The *Pancake Woman* is an early example of Rembrandt's expressive use of varying degrees of completion, or finish, in the same etching plate. The baker acquires bulk and solidity from the shading that darkens her figure as well as from the specific description of the fur

of her hat and vest. She is the weighty anchor of the hurly-burly that surrounds her. The description of the children and their mothers primarily in terms of wiry, overlapping outlines increases the suggestion of rowdy animation. The little vignette in the foreground, the grimacing child who twists away to protect his pancake from a greedy dog, is asquirm with life.

1. Reproduced in White, vol. 2, pl. 226.

2. The wealthy seventeenth-century Dutch marine painter Jan van de Capelle had in his extensive art collection a portfolio of 135 Rembrandt drawings of "the life of women with children"; see Bredius, 1892, p. 37.

3. For Brouwer's role in this tradition, see Trautscholdt, 1961.

4. Hofstede de Groot, 1906, p. 190; Strauss/Van der Meulen, 1979, pp. 348–349. Gersaint, in the first published catalogue of Rembrandt's prints, includes in his entry on this print a recipe for Dutch pancakes!

Jan Miensz. Molenaer
about 1609/10 – 1668

Jan (or Johannes) Miensz. Molenaer, the Haarlem painter of portraits and scenes from everyday life, especially low life, made only a few etchings, probably no more than two or three.[1]

Molenaer was born in Haarlem about 1609–10. His first dated paintings are from 1629. In 1636 he married the painter Judith Leyster at Heemstede, near Haarlem. Between 1637 and 1648 he is recorded as being in Amsterdam, and Jan Lievens seems to have lodged with him or shared studio space with him when he returned from Antwerp in 1644. In 1648 Molenaer bought a house in Heemstede and resided chiefly there and in Haarlem for the rest of his life. Another house was purchased in Amsterdam in 1655. These real estate transactions suggest a reasonable degree of prosperity. Molenaer was buried in Haarlem in 1668.[2]

1. Hollstein lists the prints that have been attributed to Molenaer. Holl. 1 and 6, which are signed are consistent in style with Molenaer's paintings and drawings. I have not been able to see Holl. 5, which is signed and dated 1641. It was recorded in Thieme-Becker as in the Copenhagen Print Room, but according to Erik Fischer, keeper of prints and drawings (in a letter, 1979), it is not in that collection. Holl. 2 and 7 are probably by Willem Basse, as Van der Kellen suggested. Holl. 3 is of good quality but by a contemporary of Molenaer.

2. Biography by MacLaren, 1960, pp. 256–257.

73
JAN MIENSZ. MOLENAER
Peasants Carousing before an Inn

Etching
Wurz. 3, Holl. 6
Lower center: *Jo. molenaer*
113 x 161 mm. (sheet)
Coll.: J. Sheepshanks (see L. 2333)
Lent by the Trustees of the British Museum. S. 2358

In Molenaer's *Peasants Carousing* the central cluster of figures – violin player, drinkers and those overcome by drink, a couple making love, and a bristly hog – are framed by a dark

73

foreground strip that depicts, appropriately, at left a large jug and an overturned jar and at right a celebrant relieving himself at the base of a tree. Their revels take place in the country, possibly just outside the walls of a city, for the inn in the background with its streaming pennant appears to be built into the towered defensive walls of the kind that surrounded so many Dutch cities. The Dutch were notorious at that time for the quantities of drink they consumed. Rather strong beer often replaced bad water as the common thirst quencher.[1]

The foreground and the central group are etched with firm, continuous contours, but the background trees and vista to the right are etched more atmospherically with loose open strokes or stipples. The plate is somewhat over-bitten in the darker passages, but this seems

1. See Van Deursen, 1978, pp. 38ff.

only to add to the coarse, earthy tenor of the scene.

The *Peasants Carousing* and Molenaer's *Cambyses* etching (Holl. 1) are undated. The latter, which is vigorous but rather comical, is very Lastman-like and is also generally comparable in style and conception to Gerrit Bleker's two biblical etchings of 1638 (Holl. 3 and 5). I would be inclined to place both of Molenaer's etchings in the late 1630s.

74

REMBRANDT VAN RIJN
The Good Samaritan, 1633

Etching and drypoint
G. 77, B. 90, Hind 101, Münz 196, BB. 33-A,
W.-B. 90[1]
Lower center margin in the fourth state:
Rembrandt. inventor et Feecit. 1633
243 x 202 mm. (sheet)
Wm.: Crown with castle in shield (similar to
Briquet 2291; Heawood 481)
Coll.: R.S. Holford (L. 2243)
Museum of Fine Arts, Boston, Stephen Bullard
Memorial Fund. 43.1341

The Parable of the Good Samaritan (Luke 10: 25–37), Christ's answer to the question, "Who is my neighbor?" tells of a traveler who was attacked by robbers, stripped, and beaten, and left by the wayside. A priest and a Levite, members of the victim's own faith, passed by but did not stop to offer assistance. However, a Samaritan, a man of another faith, stopped, bound up the victim's wounds, and carried him on his own mount to an inn; upon his departure the next morning, he gave the innkeeper money for the care and lodging of the wounded man.

The Good Samaritan etching, with its elaboration of detail and high degree of finish, is totally different in conception from the more spontaneous, sketch-like plates of the early 1630s such as the *Beggar Warming His Hands* (cat. no. 71) and the *Pancake Woman* (cat. no. 72). These differences are directly related to the print's function, for it is one of two large-scale etchings of 1633 in which Rembrandt reproduced his own paintings, the other being the large etching of the *Descent from the Cross* (B. 81), which reproduces Rembrandt's painting in Munich (Bredius 550), made for the stadholder Frederik Hendrik. Generally, Rembrandt's etched work paralleled but was not directly dependent on his work in painting. In these instances, however, Rembrandt apparently set out to emulate and to rival the engravings and etchings that his older contemporaries, such as Bloemaert in Utrecht or Rubens in Antwerp,

had professional printmakers make from their drawings or paintings.[1]

The *Good Samaritan* etching reproduces in reverse, with a number of variations, Rembrandt's oil painting of similar dimensions in the Wallace Collection, London (Bredius 545). Until its recent cleaning, many Rembrandt scholars rejected the painting, considering it a copy of a lost original or even a copy of the etching. Cleaning has reaffirmed the attribution and brought to light a characteristic early monogram and the date 1630.[2] Both painting and print were inspired by Jan van de Velde's engraving from the 1620s illustrating the episode of the arrival at the inn from the parable (Fr.-v.d.K. 56).[3] Van de Velde's print is a torchlit, candlelit night scene in the Goudt-Elsheimer manner and, like Rembrandt's painting and print, stresses the mundane setting in which the parable unfolds. Both Van de Velde's and Rembrandt's compositions differ from the biblical narrative in having the Samaritan pay the landlord upon arrival at the inn.

It is hardly surprising that Rembrandt, who was not a professional printmaker reproducing the work of others, should have made a number of creative changes when he translated a painting from the end of his Leyden years into the black and white of the etching medium two or three years later in Amsterdam.

Although the painting is fairly monochromatic, a few touches of brighter color – the white horse's green velvet saddle and patches of blood on the wounded man's head – assist in focusing attention on the central motif of the narrative. In the etching Rembrandt

1. In two other related instances in the 1630s, Rembrandt made monochromatic oil studies on paper as preparatory studies for etchings: the *Christ Presented to the People* in the National Gallery, London, of 1634 (Bredius 546), for his largest etching B. 77 of 1635–36, and *Joseph Relating his Dreams*, undated, in the Rijksmuseum, Amsterdam (Bredius 504), for the small etching B. 37 of 1638.

2. See Clark, 1976, for a discussion of the newly cleaned painting and the critical history of both painting and etching.

3. For a discussion of Rembrandt's choice of this episode from the parable, see Bruyn, 1959, p. 15.

strengthened the semicircle of shadow in the foreground and curved the steps, further defining the circle of light of which the wounded victim is the center. In later states he darkened the wall to the right of the victim so as to increase the focus on the central event. The etching provides far more specific detail of the inn-yard setting and lays more stress on the commonplace reality of the event, perhaps seeking to emphasize the everyday applicability of the parable.

In the etching Rembrandt made several additions to the foreground, which was rather blank in the painting. The addition of a hay trough, bucket, and barrel have never aroused controversy, but the squatting dog Rembrandt so lovingly depicted has been a point of contention for generations, some critics even going so far as to suggest that the dog was added by another hand. In the later seventeenth century classicizing critics began to object to Rembrandt's earthiness and lack of restraint or decorum when portraying subjects with morally elevated literary themes. Even Rembrandt's own pupil, Samuel van Hoogstraten, in his *Introduction to the Noble School of Painting* of 1678, criticized Rembrandt for having included two copulating dogs in his *Preaching of John the Baptist,* the monochromatic painting now in Berlin.[4]

From Bruegel on, animals and humans relieving themselves were commonplace, if usually subordinate, details in Netherlandish works of art, and the Dutch tend not to be especially squeamish about such matters even today,[5] but Rembrandt seems to have gone out of his way here to confront the viewer with this fact of life in a surprising context.

In this fine impression of the first state of the *Good Samaritan,* one fully experiences the wide range of tonalities Rembrandt has worked into the plate, from the dense shadows of the fore-

4. Cited in Emmens, 1964, p. 72.

5. The graphic symbol for "curb your dog" in Holland today is sometimes a quite explicit silhouette of a squatting dog. Rembrandt's two small 1631 etchings of a man and a woman relieving themselves (B. 190 and 191) are also relevant in this context.

ground, in which engraving reinforces heavily bitten line, to the delicate tracery of fine etched lines that suggests the atmosphere through which one sees the foliage and distant landscape.[6] Rembrandt achieves here a description of subtle nuances of light and a suggestion of color and texture (see the coats of the animals) that far surpass the coloristic achievements of the Rubens school of engravers.

6. This invented landscape with its fanciful structures anticipates Rembrandt's painted landscapes such as the *Landscape with the Obelisk* (Bredius 443) of 1638? in the Gardner Museum, Boston.

Pieter van Laer
1599 – after 1642

The Haarlem painter Pieter Bodding van Laer's some twenty etchings are as critical for the development of realism in seventeenth-century Dutch etching, particularly etchings of animal subjects, as are his scarce paintings for the development of the Italian view by Dutch artists, whether Roman street scenes or views of the southern countryside with herders. His painted Italian views, even when small in scale, are conceived with extraordinary breadth and boldness in the treatment of light and shadow, a debt he owes at least in part to the Italian painter Caravaggio and his Roman followers.

Pieter van Laer was born in Haarlem in 1599, but we have no record of his teachers or training. His earliest works show a similarity to Esaias van de Velde's cavalry subjects of the 1620s. He was in Rome from about 1625 to 1639, when he returned to Haarlem via Amsterdam. In 1642 he set out on his travels again, and from then on there is no further record of him.[1]

Van Laer was nicknamed "Bamboccio" (clumsy doll) when he was initiated into the Netherlandish artists' club in Rome, the "Bentveughels" ("Birds of a Feather") because of his ill-proportioned, hunchbacked body. Consequently, his followers, Italian as well as Dutch painters of Roman street life and of the life of the Campagna, were known as the "Bambocciante." According to his friend Sandrart, Van Laer was quite good-humored about his physical handicap.[2]

1. See biography by Blankert in Utrecht, 1965, pp. 92–94.
2. Life of Pieter van Laer in Sandrart/Peltzer, 1925, pp. 183–184.

75
PIETER VAN LAER
The Two Buffaloes and the Herdsman, 1636

From a series of eight etchings
Etching and drypoint
B. 7, Dut. 7, Wurz. 7, Holl. 7
125 x 177 mm. (platemark)
Teylers Museum, Haarlem

76
PIETER VAN LAER
The Hunter and the Dogs, 1636

From a series of eight etchings
Etching and drypoint
B. 6, Dut. 6, Wurz. 6, Holl. 6[1]
127 x 178 mm. (platemark)
Teylers Museum, Haarlem

Pieter van Laer's 1636 series of eight etchings (including title page) of various domestic animals with their herders and keepers was the groundbreaking series that became the inspiration for all the later series of animal etchings by Paulus Potter, Karel Dujardin, Nicolaes Berchem, and other Dutch painters of animals and herders. The painter Jan van Ossenbeeck based his entire style as an etcher on that of Pieter van Laer. The series is also the first translation by a seventeenth-century Dutch artist of the character and intensity of southern light into the black and white of the etching medium.

Van Laer's series is contemporary with the early etchings of Italian views by the French painter from Lorraine working in Rome, Claude Gellée, called Lorrain. Claude's earliest dated etchings are from 1634. Some of them have the harsh contrasts and scribbling directness of Van Laer's prints, while others are more delicate, more formalized, and patterned in the line work and more idealized or idyllic in conception.

75

76

The title page, as in later animal series by Dujardin and Berchem is, appropriately enough, a watering trough. Two herders, man and woman, supervise, while one of each kind of animal represented in the series drinks or peers out at us. Published in Rome, apparently by the artist, the series is dedicated to Don Ferdinando Afán de Ribera, Duke of Alcalá. Don Ferdinando, a collector, amateur artist, and patron of the Spanish painter Ribera (who painted religious and mythological subjects with the kind of radical realism that Pieter van Laer brought to southern scenes of everyday life) had been Spanish ambassador to Rome and viceroy of the Kingdom of Naples and was apparently serving at this time as viceroy of Sicily.[1] Joachim Sandrart, who was a close acquaintance of Pieter van Laer, wrote of the instant success of the series, or "little book," the high prices it sold for, and how it quickly found its way from Rome back to Amsterdam.[2]

All the plates of the series are characterized by sharp contrasts of light and shadow that convey the intensity of the southern sun. Contours are firmly defined by etched lines but pale into insignificance beside the shaggy bundles of shading strokes that not only map out broad patterns of light and shadow but also suggest the coarse textures of hair, hide, and soil. The landscape setting is often arid, the trees leafless, the soil barren.

The *Two Buffaloes* (cat. no. 75) is one of the boldest etchings of the series. The artist has heightened our sense of the ungainly bulk of the beasts by silhouetting them against the sky, water, and pale tones of the distant coastal landscape. Strong, irregular stipple patterns and short, curving, bristly strokes emphasize the coarseness of animals' coats. Their young driver, his strongly lit face contorted as he yells at the lumbering buffaloes, is dressed in cloth-

1. Du Gué Trapier, 1952, p. 50.

2. Sandrart/Peltzer, 1925, p. 184: "und auch in einem Büchlein dergleichen Stuck in Kupfer geätzt, ausgehen lassen, welche alle stark gesucht und ungeachtet des hohen Wehrts zur Zierde der Cabinetten verlangt, ja so gar die zu Rom gemachte theur erkauft und nach Amsterdam gebracht worden."

ing as shaggy as the beasts' hides. The fashion in which his figure is cut off by the border and by the crest of the hill and crowded by the hindquarters of the buffaloes represents a fresh, new vision that is intentionally graceless and clumsy but highly expressive. Much of the sky, the far shore, and the water are executed in drypoint scratches without burr, and the artist takes full advantage of drypoint's potential for jagged angularity or spikiness. The foreground soil is toned by fine drypoint scratches with some burr. These passages register effectively only in scarce, fine, early impressions such as the one exhibited here.

If we compare Van Laer's etching of the *Hunter and the Dogs* (cat. no. 76) with the etching of a similar subject attributed to Esaias van de Velde executed some twenty years earlier (cat. no. 58), we see how much more important a sense of the active play of light and shadow has become to the presentation of a vignette from daily life. Here too, as in the impression of the *Buffaloes,* fine nuances – such as the drypoint that colors the muzzle of the dog the hunter is examining – register as they do only in fine early impressions. This plate undoubtedly served as a source of inspiration for, among others, the series of dogs etched by the Flemish painter Jan Fyt (1642) and by the Dutch painter Jan Le Ducq (1661).

As in the case of many etchings by seventeenth-century Dutch painters, impressions of the series are not scarce, for the plates were printed into the nineteenth century;[3] but early impressions such as those exhibited here, untrimmed and enriched by a faint random tone of extra ink left on the plate before printing, are surprisingly uncommon.

3. According to Hollstein, the plates are still in existence, but he does not indicate where.

77 (actual size)

77
PIETER VAN LAER
Landscape with Two Trees, about 1636

Etching
B. 18, Dut. 18, Wurz. 18, Holl. 18[1]
35 x 48 mm. (platemark)
Wm.: unidentified fragment
Museum of Fine Arts, Boston, George Peabody Gardner Fund. 1972.86

A number of artists active in Italy in the first half of the seventeenth century produced small-scale, even miniaturistic, etchings, sketches as well as finished figure and landscape compositions: Jacques Callot, Claude Lorrain, Bartholomeus Breenbergh, Stefano della Bella, Karel Dujardin, and Pieter van Laer, who made four small-scale etchings (Dut. 17-20).

The unsigned *Landscape with Two Trees* may seem difficult to accept as the work of Pieter van Laer only on the basis of the traditional attribution, but a comparison with the landscape backgrounds of his animal series (Dut. 1-8; see cat. nos. 75, 76) confirms the attribution. The little landscape is very likely close in date to the animal series of 1636 and might well have been a trial (or experimental) plate related to the landscape settings of the series.

Sketchy as it is, the small plate succeeds in evoking a mood and atmosphere, perhaps of twilight, that calls to mind Sandrart's reference to Van Laer's interest in representing the times of day.[1]

1. Sandrart/Peltzer, 1925, p. 183.

Gerrit Claesz. Bleker
active 1625 – 1656

The Haarlem artist Gerrit Claesz. Bleker, whose paintings and drawings are still insufficiently known and studied, made some fourteen etchings of biblical and rural subjects. Except for the early *Raising of Lazarus* (Dut. 4), virtually all of the etchings, whether biblical or pastoral in subject, feature prominently horses, cattle, or other livestock.

We do not know Bleker's date of birth or the nature of his artistic training. In the conception of his etched works, particularly his biblical subjects, he reveals a strong affinity with Amsterdam painters of biblical and mythological subjects such as Pieter Lastman and, above all, Claes Moeyaert. Bleker's earliest dated painting is from 1625. He is mentioned by Samuel Ampzing in his 1628 description of Haarlem as a painter of landscapes with figures. In 1640 one hears of him taking on apprentices, and in 1643 he was an officer of the Haarlem artists' Guild of St. Luke. He died in Haarlem in 1656.[1]

1. See the biography by E.W. Moes in Thieme-Becker, vol. 4, pp. 111-112.

78
GERRIT CLAESZ. BLEKER
The Herdsman, 1638

Etching
B. 6, Dut. 6, Holl. 6[1]
Upper right: *GBleker f. 1638*
143 x 211 mm. (platemark)
Coll.: J. Barnard (L. 1419), A.M. Champernowne (L. 153)
Museum of Fine Arts, Boston, Anonymous Gift. 68.741

Gerrit Bleker's *Herdsman,* with its emphasis on and accurate observation of the bony architecture of cows, might appear at first glance to be a scene of contemporary Dutch rural life,[1] but

1. Blankert, 1968, p. 132, mentions the etching as a significant forerunner, like the paintings and etchings Pieter van Laer was executing in Rome at this time, of the classic Dutch animal pieces of the 1640s.

78 (actual size)

closer examination reveals the herdsman, in his slashed cap with feather, with his pipe and shepherd's crook, to be a figure from the idyllic world of the literary pastoral. When we look beyond him, beyond the dark huddled mass of sheep, we see in the distance figures gathered around a well, the most prominent wearing a turban and, to the left, a woman with a fancy headdress. The scene around the well, though admittedly difficult to read, suggests the meeting of Jacob and Rachel at the well represented in various etchings by Bleker (Dut. 2, 3, 13), one of which dates from the same year as the *Herdsman*. According to the story in the Bible, Jacob, after his vision of the ladder (see Jan Pynas, cat. no. 20) continued his travels. He encountered at a well where the flocks were watered his cousin Rachel, who was to become his wife (Genesis 29:1-2).

This is not the only one of Bleker's etched scenes of rural life that has a literary or exotic flavor. In the etching of cattle drinking (Dut. 7), undated but identical in style with the *Herdsman* of 1638, a piping herdsman, riding a donkey, drives quite commonplace cows and goats, but in the distance one sees the silhouettes of camels crossing a bridge. Bleker's etchings of rural subjects of a few years later, dated 1643, no longer contain allusions to literary subjects or to historical or exotic settings (Dut. 9-12).

The crisscrossing linear meshes that define masses of tone in the *Herdsman* are a looser, more freely drawn adaptation of the regular, crisscrossing, open linear meshes in Hendrik Goudt's first engraving after Elsheimer, the small *Tobias* of 1608, or in the prints of Jan van de Velde influenced by Goudt's tonal linear systems. Bleker immerses cattle and shepherd in a dusky, twilight chiaroscuro. The few unworked areas of blank paper function as intense patches of light, which throw the foreground figures into strong relief.

79
CLAES CORNELISZ. MOEYAERT
The Herd, 1638

Etching
V.d.K. 23 [II], Wurz. 23 [II], Holl. 24 [II]
Lower right: *Cl M fec/ 1638/ 2*
117 x 195 mm. (platemark)
Wm.: foolscap
Museum of Fine Arts, Boston, William A. Sargent Fund. 50.285

In Claes Moeyaert's *The Herd* of 1638, as in Gerrit Bleker's *Herdsman* of 1638 (cat. no. 78), cattle are featured as the principal motif, and the mood is idyllic; there is no hint of a reference, here, however, to a particular literary narrative. The crumbling ruins on the hilltop and the silhouette of a distant shepherd suggest an Arcadia similar to that of the landscape woodcut attributed to Esaias van de Velde (cat. nos. 27, 28).

The Herd forms a pair with another Moeyaert etching of 1638 similar in format and conception, *The Shepherd* (V.d.K. 22). Both relate closely to a painting by Moeyaert that features cattle in the foreground but is in fact a "history" subject, Jacob and Rachel at the well.[1] The sheep of the etching exhibited is virtually identical to the one in the center of the painting, while the cow at left in the painting matches the one at right in the *Shepherd* etching. Ruins on a wooded hill appear in the left background of the painting.

The Herd is as tonal, as nonlinear in conception as Bleker's etching, but furry masses of stipple and hairy broken strokes are employed instead of parallel lines and crisscrossing meshes. The crisp, wiry lines resembling pen lines that characterized Moeyaert's *Mercury and Argus* from before 1624 (cat. no. 69) have been replaced by the dissolution of line into a painterly softness.

1. Tümpel, p. 104, pl. 142.

79 (actual size)

80

REMBRANDT VAN RIJN
The Annunciation to the Shepherds, 1634

Etching, engraving, and drypoint
G. 43, B. 44, Hind 120, Münz 199, BB. 34–J,
W.-B. 44^{III}
Lower right: *Rembrandt F. 1634*
259 x 219 mm. (platemark)
Coll.: Three-leaved clover composed of three "C"s
Museum of Fine Arts, Boston, Anonymous Gift.
1975.279

Rembrandt's *Annunciation to the Shepherds* of 1634, one of the most ambitious prints of his early career as a printmaker, is a wonderful amalgam of soaring, operatic grandeur and earthy Dutch realism. Whereas Vinckboons's country bumpkins (cat. no. 22) are wonder-struck by the angel's appearance, Rembrandt has literally illustrated the evangelist Luke's phrase "and they were sore afraid" (Luke 2:8–14). Shepherds and herds react, not with awe but with a raw terror and sheer brute panic that have been observed with amusing accuracy. Above them a rather solid angel stands, firmly planted on an apron of cloud, and raises its hand imploring them to "Fear not." Behind the angel the sky bursts open, and robust cherubs tumble outward from the apparition of the dove of the Holy Spirit as if impelled by the radiant energy. The landscape itself responds to the startling event: the earth seems to heave, and trees to writhe about or shoot up like fire-works. It is light – "the glory of the Lord" that "shone round about them" – that unifies these disparate elements.

This, the first of Rembrandt's "dark prints," reveals his debt to the prints by Hendrik Goudt after Elsheimer (see cat. nos. 44, 45) and the engravings of Jan van de Velde from the 1620s influenced by Goudt's prints (see cat. no. 61). The distant landscape veiled in darkness with its figures around a fire and distant city are particularly reminiscent of Elsheimer. A source of inspiration closer to home were the etchings made by the Leyden printmaker Jan Joris van Vliet in the early thirties after Rembrandt's

paintings, possibly under Rembrandt's direction. In etchings such as that of St. Jerome kneeling in prayer, of 1631 (B. 13, reproduced in Rovinski), Van Vliet, often a very crude printmaker when working from his own designs, invented a dense, unsystematic mesh of lines in order to more faithfully reproduce Rembrandt's chiaroscuro.

As Christopher White has noted, in this one instance Rembrandt worked like an engraver, finishing whole areas of the plate before proceeding to the next. The working proofs (the rare first state) reveal that Rembrandt worked from dark to light, completing all the darkest areas of the background and upper right before developing the lighter areas.[1]

An unusual feature of this fine impression of the third and completed state is the discreet touches of light gray wash that have been applied to the back of the shepherd before the grotto at the right, to the roof of this grotto, and to the reflection of the distant campfire in the water. These subtle adjustments of the lights seem to indicate an artist's taste and sensibility, whether that of Rembrandt himself or of a later owner of the print.

1. White, 1969, pp. 37–39 and pl. 26.

81

JAN LIEVENS
St. Jerome in Penitence, about 1631

Etching
B. 5^1, Dut. 5^1, Rov. El. 5^1, Holl. 15^1
At left of figure: *IL*
320 x 275 mm. (sheet)
Wm.: horn (type of Heawood 2680)
Coll.: A. Hunter (L. 2306)
Museum of Fine Arts, Boston, Katherine E.
Bullard Fund in memory of Francis Bullard.
69.1060

The etching *Saint Jerome in Penitence,* in early impressions before the plate was cut down and completely reworked in engraving, is among those works of Lievens which testify to the ambition and the intensely dramatic ideas of the young artist in his Leyden period.

A good deal of the somber drama of light and darkness here appears to be the result of a happy accident of which Lievens took advantage. The plate was apparently exposed to the acid too long, so that the lines in the denser areas of shading were overbitten and broken down, thereby producing masses of dark continuous tone like a wash in a drawing. These areas have a velvety texture not unlike that of the medium of mezzotint, which was perfected in the late 1650s. An impression of an earlier state in the Albertina (H. III, 18, p. 21) reveals that some of the darkest areas were originally lighter and that Lievens reworked them with drypoint and engraving to darken them. Other areas, such as the left side of the halo or the saint's legs, were lightened by scraping the dark areas, as in a mezzotint, in which the artist works from dark to light. Traces of the scraping are quite visible in the state exhibited here, usually described as the first.

Perhaps because the overbitten areas did not stand up well to continued printing, the plate was later reduced considerably in dimensions on all sides and rather insensitively reworked with the burin. In this altered condition it was published by the Antwerp publisher Frans van den Wyngaerde, who added his address. Whether Lievens collaborated in this disap-

pointing transformation of the plate in order to give it a longer printing life is not known, but it should be noted that many of his later etched portraits contain extensive passages of engraving.

The etching, which can be dated about 1631, repeats in reverse the monochromatic oil study on paper now in the collection of the Lakenhal, Leyden.[1] The two are quite similar in scale and composition except that the painting is squarer in format. Rubens and Van Dyck prepared monochromatic oil studies as models for prints, as did Rembrandt a few years later (see cat. no. 74, *The Good Samaritan*). The figure of St. Jerome in the Lakenhal painting is similar to the figure of Job in the Lievens painting of 1631 in Ottawa; both figures seem to have been observed from the same elderly model. Like the young Rembrandt, Lievens in his early career was visually fascinated by the feathery white beard, wrinkles, and leathery skin of venerable age.

Rembrandt had executed an even larger plate of *St. Jerome Kneeling in Prayer* (B. 106) about two years before, but there seem to have been problems with the biting of the plate, and that experiment survives in only two impressions. It may, however, have stimulated Lievens to see if he could succeed where his friend Rembrandt had failed. The closest comparison with the Lievens *St. Jerome* is Jan Joris van Vliet's 1631 etching of St. Jerome kneeling in prayer after a design by Rembrandt (B. 13, reproduced in Rovinski). Both these etchings are extremely important for the evolution of dark tonalities in seventeenth-century Dutch printmaking, but the careful, rather tight, small-scale drawing of the Van Vliet only serves to emphasize the bold, scribbling freedom and breadth of the etched line in the Lievens.

1. Braunschweig, 1979, no. 24, illus.

82

JAN LIEVENS
The Raising of Lazarus, 1630–31

Etching
B. 3[1], Dut. 3[1], Rov. El. 3[1], Holl. 7[1]
Lower right (on wall): *IL*
360 x 312 mm. (sheet)
Wm.: horn (type of Heawood 2680)
Davison Art Center, Wesleyan University, Middletown, Connecticut, Gift of George W. Davison, B.A., 1892. 41-DI-II

The *Raising of Lazarus* is one of Lievens's most audacious inventions as an illustrator. It also poses problems that illuminate the extremely close interchange of ideas between Lievens and Rembrandt and the competitiveness that characterized their relationship during the Leyden years.

The miraculous raising from the dead of Lazarus, brother of Mary and Martha, followers of Christ, was a dramatic confirmation of Christ's statement, "I am the resurrection and the life" (John 11:1-44). Lievens's version of this event, the largest of his etchings, appears to combine the moment when Christ lifts up his eyes to thank God the Father for hearing his request and the slightly later moment when he cries out, "Lazarus, come forth," and the dead man rises from the grave. In Rembrandt's painting of this subject of about 1629-1631 (Bredius 538) and his related large-scale, highly finished etching of about 1632 (B. 73), Christ is shown with his arm raised in a gesture of command, while Lazarus rises head first. Lievens's solution is both more theatrical and more mystical. Christ stands isolated on the lip of the grave, which is set in a grotto or cave in accordance with the biblical text. Rather than gesturing, he clasps his hands and closes his eyes in prayer or supplication; a great oval corona of mystic light emanates from his figure. Only Lazarus's two hands are eerily visible as he rises from the sepulchre.

The etching is in reverse of the Lievens painting, dated 1631, in the Brighton Museum. Some scholars believe that the etching reproduces the painting, which has probably been cut at top and bottom, with the result that its resemblance to the print is decreased. Although the painting is poorly preserved, Christ's figure does not appear to have been surrounded by the great aureole of light of the etching, and his eyes are open rather than closed. Other scholars believe that the etching preceded the painting, pointing to Rembrandt's 1630 chalk drawing in the British Museum (Benesch 17), which parallels in its composition Lievens's undated etching. The drawing began, significantly, as a "Raising of Lazarus" and was altered to an "Entombment."[1] Other scholars see the compositional similarity between Rembrandt's drawing and Lievens's etching and painting as evidence of Rembrandt's influence on Lievens.[2] No matter which conclusion one accepts, the evidence of the complex interaction of the two artists' ideas during the Leyden years is inescapable.

Lievens's etching is relatively rare in the first state, before the plate was reworked in engraving and published by the Antwerp publisher Frans van den Wyngaerde. As one can see here, the execution of the first state is surprisingly delicate considering the scale of the plate. The extremely fine etched lines form open, transparent webs, reinforcing the ethereal effect of Lievens's conception of the subject with its all-pervading, mystic light. The drawing, however, is sometimes a bit finicky and small-scale for the breadth and monumentality Lievens appears to be striving for (see, for example, Lazarus's hands).

1. See White, 1969, pp. 29-32.
2. For a résumé of the various arguments, see Judson on the Brighton painting in Chicago, 1969, no. 79.

131

Jacob A. Duck
about 1600 – 1667

Jacob A. Duck, primarily a painter of scenes from military life and of bordello scenes, made six to eight etchings of single figures.[1] Born about 1600, probably in Utrecht, he was a pupil of the Utrecht painter Joost Cornelisz. Droochsloot (see cat. no. 60). In 1621 he is mentioned as an apprentice in the records of the artists' guild of Utrecht and as a master in the period 1626-1632. He is recorded as being in Utrecht until 1646, but from 1656 to 1660 he was in the Hague. He died in Utrecht in 1667.[2]

1. The two etchings of horsemen attributed to Duck and said to be part of a set of four, of which the other two are by Romeyn de Hooghe, do not seem to me to be by Duck. Landwehr, 1973, p. 47, rejects the other two as by Romeyn de Hooghe.

2. Biography by K. Lilienfeld in Thieme-Becker, vol. 10, p. 40.

83

JACOB A. DUCK
A Magus Kneeling in Adoration

From a set of four etchings
Etching and drypoint
Wurz. 2, Holl. 2
122 x 88 mm. (platemark)
The Metropolitan Museum of Art, The Elisha Whittelsey Fund. 67.793.33

The *Magus* is one of a set of four plates of the Virgin and Child (Holl. 1) and the Three Magi (Holl. 2-4). The *Magus Kneeling* forms a pair with the *Virgin and Child* (see illus.), which also has a blank background, while the two plates of standing Magi form pendants when facing each other, both having a delicately etched background of Italian buildings or Roman ruins.

The powerful illumination in the four prints, achieved by means of sharp variations in the strength of biting of the line, as well as the strong emphasis on the drapery folds suggest the work of an Utrecht "Caravaggist" painter, such as Hendrik Terbrugghen (about 1588-1629). The more delicate passages of etched line and the Italian vistas in Holl. 3 and 4 evoke the etchings of 1639-40 of the Utrecht painter Bartholomeus Breenbergh (see cat. nos. 115-117). On the basis of general graphic style, I would date the set in the late 1630s. They are essentially drapery studies and remind us that, as a painter, Duck is particularly known for his skillful rendering of draperies, of silks and satins. A certain wavering between two and three dimensions visible here is characteristic of the drawing in Duck's paintings.

The division of the narrative of the Adoration of the Magi into four separate single-figure plates is unusual. One earlier precedent is the Lorraine printmaker Jacques Bellange's set of three plates of the Three Magi without the Virgin and Child, datable before 1615 on the basis of the Matthaeus Merian copies.[1] The Bellange Magi are suaver and more exotically oriental than Duck's slightly scruffy, unshaven Magus, who kneels before a round-faced Virgin and a surprisingly unidealized Child.

1. Robert-Dumesnil 33-35; see Des Moines/Boston, 1975-76, pp. 59-60.

Jacob A. Duck
Virgin and Child
Etching
Institut Néerlandais, Paris

83 (actual size)

REMBRANDT VAN RIJN
The Ship of Fortune in Elias Herckmans,
Der Zee-Vaert Lof. Amsterdam, Jacob
Pietersz. Wachter, 1634.

Etching
(page 97)
G. 123, B. 111, Hind 106, Münz 256, BB. 33-E,
W.-B. 111[II]
Lower right on ship: *Rembrandt f. 1633*
112 x 165 mm. (platemark), 298 x 190 mm. (page
size), vellum
Fairfax-Murray 357, Benesch 1943, pp. 21–22,
Holl. (Basse) 49–65
Coll.: T.F. Lauson 1754, Long Island Historical
Society
Mr. and Mrs. Arthur E. Vershbow

The seaman-poet Elias Herckmans's *Der Zee-Vaert Lof (Praise of Sea-Faring)* is a somewhat long-winded narrative poem, which, to paraphrase the title page, deals with "the most notable sea voyages from the beginning to the present as they touch on the fortunes of the world's rulers." The first seafarer of the poem is Noah. The poem is dedicated to the burgomasters of the "widely famed mercantile city" of Amsterdam, whose harbor was the great international trading center of northern Europe in the seventeenth century.

All but one of the etchings in the book were executed by Willem Basse, son of the dealer and collector Jan Basse, whose etched work sometimes reflects Rembrandt's influence. Rembrandt etched only one illustration for Herckmans's poem, but it occupies a prominent position at the beginning of the third book. Though the older and more celebrated of the two artists, Rembrandt seems to have striven to accommodate himself to Basse's style of illustration, as can be seen if one compares Basse's etching representing the meeting of Alexander the Great and Neptune (see illus.), which opens the second book of Herckmans's poem.

In only three instances did etched illustrations by Rembrandt, the unsurpassed illustrator of biblical narratives, appear bound in a

book. The other instances are Rembrandt's etching for his friend Jan Six's 1648 tragedy, *Medea* (B. 112), and his illustrations for the Jewish theologian Manessah ben Israel's mystical *Piedra Gloriosa*, of 1655 (B. 36).

Rembrandt's allegorical etching has been open to many interpretations. The beginning of the third book of the poem concerns the Roman peace introduced by the emperor Augustus after the defeat of Marc Antony at the naval battle of Actium, the symbolic closing of the doors of the temple of Janus (seen in the background of Rembrandt's etching) signifying peace, and the resumption of mercantile trade by sea (the departing ship). One of the subthemes of Herckmans's long narrative touches on contemporary events, the beginning of negotiations for peace with the Spanish in 1633. The seaman Herckmans saw peace as essential to the flourishing of Holland's seaborne mercantile trade. As one of Herckmans's verses from the beginning of the third book pragmatically states, "For each one takes advantage of peace while he has it" ("Want elck gebruyckt den vreed', terwijl hy vrede heeft").

The laurel-crowned figure on the war horse that sinks to the ground is probably the emperor Augustus, whose open-armed gesture should be interpreted as signifying, "Let Peace begin." The small merchant ship sets forth, guided by the naked figure of Fortune, who clutches the sail. In the far distance is a scene of naval combat. Fortune has also been identified as a peaceful incarnation of the war goddess Bellona, for the goddess is described at the opening of the third book as removing her armor.[1]

1. For a discussion of the various interpretations of the allegory, see Benesch, 1943, pp. 21-22; De la Fontaine Verwey, 1976, pp. 130-131.

Willem Basse
Alexander the Great and Neptune
Etching in *Der Zee-Vaert Lof*
Mr. and Mrs. Arthur E. Vershbow

85

SALOMON SAVERY after JAN MARTSEN THE YOUNGER
The Procession along the Haarlemmerweg in Caspar Barlaeus, *Marie de Medicis, entrant dans Amsterdam*. Amsterdam, Jean & Corneille Blaeu, 1638.

Etching and engraving
(following page 24)
293 x 654 mm. (platemark); 415 x 280 mm. (page size); vellum
Brunet 1567; Wurz. 3(1-7); Landwehr (1971)
Coll.: Wm. Daye; Dr. Sander
Museum of Fine Arts, Boston, William A. Sargent Fund. 62.583

Marie de' Medici, mother of Louis XIII of France, was exiled from France as a result of the machinations of Cardinal Richelieu, her son's chief adviser. Rather than settling in her ancestral home of Florence, as Richelieu wished, she began a tour of Europe, seeking to arrange a reconciliation with her son. Since Richelieu would pay her no pension unless she settled in Florence, she and her retinue often lived at the expense of their hosts. Constantijn Huygens related that during her costly stay in Brussels, she was given the satirical Spanish title of "la rouïna madre" (ruinous mother), a play on her French title of "reine-mère" (queen mother). Upon her abrupt departure from the South Netherlands, Marie became the guest of the stadholder Frederik Hendrik in the Hague. On September 1, a Wednesday, she was triumphally received by the burgomasters of Amsterdam and entertained with symbolic pageants on land and water until her departure the following Sunday.

85

The illustrated book published to commemorate this controversial lady's visit, with Latin text commissioned from the famous Latinist Caspar Barlaeus, the Amsterdam professor of philosophy, was the first triumphal entry book to be published in the North Netherlands. In the South Netherlands city governments had published triumphal entry books on such occasions since the mid-sixteenth century. French and Dutch editions were also issued. Barlaeus's text is full of classical erudition. Amsterdam is elegantly referred to in the French translation exhibited here as a "ville dediée au negoce & exercices de Mercury" (city dedicated to trade & the practices of Mercury [patron of commerce]), and Marie's reception by the burgomasters compared to Athens's reception of its kings and captains, Egypt's reception of Cleopatra, Rome's of Agrippina and conquered Tyre's of Alexander the Great!

The illustration of the book was a collaborative project. The plates include an anonymous engraving after Honthorst's official portrait of Marie; Johannes Suyderhoef's engraving after Thomas de Keyser's painting of the burgomasters receiving word of the queen mother's arrival; the prints showing her reception by land designed by Jan Martsen the Younger and those showing her reception and entertainment on the water designed by Simon de Vlieger, all etched and engraved by the professional printmaker Salomon Savery (1594–after 1665). Savery was the son of Jacob Savery and nephew of Roelant Savery and one of the most prolific printmakers associated with the book trade in the mid-seventeenth century. In addition there are plates designed by Claes Moeyaert and etched by Pieter Nolpe, based on the historical and allegorical tableaux relating to the queen mother's career and the state

of France. The tableaux were presented on stages that topped the triumphal arches erected for the occasion or on floating stages in the Rokin. All the decorations and the symbolic pageantry had to be prepared in a great rush, for the Amsterdam authorities had only been advised of Marie's intended visit on August 18.[1]

The panoramic fold-out plate of the procession along the Haarlemmerweg chosen for exhibition is the least frequently exhibited, perhaps because it is the least ceremonious; on the other hand, it is splendidly Dutch in its sweep of flat terrain and in its underplaying of the pomp of the occasion: the most prominent spectators are cattle and farm folk. In the distance is the characteristic profile of the church of St. Bavo in Haarlem, where Marie had spent

1. For Marie's reception in Amsterdam, the book, and its illustration, see Snoep, 1975, pp. 39–64.

the night. At the right is the Haarlemmermeer, the great inland lake that has since been filled in. Bobbing about are the yachts that had offered to transport Marie and her retinue by water to Amsterdam and had been refused. At the head of the procession we see the trumpeters and cavaliers, the flower of Amsterdam's youth, sent out to escort the queen into the city. The plate was designed by the painter and etcher of cavalry subjects Jan Martsen the Younger (1609? – after 1647). Martsen also designed a handsome print showing the escort of cavaliers and the queen's coach arriving at the gates of the city, which Pieter Nolpe etched on several plates (Holl. 86–94). Salomon Savery's neat line work here consists primarily of etching imitative of engraving in the manner of the French seventeenth-century etchers Jacques Callot and Abraham Bosse. Many of the plates in this copy of the book are proof impressions taken before some final touches were added to the plates.

86

REMBRANDT VAN RIJN
Self-Portrait, Open-Mouthed, as if Shouting,
1630

Etching
G. 18, B. 13, Hind 31, Münz 7, BB. 30-N,
W.-B. 13 II
Upper left: [monogram] *RHL 1630*
73 x 62 mm. (platemark)
Coll.: K. Paar (L. 2009); A. Artaria (L. 33);
G.W. Vanderbilt; J. Pierpont Morgan (L. 1509)
The Pierpont Morgan Library

Rembrandt was obsessed by the recording of his own image. His painted self-portraits span his entire career, forming a remarkable portrait in time. The etched self-portraits, however, are mostly confined to his early career, and he made relatively few after the 1630s. The *Self-portrait, open-mouthed* is one of a group of etched, bust-length self-portraits dated 1630, in which Rembrandt used his own features as a convenient and inexpensive model to study the expression of emotion: glaring (B. 10), laugh-

138

86 (actual size)

ing (B. 316), wonderstruck (B. 320). Here the harsh side lighting that rakes across his features emphasizes their distortion as he calls or cries out. A painted self-portrait of 1629 in the Alte Pinakothek, Munich (Bredius 2), is quite similar in pose, expression, and lighting but in reverse. In the painting Rembrandt emphasized the wooly corona of hair by inscribing lines in the wet paint with a blunt point.

The harsh realism of this etched self-portrait is further pointed up when we discover that in the same year Rembrandt gave his own features, contorted in this expression, to the figure of a ragged beggar seated on a bank, who holds out his hand for a contribution (B. 174).

87

REMBRANDT VAN RIJN
Self-Portrait, Leaning on a Stone Sill, 1639

Etching
G. 26, B. 21, Hind 168, Münz 24, BB. 39-E,
W.-B. 21 II
205 x 164 mm. (platemark)
Wm.: letters PDB
Coll.: J. Reiss (L. 1522)
Private Collection, Boston

The etched self-portrait of 1639 is Rembrandt's answer to the debate that began at the time of the Renaissance as to whether the artist was more than a mere craftsman, whether he was in fact a person of cultivation – a gentleman. In his own time Rembrandt would have been aware of the example of Rubens, the Flemish painter who was a diplomat and friend of princes.

This portrait, which radiates self-confidence, represents the moment when Rembrandt was at the peak of his success and prosperity, one of the most sought-after portrait painters in Amsterdam. Rembrandt, who frequently painted himself in fancy dress, is here clad in Renaissance costume. The etching and the quite comparable painted self-portrait of the following year (National Gallery, London, Bredius 34) were very probably influenced by two celebrated Italian Renaissance portraits that were in Amsterdam at this time, Raphael's portrait of Baldassare Castiglione (now Louvre, Paris), whose book *The Courtier* defined the Renaissance gentleman, and the so-called portrait of Ariosto by Titian (now National Gallery, London). Rembrandt made a quick sketch (Benesch 451) of the *Castiglione* at the Amsterdam sale in which it appeared in this same year, 1639. The painting was purchased by Alphonso Lopez, a Portuguese Jew living in Amsterdam, who was an agent of the French king and who also owned the Titian portrait. The latter portrait, in which the sitter rests his full puffed sleeve on a ledge, is particularly close to Rembrandt's conception. However, as Christopher White has remarked, Rembrandt does not present himself with the cool detachment and reserve that characterize the Renaissance portraits. He confronts us eye-to-eye with a penetrating gaze and wrinkled brow.[1]

The blank background serves as a foil for the subtle description of rich textures: hair, velvet, brocade, fur, and the moss growing on the ledge. The delicate web of extremely fine etched lines and the focus on the middle range of values rather than on strong contrasts characterize many Rembrandt etchings of the 1630s.

1. White, 1969, pp. 120–122.

88

JACQUES DE GHEYN III
Grotesque Heads, 1638

Etching
B. 28, Dut. 28, Wurz. 28, Holl. 28
Lower right: *1638./DGheyn*
82 x 116 mm. (platemark)
Coll.: Arenberg (L. 567)
National Gallery of Art, Washington, D.C.,
Ailsa Mellon Bruce Fund, 1971. B-25,842

This phantasmagoria in which faces of all ages and types are discovered in rocks or clumps of earth is one of three small plates (the other two are vertical in format) fully signed by De Gheyn and dated 1638. The images call to mind Leonardo's suggestions for a new method of inventing motifs: "when you look at a wall spotted with stains, or with a mixture of stones, if you have to devise some scene, you may discover a resemblance to various landscapes, beautified with mountains, rivers, rocks, trees, plains, wide valleys and hills in varied arrangements; or, again, you may see battles and figures in action; or strange faces and costumes, and an endless variety of objects." [1]

The three etchings are related to three drawings of rocks or clumps of earth animated with faces: one in the Pierpont Morgan Library, New York; [2] one in the Institut Néerlandais, Paris (inv. 5094), and one in the Witt Collection, Courtauld Institute, London (handlist no. 4439). The clump of earth on the right in the etching exhibited here repeats in reverse, with some variations in detail, the clump of earth at the center of the Morgan sheet. The clump of earth in the drawing has roots protruding from it. The Paris drawing, with its grassy, mossy textures, ivy, and even a waterfall, makes more reference to landscape.

Although the etchings are fully signed and bear no other artist's name, Bartsch attributed them to Bartholomeus Breenbergh, perhaps because of the sharp stylistic contrast with

1. Richter, 1939, vol. 1, pp. 311–312.
2. Paris/New York, 1979–80, p. 99, no. 60, illus.

88 (actual size)

Salomon Koninck
1609 – 1656

The painter Salomon Koninck, born in Amsterdam in 1609, was the son of a goldsmith from Antwerp. He was probably a cousin of the painter Philips Koninck. In 1621 his father apprenticed him to David Colijns to learn drawing. He subsequently studied with François Venant and Claes Moeyaert, both history painters whose work, like that of Rembrandt's teacher, Pieter Lastman, was influenced by the art of Adam Elsheimer. In 1630 Koninck became a member of the Amsterdam artists' guild and began to produce history paintings and portraits. He married the daughter of the painter Adriaen van Nieulandt. In 1652, 1653, and 1654 he is mentioned in Amsterdam, where he died in 1656. [1]

Although Koninck did not study with Rembrandt, the whole of his art was formed by Rembrandt's work of the 1630s, in particular the paintings of richly garbed patriarchs and rabbis.

Salomon Koninck made a small number of etchings (four to six), which reflect the influence not only of Rembrandt but also of Lievens. [2]

1. Biography by C. Hofstede de Groot in Thieme-Becker, vol. 21, pp. 274–276.
2. Three are signed (Holl. 1–3); I find Holl. 6, though unsigned, consistent in style, but Holl. 4 and 5 seem to me to be closer to Lievens.

De Gheyn III's earlier prints (see cat. no. 49), the extreme delicacy of the line, and the date, which is close to Breenbergh's dated prints of 1639 and 1640. Van Regteren Altena initially gave both drawings and prints to De Gheyn III [3] but has recently suggested that the etchings were made by Stefano della Bella during his visit to Holland and that the drawings are late works of the elder De Gheyn. [4] The attribution of the etchings to Della Bella seems highly improbable, and I would tend to endorse Van Regteren Altena's earlier opinion that the etchings are by De Gheyn III. [5]

The separation of the drawings of father and son is still difficult. [6] The problem is aggravated by the fact that the younger De Gheyn seems to have stopped working for a few years after

his father's death. Constantijn Huygens, in his fragment of an autobiography (written about 1628–29), complains of the son's idleness after the incredible promise shown in his earlier drawings and paintings. [7]

7. Worp, 1891, pp. 114–115.

3. Van Regteren Altena, 1936, p. 108 and note.
4. Paris/New York, 1979–80, p. 99, no. 60.
5. Phyllis Massar agreed in telephone conversation that the etchings could not be by Stefano della Bella.
6. For the drawings see Möhle, 1963, pp. 3–12.

89

SALOMON KONINCK
Bust of a Man in a Turban, 1638

Etching and engraving
Rov. El. 69, Wurz. 2, Holl. 2 [1]
Upper right: *S. Koninck/An° 1638*
134 x 86 mm. (platemark)
Museum of Fine Arts, Boston, Horatio Greenough Curtis Fund. 67.15

Salomon Koninck's bust of a bearded Oriental with turban and earring is the mid-seventeenth-century equivalent of the fantasy

pen portraits in period or exotic dress produced by Hendrik Goltzius and his circle (see
Van Sichem after Matham, cat. no. 51). Both
Lievens and Rembrandt in their early careers
frequently portrayed venerable scholars, sages,
or ecclesiastics with silken beards and faces
seamed by experience. The best comparison
with Koninck's *Man in a Turban* is Lievens's
etching of a bearded, turbaned Oriental (Holl.
35), which reveals Lievens to be of equal
importance to Rembrandt for this type of
imagery. Lievens's print was apparently copied
in an etching by a Rembrandt pupil and then
retouched by Rembrandt, who annotated
the plate to this effect and dated it 1635
(B. 288). This free reverse copy embellished by
Rembrandt is one of four etched plates (B. 286–
289) of picturesque types that Rembrandt
and his pupil copied from Lievens's etchings.

The *Bust of a Man in a Turban* is virtually a
pendant to another Koninck etching (Holl. 1)
of a bareheaded old man in profile, also dated
1638 and identical in scale and format.[1] These
etchings precede by a few years Ferdinand
Bol's etchings of similar subjects.

Koninck made sensitive use of variations in
biting in this plate, suggesting by this means
the pale whiteness of the Oriental's beard.
When deeper shadows and more forceful modeling were required, as in the turban, he turned
to the engraver's burin, as did Rembrandt
in the foreground of the *Good Samaritan*
(cat. no. 74).

1. Koninck's third signed etching, a bust of an old man in
a fur cap (Holl. 3), is smaller in scale. The date, which is
reversed and difficult to read, has been read as 1628 and
1648; but given the close stylistic resemblance of Holl. 3
to the two etchings of 1638, the date should probably also
be read as 1638.

89 (actual size)

90 (actual size)

90
JAN LIEVENS
A Seated Ecclesiastic

Woodcut
B. 61, Dut. 60[1], Rov. El. 61, Holl. 102[1]
Lower right: *IL*.
167 x 131 mm. (sheet)
Coll.: W. Esdaile (L. 2617)
Lent by the Trustees of the British Museum,
Mitchell Collection. 1895-1-22-1183

Woodcut was not a common medium of
expression for Dutch painters in Jan Lievens's
time. His woodcuts, one of the most original
and vital aspects of his work as a printmaker,
undoubtedly owe their existence to his 1635–
1644 residence in Antwerp, where, from about
1631 on, Christoffel Jegher was producing
woodcuts from Rubens's designs, first book
illustrations and then single-sheet woodcuts on
a monumental scale.[1] Jegher's woodcut style
was based on the linear vocabulary of contemporary engraving. The woodcut that may be
Lievens's earliest effort in the medium, the
Cain and Abel (Holl. 99), though less regularized in its linear vocabulary, reflects the influence of Jegher's large-scale woodcuts after
Rubens such as the *Hercules* (Holl. 15).

While Lievens was stimulated by Jegher's
woodcuts, he did not ultimately model his style
on that of Jegher and soon developed his own
highly original woodcut vocabulary, which is
epitomized by the *Seated Ecclesiastic*. This stylistic independence and the unorthodox freedom
of the cutting have led some scholars to suggest
that Lievens cut his own blocks. Attractive as
this suggestion may be, it is counter to the traditional separation of roles of designer and
cutter in the making of a woodcut.

If Lievens did not cut his own blocks, he certainly encouraged the cutter to develop a new
way of working appropriate to his graphic
vocabulary. The *Seated Ecclesiastic* is characterized by a crisp, choppy angularity in the cutting that instantly calls to mind the knife and
gouge used to excavate the blank areas. There
is no reference to the vocabulary of other print-

1. See Schneider/Ekkart, 1973, p. 84.

making media. This subtractive way of working, gouging out the lights and leaving the darks in relief, is particularly effective in the irregular, spidery web that describes the crepey, parchment-like texture of the skin of the ecclesiastic's face or the pattern of highlights that gives his cap and jacket the texture of velvet.

Given the crisp precision of the figure silhouetted against the blank background, it is somewhat surprising to discover that the preparatory drawing in Rotterdam is executed in the soft medium of black chalk.[2] The style of the drawing strongly reflects the influence of Van Dyck. The seated figure in the drawing, which is in the reverse direction, is shown full length in a study surrounded by books, papers, and a globe. He appears to be a scholar and wears a long robe, light in color. The drawing was traced with a stylus to transfer the image; only the contours that relate to the woodcut image are indented. The dimensions of the areas traced are exactly those of the print.

Well-preserved examples of Lievens's woodcuts are quite rare. The impression exhibited here is unusual in that the double border has not been trimmed away.

2. Rotterdam, Museum Boymans-van Beuningen, inv. MB197; see Braunschweig, 1979, no. 57 and reproduction, p. 148.

91
Jan Lievens
Bust of a Balding Man

Chiaroscuro woodcut with light orange tone block
Rov. El. 70, Holl. 106
174 x 133 mm. (block)
Coll.: Albertina duplicate (L. suppl. 5g)
The Metropolitan Museum of Art, The Harris Brisbane Dick Fund. 25.2.61

The *Bust of a Balding Man* is Lievens's only chiaroscuro woodcut.[1] The tone block is usu-

1. Strauss, 1973, p. 342, states that this is Lievens's true chiaroscuro but then remarks cryptically that there are impressions of other woodcuts with faintly colored backgrounds. He also states that the Boston impression of the present print has more highlights cut into the tone block, but I find it on comparison to be the same as the one exhibited here.

91 (actual size)

ally printed, as here, in a light orange, a color favored by Christoffel Jegher for the printing of his chiaroscuro woodcuts after Rubens. However, a comparison with Jegher's chiaroscuro *Bust of a Bearded Man* after Rubens (Holl. 20) reveals that Lievens's woodcut is essentially independent of Jegher's way of working. Lievens did not pursue the potential of the chiaroscuro woodcut as far as Jegher. Lievens's image is essentially complete in the line block, and the single tone block only provides a few glimmering highlights. The line work of the background shading and the shading on the shirt are somewhat regularized here, but the sketchy freedom of the line work in the head of Lievens's figure is quite unlike the controlled, patterned linear systems of Jegher.

As Hind noted, there is an impression of this print in the British Museum inscribed in an early hand: "Joannes Lievens [or "Livinus"] pinxit [painted]...Francisc. du Sart sculps [engraved]."[2] This is the only recorded reference to a cutter's name in conjunction with Lievens's woodcuts; it is rather puzzling because the most likely candidate is a François Dusart who was a Flemish sculptor active in Italy, England, and Holland, but who is not recorded as a cutter of blocks.[3] As Hind pointed out, the "pinxit" reference is also puzzling because the Lievens design for the woodcut was probably a drawing.[4]

2. Cracherode D.8–95; see Hind, 1913, pp. 235, 236.

3. G.J. Hoogewerff in Thieme-Becker, vol. 10, pp. 225–226.

4. Unless the design was a chiaroscuro-style brush drawing in oil pigments, as is the *Bust of a Man* in black, red, brown, and white oil pigment on yellow paper in Berlin once attributed to Lievens but later given to Salomon Koninck. The attribution was made to Koninck because of the related etching (Holl. 5) attributed to him (see Berlin, cat. drawings, 1931, no. 5348, pl. 121). I have already suggested in Koninck's biography that the etching may be by Lievens, and I would like to advance the same suggestion with regard to the drawing.

92

92

JAN LIEVENS
Bust of a Capuchin Monk

Etching
B. 14, Dut. 14, Rov. El. 14, Holl. 27[1]
320 x 247 mm. (platemark)
Wm.: foolscap
Coll.: Friedrich August II (L. 971)
Museum Boymans-van Beuningen, Rotterdam.
BdeH 16893

The *Bust of a Capuchin Monk*[1] is the largest of Lievens's numerous etched character heads, or types, or *tronies*.[2] In his early career Lievens frequently chose monks, hermits, and anchorites as subjects. In 1629 the representative of King Charles I of England acquired in Holland two paintings by Rembrandt and one by Lievens, which he presented to the king upon his return. The Lievens work was the 1629 painting of a Capuchin monk with a rosary, now in the collection of the Marquess of Lothian.[3] The etching of the monk probably dates from the early 1630s while Lievens was still in Leyden. The drapery forms and the combination of fine sharp lines and stipple compare closely with the graphic vocabulary of the figure of Christ in the *Raising of Lazarus* etching of about 1631 (cat. no. 82). The etched line in the *Monk* is so sharp and crisp that it resembles drypoint line without the burr. The *Monk* is appealing in its largeness of conception and simplicity of execution. The blank background is often trimmed away, but in the

1. The traditional identification of the sitter as the contemporary Italian painter and etcher Giovanni Benedetto Castiglione may have arisen from Castiglione's etched heads of picturesque types and Orientals influenced by prints by Lievens and Rembrandt such as the present one.
2. With regard to the use of the Dutch term *tronie* to designate such character heads or types, a certain Jacobus Christianus published a group of the small etched character heads by or after Lievens under the title *DIVERSE TRONIKENS GEETST VAN I.L. (Various Little* Tronies [visages or mugs] *Etched by Jan Lievens); see* Dutuit, vol. 5, p. 124. I find no information on this publisher, but the edition appears to have been issued in the seventeenth century.
3. See chronology in Braunschweig, 1979, p. 36, and fig. 1, p. 15.

present superb complete impression one can see how the blank space gives the figure room to breathe and expand.

93

JAN LIEVENS
Bust of an Elderly Man

Etching and drypoint
B. (Rembrandt school), p. 108, 25, Dut. 70[1], Rov. El. 75[1], Holl. 28[1]
285 x 218 mm. (platemark)
Wm.: foolscap
Coll.: E.T. Rodenacker (L. 2438), F. Pokorny (L. 2036), unidentified (L. 2909a), P. Davidsohn (L. 654)
The Metropolitan Museum of Art, The Harris Brisbane Dick Fund. 24.1.1

One would be justified in assuming that the *Bust of an Elderly Man* was simply another of Lievens's character studies or "types" were it not for the fact that some early impressions have annotations that identify the sitter. An impression in the Albertina bears an inscription in French that identifies the sitter as Robert South, an Englishman, 112 years of age.[1] An impression in Munich and one in Rotterdam, however, are inscribed respectively "Lord digby" and "Charles Digby." We know that there was an interest in England in those who lived to an unusually advanced age. Samuel Pepys, the English diarist and print collector of the late seventeenth century, was pleased to be able to add to his portrait collection a portrait of "Mother George" of Oxford, who was reputed to have lived to the age of 120 years and who demonstrated her unimpaired faculties to visitors by threading a fine needle in exchange for a gratuity.[2] Given Lievens's visual fascination with the signs of venerable age, it is not inconceivable that he might have sought out such a wonder of nature during his stay in England, but we have as yet no firm proof.

1. Albertina, H.III.18, p. 57, no. 116. A further inscription in French identifies the handwriting of the inscription as that of the engraver Theodoor Matham (before 1606–1676).
2. See Levis, 1915, p. 91 and note.

The etching of the elderly man, which reveals a much greater interest in suggestion of color and texture than Lievens's earlier character heads, should probably be placed in his Antwerp period (1635–1644). A comparison of the etching with the chiaroscuro woodcut of a balding man (cat. no. 91), which is thought to have been executed in Antwerp, is helpful in this regard. The comparison also points up the far greater degree of specific description of the color and texture of aged skin and grizzled hair that was possible in the medium of etching and drypoint.

The frontal pose and direct gaze give the figure great dignity, but they are also typical of Lievens's etched character heads in which he frequently favored a full frontal or profile view against a blank ground.

94

REMBRANDT VAN RIJN
The Raising of Lazarus: Small Plate, 1642

Etching and drypoint
G. 73, B. 72, Hind 198, Münz 214, BB. 42-B,
W.-B. 72[1]
Lower left: *Rembrandt F. 1642* (2 reversed)
150 x 115 mm. (platemark)
Wm.: foolscap
Coll.: C.B. Brüsaber (L. 309); E. Schröter
(L. 2270)
Museum of Fine Arts, Boston, Katherine E. Bullard
Fund in memory of Francis Bullard. 1976.744

Rembrandt's 1642 *Raising of Lazarus* is a
remarkably restrained interpretation of an
extremely dramatic subject. There could
scarcely be a sharper contrast between this
plate and Rembrandt's large plate of about ten
years earlier (B. 73), with its melodramatic gestures and strong contrasts of light and darkness, or Lievens's ambitious etched version of
the subject of 1630–31 (cat. no. 82).[1] The scale
of the plate is small, and the figures are thoroughly immersed in the landscape setting;
moreover, the tonality is extremely light, the
delicate, open web of fine etched lines allowing
the white of the paper to show through. In a
fine early impression such as the present one,
the viewer can appreciate just how subtle is the
expressive distribution of dark and light accents.
In later impressions all parts of the composition tend to acquire the same weight, and the
subtle buildup of dark accents around Christ's
head that identifies him as the principal figure
is lost, as is the sense of spatial recession in the
landscape.

   Lazarus rises astonished in response to
Christ's simple gesture and compassionate
gaze. Lazarus's small figure is set off by the
blank rock face behind him. The miracle, rather
than being cloaked in dramatic shadows or sig-
naled by explosive bursts of light, is bathed in
gentle sunlight.

1. Christopher White, 1969, p. 50, pl. 50, considers a
sketch by Rembrandt in Rotterdam (Benesch 518 recto)
to be a preparatory study for the etching. The sketch, in
which Christ stands on a ledge and is more dramatically
isolated, is quite reminiscent of Lievens's earlier etching.

94 (actual size)

95
ANONYMOUS, REMBRANDT SCHOOL
The Idolatry of Solomon

Etching
Holl. 3 (Lievens)
75 x 54 mm. (sheet)
Coll.: P. Davidsohn (L. 654)
Museum of Fine Arts, Boston, Harriet Otis Cruft
Fund. M28427

This small plate illustrates the passage from the Old Testament's first book of Kings (11:4) regarding King Solomon's numerous foreign wives and their heathen beliefs: "For it came to pass, when Solomon was old, that his wives turned away his heart after other gods: and his heart was not perfect with the Lord his God, as was the heart of David his father." Solomon kneels on the steps of an altar on which an idol is enshrined, while one of his wives directs his devotions. The image is broadly conceived in terms of masses of light and dark with little attention to detail or to facial expression. This plate, which has often been attributed to Jan Lievens, differs in style of execution from the small plates in a sketchy style that bear Lievens's monogram, the *Adoration of the Shepherds* (Holl. 5) and the pair of the *Peasant Man* and *Peasant Woman* (Holl. 86, 87). These authentic small Lievens plates are less systematic in their line work and do not employ the rather regular crisscrossing grid that renders blocks of shadow in the *Solomon*.

  The *Solomon* is one of three prints virtually identical in dimensions and all executed by the same hand. The other two are the *Dismissal of Hagar* (Lievens, Holl. 1) and the *Scholar in his Study* (Lievens, Holl. 85). All of these prints derive their style from Rembrandt etchings of the early 1640s such as the 1642 *Lazarus* (cat. no. 94) or the 1641 *Angel Departing from the Family of Tobias* (B.43). A fourth plate of slightly larger dimensions representing an *Adoration of the Magi* can be added to the group (White/Boon, B. El. 4).[1]

1. A closely related version of the *Adoration of the Shepherds,* which I have not seen, is White/Boon, b, attributed by Van der Kellen to Jan van Noort.

95 (actual size)

Although attribution of these prints must remain speculative, the ornamental loops and flourishes and the shorthand notation of facial features suggest the drawings of Rembrandt's pupil and friend Gerbrand van den Eeckhout, who seems to have studied with Rembrandt in the late 1630s.[2] The one signed etching attributable with some certainty to Eeckhout's own hand, the *Bust of a Young Man with Velvet Cap* of 1646 (Holl. 5), is so different from these in scale and motif as to make comparisons difficult; but, although it is less free in execution, it does reveal a similar combination of ornamental curvilinear contours and regularized crosshatching.

2. See the Eeckhout drawings reproduced in Chicago, 1969, nos. 164–166.

Ferdinand Bol
1616 – 1680

Ferdinand Bol's life, about which we know a surprising amount, is a tale of worldly success and official approval that ends with the artist's abandoning art. Bol was born in Dordrecht in 1616, son of a surgeon. His first teacher is not known, but he may have studied with Jacob Gerritsz. Cuyp, who was the dominant artistic influence in Dordrecht at this time and father of the landscape painter Aelbert Cuyp. In 1635 Bol was still in Dordrecht and already signing himself "painter." Shortly thereafter he moved to Amsterdam, where he resided for the rest of his life. Bol entered the studio of Rembrandt, probably more as a studio assistant than as a pupil, for he was then about twenty years of age. His first independent signed and dated works are from 1642, but he remained stylistically dependent on Rembrandt until 1650.

In 1653 he married into a distinguished Amsterdam family. The family connections seem to have assisted him in gaining official commissions for group portraits and for historical and allegorical paintings for public buildings such as the stately new town hall of Amsterdam. Bol also carried out many private portrait commissions for upper-class Amsterdam families. His first wife died in 1660, and in 1669 he married the wealthy widow of a merchant. His last dated painting is from the year of his second marriage, when he seems to have abandoned art for the life of the wealthy burger and member of the ruling classes, serving as a member of the board of regents of a charitable institution and acquiring a fine house on the Keizersgracht. He died in 1680, a few months after the death of his second wife.[1]

In addition to paintings and numerous drawings, Bol made about sixteen etchings, which date from 1642 to 1651 and reflect strongly the influence of Rembrandt's etchings of the 1630s and early 1640s.[2]

1. Biography in Blankert, 1976, pp. 9–26.
2. For the etchings see Tsuritani, 1974.

96
FERDINAND BOL
St. Jerome in Penitence, 1644

Etching and drypoint
B. 3, Rov. El. 3, Dut. 3¹, Holl. 3¹
At right (on rock): *f bol. fe 1644*
286 x 247 mm. (sheet)
Museum of Fine Arts, Boston, Gift of
Mrs. Samuel Cabot. 51.2402

Ferdinand Bol's 1644 *Saint Jerome* shows no less interest in expressive illumination than Lievens's *Saint Jerome* etching of about 1631 (cat. no. 81); but Bol achieved a soft effulgence of light, whereas in Lievens's print there is a dramatic burst of light in murky darkness. This soft glow of light is close in tonality to Rembrandt's delicate, small 1632 etching of the penitent Saint Jerome kneeling in prayer (B. 101). Like Rembrandt's etching, Bol's has an arched top, and in both works Saint Jerome's faithful lion is provided with an arched den; but the space in the Bol is remarkably shallow when compared with the flow of space in the Rembrandt. The insistent double arch of the Bol emphasizes the anguished, hunched posture of the saint's upper body as he concentrates all his energies on the crucifix he holds clenched in his hands.

The contours of Saint Jerome's head and upper body are very lightly etched and meld with the lightly shaded wall of the cave behind him, evoking a soft pool of light. On the unworked areas of the saint's body a fine, irregular granular tone is visible, apparently resulting from the porosity of the etching ground. This granular tone forms an integral part of the delicate gradation of grays and the concentration on tone rather than on line that characterizes the print. Hercules Segers frequently used a porous ground that left an irregular granular tone on the plate, which he retained and which furthered the painterly aims of his etchings. In the 1640s Rembrandt repeatedly made use of such a granular bitten tone, often in a surprisingly controlled manner (see the portrait of *Sylvius,* cat. no. 97).

148

97

REMBRANDT VAN RIJN
Jan Cornelisz. Sylvius, 1646

Etching, drypoint, and engraving
G. 260, B. 280, Hind 225, Münz 68, BB. 46-E,
W.-B. 280[1]
Upper center: *Rembrandt 1646*
277 x 188 mm. (platemark)
Wm: Strasburg bend and lily (related to Heawood
141)
Coll.: Sir. E. Astley (L. 37); Earl of Aylesford
(L. 58); F. Bullard (L. 982)
Museum of Fine Arts, Boston, Gift of William
Norton Bullard. 23.1017

The preacher Jan Cornelisz. Sylvius (1563/4–
1638) was married to a cousin of Rembrandt's
wife, Saskia, and served as Saskia's guardian.
He also baptized two of Rembrandt's children.
Rembrandt had etched in 1633 a quiet, meditative portrait of Sylvius seated musing at a desk,
eyes cast down, but this posthumous portrait
of 1646 exudes greater vitality. Rembrandt
apparently wished to show that Sylvius's teach-
ings were still alive, that his eloquence had survived the grave. Sylvius, vividly gesturing,
leans out of an oval opening cut in a frame that
suggests the memorial tablets set into church
walls in Rembrandt's time. A diagonal fall of
light singles out the preacher's grave features
and his gesturing hand, throwing transparent
shadows on the opening and the frame.

    Two preparatory drawings for the etching
exist (Benesch 762a and 763). The second is
quite close in conception to the etching, but it
shows Sylvius seated with books before him
instead of holding a book that rests on the
opening of the frame; nor does he appear to
lean as far out of the frame as in the etching. In
painted portraits by Gerrit Pietersz. and Frans
Hals, Rembrandt could have seen earlier examples of the sitter in an oval frame whose gesture
intrudes into our space.[1]

1. Gerrit Pietersz.'s 1606 painting of his brother, the
organist, reproduced in Slive, 1970, vol. 1, fig. 9, and
paintings by Hals reproduced in Slive, 1970, vol. 2, pl. 14
(1615), pl. 81 (1627), and pl. 82 (1627).

In a fine early impression of the *Sylvius* such as the present one, the viewer can fully appreciate the subtle transparency of the shadows and the sense of the fleeting mobility of the lights and shadows. These qualities are in large part a product of the fine meshes of etched line and the even finer passages of drypoint, but they are also the result of a carefully controlled use of an extremely fine granular bitten tone (see detail, introductory essay).[2] This granular tone is not unlike the passages of rather grainy bitten tone seen in the second state of Werner van der Valckert's *Venus* (cat. no. 47) of 1612. Rembrandt employed such a granular bitten tone in a number of etchings of the 1640s, particularly in landscapes, where it contributes a sense of tangible water-laden atmosphere.[3] In the effect it produces it is similar to a nineteenth-century method of achieving a delicate, gray bitten tone, the sulphur tint, in which a paste of oil and flowers of sulphur was applied to the plate, corrosively pitting it.[4] It is difficult to say whether Rembrandt's method involved the use of a porous ground or the direct application of some corrosive substance to the copper plate.[5]

In the *Sylvius* Rembrandt employed this · granular bitten tone to suggest the stony texture of the frame and, far more subtly, the play of light and shadow on Sylvius's head and outstretched hand. The individual grains of the bitten tone are so fine that they read to the naked eye as a continuous tone like a fine wash. To create the highlights in these areas Rembrandt must have either masked certain parts with an acid-resistant substance (a wax or varnish) before biting the plate or scraped and burnished the granular tone after biting the plate. By these means he was able to achieve the brilliant whites of Sylvius's eyes that contribute so much to the intensity of the preacher's expression.

2. I cannot agree with Christopher White's suggestion that these granular tonal effects may be due to scraping and burnishing. The plate is clearly pitted as if bitten by a corrosive substance.

3. *Portrait of a Boy, in profile*, B. 310, 1641; *The Windmill*, B. 233, 1641; *The Three Trees*, B. 212, 1643, cat. no. 133; and *Cottages beside a Canal*, B. 228, about 1645.

4. See a sample of two strengths of sulphur tint printed from a copper plate in Frank Short, *On the Making of Etchings* (London, 1888), pl. 3, fig. 7.

5. A crackle pattern, resulting presumably from the cracking of the ground in a reticulated, mudflat-like pattern, is visible in the *Portrait of a Boy*, B. 310, in *The Windmill*, B. 233, and faintly on Sylvius's face. In one of Bartholomeus Breenbergh's etched Roman ruin views of 1639–40 (Holl. 2), he retained passages of fine, accidental crackling of the ground and used it to describe the texture of the earth and the ruins, burnishing it away in the sky.

98

REMBRANDT VAN RIJN
Christ Preaching (The Hundred Guilder Print), about 1649

Etching, drypoint, and engraving on Japanese paper
G. 75, B. 74, Hind 236 (1649), Münz 217 (1642/5), BB. 49-I, W.-B. 74, only state
285 x 388 mm. (sheet)
Coll.: Damery (L. 2862); Calonne; W. Edwards (L. 2616); W. Esdaile (L. 2617); A. Posonyi (L. 2040-1)
Museum of Fine Arts, Boston, Gift of Mrs. Horatio Greenough Curtis in memory of Horatio Greenough Curtis. 27.1392

Christ Preaching is one of Rembrandt's most ambitious religious compositions in any medium. The subject, which combines various aspects of Christ's ministry as related in the nineteenth chapter of the Gospel of Matthew, had no visual tradition and was Rembrandt's own original invention.

At the right of the etching a crowd of the sick and the crippled implore Christ's aid: "And great multitudes followed him; and he healed them there" (Matthew 19:2). At the far left are the Pharisees who engaged Christ in a debate about divorce (Matthew 19:3–12). Two mothers advance from the left, bringing their children to be blessed. One of Christ's apostles tries to restrain them, but Christ declares: "of

such is the kingdom of heaven" (Matthew 19:13–15). Between the two mothers we see the pondering figure of the rich young man who seeks eternal life, but who goes away troubled when he is told that he should sell all his possessions and give the proceeds to the poor. The camel in the gateway at the right possibly alludes to Christ's statement to his apostles after the young man's departure that it is easier for a camel to pass through the eye of a needle than for a rich man to enter heaven (Matthew 19:16–24).[1]

The chapter closes with Christ's statement that in the scheme of eternal salvation "many that are first shall be last; and the last shall be first." In Rembrandt's etching the throngs of the humble, the poor, and the afflicted are visually dominant over the rich and the powerful.

The traditional title of Rembrandt's etching, "The Hundred Guilder Print," which ironically associates this spiritual image with great monetary value, arises from traditions first recorded in the early eighteenth century about the sum for which Rembrandt sold, traded, or bought back the print at auction. In 1718 Houbraken referred to the print by this title,[2] and the first published catalogue of Rembrandt's prints,

1. The first two stanzas of a poem written by Rembrandt's contemporary H.F. Waterloos on the back of an impression of the second state in the Bibliothèque Nationale, Paris, touch on the various themes brought together here. For the complete Dutch text see Hofstede de Groot, 1906, no. 266. The following English translation of the first two stanzas is given in Bob Haak, *Rembrandt*, trans. Elizabeth Willems-Treeman (New York: Abrams, 1969), p. 214.

Thus Rembrandt's needle paints the son of
God from life,
And sets him 'mid a throng of halt and lame:
So that the World, now sixteen centuries after,
Can see the wonders he hath wrought for all them.
Here Jesus' hand is helping heal the sick. And the
children
(That's Heaven's kingdom!) he doth bless nor let be
hindered.
But (oh!) the Young Man grieves. The scribes with
arrogance
Do scorn the saintly Faith and Christ's holy radiance.

2. Houbraken, 1718, vol. 1, p. 259.

98

that of Gersaint, published in 1751, catalogued the print under this title.

It is generally agreed that Rembrandt worked on the plate over a number of years from about 1639–1640 to about 1649–1650. A large number of preparatory drawings exist for various groups or single figures.[3] Traces of Rembrandt's changes of mind about the presentation of the central figure of Christ are still visible on the plate. Contour lines filled in with shading around Christ's head and shoulders reveal that his figure was once taller. His left hand, now raised, was once lower, and traces of its original contours may be seen on Christ's robe opposite his right hand. Rembrandt's preoccupation with the conception of the head of Christ is revealed by the existence of an oil painting that is a study for Christ's features.[4] In the print Christ's head is drawn in light touches of fine drypoint without firm contours, giving his features a shimmering mobility and indefiniteness in which each viewer can discover his own image of Christ's nature.

The range of styles of drawing reflects the print's execution over a period of several years. An extraordinary aspect of the image is the varying degrees of finish – from the Pharisees at left, who are rendered mostly in outline, to the stream of the afflicted at right, described in a painterly fullness of tone, texture, light, and shadow. The Abbot Filippo Baldinucci, in his historical treatise on engraving and etching published in 1686, characterizes very well the range of degrees of finish or density of work in such a Rembrandt print: "He covered parts of his plate with intense blacks and in other places he permitted the white of the paper to play; and according to the amount of color which he wanted to give to the costume of the figures in the fore- or background, he was satisfied with using a light shadow or even a single stroke and nothing more."[5]

3. For a discussion of the preparatory drawings see White, 1969, pp. 58–61.
4. Fogg Art Museum, Harvard University. See Slive, 1965.
5. Baldinucci, 1686/1808, vol. I, pp. 197–198, as paraphrased in Slive, 1953, pp. 105–106.

In this fine early impression one can see the degree to which the expressive meaning of the print is dependent on the painterly, fluid interplay of light and shadow – from the shadows that soften the mysterious promontory in the background, which gives greater prominence to Christ's figure, to the delicate, transparent shadow cast on Christ's robe by the beseeching woman's hands and profile. This subtle play of light and shadow is abetted by Rembrandt's new, painterly manner of inking an etching plate. In some areas he left a thin film of printer's ink on the unworked areas of the plate to produce an even tone like a wash, and in other areas he wiped this extra ink from the plate with a cloth or with his hand to produce a brighter accent. This expressive use of inking is most evident in the film of ink that veils Christ's right hand and the figure of the apostle and in the subtle luminosity given to Christ's head and upper body by the wiping away of this film.

A number of impressions of this etching are printed on Japanese paper. Rembrandt was the first western printmaker to use this paper. He must have adopted its use shortly after it was first imported into Holland in 1643.[6] The Japanese papers – available to Rembrandt in a range of colors from dark buff to white and in weights from heavy to tissue thin – are very fine fibered and unusually receptive to the printer's ink. Less absorbent and less coarse fibered than European papers, they were ideal for registering every nuance of tone in impressions in which Rembrandt painted with printer's ink on the copper plate. Here the Japanese paper is quite heavy, and the film of different densities of the cool black of the printer's ink over the warmer light buff of the paper subtly enriches the image coloristically.[7]

6. Fabricated from the fibers of the *gampi* plant and available in seventeenth-century Holland as a result of the Dutch merchants' exclusive trade agreements with Japan, these papers were rarely used for prints and drawings in other European countries before the nineteenth century. Several artists around Rembrandt also used Japanese papers on occasion for their prints: for example, the landscape etchings of Philips Koninck and Pieter de With and Ferdinand Bol's *Holy Family* (cat. no. 100). Jan Lievens

frequently made landscape drawings on Japanese paper. Lievens did not customarily use Japanese paper for prints, but an impression of his rare woodcut *Bust of a Man* (Holl. 105) on Japanese paper is in the collection of the Museum of Fine Arts, Boston. In addition, most of Simon de Vlieger's etchings occur in impressions on Japanese paper. For Rembrandt's use of Japanese papers, see Sue W. Reed in Boston/New York, 1969, p. 180; see also Washington, 1977, pp. 13–15.

7. Aside from the precious connotation of the paper's silken texture, Rembrandt also undoubtedly appreciated the paper's exotic connotations. In this context it is interesting that his drawn copies of figures from Indian miniatures were usually made on Japanese paper. In Rembrandt's mind the Orient was often identical with biblical antiquity.

99

REMBRANDT VAN RIJN
Saint Jerome in a Dark Chamber, 1642

Etching, drypoint, and engraving
G. 106, B. 105, Hind 201, Münz 247, BB. 42-E, W.-B. 105[1]
Lower center: *Rembrandt f. 1642*
151 x 173 mm. (platemark)
Coll.: A. Firmin-Didot (L. 119)
Museum of Fine Arts, Boston, Gift of Lydia Evans Tunnard in memory of W.G. Russell Allen. 61.1363

In Rembrandt's 1642 etching of St. Jerome in a dark interior, the seventeenth-century Dutch artist's search for dark tonalities in printmaking reached a climax. The next step was to be the invention of the medium of mezzotint, which achieved the dense, velvety blacks of Rembrandt's print by means of a mechanical device. The first mezzotint was, in fact, produced in Amsterdam in the same year by an Utrecht-born military man and amateur artist attached to the court at Cassel, Ludwig von Siegen (1609–after 1676).[1] Von Siegen's portrait of his patroness, Amelia Elizabeth, Landgravine of Hesse (Andr. 1), a stiff, rather primitive portrait bust, does not have the overall dark tonality of the Rembrandt, but by means of the roulette (a spiked wheel on a stick) Von Siegen was able to achieve a dotted, mechanical tone, which in some of the more densely worked areas of the plate results in a

1. For Von Siegen and the beginnings of mezzotint see Hind, 1923, pp. 258ff.; Pissarro, 1956–1958.

99 (actual size)

154

deep velvety black. It was to be another fifteen years before Prince Ruprecht, a German nobleman, military leader, and amateur printmaker with close family connections to the court circles of London and the Hague, would develop the mezzotint process as we know it today. This involved the invention of another tool, the rocker or hatcher, by means of which the entire surface of the plate was roughened, producing deep, velvety blacks when printed (see Glossary). The light areas were created by scraping and burnishing the roughened surface.

Rembrandt did not use a novel tool or device to evoke the darkness in which he envelops St. Jerome's study. He simply carried further and applied less systematically the closely laid mesh of lines that had described darkness in earlier prints by Hendrik Goudt (cat. nos. 44, 45) and Jan van de Velde (61). The lines are now so fine and the mesh of lines so dense and irregular that one is scarcely conscious of line at all except in the divisions of the bright windows. The darkness is so profound that St. Jerome's lion is swallowed up by the shadows in front of the table. Only the top of the crucifix is visible in the light from the window. St. Jerome's cardinal's hat is barely discernible hanging from the spiral staircase. Only the skull, symbol of mortality, and the book are clearly visible. If it were not for one or two significant details, one might assume that the etching represented a philosopher or scholar.[2] The image in fact relates closely in conception to a 1633 Rembrandt painting of a scholar meditating in an interior with a spiral staircase (Louvre, Paris, Bredius 431).

In northern Europe, the image of Jerome, translator of the Bible into Latin, as the scholarly or humanist saint was formed to a great extent by Albrecht Dürer's brilliant engraving of 1514 (B. 60), which represents Jerome industriously writing at his desk in a study filled with sunlight. There the space of the room and every object in it are defined with crystalline clarity. Rembrandt, whose later portraits are so concerned with interior thoughts and feelings – with introspection – presents Jerome with eyes closed, his head resting on his hand, in meditation or prayer. Cloaked in darkness, its boundaries unclear, the room takes on an air of mystery. The half-seen twisting stair beneath which Jerome sits in thought becomes poetic and metaphorical, suggesting the convolutions of the human mind or soul.

A comparison of the 1642 St. Jerome with another etching of 1642, the delicate, sunlit *Raising of Lazarus* (cat. no. 94) dramatically illustrates the extreme tonal variety of which Rembrandt was capable in these years. Fine impressions of the *St. Jerome* are scarce, for, as in a mezzotint, the depth of the velvety blacks depends on the preservation of the printed surface in fresh condition. When rubbed, the denser dark areas become glossy, emphasizing the paper surface rather than the depth of the shadows.

2. As suggested by Hind, 1923, no. 201.

100
FERDINAND BOL
The Holy Family in an Interior, 1643

Etching, drypoint, and engraving
B. 4, Rov. El. 4, Dut. 4, Holl. 4
At right (in window): *F Bol 1643*
185 x 217 mm. (platemark)
Coll.: F. Rechberger (L. 2133); H.F. Sewall (L. 1309)
Museum of Fine Arts, Boston, Harvey D. Parker Collection. P8851

Ferdinand Bol's 1643 *Holy Family in an Interior* is one of his most expressive prints.[1] It was directly influenced by Rembrandt, not only by the dark interior of his *St. Jerome* etching of the previous year (cat. no. 99) but also by his 1640 painting of the *Holy Family,* in the Louvre (Bredius 563). The window, the architecture around it, as well as the motif of the nursing mother in Bol's *Holy Family* relate closely to Rembrandt's painting. In considering the influence of Rembrandt's 1642 *Jerome* on the Bol etching, it is interesting to note that in Bol's preparatory drawing for the etching in the British Museum[2] the interior is far lighter and the furnishings are far more legible than in the etching. The lines of Bol's etching are broader and the mesh lines more transparent, disclosing more domestic detail, than in Rembrandt's etching. The darkness does not have the metaphorical overtones that it has in the Rembrandt. Bol's image makes the Holy Family more accessible by emphasizing mundane domestic detail. Mary gives her breast to the Child, while Joseph solicitously hovers, holding out a towel, diaper, or swaddling cloth. A cat studies the intimate family scene from the fireplace corner. At the left rear is a Dutch bed of the built-in cupboard type and, standing on end before it, a wicker *bakermat,* a kind of legless couch or cradle that was placed on the floor for a nursing mother to sit in.

1. The date has been read as "1649" and "1645" (Hollstein). Hind in London, cat. drawings, 1915, vol. 1, p. 61, and Tsuritani, 1974, no. 4, read it correctly.
2. London, cat. drawings, vol. 1, 1915, p. 61, Bol, no. 1; Sumowski, vol. 1, Bol, no. 95.

Adriaen van Ostade
1610 – 1685

In the nineteenth and early twentieth century Adriaen van Ostade, a painter of scenes from peasant life, was probably the most acclaimed seventeenth-century Dutch etcher after Rembrandt. Ostade made fifty etchings, the dated ones ranging from 1647 to 1679. In his dated prints can be traced the broad outlines of the development of Dutch etching during this period. The early etchings are less concerned with line than with painterly textures, subtle tonal relationships, and atmospheric values. The later etchings are characterized by firm contour drawing and simple but strong value contrasts; forms have a sculptural solidity. Ostade's former concern with painterly textures or atmospheric values has been essentially abandoned. After Ostade's death in 1685 his son-in-law advertised for sale his fifty etching plates and all the surviving impressions.[1]

Ostade was born in Haarlem in 1610 and resided there throughout his life. His father, who was probably a weaver, had moved from Eindhoven to Haarlem, which was a center of the textile industry. The village of Ostade is near Eindhoven. According to Houbraken, Ostade studied with Frans Hals at the same time as Adriaen Brouwer, the Flemish painter of low-life subjects. Ostade's early paintings show no trace of Hals's influence, but they do reflect the art of Brouwer. Ostade married in 1638 and a second time in 1657. The high fees he paid for the interment of his wives (1642 and 1666) in St. Bavo suggest that he was prosperous. He was active in the artists' guild and was a member of the civic guard. Among his pupils were his brother Isaak van Ostade, Cornelis Dusart, and Cornelis Bega. He was a prolific draftsman and in his later career produced many finished watercolors. In addition to scenes of peasant life, he painted a few portraits, biblical subjects, and one or two landscapes.

1. See biographical information in Van der Willigen, 1870, pp. 233–241; MacLaren, 1960, pp. 282–283.

101
ADRIAEN VAN OSTADE
The Family, 1647

Etching
B. 46[1], Dut. 46[1], Davidsohn 46[1], Godefroy 46[1], Holl. 46[1]
Lower right: *AvOstade 1647*
179 x 159 mm. (platemark)
Wm.: foolscap
Coll.: F.S. Haden (L. 1227)
Museum of Fine Arts, Boston, Gift of Lydia Evans Tunnard in memory of W.G. Russell Allen. 63.2846

Visual pleasure in picturesque dilapidation – in things strewn about, broken, tattered, and torn reaches a high point in the interiors of Adiaen van Ostade of the 1640s. Abraham Bloemaert had already formulated this aesthetic in his paintings and drawings of farmyards and farmhouses and the etchings made after them, but Ostade takes this aesthetic of picturesque litter further, providing a vivid, painterly characterization of the worn and battered texture of things. The etching *The Family* of 1647 is one of the finest examples of this aesthetic: the barn-like interior is crammed to the rafters with hams, tubs, candlesticks, and reels for winding yarn. Everything is drawn in irregular, sketchy, broken strokes, lending surfaces an appropriately shaggy or crumbly texture.

Attention is divided equally between the details of the room's furnishings and the intimate family group at their dinner. The family is described with a good deal of tenderness. While the mother feeds the baby, the father does his part in the household duties, slicing bread or cheese. In another Ostade print of 1648, the *Father of the Family* (B. 33), the father is seated in front of the fire, feeding the child. This close family feeling is characteristic of Ostade's peasant families. The interiors themselves may be shabby and cluttered, but they are never truly squalid. Whether this rather rosy picture of peasant life reflects the relative security and prosperity of the Dutch peasantry in Ostade's time or the desire of the middle- and upper-class consumers of the images to be reassured about the state of the peasantry is difficult to say.

The etching is seen here in the relatively rare first state in etching only, fully signed and dated, before subsequent additions in etching, drypoint, and engraving. The shadows are transparent, the tonal structure consists of a delicate range of grays, and the lighting pattern is more diffuse than in the following state, with its additional work in etching and drypoint. In the second state the family group is much more clearly defined by a triangular wedge of light. Ostade's etchings characteristically go through a number of states in which the shadows and modeling become stronger, but it is frequently difficult to know where Ostade left off and the foreign hands of publishers took over after his death. The stronger contrasts and deeper shadows added by the artist or by a publisher meant a longer printing life for the image.

A pen and wash study for the etching is in the collection of the Pierpont Morgan Library.[1] It is close in scale and detail to the etching but is not in reverse and was therefore probably not the final preparatory drawing used to trace the image onto the plate.

This Ostade etching is precisely the kind of image that inspired the eccentric nineteenth-century French printmaker Rodolphe Bresdin to create prints of peasant interiors swarming with detail.

1. Paris/New York, 1979–80, no. 889

101 (actual size)

158

102
ADRIAEN VAN OSTADE
The Barn, 1647

Etching
B. 23, Dut. 23[III], Davidsohn 23[VII], Godefroy 23[VI],
Holl. 23[VI]
Lower left: *AvOstade 1647*
157 x 192 mm. (platemark)
Wm.: letters RAH? [difficult to read]
Coll.: T. Philipe? (L. 2451a); Buccleuch (L. 402);
Von Lanna (L. 2773); Hachette (L. 132)
Yale University Art Gallery, Everett V. Meeks, B.A.
1901, Fund. 1965.9.43

Adriaen van Ostade's etching of a barn, made
the same year as *The Family* (cat. no. 101), was
a radical conception for its time in that the
principal subject is the interior itself – its space,
light, and texture. The anonymous figure of a
peasant woman bends over in a far corner
while chickens roost or scratch in the foreground, but they are subordinate to the mood
of the interior as a whole; the latticed pattern
of light and shadow and the shaggy textures of
hay and thatch.

Ostade had been anticipated in his choice of
motif by Pieter van Laer in an etching from his
animal series, published in Rome in 1636. In
Van Laer's rather startling and quirky conception we find ourselves in a dark interior strewn
with farm implements. We look toward the
bright rectangle of a doorway through which
we are stared at curiously by two donkeys and a
dog (see illus.). Pieter van Laer's line work is
somewhat dry and bristly, however, and lacks
the depth of texture of the Ostade – the sense
of layer upon layer of things mossy, shaggy,
and frayed.

Ostade made a number of drawn studies of
barn interiors comparable to that in the
etching.

102

Pieter van Laer
The Mules, 1636
Etching and drypoint
Museum of Fine Arts, Boston

159

Simon de Vlieger
about 1600/01 – 1653

Simon de Vlieger, one of the leading Dutch painters of marine subjects, made some eighteen to twenty etchings,[1] none of which are true marine views in the sense of Zeeman's or Bakhuizen's etchings. They consist of woodland and river views, a village street, a beach scene with fisherfolk, a southern view with ruins (cat. no. 121), and a set of ten etchings of animals.

De Vlieger was born in Rotterdam about 1600–01. Nothing is known of his artistic education. He married in Rotterdam in 1627, and in 1634 he was in Delft, where he was enrolled that year as a member of the artists' guild. In 1638 he moved to Amsterdam, where he became a citizen in 1643. In 1650 he bought a house in Weesp, near Amsterdam. He died there in 1653.[2] He was the teacher of the important marine painters Willem van de Velde II and Jan van de Capelle. His son-in-law was the animal painter and etcher Paulus van Hillegaert.

In addition to marine views, De Vlieger painted landscapes, scenes from everyday life, and portraits. There are records of official commissions; in 1640 and 1641 he was paid for tapestry designs for the city of Delft, in 1642 he was commissioned to paint the wings of the organ of the Groote Kerk in Rotterdam, and in 1645 he contracted to design windows for Amsterdam's Nieuwe Kerk. He also made drawings for book illustration (see cat. no. 85).

1. Dutuit 1 and 2, although both eventually receive an engraved "S.D.V." monogram, are so different in style from the other etchings that one questions whether they are by De Vlieger or whether they are works by another hand added by a publisher to De Vlieger's prints after the artist's death.

2. Biography in MacLaren, 1960, pp. 442–443.

103
SIMON DE VLIEGER
The Two Hogs

From a series of ten etchings
Etching and drypoint
B. 16, Dut. 16
Upper left: [monogram in reverse] *S DE V*
132 x 157 mm. (platemark)
Wm.: undecipherable fragment
Museum of Fine Arts, Boston, Stephen Bullard Memorial Fund. 1972.214

After Pieter van Laer's series of animal etchings published in Rome in 1636, the series of ten animal etchings by Simon de Vlieger is perhaps the most significant and influential such series by a seventeenth-century Dutch painter.[1] In Van Laer's series the herders still play an important role, but in De Vlieger's etchings human beings rarely appear, and the animals are generally placed in the immediate foreground. They are not scenes from daily life with animals in a landscape setting; they are full-fledged animal pieces. The series includes birds (geese and turkeys) as well as mammals. All the animals are domesticated except the mountain goats of Dut. 19.

1. Taking into account the overall development of tonality and graphic style in Dutch printmaking of this time, I have placed this undated series with etched works of the 1640s. Jan Kelch, who prepared a dissertation on Simon de Vlieger (Berlin, 1963), suggested to me in conversation that the animal etchings might be as early as the 1630s. A date in the 1630s is also suggested in the catalogue of the Lugt drawings, New York/Paris, 1977–78, no. 123, p. 181, on the basis of the Lugt 1629 black chalk drawing of goats and the Berlin chalk drawing of goats dated in the 1630s (last digit difficult to read; Berlin, cat. drawings, 1931, no. 12505). In my opinion, however, the use of line in these drawings is too ornamental to serve as a valid comparison with the etchings, which are more tonal in conception.

The first dated work by De Vlieger from the 1630s that seems to provide some analogy with the animal etchings is the 1637 painting of the *Falconer's Return* in the Rijksmuseum (inv. no. A 1981, reproduced in Bernt, 1970, vol. 3, no. 1317), which is closely related to Rembrandt's *Good Samaritan* etching (cat. no. 74) in motif and illumination. The horse and dogs of the painting are reasonably close in conception to those in the etched series.

The sleepy bulk of the two hogs is wonderfully described. De Vlieger has used drypoint with and without burr to characterize the bristly coat of the nearer of the two. Apart from Rembrandt, De Vlieger was one of the few artists who used drypoint with burr. Drypoint without burr can achieve an incredibly fine line and was employed by many seventeenth-century Dutch printmakers to add fine supplementary detail or to lightly sketch in the distance seen through a haze of atmosphere or the clouds of the sky.

Like Adriaen van Ostade in his etching of a barn interior (cat. no. 102), De Vlieger is here concerned more with painterly texture than with contour drawing. Everything is fibrous: hog bristles juxtaposed against reeds, against wickerwork, hay, and coarse wood grain.

This series can also be found printed on warm-toned Japanese paper (British Museum, Sheepshanks Collection) as can the majority of De Vlieger's etchings. De Vlieger was one of a very small number of Dutch printmakers (Ferdinand Bol, Philips Koninck, and Pieter de With), apart from Rembrandt, who used Japanese paper.

103 (actual size)

104 (actual size)

104

ADRIAEN VAN OSTADE
Slaughtering the Hog

Etching, drypoint, and engraving
B. 41^I, Dut. 41^{III}, Davidsohn 41^V, Godefroy 41^V,
Holl. 41^V
Lower left: *Av Ostade*
117 x 116 mm. (platemark)
Coll.: Buccleuch (L. 402); Von Lanna (L. 2773);
Brayton Ives; P.J. Sachs (L. 2091); H.G. French
(L. 1307a)
Cincinnati Art Museum, Bequest of Herbert Green
French. 1943.338

In the Netherlands, hog slaughtering was one
of the activities traditionally associated with
the cycle of the months. The name for November in Dutch is *slachtmaand* (slaughtering
month), the month when provisions were laid
up against the winter.[1] Ostade's print is a single
image, however, and does not form part of a
series.

Here an entire peasant family is gathered in
a ring to witness and participate in this important event. The circular format echoes the circle
of spectators. As a man kneels to cut the pig's
throat, a woman holds out a long-handled pan
to catch the blood.[2] Ostade handles this with a
good deal of discretion, whereas his pupil
Cornelis Dusart, in *November* from his mezzotint cycle of the months (Holl. 30), shows us
the same from the other side, with crude gusto
and sparing no detail.

On the basis of comparison with Ostade's
dated prints, this etching can be dated to the
period 1647–48 to 1652–53. In the successive
states the shadows of this night scene become
progressively denser. In the state shown here
they have depth but are still fairly transparent.
Ostade's scribbling, unsystematic web of lines
that defines the darkness is far removed from
the regularized, systematic vocabulary of
Goudt (cat. nos. 44, 45) and Jan van de Velde
(cat. no. 61).

1. In Pieter Bruegel's drawing of *Prudentia,* hog slaughtering is one of the symbols of prudence or foresight.
See De Jongh in Amsterdam, 1976, no. 24, p. 117.

2. Probably to make blood sausage.

105

REMBRANDT VAN RIJN

The Hog, 1643

Etching and drypoint
C. 152, B. 157, Hind 204, Münz 265, BB. 43-A,
W.-B. 157[1]
Lower right: *Rembrandt f. 1643*
144 x 184 mm. (platemark)
Wm.: fragment of coat of arms with fleur-de-lis
(see Wibiral 8)
Coll.: Maberly; Galichon; Gutekunst; G. Hibbert
(L. 2849); Th. Irwin (L. 1540); Th. M. Whitehead
(similar to L. 2449)
The Pierpont Morgan Library, New York

Rembrandt's 1643 etching may at first sight
seem to be only a study of a trussed pig, but a
closer reading of the lightly sketched activities
of the background suggests that it is related in
subject to Adriaen van Ostade's etching (cat.
no. 104). The father of the family holds a basket and possibly an axe cradled in his right arm,
while his left hand grasps a curved yoke from
which to suspend the hog's carcass. Before him
a trough to be used in the slaughtering leans
against the wall.[1] At left the mother of the family shows the baby, who wears a helmet-like
head protector, the source of their winter's
food. The boy at right, in front of the trough,
holds an inflated pig's bladder and a straw to
blow it up or a pin to puncture it. The latter
motif, like the related one of the child blowing
fragile soap bubbles (see cat. nos. 178 and
194), was a seventeenth-century Dutch
emblem of mortality.[2] Thus, it is very likely not
just the fate of the hog that is alluded to but
also the brevity of life in general.

The individual, almost portrait-like characterization of the trussed animal dominates the
print. There are a number of drawn studies of
hogs by Rembrandt from this time, including a
sheet with a trussed hog (Benesch 777), which

1. Many of these implements, such as the curved yoke and
bladder and the trough, are present in Dusart's *November*
mezzotint (Holl. 30).

2. See De Jongh's discussion of Barent Fabritius's painting of an interior with a slaughtered hog and children
inflating bladders, in Amsterdam, 1976, no. 24,
pp. 117–119.

105

163

may be related to the evolution of the etched image. In the etching, only the hog is described with a full range of textural and coloristic suggestion. It is interesting that Rembrandt should have chosen the moment just before the animal is slaughtered; the usual motif in prints and paintings of the Dutch seventeenth century is either the slaughtering itself, as in the Ostade etching, or the dressed carcass hanging from a yoke and ladder. Although one is wary of imposing an anachronistic or falsely sentimental interpretation, Rembrandt has so structured the image that it is difficult not to feel a certain identification with the fate of the animal.

106

REMBRANDT VAN RIJN
A Sheet of Sketches (Saskia ill in bed, beggars), about 1641–42

Etching
G. 335, B. 369, Hind 163 (1639), Münz 96 (1641/2), BB. 38-2, W.-B. 369, only state
138 x 150 mm. (platemark)
Coll.: C. Delanglade (L. 660)
Fogg Art Museum, Harvard University, Purchase, Hyatt and Prichard Funds

On several occasions Rembrandt treated the etching plate like a sketch page, bringing together on the same surface loosely associated sketches or studies.[1] Perhaps the most radical example is the present etching, which can be read either vertically or horizontally. Two different groups of studies are juxtaposed here: sketches of a woman, possibly the artist's wife, Saskia, reclining in bed, ill or recovering from childbirth. Rembrandt made a number of drawings of Saskia in bed on such occasions until her death in 1642. The plate shown here is usually dated in the period 1639–1642. The studies of the woman in bed have some of the extreme delicacy of line that we see in the little etched plate of a bust of a sick woman, presumed to be Saskia in her last illness (B. 359).

The other studies on the plate are of beggars or lepers, who announce their coming with a clapper. In this fine impression the contrast between the more heavily modeled and shaded figures of the beggars at the lower left and the more delicate sketches is very apparent. The sketches on the plate may at first sight seem ill-sorted, but the likelihood that the woman in bed is recovering from an illness combines with the miserable plight of the beggars to give a kind of melancholy emotional unity to the whole.

Aside from his own constant sketching activity, Rembrandt could have been stimulated to treat the etching plate as a sketch sheet by the example of the series of plates with assorted studies, intended as models for young draftsmen, by artists such as the Italian painter Palma Giovane (first published 1611)[2] or the Spanish painter working in Naples, Jusepe Ribera (B. 15, 16, 17, about 1622).[3] The Italian etcher Stefano della Bella published various etched series of models for beginning draftsmen or "sketches" (*griffonnements*) in Paris in the 1640s and early 1650s.

2. Vienna, 1966, pp. 157–158.
3. Princeton/Harvard, 1973–74, pp. 69–71.

1. See also B. 363, 365–370, 372, 374.

(actual size)

Geertruydt Roghman
born 1625

Professional women printmakers were relatively rare in Holland in the seventeenth century. Like Magdalena van de Passe or Geertruydt Roghman, they were usually members of families of professional printmakers.[1] There were also amateur or dilettante women printmakers such as the learned Anna Maria Schurman and the poet Anna Maria de Koker.

Geertruydt Roghman was the daughter of the engraver Hendrik Lambertsz. Roghman and sister of the painter and etcher Roelant Roghman. Her mother, Maria, was the sister of the painter Roelant Savery. Geertruydt's sister Magdalena also engraved. Geertruydt was born in Amsterdam in 1625, but we have no other information about her life. She signed her name or initials to about thirteen engravings and etchings, including part of a series of landscapes etched after designs by her brother (Holl. 9–22). The Amsterdam printmaker Claes Jansz. Visscher was usually her publisher.[2] Though less skilled as an engraver than Magdalena van de Passe, Geertruydt engraved one series of the household tasks of women after her own designs that was exceptionally original in subject and conception.

1. For other women printmakers of the sixteenth through the eighteenth century, see Rotterdam, 1975–76, pp. 27–31.
2. Biographical information in Hollstein, vol. 20.

107

GEERTRUYDT ROGHMAN
Woman Spinning

No. 4 from a series of five engravings
Engraving
Nag. 17, Dut. vol. 6, p. 21, no. 4, Wurz. 5, Holl. 5[1]
Lower left: *Geertruyt Roghman / invenit et Sculpsit;*
lower right: *4*
207 x 166 mm. (platemark)
Rijksmuseum, Amsterdam. OB4231

One of our most common images of
seventeenth-century Dutch painting is the
light-filled interior of a house with women
going about their household tasks. Such
imagery is, however, extremely uncommon in
printmaking outside the sphere of book illustration. It is interesting that a series of five
engravings of household tasks of women designed and engraved by a woman, Geertruydt
Roghman, should prove to be an exception.
These are the only original designs we know
by Geertruydt Roghman.

All of the engravings in the series present
scenes of domestic activities in quite an objective manner except for the second engraving,
which represents a mournful-looking young
woman seated reading a letter (probably a love
letter), while on the wall can be seen a clock
and on the floor behind her chair a skull. The
eternal Dutch *Vanitas* theme has surfaced once
again!

The engravings are executed in a conventional engraving style, and the drawing is
sometimes a bit clumsy in the academic sense
(see, for example, the foreshortening of the
spinner's head), but the overall conception is
usually quite bold. All of the engravings
include strong indications of light falling into
the interior or being cast by a fire. Here the
spinner turns her back to us, and her features
are in shadow, while the little girl's frank,
examining stare is dramatized by the wedge of
light that singles her out. The child is seated on
a footwarmer, a wooden box pierced with holes
in which a dish of hot coals was placed.

107

166

Herman Saftleven
1609 – 1685

The etchings of the painter Herman Saftleven are more consistently high in quality than his paintings and show the same diversity of style as the paintings. Saftleven's etchings number about forty and range in date from 1627-1669. The earliest are landscapes that reveal the influence of Willem Buytewech; the latest are Rhineland views that, surprisingly, show the influence of the later Flemish followers of Pieter Bruegel. Many of his best works of the 1640s reflect the landscapes of Jan Both, the Utrecht painter and etcher of idyllic southern views. Most of Saftleven's etchings are landscapes or topographic views, but the series of small proverbial figures from daily life (Dut. 2–11) and the large etching of *Elephants* are lively exceptions.

A member of the third generation of a family of painters, Herman Hermansz. Saftleven was born in Rotterdam in 1609. By 1633 he was in Utrecht, where he was married in that year. He lived in Utrecht for the rest of his life except for a period of residence in the Rhineland (in 1667 he was resident in Elberfield). He was active in the artists' guild of Utrecht and received topographical commissions from the city. He died there in 1685.[1]

1. For Saftleven's biography see Wolfgang Stechow in Thieme-Becker, vol. 29, pp. 310–311; MacLaren, 1960, pp. 310–311. For Saftleven's development as a painter, see Nieuwstraaten, 1965, pp. 81ff.

108–111
HERMAN SAFTLEVEN
Four genre figures from a series of nine etchings, 1647
Museum Boymans-van Beuningen, Rotterdam

108 (actual size)

109 (actual size)

110 (actual size)

111 (actual size)

108
Vloije vanger (Flea catcher)

Etching and drypoint
B. 10, Dut. 10
Lower left: *HS 1647*
49 x 38 mm. (platemark)

109
Liefde (Love)

Etching and drypoint
B. 7, Dut. 7
Lower right: *HS 1647*
48 x 36 mm. (platemark)

110
Hennetaster (Hen feeler)

Etching
B. 5, Dut. 5
Lower right: *HS 1647*
49 x 36 mm. (platemark)

111
Gorttentelder (Barley counter)

Etching
B. 4, Dut. 4
Lower right: *HS 1647*
50 x 37 mm. (platemark)

In Saftleven's series of single figures from daily life each one embodies or acts out a certain quality, action, or popular expression.[1] A young man fleas his dog (*vloije vanger:* "flea catcher") or a robust peasant mother nursing her strapping child represents love (*liefde*). The *Hennetaster* and the *Gorttentelder* represent more proverbial expressions. A *hennetaster* is literally a person who feels the hen to assure himself that it is laying an egg,[2] but the phrase can also mean a man who busies himself with domestic details of house and kitchen or a man dominated by his wife (hen-pecked).[3] A *gort-tentelder* is a man who counts every grain of barley, a miserly person or nit-picker,[4] and like *hennetaster,* the word can refer to a man dominated by his wife.[5] Both are figures of fun and ridicule.

The firmly drawn, solidly modeled, stocky figures in this series are in the tradition of Pieter Bruegel's sturdy barrel-like peasants. They are not executed with the sketchy freedom of Rembrandt's 1630 *Beggar* (cat. no. 71) but have a sculptural solidity. Distant background details are scratched in with fine drypoint lines. Small drawings by Saftleven of peasant figures executed in black chalk and watercolor on the backs of playing cards compare closely in style.[6]

Aside from providing amusement, etched or engraved series of single figures such as these, from the life of the streets or the working classes, probably provided other artists with a ready fund of figures with which to people their compositions when they lacked inspiration or were incapable of drawing figures well. Similar series were executed or designed by Pieter Quast, Salomon Savery, Gillis van Scheyndel, Jan Porcellis, J.J. van Vliet, and by Herman's brother, Cornelis Saftleven.

1. Dut. 11, an undated etching of a peasant carrying a bundle of brush on a stick, is not part of the series. Though close in style, it is smaller in scale and lacks an engraved title.

2. Ter Laan, 1963, p. 142.

3. Van Dale, 1970, p. 781.

4. Ter Laan, 1963, p. 118.

5. Van Dale, 1970, p. 696.

6. See examples in the Ashmolean collection, Oxford, cat. drawings, 1938, vol. 1, nos. 212, 213.

112
ADRIAEN VAN OSTADE
The Dance under the Trellis, 1648–1652

Etching
B. 47, Dut. 47[II], Davidsohn 47[II], Godefroy 47[III], Holl. 47[III]
Lower right: *Av ostade*
123 x 175 mm. (platemark)
Wm.: phoenix in laurel wreath (probably Heawood 200, Churchill 499, Godefroy 33)
Museum of Fine Arts, Boston, Gift of Mrs. Lydia Evans Tunnard in memory of W. G. Russell Allen. 63.2847

In the *Dance under the Trellis,* Ostade seems to have been more interested in conveying a sense of the continuous flow and deep recession of space and of the immersion of figures, buildings, and vegetation in light and atmosphere than in the antics of individual participants. The most distant details dissolve completely in the haze. These preoccupations are pointed up when one compares Ostade's etching with Molenaer's etching of carousing peasants before an inn (cat. no. 73), in which the various elements are not unified by enveloping light and atmosphere and in which there is a robust pleasure in the coarse details of the drinking party.

This undated etching should be placed between Ostade's *Charlatan* of 1648 (B. 43) and his *Woman Spinning* of 1652 (B. 31). Godefroy proposed a tentative date of 1652, but I would suggest an earlier date because of the tonal refinement of the print. This is especially evident in the present impression, in which the plate has been printed with a light grayish film of extra ink.

There is a pen and wash preparatory drawing in reverse for the etching in the Lugt collection of the Institut Néerlandais, Paris.[1]

1. Inv. 3523, reproduced in Godefroy, 1930, no. 47.

112 (actual size)

Anthonie Waterloo
about 1610 – 1690

About 126 etchings by the draftsman and printmaker Anthonie Waterloo survive in great numbers of impressions,[1] but only rarely does one have the opportunity to see early impressions or to separate them from the overwhelming mass of later or posthumous impressions that distort the image of Waterloo's work in etching. The aesthetic confusion is not helped by the fact that Waterloo was fond of using, particularly in his later prints, rather harsh drypoint and burin lines to supplement the etched line and thereby achieve strong lighting and modeling. It is sometimes difficult to separate Waterloo's own harsher passages from insensitive reworking by later publishers.

Anthonie Waterloo was born in Lille about 1610. His artistic training is not known, and he may have been self-taught. Waterloo moved about a great deal, first settling near Utrecht. In 1640 his marriage was registered in Amsterdam. He is next found in Leeuwarden in Friesland, where he became a citizen in 1643. After another period in Amsterdam he was back in Leeuwarden in 1654. He finally settled in Utrecht, where he died in 1690. He not only shifted his place of residence frequently but also traveled a great deal in northern and southern Germany, the South Netherlands, and possibly in Italy.[2]

Waterloo was almost exclusively a landscape artist. Only a small number of paintings are known, but a large number of drawings as well as prints survive. The great popularity of his woodland views in the late eighteenth and early nineteenth century and their imitation by artists of that time have sometimes made it difficult for modern viewers to see his work with fresh eyes.

113

ANTHONIE WATERLOO
The Cart on the Road before a Coastal Village

Etching and drypoint
Dut. 15[1], Wessely 15[1]
97 x 140 mm. (platemark)
Coll.: J. Sheepshanks (see L. 2333)
Lent by the Trustees of the British Museum

Not a single print in Anthonie Waterloo's large and varied production of landscape etchings is dated.[1] There is, however, an early group of etchings, small in scale and horizontal in format, that parallel the drawn and painted landscapes of Jan van Goyen dating from the 1630s and 1640s in their concern with a tangible sense of atmosphere and broad but subtly graded tonal effects.[2] *The Cart on the Road*[3] belongs to this group and, in a rare early state before reworking such as the present one, conveys much the same sense of Holland's frequently misty, water-charged atmosphere as does Ostade's *Dance under the Trellis* (cat. no. 112). The conception of the subject as a whole is remarkably similar to that of Jan van Goyen's 1646 painting of the *Beach at Egmond aan Zee* in the Louvre.[4]

Waterloo's black chalk study for the etching in the same direction, in the collection of the British Museum, shows a style of drawing that is close to Van Goyen's.[5] The study is even lighter, softer, and grayer in tonality than the etching. The sky is less fully developed than in the print, the church steeple is less acute, and there is a slightly different disposition of the houses of the village. In the print fine drypoint lines have been used to convey the feathery softness of the clouds.

5. London, cat. drawings, 1931, vol. 4, p. 106, no. 24.

1. Dutuit lists 136 etchings. He rightly noted that Dutuit 17 is a print by Barent Graat that a later publisher added to Waterloo's prints when republishing them. To the confusion of cataloguers, Waterloo himself seems to have reworked and republished nine of Johannes Ruisscher's etchings (Dutuit 1, 2, 19, 20, 39, 40, 90, 91, and 93) with the inscription "A. W. ex." In the Amsterdam Segers exhibition catalogue of 1967 and in Eduard Trautscholdt's catalogue of Ruisscher's etchings in Haverkamp-Begemann, 1973, pp. 113ff., these prints were reclaimed as Ruisscher's work.

2. Biography by Hans Vollmer in Thieme-Becker, vol. 35, pp. 181-182.

1. The selection reproduced in De Groot, 1979, pls. 148-162, gives a good idea of the diversity of scale, format, and style to be found in Waterloo's etched work.

2. For the early prints see the series in which the present print is included, Dut. 7–18, 21–32.

3. The etching has been traditionally catalogued as *The Cart on the Road to Scheveningen,* but the church tower in the etching is not that of Scheveningen's church.

4. Stechow, 1966, pl. 203.

113 (actual size)

HERMAN SAFTLEVEN
The Wittevrouwen-poort, Utrecht, 1646

Etching and drypoint
B. 29, Weig. 29^{I}, Dut. 29^{II}
Below: *HS…A.º 1646.*
273 x 231 mm. (platemark)
Wm.: double C (of the type shown in Heawood
2892) with letters PI ? below
Rijksmuseum, Amsterdam. OB4630

Herman Saftleven's 1646 etching of one of the
city gates of Utrecht, the *Wittevrouwen-poort,* is
one of the most aesthetically rewarding of
Dutch topographical prints from the seventeenth century, not only because of the relationship between the upright rectangular
blocks of the architecture and the novel upright
format but also because of the recording of the
intense play of light and shadow, which is of
equal importance to the accurate recording of
the motif itself. The principal gates in the fortified walls that encircled Dutch cities were conspicuous landmarks and popular motifs for
Dutch painters of this time. Saftleven, who
received commissions from the city government to make topographical drawings of
Utrecht, etched two large, panoramic profile
views of the city, one, consisting of three
plates, in 1648 (Dut. 35) and the second, composed of four plates, in 1669 (Dut. 36).

The strong, almost southern light that characterizes the print probably reflects Saftleven's
contact with the work of Jan Both, the Utrecht
painter of idyllic Italian landscape views, who
had returned to Utrecht from Italy in 1641 (see
cat. no. 118). This is particularly true of the
print in this state, in which the sky is virtually
blank save for a few fine drypoint shadings and
light indications of clouds. In the following
state Saftleven added a heavy blanket of cloud
to the sky. Even though Rembrandt had etched
a number of landscapes with completely blank
skies in the early 1640s, Saftleven perhaps
found the blankness disturbing and wished to
fill it in; or perhaps he simply found the effect
inappropriately southern. The fine drypoint
touches in the sky of the present state would in

De Cwittevrouwven-poort. A.º 1646.

114

any case have worn quickly away. The next state with its heavy sky is undoubtedly more Dutch in appearance, but it is also more mono-tone and less atmospheric in feeling. Both states give a sense of late afternoon light or sunset.

A preparatory black chalk and wash drawing in reverse direction for the print, in Berlin, has a blank sky, but the effect of sunlight and shadow is less strong than in the etching.[1] The calligraphic inscription at the bottom is similar to that in the print. Another Saftleven drawing in the Archives of the Royal House in the Hague shows the gate from the same view-point but in winter, with the moat frozen over.[2]

1. Berlin, cat. drawings, 1930, no. 2900.
2. Koninklijk Huisarchief, Atlas Munniks van Cleef, no. 125.

Bartholomeus Breenbergh
about 1598-1600 – 1657

Bartholomeus Breenbergh, a painter of land-scapes with Roman ruins and of history sub-jects, made about thirty etchings; most of them date from 1639–40, and most are quite small in scale, as are his "cabinet-picture"–scale paintings.

Breenbergh was born in Deventer between 1598 and 1600. His teachers are not known, but his earliest works are close to those of the Amsterdam painter Jacob Pynas. In Rome Breenbergh was part of the circle of the Flem-ish painter Paulus Bril. Breenbergh arrived in Rome in 1619 and remained until the end of the 1620s. In Rome he must also have been in close contact with the Utrecht painter Cornelis Poelenburg, the originator of the idealized Italian view in seventeenth-century Dutch painting. Breenbergh was a founder of the Netherlandish artists' fraternity in Rome in 1623. In 1625 he was sharing a studio in the Via del Babuino in the artists' quarter of Rome. In 1633 he married into an upper-class Amster-dam family. After 1644 he turned away from landscape and devoted himself to painting lit-erary or "history" subjects. He is documented in Amsterdam in the 1640s and 1650s, and in 1652 and 1653 he is referred to as a merchant. His production of paintings was smaller in his later years. He died in Amsterdam in 1657.[1]

1. See biographies in Blankert, 1965, pp. 75–76; Röthlisberger, 1969. For Breenbergh's stylistic develop-ment as a painter, see Stechow, 1930.

115 (actual size)

115
BARTHOLOMEUS BREENBERGH
A Grotto, 1640

From a series of seventeen etchings, "Various ruined buildings within and without Rome" Etching and drypoint
B. 12, Weig. 12, Dut. 12
101 x 63 mm. (platemark)
Coll.: F.S. Haden (L. 1227), H.F. Sewall (L. 1309)
Museum of Fine Arts, Boston, Harvey D. Parker Collection. P8186

116
BARTHOLOMEUS BREENBERGH
Ruins of an Aqueduct, 1640

From a series of seventeen etchings, "Various ruined buildings within and without Rome" Etching and drypoint
B. 8, Weig. 8, Dut. 8, Holl. 8
Lower right: *BB. f. 1640*
102 x 64 mm. (platemark)
Museum of Fine Arts, Boston, Stephen Bullard Memorial Fund. 53.459

Bartholomeus Breenbergh's 1640 series of sev-enteen etchings[1] of "Various ruined buildings within and without Rome"[2] may come as a surprise to those accustomed to thinking of etchings of Roman ruins in terms of the scale and format of the prints of the eighteenth-century Venetian etcher Piranesi. Breenbergh's etchings are not only miniaturistic in scale but also vertical in format and etched with an extremely fine line. Although they have their own distinct personality, they also form part of a tradition of etched series of Roman ruins. The grandfather of all such series by Netherlandish artists is that of Hieronymus Cock of 1551 (Holl. 22 – 47). The next signifi-cant series by a Netherlandish artist is that of Willem van Nieulandt, of which Claes Jansz. Visscher published copies in 1618 (Holl. 10 –

1. The print reproduced in Hollstein as Dut. 12 is a copy in reverse of Dut. 11. The number 12 described by Bartsch and Dutuit is the one with a grotto-like interior shown here.

Three of the unsigned, undated prints usually cata-logued with the series seem to me different in style and motif from the rest of the series: Holl. 4, 5, and 7. The first two could as easily be described as Dutch farmyard scenes as Roman ruins; the third is more ambiguous in motif. All three view their subjects from a closer vantage point than the signed and dated prints in the series and are executed with a broader touch and in a different handwriting. It seems to me very likely that they were added to the series at some point and that either they are by another artist or they were executed in another period of Breenbergh's career.

2. Title engraved on title plate: "Verscheyden/vervallen gebouwē/Soo binnen als buyten/ROMEN./ Geteykent en Ghe-ets/Door/Bartholomeus Breenbergh/Schilder./ Gedaen in't Jaer 1640."

116 (actual size)

29).[3] These, like Breenbergh's, are quite modest in scale and reflect Nieulandt's contact with Paul Bril, the Flemish painter and etcher living in Rome.

Breenbergh's etchings emphasize more than any of his precursors' the intensity of the southern light. In spite of their miniaturistic scale, they are conceived in broad patterns of

light and shadow. A number of drawings related to the prints are brush and wash drawings that emphasize the essential patterns of light and shadow.[4]

The etching of two monks in a grotto or grotto-like ruin[5] introduces one of the favorite motifs of seventeenth-century Dutch artists representing Italian subjects: a view from a dark interior or grotto-like space toward the brilliant light outside.

In the etching of a ruined aqueduct Breenbergh seems more interested in the light and in the sharply receding space created by the aqueduct than in topographical accuracy.[6] The entire series, apparently based on drawings made in Rome but etched in Amsterdam several years later, suggests poetic fantasies or variations on the theme of Roman ruins rather than documentary images.

3. The Italian etcher G.B. Mercati published an extended series of etchings of Roman ruins possibly inspired by Nieulandt's series in 1629 (B. XX. 12–63). They are also modest in scale and include engraved identifications of the ruins represented. The ruin etchings of Carel de Hooch, a painter of Roman ruin subjects active in Haarlem and Utrecht, are also important forerunners of Breenbergh's series. The undated series of etchings in a larger format by J.G. Bronchhorst after Cornelis Poelenburg form an interesting parallel to Breenbergh's series. Herman Saftleven's 1640 series of small landscapes (Dut. 12–17) seems to reflect Breenbergh's influence in its ruin subjects.

4. See, for example, Röthlisberger, 1969, nos. 27, 124, 144.

5. The traditional title cited by Weigel in his supplement to Bartsch and based on the catalogues of the Prévost and Rigal collections is "One of the grottos of Valmontone." A wash drawing of a grotto with figures, in a private collection, though horizontal in format, seems close in conception to the motif of the etching; Röthlisberger, 1969, no. 113, illus.

6. Weigel's title is "The Aqueduct of Meza Via, between Rome and Albano." On the verso of a drawing, in Amsterdam, that is related to the print and in the reverse direction is an old Italian inscription identifying the subject as an aqueduct between Rome and Frascati; see Röthlisberger, 1969, no. 124. The etching, made in Holland, shows many differences from the drawing, not only in detail but also in general pattern of lighting. Röthlisberger places the drawing in the late Roman period.

117
BARTHOLOMEUS BREENBERGH
The Hasting Man before the Ruins of the Baths of Caracalla, 1639–40

Etching and drypoint
B. 22, Weig. 22, Dut. 22, Holl. 22
Upper right: *BB f*
92 x 155 mm. (platemark)
Coll.: R. Gutekunst (L. 2213a), F. Rumpf (L. 2161)
Allen Memorial Art Museum, Oberlin College, Oberlin, Ohio, Gift of Richard Zinser. 65.7

This delicate etching is a companion piece to another etching of the same dimensions and panoramic format in which ruins identified as those of the Colosseum dominate the background (Holl. 21).[1] Both emphasize the landscape aspect of the crumbling, overgrown ruins, a pastoral scene that has been banished by the excavations of modern archaeology and is perhaps in part the product of Breenbergh's poetic imagination. The scene is strewn with fragments of monuments. A stream lined with rushes cuts its way through the ruins. As in Breenbergh's series of small, upright ruin landscapes (cat. nos. 115, 116), the most distant elements of the landscape, paled by an intervening haze of light and atmosphere, have been indicated with drypoint lines even finer than the remarkably slender etched lines.

Although both etchings are undated, they are close in style to the etchings of 1639–40 and should be assigned the same date.

1. Although it is difficult to confirm that the ruins are indeed those of the Baths of Caracalla, the great arched vault resembles those of the monumental Roman thermal baths. I would like to thank Miriam G. Braverman, of the Classical Department, for discussing with me the various views of Roman ruins in this catalogue.

117

Jan Both
about 1615-1618 – 1652

One of the central figures in the second wave of Dutch artists who painted idyllic views of Italy, Jan Both made about fifteen etchings.[1] Most of these are idealized Italian landscape views with the exception of the series of the "Five Senses" (in the guise of scenes from peasant life) after designs by his brother, Andries Both (Holl. 11–15),[2] and two rare copies after Rembrandt's etching of his mother of 1628 (Holl. 18, incorrectly titled "Head of an Old Man") and Rembrandt's etching of Saskia as St. Catherine of 1638 (Holl. 17). Two painters whose landscape etchings were strongly influenced by Both's style of etching were Willem de Heusch and Jan van Nikkelen.[3]

Probably born in Utrecht between about 1615 and 1618, Jan Both was said by Sandrart to have first studied with his father, a glass painter, and then, like his brother, Andries, with the Utrecht painter Abraham Bloemaert. Andries Both, who painted scenes from peasant life and low-life scenes, was in Rome by 1635. Jan is recorded there in 1638, 1639, and 1641, sharing living quarters with his brother. Sandrart reports that Andries painted the figures in Jan's paintings. In Rome Jan was in contact with Herman van Swanevelt and Claude Lorrain, the Dutch and French painters of idyllic southern landscapes. In 1636–1640 Claude Lorrain and Jan Both were commissioned by Philip IV of Spain to paint a series of landscapes for the palace of Buen Retiro. In 1641 Andries Both, while returning home by night in Venice, fell into a canal and drowned. After his brother's death Jan returned to

1. The first "wave" or generation of Dutch "Italianate" or "Italianizing" painters of idealized views was that of Cornelis Poelenburg and Bartholomeus Breenbergh; see Stechow, 1966, pp. 147ff., "The Italian Scene."

2. Andries's own style of etching (see Hollstein, vol. 3, pp. 151ff.) was much more stylized and ornamental in the use of line and reminiscent of Jacques Callot, Claes Jansz. Visscher, or J.C. Drooghsloot (cat. no. 60).

3. A selection of their etched work is reproduced in De Groot, 1979, pp. 188–191, 240–241.

Utrecht, where his "Italianate" style developed more fully. The majority of his surviving idealized visions of Italy seem to have been painted in Utrecht, where he died in 1652.[4]

4. See biographies in Sandrart/Peltzer, 1925, pp. 184–185; Blankert, 1965, pp. 112–115; Burke, 1976, pp. 34–39.

118

JAN BOTH

Landscape with Ruins and Two Cows at the Waterside

From a series of etchings (4–6)
Etching
B. 8, Weig. 8[II], Dut. 8[II], Holl. 8[III], Burke 8[II]
200 x 275 mm. (platemark)
Wm.: crowned shield with fleur-de-lis, letters PR and countermark WK (related to Heawood 1664, 1666)
Coll.: St. J. Dent (L. 2373); T.W. Waller (L. 2472)
Museum of Fine Arts, Boston, Gift of Miss Ellen Bullard. 25.1142

The *Cows at the Waterside* is one of four horizontal landscapes by Both based on sites in the vicinity of Rome, three of the four featuring Roman ruins.[1] The ruins in the present etching are also to be seen in a Both painting in Edinburgh, in a Breenbergh drawing in Chantilly, and in a Breenbergh etching (Holl. 16).[2] The painting, upon which the etching may be based, is in reverse of the etching and quite similar in the arrangement of the landscape but is animated with different figures. The four etchings, which are in Both's mature style,

1. Like James Burke, 1976, p. 287, I consider the two landscapes usually catalogued with these four, Holl. 9 and 10, to be after Both rather than by his hand. Mrs. de Hoop Scheffer, 1976, p. 181, expressed skepticism about Burke's rejection of the two etchings as part of the series in her useful article on early states of Both's etchings. However, there is a genuine difference of style between these two prints and the other four. They are less varied and spontaneous in the use of line, less varied in tonality, and, though very competent, generally more mechanical in execution. I do not believe that these differences can be accounted for by assuming them to represent another phase of Both's activity as an etcher; I would suggest that they were added to the series by an early publisher.

2. For the painting see Burke, 1976, pp. 305–306 and no. 28, with small illus. Burke mentions the possibility that the ruins may be those of the baths of ancient Albano near Rome. For the Breenbergh drawing in Chantilly see Röthlisberger, 1969, no. 52. Röthlisberger questions the authenticity of the Breenbergh drawing of the same ruin in the Louvre mentioned by Burke (Paris, cat. drawings, 1929–1933, vol. 1, no. 173, illus.). Lugt and Röthlisberger identify the ruins as being near Tivoli. The ruins in the Breenbergh drawing are in reverse of those in the Both etching.

were almost certainly done in the Netherlands after his return from Italy in 1641 and most likely in the second half of the 1640s.[3]

In the etchings one finds Both searching for the black and white equivalent of the golden haze of southern light that vaporizes or makes the forms of the landscape translucent in the artist's paintings. Here the slanting open parallel shading lines of the bank and the vegetation suggest not only the translucency of the shadows but the path of the sun's rays.

Passages of bitten granular tone comparable to that which occurs in some of Rembrandt's etched landscapes of the 1640s (see Rembrandt, B. 212, 228, 233, for example) combine with Both's masses of fine scribbling lines to lay stress on the broader patterns of southern light and shadow rather than on contour drawing.

3. With regard to the dating of the related series of vertical landscape etchings (Holl. 1–4), see Blankert in Utrecht, 1965, no. 52; Burke, 1976, p. 288.

118

Jan Baptist Weenix
1621 – about 1660/61

Of the small group of etchings attributed to Jan Baptist Weenix, a versatile painter of Italian views, game pieces, portraits, and genre scenes, only two fully signed etchings can be attributed with any certainty.[1]

The early eighteenth-century biographer of Dutch artists Arnold Houbraken was unusually well informed about the facts of Weenix's life because he had interviewed Weenix's son and pupil, the still-life painter, Jan Weenix. Jan Baptist Weenix was born in Amsterdam in 1621. He first studied with Jan Micker, to whom he was related by marriage, subsequently with Abraham Bloemaert, and, for a period of two years, with Claes Moeyaert. At age eighteen he married the daughter of the painter Gillis d'Hondecoeter. Four years later, in late 1642 or early 1643, he departed for Italy, where he remained for about four years. In Rome his patron was Cardinal Giovanni Battista Pamphili, who in 1644 became Pope Innocent X. Weenix changed his name from Johannes or Jan to Giovanni Battista Weenix while in Italy, probably in honor of his patron, and signed himself this way for the rest of his life. When inducted into the Netherlandish artists' fraternity in Rome, the "Bent," he was given the nickname "Ratel" (Rattle), a reference to a speech defect.

He was back in the Netherlands in 1647 and settled in Utrecht. Three years before his death (in about 1660–61) he moved to a house outside Utrecht.[2]

1. *The Bull,* B. 1, and *The Bull* or *The Cow,* Weig., Dut. 3 and 4, which are apparently the same print, as pointed out by Nagler (vol. 21, p. 203), in his discussion of Nag. 3. In the unsigned etching of *The Seated Man and His Dog,* B. 2, which appears to be an unfinished sketch, the figure-drawing style is very close to that of J.B. Weenix. Stechow (1948, p. 196) noted that *The Fountain,* Nag. 5 (Weig., Dut. 6) is by the son, Jan Weenix, and bears his signature.

2. See biographies by Stechow, 1948, pp. 181–182; MacLaren, 1960, pp. 448–449; Blankert in Utrecht, 1965, pp. 174–176.

119 (actual size)

119

JAN BAPTIST WEENIX
The Bull, 1649

Etching
B. 1, Weig. 1, Nag. 1, Dut. 1, Wurz. 1
Lower right: *Gio Battā Weenix*
162 x 112 mm. (platemark)
Coll.: J. Sheepshanks (see L. 2333)
Lent by the Trustees of the British Museum. S. 2785

The Bull forms a pair with the etching of a similar bull, cow, or ox that faces the viewer (Nag. 3; see illus.) The latter is inscribed in reverse in Italian above the borderline at top (here cropped from photo): "Gio Batta Weenix a° 1649 di 19 ottobre." *The Bull* should undoubtedly be assigned the same date. Weenix's inscription in Italian on a print made after his return to Holland points up – as does his adoption of an Italian form of his name – how deep an impression the Italian experience had made on him. The ungainly conception of the beasts is indebted to the animals of Pieter van Laer (see the buffalos, cat. no. 75), who also influenced Weenix's figure-drawing style, but the line is freer, more scribbling than Pieter van Laer's and closer to Jan Both's etchings. There is also a greater interest in the dissolution of forms in a haze of light than in Van Laer's etched work.

One wonders if Weenix contemplated a series of animal etchings that would have served as models for other painters. Here one sees three foreshortened figures of bulls or cows pointing the way into the landscape, a conception that is more schematic than naturalistic.

Jan Baptist Weenix
A Bull
Etching
Musée du Petit Palais, Paris

Nicolaes Berchem
1620 – 1683

Nicolaes (or Claes) Pietersz. Berchem, the most famous of the Dutch painters of idyllic Italian views in the eighteenth and nineteenth centuries, made a little over fifty etchings, all of them pastoral subjects dealing with herders and the animals in their charge.

Born in Haarlem in 1620, Nicolaes was the son of a still-life painter, Pieter Claesz. Houbraken gives an astonishingly long list of teachers: first his father, then Jan van Goyen, Claes Moeyaert, Pieter de Grebber, Jan Wils, and Jan Baptist Weenix. Some of them, such as the younger Jan Baptist Weenix, would have been unlikely candidates; the most likely and most significant in terms of influence on Berchem's early development would have been Claes Moeyaert. In 1642 Berchem entered the Haarlem guild as a master and began taking pupils. He was first married in 1646. His second wife was the daughter of his teacher Jan Wils. He resided primarily in Haarlem until he moved to Amsterdam in 1677, where he died in 1683.

It is assumed by most writers on the basis of Berchem's subject matter that the artist visited Italy, and some authors mention as many as three visits, but there is no firm documentation for even one journey. Berchem, who was extremely productive, was one of the most successful of seventeenth-century Dutch painters during his lifetime. His many pupils included Karel Dujardin, Jan van der Meer the Younger, and Dirck Maas.[1] The painter Abraham Begeyn made etchings in Berchem's manner.

1. Biographies by E. W. Moes in Thieme-Becker, vol. 3, pp. 370–372; MacLaren, 1960, pp. 20–21; Blankert in Utrecht, 1965, pp. 147–149.

120

121

120

NICOLAES BERCHEM
The Bagpiper, about 1644–45

Etching and drypoint
B. 4, Weig. 4[II], Dut. 4[II], Wurz. 4[I], Holl. 4[II]
Upper left in the next state: *N Berghem fe.*
161 x 233 mm. (platemark)
Wm.: foolscap with letters CPG
Coll.: F. Debois, 1833 (L. 985); St. J. Dent
(L. 2373); A. Hubert (L. 130); C. Buckingham
(L. 497)
The Art Institute of Chicago, The Clarence
Buckingham Collection. 1938.1365

Although the figures in Berchem's early etching *The Bagpiper* were inspired by Pieter van Laer's conception of the Italian peasantry, one sees already in the almost languid grace of the rider's pointing arm the ornamental elegance Berchem brought to "Italianate" pastoral themes. The transfiguring southern light is the principal subject. The group of rider and bagpiper placed boldly at dead center is etched with stronger contrasts so that it seems almost to float against the paler cloudy forms of the landscape vaporized by the light. The fine tonal meshes of short, broken strokes and crisscrossing lines that compose these soft landscape forms are a further refinement of the tonal meshes or masses of stipple seen in the 1638 herdsman subjects of Bleker and of Berchem's teacher Claes Moeyaert (cat. nos. 69, 79).

When compared with Berchem's dated prints, *The Bagpiper* appears to be close in style to the etchings of 1644, *The Man on a Donkey,* Holl. 5, and the series of small plates of cows, Holl. 23–28, which also employ tonal meshes of line but less densely woven. I would date *The Bagpiper* shortly after 1644, like the *Shepherd Playing the Flute,* Holl. 6, which it so closely resembles.

The print acquired a considerable reputation with French eighteenth-century collectors, among whom it was known as "Le Diamant" (The Diamond), while *The Man on a Donkey,* Holl. 5, was known as "La Perle" (The Pearl). Berchem's elegant treatment of humble subjects was in tune with a century and a country that conceived of shepherds and herders in terms of the paintings of Watteau and Boucher.

121

SIMON DE VLIEGER
The Inn in the Ruins

Etching, drypoint, and engraving
B. 8, Dut. 8, Wurz. 8
190 x 285 mm. (sheet)
Wm.: crowned shield with fleur-de-lis
Rijksmuseum, Amsterdam. A6071

From the 1640s on, it became evident that it was not essential for Dutch artists to make the Italian journey in order to represent Italian views. As far as we know, Simon de Vlieger never visited Italy, but his ambitious etching of a ferryboat with a coach arriving at an inn built into overgrown antique ruins combines many motifs popular with "Italianate" painters.[1] Other artists who painted Italian or Mediterranean motifs or southern lights without having made the Italian journey were Adriaen van de Velde and Aelbert Cuyp.

One of the familiar sights that greeted the artists who went to Italy and who drew the ancient ruins there were modern dwellings and shops built into the ruins, which gave a sense of the long history and continuity of Mediterranean civilization.[2]

The print is shown here in a rare early state, which emphasizes the middle range of grays. This tonality, in combination with the cloud-filled sky, gives the Italian view a rather Dutch atmosphere. In the following state a clearer, more brilliant, more southern light and atmosphere was created by scraping and burnishing the clouds away, by darkening the foreground, and by adding deeper shadows to the ruins.[3]

3. The present state is sometimes described as the first; but an impression in the Kupferstichkabinett, Berlin (inv. 250–1896), was printed before some work on the arbor and the figures around it, with more drypoint shading in the sky, and before the addition of the heavier, more continuous borderline.

Jan Kelch's suggestion, in conversation, of a date in the 1640s seems quite consistent with the overall development of graphic style and tonality in the printmaking of this period.

1. An undated pen drawing by Simon de Vlieger in Rotterdam (inv. 5) represents a similar inhabited ruin.

2. The ruins of the theater of Marcellus in Rome were occupied by shops and dwellings until the late 1920s. See Scherer, 1955, pp. 113–114 and pl. 185.

122

Paulus Potter
1625 – 1654

Paulus Potter, the Dutch painter who fully defined the animal piece as a separate artistic genre, made about eighteen etchings, all dealing with animals and herders. The dated etchings range from 1643 to 1652.

Born in Enkhuizen in 1625, Paulus was the son of the painter Pieter Simonsz. Potter. According to Houbraken, he studied with his father. Claes Moeyaert has also been suggested as Potter's teacher. Since his father moved to Amsterdam in 1631, Paulus probably spent his youth in that city. In 1646 he was received into the artists' guild in Delft. By 1649 he was in the Hague, where he married the daughter of an architect in 1650. He moved to Amsterdam in 1652, possibly at the insistence of the burgomaster Nicolaes Tulp, whose son Dirk was portrayed by Potter in an equestrian portrait. He died in 1654 at the age of 29.[1]

1. Biographies by Rudolf von Arps-Aubert in Thieme-Becker, vol. 27, pp. 306–307; MacLaren, 1960, pp. 298–299.

122
PAULUS POTTER
The Shepherd, 1644

One of a pair etchings
Etching and drypoint
B. 15, Weig. 15[II], Dut. 15[II], Wurz. 15, Holl. 15[II]
Lower right: *Pauwelus Potter. inv. et f. aᵒ 1644;*
lower left: *2*
183 x 270 mm. (platemark)
Coll.: A.M. Champernowne (L. 153); J. Barnard (L. 1419)
The St. Louis Art Museum, The Sidney and Sadie Cohen Foundation, Inc., Print Purchase Fund. 49:69

The Shepherd was executed when the artist was nineteen years of age. Although the piping shepherd suggests Arcadia and pastoral literature, most of the image is characterized by a new and rather startling realism, both in the description of the surfaces of things and in the brilliant light that slashes across the foreground. We confront the sheep close up, and one of them peers straight out at us. Potter's observant eye and fine, wiry line delineate every scruffy clump of wool. Everything is drawn with firm, closed contours that lend a crystalline precision to the forms, but the contours are so fine that, when viewed at a slight distance, they meld into the bold pattern of light and shadow. The strong foreground light both pitilessly illuminates and abstracts forms. Shadow lops off the lower legs of shepherd and dog.

Only in such a fine early impression does one fully experience the intervening space between the foreground sheep and the distance, paled by light and atmosphere. In later impressions the background, dunes, church, plowing team, and delicate clouds become heavier and push forward, collapsing the space. The motif of the man plowing is relatively rare. Peasants may labor in the fields in the nineteenth-century art of Millet and the Barbizon artists, but in seventeenth-century Dutch art they are usually seen relaxing or carousing rather than laboring, unless the image is part of a cycle of the activities appropriate to the months.[1]

The Shepherd of 1644, which is numbered "2," was probably intended to form a pair with Potter's *Cowherd* etching (Holl. 14), which in the early states is dated 1643 and numbered "1." *The Cowherd* is very close in format and style to *The Shepherd.*

1. I would like to thank Alison Kettering for her suggestions regarding the imagery of this print. She is engaged in writing a book on pastoral imagery in seventeenth-century Dutch art.

Jacob van Ruisdael
about 1628/29 – 1682

A painter of landscapes, marines, and city views, Jacob Isaacksz. van Ruisdael made about twelve etchings, all landscapes.

Ruisdael was born in Haarlem about 1628–29, the son of a frame maker, art dealer, and landscape painter. He probably studied with his father and possibly also with his uncle, the painter Salomon van Ruisdael. His earliest dated work is from 1645–46, but he did not join the Haarlem guild as a master until 1648. In 1650 he visited Bentheim, just over the Dutch border in Germany, possibly in the company of his friend Nicolaes Berchem, the painter of Italianate views. A number of Ruisdael's works have motifs taken from this area.

In 1657 Ruisdael, who was of Baptist background, was baptized in Amsterdam as a member of the Reformed Church. By June 1659 he had settled in Amsterdam. He seems to have been reasonably prosperous, and he supported his father financially. His paintings of waterfalls, possibly inspired by Allart van Everdingen's Scandinavian views, enjoyed great success.[1] In 1676 a Jacob Ruisdael received the degree of doctor of medicine at Caen in France and was registered as a doctor in Amsterdam.[2] He seems to have lived in Amsterdam until his death in 1682, but he was buried in Haarlem.[3]

1. Rosenberg, 1928, p. 9, mentions the valuation of the collection of a wealthy Amsterdam art lover in 1669, which contained three Ruisdael waterfall paintings. Houbraken, 1721, vol. 3, pp. 65–66, singles out for particular praise the waterfalls, which are less appreciated in our own time and often cited as examples of Ruisdael's "decline."

2. According to Houbraken, Ruisdael performed many successful operations. Rosenberg and Slive (Rosenberg/Slive/Ter Kuile, 1966, pp. 154–155) express extreme skepticism about the likelihood of Ruisdael's having pursued a medical career.

3. See biographies by MacLaren, 1960, pp. 353–355; K.E. Simon in Thieme-Becker, vol. 29, pp. 190–193; Rosenberg, 1928, pp. 6–11.

123
JACOB VAN RUISDAEL
Cottages and Clump of Trees near a Small Stream, 1646

Etching and drypoint
B. 7, Weig. 7, Dut. 7, Wurz. 7, Keyes 1[II], Holl. 7[II]
Upper right: *JvRuisdael f 1646*
205 x 280 mm. (sheet)
Rijksmuseum, Amsterdam. OB4637

Many of Ruisdael's early paintings and early etchings such as the present one, made when he was seventeen or eighteen years old, feature dense thickets and tangles of foliage. In the paintings this is often expressed in tacky, prickly paint surfaces: here the dense accumulation of texture upon texture is expressed by a different type of stroke for each kind of foliage: spiky, curly, zigzag. Conventional contour drawing is ignored, the landscape being gradually built up from masses of these short strokes with their strong implications of color and texture. The short, broken strokes and stipples no longer have the decorative, pattern-making function they assumed in the work of earlier landscape etchers, such as, for example, Willem Buytewech's etching of the ruins of the Huys te Kleef (cat. no. 37). The dotted lines that suggest atmosphere in the sky of Ruisdael's etching follow no regular pattern. The primitive cottages are of the same substance as the surrounding landscape and seem on the verge of dissolving into the fabric of nature. The two little figures in the far distance are barely identifiable as human presences. Nature's burgeoning, vegetative power is dominant.

George Keyes, in his catalogue of Ruisdael's etchings, suggested that only the unique first state, in the collection of the Fondation Custodia of the Institut Néerlandais, Paris, was by Ruisdael.[1] However, the changes in the second state exhibited here seem to me consistent with Ruisdael's hand. He shaded in the lower margin, obliterating his original signature and date so that the lower margin now has the appearance of a weathered board. A new signature and date were etched in the sky at upper right. More foliage was added to the tallest tree in the clump of trees, increasing its density and height. Shading was added to the end wall of the far cottage and the trees behind it. It is only in the third state, in which the plate was cut down and rather meaningless strokes of drypoint were added, that one is conscious of the intervention of a hand other than Ruisdael's.

1. Keyes, 1977, p. 15, no. 1.

123

124 (actual size)

124
JACOB VAN RUISDAEL
The Wheatfield, 1648

Etching and drypoint
B. 5, Weig. 5, Dut. 5, Wurz. 5[II], Keyes 4, Holl. 5[II]
Lower right (in the grass): *JvRuisdael 1648*
102 x 152 mm. (platemark)
Wm.: crowned shield with fleur-de-lis
Coll.: K.F.F. von Nagler (L. 2529)
National Gallery of Art, Washington, D.C.,
Rosenwald Collection. B-4782

Ruisdael was the seventeenth-century Dutch
landscape painter most deeply identified with
forest views. Here we find ourselves on the
edge of a wood, the only token of human
presence the field of grain.

In this small etching, made two years after
that of the cottages and clump of trees of 1646
(cat. no. 123), nature has acquired greater
solidity and density. The thickets have become
so prickly as to suggest brambles. The etched
line is very fine, and the foliage less diversified
than in the earlier print. The field of grain is a
pool of light ringed about by dark vegetation.
Ruisdael's theme of the heroic tree, which he
developed further in the 1650s, is already visible in the twisted limbs of the great oak.

In the subsequent state, which bears the initials of the Antwerp publisher Frans van den
Wyngaerde and the engraved name of the artist, an unimaginative attempt was made to
bring clarity to Ruisdael's dense tangle of vegetation. Engraving was used to make the fallen
tree limb of the foreground emerge from its
nest of grasses and brush, whereas in the first
state it had been inextricably woven into
nature's dense web.

Johannes Ruisscher
about 1625 – after 1675

The landscape painter and draftsman Johannes
Ruisscher (or Rauscher) made about twenty-
nine landscape etchings. He was known in
Holland as "de jonge Hercules" ("the young
Hercules") apparently because of certain of his
prints that show the influence of Hercules
Segers's technical innovations. Ruisscher occasionally printed in a color or on a prepared colored ground or colored and varnished his
prints after printing. Also, in one rare instance,
he employed a resist or stop-out (Trautscholdt
19), as did Segers in his *Large Tree* (cat. no.
68). His later prints, made in Germany, are less
experimental and appear to be primarily topographical views. Considerable confusion about
the cataloguing of his work has arisen from the
fact that Anthonie Waterloo reworked a number of Ruisscher's prints and republished them.
Eduard Trautscholdt's admirable catalogue
appears to have finally clarified the majority of
the attribution problems.[1]

Born in Franeker in Friesland about 1625,
Ruisscher was possibly the son of the German
painter Johannes Rauscher II, who died in
Dresden in 1632. His drawings of around 1648
reflect the influence of Rembrandt and his circle. Ruisscher married in Dordrecht in 1649,
and in 1650 a child was baptized. He left
Dordrecht in 1651 but was there again in 1657.
After a period of activity in the area of Cleves,
he was, until 1661, landscape painter at the
Brandenburg court in Berlin. From 1662 until
1675 he was court painter for the elector
Johann Georg of Saxony. In 1675 his wife
pleaded for the payment of four years' back sal-
ary, explaining that her husband had been
forced to pursue his fortunes elsewhere. The
exact date of Ruisscher's death is not known.[2]

1. Trautscholdt, 1973.
2. For Ruisscher's career and work see the series of articles by A. Welcker, 1932, 1933, 1934, 1936, and 1940; see
also the biography by Welcker in Thieme-Becker, vol. 29,
p. 244.

125
JOHANNES RUISSCHER
Edge of a Wood with Houses among Trees,
1649

Etching
V.d.K. 1, Wurz. 1, Trautscholdt 1[Id]
Upper right: *JRuischer. Fecit./.1649.*
156 x 238 mm. (sheet)
Wm.: monogram PH (countermark)
Museum of Fine Arts, Boston, Anonymous Gift.
1979.392

One of two Ruisscher etchings dated 1649,
The Edge of a Wood, though lacking in subtle
tonal gradations or atmospheric qualities, is
characterized by the tremendous vitality of the
coarse wiry lines that delineate dense tangles of
foliage and bristly grasses. It is seen here in the
rare first state before the plate was cut down,
before rather conventional parallel shading
lines were added to the sky at upper right, and
before the foliage and the log in the foreground were retouched. The image of a road
leading to houses among trees is very closely
related to three of Hercules Segers's etchings,
The House in the Woods, Haverkamp-Begemann
35, *Country Road near the Gate of a Farm
Building,* Haverkamp-Begemann 36, and, in
particular, *Country Road with Trees and Buildings,* Haverkamp-Begemann 37. All three
Segers's etchings show a comparable freedom,
vigor, and directness in the use of line. The
motif of a fringe of wood encircling an area of
open fields is also related to Ruisdael's 1648
Wheatfield (cat. no. 124), but the boldly scribbled "steel-wool" masses of Ruisscher's foliage
are quite different from Ruisdael's prickly web
of finer, more controlled lines.

The printing is somewhat uneven as a result
either of careless inking or of overbiting of the
darker passages. Ruisscher's early impressions
are often printed somewhat casually rather
than with professional precision. Impressions
of the first state also occur printed in black on
brown-tinted paper (Trautscholdt 1[Ia,]
Amsterdam, and 1[Ib,] Dresden).

125

188

Jan de Lagoor
active 1640s and 1650s

Very little is known about the Haarlem landscape painter Jan de Lagoor. His six etchings
(Holl. 1–6), five of them signed, constitute
some of the firmest evidence of his activity.[1] He
joined the Haarlem artists' guild in 1645 and
was one of the officers of the guild in 1649.
His insolvency inventory in Amsterdam in
1659 suggests that he was a wine dealer as well
as a landscape painter.[2] His signed paintings
are few in number, and no certain drawings are
known. His paintings reveal him to be a follower of Jacob van Ruisdael.

1. Hollstein 7 and 8 are by other hands. Although
Hollstein 7 is not by Lievens, it is strongly suggestive of
Lievens's painted landscapes.

2. Biographies by M.D. Henkel in Thieme-Becker, vol.
22, p. 219; MacLaren, 1960, p. 214.

126 (actual size)

126
JAN DE LAGOOR
The Houses behind the Trees

Etching, touched with gray wash
V.d.K. 1, Wurz. 1 Holl. 1
Upper left: *J. Lagoor*
90 x 95 mm. (platemark)
Coll.: J. Sheepshanks (see L. 2333)
Lent by the Trustees of the British Museum. S. 5732

Lagoor's landscape etchings are among the
most simply executed of seventeenth-century
Dutch etchings. The line is relatively unmodu-
lated, and forms are delineated with an easy,
scribbling stroke. The *Houses behind the Trees* is
the only etching in which Lagoor used a square
format.

The motif of a winding road leading to
houses among trees, which may also be seen in
Ruisscher's etching (cat. no. 125), was first
introduced by Hercules Segers in etchings
such as *The House in the Woods,* Haverkamp-
Begemann 35, which is also very simple in
execution.

The etching is lightly and unevenly bitten.
Touches of gray wash have been added to the
bank and tree trunk to compensate for the lack
of darker tones. Whether these were by the artist's hand or by a later owner of the print it is
difficult to say.

127
JAN LIEVENS
Landscape with a Group of Trees

Woodcut, touched with brown wash
B. 63, Dut. 62, Rovinski 63, Holl. 100
Lower center: *IL.*
240 x 150 mm. (block)
Rijksmuseum, Amsterdam. OB4634

189

127

The mid-seventeenth century in the North Netherlands was a period in which andscape prints were produced in extraordinary quantity and quality, but this print by Lievens is the one instance of a landscape in woodcut. While the woodcuts of Titian and his circle, those of Goltzius (see cat no. 14), and the "Arcadian" landscape attributed to Esaias van de Velde (cat. no. 27) had prepared the way for Lievens's use of woodcut as a medium for landscape, none of the landscape woodcuts that preceded Lievens presented the landscape entirely without human presence or with such sketch-like freedom.

Lievens's choice of the woodcut medium for a landscape may have been more immediately inspired by the woodland landscape background in Christoffel Jegher's chiaroscuro woodcut after Rubens's *The Flight into Egypt* (Holl. 4). But Lievens's use of woodcut is freer, more suggestive, particularly in the passages that suggest foliage moving and shimmering in an envelope of light and atmosphere. Where Jegher still quotes from the systematic linear crosshatching vocabulary of engraving, Lievens's woodcut has passsages of dynamic, choppy, angular cutting (see the vegetation at lower right) that seem to prefigure the self-consciousness about the medium seen in twentieth-century woodcuts, the desire to proclaim to the viewer that the image has been cut and gouged from a plank of wood. This is the opposite extreme from the woodcut as a skillfully executed facsimile of another medium – of a calligraphic pen drawing, for example, such as the Christoffel van Sichem woodcut after Jacob Matham (cat. no. 51). As pointed out earlier (cat. no. 90), it is impossible to prove that Lievens cut his own blocks, but the originality of the cutting in a woodcut such as the present one certainly inclines one to believe that he did.

In the North Netherlands in the 1640s and 1650s a single tree or clump of trees was frequently the central motif of a landscape print. Hercules Segers's etching of the *Large Tree* (cat. no. 68) was one of the forerunners of this development. Wolfgang Stechow dated

Lievens's woodcut about 1640–1645, that is, in the period when Lievens was still in Antwerp or shortly after his return to Holland in 1644.[1] The print relates closely in style and conception to Lievens's landscape drawings in pen and brown ink, often executed on warm-toned Japanese paper. Two landscape drawings by Lievens that are also upright in format and feature a section of woodland interior with tree trunks provide a useful comparison with the print: the *Wooded Landscape with Large Tree*, in Rotterdam (inv. no. H. 34),[2] and the *Group of Trees with Shepherd and Sheep*, in Berlin (Berlin, cat. drawings, 1931, no. 2622).[3] The fact that Lievens usually used a broad point when drawing these landscapes makes the analogy even closer.

Pale brown wash has been added to this impression of the woodcut. At first sight it is disconcerting, and one immediately assumes that it was applied by a foreign hand, but the pattern of the wash's application is, in fact, fairly sensitive rather than disfiguring. It is applied chiefly to areas of blank sky, causing the pale trunks of the trees to stand out in greater relief and adding a few streaks of cloud or atmosphere to the sky. It is not totally out of the question that Lievens himself might have added these touches to a print that was probably a personal experiment, for so few examples survive. Perhaps he was exploring the possibility of a chiaroscuro version of the landscape.

1. J.G. van Gelder, 1959, p. 23, dates the woodcut "after 1640," when Lievens was back in Holland. R.E.O. Ekkart in Braunschweig, 1979, no. 116, p. 214, suggests, perhaps on the basis of the relationship with Jegher's woodcuts, that it was probably executed in Antwerp.

2. Paris, 1974, pl. 44.

3. See also the exhibition of Dutch seventeenth-century landscape drawings, Berlin, 1974, no. 112, pl. 72.

Jan van Brosterhuisen
about 1596 – 1650

One of the most original of seventeenth-century Dutch landscape etchers, Jan van Brosterhuisen was a dilettante whose interests and activities included poetry, music, architecture, painting, etching, and botany. He made sixteen landscape etchings, the majority of which exist in a very small number of impressions.[1] He also etched a number of illustrations after drawings by Frans Post for Caspar Barlaeus's book *Rerum per octennium in Brasilia...*, published in 1647, concerning the Dutch colonial venture in Brazil under the governorship of Count Johan Maurits of Nassau-Siegen.

Born in Leyden about 1596, Brosterhuisen was already enrolled at age fourteen as a student at the University of Leyden. He first attracted the attention of leading poets and scholars with his poems in Dutch. Caspar Barlaeus attempted to win him over to the cause of Latin poetry, but Constantijn Huygens defended his writing in Dutch. After studying at the university, he lived with his parents while he sought an appropriate position, through his protector Huygens. In 1639 he was in Heusden, apparently employed in some capacity by the bailiff of the castle. 1642 found him in Amersfoort, where he was in close contact with the architect of the monumental town hall of Amsterdam, Jacob van Campen. Brosterhuisen was perhaps studying architecture with Van Campen, but he was certainly engaged in translating architectural works by Vitruvius and Palladio for him. He seems also to have been occupied with painting, drawing, and etching in Amersfoort, and he sent Huygens a

1. The one exception is the series "Praedia" ("Farms"), V.d.K. 11–16, which seems to have appeared as a regular published edition. The second and third landscapes in the series are different in format and conception, contain no farm buildings, and were probably originally conceived apart from the series.

view of Amersfoort.[2] He looked about for a position as organist, but in 1646 Huygens finally found him a position at the newly founded Illustre School in Breda, where he was in charge of the botanical garden and taught botany and literature.

In Breda he was harshly criticized by Protestant ministers connected with the school, with regard to both his teaching and his personal conduct. They attempted to blacken his name with Huygens, but Huygens continued to support him. Brosterhuisen, who had been sickly for many years, died in Breda in 1650.[3]

2. In a letter to Huygens written from Amersfoort in June 1645 (Huygens/Worp, 1915, vol. 4, no. 3985, pp. 160–161), Brosterhuisen speaks of his topographical landscape activities, including etching. In another letter to Huygens, written in November of that year, from the Hague (Huygens/Worp, 1915, vol. 4, no. 4186, pp. 247–248), Brosterhuisen enclosed landscape etchings and speaks of publishing others.

3. See biographies by Van der Kellen, 1867–1873, pp. 129–132; E.W. Moes in Thieme-Becker, vol. 5, p. 71.

128
JAN VAN BROSTERHUISEN
Landscape with the Two Dead Fir Trees, about 1645

Etching, touched with gray wash
V.d.K. 3, Wurz. 3, Holl. 3
97 x 108 mm. (platemark)
Rijksmuseum, Amsterdam. B.I. 4916

The *Landscape with the Two Dead Fir Trees* does not correspond to one's conventional idea of the kind of landscape a botanist might produce, but Brosterhuisen was a painter and a poet as well as a botanist. His landscape etchings show an unusual sensitivity to trees and their soft, translucent masses of foliage. Here we find ourselves in the midst of a forest of conifers: the forest floor is barely visible, and no vista opens beyond. No human presence is indicated.

In his landscape etchings Brosterhuisen made unusually expressive use of variations in strength of biting; in this print there is a range

128 (actual size)

from the strong blacks of the screen of dead and living vegetation of the immediate foreground to the almost imperceptible haze of foliage in the far distance at center. Little use is made of contour drawing. The drooping branches are composed of loosely associated, short, delicate strokes, so that the foliage seems to breathe, enveloped in atmosphere. The system of strokes for each individual tree is subtly varied. This open system of broken strokes and stipples suggests Brosterhuisen's debt to his predecessors such as Willem Buytewech (cat. no. 37) and Hercules Segers (cat. no. 66).[1]

1. The only Brosterhuisen drawing with which I am familiar, the monogrammed pen and ink drawing of a castle and moat in the Rijksprentenkabinet, Amsterdam (inv. A 3375), makes extensive use of a fine stipple and evokes the Bruegel tradition of draftsmanship.

Some of the tree trunks show touches of gray wash. A few of the impressions of Brosterhuisen etchings in the Rijksmuseum collection show touches of hand-applied wash; one small etching (V.d.K. 2) has a veil of gray wash over the entire image.[2] It is quite likely that in these rare etchings, which were apparently never published, Brosterhuisen applied a few touches of pen or wash to achieve the effect he desired. Here the touches of wash give the tree trunks slightly more substance without being obtrusive.

2. Another impression of the etching exhibited here (V.d.K. 3), in the collection of the Albertina, Vienna, appears either to be printed in a dark gray ink or to have a milky overlay.

129

JAN VAN BROSTERHUISEN
after FRANS POST
Obsidio et expugnatio Portus Calvi (The Siege and Taking of Porto Calvo) in Caspar Barlaeus, *Rerum per octennium in Brasilia....* Amsterdam, Joannis Blaeu, 1647.

Etching and drypoint
(plate 8)
439 x 305 mm. (page size); vellum
F.M. 1822; Tiele, p. 18; Wurz. vol. 1, p. 193, vol. 2, p. 347; Holl. vol. 3, p. 245.
Rijksmuseum, Meermano-Westreenianum, The Hague. 116.A21

Caspar Barlaeus's book *Rerum per octennium in Brasilia* ..., published in 1647, describes the 1636–1644 governorship of Count Johan Maurits of Nassau-Siegen over the rich sugar-producing lands on the northeast coast of Brazil, which the Dutch West India Company had taken by force from the Portuguese. In his attitude toward these Brazilian territories Johan Maurits was enlightened and full of scientific curiosity rather than merely exploitative, and he eventually fell out with the directors of the West India Company, finally resigning in 1644. After Johan Maurits's departure, a series of Portuguese uprisings led to the West India Company's eventual loss of the territories. When Maurits arrived in Brazil in 1637, he was accompanied by a naturalist, a map maker, an architect, Pieter Jansz. Post, and the latter's brother, the painter Frans Post – an entourage testifying to the prince's desire to document the unique qualities of the Brazilian terrain and its flora and fauna and his intention of making improvements there. Barlaeus's book was undoubtedly intended to justify Johan Maurits's actions in the light of his disagreements with the West India Company.[1]

The many large plates of Brazilian views that illustrate the book were etched and engraved from drawings by Frans Post dated 1645, that is, after Johan Maurits's party's return to

1. Cleves, 1979, p. 332.

OBSIDIO ET EXPUGNATIO
PORTUS CALVI.

A. Caſtrum Piracon.
B. Vrbs.
C. Baſilica.

D. Acceſſus Comitis ad urbem.
E. Suggeſtus tormentarius.
F. Statio Comitis.

G. Suggeſtus torm. gubernatoris Scoppy.
H. Suggeſtus torm. Admiraly fiſtarty.
I. Caſtella duo hoſti derelicta.

Holland. The names of the etchers of these views are not given, but a number are quite plausibly attributed to Salomon Savery, who etched the plates for Barlaeus's 1638 book on the reception of Marie de' Medici (cat. no. 85) in Amsterdam. A number of the plates, including the plate exhibited here, showing the siege and taking of the Portuguese Fort of Porto Calvo by Johan Maurits's forces, were etched by Jan van Brosterhuisen. In a letter to Constantijn Huygens written from Amersfoort in June 1645, the botanist-poet Brosterhuisen mentions that he is busy etching some "West Indian" landscapes for Count Maurits.[2] Barlaeus had taken an active interest in Brosterhuisen's career from the time that the precocious poet Brosterhuisen was attending the University of Leyden.

The fortress of Porto Calvo was surrounded by sugar mills. Post's drawing for the print was based on a painting that he had made in Brazil, now in the Louvre, Paris.[3] In the middle distance in the etching one sees a defile of Brazilian Indian troops and their wives coming to the support of Johan Maurits's attack on the fort. The key in the lower margin indicates the principal events of the siege and the position of the combatants.

Here Brosterhuisen's personal touch is revealed in the fluid, sketchy rendering of the transparent foliage of the great wild fig tree at the left and in the free, painterly use of stipple to convey the softness of the masses of vegetation in the middle distance.

2. Huygens/Worp, 1915, vol. 4, no. 3985, pp. 160–161.
3. Inv. no. 1729; see The Hague, 1979–1980, p. 107, pl. 100.

130

130
SIMON DE VLIEGER
The Wood near the Canal, 1640s

Etching
B.6, Dut. 6
Lower left: *S. de V.*
137 x 157 mm. (platemark)
Wm.: foolscap (fragment)
Coll.: St. John Dent (L. 2373)
The Art Institute of Chicago, Albert H. Wolf Fund.
1975.49

In Simon de Vlieger's *Wood near the Canal*
human life and activity are thoroughly integrated with nature. Light, atmosphere, and the
foamy softness of the foliage dominate, but as
one studies the image more closely, one discovers small figures chatting at the gate, a cottage, a boat with a fisherman.

The trees rise from a narrow strip of land
bordering a waterway to occupy most of the
space of the print, profiled against the blank
sky and merging with its atmosphere. There is
a sense of an infinite range of fine tonal gradations and of the enveloping haze of atmosphere, as in Adriaen van Ostade's *Dance under
the Trellis* (cat. no. 112). De Vlieger's interest in
an extended range of tonal gradations is visible
in the heavily bitten, almost overbitten right
foreground. This deeply bitten vegetation does
not stand out in silhouette as a distinct zone,
however, but fuses in painterly fashion with the
vegetation behind. The luxuriant foliage of the
trees is no longer seen as the decorative patterns or stylized "cauliflower" clumps that
characterized landscape etchings of the second
and third decade of the century, such as Esaias
van de Velde's *Square Landscape* (cat. no. 41),
but, rather, as soft, feathery masses suspended
in light and atmosphere.

Squarish or vertical formats for landscape
etchings were quite popular in the 1640s,[1] the
choice of format apparently being directly
related to the choice of trees and woodlands as
favored landscape themes.

1. Jan Kelch, in conversation, dated the De Vlieger etching in the second half of the 1640s.

Moses van Uyttenbroeck
about 1595-1600 – about 1646/47

Moses van Uyttenbroeck, a painter of idealized
landscapes enlivened with mythological scenes
and Arcadian herders, made over sixty etchings. They range in date from the earliest dated
etching of 1615 to the 1640s.[1] The earlier
prints are generally executed in pure etching;
the later ones make highly original use of
engraving in combination with etching.

Although we are ill-informed about many
aspects of Uyttenbroeck's life and career, all his
known activity is centered in the Hague. Born
about 1595-1600, he was admitted to the
Hague's guild of St. Luke in 1620 and was
active in it until 1638; he was an officer of the
guild in 1627. His elder brother, Jan, was also a
painter. He married in 1624 and had a family of
four children, one son being an engraver in his
youth. In spite of the obvious relationship of
Uyttenbroeck's work to the Arcadian landscapes of Adam Elsheimer, there is no definite
record of an Italian journey or of who his
teachers were. He seems to have been very successful. Dutch painters working in an international mode were often more popular in
Holland in the seventeenth century than in our
own time. Uyttenbroeck's work was purchased
by the stadholder Frederik Hendrik, and he
received commissions for extensive decorations
for one of Frederik Hendrik's palaces. His presumed prosperity is supported by his purchases
of real estate. He died about 1646-47, his wife
being mentioned as a widow in 1647.[2]

1. One possible source of confusion about the dating of
Uyttenbroeck's prints is that the etchings dated 1620 and
1621 were republished by Hendrik Hondius with his
publication date of 1646.

2. See biographies by Weisner, 1964, pp. 189-191; and
Tümpel in Sacramento, 1974, p. 115.

131
MOSES VAN UYTTENBROECK
Bather Emerging from a Forest Pool

Etching and engraving
B. 39, Weig. 39[1], Wurz. 39
125 x 146 mm. (platemark)
Wm.: letter H
Rijksmuseum, Amsterdam. OB4631

The majority of Uyttenbroeck's etchings are
landscapes in which a mythological, biblical, or
pastoral figural group, often accompanied by
flocks and herds, is prominently featured, as
in Moeyaert's landscape *Mercury and Argus*
(cat. no. 69). Here the central figural incident
is a nymph-like bather emerging from a sylvan
pool while turning her head toward the viewer.
As in many of Uyttenbroeck's later paintings,
the figural motif is provided with its own dramatic lighting, separate from the daylight of
the landscape, so that the pale nude figure
stands out vividly in relief against the darker
foliage behind. At the left, a vista opens into
the landscape, and we glimpse cattle at a watering place, suggesting an Arcadian world of
shepherds and shepherdesses.

In his later prints Uyttenbroeck made extensive use of very freely handled engraved passages to give greater sculptural force to
foreground motifs and to create the darkest
values. Here engraving supplements etching in
the foreground, modeling the bather's figure
and, in the form of flicks and dots, suggesting
the texture of her flesh. Freely engraved crosshatching lends an undulant rhythm to the great
tree trunk that forms a background for her
figure.

131 (actual size)

132

HERMAN SAFTLEVEN
The Great Tree, 1647

Etching
B. 28, Dut. 28
Lower left: *HS 1647*
256 x 235 mm. (platemark)
Wm.: foolscap
Museum of Fine Arts, Boston, Visiting Committee
Funds. M25870

Herman Saftleven's 1647 etching *The Great Tree* is one of the finest examples in Dutch printmaking of the 1640s and 1650s of the isolated tree or clump of trees as the dominant motif of a landscape. Saftleven's tree, a gnarled and weatherbeaten old giant, missing limbs but still putting forth luxuriant foliage, fills nearly the whole field of the print. The stump of a hacked-off trunk to the right emphasizes its struggle for existence. Its fan of lacy, translucent foliage is spread out against the blank sky. Below the giant's arching branches the land drops away, and the eye pursues a wandering road and stream deep into a distant river valley. The atmospheric depth of the landscape accentuates the tree's dramatic isolation and emphasizes the relative two-dimensionality of the pattern formed by the tree's splayed-out foliage. This river valley landscape prefigures the many Rhine valley landscapes that Saftleven was to paint after 1650.[1]

In the discussion of Saftleven's etching of the Wittevrouwen-poort (cat. no. 114), it was noted that the light of the print resembled the southern light that Jan Both brought back to Utrecht from Italy. Here Both's influence is visible in the translucent foliage spread out against the sky. Similarly conceived and drawn foliage may be seen in the trees in Both's landscape etchings of vertical format (Holl. 1–4), but the trunks of Saftleven's trees are less slender and willowy and the rhythms of his foliage much more elaborated and intricate than Both's.

1. For Saftleven's development as a painter before 1650, see Nieuwstraten, 1965.

As Dutuit pointed out,[2] *The Great Tree* is virtually a pendant to the etching of roughly similar dimensions, *The Wood* of 1644 (Dut. 27), in which a distant landscape is viewed through a screen of trees high on a hillside.[3]

2. Dutuit, 1885, vol. 3, p. 294.

3. A number of Saftleven's drawings relate in style or conception to these etchings. The studies from nature labeled as being made in the "Hooge-Soerder bos" (a wood in the Veluwe) relate closely in motif to the trees of the etchings but are virtually all closed views of a wood interior. One of these drawings, a study used for a painting of 1647, is reproduced in Nieuwstraten, 1965, p. 106, pl. 32. A chalk and wash drawing, in the Louvre, with two figures conversing in a wood, whose trees are silhouetted against a distant landscape, is quite similar in basic conception to the etchings; Paris, cat. drawings, 1931, vol. 2, no. 691, illus.

132

133

198

133

REMBRANDT VAN RIJN
The Landscape with the Three Trees, 1643

Etching, drypoint, and engraving
G. 204, B. 212, Hind 205, Münz 152, BB. 43-B,
W.-B. 212, only state
Lower left (barely visible): *Rembrandt f. 1643*
215 x 283 mm. (platemark)
Wm.: Strasburg lily in shield (related to Heawood
1663) with letters PR (?) below and countermark
WK (?)
Coll.: F. Bullard (L. 982)
Museum of Fine Arts, Boston, William Norton
Bullard Collection. 31.1287

The most ambitious of Rembrandt's some
twenty-five etched landscapes of the 1640s and
early 1650s, the *Landscape with the Three Trees*
brings to the outdoors the profound etched
chiaroscuro that Rembrandt had developed in
the *Saint Jerome in a Dark Chamber* (cat. no.
99) of the year before. The intensely dramatic,
shifting light is that of a passing or approach-
ing rainstorm. In the Netherlands the winds
are unimpeded by hills or mountains, and the
clouds move very rapidly overhead, often
resulting in abrupt changes of weather.

Ever since the publication of Gersaint's catalogue in the eighteenth century, this landscape
has been referred to as the *Three Trees,* a perfectly explicable title, given the dramatic play
of shadows around the group of trees, which
stand out, their foliage ruffled by the wind,
against a light patch of sky. The traditional
title, however, is limiting in that it draws attention away from the full scope of this complex
landscape. Based on observations made during
Rembrandt's sketching expeditions in the
vicinity of Amsterdam,[1] the landscape is virtually unique among Dutch landscape etchings of
the first half of the seventeenth century in

representing nature in a state of change.[2] The
notion of nature as dynamic and ever changing
was eloquently conveyed in the landscape
paintings of the Flemish painter Peter Paul
Rubens (1577–1640), with their rainbows,
rainstorms, and simultaneous sunsets and
moonrises. The Dutch engraver Schelte A.
Bolswert made numerous engravings after
Rubens's landscapes.[3] The sense of nature as a
dynamic process is suggested here by the
mobility of the light, by the towering clouds in
the distance that seem to be drawing up water
from the earth, and by the visible streaks of falling rain – a new motif in landscape
printmaking.[4]

Although the broad patterns of light and
shadow – the larger movements of nature – are
dominant, one gradually discovers that this is
an inhabited landscape. In this respect
Rembrandt's landscape continues the tradition
established by Pieter Bruegel's sixteenth-
century painted landscapes, which teem with
varied human activity; but, whereas Bruegel
delineates everything with great clarity,
Rembrandt intentionally half-obscures much
of the human detail, subordinating it to
nature's larger patterns, and giving the viewer
the pleasure of gradually discovering it. In a
bower-like gap in the shrubbery at lower right
two lovers are barely discernible. At left, at the
edge of the foreground body of water, are a
fisherman and his wife. In a dale beyond the
three trees nestles a cottage, while at the crest
of the dike one sees a wagon filled with travelers and, at far right, a seated draftsman
engaged in delineating the landscape. The panorama that opens at the left is dotted with cattle and herders, and at the horizon one
discovers the profile of the distant city, reduced
to insignificance by the grand movements in
the sky above it.

The landscape's rich complexity of conception is equaled by its complexity of execution.
As in the *St. Jerome* of 1642, some of the denser
passages of the right foreground are so impenetrable that one cannot determine precisely
what ingredients produced them, but it is
probably a combination of etching, drypoint,
and engraving. As Christopher White noted,
this is the first landscape in which drypoint was
used extensively.[5] It is employed boldly to
define the heavier clouds that frame the landscape at the top and the slashes of falling rain.
Finer meshes of drypoint are used to create the
translucent shadows of the rising clouds that
dwarf the city and those of the dike and the
dale below it. The fine granular bitten tone
that Rembrandt used so expressively in the
portrait of *Sylvius* is used on the fields in the
middle distance at left, contributing a subtle
sense of cloud shadows moving over the land.

Schelte A. Bolswert after Rubens, e.g., Dut. 27
(Rubens), no. 7, and the landscape etching with a distant
rainstorm, B. 47, by the Flemish painter Lucas van Uden
(1595–about 1672/73). None of these prints show the
veil of rain falling in the immediate foreground as
Rembrandt's etching so boldly does.

5. White, 1969, p. 200.

1. The city in the distance is generally identified as
Amsterdam or as inspired by Rembrandt's observations
of the city from a distance. The dike at the right has been
identified as the Diemerdijk or St. Anthonisdijk (Filedt
Kok, 1972, p. 126).

2. Other contemporary views of nature in a state of
change are the storms at sea etched by Hercules Segers
(Haverkamp-Begemann 48, 49) and by Reinier Nooms,
called Zeeman (the element of *Water,* Dut. 21).

3. White, 1969, p. 200.

4. Other contemporary prints in which streaks of falling
rain are represented are certain landscape engravings of

134
REMBRANDT VAN RIJN
The Goldsmith 1655

Etching and drypoint on Japanese paper
G. 119, B. 123, Hind 285, Münz 277, BB. 55-D,
W.-B. 123[1]
Lower left: *Rembrandt F. 1655*
76 x 56 mm. (platemark)
Coll.: J. Benedict (not in Lugt)
Private collection

In Rembrandt's etching *The Goldsmith,* of 1655,
the sculptor in metal embraces his allegorical
figure of Charity as tenderly as Charity
embraces her children.[1] Etched the year before
Rembrandt's portrait of the great silversmith
Jan Lutma (cat. no. 137), this intimate, small-
scale etching constitutes a moving commentary
on the relationship between an artist and his
work. The sculptor is possibly engaged in fas-
tening the sculpture to its scrolled base.[2]
Behind him we see the glow of the hooded
forge and to left and right on his workbench
other tools of his trade such as a pair of pincers
and an anvil.

    The impression exhibited here is one of a
number from this plate that Rembrandt chose
to print on a warm-toned Japanese paper. Here
the color of the paper contributes a muted
glow to the light of the interior. When one
compares this late work of Rembrandt the
etcher with an early work such as the *Pancake
Woman* of 1635 (cat. no. 72), one is conscious
of how much Rembrandt's etching style has
evolved. Sketchy freedom and restless vitality

1. No metalwork sculpture of Charity on this scale by a
Dutch metalsmith of this period is known, but a contemporary sculpture in wood on a much larger scale is very
close in motif. Attributed to Jan Hardewel, who died in
1659–60, this sculpture group in a classicizing style
adorned one of Amsterdam's public charitable institutions, where food and fuel were doled out to the poor;
reproduced in Carosso-Kok, 1975, p. 114.
2. As H. van de Waal, 1974, pp. 233–234, points out,
the pedestal, from Gersaint on, has been interpreted as an
anvil. If it is an anvil, it deviates a good deal, as Van de
Waal makes clear, from the usual forms assumed by metal
workers' anvils in the seventeenth century.

134 (actual size)

have been replaced by measured order and
calm. In the shallow space of the room the
group of sculptor and sculpture are firmly
locked into the background with its carefully
calculated right-angle divisions. There is an
architectural order and stability in such works
by Rembrandt of the 1650s that has led modern historians to speak of Rembrandt's classical
or classicizing style as one would designate as
classical or classicizing the high degree of
geometrical organization in the later works of
the contemporary French painter, Nicolas
Poussin. Even the shading lines have become
more orderly and now consist primarily of
regularized, almost systematic parallels.

Willem Drost
active 1650s

About the painter Willem (Wilhelm ?,
Wilhelmus ?) Drost, a follower of Rembrandt,
we know extraordinarily little. Houbraken
mentions by last name only a Drost who studied with Rembrandt and who spent a long
period in Rome.[1] The first name of his signature on one of his few signed paintings has
been read as "Wilhelm," leading to speculation
that he was German. It has also been interpreted as "Wilhelmus," the Latin version of the
Dutch Willem. A Willem Drost, who may or
may not be identical with the painter, was
present during an inventory in Rotterdam in
1680. His study with Rembrandt is not documented, but as his signed works show a clear
relationship to Rembrandt's works of the late
1640s and early 1650s, a period of study with
Rembrandt is generally acknowledged.[2]
    At least six etchings can be accepted as by his
hand,[3] two of them signed. Most impressions
of these prints show signs of experiment with
tonal printing or the imitation thereof by
washes applied after printing.

1. Houbraken, 1721, vol. 3, p. 61.
2. Biographies by MacLaren, 1960, p. 107; and Judson in
Chicago, 1969, p. 53.
3. Reproduced in Münz, 1952, pl. 30a., pl. 31 a. – e. See
also further attributions by Münz. The *Woman Reading,*
Holl. 3, is by another hand.

135
WILLEM DROST
The Painter at His Easel, about 1652

Etching with tone and touched with black pigment
B. 328 (Rembrandt), Rov. El. col. 67, Atlas 401;
Hind †355, Münz 342, Holl. 2
69 x 63 mm. (platemark)
Coll.: J. Sheepshanks (see L. 2333)
Lent by the Trustees of the British Museum.
BM307

At least two of Drost's etchings are portraits of
artists. The first (Holl. 1) is a bust-length etching of a man in a broad-brimmed hat who

135 (actual size)

looks directly out at us as he draws his own image. That etching, probably dated 1652 (the last digit is somewhat unclear), is very likely a self-portrait. The present bust-length portrait of an artist painting at an easel has been identified variously as a portrait of Drost by Rembrandt (Bartsch), a portrait of Rembrandt by Drost (Valentiner),[1] and a self-portrait (Münz, Hollstein). It is difficult to determine on the basis of the probable self-portrait (Holl. 1), etched in full face, whether the profile portrait shown here could be a self-portrait. Because of the difficulties presented to the artist, self-portraits in profile are necessarily rare.

Like the Rembrandt follower Philips Koninck (cat. nos. 159–162), Willem Drost was apparently inspired by Rembrandt's use of tonal inking, by his manipulation of a film of printer's ink on the smooth unworked areas of the etching plate. He emulated Rembrandt's expressive use of inking by the application of ink or pigment before printing or by the application of wash by hand after printing.[2] Each of the four impressions of *The Painter at His Easel* that I have examined (London, Vienna) is

1. Valentiner, p. 308.

printed or retouched in a very personal fashion and, like a drawing, is essentially unique.[3] The British Museum impression exhibited here appears to have been printed in grayish ink or overlaid with a somewhat opaque grayish ink or pigment. It was certainly touched with black pigment after printing. The two impressions in the Albertina, Vienna, have, respectively, a dark gray tone and a light gray tone applied to the image, probably before printing.[4] In these three impressions most of the tone has been added to the figure of the painter and to his easel. The background above the painter's head and between painter and easel is lighter, having been wiped free of excess pigment or touched less heavily.

The Painter at the Easel is rather loosely sketched and lightly bitten, but it has the blocky character of the drawing in Rembrandt's etchings of the late 1640s and 1650s. It was probably executed around 1652, the date of Drost's etched self-portrait (Holl. 1).

2. The pigment Drost used often seems cloudier and more opaque than conventional printer's ink, resembling watercolor with opaque white in it. Marks that suggest the manipulation of the pigment on the smooth surface of the plate, or that it was wiped from this surface, point to the probable application of the pigment before printing, as do occasional passages of dry, granular, or blotted textures.

3. Münz, 1952, p. 184, no. 342 describes the impression of head alone, in the British Museum (an impression in which the platemark has been clipped away), as a first state. This is perhaps correct, but one wonders if this could be an impression taken by hand, by rubbing, in which the rest of the image did not register. The portion that did print is accompanied by a veil of splotchy tone. An intermediate state may also exist. An impression in the Albertina (inv. 1930/540) appears to have been printed before the addition of heavier drypoint contours to the upper sleeve.

4. An impression of the self-portrait (Holl. 1) in the Rijksmuseum is printed in a brownish ink.

Cornelis Visscher
1629–1658

The professional engraver and draftsman Cornelis Visscher was born in 1629, most likely in Haarlem. He probably studied with the Haarlem painter and etcher Pieter Soutman, one of the printmakers who had reproduced the work of Rubens in Antwerp. At the beginning of his career, in 1649 and 1650, Visscher was active as an engraver for Soutman, engraving series of historical portraits designed and published by Soutman. In 1653 Visscher joined the Haarlem artists' guild. His father, who was from Delft and who owned property there, was also a member of the Haarlem artists' guild. Cornelis moved to Amsterdam and died there in 1658, at the age of twenty-nine. His brothers, Jan and Lambert, were also engravers.[1]

Cornelis made almost two hundred engravings, many of them portraits and genre scenes from his own designs. He also produced a large number of finished drawings in chalk on vellum, both portraits and scenes from daily life.

1. Biographical information on Cornelis Visscher was supplied, in conversation, by Mary E. Smith, who is preparing a dissertation on this artist.

136
CORNELIS VISSCHER
Gellius de Bouma, 1656

Engraving
Wussin 8[II], Dut. 89[II], Wurz. 8
Lower left: *C. de Visscher / ad viuum deli. / et sculp.*
Lower center in the third state: *1656*
402 x 290 mm. (platemark)
Wm.: crowned shield with fleur-de-lis and countermark P ?
Coll.: H.F. Sewall (L. 1309)
Museum of Fine Arts, Boston, Harvey D. Parker Collection. P7782

Among the many printed portraits produced in the Netherlands in the seventeenth century, portraits of preachers, like those of admirals, occur in great numbers, reflecting the importance of these professions in the society of the time. The career of Gellius Petri de Bouma (about 1579–1658), a preacher of the Reformed Protestant Church from Zutphen, near Arnhem, was remarkable only for his long and steadfast service.[1] His venerable age of seventy-seven and his fifty-five years of service to the Church are alluded to in the inscription in the lower margin. The rhetorical Dutch verses by J. Visscher (possibly Jan Visscher, the artist's brother) begin: "Live long, oh worthy man, who has dedicated fifty-four years of life, voice, and pen to Christ's flocks."

Bouma, robust and vital, looks us in the eye, lips parted, and gestures to reinforce his theological point. At his side are a lectern with open book and writing materials. Visscher's Latin inscription on a scrap of paper next to the quill pen and open inkwell indicates that the artist not only engraved the preacher's portrait but also drew him from life.

This engraving, dated 1656 in the following state, is one of the most celebrated of portrait engravings, not so much for the person it represents as for the vividness with which he has been represented. Gellius de Bouma does not lean out of a window, as does Rembrandt's Sylvius (cat. no. 97); nevertheless, he is very much a living presence. The tendency toward suggestion of color and texture in engraving, which was noted in De Gheyn's *Vanitas* (cat. no. 11), here reaches a climax in the depiction of the preacher's ruddy flesh, silken beard, and the glossy fabric of his garments. Visscher's immediate source of inspiration would have been the coloristic engravers around Rubens, among whom was his probable teacher Pieter Soutman. A comparison with the powerful sculptural emphasis in Hendrik Goltzius's head of his teacher Coornhert (cat. no. 5) makes clear the degree of coloristic suggestion in Visscher's portrait of the preacher.

1. See biography by Knipscheer in *N.N. Biografisch Woordenboek*, vol. 6, p. 176.

GELLIUS DE BOVMA ECCLESIASTES ZUTPHANIENSIS OVT INT 77 IAER EN INT 55 IAER VAN ZYN BEDIENINGHE.

Ora viri vultumq, vides, quæ pinxit Apelles,
Ingenium doctum pingere non potuit—
Quale fit hoc noscit Zutphania, scripta loquuntur.
Noscis Bouma senem? noscis et ingenium.

Leer' sang, ò weeede Man, die vier en vijftigh jaren
Met leven, stemm; en schrift, geweit hebt Christi scharen,
Gaet voort tot 's levens end, verflauwt noit in uw weeck.
Leer' lang, tot vreughd van ons, en dienst van Godes keeck.

J: Visscherus.

REMBRANDT VAN RIJN
Jan Lutma the Elder, 1656

Etching and drypoint
G. 256, B. 276, Hind 290, Münz 77, BB. 56-C,
W.-B. 276[1]
Upper center in the second state: *Rembrandt F. 1656*
197 x 150 mm. (platemark)
Wm.: foolscap (related to Churchill 355) with the
letters DC
Coll.: W. Esdaile (L. 2617); H. Brodhurst (L.
1296)
Museum of Fine Arts, Boston, Harvey D. Parker
Collection. P1607

While Cornelis Visscher's portrait of the
preacher Gellius de Bouma (cat. no. 136) represents the summit of achievement in professional portrait engraving at midcentury,
Rembrandt's 1656 portrait in etching and drypoint of the great Amsterdam goldsmith Jan
Lutma the Elder (1587–1669)[1] personifies the
mature Rembrandt's unconventional approach
to portraiture. In Visscher's print one has a
sense of light actively playing over the subject,
a light that clarifies and makes things explicit;
Rembrandt's sitter, on the other hand, is partly
veiled by an ellipse of shadow. In this fine,
well-preserved impression of the first state, the
areas of deepest shadow in many passages are
fortified by heavy accents of velvety drypoint
burr (see the deep folds of the sitter's right
sleeve.) Even the silver bowl, containing
punches, and the hammer that proclaim Lutma's
profession are half-enveloped by shadow. The
silver dish closely resembles the splendidly grotesque one in the lobate style (for the lobate
style, see Adam van Vianen's model book [cat.
no. 138], dated 1641, now in the collection of
the Rijksmuseum, Amsterdam).[2]

Like Rembrandt's painted portraits of
Nicolaes Bruyningh of 1652 (Bredius 268) and
Jan Six of 1654 (Bredius 276), the *Lutma* is
one of his later introspective portraits. Whereas
the preacher Gellius de Bouma in Visscher's

1. See biography in Amsterdam/Toledo/Boston, 1980,
p. 359.
2. Ibid., pp. 84–85, no. 40.

137

engraving directly engages our attention with his glance, Lutma, who holds an example of his work in his hand, looks downward or inward, his brow wrinkled in thought.[3] Shadow makes Lutma's expression ambiguous and mobile, suggesting a range of possible interpretations and hinting at human complexity. This sense of interior meditation and intellectual life is one of Rembrandt's most remarkable contributions to portraiture.

In the second state Rembrandt added a window in a deep embrasure behind Lutma, giving a greater sense of reality to the setting and somewhat diminishing the meditative atmosphere.

3. The subtlety and ambiguity of the expression of Lutma's eyes is pointed up when one compares the portrait of him etched by his son, Jan Lutma the Younger (see biography and cat. no. 195), in the same year (Holl. 5). Inspired by Rembrandt's portrait, the head in this interesting pastiche is a reversed copy of that in Rembrandt's etching. The eyes in Lutma's etching are rigid, mask-like slits. Although lighter in tone, Lutma's print with its mixture of techniques reveals the artist's interest in various methods of achieving tone in a print; among these is scoring the plate with a toothed goldsmith's tool, which gives the effect of a light gray wash.

23

Adam van Vianen
about 1569 – 1627

The goldsmith and silversmith Adam van Vianen, brother of Paulus van Vianen (cat. no. 17), was born in Utrecht about 1569. Like Jan Lutma the Elder (see cat. no. 137), he was one of the most important silversmiths working in the lobate style. While his brother, Paulus, had a particular gift for subtle work in low relief, Adam had a strong feeling for sculpture in the round. Paulus spent most of his career outside the Netherlands, but Adam remained in Utrecht, where he died in 1627. His son Christiaen (1600–1667), who was active as a silversmith for the courts of Charles I and Charles II of England, was his apprentice.[1]

1. See biographies by J.R. ter Molen, pp. 365–367, in Amsterdam/Toledo/Boston, 1980.

138
THEODOR VAN KESSEL
after ADAM VAN VIANEN
Candlestick, in *Constighe modellen van verscheijden silvere vasen…(Artistic Models of Various Silver Vases…)*. Utrecht, Christiaen van Vianen [about 1650].

Etching
(plate 23)
Lower left: monogram *AV;* upper right: *23*
257 x 196 mm. (platemark); 355 x 240 mm. (page size); red leather
Wm.: crowned shield with fleur-de-lis (type of Heawood 1800)
Guilmard, p. 506, 17; Berlin Orn. 1939, 1021
Museum of Fine Arts, Boston, Horatio Greenough Curtis Fund. 59.198

Published by Christian van Vianen about 1650, long after the death of his famous father, Adam, in 1627, the plates in the *Constighe modellen…(Artistic Models…)* were etched by Theodor van Kessel[1] from Adam's drawings.

1. Theodor van Kessel, who was born in Holland (?) about 1620, settled in Antwerp in 1652. He died after 1660. He was active in reproducing the work of Flemish painters for Antwerp publishers. He often used etching as a base for his engraving. See M.D. Henkel in Thieme-Becker, vol. 20, pp. 203–204.

Theodor van Kessel after Adam van Vianen
Lids and Spouts for Tankards and Ewers
Etching
Museum of Fine Arts, Boston

The fluid line of the etching medium was peculiarly appropriate for reproducing this grotesque biomorphic style, designated today by such terms as lobate, auricular, and cartilage.[2] Plate 13 (see illus.), with its various designs for spouts and for lids of tankards and ewers, epitomizes the playful inventiveness of this style, of which Adam van Vianen was perhaps the leading practitioner.

The title page bears inscriptions in Italian, French, and Dutch and announces eight parts, of which only three were published. The volume shown is one of the very few complete copies with all forty-eight plates. Like many printed pattern books, it probably became rare through popularity and use. The title page announces proudly that many of the intricate pieces were beaten from a single piece of silver.

This was not the only series of printed models for silversmiths in this style so full of surprising metamorphoses. Designs by Jan Lutma the Elder and by the Rembrandt pupil Gerbrand van den Eeckhout (whose father and brother were goldsmiths) were also engraved and published.[3]

The etching of a candlestick shown here is one of the handsomest of the plates. The design spans the copper plate precisely from edge to edge and is accompanied by Adam van Vianen's monogram. Beginning with the recognizable snails that form the base and moving upward, one sees how natural forms were transformed into virtually abstract ornament that is nevertheless curiously alive and organic; this lifelike quality is enhanced in the finished pieces by the slippery reflections on the polished metal surfaces. The candlestick is provided with a basin, apparently intended to catch the candle drippings. One can imagine how well the flowing forms of the candle drippings would have echoed the dewlap-like forms of the candlestick.

2. Ironically, many of the plates show signs of the imitation of the swelling line of engraving in the manner of the contemporary French etcher Abraham Bosse.

3. See Jessen, 1920, pp. 189–190.

139

FERDINAND BOL

The Woman with the Pear, 1651

Etching and drypoint
B. 14, Dut. 16, Rov. El. 14[III], Holl. 15[III]
Lower left: *Bol 1651*
145 x 118 mm. (platemark)
Coll. E. Astley (L. 2775)
Cincinnati Art Museum, The Albert P. Strietmann
Collection. 1960.612

The illusionistic image of a figure who confronts the viewer through a window embrasure is a familiar one in the paintings of Rembrandt as well as in those of his pupil Gerrit Dou and Dou's Leyden followers. Ferdinand Bol's etching of a woman with a veil who regards the viewer with a somewhat enigmatic look while holding out a pear by its stem is a fine example of such compositions in which the picture plane becomes a window opening.[1] A preparatory drawing in reverse for the print, indented for transfer, is in the Fogg Art Museum, Harvard University.[2] The expression of the woman's features is a bit fixed in the drawing and has greater mobility in the print than in the drawing. This is in part owing to the greater complexity of the play of light and shadow over her features in the print, including the subtle nuance of the translucent shadow cast by the woman's veil onto her brow. The fine meshes of shadow and the plush textures of the woman's garments are enhanced by velvety drypoint burr.

In recent years there has been a reevaluation of seventeenth-century works that critics in the nineteenth and earlier twentieth century chose to regard as straightforward vignettes from daily life. Scholars, led by Mr. E. de Jongh, have pointed to emblematic and allegorical content in such works that would have been evident to a seventeenth-century public well

1. Rembrandt's painting of the same year, in Stockholm, of a young girl resting her arms on a window ledge, while gazing directly out at the viewer, is a fine example of such a motif in his work (Bredius 377).

2. Reproduced in Sumowski, vol. 1, no. 105, p. 234.

139 (actual size)

versed in emblem literature.[3] The woman with the pear is very likely such an image but its emblematic meaning has not as yet been clarified.[4]

3. See, for example, De Jongh, 1967, and the catalogues of the exhibitions Amsterdam, 1976, and Braunschweig, 1978.

4. Mr. E. de Jongh informed me, in correspondence, that another writer is preparing an article on the emblematic meaning of the print. The interpretation will apparently focus on an emblem in Jacob Cats's *Speigel van den Ouden en Nieuwen Tijt (Mirror of Ancient and Modern Times)*, 1632 (p. 27 in the 1657 edition of the collected works of Cats) in which a seated woman, eyes modestly cast down, peels a pear, while a standing maid servant holds a bowl of pears. The motto and text concern silence as a virtue in women. There is, however, no direct visual correlation between image and gesture in Bol's etching and Cats's emblem. In emblem literature the same object or article can lend itself to several quite different meanings. In the same book by Cats (1657 edition, p. 24) is an emblem in which a seated unmarried woman offers a bowl of plucked pears to a bachelor, who rejects it and climbs a tree to pluck for himself fruit more difficult of access. Another emblem (1657, p. 48) shows a farmer in the foreground bemoaning a ripe pear that has "fallen easily into the mud," while in the background a woman berates a young pregnant woman.

Levi d'Ancona, 1977, p. 296, indicates that in antiquity the pear was the fruit of Venus and that its general meaning in the Italian Renaissance was that of affection and well-being. A pear is included in Lucas van Leyden's engraving of the allegorical figure of Virtue or Charity or Love (B. 129). I would like to thank William Robinson for discussing this iconographical problem with me.

Aelbert Cuyp
1620 – 1691

Aelbert Cuyp, who painted pastoral scenes and river views transfigured by morning or evening light, made eight small etchings representing cows and herders in landscape settings.

Born in Dordrecht in 1620, he resided there throughout his life, but the motifs of his landscape paintings show evidence of his travels within the Netherlands. He studied with his father, Jacob Gerritsz. Cuyp, a painter of pastoral subjects and portraits, as did his uncle, the painter Benjamin Gerritsz. Cuyp. Aelbert's earliest dated work is from 1639. When his father and mother died in 1651 and 1654, respectively, he was their sole heir and seems to have inherited considerable wealth. His work was well received in upper-class Dordrecht circles, and in 1658 he married a widow from the upper class. In later years he was a distinguished citizen of Dordrecht, filling many official positions in the Reformed Church and in the community. His sudden affluence seems to have led to a decline in the quality and quantity of his work as a painter.[1] Dated works are rare, and there are none after 1655. Aelbert's wife died in 1689, and he in 1691.[2]

Aelbert Cuyp never traveled to Italy. The light that irradiates his landscapes, gilding forms or making them transparent, was inspired by the southern light in the paintings of Jan Both, who returned to Utrecht from Italy in 1641–42. Besides his celebrated landscapes Aelbert Cuyp also painted portraits and poultry pieces.

1. See Stechow, 1966, pp. 61–64.

2. See biographies by Veth, 1884, pp. 256ff.; MacLaren, 1960, pp. 82–83; Blankert in Utrecht, 1965, pp. 171–173.

140 (actual size)

140
AELBERT CUYP
Two Cows at the Water's Edge

From a series of eight etchings
Etching
V.d.K.4[1], Dut. 1[1], Holl. 4[1]
Lower right: *AC*
68 x 74 mm. (platemark)
Coll.: J. Sheepshanks (see L. 2333)
Lent by the Trustees of the British Museum. S.7314

Aelbert Cuyp's eight etchings of cows and herders are often underrated because one normally sees only the pale, uneven, or harsh impressions of six of them (Holl. 1–6) issued by later publishers. Early impressions such as the present one, in which the image is enriched by a light film of extra ink that gives the landscape atmosphere, are extremely rare. All eight prints are similar in scale and format.

A series of prints of this kind, like Berchem's six small etched plates of cows of 1644 (Holl. 23–28), would have been extremely useful to landscape painters less skillful in drawing animals or looking for new motifs involving cattle. One of the earliest dated etched or engraved series of animal prints was engraved by Reinier van Persijn after designs by Aelbert's father (published in 1641, Holl. 11–23). In the landscape paintings of seventeenth-century Holland it was fairly common for figures or animals to be added by another artist. Perhaps the landscape painter was less skilled in drawing figures or animals, or he wanted more fashionable and marketable figures and animals to animate his landscapes. The figures in Jacob van Ruisdael's landscape paintings, for example, were frequently painted by artists such as Adriaen van de Velde, who specialized in painting such "staffage" figures in other artists' paintings.

The drawing of cattle and figures in Cuyp's eight etchings relates in style to that in his mature paintings of the late forties and early fifties. I have grouped the etchings with works of the 1650s.[1] The cattle and the foreground grasses are drawn with a calligraphic feeling that parallels the ornamental rhythms in Nicolaes Berchem's pastoral etchings.

1. A chalk and wash sheet of studies by Cuyp in Berlin of two cows relates closely in style and motif to the etching. The cow lying down is nearly identical to the one in the etching but in reverse. See Berlin, 1930, cat. drawings, p. 112, no. 10345, pl. 85.

Karel Dujardin
about 1622 – 1678

Karel Dujardin, a painter of Italian views with herders and their animals, produced a substantial body of work in etching, some fifty-two prints, the dated works ranging from 1652 to 1600. They are primarily Italian landscapes and animal subjects.

Karel Dujardin was born about 1622 in Amsterdam. His father was probably the Amsterdam painter of history subjects Guillaum Dugardin. The Du Gardyn family was an important patrician family that held many official positions.

As Houbraken stated, Karel Dujardin probably studied with Nicolaes Berchem. Dujardin is presumed to have made an Italian journey in the period 1640–1652, but it is not firmly documented. In 1650 someone of his name described as a "coopman" (merchant) was preparing to travel from Amsterdam to Paris. There is some evidence that Dujardin did visit Paris. His wife was apparently from Lyons, a popular stop for Dutch artists on the Italian journey. In 1652 he was in Amsterdam and sickly, making out his will with his wife as sole inheritor. In 1656 he was in the Hague, where he was a founding member of the painters' association "Pictura," which had broken off from the artists' guild of St. Luke. In 1659 he was again in Amsterdam, where his portrait was painted by Ferdinand Bol and by Bartholomeus van der Helst. Dujardin himself painted portraits of distinguished citizens of Amsterdam and etched a portrait of the prominent poet Jan Vos that was used as a frontispiece for a book of Vos's poems. Dujardin lived in a fashionable neighborhood of Amsterdam, on the Heerengracht, and owned property. He was friendly with the family of the collector of Italian paintings Gerrit Reynst and had a good knowledge of Italian painting. In 1674 he was still in Amsterdam, but 1675 found him in Rome. He seems to have visited Tangiers in North Africa on his way to Italy. He was very productive as a painter in Rome and was in

contact with the classicizing Dutch painter Jan Glauber. Dujardin was nicknamed by his Dutch artist colleagues "Bokkebaart" ("goatbeard"). In 1678 he moved to Venice, where he died in that year; his wife had died shortly before in Amsterdam. The inventory of the household reveals great prosperity.

In addition to Italian landscapes with herders, Italian genre scenes, and portraits, Dujardin painted religious subjects. His late work in Italy shows strong traces of the international classicizing style whose central figure was the French painter active in Rome, Nicolas Poussin.[1]

1. See biographies by Brochhagen, 1958, pp. 1–9; Blankert in Utrecht, 1965, pp. 195–197.

141
KAREL DUJARDIN
The Cow and the Calf, 1652

From a series of eight etchings
Etching and drypoint
B. 3, Dut. 3[1], Wurz. 3, Holl. 3[1]
Upper left: *.K.DV.I fe*
152 x 136 mm. (platemark)
Coll.: R. Peltzer (L. 2231)
Prints Division, The New York Public Library, Astor, Lenox and Tilden Foundations. 57140

Most, if not all, of Karel Dujardin's etchings with Italian settings or subjects seem to have been executed in the Netherlands. Quite a large number of painters specializing in Italian or southern subjects made etchings. This may reflect not only a popular demand for these exotic foreign views, in which the light was so different from that of the Netherlands, but also the profound impression made on these artists by their Italian experience.

Many of Karel Dujardin's animal etchings have a southern setting. The present series of seven animal etchings with title plate (Holl. 1–8) is close in conception to Pieter van Laer's ground-breaking Roman series of animal etchings of 1636 (cat. nos. 75, 76), which was the point of departure for all such series. The title plate of Dujardin's series (Holl. 1), like Van Laer's, is a watering trough, but without the flock of animals and herder seen in Van Laer's. The inscription on the title plate indicates that Dujardin served as his own publisher.

Dujardin's squarish format for his series is quite different from Van Laer's, but the most significant difference is Dujardin's greater interest in the rendering of light and atmosphere. This is particularly evident in the etching shown here, in which the play of light and shadow over the forms of the cow on the right is so boldly abstract that one might be forgiven for not recognizing the cow as a cow. In very early impressions of the plate, such as the present one, it can be seen how Dujardin made highly original use of bundles of extremely fine drypoint strokes to create areas of continuous tone that read like a gray wash. These lines are most legible along the edges of the rooftops and in a patch of tone in the clouds above the branches, but they are most effectively used in casting a transparent shadow over the calf and the underside of the cow's body and in defining a band of shadow in the middle ground behind the calf. These delicate passages of tone were rapidly diminished by further printing.

The upper body of the cow, the background buildings with smoking chimney, and the sky show Dujardin's characteristic use of open patterns of stipples and short broken strokes to represent surfaces suffused with light or forms made transparent and weightless by light and atmosphere.

141 (actual size)

142

42

PAULUS POTTER
The Frisian Horse, 1652

From a series of five etchings
Etching, drypoint, and engraving
B. 9^{II}, Weig. 9^{II}, Dut. 9^{II}, Wurz. 9, Holl. 9^{III}
262 x 241 mm. (platemark)
Wm.: foolscap
Yale University Art Gallery, Everett V. Meeks, B.A.
1901, Fund. 1966.9.58

43

PAULUS POTTER
The Worn-Out Horse, 1652

From a series of five etchings
Etching and engraving
B. 13, Weig. 13, Dut. 13, Wurz. 13, Holl. 13^{I}
262 x 242 mm. (platemark)
Wm.: letters bi (?)
Coll.: C. Josi (L. 573)
Rijksmuseum, Amsterdam.

Paulus Potter's 1652 series of five etchings of horses in landscape settings consists of three plates representing different types of horses in the prime of life (B., Holl. 9–11; see the *Frisian Horse*, cat. no. 142), a plate representing rather battered work horses (B., Holl. 12), and one of lying horses (B., Holl. 13; cat. no. 143). As Jan Verbeek has noted, the reference to the life cycle of the horse is inescapable.[1] Verbeek also suggests that the landscapes represent the cycle of the seasons,[2] but this suggestion seems less convincing.

Pieter van Laer etched an undated series (Holl. 9–14) of six small plates representing various aspects of a horse's life. The series, which is probably close in date to the 1636 animal series (Holl. 1–8), is unusual in that the numbers of the sequence appear to have been etched on the plates by Van Laer's hand and represent his original sequence rather than a publisher's. In most etched series of this kind

1. Verbeek, 1974–75, pp. 854–861.
2. Ibid.; Verbeek suggests a new sequence for the series in accordance with his theories: B. 11, B. 10, B. 9, B. 12, B. 13.

published in the Netherlands in the seventeenth century, the numbers are engraved, and one is frequently uncertain whether the sequence represents the artist's intentions or those of a publisher who later acquired the plates. In Van Laer's sequence the horse drinks in one plate (3) and makes water in the next (4), or grazes and frisks in one plate (5), and lies dead in the next, and final plate (6).

The lighting in the Potter series of horses is much simplified compared with that in his 1644 *Shepherd* (cat. no. 122). The accurate delineation of the horses themselves was apparently of greater interest to Potter than the detailed description of a specific light or atmosphere. Even the most dramatically lit of the series, *The Frisian Horse* (cat. no. 142), consists of a simple juxtaposition of the dappled horse with its light coat against a sky darkened by an impending storm. In *The Neighing Horse* (B., Holl. 10) Potter reverses this arrangement by silhouetting a dappled horse with a dark coat against a lighter sky.

Potter shows considerably less interest in specific description of texture than in the *Shepherd* of 1644. In the earlier etching, contours were continuous and firm but so fine that they were usually subordinate to the bold pattern of light and shadow or fused with the white of the blank paper to represent the dissolution of distant forms in atmosphere. In *The Frisian Horse* the line is heavier, and one is more conscious of contour drawing. Shading and crosshatching are often quite regularized, almost systematic, as in the shadow on the distant fields and the dark areas of the sky. Distant forms are perfectly distinct and firmly delineated rather than dissolved in atmosphere. In this completed state of the print Potter had lengthened the horse's tail, perhaps to give more stability to the horse's figure and to emphasize the magnificence of the specimen.

Instead of the vigorous contrast of the light horse against a stormy sky in *The Frisian Horse*, the tonality of *The Worn-Out Horse* is pale, monochromatic, and bleached out. The landscape has a desert-like aridity. In the working

drawing for the print, in Rotterdam (inv., Potter, no. 3), the image is slightly less bleak. A cottage surrounded by taller trees and bushes occupies the background, and the horse lying on the ground raises its head, whereas in the etching it appears to be dead. *The Worn-Out Horse* is one of the earliest dated examples of a seventeenth-century Dutch etching outside the work of Rembrandt that reflects the light monochromatic tonality and linear simplicity of many contemporary Italian etchings. This tendency toward less tonal variety, a light monochrome tonality, and linear economy was to be of great importance for Dutch etching during the rest of the century. Similarly, Potter was one of the first to introduce, in his later paintings, a cooler palette with grayed blue-greens, which was to be of great significance for Dutch painting during the second half of the century.

143

144

KAREL DUJARDIN
Sheep and Goats, 1655

Etching
B. 33, Dut. 33[1], Wurz. 33, Holl. 33[1]
Upper right: *K.Dv.IARDIN.1655*
195 x 222 mm. (platemark)
Wm.: foolscap and letter H
Museum of Fine Arts, Boston, Horatio Greenough
Curtis Fund. 1972.215

It would be reasonable to assume that Karel
Dujardin's 1655 etching of *Sheep and Goats,*[1]
with its huddle of animals placed in the immediate foreground, was concerned only with the
accurate portrayal of domestic animals, but the
artist seems to have been equally concerned
with the portrayal of light and space. A great
deal of the sky is completely blank, representing a clear atmosphere; Dujardin has emphasized the intervening space between the animals of the immediate foreground and the
shepherd and flocks on the far hillside.

Dujardin was undoubtedly conscious of
Potter's animal pieces such as *The Shepherd* of
1644 (cat. no. 122) and, like Potter, conveys a
strong sense of the textures of the coats of the
animals, but his realism is softer, less brutal
than Potter's. In the standing goat at the left
Dujardin manages to suggest not only the
color and texture of the animal's coat but also
the subtle play of light over these surfaces.

The *Sheep and Goats* was probably intended
to form a pair with the undated *Cow, Bull, and
Calf* (B., Holl. 34), which is similar in dimensions and also places animals on a hilltop
against open space.

1. A painting on copper panel in the National Gallery,
London, bearing Dujardin's signature and a date of 1673,
is quite close in motif and dimensions to the print. Only
the sky is noticeably different, being filled with cumulus
clouds. See MacLaren, 1960, p. 203, no. 985, and Plates,
1958, vol. 1, p. 170. Dujardin apparently repeated the
composition of his etching with few changes.

244 (actual size)

213

145

145

KAREL DUJARDIN
The Battlefield, 1652

Etching and drypoint
B. 28, Dut. 28¹, Wurz. 28, Holl. 28¹
Upper left: *K.DV.I fe /1652*
167 x 197 mm. (platemark)
Wm.: Strasburg lily (similar to Heawood 1732)
Coll.: P. Davidsohn (L. 654)
The Art Institute of Chicago, The John H. Wrenn
Memorial Collection. 1965.511

In Karel Dujardin's scene of foreign conflict,
mounted troops sweep past in the background,
banners flying, while in the foreground a
mounted officer, his horse shying warily,
inspects the dead or dying. The man in the
foreground has possibly been plundered of his
clothing after death: behind the mounted officer a man carries a bundle of cloth on his back.
The prostrate naked figure has the appearance
of an academic study made in the studio; its
pitiful nakedness is emphasized by the harsh
light that falls on the body.

Prints that have cavalry engagements as their
subject are relatively rare at this time. Earlier
etchers, such as Jan Martsen the Younger and
Willem van Lande, inspired by the cavalry
engagements painted by Esaias van de Velde in
his later career, made etchings of such subjects.
Later in the century, during the period of
Willem III's struggle with the French, Dirck
Maas and Jan van Huchtenburgh made etchings or mezzotints on similar themes.
Dujardin's conflict, apparently taking place on
foreign soil, is related in conception to the
undated etchings of cavalry combats by the
French painter of military subjects active in
Rome, Jacques Courtois (or Giacomo Cortese,
1621–1675).[1]

The twentieth-century English etcher Walter
Sickert admired this etching for its directness
and lack of dependence on tricks of printing to
disguise bad drawing: "Technically, this plate,

1. See Courtois's series R-D. 1–6. Although these prints
are undated, Courtois is known to have etched battle
scenes for a book that appeared in 1640 and again in
1647.

of which there is no proof in the British Museum, is perhaps *the* etching of the world. It is impossible for clarity, concision and vivacity to go further. For the sake of his drama, the artist knew that it was necessary to throw the mass formed by the carcase of the charger, the bank, and the receding troop into penumbra. A baser modern would have left the mass flimsy and empty, and called it atmosphere, or downed it with dirt. Not so the master....Enlarged photographs of the naked corpse should be in every art school as a standard of drawing from the nude. As in Vandyke, the approaches of the shadows are felt with a sensitive stipple that gives way, at the definite transition into shadow, to expressive line work."[2]

2. Sickert, 1911–12, p. 308.

Constantijn Daniel van Renesse
1626 – 1680

Constantijn Daniel van (or à) Renesse, painter, draftsman, and bureaucrat, made about seventeen etchings.[1] The dated etchings range from 1649 to 1653. Extremely varied in subject, they include portraits, scenes from daily life, and biblical themes.

Born in Maarssen, near Utrecht, in 1626, Constantijn was the son of a Reformed Protestant preacher, who served the house of Nassau as an army chaplain and who, in 1646, became rector of the Illustre School in Breda, the institution at which Jan Brosterhuisen taught botany and Greek. The family moved to Breda in 1638. In 1639 Constantijn was enrolled at Leyden University, studying first letters and then, in 1642, mathematics. He began drawing while at the university and around 1649 had some instruction in drawing from Rembrandt in Amsterdam. In 1653 he became secretary of the town of Eindhoven, remaining in the post until his death from cholera in 1680. There are no dated prints after this appointment, but he continued to make drawings, the last dated drawing being from the early 1670s.[2] Renesse should probably be considered a gifted amateur rather than a professional artist.

1. An etching of a seated boy drawing, Holl. 10, seems very inconsistent with Renesse's style and is probably not by him. Nor does an etching of a tramp and his family, Holl. 9, seem very convincing. On the other hand, the oval bust of a boy, Wurz. 11, is consistent in style with Renesse's other portraits and should have been included with Renesse's authentic etchings in Hollstein. It is reproduced in Waller, 1938, pl. XLVI, where it is identified as a self-portrait. This identification is not too implausible if one compares Wurz. 11 with Renesse's painting of a family concert of 1651, in which Vermeeren, 1978, pp. 8–9, illus., has identified the boy drawing at the left as a self-portrait.
2. See biographies by E. Trautscholdt in Thieme-Becker, vol. 28, pp. 160–161; Karel Vermeeren, 1978 and 1979.

146
CONSTANTIJN DANIEL VAN RENESSE
Village Fair with Charlatans, about 1650

Etching and drypoint
B. (Rembrandt school), p. 104, 18; Nagler 6; Rovinski (Anon.) 18[II]; Wurz. 4[III]; Holl. 7[III]
128 x 200 mm. (sheet)
Wm.: Cockatrice (related to Heawood 845)
Davison Art Center, Wesleyan University, Middletown, Connecticut, Gift of George W. Davison, B.A., 1892. 42-D1-156

Constantijn van Renesse's lively, anecdotal etching represents a fair with a row of tents, a large painted poster advertising a quack doctor's wares, and in the foreground a theatrical performance on a rickety, improvised stage set up in front of ruins.[1] One of the players is dressed in Italian *commedia dell' arte* costume. Behind him a head peeks out through the painted curtain to inspect the audience. At the top of the curtain one sees the silhouettes of puppets. The spectators include (center foreground) a vendor resting on his one-legged stool and (far right) a seller of rat poison holding a pole topped by a cage on which a rat scampers.

The arrangement of the space in Renesse's print is quite close to that in Ostade's *Dance under the Trellis* (cat. no. 112), but Renesse gives racy narrative detail precedence over the painterly atmospheric unity and the continuous flow of space visible in Ostade's etching. There are signs that Renesse was striving for a unity of light and atmosphere that he did not wholly achieve. In the second state and in the completed state, shown here, he added passages of irregular drypoint scratches that cast a shadow over the distant tent tops, trees, and churchtower and the quack's conical umbrella and poster, as well as modeling various figures in the crowd of spectators. These tonal passages do not, however, produce a unified sense of atmosphere.

The etching should probably be dated about 1650, between Renesse's *Charlatan* of 1649 (Holl. 8) and the *Violin Player* of 1651 (Holl. 5).

1. The church tower of the background has been identified as that of Eindhoven; see Hollstein, vol. 20, p. 14.

215

146 (actual size)

Adriaen van de Velde
1636 – 1672

The painter Adriaen van de Velde made some twenty-five etchings,[1] the dated ones ranging from 1653 (age 17) to 1670. Their subjects are animals in landscape settings and landscapes with travelers or peasants. Born in Amsterdam in 1636, Adriaen was the son of the marine painter Willem van de Velde the Elder and brother of the marine painter of the same name. Adriaen probably studied with his father. According to Houbraken, he studied with Jan Wynants in Haarlem. He was married in Amsterdam in 1657 and continued to reside and work there until his death in 1672.

Although the majority of Adriaen's paintings are landscapes, including coastal and winter scenes, the human figure is prominently featured in them. One of the most gifted of seventeenth-century Dutch figure draftsmen, Adriaen was often asked to paint the figures in the landscapes of other artists, such as Philips Koninck or Jacob van Ruisdael. He also painted biblical and mythological themes as well as portraits.[2]

1. Two undescribed etchings should be added to Dutuit's list: a small etching, in the Rijksmuseum, of a dog curled up by a board fence, signed "AVV" in reverse; and a square sketch plate, in the British Museum, with studies of heads of two goats, a sheep and a man's head, signed "A.V.V." and dated "165[9?]."

2. See documents in De Vries, 1886, pp. 143–144; biography in MacLaren, 1960, p. 413.

147 (actual size)

147
ADRIAEN VAN DE VELDE
The Town Gate, 1653

Etching
B. 18, Dut. 18, Wurz. 18
Upper left: *A.V. Velde: f. / 1653*
123 x 122 mm. (platemark)
Rijksmuseum, Amsterdam. OB4638

The Town Gate, showing an inn and travelers inside the gate of a southern town, is one of a number of etchings Adriaen van de Velde made in 1653 at the age of seventeen. These 1653

etchings and the drawings for two of them are Adriaen van de Velde's earliest documented works.[1] This etching of square format, together with its companion etching of similar dimensions, representing hunters pausing for a drink beside antique ruins (B. 19), were very likely inspired by Karel Dujardin's etchings such as the animal series of 1652 (see cat. no. 141).

Van de Velde, who apparently never went to Italy, had to "travel" by means of the motifs he

1. For Adriaen van de Velde's preparatory drawings, see Robinson, 1979.

saw in the works of other artists. His 1653 etchings, with their sketch-like freedom and zigzag strokes, are less complex in conception and execution than Dujardin's prints with their sensitive use of stipple, but their simplicity and directness are part of their appeal. Beginning in the later 1650s Adriaen van de Velde's drawing in his etchings became firmer and tighter, more reminiscent of Paulus Potter's etching vocabulary.

148

Gerrit Battem, a painter known primarily for his brightly colored or monochromatic gouache landscapes animated with figures, made only one etching, dated 1658, which is extremely rare.

Gerrit Battem was born about 1636 in Rotterdam. In 1640 his mother died, leaving Gerrit an orphan. The painter Jan Daemen Cool was appointed his guardian. His teacher may have been Cool or the landscape painter Abraham Furnerius, who was related to Battem's family and who probably studied with Rembrandt. In 1666 Battem was appointed by Johan Furnerius, Abraham's father, as tutor to his children. (Johan's son-in-law was the landscape painter Philips Koninck [see cat. nos. 159–162].) In 1667 Battem was married in Utrecht and was still living there in 1668. 1669 found him back in Rotterdam, where, in 1678, he restored a painting for the city government. He died in Rotterdam in 1684. His oil paintings are rare, but his gouaches numerous. Until recently a number of his monochrome gouache landscapes were regarded as works of Adam Elsheimer.[1]

1. See biographies by Haverkorn van Rijsewijk in Rotterdam, cat. paintings, 1892, p. 5; idem, Thieme-Becker, vol. 3, p. 43.

148

KAREL DUJARDIN

Italian Landscape (An Ass between Two Sheep), 1653

Etching
B. 32, Dut. 32^1, Holl. 32^1
Upper right: *K.DV.Iardin fe / 1653*
190 x 218 mm. (platemark)
Wm.: foolscap
Rijksmuseum, Amsterdam. OB4641

One of Dujardin's largest etched landscapes, the *Italian Landscape* of 1653 is perhaps the most lyrical southern landscape etched by a Dutch artist in the seventeenth century. The dark foreground, with animals resting in the cool shadows, acts as a foil for the sea of light beyond. Never did Dujardin use stipple with such suggestive power as in the slopes of the mountain vaporized by the flood of light.

149

GERRIT BATTEM
Rocky River Valley with Storm, 1658

Etching and drypoint
B. (Rembrandt El.) p. 123, 54; Rov. El. 54, Holl. 1
Lower right: .G. BATTEM 1658
170 x 193 mm. (platemark)
Graphische Sammlung Albertina, Vienna. H. III,
20, p. 59.

Gerrit Battem's 1658 *Rocky River Valley with Storm,* like Jan Pynas's *Jacob's Dream* (cat. no. 20), is an example of a Dutch painter's single experiment with etching that is so original and so expressive that one regrets that the artist abandoned the medium. Seventeenth-century Dutch painters seem to have often made prints at the beginning of their career, probably with the intention of publicizing their work by giving it greater circulation. Gerrit Battem was about twenty-two when he made the present landscape etching.

It is likely that very few impressions of the *Rocky River Valley* were printed, for I have seen only two impressions in the major printrooms. Fortunately, this example is untrimmed and is printed with an extra tone of ink that gives a more painterly character to the etching. The landscape with high cliffs lining a river valley is reminiscent of paintings of similar motifs by Hercules Segers, such as the *River Valley with Houses,* in Rotterdam,[1] or by Roelant Roghman, such as the two mountainous landscapes in Amsterdam.[2]

Freely drawn in a very fine etched line, the landscape is viewed from a considerable distance. The ledge at bottom, which bears the signature and date, and the double borderline at the sides suggest a window opening through which one views the landscape.

There is a strong sense of changing light, of cloud shadows moving over the land, as in Rembrandt's painted fantasy landscapes of the

1. Rowlands, 1979, color plate 2.
2. Amsterdam, cat. paintings, 1976, nos. A 760, A 4218, pp. 478–479.

149

1630s and his etched *Landscape with the Three Trees* (cat. no. 133) of 1643. The light film of ink that has been left on the plate in some areas has been wiped from the river surface, giving the impression that the water reflects the light of the sky.

This fully signed and dated etching should prove useful in identifying Gerrit Battem's pen landscape drawings (often executed on Japanese paper), which have hitherto been attributed to members of Rembrandt's circle such as Abraham Furnerius.[3]

3. Two drawings in Rotterdam published as Furnerius fall into this category; see Rotterdam cat. drawings, Rembrandt, 1969, Furnerius inv. V 40 and H 38, pls. 101, 102. Inv. H 38 is particularly close in style and motif to the etching. Inv. V 40 is inscribed on the back with Battem's name; see Paris, 1968–69, p. 61, n. 7. I would like to thank Jeroen Giltay for discussing this problem with me.

Den Bergh

R. Roghman fe.

150 (actual size)

Roelant Roghman
active 1646–1651

Roelant Roghman, a painter of mountainous landscapes and a topographical draftsman, made about forty etchings. Most of these are topographical views of the Dutch countryside and its villages, except for a series of Alpine views published in Augsburg[1] and the etching of a dike break that occurred in 1651.

Houbraken records that Roghman was born in Amsterdam in 1597, but about 1620 is a more probable date. We know nothing of his artistic education. According to Houbraken, he was a friend of Rembrandt and of Rembrandt's pupil Gerbrand van den Eeckhout. Roghman was apparently active in Amsterdam and is mentioned there in 1661 and 1664, the last occasion being the making of his will. An Italian journey is presumed on the basis of the subject matter of certain works but is not otherwise documented. According to Houbraken, Roghman never married and in 1686 was living in the "Old Man's House." He may have died in 1687.[2]

Roghman's paintings of invented mountain views related to those of Hercules Segers have received an increasing amount of attention in recent decades. His drawings fall into two categories: invented rocky or mountainous views and topographical drawings made in the Netherlands. In 1646–47 he made a series of 241 large drawings of Dutch castles and manor houses. He perhaps intended to publish these, but only one was engraved by his sister Geertruydt (Holl. 7).

1. Some doubt is expressed in Hollstein, vol. 20, p. 78, about whether these mountain views were executed by Roghman, but if one compares them with the 1651 etching of the dike break (Holl. 39), the qualities of line and illumination are extremely similar.

2. Biographies by Houbraken, vol. 1, pp. 173–174; R. Juynboll in Thieme-Becker, vol. 28, p. 518; MacLaren, 1960, p. 353.

150
ROELANT ROGHMAN
The Church at Nederhorst den Berg, about 1651

From a series of eight views of Holland
Etching
B. 24, Dut. 24[II], Holl. 24
Lower right: *R. Roghman fe;* upper right: *Den Bergh*
123 x 203 mm. (platemark)
Coll.: S.S. Scheikevitch (L. 2264); P.J. Sachs (L. 2091)
Museum of Fine Arts, Boston, Gift of Paul J. Sachs. M26296

Roelant Roghman's etching of the church at Nederhorst den Berg, on the river Vecht in the province of Utrecht,[1] is one of a series of eight landscape views in different provinces of the Netherlands (Holl. 17–24). Two other topographical series, of eight etchings each, are very similar in conception (Holl. 1–8, 9–16). Most of these views are remarkably simple, reflecting faithfully the undramatic nature of the Dutch landscape.

The church on a sand hill (*Bergh:* mountain), with a stork's nest constructed on its roof to bring good fortune, is one of the more dramatic images in these series. Roghman's etchings are often characterized, as here, by powerful illumination from the side. The intensity of the lighting, comparable to that in Herman Saftleven's *Wittevrouwen-poort* etching of 1646 (cat. no. 114), can only be experienced to its fullest in early impressions, such as the present one. The etched line is very fine but wiry. Contours are firm and continuous, except for the stipple that suggests the grass of the hillside. The cumulus clouds share much of the solidity of the earth below.

In style *Den Bergh* relates to certain of Roghman's castle drawings of 1646–47, but it is closest of all to the etching of the 1651 dike break.

1. For assistance in identifying the site, I would like to thank the Topographical Section of the Rijksbureau voor Kunsthistorische Documentatie, the Hague.

Reinier Nooms, called Zeeman
about 1623–1667

The marine painter Reinier Nooms, called Zeeman, was perhaps the most significant etcher of shipping and marine views in seventeenth-century Holland. His etched city views also are pictorially superior to the etched and engraved topographical views of his contemporaries. Generally working in series of "ports," "ships," and "views," dated from 1650 to 1656, Zeeman produced about 170 etchings.

Remarkably little is recorded about the life and career of this prolific etcher, who was probably born about 1623 in Amsterdam. His artistic education is unknown. On the basis of his signature "Zeeman" (seaman) and the presence in his widow's estate of books on navigation, he is presumed to have been part of a ship's crew at some time in his life. His first and second dated series of etchings (Dut. 6–18, 39–46) were issued in Paris in 1650 and 1652. These facts, together with his etched series of views in and around Paris (Dut. 55–62) confirm a period of residence in Paris around 1650. In a similar fashion, his painted views of North Africa, though unsupported by other documents, suggest at least one visit to that region. Zeeman also painted views of Mediterranean harbors. In Holland he seems to have been active exclusively in Amsterdam, which he portrayed in etched series such as that of the city gates (Dut. 119–126). He died in Amsterdam in 1667.

151

REINIER NOOMS, called ZEEMAN
Ships at Anchor

From a series of twelve marine views
Etching
Weig. 116[1], Dut. 116[1]
206 x 300 mm. (platemark)
Wm.: foolscap
The Metropolitan Museum of Art, Harris Brisbane
Dick Fund. 26.72.192

152

REINIER NOOMS, called ZEEMAN
Harbor View with Ships Careened

From a series of twelve marine views
Etching
Weigel 118[1], Dut. 118[1]
204 x 302 mm. (platemark)
Wm.: foolscap
Coll.: C. Josi (L. 573); J. Reiss (L. 1522)
Prints Division, The New York Public Library,
Astor, Lenox and Tilden Foundations. 52513

Zeeman's series of twelve views, with title plate, of various types of vessels in harbors and shipyards (Dut. 107–118) has the largest format of any of his series. The mood of these etchings, with their still, mirror-like sheets of water and ships at rest, is the becalmed mood of many of Simon de Vlieger's and Jan van de Capelle's marine paintings of the late 1640s and 1650s. The strong, clear light and atmosphere in which ships and figures are immersed has the intensity of the light in prints by contemporary Dutch etchers of idyllic Italian views such as Karel Dujardin. There is also a subtle sense of the shifting play of light and cloud shadow on the water's surface.

Zeeman's series of Dutch ships were anticipated by the series of Dutch ships in harbor and dry dock etched by the prolific etcher from Prague, Wenzel Hollar (Parthey 1261–1272), and published in 1647. One of the first publishers of Hollar's series was the Amsterdam publisher Clement de Jonghe, who also published some of Zeeman's series. Hollar, who was active in England, was residing at this time in Antwerp to avoid the disturbances of the English civil war. On the basis of comparison with Zeeman's dated etched series, one can place his series of large ships in the mid-1650s (compare his series of foreign seaports published in 1656).

Plate 7 from Hollar's series (see illus.) represents the same subject as cat. no. 152, ships in a shipyard being repaired and refurbished for another voyage. The contrast with Hollar's print, with its sculptural feeling for the form of the ships and its representation of sky and water in terms of regularized, virtually ruled, parallel lines, makes one aware that Zeeman's emphasis on the pictorial values of light and atmosphere was as strong as his mariner's desire to accurately describe what was taking place. In Zeeman's print all the ships have been careened, their hulls are being cleaned of growth, and the seams between the planks filled with caulking material to make them watertight. Fires fueled by bundles of reeds were used to dry the hulls, and the caulking materials hammered into the seams consisted of materials such as moss, brown paper, tow, and cloth.[1]

Although the intricate linear patterns of the ships' rigging silhouetted against the blank sky are integral to the pictorial appeal of these prints, most of the image is defined by bundles of freely drawn, parallel shading lines that stress the tonal rather than linear conception of the image. In the etching of the ships at anchor (cat. no. 151), the perpendicular relationship between the shading lines of the sails and the shading lines of still water and sky reinforces the mood of calm.

In 1675 Arthur Tooker, a London publisher, issued a new edition of the plates. An advertisement at the end of the appendix (p. 39) to the 1675 edition of Alexander Browne's art manual *Ars Pictoria* (published by Arthur Tooker) informs the reader: "Since the Printing of the following Catalogue there is happily fallen into Mr. Tooker's hands the best Book that ever Zeeman did, consisting of Men of War, Merchant Ships, Fly-Boats, Ships Building and Careening, etc."

1. See *Maritieme Encyclopedie,* 1970, s.v. "breeuwen" and "kalfaten"; Van Beylen, 1970, pp. 29, 42–43.

151

Wenzel Hollar
Dutch East India Merchantman under Repair
Etching (Parthey 1267)
Museum of Fine Arts, Boston

152

Claes van Beresteyn
1629 – 1684

Like Jan van Brosterhuisen (see cat. no. 128), the Haarlem draftsman and etcher Claes van Beresteyn was a gifted amateur artist who portrayed woodland views. The woodlands of his eight or nine etchings[1] consist of dense thickets inspired by the early painted and etched landscapes of Jacob van Ruisdael. Six of the etchings are signed, and two are dated 1650.

A member of a wealthy and distinguished family, Beresteyn was born in Haarlem in 1629. He was inscribed in 1644 as a pupil of the Haarlem painter Salomon de Bray. His brother-in-law was the painter and etcher Pieter Verbeeck. The one surviving painting by Beresteyn may portray Verbeeck and one of the horses the latter liked to paint. Beresteyn died in Haarlem in 1684. A small number of drawings are known. They also represent the twisted, rotting trunks and spiky vegetation seen in the etchings.[2]

1. The unsigned etching, Gerson 2, is so different in style from the other etchings that it is either from another phase of Beresteyn's activity as an etcher or from another hand, probably the latter.

2. For Beresteyn's life and work see Gerson, 1940. Although many drawings included in Gerson's catalogue are now attributed to Adriaen Verboom or Cornelis Vroom, the monogrammed and signed drawings reproduced there provide a firm foundation for further attributions of unsigned drawings.

153
CLAES VAN BERESTEYN
Landscape with a Clump of Oaks and Peasant Resting, about 1650

Etching
Gerson 9, Holl. 9
Lower center: *c.v. beresteyn.f.*
200 x 217 mm. (sheet)
Wm.: foolscap
Coll.: N.C. de Gijselaar (L. 1967)
Rijksmuseum, Amsterdam. B.J. 1061

153

Beresteyn's space is primitive and shallow: there is little sense of a free flow of space into depth. The shallowness of the space only serves to emphasize the claustrophobic density of the thickets of vegetation and the decorative two-dimensional patterns formed by the writhing, flame-like branches silhouetted against the blank sky. Beresteyn's etchings, some of which are dated 1650, are intensely expressive exaggerations of the thicket and bramble imagery seen in Jacob van Ruisdael's early paintings and etchings, such as *The Wheatfield* (cat. no. 124) of 1648. Beresteyn's etching of a grain field ringed by gnarled trees, Gerson 5, is a free variation in reverse of Ruisdael's etching.

The squarish format of the present etching serves to focus our attention on the central pyramidal clump of trees. The trunks of these trees are composed of loose, tangled skeins of etched lines, while the prickly foliage is rendered by open clusters of broken spiky lines. The single human inhabitant of the landscape is drawn with the same vocabulary of etched lines and is consequently almost invisible, absorbed into nature's living web.

225

154

226

154

JACOB RUISDAEL
The Wooded Landscape with a Great Tree,
about 1651–1655

From a series of four etchings
Etching
B. 2, Weig. 2[I], Dut. 2[I], Wurz. 2[I], Keyes 9[I], Holl. 2[I]
Lower center: *.Ruisdael. f.*
189 x 275 mm. (sheet)
The Metropolitan Museum of Art, Harris Brisbane
Dick Fund. 26.72.10

The Wooded Landscape with a Great Tree is one
of four etchings of similar format and dimensions (B. 1–4) that were never published as a
numbered set but were undoubtedly executed
at the same time. They are Ruisdael's last works
in the etching medium. On the basis of comparison with dated paintings, they should
probably be dated in the first half of the 1650s,
at the earliest about 1651.[1]

A remarkable change has occurred in
Ruisdael's conception of the etched landscape
in the few years since the landscape etchings
of 1646 and 1648 (cat. nos. 123, 124). Forms
are more broadly conceived and drawn, and
there is less sense of specific texture or varie-
gated color. Ruisdael now suggests rather
than specifies. The lighting is more diffuse, the
shadows less deep. A sense of depth in the landscape is simply and efficiently created by two
bitings of the plate of different strengths. The
overall tonality is light and somewhat monochromatic, evoking the tonalities of many
seventeenth-century Italian etchings.

The theme of the heroic tree or group of isolated trees entered Ruisdael's paintings about
1651. Ruisdael's scarred old giant has a serene
majesty quite different from that of the trees
locked in a jungly struggle for life in Roelant
Savery's etching *Gnarled Trees in a Swamp* from
the first decade of the century (cat. no. 19).
Ruisdael's tree stands in proud isolation, light
and air flowing around it, its roots firmly
anchored in the soil. Between the limbs of the

trees one glimpses, half-concealed behind a
hill, a half-timbered cottage of the kind
Ruisdael would have seen during his visit to
Germany, near Bentheim.

Impressions of the first state of the print,
before the plate was reworked by other hands,
are comparatively rare. In the next state, stiff,
puffy cumulus clouds and parallel shading were
added to the sky, crowding the space of the
landscape and diminishing the sense of light
and atmosphere. The clouds resemble those in
some of the later landscape paintings of
Ruisdael but are clumsily executed. They also
resemble the rather rigid, puffy clouds in many
of the etched landscapes by Allart van Everdingen, whose paintings of Scandinavian
waterfalls inspired Ruisdael's highly successful
waterfall paintings. The lower right corner of
The Wooded Landscape was also reworked in the
second state. Heavier etched shading outlines
the fallen tree trunk and the rock, so that they
stand out as separate entities rather than forming part of a painterly unity. All four of the
landscapes made at this time (B. 1–4) were
reworked in a similar fashion, the first three in
the second state, B. 4 in the fourth state.

1. Rosenberg, 1928, pp. 23–24.

155

JACOB VAN RUISDAEL
The Cottage and Footbridge,
about 1651–1655

From a series of four etchings
Etching
B. 1, Weig. 1[I], Dut. 1[I], Wurz. 1[I], Keyes 8[I], Holl. 1[I]
Lower right: *Ruisdael f*
196 x 278 mm. (platemark)
The Art Institute of Chicago, The Clarence
Buckingham Collection. 44.606

The Cottage and Footbridge is part of the same
group of four etchings as the *Wooded Landscape
with a Great Tree* (cat. no. 154). Although
Ruisdael's vocabulary of etched line has totally
changed in this print, the sense of humble
human dwellings about to reenter the cycle of
nature is similar to that in the earlier *Cottages
by a Stream,* of 1646 (cat. no. 123).

In this fine, well-preserved impression of the
first state – before the disturbing additions by
another hand in the second – the battered
boards and tattered thatch of the half-timbered
cottage fuse pictorially with the surrounding
foliage. In the more common second state conventional shading and wiry cumulus clouds
were added to the sky, and each object of the
foreground was made more distinct and separate by conventional and heavy-handed shading: the roof line of the cottage, the log in the
water, and the crooked willow. In this impression of the first state a light film of printer's ink
left on the plate contributes a sense of tangible
atmosphere and subtly collaborates in the pictorial harmony.

Ruisdael's awareness of the visual appeal –
even poetry – of the battered, dilapidated, and
tumbledown is related to that of Adriaen van
Ostade in his interiors of 1647, *The Family* and
The Barn (cat. nos. 101, 102), but his description is less specific. A rural cottage or farmhouse as the dominant motif of a landscape is
familiar from Rembrandt's landscape etchings
of the 1640s such as the *Landscape with a
Cottage and Large Tree* (B. 226) of 1641.

155

228

156

ANTHONIE WATERLOO
Wooded Landscape with Resting Travelers

From a series of six etchings
Etching and engraving
B. 122, Dut. 122[1]
Lower right: *AW.f.*
294 x 239 mm. (platemark)
Wm.: foolscap
Museum of Fine Arts, Boston, Katherine E. Bullard
Fund in memory of Francis Bullard. 65.972

In Waterloo's etching a woman and three children, including a baby in a wicker backpack, rest beside a road before a house buried in trees. The landscape forms are more solid, more powerfully modeled and lit than in Waterloo's earlier *Cart on the Road,* with its delicate line and soft atmospheric feeling. Although Waterloo's prints are all undated and extremely difficult to place in chronological sequence, this etching, one of a series of six landscapes in an upright format (Dut. 119–124) and comparable in scale and format to Herman Saftleven's *Great Tree* of 1647 (cat. no. 132), is stylistically compatible with Dutch landscape printmaking in the 1650s.

  In all six of the etchings in this series, anecdotal incidents from daily life are prominently featured. Two other etched landscape series of vertical format, comparable in scale and style, feature episodes from mythology (Dut. 125–130) and from the Old Testament (Dut. 131–136). These last two series parallel in conception Herman van Swanevelt's landscapes of the 1650s animated with mythological or biblical figures.

  In his prints Waterloo frequently used drypoint and engraving to supplement etching in order to achieve the maximum strength of modeling or depth of shadow. In a fine early impression such as the present one, these harsher accents are perfectly integrated (see the dark engraved tips of the grasses or rushes around the woven fence at center). Waterloo's bold contrasts, strong lighting, and solid forms, often achieved by means of engraving, are paralleled in the landscape prints of Roelant

Roghman; see, for example, Roghman's series of views of the Hague wood (Holl. 33–38) which, even in the rare first state, make extensive use of engraving. Waterloo's own use of engraving in the early printings of the plates is often difficult to distinguish from the reworking of the plates in engraving by other hands at a later date, when the effect of the more delicate etched passages was beginning to diminish. In the present impression the strong contrasts are muted by the pictorially unifying transparent film of ink left on the plate before printing.

Mid-seventeenth-century Dutch wooded landscapes of this type were so widely imitated in Germany, France, and England in the late eighteenth and early nineteenth centuries that it is often difficult to see them with fresh eyes.

Jan Hackaert
about 1629 – after 1685

Jan Hackaert, painter of idyllic woodland lanes with warm, southern light filtering through tall trees, made a series of six etchings of wooded landscapes with bodies of water.[1]

Hackaert was born in Amsterdam about 1629. We know nothing of his artistic education. Certain of his paintings and drawings reflect the influence of Jan Both. Hackaert's travels in Switzerland in the period 1653–1656 are documented by dated drawings. He may also have visited Italy. There are dated paintings from 1657–1685. He was probably active in Amsterdam. His death date is unknown, but there is no record of him after 1685.[2] The figures and animals in his paintings were often painted by other artists such as Adriaen van de Velde and Nicolaes Berchem.

1. A seventh landscape etching attributed to Hackaert (Weig., Holl. 7) is most likely not by him, but it is one of the most beautiful unattributed etchings of the Dutch seventeenth century; see De Groot, 1979, p. 231.

2. Biographies in MacLaren, 1960, p. 141; Blankert 1965, p. 217.

157

JAN HACKAERT
The Winding Road, about 1653

From a series of six etchings
Etching and drypoint, touched with gray wash
B. 2, Weig. 2^I, Dut. 2^I, Holl. 2^I
Lower right: *I.H*
192 x 218 mm. (sheet)
Wm.: crowned shield with fleur-de-lis
Coll.: C.H. Hodges (L. suppl. 552); E. and A. Dutuit (L. suppl. 709a)
Musée du Petit Palais, Paris. Dut. 5471

Impressions of the expressive first states of Hackaert's series of six wooded landscapes (Dut. 1–6) are extremely scarce. In the second state, published by the Amsterdam publisher Clement de Jonghe, the plates were completely reworked in rather tight, conventional engraved shading, which suppressed the immediacy of drawing and vibrant atmospheric feel-

ing of the first states. The first states, which bear the artist's monogram, are executed mostly in etching.[1] Perhaps the publisher felt that the more delicate etched lines would not survive a large printing.

The first state of *The Winding Road,* shown here, shares some of the short-hand power of suggestion and continuous flow of space seen in Rembrandt's *View toward Haarlem (The Goldweigher's Field)* of 1651 (cat. no. 158). The delicate broken lines (probably drypoint) of the sky contribute a subtle atmospheric shimmer that was lost when they were scraped away for the publisher's edition. In another landscape from this series, Dut. 3, the sky in the first state was full of freely drawn, fleecy clouds that were subsequently scraped away, leaving the sky blank.

The series was probably executed in the 1650s, the nearest comparison in style and motif being a drawing dated 1653, in the British Museum.[2]

1. Touches of gray wash on tree trunks and brush in this print, however, may be related to the artist's plans for further development of the image.

2. London, cat. drawings, 1926, vol. 3, Hackaert, no. 1.

157 (actual size)

158

158

REMBRANDT VAN RIJN
*Landscape with a View toward Haarlem
(The Goldweigher's Field),* 1651

Etching and drypoint
G. 226, B. 234, Hind 249, Münz 167, BB. 51-A,
W.-B. 234, only state
Lower left: *Rembrandt 1651*
120 x 317 mm. (platemark)
Wm.: fragment of Paschal Lamb (Heawood 2843)
Coll.: L.J. Rosenwald (L. suppl. 1760b)
National Gallery of Art, Washington, D.C.,
Rosenwald Collection

Rembrandt's etching is the ultimate expression
of the development of the panoramic Dutch
landscape in print form that began with the
engravings of cities in profile by Pieter Bast
around 1600 and includes landscape etchings
by Esaias van de Velde (cat. no. 40), Jan van de
Velde (cat. no. 42), as well as Hercules Segers
and Johannes Ruisscher.

The print has been known since the eighteenth century as "The Goldweigher's Field,"
because it was thought to represent the estate
of Jan Uytenbogaert, the tax receiver (who was
represented by Rembrandt in an etching as a
goldweigher, B. 281). It has been persuasively
identified by Van Regteren Altena, however, as
a view of Saxenburg, the estate of Christoffel
Thijsz., with the city of Haarlem and the characteristic profile of its great church of St. Bavo
in the distance.[1] Christoffel Thijsz. had sold
Rembrandt the house in the Breestraat several
years earlier, in 1639, and the artist still owed
money on the purchase. Standing on the
dunes – as Jacob van Ruisdael did when con-
ceiving his painted views with Haarlem in the
distance – Rembrandt made a drawing
(Benesch 1259) that is related to but not identical with the etching. He also made a painting
of the view.[2] The etching reverses the view in
the drawing and painting.

Rembrandt's etching is the most expansive

seventeenth-century Dutch landscape in print
form. Hyatt Mayor captured the peculiar originality of the space of the landscape in his
description in *Prints and People:* "It is the only
landscape in all art that wheels under the drive
of invisible wind around a pivot on the horizon, as level lands seem to wheel when watched
from a fast train."[3] Rembrandt has ignored
the conventional schematic devices to define
space used by Jan van de Velde in his large panoramic view toward Haarlem (cat. no. 42).
Inventive draftsman that he was, he used frag-
mentary etched lines and strategically placed
clumps of drypoint with burr to give definition
to the intangible. In the beautifully balanced
impression shown here, the drypoint burr has
the proper weight to fully define the sweep of
space. In some of the earliest impressions, distant drypoint accents are too heavy and leap
forward, optically distorting the space; in later
impressions, in which the burr is completely
worn away, the space collapses.

1. Van Regteren Altena, 1954, pp. 1–17.
2. Not included in Bredius/Gerson, 1969. Reproduced
in color in Van Regteren Altena, 1954, facing p. 1.

3. Mayor, 1971, pl. 504.

Philips Koninck
1619 – 1688

The great landscape painter Philips Aertsz. Koninck made about eight etchings, all landscapes.[1] The majority of these were originally assigned by Bartsch to Rembrandt, whose influence they strongly reflect. Most impressions of Koninck's prints were worked up in gray, black, and brown washes after printing, possibly in emulation of Hercules Segers's procedures but certainly in emulation of the tonal patterns of Rembrandt's landscapes in etching and drypoint.

Born in Amsterdam in 1619, Philips Koninck was the son of the prosperous goldsmith Aert de Koninck. He studied with his brother, the painter Jacob Koninck, in Rotterdam in 1640 and perhaps as early as 1637. According to Houbraken, he was a pupil of Rembrandt, but this is not documented; it is known, however, that he was a friend of Rembrandt's after he moved to Amsterdam. In 1640 he married in Rotterdam Cornelia Furnerius, sister of Abraham Furnerius, a Rembrandt follower whose drawings are closely related to his own. In 1641 Koninck moved to Amsterdam, where his wife died in 1642. He lived the life of a well-to-do member of the middle class and was acquainted with many prominent citizens of Amsterdam, such as the poet Vondel. Like many Dutch artists of his time, he had two professions, being also proprietor of a passenger-boat service between Amsterdam and Rotterdam. He married a second time in 1657. He died in Amsterdam in 1688.[2]

In his own time Koninck was better known for his portraits, genre scenes, and paintings on literary themes than for his landscapes, which are regarded today as among the finest produced in the seventeenth century.

1. Holl. 9 is not by Philips Koninck but probably by Pieter de With or Jacob Koninck.

2. See biographies by Gerson, 1936, pp. 8–14; MacLaren, 1960, p. 210.

159
PHILIPS KONINCK
The Landscape with a Coach

Etching touched with gray and black washes
Gersaint 207, B. 215, Middleton R. 1, Dut. 212, Hind 325, Münz 362, Biörklund-Barnard rej. 23, Holl. 4
63 x 173 mm. (sheet)
Coll.: Aylesford (L. 58); Buccleuch (L. 402); M.J. Perry (L. 1880)
Yale University Art Gallery, The Fritz Achelis Memorial Collection, Gift of Frederic George Achelis, B.A., 1907. 1925.140

160
PHILIPS KONINCK
The Landscape with a Coach

Etching touched with gray, black, and greenish gray washes
Gersaint 207, B. 215, Middleton R. 1, Dut. 212, Hind 325, Münz 362, Biörklund-Barnard rej. 23, Holl. 4
63 x 177 mm (sheet)
Coll.: W. Esdaile (L. 2617); G. Biörklund (L. suppl. 1138c); A. Artaria (L. 33)
Museum of Fine Arts, Boston, Horatio Greenough Curtis Fund. 58.21

161
PHILIPS KONINCK
The Landscape with a Coach

Etching on Japanese paper, touched with gray and black washes
Gersaint 207, B. 215, Middleton R. 1, Dut. 212, Hind 325, Münz 362, Biörklund-Barnard rej. 23, Holl. 4
61 x 175 mm. (platemark)
Teylers Museum, Haarlem

This panoramic etching of a coach rolling along a dike, with a city visible in the distance, was once, like the majority of Philips Koninck's etchings, catalogued by Bartsch as Rembrandt. Charles Middleton, in his 1878 catalogue of Rembrandt's etchings was the first to attribute it to Koninck.[1] By means of comparisons of Koninck's drawings and of the early manuscript signatures and annotations on individual impressions of the etchings, scholars have arrived at the group of prints now considered to be by Koninck's hand. Confusion of Koninck's work with the etchings of his brother, Jacob, and those of Pieter de With, another landscape etcher in the Rembrandt circle, still presents problems.

A few impressions of Koninck's etchings are untouched with wash, but the majority were worked up by hand after printing. The passages of wash are consistent in style with the passages of wash in Koninck's drawings and were not added by another hand. Hercules Segers had provided a precedent for this practice of treating each impression as a unique object, like a drawing. Three impressions of the *Landscape with a Coach,* one printed on Japanese paper, are shown here to illustrate this aspect of Koninck's etchings. As in Willem Drost's prints (see cat. no. 135), Koninck's use of wash was undoubtedly inspired in part by Rembrandt's tonal inking of his prints from the late 1640s onward (see cat. no. 167). The use of wash in impressions of the *Landscape with a Coach,* however, most closely resembles the pattern of drypoint accents in a Rembrandt landscape etching such as the *Landscape with a Flock of Sheep* of 1652 (cat. no. 163). The etched lines of Koninck's prints often consist solely of the outlines of the landscape forms, as if he were already planning to add the tonal passages later by hand. In the landscape with the coach, as in some of the other etchings, Koninck's etched line is very fine and rather soft and granular, blending all the better with the areas of wash. The applied washes range from opaque white to gray to deep black as well as brownish

1. Middleton, 1878, pp. 308–310.

233

159 (actual size)

160 (actual size)

161 (actual size)

hues. In some areas the wash has a grainy, blotted texture, suggesting either application to the plate *before* printing or, more likely, blotting immediately after application.

The variations in the application of the wash to different impressions subtly alter the pattern of light and shadow, the definition of the space, and the prominence given to individual objects.

Koninck, like Rembrandt from the later 1640s on (see cat. no. 98), often printed his etchings on Japanese paper, usually of a fairly heavy weight and yellowish in color. Pieter de With was another landscape etcher around Rembrandt who touched his prints with wash and whose etched work is often confused with Koninck's; De With also used Japanese paper for prints. In the Teylers Museum impression exhibited here, the Japanese paper is a light buff color.

Koninck's prints are not dated. One or two impressions of the *House with a Picket Fence* (cat. no. 162) are known that bear an early inscription with Koninck's initials and the date 1659. Gerson discussed the etchings in relation

to drawings dated 1660–1663.[2] They should probably be placed in the late 1650s or early 1660s. I have chosen to juxtapose them here with Rembrandt etchings of the 1650s, their immediate source of inspiration.

2. Gerson, 1936, pp. 63–64.

162

PHILIPS KONINCK
The House with a Picket Fence, 1659?

Etching and drypoint on Japanese paper touched with black, gray, and white washes
Gersaint 234, B. 242, Middleton R. 11, Dut. 239, Hind 333, Münz 361, Biörklund-Barnard rej. 31, Holl. 3[II]
90 x 157 mm. (platemark)
Teylers Museum, Haarlem

The *House with the Picket Fence* is one of the rare instances in which Koninck worked the tonal passages into the printing plate itself. Drypoint shades the house and trees, the first row of pickets, and the ground at right. Over this tone scratched into the plate, Koninck applied washes of black, gray, and white. Some

of this supplementary tone may have been spread on the smooth surface of the plate before printing. The drag marks in the film of tone in the right foreground suggest marks made during the inking and wiping of a plate rather than during application after printing.

Shown here is an intermediate state of the print before Koninck added the horizon at right in drypoint and before he created a doorway with a half-door and a figure in the facade at left. This impression of the *House with a Picket Fence* is apparently printed on a cream-colored Japanese paper with bamboo laid lines (unlike European laid paper, it has no connecting chain lines).

Frits Lugt identified the site as a house in one of the bulwarks of Amsterdam's fortifications, the "de Rose" or "Rijck" bulwark. According to Lugt, Rembrandt also drew this house and others in this area (Benesch 1263, 1264).[1]

1. Lugt, 1920, pp. 76–79.

235

162

163
REMBRANDT VAN RIJN
Landscape with a Haystack and a Flock of Sheep, 1652

Etching and drypoint
G. 216, B. 224, Hind 241 (1650), Münz 159 (1650), BB. 52-A, W.-B. 224^II
Lower left: *Rembrandt f. 1652*
82 x 175 mm. (platemark)
Wm.: foolscap (fragment)
Coll.: Arnold Knapp (not in Lugt)
Fogg Art Museum, Harvard University. 12.901

A number of Rembrandt's etched landscapes were based on observations made during sketching excursions in the countryside just outside Amsterdam. Frits Lugt identified the site of this etching and that of the *Landscape with the Milkman* (or *Fisherman,* B. 213) as a farmstead along the Diemerdijk or St. Anthonisdijk outside Amsterdam.[1] The same area and the dike may also have been the setting for the *Landscape with the Three Trees* (cat. no. 133). A drawing of the same period (Benesch 1226) seems to represent the farmhouse nestled in trees that is shown reversed in the etching. In the Dutch countryside one can still see in the midst of the flat expanse of land such islands of greenery sheltering a farmhouse. The design of the haystack has not changed, but the adjustable roof that protects it may be aluminum rather than thatch.

The plate curves in a low arch at the top. Rembrandt occasionally used this format in paintings and favored it when inventing architectural backgrounds for literary subjects from the Bible or ancient history. Like the *Landscape with the Three Trees,* the *Landscape with a Haystack and Flock of Sheep* is a landscape animated by incidents of human and animal life that only fully reveal themselves after prolonged study. Many viewers have never noticed in Rembrandt's print the lively detail of the horse in the middle of the meadow, joyously rolling on its back and kicking its legs in the air, but no

1. Lugt, 1920, pp. 139–140.

163 (actual size)

one would overlook the frisking horse in Claes Jansz. Visscher's etching of the Huys te Kleef (cat. no. 36). These details, which are subordinated to the total unity of space, light, and atmosphere and only gradually reveal themselves, are one of the most lasting and intimate sources of pleasure in Rembrandt's landscape prints.

The Landscape with a Haystack and Flock of Sheep is based on a framework of etched lines, but the essential tonal passages, both the most subtle and the most forceful, were added in drypoint.[2] The delicate parallel lines that shade the hillside behind the kicking horse and cause it to stand out white against the slightly darker slope are drypoint, as are the fine scratches that suggest the distant horizon seen through a haze of atmosphere at left. The deeper accents that define the masses of the landscape, the bank of the stream in the foreground, the flock of sheep, and the deep shadows under the trees

2. For a study of the development of the design of this landscape and its manner of execution on the plate, see Morse, 1966.

are also drypoint. As in the view toward Haarlem ("The Goldweigher's Field") of 1651 (cat. no. 158), when the fragile drypoint diminishes in effect, the landscape is deprived of its characteristic space and atmosphere.

164

REMBRANDT VAN RIJN
The Flight into Egypt: Altered from Segers, about 1653

Etching, drypoint, and engraving
G. 56, B. 56, Hind 266 (1653), Münz 216 (1643/4), BB. 53-2, W.-B. 56[IV]
211 x 283 mm. (sheet)
Wm.: fleur-de-lis (related to Heawood 1769)
Museum of Fine Arts, Boston, Gift of the Visiting Committee through George Peabody Gardner, 1916. M26200

The *Flight into Egypt* is the last link in one of the most tightly interlocking chains in the history of art. Rembrandt, who owned several paintings by Hercules Segers, also acquired the copper plate of Segers's etching of *Tobias and*

the Angel (Haverkamp-Begemann 1). Segers's etching was a creative variation on a painting by Adam Elsheimer. Segers probably saw not Elsheimer's original painting but, rather, the translation of the image into black and white in Hendrik Goudt's engraving of 1613 (Holl. 2). Rembrandt took Segers's plate and transformed it into a *Flight into Egypt,* retaining whole passages of Segers's original etched work at left and in the distance at center.[1] Such a "collaboration" across the generations between two great printmakers – one living, one dead – was without precedent in the history of printmaking and is still a surprising and moving event. Rembrandt also made creative alterations, involving a shift in scale and a change in patterns of illumination, in one of Segers's paintings, the great *Mountain Landscape,* now in the Uffizi, Florence.[2]

1. The only two surviving impressions of Segers's etching before Rembrandt's creative alteration are printed in olive green.

2. Reproduced in color in Rowlands, 1979, pl. 3.

237

164

Rembrandt radically revised the right side of Segers's plate, scraping away the large figures of Tobias and the angel and replacing them with the Holy Family seen against a screen of dark vegetation. Traces of the angel's wing feathers can be seen in the trees at upper right. Segers's plate was executed in the same vocabulary as his *Large Tree* (cat. no. 68): a combination of dots of resist painted onto the plate, resulting in a light pattern on a dark field (as in the "cauliflower" trees at the left), and a regularized tonal mesh of crisscrossing lines, most clearly visible in the far distance. A few traces of Segers's work are still visible on the right side of the plate: for example, the light-colored lizard in the immediate foreground. Rembrandt's discreet additions to the landscape of the left side can be seen in the curving, parallel drypoint strokes at the left margin and in the wiry drypoint lines added to the clumps of trees profiled against the sky.

Rembrandt took the revision of Segers's plate through many stages, beginning by sketching in the additions with drypoint and then overlaying them with heavily bitten etched lines supported by engraving. Impressions were taken on both vellum and Japanese paper. This stage in the development of the plate is characterized by deep chiaroscuro around the figures. Rembrandt developed the plate further, however, lightening the figures of the Holy Family and the ground around them.[3] The bold, roughened areas, resulting from the scraping and burnishing of Segers's work from the plate, parallel the broad brush and palette knife passages in Rembrandt's later paintings.

3. See White, 1969, pp. 218–220.

Herman van Swanevelt
about 1600 – 1655

A painter of idyllic Italian views, Herman van Swanevelt made about 115 etchings, representing Italian landscapes with peasants, ruins in the vicinity of Rome, and landscapes with biblical and mythological themes. Many of these were published in series, some of which bear dates of 1652, 1653, and 1654. Swanevelt seems to have often served as his own publisher.

Swanevelt was probably born about 1600, most likely in Woerden near Utrecht. His artistic education is not known. He spent much of his apparently highly successful career in France and Italy. In 1623 he was in Paris. From 1629 to 1641 he was active in Rome; there he shared living quarters with the French printmaker Charles Audran, whose name as publisher occasionally appears on Swanevelt's prints, and with Michelangelo Cerquozzi, the Italian follower of Pieter van Laer. He acquired the nickname "Hermit" because, relates Sandrart, he haunted the ancient ruins and deserted places in the vicinity of Rome and Tivoli. He received official commissions in Italy, painting Italian views in the loggias of the Vatican and religious subjects and landscapes at the monastery of Monte Cassino.

In 1643 he was back in Woerden, which he was to revisit during the next years, and in 1644 he settled in Paris, where he was appointed "peintre ordinaire du Roy." He married at this time a woman to whom he was related. Together with other artists he executed decorations for the Hotel Lambert, and in 1651 he was made a member of the Royal Academy. He died in Paris in 1655.[1]

Swanevelt was once described as being totally under the influence of the French painter living in Rome, Claude Lorrain, but it is now conceded that in their early careers as painters the two artists probably developed parallel to each other, each influencing the other. Swanevelt's art forms a bridge in the

1. See biographies in Thieme-Becker, vol. 32, pp. 339–341; Utrecht, 1965, pp. 98–99.

development of the Dutch idealized Italian view between the generation of Breenbergh and Poelenburg and that of Both, Berchem, and Weenix.[2]

2. See Stechow, pp. 151–152.

165
HERMAN VAN SWANEVELT
The Rest on the Flight into Egypt,
about 1652–1654

From a series of four etchings
Etching, drypoint, and engraving
B. 100, Weig. 100[II], Dut. 100[II]
Lower left: *Herman van Swanevelt Inventor et fecit excuditg;* lower right: *cum privilegio Regis*
210 x 274 mm. (platemark)
Wm.: coat of arms (of the type seen in Heawood 717–720, 722)
Cleveland Museum of Art, Mr. and Mrs. Lewis B. Williams Collection. 43.628

Herman Swanevelt's serene etching of the Holy Family resting near a grotto while angels adore the child, is one in a series of four etched landscapes with scenes from the Flight into Egypt (Dut. 97–100). Other etchings from the set show the Holy Family on the road, Joseph helping Mary to dismount while an angel adores the child, and Mary changing the child while Joseph leads the donkey to water. In the eighteenth century the Venetian painter Domenico Tiepolo etched an extended series of variations on this theme.

Swanevelt had already formulated landscapes of this type in his painting by the end of his Roman period in 1641,[1] but the style of execution of the etching, with its strong lights and extensive use of engraving, relates it to the prints executed and published in Paris in the period 1652–1654 (the various Roman views of 1652–53, see Dut. 53–65, or, more particularly, the Adonis series of 1654, Dut. 101–106) with their extensive use of engraving and strong illumination from the side.

1. See Waddingham, 1960.

Herman van Swanevelt Inventor et fecit excudit)   cum privilegio Regis

165

In a fine early impression such as the present one, in which the etched passages are still strong and well integrated with the engraved ones, one can fully experience the clarity of Swanevelt's version of the southern light and the dense texture of the verdant landscape. Short flicks of engraving add to the vibrancy of the foliage, and stipple defines the soft cloud forms. The strong, raking illumination is comparable to that in etchings published in the Netherlands in the 1650s by Roelant Roghman, Reinier Nooms (Zeeman), and Anthonie Waterloo.

The clarity and order of this landscape, in which everything unfolds parallel to the picture plane, is abetted by the insistent engraved parallels of the sky. It is easy to comprehend how such a serene and well-ordered vision of landscape would have appealed to the French classicizing taste of the mid-seventeenth century, which admired Claude Lorrain and Nicolas Poussin.

A pen and wash preparatory drawing for the print is in the collection of the Uffizi (inv. 716), one of a number of drawings in that collection for the prints Swanevelt published in the 1650s.[2]

2. Florence, 1964, no. 84, pl. 89.

166
REMBRANDT VAN RIJN
Saint Jerome Reading in a Landscape, about 1654

Etching, drypoint, and engraving on oatmeal paper
G. 104 and 105, B. 104, Hind 267 (1653), Münz 249 (1651/2), BB. 53-3, W.-B. 104[II]
258 x 210 mm (platemark)
Coll.: Cabinet Brentano-Birckenstock (L. 345); M. Holloway (L. 1875); H.F. Sewall (L. 1309)
Museum of Fine Arts, Boston, Harvey D. Parker Collection. P496

The usual sixteenth- and seventeenth-century conception of St. Jerome in a landscape setting involved a half-nude saint of heroic build or leathery strength in an austere, rocky setting engaged in penitential prayer or self-chastiseme

Rembrandt's *St. Jerome,* of about 1654, on the contrary, shows the saint cozily at home in the landscape, reading, one sandal off, his faithful lion alertly defending his peace and quiet. Rembrandt had already created an image of St. Jerome "at home" in the landscape in his 1648 etching *St. Jerome by the Pollard Willow* (B. 103), in which the gentle-looking, bespectacled saint writes at a makeshift desk carpentered onto a pollard willow.

This landscape has often been referred to as "Italian" because the buildings on the far hill, which include a church or monastery chapel, resemble in structure and drawing buildings in the landscape drawings and prints of the sixteenth-century Venetian painter Titian and his circle, particularly those in the drawings and engravings of Domenico Campagnola. About the same time Rembrandt made revisions in a landscape drawing by Domenico Campagnola that contained buildings related in conception and drawing to those in Rembrandt's etching.[1]

The print is a splendid example of Rembrandt's use of varying degrees of finish in the same etched plate. The distant buildings are fully defined and modeled, while the foreground, except for St. Jerome's hat and attentive features, is only sketchily defined. The sketchy definition of St. Jerome's figure serves to heighten his fusion with the landscape. For this reason Gersaint, in the first published catalogue of Rembrandt prints, considered the print unfinished, and Bartsch adopted his opinion. Rembrandt has used freely drawn passages of drypoint with burr to describe the fur of the lion's mane and soft tufts of foliage. A fringe of strong drypoint accents defines the division between foreground and background. The slanting thatch roof of St. Jerome's lean-to has been suggested by scraping or burnishing lines already etched into the plate.[2]

A few impressions of the *St. Jerome Reading* were printed on *cardoes* (cartridge paper). This coarse gray-brown paper, full of undigested colored fibers, is also referred to as "oatmeal" paper. Rembrandt used it to print impressions of a few of his later prints, but it was rarely used by other Dutch printmakers.[3] It was frequently employed, however, by Dutch draftsmen, for whom it provided a ready-made middle tone. Here it gives the landscape a muted light, as if filtered through an overcast sky. Rembrandt also printed the etching on warm-toned Japanese paper, which contributes a glow of sunlight to the landscape.

1. See White, 1969, p. 220, pl. 339.

2. A reed pen preparatory drawing for the print, giving the broad outlines of the composition, is in Hamburg (Benesch 886).

3. I have seen impressions of Jacques de Gheyn III's *St. Matthew* etching (Holl. 21a) and Esaias van de Velde's etching *Fishing before the Fortifications* (Bur. 15) on *cardoes* paper, the former in Amsterdam, and the latter in the Metropolitan Museum, New York.

167

REMBRANDT VAN RIJN
The Entombment, about 1654

Etching, drypoint, and engraving
G. 87, B. 86, Hind 281 (1654), Münz 241 (1658/9), BB. 54-2, W.-B. 86[II]
210 x 162 mm. (platemark)
Wm.: Foolscap (similar to Churchill 337)
Coll.: E.P. Otto; W. Koller, 1852 (L. 1583); F. Bullard (L. 982)
Museum of Fine Arts, Boston, Gift of William Norton Bullard. 23.1013

The Entombment is one of four etchings, two dated 1654, of similar format and dimensions that illustrate episodes from the life of Christ; the other three are *The Presentation in the Temple,* B. 50; *The Supper at Emmaus,* B. 87; and *The Descent from the Cross,* B. 83. It is not clear whether Rembrandt was contemplating a more extended series on the life of Christ, but these four etchings are quite compatible in style. In three of the etchings the events unfold in profound darkness. In the fourth, the *Supper at Emmaus,* a moment of sudden revelation, the scene is flooded by a burst of light.

The *Entombment* takes place in an arched, rock-cut tomb.[1] Joseph of Arimathaea, who claimed the body of Christ and paid for its burial looks on solemnly at left, leaning on his stick, while below him Mary, Christ's mother, clasps her hands and closes her eyes in sorrow as her son's body is lowered into the grave. Above, on a ledge, rest two skulls.

The *Entombment* is known in four states; in each successive state Rembrandt added work to the plate, deepening the encroaching shadows. The first state is executed almost exclusively in etching, in a simple but lucid vocabulary of long, parallel shading lines that is Rembrandt's personal adaptation of the graphic vocabulary of the Italian Renaissance painter, draftsman, and engraver Andrea

1. The tomb, with its arch and skulls, as well as the semicircular disposition of the figures were probably inspired by a drawing, now in the Fogg Art Museum, Harvard University, attributed to Perino del Vaga, a follower of Raphael; Rembrandt copied the drawing about this time (Benesch 1208).

Mantegna.[2] In the second and third states Rembrandt successively darkened the scene with additions in drypoint and engraving. In many impressions of these two states, Rembrandt experimented with various degrees or patterns of expressive illumination and darkness, painting with a film of printer's ink on the surface of the copper plate before printing. The fourth state, in which the web of darkness was finally etched, scratched, and gouged into the plate itself, he sometimes printed in a conventional manner, with the surface of the plate wiped free of all excess ink and, on other occasions, with a heavy film of printer's ink.[3] In the first three states Rembrandt printed a number of impressions on Japanese paper and on vellum; in the fourth, he used white European paper.

The impression of the second state shown here is one of the darker impressions of this state. The translucent gray-black veil of ink shrouds all but a glimmer of light from a concealed source, which partly illuminates Christ's upper body but leaves his face in darkness. The pattern of expressive inking becomes a metaphor for the extinguishing of life. The ridged marks made by the artist's fingers or palm as he wiped away the film of ink are still visible in this area.

2. White, 1969, pp. 80–83.

3. For the successive states of this print and the experiment with inking, see Boston/New York, 1969–70, pp. 123–135; Christopher White in London, 1969, pp. 21–22. There are two known impressions of the fourth state printed with a heavy tone of ink in which the artist added touches of opaque white watercolor to create lights; White, 1969, p. 84.

167

168 (actual size)

168

REMBRANDT VAN RIJN
Christ Appearing to the Apostles, 1656

Etching on Japanese paper
G. 68 and 76, B. 89, Hind 237 (1650), Münz 220
(1650), BB. 56-A, W.-B. 89, only state
Lower center: *Rembrandt f. 1656*
163 x 208 mm. (platemark)
Coll.: F. Bullard (L. 982).
Museum of Fine Arts, Boston, Gift of Miss Ellen
Bullard. 25.1146

In contrast to the impression of the second
state of *The Entombment* shown here (cat. no.
167), with its profound depth of shadow and
somber mood, the *Christ Appearing to the
Apostles,* of 1656,[1] like the etching of the *Supper
at Emmaus,* of 1654 (B. 87), is extremely light
in tonality and more than usually dependent on
the white of the paper for its effect.

Very freely and lightly sketched, with open,
broken contours, the plate represents, as Christopher White has persuasively argued,[2] the
appearance of Christ to the assembled apostles
after the Resurrection: "And as they thus
spake, Jesus himself stood in the midst of them,
and saith unto them, Peace be unto you. But
they were terrified and affrighted, and sup-
posed that they had seen a spirit. And he said
unto them, Why are ye troubled? and why do
thoughts arise in your hearts? Behold my
hands and my feet, that it is I myself: handle
me and see; for a spirit hath not flesh and
bones, as ye see me have. And when he had
thus spoken, he shewed them his hands and his
feet" (Luke 24: 36–40). Christ reveals himself
in a blinding burst of illumination, a white
light like a magnesium flash that vaporizes and
dematerializes forms. Rembrandt has stressed
Christ's spirituality, not only in the dissolution
of his figure into radiant light but also in his
ambiguous, half-hovering stance and the
clouds that seem to billow out from around his
feet. Christ's gesture toward the wound in his
side simultaneously stresses his physical nature,
his humanity.

These etchings of Rembrandt – lightly
sketched, economical images in which the
printed line fuses optically with the white of
the paper to create an overall light tonality – are
linked in their manner of execution to the
prints of North Italian and Bolognese printmakers such as Guido Reni (1575–1642) or
Reni's follower Simone Cantarini (1612–1648)
(see illus.).[3]

Rembrandt's *Christ Appearing to the Apostles*
is more radical in conception than the majority
of prints executed in this international, often
serenely classicizing style; in his economy of
line and power of suggestion Rembrandt is
more audacious. He further dematerialized
many of the etched lines by going over them
with a burnisher or another tool, breaking
them down into dots and dashes.

Judging quality of impression in seventeenth-century etchings executed in this manner can be deceptive if one assumes that the
stronger, darker impression is automatically the
finer one, for the printed lines should meld
with the light tone of the paper. The delicate
impression of *Christ Appearing to the Apostles*
shown here is printed on a thin, white Japanese
paper with a faintly shimmering surface that
fully expresses the immaterial, spiritual nature
of the image.[4]

3. The relationship of Rembrandt's etching style to that
of the Italian Renaissance and Baroque is discussed by
Münz, 1952, pp. 40–42.

4. This catalogue entry is based on an article, Ackley,
1977, pp. 6–7.

1. The date etched into the plate is difficult to read and
has frequently been incorrectly read as "1650" (see, for
example, Hind, 1912). Recent cataloguers, such as
Biörklund and Barnard, 1955 and 1968, and White and
Boon, 1969, record it as "1656," not only on the basis of
style but also on the basis of a more legible date on an
impression from the de Bruijn collection, now in the
Rijksmuseum, Amsterdam.

2. White, 1969, pp. 95–96.

Simone Cantarini
Rest on the Flight into Egypt
Etching
Museum of Fine Arts, Boston

169, 170

REMBRANDT VAN RIJN
Christ Crucified (The Three Crosses),
1653 – about 1660

G, 80, B. 78, Hind 270, Münz 223, BB. 53-A,
W.-B. 78
Lower center in third state only: *Rembrandt f. 1653*

Second state, 1653
Drypoint
385 x 450mm. (platemark)
Wm.: Strasburg bend in shield surmounted by lily
(close to Heawood 145)
Coll.: Duc d'Arenberg (L. 567); A.L. Blum
(L. 79b)
Museum of Fine Arts, Boston, Katherine E.
Bullard Fund in memory of Francis Bullard and
Bequest of Mrs. Russell W. Baker. 1977.747

Fourth state, about 1660
Drypoint and engraving
385 x 450 mm. (platemark)
Coll.: J. Webster (L. 1554 and 1555); G. Cognacq
(L. 538d)
Private Collection

Rembrandt's two large plates executed in dry-point, the *Christ Crucified* of 1653 – 1660 and the *Christ Presented to the People* of 1655 (B. 76), can be seen as the climax of his career as a printmaker. Both have the scale of paintings, and in both instances Rembrandt made radical changes in the image that dramatically trans-formed the expressive meaning of the work. The medium of drypoint, in which the fragile burr rapidly disappears with the pressure of repeated printing, encouraged constant reworking of the plates. Prints on this scale executed in drypoint – a medium that is diffi-cult to control – were unprecedented then and still constitute a challenge to printmakers. In this medium the image is directly scratched and gouged into the soft copper without the inter-vention of an etching ground. Rembrandt's use of the drypoint medium gives the image of *Christ Crucified* a sense of directness and imme-diacy comparable to one of his late drawings. The angular rhythm of the drypoint line accords well with the blocky stylization charac-

teristic of Rembrandt's late drawing style. Because of the fugitive nature of the drypoint burr each impression was essentially unique. Rembrandt's constant experimentation with selective painterly inking of most impressions, particularly in the first three states, further con-tributed to the uniqueness of each impression.

The *Christ Crucified* involves one of the most radical revisions of a plate in the history of printmaking. After having signed and dated the plate "1653" in the third state, which follows the second state shown here, Rembrandt seems to have put the plate aside. Taking it up again several years later (probably about 1660), he scraped most of the previous work from the plate and reworked it, completely revising his conception of the subject.

The first three states of the *Christ Crucified* appear to illustrate the passage in Luke 23: 44 – 48: "And it was about the sixth hour, and there was a darkness over all the earth until the ninth hour. And the sun was darkened, and the veil of the temple was rent in the midst. And when Jesus had cried with a loud voice, he said, Father, into thy hands I commend my spirit: and having said thus, he gave up the ghost. Now when the centurion saw what was done, he glorified God, saying, Certainly this was a righteous man. And all the people that came together to that sight, beholding the things which were done, smote their breasts and returned."

In the first three states Rembrandt shows much greater concern with details of the narra-tive than in the fourth state, in which the "darkness over all the earth" obscures most of the participants. See, for example, the impres-sion of the second state shown here. Revealed in a great cone of light, Christ's cross is flanked by the two crucified thieves. At the right are gathered Christ's followers: Mary Magdalene embraces Christ's feet, John raises his clenched hands to his head, and Mary swoons, sup-ported by another woman. At the left are the soldiery – the executioners. The centurion kneels, arms outspread, in reverent wonder. In the foreground the spectators move, sorrowing or covered with shame and confusion; in the

midst of them is a barking dog. At the right a dark grotto prefigures the entombment of Christ's body.

The second state, which is known in only a small number of impressions, is very similar to the first except for the further definition of the head of the spectator at the far right of the plate. A number of impressions of the first state and at least one of the second were printed on vellum.[1] By the second state the effect of the drypoint burr was somewhat diminished, but in impressions such as the present one (cat. no. 169) Rembrandt compensated for the reduced strength of the drypoint by his expressive ink-ing of the plate. Here a heavy veil of ink shrouds most of the plate except the figure of Christ and the area around the foot of the cross, which are illumined by a shaft of light. There is a sense of diffuse, filtered light, of twi-light. This pattern of inking anticipates the deep well of shadowy light that Rembrandt would create when he revised the plate a few years later.

In the past much discussion was devoted to the question of which version of the print – that of the first three states (1653) or that of the revised fourth state – was the more expressive, but for the twentieth-century viewer this issue is perhaps less important than the fact that the two versions provide an opportunity to partici-pate in the artistic process, the unfolding of a great artist's ideas in his dialogue with the medium.

The fourth state, seen here in a very strong impression in which the darkness has its full power, presents a scene of chaos and confusion as darkness streams down from above or radi-ates outward. Never before in a work on this theme had the "darkness over all the land" been so tangible or such a violently active partici-pant. At right the hail of deeply gouged dry-point lines threatens to obliterate the figures of Christ's followers, and the thief on his cross is

1. I once had the opportunity to examine an album of prints on religious themes from the collection of the late-seventeenth-century diarist and print collector Samuel Pepys. The centerfold of the album was Rembrandt's *Three Crosses* printed on vellum.

247

248

170

totally swallowed up by the darkness. Many figures have been completely scraped from the plate, or their attitudes radically altered. At left a man reins in a rearing horse, while at right John flings out his arms in a gesture of despair. The departing figure in the right foreground, who remains from the third state, now breaks into a run, plunging into the darkness. At left a new and stately figure of the centurion, mounted and holding his lance, has been added, based on the image on a medal by Pisanello.[2] Not one area of the plate has been left unshaded; the brightest accent is the dim light from Christ's halo. Christ's figure has been redrawn; his figure is the only one given full sculptural definition.

This scene of anguish and murky confusion has been interpreted by Christopher White as illustrating Christ's moment of despair as related by the evangelists Matthew and Mark: "Now from the sixth hour there was darkness over all the land unto the ninth hour. And about the ninth hour Jesus cried with a loud voice saying…My God, my God! Why hast thou forsaken me?" (Matthew 27: 45–46).[3]

2. It has been noted that the man restraining the rearing horse was probably inspired by one of the Horse Tamers, the antique sculptures on the Quirinal in Rome. That Rembrandt should have included such direct quotations in one of his most startlingly original works only points up his omnivorous interest in whatever he could put to use artistically.

3. White, 1969, p. 102.

171
REMBRANDT VAN RIJN
St. Francis beneath a Tree, Praying, 1657

Drypoint with etching and engraving on Japanese paper
G. 107, B. 107, Hind 292, Münz 250, BB. 57-A, W.-B. 107[II]
Lower right: *Rembrandt f. 1657*
184 x 242 mm. (platemark)
Coll.: Dukes d'Arenberg (L. 567)
Museum of Fine Arts, Boston, 1951 Purchase Fund. 51.703

In the *St. Francis* the Protestant Rembrandt presented his personal interpretation of an intensely Catholic subject. Francis, founder of the Franciscan order, retired to Mount Alverno for a period of fasting and prayer, accompanied by a brother monk (whose hooded figure can be seen kneeling before an open book in the shelter at the right).[1] During Francis's retreat a seraphic vision of the crucified Christ appeared to him and imprinted on his body the stigmata, the wounds of Christ. Instead of following the visual tradition and representing the dramatic moment of Francis's stigmatization, Rembrandt shows Francis kneeling, eyes closed and hands clasped in prayer. The mighty trunk of a tree divides Francis's figure from the nearly life-size crucifix. In the distance is the belfry of a monastery or hermitage.

Rembrandt began the print as a bold sketch in drypoint and then completed it in etching, reversing the normal procedure of etching a plate and adding details in drypoint. Rembrandt's complex interweaving of the media may be observed in the foreground leaves at right: those at far right are etched, and those nearest Francis are executed in drypoint. Lines half-erased with the scraper or burnisher describe the thatch of the shelter's roof.

In impressions of both the first and second states Rembrandt experimented with various patterns of inking and a variety of printing sur-

1. White, 1969, p. 223, read the kneeling figure of the companion monk and the shelter supports as a massive armchair with clothes flung over it.

faces: vellum, an Indian paper with colored fibers, and, as here, Japanese paper. In this impression a veil of printer's ink shadows both Francis and the crucifix, bringing them into closer communion. Francis's closed eyes and the mysterious shadows that envelop the crucifix and make it seem to hover suggest that the crucifix may be not merely a carved figure but also Francis's inner vision of the crucified.

172
REMBRANDT VAN RIJN
The Woman with the Arrow
(Venus and Cupid?), 1661

Etching and drypoint
G. 194, B. 202, Hind 303, Münz 144, BB. 61-A, W.B. 202.[II]
Lower left: *Rembrandt f. 1661* (*d* reversed)
205 x 124 mm. (platemark)
Wm.: Crown over Strasburg lily in shield (related to Wibiral III, 8d)
Coll.: H.F. Sewall (L. 1309).
Museum of Fine Arts, Boston, Harvey D. Parker Collection. P587

The Woman with the Arrow of 1661 is Rembrandt's last print except for the commissioned portrait of Jan Antonides van der Linden (B. 264). The print was first referred to as "The Woman with the Arrow" ("het vrouwtje met de pijl") in a list (about 1731) of Rembrandt's etchings in the collection of the Delft collector Valerius Röver.[1] Based on one of Rembrandt's several drawn studies of the female nude from the 1650s and 1660s (Benesch 1147), the original study from life has clearly been transformed into a subject with literary overtones. The nude model of the drawing, wearing an everyday Dutch cap, is posed against a mound of drapery and grasps a sling to keep her arm elevated during the pose. The nude woman of the print sits on the edge of a canopied bed, holding an arrow aloft, while she turns to look in the direction of a boyish face hidden in the depths of the bed. Her elaborate coiffure suggests classical antiquity. The

1. Van Gelder, 1938, p. 12.

171

subject has been variously identified by modern writers as Venus and Amor, Anthony and Cleopatra, and King Candaules showing his bodyguard Gyges the beauty of his wife.[2] The most plausible of these identifications would seem to be Venus and Amor (Cupid), Venus either arming Amor or taunting him, having wrested the dangerous love-dart from him.[3]

Like the majority of Rembrandt's female nudes, the woman portrayed here is anything but goddess-like in proportion and drawing. Yet this is one of the tenderest studies of the nude in the history of printmaking. In a highly expressive impression such as the one shown here, the woman's flesh gives off a soft glow of light. Beginning with a base of etched lines, Rembrandt built up the image with fine, unsystematic scratches, flicks, and dots of drypoint without burr that give the flesh its softness. Stronger strokes of drypoint with burr model the folds of the plush drapery or define the coiffure. In the foreground the patches of parallel shading lines were broken down by being worked over with a burnisher or scraper, which gave them a soft, grainy quality. The painterly execution of the image worked into the plate was supported in a number of impressions of the first and second states by Rembrandt's careful selective inking of the plate. Here the curtains of the bed and its shadowy recesses as well as the foreground are veiled by a tone of printer's ink. The film of ink has been removed before printing from the edge of the woman's torso, her thigh, and the bedclothes around it, causing the flesh to glow as if illuminated from within.

2. See the bibliography on the iconography in White and Boon, 1969, p. 98. See also Boon, 1972, and Rifkin, 1972, p. 124. It has been suggested that the woman is closing a gap in the bed curtains rather than holding an arrow.

3. See, for example, the early seventeenth-century Venetian etcher Odoardo Fialetti's etched series "Scherzi d'Amore" (B. 5–19), in which Venus plays with her son, Cupid, and teases or punishes him (see especially B. 7, in which Venus has taken the powerful arrow from Cupid and taunts him with it).

Gerard de Lairesse
1641 – 1711

A classicizing painter of allegories and subjects from ancient history, mythology, and the Bible, Gerard de Lairesse made nearly one hundred and thirty etchings and engravings and four mezzotints on similar themes;[1] these include title pages and book illustrations.

Born in Liége in 1641, Lairesse first studied with his father, Renier, a painter, and then, in 1655, with a Liége painter in close touch with the fashionable French academic taste of the day, Bertholet Flémalle. He also studied the Greek and Roman literature of classical antiquity and showed a precocious gift for the invention of allegories. While in Liége he studied printmaking with the engraver Michael Natalis and had the opportunity to study French etchings and engravings after the painter Simon Vouet. In 1660 Lairesse, then an independent master, journeyed to Cologne, stopping in Aachen, where he executed a commission for the cathedral. His disastrous entanglement with two sisters who served him as models ended in an exchange of knife thrusts and caused his family to arrange his marriage to a relative in 1664. The incident also caused his emigration, in the same year, north to Utrecht, where he came to the attention of the Amsterdam art dealer Gerrit van Uylenburgh. He settled in Amsterdam in 1665, first working briefly for Uylenburgh and then independently. He became a citizen of Amsterdam in 1667.

Lairesse's literary subjects with their idealized nudes appealed to the classicizing taste of Amsterdam's patricians, and he received many private and public commissions. He was perhaps most successful as a painter of decorative schemes for ceilings and walls, executing decorations for the palaces of Willem III as well as for the council chamber of the Court of Justice in the Hague. He collaborated with his friend

the classicizing landscape painter Jan Glauber, painting figures in his landscapes. He also ran a drawing academy and drew regularly from the nude model.

Lairesse's career as a visual artist came to an end in 1689-90, when he lost his sight. He suggested that etching by candlelight might have been one of the causes. After Lairesse became blind, he initiated a series of lectures and lessons on the theory and practice of art, addressing them to the art association Ingenio et Labore. These were transcribed by his artist son, Abraham, and served as the basis for two books, one on drawing published in 1701, and *Het Groot Schilderboek (The Great Painter's-Book)* published in 1707. These did not enjoy their greatest success until after his death in 1711. Lairesse's rather grotesque, snub-nosed appearance can be studied in Rembrandt's painted portrait of the artist (Bredius 321) in the Lehman collection of the Metropolitan Museum, New York.[2]

2. See biographies by M.D. Henkel in Thieme-Becker, vol. 22, pp. 233-237; Timmers, 1942, pp. 1-18.

173

GERARD DE LAIRESSE
The Sacrifice of Polyxena, 1667

Etching and drypoint
Le Blanc 61, Timmers 52[1], Holl. 52
Lower right: *Gerardus Lairesse inūentor/fecit et excudit Amstelodami;* at left, on vessel: [monogram] *GL;* at center, on offering stone: *1667*
303 x 387 mm. (platemark)
Wm.: crowned shield with fleur-de-lis and countermark including letter H
Teylers Museum, Haarlem

Though traditionally described as the sacrifice of Iphigenia, the subject of Lairesse's early etching of 1667 is probably, as Henkel noted,[1] the sacrifice of Polyxena. After the fall of Troy, the Trojan women were divided among the Greeks. Not to be denied his share in the war booty, the ghost of Achilles arose from his grave and demanded that Polyxena, the daugh-

ter of King Priam and Queen Hecuba, be slain on his tomb so that her shade could join his. Behind the blindfolded Polyxena and the officiating priest can be seen a tomb and the shadowy figure of a warrior on a rearing horse, the ghost of Achilles.

Lairesse's combination of strong, dramatic lighting and regularized engraving-like use of line suggests the style of the printmakers such as Michel Dorigny (1617-1665) who etched and engraved after Simon Vouet. The striving for archaeological accuracy and the broad, rhetorical gestures of the participants suggest the etchings of the Italian painter Pietro Testa (1611-1650). This early etching employs more dynamic lighting and more dramatic spatial relationships than many of Lairesse's later prints.

In his writings Lairesse designated etching as the painter's print medium because, unlike engraving, it is so closely akin to drawing. He also stated that one values a plate, however cursorily etched, by the painter's hand more than the best etching and engraving made after his design.[2]

As a result of Lairesse's devotion to a classicizing aesthetic, his own etchings generally show more interest in the firm definition of strongly modeled sculptural figures in a clearly defined space than in coloristic or tonal variety, atmospheric values, or spontaneity of execution. His etchings were frequently based on his painted compositions. His feeling for allegorical invention was expressed in etched title pages and in his large etched political allegories devoted to the exploits of Willem III.

2. Lairesse/Davaco, 1740/1969, pt. 2, pp. 374-376.

---

1. If one attributes to Lairesse, as Timmers does (1942, pp. 129-131), the etchings of antique sculptures in the Reynst collection, one must add 110 etchings to Lairesse's etched work.

1. Thieme-Becker, vol. 22, p. 235.

Gerardus Latresse inventor
fecit & excudit Amstelodami

173

Leendert van der Cooghen
1610 – 1681

The draftsman and etcher Leendert van der Cooghen, who came from a wealthy family related to the Beresteyn family, was essentially a dilettante rather than a professional artist. He made about fourteen etchings, of which four are copies after Salvator Rosa. His etchings, many of which are single figures, are diverse in subject: the Man of Sorrows, saints, Roman soldiers, a milkmaid, a backgammon game with players in historical dress. They range in date from 1664 to 1666.

Born in Haarlem in 1610, Van der Cooghen studied in Antwerp with the painter and etcher Jacob Jordaens. His numerous drawings – figure studies, portraits, and genre scenes – are close in style to those of his friend Cornelis Bega. His paintings are rare. In 1648 he became a member of the Haarlem militia and in 1652 entered the artists' guild. He died in Haarlem in 1681.[1]

1. See biographies by Houbraken, 1718, vol. 1, pp. 350–354; E.W. Moes in Thieme-Becker, vol. 7, p. 345.

174
LEENDERT VAN DER COOGHEN
St. Bavo, 1664

Etching
B. 3, Holl. 3
Upper right: *1664;* lower center: *S:BAVO*
190 x 133 mm. (platemark)
Museum Boymans-van Beuningen, Rotterdam.
BdH 10913

St. Bavo (or St. Allowin) was a wealthy pagan landowner of seventh-century Brabant who, after his wife's death, gave away his possessions, converted to Christianity, and lived a life of monastic poverty and, later, of hermit-like seclusion.[1] As in Jacob Matham's engraving of St. Bavo (B. 12), he is shown here with his

1. See Attwater, s.v. "Bavo."

174

attributes of sword and falcon. Unlike Matham, however, Van der Cooghen portrays him in the uniform of a Roman soldier, standing in a landscape, the sketchy profile of Haarlem's great church of St. Bavo visible in the distance. The fallen antique column may allude to the end of the pagan tradition.

The largest and most articulately drawn of Van der Cooghen's etchings, *St. Bavo* relates closely in its simplicity of execution and light tonality to contemporary Italian etchers, specifically Salvator Rosa in his "Figurine" series, dated by Wallace about 1656–57.[2] Van der Cooghen's 1665–66 set of four etchings of Roman soldiers (Holl. 4–7) which resemble academic figure studies are also close in conception to the Rosa series. Houbraken recognized the relation of Van der Cooghen's prints to Italian etchers, but the name he mentions is Carracci.[3] The drawing vocabulary of the *St. Bavo,* however, with its diagonal parallel shading, is Van der Cooghen's own. A pen and wash drawing for the print, in the reverse direction, is in the Teyler's Museum, Haarlem, and is dated 1662.[4]

2. See the etching of a Roman soldier with a staff, B. 31; Wallace, 1979, pl. 14.

3. Houbraken, 1718, vol. 1, p. 350: "Hy heeft ook eenige platen geetst in koper, redelyk fraay en kloek maar wat ruuw op de wyze als die van Carrats" ("He also etched a few copper plates, rather handsome and vigorous but somewhat rough in the manner of those of Carracci").

4. Teylers Museum, Haarlem, portfolio no. 100.

Jan de Bray
about 1626/27 – 1697

The Haarlem portrait painter Jan Salomonsz. de Bray made a small number of etchings, but there exists considerable confusion between them and the etchings of his artist brother Dirk, whose style and monogram are very closely related to Jan's.[1]

Jan, Dirk, and their other artist brother, Joseph, were the sons of the painter and architect Salomon de Bray. Born about 1626–27 in Haarlem, Jan probably studied with his father. His earliest dated works, a portrait drawing and a portrait painting, are from 1648 and 1650, respectively. He was active in the Haarlem Guild of St. Luke from 1667 to 1684. He married three times. Although he spent most of his life in Haarlem, he apparently resided in Amsterdam for two years, about 1686–1688. In 1688 he returned to Haarlem. In 1689 he went into bankruptcy, and his paintings were ordered to be sold. He died in Haarlem in 1697. Like his father, Jan was an architect as well as a painter.[2] In addition to portraits, he painted biblical and mythological subjects, as well as group portraits, in which the sitters assume the roles of figures from history or literature.

1. For example, the beautiful etching of St. John the Baptist catalogued as Jan's in Hollstein (Holl. 3) is probably by Dirk after Jan.
2. See biographies by E.W. Moes in Thieme-Becker, vol. 4, p. 555; and MacLaren, 1960, p. 57.

175
JAN DE BRAY
The Chess Player

Etching
Vis Blokhuyzen 27, Wurz. 5, Holl. 19
At right: *JDBray fe./a Haerlem*
186 x 130mm. (platemark)
Coll.: E. Peart (L. 891); J. Sheepshanks (see L. 2333)
Lent by the Trustees of the British Museum. S. 4815

Jan de Bray's chess player, possibly a portrait of a friend or brother, invites us to seat ourself on the cushioned stool provided and engage in a contest, the winner of which will be rewarded with the wreath of honor hanging on the wall. The unsigned Dutch verses may be freely translated as follows: "Seat yourself at the noble chess board, The contest gives a wreath of honor." Jan de Bray's fondness for a direct confrontation of sitter and viewer may be seen in his painted group portrait of 1663 in the Frans Hals Museum, in which all six men portrayed look directly out at us, even if they have to turn to do so.[1]

The etching is closely related to a drawing made by Jan de Bray in 1661 for the friendship album of Jacques Heyblocq (Royal Library, The Hague).[2] The album drawing is horizontal in format, omits the stool and wreath of honor, and is in the reverse direction. It has the feeling of a drawing from life, while the etching is more emblematic in character.

The etching is executed with firm, continuous contours and the lucid, regular diagonal parallel shading strokes familiar from the drawings of Jan de Bray and other classicizing artists of Haarlem such as Leendert van der Cooghen (cat. no. 174).

1. Inv. no. 36; see Bernt, 1970, vol. 1, pl. 179.
2. See Von Moltke, 1938–39, Z 100, pl. 73.

175

Cornelis Bega
about 1631/32 – 1664

Cornelis Bega, a painter of scenes of peasant life and the low life of taverns, made about thirty-five etchings with the same subject matter.[1]

Born about 1631–32 in Haarlem, Cornelis Pietersz. Bega was the son of Pieter Jansz. Begijn, or Bega, a wood carver and silversmith, and of Maria Cornelisdr., an illegitimate daughter of the Mannerist painter Cornelis van Haarlem. According to Houbraken, Bega was a pupil of Adriaen van Ostade, which is quite credible given the nature of his work. As we know from the travel journal of the Haarlem painter Vincent Laurensz. van der Vinne, Bega joined him on his travels in Germany and Switzerland for about two months in 1653. In 1654 Bega was admitted to the Haarlem artists' guild. He died in 1664.[2] His drawings, both studies from the model and finished drawings of peasant subjects, are close in style to those of other Haarlem contemporaries such as his friend Leendert van der Cooghen and Dirk Helmbreker and are often confused with their work.

1. Holl. 36–40 are probably not from Bega's hand. Holl. 37 and 38 are based on Bega's etching style but are not executed by him.

2. See biographies in Houbraken, 1718, vol. 1, pp. 349–350; Van Hees, 1956; MacLaren, 1960, pp. 16–17.

176

176
CORNELIS BEGA
Tavern Scene, 1661–1664

Etching and engraving
B. 32, Weig. 32[I], Dut. 32[II], Holl. 32[II]
178 x 133 mm. (platemark)
Rijksmuseum, Amsterdam. A19670

The *Tavern Scene* is Cornelis Bega's most ambitious etching. On the basis of comparison with Bega's datable drawings and paintings, this etching should be dated about 1661–1664. Bega's later tavern scenes do not have the cozy mood of his teacher Ostade's works of the 1640s on. They are characterized by a harsher mood, a furtive, even sinister air.[1]

A minimum of props indicate the tavern setting; the background is composed of murky, impenetrable darkness. The figures are either types or totally anonymous, backs turned, caps pulled down. These barrel-like figures are related to the robust, roughhousing types seen in Adriaen van Ostade's early paintings of the 1630s or the tavern scenes of the Flemish painter Adriaen Brouwer. They are descendants of Pieter Bruegel's sturdy peasants.

In many of Bega's later works his rather depersonalized figures are tightly locked together, as here, in patterns of a geometric stringency worthy of classicizing French painters such as Nicolas Poussin and Sebastien Bourdon. The central cube of figures, particularly the figure whose back, turned toward us, projects like a cornerstone, stands out against the darkness, illuminated by a strong side light like that from an open door. Bega's formalism is surprising, given his choice of subject matter, but scenes from daily life are frequently firmly, even architecturally structured in Dutch art of the second half of the seventeenth century.

1. The article on Bega's etchings by Knoef, 1920, skillfully characterizes their mood and formal qualities.

Romeyn de Hooghe
1645 – 1708

The great illustrator Romeyn de Hooghe made over 3,500 etchings, of which more than 2,000 were frontispieces and book illustrations. Many of his single-sheet prints were political broadsheets, allegories, and satires. Together with the book illustrators Jan and Caspar Luyken (see cat. no. 210), he was responsible for a flood of images that poured forth from Amsterdam, the late-seventeenth-century book publishing center of Europe. Romeyn de Hooghe's richly detailed and decorative illustrations concerned the most diverse subjects: wrestling, comparative religion, contemporary atrocities of war. He illustrated the works not only of Dutch writers but also of foreign authors such as La Fontaine and Boccaccio, as well as his own writings. Collectively, his illustrations paint a broad picture of the political and intellectual life of Northern Europe in the late seventeenth century.

Romeyn de Hooghe was born in Amsterdam in 1645, the son of a button maker. Nothing is known of his artistic education. His earliest dated echings (1662) are copies after Nicolaes Berchem. His brother-in-law, Pieter Fris, was a painter and art dealer and might also have given him instruction. In 1668 he made a journey to Paris. Despite De Hooghe's later virulent attacks on Holland's invading enemy Louis XIV, his printmaking style shows much evidence of the influence of contemporary French printmakers, including the followers of Jacques Callot. In the early 1670s he became a propagandist for the cause of Prince Willem of Orange, the "Stadholder King," who became King of England in 1689. On this occasion Willem III rewarded De Hooghe by making him commissioner of mines for the county of Lingen, in Germany. De Hooghe continued to be a supporter of Willem III until the latter's death. He was ennobled by the King of Poland for a series of prints representing the defeat of the Turks. He married in 1673. In 1675 he is first mentioned as an art dealer. Beginning in the late 1670s he began to train large numbers of pupils in printmaking.

About 1680-1682 he moved with his wife and daughter to Haarlem. De Hooghe, who sometimes indicated by his signature that he had a law degree, served on a court of justice there in 1687 and 1688. In 1688-1690 he served as a member of the board of regents of a Haarlem charitable institution. He also gained official support in founding a drawing academy in Haarlem and published an elaborate etched map of the city.

In 1690 a conflict over the political power of Willem III in the province of Holland led to a savage exchange of slanderous and satirical pamphlets between Willem's supporters (De Hooghe was one of his principal adherents) and the government of Amsterdam. De Hooghe was accused of, among other things, atheism, etching pornographic illustrations, and incest with his daughter. The mayor of Haarlem was persuaded to hear the testimony against De Hooghe, but the artist was not prosecuted. Haarlem placed a ban, however, on further publication of these satires. The accusations against De Hooghe blackened his reputation with later biographers such as Arnold Houbraken. While in Haarlem, Romeyn de Hooghe continued to work for Amsterdam publishers. In 1700 the city of Rotterdam commissioned a series of paintings from him. He died in Haarlem in 1708.[1]

A learned and witty man, De Hooghe's artistic activity was very diverse; in addition to etching, he painted and made designs for coins and medals, sculpture, and decorations for triumphal entries. A small number of his drawings survive.

1. See biographies by M.D. Henkel in Thieme-Becker, vol. 17, pp. 458-461; Wilson, 1974, pp. 20-52.

177
ROMEYN DE HOOGHE
Mother Offering Her Child a Choice betweeen a Jewel and a Fruit (Illustration to "But they that will be rich fall into temptation," 1 Tim. 6:9) in Fransois van Hoogstraeten, *Het Voorhof der Ziele, Behangen met leerzaeme Prenten en Zinnebeelden.* Rotterdam, Fransois van Hoogstraeten, 1668.

Etching
(page 88)
91 x 118 mm. (platemark); 180 x 143 mm. (page size); brown leather
De Vries (1899) 217, Landwehr (1962) 95a, Landwehr (1970) 3, Praz (1975), p. 372
Coll.: A. Decorte
Mr. and Mrs. Arthur E. Vershbow

Romeyn de Hooghe's first book illustrations were the etched frontispiece and sixty etched plates for the Rotterdam bookseller Fransois van Hoogstraten's moralizing emblem book *Het Voorhof der Ziele (The Forecourt of the Souls)* of 1668. The Dutch text of the title page speaks of the "Forecourt of the souls, hung round with instructive prints and emblems." The work is made up of texts and pictures that constitute a guide to proper moral conduct and to the soul's salvation. The frontispiece represents the soul personified as a young man crowned with laurel, escorted toward the open arms of the figure of Christ by a guardian angel who tramples on the figures of Death and the Vices. Behind them, steps ascend to a vision of the Holy Spirit and the Name of God. The etched images, except for one or two landscapes, are all figural scenes, many drawn from contemporary Dutch life and others from literature and the Bible.

The etching shown here illustrates a motto from the New Testament, which is printed on the preceding page: "But they that will be rich fall into temptation and a snare" (1 Tim. 6:9). As the text of the commentary elucidates, a wealthy mother dangles before her young child (the leading straps hang from its dress) a rich

Wat anders, dan het doen des menfchen, die 't gefteente
Des Hemels, 't eeuwigh heil, dat Godt aen zijn Gemeente
(c) *Qui ter-* En Kinderen, zijn jock opnemende, belooft,
renarum re- Zoo reukeloos verfmaet, om een verganklijk ooft
rum amore Van weelde en rijkdom te genieten hier op aerde.
vincitur, Den (c) Hemel reeckent hy van een geringe waerde,
nullatenus Die op den rijkdom vlamt. Ik toon dit: zoo men Godt
in Deo de- Genieten wil, en met de zaligen een lot
lectatur. Deelachtigh worden, is het noodigh, zijn gedachten
Greg. Mo- Naer Godt te wenden, en de (d) winft der werelt achten
ral lib.18. Voor louter fchade: maer (e) wie gelt en goet bemint,
(d) *Ik achte* Is nacht en dagh daer meê bekommert, en hy vind
alle dingen
verlies te
zijn om de overhooge kenniffe Jefu Chrifti onfes Heeren. Phil. 3: 8. (e) *Qui diviarum*
fervus eft, divitias cuftodit ut fervus. Hieronymus.

Noit

Noit meer genoegen, dan wanneer hy zijn vermogen
Gelijk een volle Maen ziet waffen. Zoo beoogen
Des rijcken driften dan geen zaligheit; zoo ftaet
De Hemel, Godts Paleis, in eenen leegen graet
By hem; zoo wenfcht hy 't heil der Engelen te miffen
Voor een' onnutten klomp van Goud. Wat duifterniffen
Bedwelmen het gezicht van zijne ziel! Helaes,
Wanneer de menfch geen licht uit Gode fchept, hoe (f) dwaes
Is al zijn poogen en bedrijven in dit leven!
Een Valk, indien men hem veel fpijze komt te geven,
Is zijnen Meefter niet gehoorzaem: zoo en ziet
Een Man van middelen na (g) Godts bevelen niet.
Geen rijkdom baete den verloren Zoon: hy fcheide
Uit dat gezaligt huis zijns Vaders, en vermeide
Zich in de dertelheit en weelde; maer wanneer
Hy al zijn gelden had verloren, van een' Heer
Geworden was een flaef, die vuile zwijnen hoede,
Zoo (h) openbaerde zich de kennis. d'Arremoede
Bekeerde hem, die van den rijkdom was verleit.
Wie zou om rijkdom dan noch wenfchen, die befcheit
En reden plaetfe gunt? De rook des vyers, gedreven
Uit eenen Schoorfteen, zal ons in 't gezichte zweven
Voor eene korte wijl: de rijkdom en het goet,
Al maekt het iemant zoo hovaerdigh van gemoed,
Is (i) onbeftandigh en verdwijnende. Wie heden
Gegoet is, en van elk geëert wort, en gebeden
Dat hy zijn dienaer flechts genoemt magh wezen, zal,
Eer noch de Morgenzon gerezen is, ten (k) val
Geraecken, ja een kleed voor zijne naektheit hoeven.
Maer fchoon al dracide zijn geluk op vafte fchroeven,
De rijkdom fchaft hem zorge. Een dienaer, die getrouw
Zich in den dienft quijt van zijn' Huisheer, en den bouw
Van zijnen Acker helpt bevorderen, vermindert
Zijns Heeren kommer, die te voren was verhindert
Met al dien ommeflagh in zijn' gewoonen flaep:
Maer grooten rijkdom is een ongetrouwen knaep,

(f) *Nihil mi-*
ferius eft,
quam prop-
ter num-
mum Deum
contemnere.
Idem.
(g) *Nifi va-*
caveritis à
terreftribus,
nihil cognof-
cere poteri-
tis de cœle-
ftibus. Am-
brofius.
(h) *Ik zal*
opftaen, ende
gaen tot mij-
nen Vader,
ende hem
zeggen: Va-
der, ik heb-
be gezon-
dight in den
Hemel ende
voor u. Luc.
15: 18.
(i) *Het is*
een damp,
die een lut-
tel tijts ge-
zien wort.
Jac. 4: 15.
(k) *Divi-*
tiarum &
formæ gloria
fluxa atque
fragilis eft.
Saluft. in
Catil.

M Dewijl

jewel and a piece of fruit. The child, still uncorrupted, instinctively reaches for the piece of fruit rather than the jewel.

Such a scene of upper-class life is rare in Dutch prints outside book illustration but is familiar in Dutch paintings of the time, such as those made by Pieter de Hooch in Amsterdam in the 1660s.

Romeyn de Hooghe's uncomplicated and efficient use of etched line contributes to the moral point by evoking the shimmer of light on rich fabrics. The parallel shading is comparable to that in Jan de Bray's *Chess Player* (cat. no. 175) though somewhat more loosely handled.

Dirk de Bray
active 1658 – 1678

The cutter of woodblocks and painter Dirk de Bray made about 150 prints of which about 30 are etchings and the remainder are woodcuts. Both etchings and woodcuts are varied in subject matter; they range from religious themes and Catholic devotional prints to scenes from everyday life, allegories, different types of birds, coats of arms, and merchants' labels. Some of the devotional woodcuts are printed in red and black, and there is one chiaroscuro woodcut. The dates on prints or related drawings range from 1658 to 1677.

Dirk de Bray was the son of the Haarlem painter and architect Salomon de Bray and brother of the painter Jan (cat. no. 175). His birth and death dates are not recorded. It is probable that Dirk first received instruction from his father. In 1651 he was inscribed as an apprentice to the Haarlem bookbinder Passchier van Wesbusch. An illustrated manuscript treatise on bookbinding in Dirk's hand is dated 1658. The majority of his work in woodcut was probably done on commission for publishers such as the Haarlem publisher Abraham Casteleyn. His best known woodcut is the portrait of his father, Salomon, after a drawing by his brother Jan (Vis Blokhuyzen 122). Many of Dirk's original blocks are today in the possession of the Haarlem publishers Enschede and Sons. The Haarlem artist Isaak van de Vinne (1665–1740) designed woodcut vignettes in a similar style.

In 1671 Dirk was secretary of the Haarlem Guild of St. Luke. He was active as a painter in his later years, painting both portraits and flower pieces. His last dated painting is from 1678. There is a tradition reaching back to the seventeenth century that Dirk de Bray became a monk. He is said to have died at a monastery in Brabant, in the South Netherlands.[1]

1. See biographical information in Vis Blokhuyzen, 1870, pp. vi–viii; Van der Willigen, 1870, pp. 90–98; E.W. Moes in Thieme-Becker, vol. 4, p. 554.

178 (actual size)

179 (actual size)

178
DIRK DE BRAY
The Month of May (Children Making Soap Bubbles), 1666

Illustration to an almanac
Woodcut after Jan de Bray
Vis Blokhuyzen 50, Holl. 50
62 x 110 mm. (borderline)
Gemeentearchief, Haarlem. V.S. XI, 231

179
DIRK DE BRAY
The Month of July (Haying), 1666

Illustration to an almanac
Woodcut after Jan de Bray
Vis Blokhuyzen 52, Holl. 52
62 x 110 mm. (borderline)
Gemeentearchief, Haarlem. V.S. XI, 232

Three series of woodcut vignettes of the months, intended for an almanac or calendar,

259

have been attributed to Dirk de Bray: the series shown here, with scenes from everyday life; a series with cupids, or *amorini*, indulging in activities appropriate to the month (Vis Blokhuyzen 57–68); and a series of tiny still lifes of food associated with the different months (Vis Blokhuyzen 69–80).

Although Vis Blokhuyzen attributed the design of the present series to Dirk, the monogram cut on the block for *January* is that of his brother Jan, who probably designed the entire series. Two of the months, *April* and *November,* bear the cutter's monogram of Christoffel van Sichem IV and are cut in a distinctly different style from the remaining blocks, which all seem to be cut by Dirk de Bray. Dirk's simple "B" monogram followed by the date "66" occurs on the block for *September.*

Dirk's own cutting style is delightfully crisp and fresh, as may be seen in the woodcuts representing the months of *May* and *July* shown here. *May* is represented by children on a dune top, making soap bubbles that are quickly borne away by the high wind. Behind them unfolds a panorama of the flat land of the Netherlands; a serpentine river, its banks lined with windmills, is crowded with boats under full sail. The image of children making fragile, evanescent bubbles was a popular symbol of the brevity of life in seventeenth-century Holland. Jan de Bray's design is an unusually fresh, naturalistic conception of the theme. By giving the bubbles a broken, dotted contour, Dirk de Bray's skillful knife emphasizes their fragility.

As noted earlier, in reference to the plowman of Paulus Potter's *Shepherd* of 1644 (cat. no. 122), scenes of peasants or farmers laboring in the fields were rare in seventeenth-century Dutch prints outside of book illustration. The haying scene in *July* would have been common in mid-nineteenth century France in the work of Millet and other artists, but it was seldom encountered at this time unless in the context of these traditional cycles of the activities of the months. Dirk de Bray's cutting succeeds once again in capturing the spontaneity of a freely sketched drawing; short, chopped-off lines evoke the stubble of the hay.

Allart van Everdingen
1621 – 1675

A painter of rocky Scandinavian views with cascades and log cabins, Allart Pietersz. van Everdingen made about one hundred and five single etchings and one or two mezzotints as well as some fifty-seven etched and mezzotinted illustrations for *Renard the Fox.* Most of Everdingen's prints, with a few exceptions such as the set of four views of mineral springs at Spa, represent rocky or mountainous landscapes with Scandinavian motifs.

Allart was born in Alkmaar in 1621. His father was a notary and solicitor. Allart's older brother, Cesar, was a painter of literary and allegorical themes, and his brother Jan, a notary and solicitor like his father, also painted still lifes. Houbraken records that Allart was a pupil of Roelant Savery (who died in Utrecht in 1639) and of Pieter Molijn in Haarlem. A period of study with Roelant Savery seems very likely, because Everdingen was to see Scandinavia in the light of Savery's Tyrolean views. He visited Norway and Sweden about 1644. The landscapes he subsequently painted on Scandinavian themes seem to have enjoyed great popularity and brought good prices. Jacob van Ruisdael's later paintings of cascades and waterfalls appear to have been influenced by them.

In 1645 Allart married in Haarlem and joined the artists' guild there the same year. He is traceable in Haarlem in 1646–1648, 1651, and 1655. He afterwards settled in Amsterdam where he became a citizen in 1657. He died there in 1675.

Like many other seventeenth-century Dutch artists, Allart seems to have supported himself by dealing in art.[1] His earliest paintings were marines. In addition to Scandinavian landscapes, he painted Dutch landscapes and city views.

1. See biographies in Houbraken, 1718, vol. 2, pp. 95–96; MacLaren, 1960, pp. 119–120; Davies, 1973/1978, pp. 28–43.

180

ALLART VAN EVERDINGEN
*A Mineral Spring at Spa
(The Fourth Spring)*

From a series of four etchings
Etching and drypoint
B. 98, Drugulin 101, Dut. 98[1], Holl. 98
Lower left: *AVE*
132 x 178 mm. (platemark)
Wm.: foolscap
Coll.: H.F. de la Motte-Fouquet (L. 778); C. Schlösser (L. 636); E. Schröter (L. 2270)
Museum of Fine Arts, Boston, Otis Norcross Fund. M25473

Although most of Everdingen's etchings are landscapes inspired by scenery observed during his Scandinavian journey, the etching shown here is one of four representing mineral springs at the watering place of Spa, near Liége, in the South Netherlands. This spring has been identified as the Watroz spring.[1]

Everdingen's etchings are undated, and their relative stylistic unformity makes it difficult to place them in chronological sequence. The present etching, however, cannot be earlier than the 1660s, because some of the doll-like figures of the pilgrims to the health-giving waters are dressed in costumes that were in the height of fashion at that time.[2]

There is a study for the Watroz spring etching in pen and monochromatic oil colors on paper in Hamburg. This is one of three such oil-on-paper studies for the Spa etchings that survive, two of which are directly related to the images of the etchings as executed.[3] It has been suggested that these studies were made on the spot. The general disposition of elements in the Hamburg oil study of the Watroz spring is similar to the completed etching, but the tonal structure is different; in the oil study the trees

1. Davies, 1973/1978, p. 258.

2. Observed by Davies, 1973/1978, p. 40. See the fashionable young people in the garden playing skittles in Pieter de Hooch's painting of about 1663–1666 at Waddeson Manor (Sutton, 1979, pl. 64).

3. The other two oil studies are in the British Museum.

are dark against a light sky, whereas in the etching they are light against a sky darkened with fine strokes of drypoint.

The impression shown here is an early state before the reworking of the plate in engraving. It is printed with a light film of ink left on the plate surface, which has been wiped away from the brighter areas of the foreground in order to intensify the sunlight.

181

ALLART VAN EVERDINGEN
Landscape with Sailing Boat
(The Broad River)

Etching
B. 82, Drugulin, 86, Dut. 82¹, Holl. 82¹
Lower left: *AVE*
125 x 160 mm. (platemark)
Coll.: R. Peltzer (L. suppl. 2231)
Museum of Fine Arts, Boston, Gift of Mrs. T. Jefferson Coolidge. 29.1994

If the large numbers of etchings of Scandinavian views made by Everdingen are any token, these exotic northern views seem to have enjoyed a popularity in seventeenth-century Holland comparable to that of idyllic views of Italy. Everdingen's etched Scandinavian views sometimes strike one as somewhat schematic and repetitious when seen in quantity. The present example, representing a wide river or inlet from the sea, is particularly attractive for the fluency and freedom with which it is drawn. This is particularly evident in the first state shown here, executed in etching alone before the addition of half-tones in drypoint or engraving in the next state. The light tonality and the drawing of the distant mountain evoke classicizing landscape etchings of the seventeenth-century Bolognese school inspired by the landscapes of Titian, such as those of Giovanni Francesco Grimaldi (1606–1780).

180

181 (actual size)

Adriaen Verboom
about 1628 – about 1670

The landscape painter Adriaen Hendricksz. Verboom, a follower of Jacob van Ruisdael, made about six etchings of landscapes.[1] Little is known of Verboom's life. He was born in Rotterdam about 1628. He was first active in that city and then in the period around 1650–1660 in Haarlem. He was later in Amsterdam, where his wife was buried in 1667. He died, probably in Amsterdam, about 1670.[2] His brother Willem was also a landscape painter.

1. Including two undescribed etchings, one signed and one unsigned. A landscape with an inn and a water mill, in the Rijksmuseum, is fully signed. An unsigned etching of ruins in a landscape, in the British Museum, corresponds in style to *The Castle in Ruins,* Dut. 4.

2. Biography by M.D. Henkel in Thieme-Becker, vol. 34, pp. 227–228.

182

ADRIAEN VERBOOM

The Hamlet, about 1663

One of a pair of etchings
Etching
B. 1, Dut. 1[1], Wurz. 1[1]
Upper left: *V boom.f.*
133 x 181 mm. (platemark)
Wm.: letters IB
Coll.: J. Barnard (L. 1417)
Davison Art Center, Wesleyan University, Middletown, Connecticut, Gift of George W. Davison, B.A., 1892. 41-D1-67

The Hamlet forms a pair of landscape etchings with *The Pond* (Dut. 2). Similar in dimensions, both represent a low strip of land with trees in the immediate foreground that frame a vista opening into the landscape at center.

The Hamlet is etched with great delicacy, the trees and their foliage having a feathery lightness and lyrical, ornamental rhythm comparable to the trees in the landscapes painted by Meindert Hobbema in the 1660s. The softness of the landscape forms is due chiefly to the fineness of the etched line and the execution of much of the image in terms of masses of short

182

strokes, stipples, and squiggles rather than in continuous contour drawing. The clouds have an appropriately indefinite, aerial quality.

Shown here is one of the scarce impressions taken before the plate was reworked in engraving, probably at the hands of a publisher who acquired the plates. In this reworking, engraved parallel shading lines, mechanical in character, were added to the sky, robbing it of its aerial feeling and making nonsense of the evanescent clouds.

Verboom's dated drawings suggest that this pair of etchings may have been executed around 1663.[1]

1. See, for example, the brush drawing, annotated 1663, from the Lugt collection, in Paris, 1968–69, no. 161, pl. 128, and the Teylers Museum, cat. 1904, p. 228, Port. Q+, no. 44, dated 1663.

263

Adam Pynacker

1621–1673

Only one etching can be attributed with certainty to Adam Pynacker, a painter of idealized Italian views transfigured by the glow of southern light.

Adam Pynacker was born in 1621 in the village of Pijnacker, near Delft. His teachers are not known, but Jan Both has been suggested, since Pynacker's vision of Italy is clearly indebted to Both's. According to Houbraken, he spent three years in Italy. The visit probably took place about 1645. In 1649 Pynacker was living in Delft and in 1658 in Schiedam. He died in Amsterdam in 1673.[1]

Many of the painters of idyllic Italian views executed suites of painted wall decorations to warm the interiors of fine Dutch houses. Houbraken singles out Pynacker's wall decorations for special mention. Today he is particularly appreciated for his views of still, southern harbors with their magical light.

1. See biographies by Houbraken, 1718, vol. 2, pp. 477–478; Blankert in Utrecht, 1965, pp. 184–185.

183

ADAM PYNACKER
Hilly Landscape

Etching and drypoint
Wurz. 1, Holl. 1
119 x 146 mm. (platemark)
Wm.: foolscap (fragment)
Rijksmuseum, Amsterdam. OB4633

Adam Pynacker's only etching is a fantasy based on familiar Italianate themes: the herdsman, the ruins, the stream in the gorge that springs from a dark, cool grotto.

In his works after 1660 Pynacker is allied to Nicolaes Berchem (cat. no. 120) in his feeling for decorative, rhythmic use of line. The silhouetted branches and the edges of forms in this etching have the scalloped rhythm characteristic of Pynacker's later paintings and his drawings dating from the 1660s. These ornamental

183 (actual size)

tendencies are particularly evident when one compares this etching with an etching representing similar motifs by Jan Both (*Cows at the Waterside,* cat. no. 118).

The landscape is freely sketched in etched line as fine as Bartholomeus Breenbergh's. Skillful use is made of changes of direction in the loose bundles of parallel shading strokes to model the landscape's hills and vales. Unworked patches of blank paper evoke the intensity of the southern light. This impression has been printed with a light film of ink that has apparently been intentionally wiped or graded so as to suggest a glow of light entering the sky from the right.

Thomas Wyck
about 1616 – 1677

A painter of Mediterranean harbor views and cluttered interiors, Thomas Wyck made about twenty-five etchings, none of which are dated. Small in scale, they represent Italian architectural views, courtyards, and street scenes, the last in the manner of Pieter van Laer.[1]

Born in Beverwyck near Haarlem about 1616, Thomas Wyck joined the artists' guild of Haarlem in 1642. His teachers are not known. In 1644 he married in Haarlem. He is traceable there between 1656 and 1660. From about 1660 he spent several years in England, where he painted the great London fire of 1666. In 1677 he died in Haarlem. Houbraken reports that Wyck was in Italy, but the journey is not documented.[2]

In addition to views of Italian harbors and streets, Wyck painted northern interiors (such as alchemists' laboratories), full of colorful but strictly regimented clutter.

1. There is one undescribed oblong etching of stairs descending into a courtyard in the collection of the Rijksmuseum. Less certainly by Wyck's hand but in his style are three undescribed etchings of vertical format in the Albertina: *Figures under an Arch, A Grotto, Bridge and Ruins* (all H. III, 31, p. 3).

2. Biography by Blankert in Utrecht, 1965, pp. 144–145.

184 (actual size)

184

THOMAS WYCK
House Built into the Ruins

Etching
B. 18, Dut. 18[II]
Upper left: [monogram] TW
113 x 119 mm. (platemark)
Wm.: foolscap (fragment)
Museum of Fine Arts, Boston, Gift of Richard Zinser. 1971.27

Thomas Wyck's etched Italian views reveal not only his interest in recording the strong southern light that rakes the scene and illuminates even the shadows but also his desire to impose a firm, rectilinear order on the scene. In this self-conscious striving to impose a lucid architectural organization on subjects drawn from daily life, Wyck resembles his Haarlem contemporary Cornelis Bega in his later works. He also shares with Bega a certain tendency toward two-dimensionality and collapsible space, as in the etching shown here, in which the far buildings tend to fuse with those of the middle ground. The square format that Wyck favored in a few etchings is well suited to his stringently formal organization.

185

ALLART VAN EVERDINGEN
Nocturnal Landscape with House and Church Spire

Mezzotint and drypoint
B. 91, Drugulin 93, Dut. 91, Holl. 91[I-II]
125 x 162 mm. (platemark)
The Art Institute of Chicago, Mr. and Mrs. James
W. Alsdorf Fund. 1955.1025

185

The medium of mezzotint as we know it today saw its final development in the period 1657–1661 at the hands of a dilettante, the military leader Prince Ruprecht (or Rupert) of Bohemia, Count Palatine. During these years Ruprecht developed the mezzotint "rocker," a tool with a ridged steel blade used to roughen the surface of the copper plate to achieve a continuous, deep velvety tone (see Glossary).

Ruprecht learned of Ludwig von Siegen's experiments with a spiked wheel or roulette to produce tonal areas in portraits (see the discussion of Rembrandt's *St. Jerome in a Dark Chamber,* cat. no. 99) when he visited his cousin Landgrave William VI at Cassel in 1657. Upon returning to Frankfurt in that same year, Ruprecht, who had done some etching during his childhood at the court in the Hague, began to experiment with improving Von Siegen's method, hiring the Dutch portrait painter Wallerant Vaillant to work with him. Vaillant, who later developed into one of the most important Dutch mezzotint artists (see cat. nos. 190, 191), was experimenting in portrait engravings dating from around 1656–1658 (Wessely 2 and 7, for example) with a variety of tonal effects: dotted lines, roulette, close-laid parallel lines, and granular bitten tone. It is impossible to know how much the professional artist Vaillant contributed to the first mezzotints of the amateur Prince Ruprecht.

In February 1661 the English amateur of prints John Evelyn recorded in his diary that Prince Ruprecht had shown him "how to Grave in M[e]zzo Tinto." In his book on the history of engraving, *Sculptura,* published in the next year, Evelyn included a description of

a mezzotint by Prince Ruprecht in the book but coyly withheld information regarding the tools necessary to create the effects he described. In recent years Orovida Pissarro has published a passage in a manuscript by John Evelyn, preserved at Christ Church, Oxford, that includes a description and sketches of the mezzotint rocker and scraper, or "Hatcher" and "Style," as Evelyn called them. Evelyn's sketches served as the basis for the drawings of the rocker and scraper included in the Glossary in this catalogue.[1]

1. For Prince Ruprecht and the early history of mezzotint, see Pissarro, 1960; Yale University, 1976.

The year in which Vaillant settled in Amsterdam, 1665, provides a firm date for the introduction of the fully developed form of mezzotint into Holland. The first dated mezzotints by Dutch artists, however, are generally from the 1670s and 1680s. As Everdingen's efforts in mezzotint have a somewhat experimental character, I have taken the liberty of placing his mezzotints in the early years of the Dutch mezzotint, in the 1660s. Everdingen's free, unsystematic roughening of the plate surface is perhaps responsible for the suggestion that he used a rat-tail file instead of a rocker to prepare the surface.[2]

2. Rotterdam, 1942–43, p. 8.

The landscape shown here is the only pure mezzotint securely attributed to Everdingen. In one instance he used passages of mezzotint to convert an etched landscape into a twilight or nocturnal landscape (B. 31), and in a number of his etched illustrations to *Renard the Fox* he used mezzotint for nocturnal effects. Here the marks of Everdingen's scraping of the plate to create the light are very evident and lend a sense of spontaneity of execution to the image. A few supplementary details were added in drypoint.

Impressions of Everdingen's nocturnal landscape survive, taken at different stages of the scraping-out of the image on the plate. John Evelyn mentioned in his Christ Church manuscript the necessity of taking frequent proofs to see how the work was progressing,[3] and the many surviving working proofs of seventeenth-century Dutch mezzotints confirm this practice. States in mezzotints are unusually difficult to describe because one is dealing with broad areas of tone rather than line, and variations in inking can easily be mistaken for changes of state. The impression of Everdingen's landscape shown here appears to be intermediate between the published descriptions of the first and second states. I have seen a very dark impression in a private collection that seems to precede the first state as described by catalogers.

Landscapes in pure mezzotint were rare in the seventeenth century. I have also seen in Rotterdam a moonlit landscape in mezzotint attributed to Isaac van der Vinne (1665–1740). It is printed in greenish-black, and the moon was added by hand in opaque white watercolor.

3. Pissarro, 1960, p. 5.

186 (actual size)

186
Attributed to ALLART VAN EVERDINGEN
Three Monks

Mezzotint
B. 105, Drugulin 109, Dut. 105, Holl. 105
100 x 147 mm. (platemark)
Coll.: unknown (L. 2794); Arenberg (L. 567)
The Metropolitan Museum of Art, The Harris Brisbane Dick Fund, Rogers Fund, Joseph Pulitzer Bequest and Henry Walters Gift, by Exchange. 1970.599.39

This small mezzotint of three monks – one reading, one explicating, one sleeping – is difficult to attribute firmly to Everdingen because of the surprising choice of subject. Monks appear in the etching of the Watroz spring at Spa, but not in the tenebrous, mysterious atmosphere that suggests a seventeenth-century Italian painter such as Salvator Rosa. The texture of the prepared plate surface, however, is very similar to that in Everdingen's *Nocturnal Landscape* mezzotint (cat. no. 185). The lower margin is blank as if ready to receive an engraved inscription.

A third mezzotint attributed to this artist, representing *Venus and Cupid on Clouds* (Dut. 104), is certainly not by Everdingen but, rather, is by a painter of mythologies such as his brother, Cesar van Everdingen, or perhaps a member of the Utrecht painter Cornelis Poelenburg's circle. The texture resulting from the roughening of the copper plate is quite different from that in the other two mezzotints given to Allart van Everdingen.

Abraham Storck
1644 – after 1695

The marine painter Abraham Storck made six etchings (Wurz. 1-6), which are not represented in most collections. Four are fantasy views of Mediterranean harbors or the figures who inhabit them. One is a Dutch river view with ships, and another is a southern river view with a gateway leading to an Italian garden.

Abraham Jansz. Storck was born in Amsterdam in 1644. His father, the painter Jan Sturck, or Sturckenberg, had emigrated to Amsterdam from the town of Wesel, near the eastern Dutch border. Abraham's two brothers, Johannes and Jacob, were also marine painters. All three brothers painted, among other specialities, fantasy views of Mediterranean harbors.

Abraham was a member of the artists' guild of Amsterdam and seems to have remained in that city all his life. It is possible that he made an Italian journey, but it is not documented. He is last mentioned in 1697, but according to Houbraken, he painted the reception of Marlborough on the Amstel, an event that took place in 1704.[1] In addition to fantasy views of southern harbors, he painted northern harbor views and topographical views, especially around Amsterdam. His paintings have an enamel-like finish and a bright palette.

1. See biographies by MacLaren, 1960, p. 408; Jacob Olibeeck in Bol, 1973, pp. 315-318.

187

ABRAHAM STORCK
Harbor with Classical Ruins, about 1675

Etching
B. 6, Wurz. 6
Upper right, on temple entablature: *A Storck*
100 x 138 mm. (platemark)
Graphische Sammlung Albertina, Vienna.
HB 73(6), p. 27, 3

187 (actual size)

In Abraham Storck's etched fantasy on the theme of Mediterranean harbors, we see at left a galley of the Italian type and, in the distance at center, a Dutch ship. The appearance of Dutch ships in foreign harbor views of this type celebrated Holland's far-reaching seaborne mercantile trade as well as her military might on the sea. Storck's etching relates closely to drawings of such harbors by Storck dated in the 1670s, some of them watercolored; see, for example, the drawing signed and dated 1674 in Berlin (Berlin, cat. drawings, 1931, no. 5611). An even more closely related pen and wash drawing, signed and dated 1675 (see V.A. Heck, stock cat. no. 68), shows a galley and ruined temple in the same relationship but in reverse. The other elements are different.

188

ADRIAEN VAN OSTADE
The Cobbler, 1671

Etching, drypoint, and engraving
B. 27, Dut. 27[IV], Davidsohn 27[IV], Godefroy 27[IV],
Holl. 27[IV]
Lower right: *Av Ostade 1671*
189 x 151 mm. (platemark)
The Art Institute of Chicago, The Clarence Buck-
ingham Collection. 1938.1671

In Adriaen van Ostade's etching of 1671, a cob-
bler, clutching an awl, works on a shoe in his
cellar shop. The ingenious shutters open to
admit the sun and form both a counter and a
roof to shelter it. A passerby seated on a three-
legged stool "kibitzes" with the shoemaker,
gesturing with his clay pipe. On the roof a dog
is curled up, dozing in the sun.[1]

   In this fine impression of an early state of
one of Ostade's latest dated etchings, one can
observe how greatly Ostade's style has changed
since the 1640s (see cat. nos. 101, 102, 112).
The contours are firm and continuous; the
forms are solid, rather than being dissolved in
atmosphere. There is relatively little interest in
textural description. As in Ostade's late watercolors, the tonality is light, high-keyed.

1. A pen and ink preparatory drawing in reverse, indented
for transfer, is in the collection of the Metropolitan
Museum of Art, New York; see Franklin W. Robinson,
*Seventeenth Century Dutch Drawings from American Col-
lections* (Washington, D.C.: International Exhibitions
Foundation, 1977), no. 47, illus.

188

Jan van Huchtenburgh
1647 – 1733

The battle painter Jan van Huchtenburgh made nearly eighty prints, including seven mezzotints. A number of the etchings reproduce the work of the Flemish battle painter Adam Frans van der Meulen. The majority of the subjects in both print media are concerned with warfare.

Jan (or Johan) van Huchtenburgh was born in Haarlem in 1647. He was probably a pupil of Thomas Wyck, whose son, Jan, was a friend of his. He was also influenced by the work of Nicolaes Berchem and Philips Wouwerman. He is said to have traveled to Rome in 1667, where he visited his painter brother, Jacob. In 1667 he also began to work at the Gobelins tapestry factory in Paris under Adam Frans van der Meulen and Charles Le Brun. At this time Huchtenburgh's friend Abraham Genoels, the classicizing Flemish landscape painter and etcher, accompanied him on his travels. By 1670 he was back in Haarlem, where he was married in that year. In the next years he was alternately active in Haarlem and Amsterdam. In 1708–09 he painted a series of paintings for Prince Eugene of Savoy in Italy. Huchtenburgh also worked for Elector Johann Wilhelm von der Pfalz, who presented him in 1711 with a gold chain and medal. In 1719 he joined the painters' confraternity in the Hague. He died in Amsterdam in 1733.[1]

Besides battle scenes, Huchtenberg painted hunts and other subjects involving horses. The horse painter, etcher, and mezzotinter Dirck Maas was his pupil (see cat. nos. 199, 200).

1. See biographies by H. Schneider in Thieme-Becker, vol. 18, pp. 29–30; MacLaren, 1960, p. 195.

189
JAN VAN HUCHTENBURGH
Robbers and Peasants

Mezzotint
B. 1, Holl. 1
Lower right: *Huchtenburg*
224 x 300 mm. (platemark)
Wm.: crowned circle
National Gallery of Art, Washington, D.C., Andrew W. Mellon Purchase Fund, 1976. B-29.036

Jan van Huchtenburgh's powerful mezzotint of bandits, probably soldiers, stealing provisions from peasants is part of a set of four mezzotints dealing with subjects relating to warfare. Another mezzotint in the series (B. 2) represents a meal in a soldier's encampment; a serving woman bearing a platter of meat looks disdainfully at a ragged woman with children in tattered clothing who sits by the fire and begs for food.

In the mezzotint shown here the sculptural group of the pleading, sorrowing, and fearful peasant family is treated with a surprising grandeur of rhetorical gesture and nobility of illumination. The pears spilling from the market basket onto the ground is a beautifully expressive detail. The loyal family dog barks bravely at the robbers. The older soldier is in the act of pulling a pig out of the wicker hamper and has already tied a kid and a rooster to his saddle. To judge from their expressions, the robbers, particularly the younger man, seem to have mixed feelings about the deed to which they have been driven.

The dramatic but nuanced lighting of which the mezzotint medium is capable reinforces the tragic overtones of the encounter. The idealized Italianate landscape of the background and the sky streaked with morning light suggest the etched landscapes of Herman van Swanevelt from the early 1650s.

Seventeenth-century Dutch mezzotints are often lighter in tonality, more concerned with the middle range of values, than the eighteenth-century English mezzotints one thinks of as setting the standard for this medium. It is therefore easy to misjudge quality of impression in these early Dutch examples of the medium and to consider a perfect impression too pale. These lighter tonalities were sometimes reinforced by printing with a greenish or brownish ink. Huchtenburgh frequently used a greenish black ink to print his mezzotints.

189

271

Wallerant Vaillant
1623 – 1677

The portrait painter and draftsman Wallerant Vaillant made seven etched and engraved portraits from his own designs and over two hundred and thirty mezzotints from his own designs and those of others. The mezzotints range in subject from portraits of members of the Vaillant family, to literary subjects, to scenes from daily life. Vaillant was one of the most important early practitioners of the mezzotint. Sandrart observed that no other artist had brought the art of mezzotint to a higher perfection and noted that amateurs of art everywhere sought examples of Vaillant's *Schwarze Kunst* (literally, "black art") for their albums and paid good prices for them. [1] The mezzotints of Wallerant's half-brother Bernard are sometimes confused with his.

Born in Lille (then a Flemish city) in 1623, Vaillant was the son of a merchant, who settled in Amsterdam in 1642–43. He was the eldest of five artist brothers and is said to have studied with Erasmus Quellinus in Antwerp. In 1647 he joined the artists' guild of Middelburg in Zeeland. He was probably in Amsterdam by 1649, for he painted Rembrandt's friend Jan Six in that year. He is also recorded there in 1651 and 1652. In 1658 he was in Frankfurt, where he was busy drawing and etching portraits of the dignitaries assembled for the coronation of Emperor Leopold I. At this time he met Prince Ruprecht von der Pfalz and assisted him with the development of the mezzotint process.

Vaillant was in Paris from 1659 to 1665 and in the latter year settled in Amsterdam, which remained his principal place of residence. In 1675, however, he still paid dues to the Middelburg artists' guild. He died in Amsterdam in 1677.

Sandrart mentions as Vaillant's first claim to fame his paintings of literary subjects, or "histories," and next his portraits. Of the latter he singles out for special mention Vaillant's life-size portraits drawn in black and white chalks on blue paper. [2] These bust-length portraits executed in the manner of pastels are Vaillant's best-known works today. Their textures and their value structures parallel closely the artist's work in the medium of mezzotint. Wallerant's brother Jacques and his half-brothers Bernard and Andries produced similar portraits in a pastel manner. As a painter Wallerant also executed still lifes and scenes from daily life. His half-brother Andries was his pupil. [3]

2. Wallerant's etched portraits from the 1650s were sometimes printed on blue paper.

3. See biographies by Vandalle, 1937, pp. 347–351; MacLaren 1960, p. 410.

190
WALLERANT VAILLANT
The Young Draftsman

Mezzotint after Michiel Sweerts
Wessely 23, Wurz. 23
332 x 270 mm. (platemark)
Lent by the Trustees of the British Museum.
1874–8–8–1051

Wallerant Vaillant's mezzotint reproduces a painting by the Flemish painter Michiel Sweerts that has recently been acquired by the Minneapolis Institute of Arts. [1] A young art student is shown absorbed in drawing from a plaster cast of a sculptured head of the Roman emperor Vitellius. The sheet on which he draws rests on a portfolio that serves as a drawing board. On the floor beside the youngster's foot is a knife to sharpen the sticks of chalk or charcoal, a container for the shavings, and a bird's wing to brush away loose chalk granules. The plaster head is steadied by an open song book. Waddingham, in his article on Minneapolis's newly acquired Sweerts, notes the contrast between the innocent child and the gross features of the gluttonous Roman emperor. [2] The contrast is heightened in Vaillant's mezzotint, in which the features of the battered plaster head seem animated, almost alive.

The Vaillant mezzotint, which reverses the image of the Sweerts painting, differs slightly in detail from the painting but is essentially faithful to it. Waddingham, struck by the painting's closeness in style to that of contemporary Dutch painters such as Gerard ter Borch, dates it around 1661, during Sweerts's brief stay in Amsterdam. [3] The mezzotint was probably done several years later, after Vaillant's return to Amsterdam in 1665. The only dated mezzotints by Vaillant known to me are from the 1670s.

Drawing from plaster casts of antique sculpture was as much a part of the apprentice art-

1. Reproduced in color in Waddingham, 1976–77, p. 56. Waddingham's article does not mention the Vaillant print but does discuss related paintings by Vaillant.

2. Ibid., p. 57.

3. Ibid, p. 59.

1. Sandrart/Peltzer, 1925, p. 264.

ist's education in seventeenth-century Holland as drawing from prints. The chiaroscuro print by Frederick Bloemaert that forms the frontispiece to the first part of Abraham Bloemaert's drawing book (first published about 1650) represents a somewhat older student drawing from a cast of a reclining river god surrounded by other plaster casts, including casts from life.[4]

Both Sweerts and Vaillant represented in their paintings young art students learning by drawing from plaster casts, flayed anatomical figures (*écorchés*), or other works of art.[5] A Vaillant painting known in two versions (in the Louvre, Paris, and in the National Gallery, London) represents a young boy studying a book of drawings; behind him are plaster casts after the Christ Child of Michelangelo's Bruges Madonna and after the antique, including a cast of the head of Vitellius seen here. This painting was also reproduced in mezzotint by Vaillant (Wessely 21).

Since Vaillant did not always indicate the sources of his images in his prints that reproduce the work of others, one would be forgiven for assuming that the print shown here, like the one just described (Wessely 21), was one of Vaillant's own design. When the mezzotint after Sweerts's painting is compared with that after Vaillant's own painting, one sees that the forms in the latter are broader, softer, and more rounded than the forms in the mezzotint after Sweerts, which are more crisply defined.

The Young Draftsman is seen here in a fine impression in which the fresh tracks of the scraper and burnisher are evident, and all the finely nuanced gradations of modeling and illumination are present. In some later impressions of Vaillant's mezzotints (which bear the address of the publisher De Wit) it is clear that the plates have been rerocked and rescraped.

4. Reproduced in Strauss, 1973, no. 164.

5. See, for example, Sweerts's painting, in the Rijksmuseum (inv. A 1957), of an artist's studio with a student drawing, plaster casts after the antique, and an *écorché* figure.

190

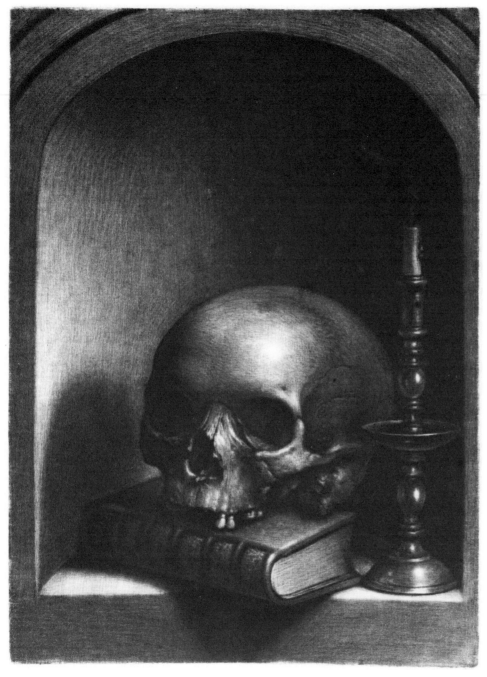

191

191

WALLERANT VAILLANT
Vanitas Still Life (Memento Mori)

Mezzotint
Wessely 117, Wurz. 117
222 x 163 mm. (platemark)
Lent by the Trustees of the British Museum.
1874–8–8–1064

Still lifes in print form are quite rare in the late sixteenth and seventeenth century in the North Netherlands, a period when still-life painting flourished. The majority of the still lifes that were executed in print media were *Vanitas* subjects. Rembrandt's etching of a cone shell (B. 159) is an exception, but, as one can read in Roemer Visscher's *Sinnepoppen* (cat. no. 54), these costly exotic shells could also have overtones of folly and *Vanitas*.

Vaillant's mezzotint *Vanitas* still life in a niche with a skull resting on a book and a recently extinguished candle, its wick still smoking, is probably from his own design. It reveals, however, an extreme, even conservative consciousness of tradition in its allusion to the kind of skull-in-niche still lifes that Barthel Bruyn the Elder, the sixteenth-century Cologne painter, painted on the back of portrait panels as a moralizing reminder to the sitter.[1]

The subtle illumination and coloristic suggestion that the medium of mezzotint was capable of in Vaillant's hands give these simple objects a grim and powerful presence. This fine impression was printed before the engraved inscription "Memento Mori" and the artist's signature and "Fecit" were added to the plate.

A number of *Vanitas* still lifes were engraved or etched by other Dutch artists: Jan Saenredam after Abraham Bloemaert, Hendrik Hondius, Theodor Matham, and Leonart Bramer.[2]

1. See the pair of portraits of Gerhard and Anna Pilgrum by Barthel Bruyn, in the Wallraf-Richartz Museum, Cologne (nos. 230, 231).
2. Many of these *Vanitas* still-life prints are reproduced in the exhibition catalogue of "Still Life in Europe," Münster and Baden-Baden, 1980, pp. 194–208.

Samuel van Hoogstraten
1627 – 1678

The painter, playwright, and poet Samuel van Hoogstraten made about ten single etchings and provided part or all of the illustrations for about seven books, including the portraits for Balen's description of Hoogstraten's native city of Dordrecht (1677) and the charming illustrations for his own *Pretty Roselin* (*Schoone Roselin*). Hoogstraten's earliest dated print of 1648 (Holl. 2) reflects his study with Rembrandt, whereas his last prints, the illustrations for his 1678 book on the rules of art, are closer to the classicizing etchings of Gerard de Lairesse in style and spirit.

Samuel Dircksz. Hoogstraten was born in Dordrecht in 1627. He first studied with his father, the painter and engraver Dirck Hoogstraten, and, after his father's death in 1640, with Rembrandt in Amsterdam. His fellow pupils in Rembrandt's studio were Carel Fabritius and, probably, Abraham Furnerius. He was back in Dordrecht in 1648 and was baptized a Mennonite (or Baptist) in that year.

In 1651 Hoogstraten arrived in Vienna after a journey through Germany. The emperor Ferdinand III purchased a still life from him and presented him with a gold chain and medal, of which Hoogstraten was very proud. In 1652 he visited Rome. He returned to Vienna, where he remained until at least 1653. In 1654 he was again in Dordrecht. In 1656 his marriage to Sara van Balen, an outsider, led to his expulsion from Dordrecht's Mennonite community. He worked in Dordrecht until his departure for London in 1662. In 1666 he witnessed that city's great fire. He returned to the Hague, where one of his plays was performed in 1668 and where he joined the painters' confraternity. He was still in the Hague in 1671. In 1673 he returned to Dordrecht, where he became one of the provosts of the mint. He died there in 1678.[1]

1. See biographies by Hofstede de Groot in Thieme-Becker, vol. 17, pp. 463–465; MacLaren, 1960, pp. 191–192.

Hoogstraten's production as a painter was unusually varied: biblical and mythological subjects, portraits, subjects from daily life, architectural views, landscapes, seascapes, flower pieces, still lifes, *trompe l'oeil* (fool-the-eye) pictures, and perspective peep boxes.

192
SAMUEL VAN HOOGSTRATEN
The Muse Urania (Urania de Hemelhefster) in Samuel van Hoogstraten, *Inleyding tot de Hooge Schoole der Schilderkonst; Anders de Zichtbaere Werelt.* Rotterdam, Fransois van Hoogstraeten, 1678.

Etching, drypoint, and engraving
(opposite page 325)
163 x 125 mm. (platemark); 201 x 157 mm. (page size); vellum
LeBl. 1, Wurz. vol. 1, pp. 720f., Holl. 31
Museum of Fine Arts, Boston, William A. Sargent Fund. 1973.612

Samuel van Hoogstraten's *Introduction to the Noble School of Painting; otherwise the Visible World* was published in Rotterdam in the year of his death by his brother Fransois. The title page of this treatise on the rules of painting, which provides advice for artists and dilettantes, informs the reader that it is divided into nine instructional workshops (*Leerwinkels*), each presided over by one of the nine Muses. The book was illustrated with Hoogstraten's own etchings, which include a self-portrait, a frontispiece to the book as a whole, and frontispieces to the nine individual books. In the frontispiece to the book as a whole the nine Muses cluster round the artist, who carries a maulstick and palette and is clad in the dress of an antique Roman soldier. He is winged at head and heel like Mercury, patron of artists and artisans. The Muses crown him with laurel and direct his attention to the orb of the "visible world."

The frontispiece to the ninth and last book is presided over by the "heavenly" Muse, Urania, patroness of astronomy, her lovely face encircled by stars. Hoogstraten dubs her the "Hemelhefster" (literally, the one who elevates to heaven), alluding to the theme of the ninth book: the artist's rewards for his efforts – fame and enduring posthumous reputation. The cartouche on which Urania's name and title are inscribed is enframed in medals, crowns of laurel, money bags, a sword betokening elevation to the nobility, and the palm of victory. Hoogstraten's verses on the facing page set the theme of the ninth book and explicate the imagery of the print. The verses explain that she (Urania) who can cause the spirit to strive for heaven is appropriately crowned with stars. The three children of the etching are identified. Honor, crowned with laurel, reaches up to pluck further laurels (in the etched frontispiece to the book as a whole Urania is the Muse who crowns the artist with laurel). A second child, Wealth, holds money bags. The third child holds out the fruit of satisfaction, or contentment, which is another reward for the artist's striving. In the foreground a memorial slab, with a snake slinking from beneath it and toadstools growing beside it, refers to the body's mortality. Tokens of the immortality of the artist's fame or reputation are seen in the image on the scroll held by Urania and in the phoenix reborn from flames behind her. The image on Urania's scroll represents a skull and bones, but the skull is topped by a steadily burning lamp rather than accompanied by a guttering or extinguished light and is enframed with palms of victory. In the middle distance at left, an artist, clutching palette and brushes, climbs the ladder that leads to heaven, to fame and glory. In the far distance a ruler ennobles with a sword the artist who kneels before him.

The theme of the artist's strivings, motivations, and rewards is taken up again by Hoogstraten in the painted decorations of three of the exterior sides of a perspective peep box now in the National Gallery, London. On each of the three sides Hoogstraten represents one of the artist's motivations for working: Gain (as the artist paints a portrait, gold pours from the cornucopia held by a crowned putto);

275

192 (actual size)

Glory (a putto crowns the artist with laurel and places a gold chain around his neck) and Love (the artist draws the image of the Muse Urania, to whom the putto leaning over his shoulder points).[1]

Hoogstraten's etched allegories, like so much Dutch classicizing art of this time, are a lively, if sometimes uneasy, combination of idealization and earthy realism: the ladder that the aspiring artist ascends is prosaically and amusingly literal, the symbolic putti have chubby, gamin-like faces.

When seen in ordinary impressions, Hoogstraten's etchings for his *Inleyding* ... strike one as dry and academic in the worst sense, but in fine impressions such as those in the volume shown here, they have a surprising degree of coloristic suggestion and sparkle.

1. See MacLaren, 1960, pp. 192–195, and Plates, 1958, vol. 1, pp. 158–160.

Attributed to PIETER and
PHILIP VAN GUNST
after GERARD DE LAIRESSE
The Muscles of the Arm in Govert Bidloo,
*Ontleding des Menschelyken Lichams (Dissec-
tion of the Human Body)*. Amsterdam,
By de Weduwe van Joannes van Someren,
de Erfgenaamen van Joannes van Dyk,
Hendrik en de Weduwe van Dirk Boom,
1690. (First edition in Latin, 1685.)

Etching and engraving
(plate 70)
470 x 330 mm. (platemark); 520 x 350 mm.
(page size); brown leather
Choulant/Frank (1920), pp. 250–253
Coll.: Oettingen-Wallerstein; Philip Hofer
The Houghton Library, Harvard University,
Department of Printing and Graphic Arts, Gift of
Philip Hofer

The *Dissection of the Human Body,* by the anatomy professor and surgeon Govert Bidloo,
with illustrations designed by Gerard de
Lairesse, is one of the most visually splendid of
the many illustrated volumes on science, natural history, and medicine published in Holland
in the seventeenth century.

The frontispiece shows Time pushing back a
curtain to reveal, enthroned on a sarcophagus,
the draped female figure of Anatomy, or Dissection, who holds a knife and book. Beside
her the statue of a putto, its head cloaked,
holds up a dissected arm. Behind them Fame
sounds a trumpet. In the foreground putti
study a skull, an arm, and an anatomical print.
The author's bust-length portrait in an oval,
also designed by Lairesse, was engraved by the
skilled professional engraver Abraham
Blooteling. Its format and style of engraving
suggest seventeenth-century French engravers
such as Robert Nanteuil.

The plates begin with Lairesse's conception
of the ideal man and woman. The ideal man
(patterned on Dürer's Adam from his engraving of *Adam and Eve,* B. 1) stands before a

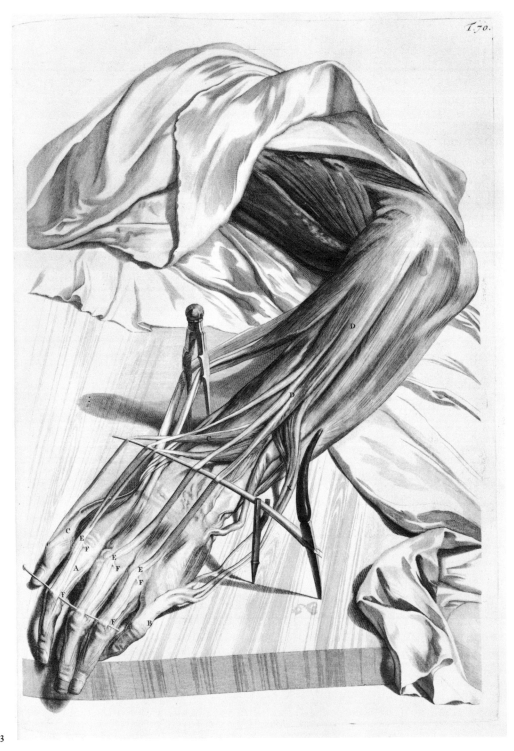

background composed of a draped antique urn and antique reliefs.

Thus far everything conforms to one's preconceptions about Lairesse's style, but many of the plates, which have the candid realism of a still life, force us to expand our notion of the artist's potential. The unsigned plates are traditionally attributed to the professional engravers Pieter and Philip van Gunst. Lairesse's drawings are said to be preserved in the Ecole de Médicine, Paris. The engraver's highly successful melding of delicate etched lines and bolder engraved lines accounts in part for the strong sense of coloristic suggestion, as in the grained blond wood of the dissection table. The still-life character of many of the plates is heightened by the near life-size scale and the meticulously described play of light and shadow. The almost brutal Dutch realism of some of the illustrations is epitomized by the inclusion of a fly in one of the plates. The anatomy has been said to be inaccurate,[1] but the immediacy of the plates is so persuasive that one finds this judgment hard to credit.

In his preface Bidloo indicates that the book is intended for the use of artists as well as medical students. In the seventeenth century it was not easy for the artist who was a devoted student of anatomy to have access to cadavers or dissections. Bidloo even indulges in a bit of art criticism, criticizing some painters and sculptors for defining the separate muscles too sharply, making the figures look as if they were flayed. Possibly Bidloo had Goltzius and the Dutch Mannerist artists in mind.

The present illustration, showing the muscles of the arm, is from the section on the limbs, the fifth of the book's six sections. The explication of the muscles, following the alphabetical indicators, is printed on the facing page.

1. Choulant/Frank, 1920, p. 250.

Michiel van Musscher
1645 – 1705

The portrait painter Michiel van Musscher made about eight prints, of which the majority are mezzotints and one or two are etchings. All are portraits or heads.

Born in Rotterdam in 1645, Musscher had a number of teachers: in 1661 Martinus Saagmolen and Abraham van den Tempel, in 1665 Gabriel Metsu, and in 1663 and 1667 Adriaen van Ostade. In 1668 Musscher was in Rotterdam. He married Eva Visscher in 1678, and in 1688 he became a citizen of Amsterdam. He died in that city in 1705.[1]

1. See biography by M.D. Henkel in Thieme-Becker, vol. 25, pp. 293–294.

194
MICHIEL VAN MUSSCHER
Self-Portrait, 1685

Mezzotint
Wurz. 1, Holl. 1[1]
314 x 283 mm. (platemark)
Wm.: shield (?)
Museum of Fine Arts, Boston, Stephen Bullard Memorial Fund. 69.1237

In Michiel van Musscher's mezzotint self-portrait of 1685, the artist looks us straight in the eye, exuding self-confidence. Musscher has employed the illusion of leaning through a window, as Rembrandt did in his etching of Sylvius (cat. no. 97). The portrait image is surrounded with an elaborate allegorical frame, which alludes to time, transience, and the artist's immortality through fame. The verses engraved on the tablet at bottom in the next state imply that Time raises the curtain to reveal Musscher's greatness but also extends the hourglass to show that much sand has already run through it, that life is fleeting.[1] The soap bubbles blown by the putto at left were for the Dutch in the seventeenth century the archetypal symbol of the fragility of life. The portrait is pervaded by feeling for pomp and

for ornamental elaboration, expressed in such details as the oval, lobate-style frame, the silken-textured and fringed curtain, and the artist's neatly curling wig.

The modello for the mezzotint is one of a pair of portraits of Musscher and his wife painted by the artist in the same year as he made the print. The painting, in which the portrait is in color and the allegorical frame in *grisaille,* is smaller than the print and less elaborately worked out in detail. The painting bears the same inscription as the print, with slight variations in spelling.[2]

The rocking of the plate in Musscher's print, in contrast with that in the first mezzotint discussed here, the landscape by Everdingen (cat. no. 185), is extremely regularized in pattern and fine in texture. The scraping out of the image in this print is also very careful and smooth, leaving scarcely a trace of the action itself.

Two of the most attractive seventeenth-century Dutch mezzotints with effects of artificial light were designed by Musscher and executed by Gerard Valck: a maidservant sleeping and a maidservant searching for fleas (Nag. 41, 42).

A mezzotint self-portrait dated 1690 by Carel de Moor (see biography and cat. no. 196) also has an oval format. Two other contemporaries of Musscher who produced mezzotint portraits in a style that paralleled his were Jacob Gole (see the discusssion at cat. no. 201) and Abraham Blooteling.

1. "Dus heeft hier Musschers hand, dees omtreks zelfs gegeven/Tot een geheugenis, hoe zyn gedaante was./ Den Tyd ontdekt hem wel, maar thoont ook dat zyn glas,/ Al veel verloopen is, en leerd ons 't brosze leven."
2. Van Thiel, 1974, pp. 131ff.

Jan Lutma II
1624 – 1689

The silversmith Jan (or Johannes) Lutma II made about twenty-four prints, of which about half are ornament prints after the designs of others. In his earliest dated prints of 1656 Lutma was already supplementing etching with tonal passages achieved by mechanical punch or roulette work. In his later hammer or punch prints (*opere mallei* [literally, hammer works] was the Latin term used by Lutma to refer to these works) of around 1681, he employed a variety of punches to achieve tonal effects comparable to those of a wash drawing.

Jan Lutma was born in Amsterdam in 1624, the son of the famous silversmith portrayed by Rembrandt in his etching of 1656 (cat. no. 137). He became a master in 1643. In 1651 he was in Rome. He died in 1689.[1] There is considerable uncertainty about attribution to his hand of works in silver. A small number of drawings are known, one of them inscribed "Roma 1651."[2]

1. Biographies by C.J.H. in Thieme-Becker, vol. 23, pp. 481–482; J. Verbeek in Amsterdam/Toledo/Boston, 1980, p. 360.

2. At least two drawings bear Lutma monograms that make it clear that the monogram on the 1656 etched view of a Roman fountain (Holl. 10) is Lutma's rather than Bernini's, as mentioned in Hollstein.

195
JAN LUTMA II
Self-Portrait, 1681

Punch engraving, touched with gray wash
F.M. 3346, Wurz. vol. 2, p. 72, 3, Holl. 4
Below: *IANUS. LUTMA. BATAVUS./Per Se Opere Mallei. 1681.*
300 x 220 mm. (platemark)
Wm.: letters DI
Coll.: J. Barnard (L. 1419)
Davison Art Center, Wesleyan University, Middletown, Connecticut, Gift of George W. Davison, B.A., 1892. 42.DI.149

When Ludwig von Siegen (see cat. nos. 99, 185) wrote in 1642 to his patron William VI of Cassel about his new method of obtaining a continuous tone in an engraved portrait by scoring the copper plate with a spiked wheel or roulette, he stated that there were three methods of creating an image on a copper plate: engraving, etching, and "a method very little used, executed in small dots made with punches, but which is difficult and so arduous that it is seldom practised."[1]

As noted earlier, in the discussion of the punch engraving attributed to Paulus van Vianen (cat. no. 17), this dotted method of engraving was employed mostly by goldsmiths and silversmiths accustomed to the use of punches. Thus, it is not surprising that the silversmith Jan Lutma II should have employed such a method to produce the engravings in what he termed *opus mallei* (hammer work). Jan's goldsmith father had executed in 1641 an ornament print with a punched dotted outline in the sixteenth-century German manner (Holl. 1). The younger Lutma used punchwork, however, in a broad tonal manner imitative of drawings made with ink washes of varying degrees of intensity. His tonal use of punch work from 1656 to 1681 parallels the perfecting and flourishing of the ultimate tonal method of engraving: mezzotint.

The younger Lutma's self-portrait, like Michiel van Musscher's mezzotint self-portrait, (cat. no. 194) toys with *trompe l'oeil* (fool-the-

1. Pissarro, 1956–1958, p. 2.

eye) illusionism; the base of the artist's bust juts out of the niche and casts a shadow on his name engraved in Roman letters below. The conception of Lutma's self-portrait, that of a "living classical bust" in a niche, is probably derived from similar images by Rubens. The allusion to classical antiquity is extended by the Latin inscription, "Ianus Lutma. Batavus" (Jan Lutma. Batavian.") and the Latin motto "Ne te quaesiveris extra" ("Question yourself no further").

The younger Lutma's self-portrait was very likely intended to form a pair with the posthumous portrait in punchwork of his father, which is similar in scale and conception. He also "punched" in this scale and format the "living classical busts" of two leading contemporary Dutch poets, P.C. Hooft and Joost van den Vondel (Holl. 7, 8). In accordance with the classical theme, Hooft wears a laurel crown, and Vondel is accompanied by a lyre. It is conceivable that Lutma intended to engrave a pantheon of notable individuals of his time, for there is in the Dresden collection a posthumous portrait drawing (dated 1683) by him of Hendrick Dircksz. Spieghel, burgomaster of Amsterdam, which is similar to the Hooft and Vondel portraits in format and conception, but which was never made into an engraving.

The fine impression of the self-portrait shown here has been extensively touched with gray wash, adding creases to the neck and deepening shadows. One might assume that these touches were applied by a later hand, but I have seen numerous good-to-fine impressions of Lutma's punchwork portraits that have been touched with wash in this fashion. These additions, possibly by the artist's own hand, blend so well with Lutma's punchwork imitative of graded ink washes that it is often difficult to tell them apart.

NE TE
QUÆSIVERIS
EXTRA.

IANUS. LUTMA. BATAVUS.

Per se Opere Mallei. 1681.

Carel de Moor
1656 – 1738

A painter of portraits, scenes from daily life and literary subjects, Carel de Moor made about twenty prints, including four or five mezzotints. A few of his etchings are after artists such as Terborch, Gerrit Dou, and Frans van Mieris, but many are from his own design. The latter represent primarily fantasy heads and busts, executed in a sketchy manner.

Born in Leyden in 1656, Carel de Moor was the son of a painter, frame carver, and art dealer of the same name. He studied with Gerrit Dou and Frans van Mieris in Leyden, with Abraham van den Tempel in Amsterdam, and with Godfried Schalken in Dordrecht. His style is indebted to Frans van Mieris and Gabriel Metsu. In 1683 he was admitted to the Leyden artists' guild. A highly successful portrait painter, De Moor was knighted by the emperor Karl VI in 1714. He died in Warmond in 1738. His son, Carel Isaak de Moor, was also a painter.[1]

1. See biography by M.D. Henkel in Thieme-Becker, vol. 25, p. 104.

196

CAREL DE MOOR

Portrait of Jan van Goyen

Etching and drypoint after Gerard Terborch
V.d.K. 1[1], Dut. 1[1], Wurz. 1, Holl. 1[1]
Lower left: *TB CDM*
217 x 167 mm. (platemark)
Wm.: foolscap
Coll.: A.N. Alferoff (L. 1727);
Dutuit (see L. 708, 709)
Musée du Petit Palais, Paris. Dut. 6415

As indicated by the monograms etched on the
balustrade, Carel de Moor's etching reproduces
(in reverse) Gerard Terborch's painted portrait
of Jan van Goyen in the Liechtenstein Collection, Vaduz.[1]

This superb impression is apparently the
very earliest state printed before De Moor
began to add in stages darker tones to the
image by means of a mezzotint rocker or a roulette. Here one experiences to the fullest the
easy fluidity of draftsmanship that is associated
more readily with original etchings than with
etchings made after designs of other artists.

Besides giving a sense of color to the image,
the rocker or roulette tonal passages describe
the velvety texture of Van Goyen's lapels.
Carel de Moor also used rocker or roulette to
describe the velvet cloak in his etching after
his teacher Frans van Mieris's self-portrait
(Holl. 3). He combined rocker or roulette work
with granular bitten tone to achieve tonal
effects in his plate of studies for a composition
portraying the beheading of John the Baptist
(Holl. 15).

The shimmering highlights of the sitter's
cloak in De Moor's etching of the Van Goyen
portrait express the love of sumptuous fabrics
such as silk, satin, and velvet to be found in
the works of Dutch painters of portraits and
elegant genre in the second half of the seventeenth century.

1. See Gudlaugsson, 1959, pl. 93.

IOHANNES·A·GOYEN. *Natione Batavus*
Genuinus Pictor Regionum

Jan Verkolje
1650 – 1693

A painter of portraits, scenes of daily life, and
mythological subjects, Jan Verkolje made
about fifty mezzotints, which have the same
diversity of subject matter as his paintings.
Some of these reproduce the works of others,
but a good number are after his own design.
Houbraken claims that Verkolje taught himself
to make mezzotints.

Verkolje was born in Amsterdam in 1650.
He is said by Houbraken to have studied for
six months with Jan Lievens. After his marriage in 1672, he settled in Delft, joining the
artists' guild there in 1673. He died in that city
in 1693.[1] Two sons, Jan and Nicolaes, were
painters who also produced mezzotints.

1. See biographies by Houbraken, 1718, vol. 3, pp. 282–
285; K.G. Boon in Thieme-Becker, vol. 34, p. 257.

197
JAN VERKOLJE
Venus and Adonis

Mezzotint
Nag. 16, Wessely 31^{II}, Wurz. 31
Lower left: *I. Verkolje inv. et fec.*
385 x 300 mm. (platemark)
Wm.: crowned shield with fleur-de-lis
Coll.: Van Leyden (see L. 12, 240)
Rijksmuseum, Amsterdam. OB4628

Adonis was one of the mortals for whom
Venus, goddess of love, conceived a passion.
Here they are shown dallying in a forest glade.
Venus's swan-drawn chariot is parked on
clouds behind them. Cupid tugs at Adonis's
cape while an *amorino* holds the leashes of
Adonis's swift hunting dogs. Hunting gear
hangs from the tree at right and lies strewn on
the ground before the lovers. This hunting paraphernalia hints at impending tragedy. Venus
had warned Adonis not to pursue dangerous
quarry, but he ignored her advice and was slain
by a wild boar. Venus caused the scarlet anem-
one to spring from his blood.

197

Houbraken mentions Verkolje's celebrated painting of *Venus and Adonis* and the mezzotint after it.[1] A comparison of this work with Verkolje's dated mezzotints of the 1680s suggests that it should also be dated in the 1680s. In Verkolje's skillful hands the mezzotint medium lends itself superbly to the description of the soft clouds on which Venus's chariot rests and the silks and velvets so beloved of artists of this period. One perceives here again the Dutch classicizing artist's lack of ease in portraying idealized beauty: Venus has the robust vitality of a Dutch milkmaid. A number of Dutch classicizing artists made mezzotints of mythological or biblical "histories": Gerard de Lairesse, Johannes Glauber, Caspar Netscher, Carel de Moor, and even Arnold Houbraken.

This fine impression is printed in a brownish black ink. The Rijksmuseum also has a fine early impression printed in brown.

1. Houbraken, 1718, vol. 3, p. 285.

198 (actual size)

198

JAN VERKOLJE
Sleeping Spaniel

Mezzotint
Nag. 31, Wessely 48[II], Wurz. 48
Lower left: *J. Verkolje fecit.*
95 x 109 mm. (platemark)
Wm.: indecipherable fragment
Yale Center for British Art, Paul Mellon Fund.
B1970.3.1282

Many Dutch artists of the second half of the seventeenth century alternated between painting idealized mythologies or biblical subjects and closely observed scenes of daily life. This versatility is illustrated by Verkolje's *Venus and Adonis* with its grandiloquent love scene (cat. no. 197) and the charming little mezzotint of a sleeping spaniel shown here.

Like the *Venus and Adonis,* the mezzotint of the sleeping spaniel probably dates from the 1680s. It compares closely with *The White Dog,* dated 1680 (Wessely 46), and the *Spaniel Running,* dated 1684 (Wessely 49). Verkolje's mezzotint is in the tradition of Rembrandt's small etching of a sleeping puppy of about 1640 (B. 158). The mezzotint medium was perfectly suited to the description of the spaniel's soft, glossy coat. Other seventeenth-century Dutch artists who produced similar prints of household pets such as dogs and cats were Cornelis Saftleven, Cornelis Visscher, Karel Dujardin, Adriaen van de Velde, and Frans van Mieris.

Dirck Maas

1659 – 1717

Dirck Maas, a painter of equestrian subjects, made about thirty prints, which include a series of figures of soldiers and fallen horses derived from Philips Wouwerman (probably intended for the use of other artists when designing battle scenes), celebrated battles of Willem III of Orange, and riding-school subjects. The majority of the prints are etchings, but among them are two fine mezzotints.[1]

Dirck Maas was born in Haarlem in 1659. His teachers were Hendrik Mommers and Nicolaes Berchem. In 1678 he was admitted to the Haarlem artists' guild and, in 1697, to the guild in the Hague. He worked a good deal for Willem III of Orange, King of England, and traveled to England as part of his entourage in 1690. In 1700 he executed a chimney-piece painting, a stag hunt, for Willem's palace of Het Loo. He died in Haarlem in 1717. Like his friend Jan van Huchtenburgh, Dirck Maas painted a great variety of equestrian subjects: hunting scenes, cavalry engagements, and military encampments.

1. Holl. 17 (British Museum), described by Hind as a proof of an etching touched with red chalk, appears to be a drawing in pen and black ink and red chalk rather than an etching. It is drawn, however, in the style of Maas's etchings.

199
DIRCK MAAS
Horse and Rider Performing a Volte

Mezzotint
V.d.K. 27[1], Wurz. 27, Holl. 29[1]
Lower left in the second state: *T. Mass inv: et fecit. J. Gole exc: cum Privilegio Amstelodami*
248 x 177 mm. (platemark)
Wm.: crowned shield with fleur-de-lis
Rijksmuseum, Amsterdam. 08:371

Only two mezzotints by Maas are known, but they are among the most accomplished executed in Holland in the seventeenth century. The two mezzotints, *Volte* and *Volte Renversée* (Holl. 29, 30), form a pair, illustrating riding-

school maneuvers in fancy horsemanship. The impression of *Volte* shown here is an early one, printed before the engraved title was added in the lower margin. In such an impression the glossy sheen of the horse's coat and the rippling power of its muscles are experienced to the fullest, as is the subtle play of light over the foliage of the park and the cloud-filled sky.

200

DIRCK MAAS
Horse and Rider Performing a Curvet

From a series of nine etchings
Etching
V.d.K. 7[II], Wurz. 7, Holl. 7[II]
Lower left: *D: Mass. inv: et Fecit.*
209 x 231 mm. (platemark)
The Metropolitan Museum of Art, The Elisha Whittelsey Fund. 51.501.1290

Dirck Maas's riding-school series is characterized by the light tonality of the international classicizing style of etching. A comparison of the etching from this series shown here with the mezzotint *Volte* (cat. no. 199), similar in style and motif, points up the degree to which the mezzotint medium tended to dictate dark tonalities to the artist.

The park-like backgrounds of Maas's riding-school etchings are among the most sophisticated etched landscapes by a Dutch artist in the international classicizing style. They suggest in their neat calligraphy the etched classicizing landscapes by the Flemish painter Abraham Genoels. They also call to mind the undated etchings (around 1700?) of antique parks made by the Dutch painter Isaac de Moucheron after his painted wall decorations. When comparing Dirck Maas's etching, probably executed in the 1680s, with Paulus Potter's *Frisian Horse* of 1652, one is conscious of the calligraphic and ornamental character of Maas's etched line.

The riding-school etchings are close in general style to drawings by Dirck Maas in the British Museum that are dated 1680 and should probably also be dated in the 1680s.[1]

1. London, cat. drawings, 1926, vol. 3, p. 140, nos. 18, 19.

200

Cornelis Dusart
1660 – 1704

Cornelis Dusart, a painter of scenes of peasant life, made about fourteen or fifteen etchings[1] and a large number of mezzotints. It is difficult to determine how many mezzotints were executed by Dusart himself because of his close collaboration with his friend Jacob Gole, the Amsterdam mezzotinter and publisher, who made a number of mezzotints after Dusart's designs. Most of the etchings are dated 1685, as are a few of the mezzotints. The subjects of Dusart's prints primarily represent robust and rowdy scenes from the life of the lower classes.

Dusart was born in Haarlem in 1660. He was a favored pupil of Adriaen van Ostade and seems to have inherited many of the contents of Ostade's studio, for the 1704 inventory of Dusart's estate lists quantities of drawings by Adriaen and his brother Isaak, arranged according to various categories. There is also reference in the inventory to unfinished paintings by Isaak and Adriaen completed by Dusart. Dusart's style was primarily formed by his teacher's art and by the more caricatural, satirical art of the painter Jan Steen. In 1679 he was admitted to the Haarlem artists' guild. Dusart did not marry and lived from 1693 to 1704 with two aunts. He was related by marriage to the painter Jan van der Meer III of Haarlem. Apparently frail in health from an early age, he died in Haarlem in 1704.[2]

1. Although it is conceivable that the etching *The Two Singers in the Inn*, Holl. 3, is simply another version of Holl. 4, it is more likely a copy of the latter by another hand.

2. See biographies by K. Lilienfeld in Thieme-Becker, vol. 10, pp. 224–225; Trautscholdt, 1966, pp. 172–174.

201
CORNELIS DUSART
February

From a series of twelve mezzotints
Mezzotint
B. 21, Weig. 21[1], Dut. 21[II], Wurz. 21, Holl. 21
Lower left: *C. Dusart inv: J. Gole exc. Amstelod: cum Privilegio.*
215 x 154 mm. (platemark)
Coll.: H.F. Sewall (L. 1309)
Museum of Fine Arts, Boston, Harvey D. Parker Collection. P3263

Dusart's mezzotint series of the twelve months, like the small almanac woodcuts of Dirk de Bray (cat. nos. 178, 179), represent the months in terms of the characteristic activities associated with them. February, shown here, is represented by the raucous celebrants of the Shrovetide carnival, which took place before Lent. The grotesquely masked figure at center wears a woman's wig and fashionable French-style headdress, while brandishing a torch and a waffle iron. The small figure at right, wearing a clay pot on his head, vigorously works a *rommelpot*, a noisemaker associated with Shrovetide, which consists of a pig's bladder with a reed through it stretched over a clay pot half-filled with water.[1]

As one can see here, mezzotint lent itself splendidly to the representation of nocturnal scenes with artificial illumination. In another plate from the series, *March* (Holl. 22), the mezzotint medium, with its subtractive method of scraping lighter areas out of a darker field, encouraged Dusart to represent a rare motif in the seventeenth century: falling snowflakes.

Dusart's "Twelve Months" series poses certain attribution problems. February is one of four months (the others are April, June, and December) that, since the publication of Bartsch's first catalogue, have been believed to be by Jacob Gole after Dusart's drawings. This attribution is based on the French inscription engraved on *January* (Holl. 20), which serves

1. For Shrovetide and *rommelpot* see Slive, 1970, vol. 1, pp. 34–37.

as a titlepage: "invanté et gravé par Corñ: Dusart et terminé par J. Gole" ("invented and engraved by Cornelis Dusart and finished by Jacob Gole") and the fact that the four prints in question omit "fecit" ("made it") from their inscriptions. It is known that Dusart and Gole, the publisher of the "Twelve Months," were closely associated, apparently even keeping a journal together.[2] Gole's handling of mezzotint, however, is generally less skillful than Dusart's.

An edition of the "Twelve Months" was very likely printed before Dusart's death, for one finds in the 1704 inventory of his possessions, under the category of "Mezzotints": "50 maal de 12 maanden door Corn. Dusart compleet" ("50 times the 12 months of Cornelis Dusart complete").[3] This is interesting in the light of Joachim von Sandrart's statement that a mezzotint plate would yield only 50 or 60 good impressions.[4]

It is difficult to discern stylistic differences between the four plates said to be by Gole and those said to be by Dusart. The "Gole" plates are inscribed not "Gole fecit" but "Gole exc.," identifying Gole as the publisher. I am inclined to think that all are executed mostly by Dusart, including *February*, one of the most successful in the series. Perhaps Gole's "finishing" of the plates consisted only of a few final touches and the addition of inscriptions to the plates. The impression shown here is from a set printed before the addition of the engraved name of the month.

Many drawings for Dusart's mezzotints survive, most of them broad wash drawings. The study for *February* is in Rotterdam (inv. Dusart no. 8). In the drawing the central figure holds a frying pan rather than a torch, and the scene is illuminated from outside rather than by the flare of the torch.

Dusart's involvement in the mezzotint medium is evident from the inventory of his estate, which includes not only the necessary

2. Bredius, *Künstler-Inventare*, vol. 1, p. 51.

3. Ibid p. 38.

4. Sandrart/Peltzer, 1925, p. 300. "Diese Arbeit gibt etwan [sic] 50 oder 60 saubere Abdrücke."

C. Dusart juv: J. Gole exc: Amstelod: cum Privilegio.

February

tools but also a portfolio of 129 English mezzotints and a collection of mezzotints by Dutch artists: Huchtenburgh, Lairesse, Vaillant, and Valck.[5] Dusart also added tone to a later state of at least one of his etchings, *The Violin Player*, B. 15, by means of the mezzotint rocker or roulette, as did Carel de Moor in his etched portrait of Van Goyen (cat. no. 196).

I have placed the "Months" in the 1680s on the basis of comparison with Dusart's dated prints, but it is equally conceivable that they may date from the 1690s. The chronology of Dusart's mezzotints still needs to be determined.

5. Bredius, *Künstler-Inventare*, vol. 1, pp. 27–73.

202

CORNELIS DUSART
The Village Festival, 1685

Etching
B. 16, Dut. 16[II], Wurz. 16, Holl. 16[II]
Lower left: *Corn. duSart fe. / 1685*
253 x 337 mm. (sheet)
Wm.: grapes
Coll.: J.M. (unidentified)(L. 1493); H.G. French (L. 1307a)
Cincinnati Art Museum, Bequest of Herbert Greer French. 1943.323

Dusart's rowdy *Village Fair* of 1685 is conceived on a monumental scale. The artist has imposed on the lively, anecdote-filled scene the rational order of a Renaissance stage setting with a deep perspective. The inn's banner identifies it as the "Gulde Schenk Kan" ("Golden Tankard"), and many of the celebrants appear to have drunk deeply from the tankard. In the middle distance at center can be seen the umbrella of a medical quack and at right a stage with acrobats.[1]

1. A traced reverse study for the print is in the Albertina, Vienna (VI. XXXVII, no. 10394). In the drawing the clouds in the sky are rendered in wash, and the sky is not ruled with parallel lines.

202

289

203

Jan van der Meer III
1656 – 1705

A painter of landscapes and animal pieces, Jan van der Meer III was one of four generations of Haarlem painters of the same name. He made about four etchings; two etchings of sheep are dated 1685. Van der Meer frequently painted Italianizing subjects. He was also a prolific draftsman.

Born in Haarlem in 1656, he first studied with his father and then with Nicolaes Berchem. After making an Italian journey, he and his painter brother, Barent, joined the Haarlem artists' guild in 1681. In 1683 he married Cornelis Dusart's sister, Maria. In 1700 the bankruptcy sale of his furniture and paintings brought only a pitiful 96 guilders. He died in Haarlem in 1705.[1]

1. See biography by E. Trautscholdt in Thieme-Becker, vol. 34, p. 263.

203
JAN VAN DER MEER III
Stormy Landscape with Shepherd and Flock,
1685 or 1688

Etching and engraving
Weig. 4, Dut. 4, Wurz. 4, Holl. 4
Lower left: *J v der meer/jonge f 16(?) 8 (d* reversed)
130 x 199 mm. (sheet)
Graphische Sammlung Albertina, Vienna. H.III, 46, p. 70

204
JAN VAN DER MEER III
River Landscape with Donkeys, Sheep and Shepherds

Etching
Weig. 3, Dut. 3, Wurz. 3, Holl. 3
133 x 180 mm. (platemark)
Coll.: J. Barnard (L. 1419)
Museum Boymans-van Beuningen, Rotterdam.
BdH5150

Although these two landscapes are not absolutely identical in dimensions, they are close enough in format and style to form a pair. The *Stormy Landscape* is signed and dated, but the date is difficult to interpret: the third digit is hard to read, and the last digit is an "8." Deciphering the date is further complicated by the fact that in at least one of Van der Meer's etchings the signature and date are etched in reverse, and it is not inconceivable that the last two digits are reversed here. The style of the landscapes is compatible with a number of Jan van der Meer landscape drawings dating from the 1680s and with the landscape background of Van der Meer's two sheep etchings of 1685. I would propose reading the date as either "1685" or "1688."[1]

These two ideal, or classicizing, landscapes are so international in style that one might take them to be the works of a French or Italian artist such as the Roman landscape painter-etcher Gaspard Dughet.

The *Stormy Landscape* exists also in a working proof (in Rotterdam) touched with gray wash (probably by the artist) before some of the heavier accents were added to the plate. The two etchings are more accomplished in the drawing and more successful in the rendering of the landscape spaces than the majority of the etched landscapes by other Dutch classicizing artists of this time, such as Johannes Glauber or Albert Meyeringh. The etchings of Adriaen van Diest, who worked in England, are quite close in style.

1. The date has also been interpreted as 1678 (Dutuit, Hollstein) and as 1691 (Rotterdam, 1943–44, p. 24).

204

205

205
NICOLAES BERCHEM
The Cows at the Watering Place, 1680

Etching and drypoint
B. 1^I, Weig. 1^I, Dut. 1^{II}, Holl. 1^{II}
Lower left: *NBerghem. f. 1680.*
280 x 376 mm. (platemark)
Wm.: coat of arms of Amsterdam (similar to
Churchill 15)
Coll.: F. Debois (L. 985); J. Reiss (L. 1522)
The Art Institute of Chicago, The Clarence
Buckingham Collection. 38.1478

The balletic grace with which Berchem has
treated a trivial incident at an Italian watering
hole explains his appeal for eighteenth-century
French Rococo artists such as François
Boucher. This etching of 1680 also reveals the
changes that have taken place in Berchem's
etching style. Strong contrasts and rhythmic,
calligraphic contours have replaced the tonal,
atmospheric approach seen in the *Bagpiper* of
the mid-1640s (cat. no. 120). As in Dusart's
Village Fair of 1685 (cat. no. 202), an incident
from daily life is presented on a monumental
scale.

An essential aspect of the idyllic Italian view,
reference to classical antiquity, has not been
omitted here; a crumbling, overgrown antique
sarcophagus with a sculptured relief of a scene
of combat forms a backdrop for the drinking
herd.

Adriaen van der Cabel
1630/31 – 1705

A painter of classicizing landscapes and harbor
views, Adriaen van der Cabel made sixty to seventy etchings of similar subjects.

Born in 1630 or 1631 in Rijswijk, Van der
Cabel studied with Jan van Goyen in the
Hague. In 1660 to 1665 he was in Rome, where
he was a member of the Netherlandish artists'
club, the "Bent." On the basis of Van der
Cabel's drawings of Sicilian sites, it is presumed that he traveled to Sicily. In 1668 he settled in France, marrying in 1669 in Lyons,
which remained his permanent residence. Van
der Cabel painted decorations for various private houses there. In 1670 to 1672 the Dutch
classicizing landscape painter Johannes
Glauber was active in Van der Cabel's Lyons
studio. Lyons was a frequent stopping place
for Dutch artists making the Italian journey.
During his life Van der Cabel was very influential; in recent times he has often been omitted
from discussions of Dutch Italianizing artists
because he remained an expatriate.[1]

1. See biography by Hofstede de Groot and H. Schneider
in Thieme-Becker, vol. 19, pp. 403–405.

206
ADRIAEN VAN DER CABEL
A Mediterranean Harbor

Etching
B. 55, Wurz. 65, Holl. 65
108 x 157 mm. (platemark)
Wm.: unidentified name (?)
Coll.: R. Peltzer (L. 2231)
The Cleveland Museum of Art, The Mr. and Mrs.
Lewis B. Williams Collection. 43.559

This harbor view, with galleys of the Mediterranean type in the foreground and a northern
merchant ship in the distance, is part of a set of
four landscape views issued by the Parisian
print publisher Nicolas Robert. The present
impression is an unusually rich working proof
taken before the plate edges were evened up,
before the completion of the borderline, and

before a small number of fine lines were added
to complete the image.

The harbor view, probably based on Van der
Cabel's impressions of Sicily, is close in motif
to the Netherlandish painter Abraham
Casembrot's series of etchings of the harbor of
Messina (Holl. 1–13). Van der Cabel's harbor
view, however, is much more rationally and
lucidly ordered, with ships lined up parallel to
the picture plane and stepping back into depth
like stage flats.

The style of Van der Cabel's landscape etchings closely parallels that of classicizing Italian
and French landscape etchers active in Rome
such as Giovanni Francesco Grimaldi. The
standard publishers' editions of Van der Cabel's
etchings were generally printed much more
cleanly and dryly than the present working
proof, which is enriched by a random tone of
ink left on the plate before printing.

206

Ludolf Bakhuizen
1631 – 1708

The marine painter Ludolf Bakhuizen made
about fourteen etchings, all marine views
except for a splendid but scarce self-portrait
(Holl. 13).

Bakhuizen was born in Emden in Friesland
in 1631. About 1649–50 he came to Amsterdam
as a merchant's clerk. He taught calligraphy
but eventually turned to making drawings of
shipping. In 1656 he is referred to as a calligrapher and in 1657 as a draftsman. He took
up painting late, studying first with Allart
van Everdingen (who also painted marines)
and then with the marine painter Hendrick
Dubbels. Bakhuizen's mature work as a painter
shows the influence of the younger Willem van
de Velde. His earliest dated painting is from
1658, but his profession is not given as
"painter" until 1664. After both the elder and
younger Willem van de Veldes moved to England in 1672, Bakhuizen became Holland's
leading marine painter and enjoyed much success. That he was already renowned prior to
the emigration of the Van de Veldes is demonstrated by the 1666 commission he received
from the Amsterdam city fathers to paint a
view of shipping in the port of Amsterdam
for presentation to one of the ministers of
Louis XIV. Bakhuizen was handsomely paid
for this commission. In his later career
Bakhuizen received the attention of German
princes and is said to have instructed Peter the
Great of Russia in drawing. In addition to
marines he painted a few portraits. He married
four times. He died in Amsterdam in 1708.[1]

1. See biographies by MacLaren, 1960, pp. 5–6;
E.W. Moes in Thieme-Becker, vol. 2, pp. 325–326; Bol,
pp. 301–307.

208

207

LUDOLF BAKHUIZEN
*The Personification of Amsterdam Riding in
Neptune's Chariot,* 1701

From a set of etchings, "The River IJ and
Seascapes"
Etching
B. 1, Dut. 1, Holl. 1[1]
Incomplete working proof
Lower right on barrel: L BAK (in reverse)
199 x 264 mm. (platemark)
Wm.: Pro patria and countermark letters AI
(Churchill 127)
Private Collection

208

LUDOLF BAKHUIZEN
Shipping off Amsterdam, 1701

From a set of etchings, "The River IJ and
Seascapes"
Etching
B. 4, Dut. 4, Holl. 4[1]
Proof before letter
179 x 240 mm. (platemark)
Wm.: Pro patria and countermark letters DG (?)
(Churchill 129)
Private Collection

The first plate of Bakhuizen's series of ten
marine etchings, an allegory of Amsterdam's
seaborne mercantile power, serves as a frontispiece for the series. In the foreground the Maid
of Amsterdam rides in triumph in Neptune's
chariot, drawn by sea horses (one a "unicorn"),
while water folk brandish oars and palms of
victory and sound shell trumpets. At the right
can be seen the richly decorated stern of the
warship *Amsterdam,* with Atlas bearing the
world on his shoulders, the symbolic figure
that also crowns the west pediment of Amsterdam's classical town hall. In the distance we see
the long silhouette of the warehouse of the
East India Company. In the published edition a
separate small plate with verses signed by
Bakhuizen was printed beneath the image,
making the mercantile allegory even more

explicit. The last two verses allude to a balance
of trade that consisted of the importation of
pearls from far lands and the export of
Christian teaching![1]

Bakhuizen's background as a calligrapher is
evident in the swirling baroque rhythms of the
frontispiece. Preparatory drawings for the
frontispiece are to be found in the Dutuit Collection of the Petit Palais, Paris, and in the
British Museum, London. The impression
shown here is a working proof taken before the
execution of a few final details. The impression
of *Shipping off Amsterdam* was taken before the
addition of the engraved signature and copyright in the lower margin at left. Both of these
delicately nuanced proofs taken before the edition convey a vivid sense of the water-charged
atmosphere. Bakhuizen, who gave his age as
seventy-one on the typeset title page of the
series, served as his own publisher.

1. "Zoo bouwt men hier aan't Scheepryk Y/ De Moerbalk
van den Staat en Steeden,/ Ten besten van 't gemeen en
Leeden/ Van de Indiaansche Maatschappy:/ Zoo brengt
men peerlen, wyd vant een in 't ander Landt;/ Daar Kris-
tus Leer, geleert, gesticht werd, en geplant." A literal
translation might read: "So one builds here on the
[River] Y rich in shipping/ The centerbeam of the state
and cities/ For the benefit of the community and the
members/ Of the East India Company/ So one brings
pearls from far-flung lands/ There Christ's teaching is
learned, established, and planted."

209

ROMEYN DE HOOGHE
*Reception of His Majesty William III of
England at Westeinde Bridge (Inhaling van
S.K. Maj. aende Westeynder brug)* in Govert
Bidloo, *Komste van Zyne Majesteit Willem
III Koning van Groot Britanje, enz. in
Holland.* The Hague, Arnoud Leers, 1691.

Etching
(following page 30)
325 x 435 mm. (platemark); 405 x 260 mm. (page
size); vellum
Holl. 168–185, Landwehr (1970) 79
Museum of Fine Arts, Boston, William A. Sargent
Fund. 62.684

Willem III of Orange, who in 1689 had
become King of England, set out on January
26, 1691, by ship for the Hague to attend a
conference of allies leagued against Louis XIV.
With his military skills, Willem was the natural
leader of the allies. The crossing from Graves-
end was slow and shrouded in a chill fog, and
Willem and other members of his party set out
in rowboats, impatient to reach land more
quickly. After unanticipated and uncomfort-
able hours on the water, Willem and his party
finally stepped ashore the next morning at the
Oranjepolder where he was greeted by Dutch
peasants. The stadholder-king proceeded in
haste to the Hague, taking by surprise the city
fathers, who had been making elaborate and
costly preparations for his formal reception,
involving triumphal arches, lighted transparen-
cies, and fireworks. Willem was at first luke-
warm to the idea of reentering the city in
which he had already arrived, but he was finally
persuaded to cooperate. Thus, on February 5,
1691, Willem's procession departed from the
Binnenhof, the government center in the middle of the Hague, drove outside the city, and
reentered it, as shown here, at the West End
bridge.

Romeyn de Hooghe's splendid double-page
etching represents the moment when the king's
coach paused to receive the welcoming
addresses of the city fathers before reentering
the city. The noise of the throngs drowned out
these fine speeches. On the frozen canal we see
some of the many spectators who arrived by
ice, some riding in fancifully carved sledges
drawn by plumed horses. Other spectators
crowd the gallery of a windmill to gain a better
vantage point. The temporary festival arch
under which Willem's coach is about to pass is
topped, as the text informs us, by a figure of
Bellona (*Krijgsdeugd,* literally, "War-Virtue"),
supporting Willem's initial and an imperial
crown. She is flanked by the allegorical figures
of "Patriotic Duty" and "Happiness," which
are in turn flanked by symbolic orange trees in
urns. The fabric of the arch had the appearance
of blue stone but was probably made of lath,
plaster, and paint. We know that Romeyn de

INHALING VAN S.K.MAJ.
aende Wefteynder brug
door de E.A. MAGISTRAET
van S GRAVENHAGE.

RECEPTION DE
MAJESTÉ AU
ONT DU WESTEN

209

298

Hooghe not only designed and etched the plates describing this triumphal entry but also participated in the planning of the decorations sponsored by the city fathers, as is indicated by the payment he received from the Hague painters' association, "Pictura."[1]

In the plate illustrated, the inherently decorative character of the linework of Romeyn de Hooghe's mature etching style further enhances the pomp of the occasion.

1. For the events and the book, see Wilson, 1974, pp. 262–274; Snoep, 1975, pp. 91ff.

Jan Luyken
1649 – 1712

The etcher and illustrator Jan Luyken and his son Caspar (1672-1708), like Romeyn de Hooghe, were part of the booming late seventeenth-century and early eighteenth-century book publishing industry in Holland. They rivaled De Hooghe in their prolific output; about 3,275 etchings have been attributed to Jan, and about 1,187 to Caspar.

Jan Luyken was born in Amsterdam in 1649, the son of a pious schoolmaster who wrote books on theological or moral themes. The young Jan first made his name as a poet, publishing a volume of love poetry in 1671. He seems to have reacted against parental piety, and his circle of friends and associates was worldly and pleasure-loving. He had studied painting with a certain Martinus Saagmolen and in 1672 is referred to as a "painter." No certain paintings by Luyken are known. His teacher in etching was possibly Cornelis Decker, who etched most of the plates in Jan's first illustrated book. In 1673, a year after his marriage, Jan joined a Baptist community. Shortly thereafter the sudden death of one of his boon companions seems to have precipitated his religious conversion. His first pietistic text on a print dates from 1677. In 1699–1703 he was resident in Haarlem. He died in Amsterdam in 1712.

Only at the beginning of his career did Jan etch from the designs of others. His best illustrations were for books for which he also wrote the texts. Caspar, whose figures were less elegantly elongated than those of his father, illustrated literary texts of a more worldly character, such as novels and plays.[1]

1. See biographies by M.D. Henkel in Thieme-Becker, vol. 23, pp. 488–489; Van Eeghen, 1905, vol. 1, pp. V-LVIII.

210

JAN AND CASPAR LUYKEN
The Engraver (De Plaatsnyder) in Jan and Caspar Luyken, *Het Menselyk, Bedryf.* Amsterdam, Johannes en Caspaares Luiken, 1694.

Etching
(plate 85)
Van Eeghen 1446
138 x 80 mm. (platemark); 192 x 154 mm. (page size); vellum
Van Eeghen 244, Landwehr (1962) 140a, Holl. 244, Praz (1975), p. 406
The National Gallery of Art, Washington, D.C., Rosenwald Collection, 1962. B-23,741

Jan and Caspar Luyken's *Het Menselyk Bedryf* (literally, *The Human Profession)* is both a book of trades, offering a highly detailed peep into the shops of various craftsmen and a pious emblem book. The title page informs us that the book is by both Jan and Caspar. The drawings were made by Jan, but it is very difficult to separate the hands of father and son in the execution of the plates.

The motto above the image of the *Engraver (Plaatsnyder)* is apparently a play on the retouching and wearing down of the image on the copper plate: " 't Herstellen als 't vervallen, Dat komt van een op allen" ("Recovery as well as decline, that is everyone's fate"). The verses below the image play upon the thousands of impressions a copper plate can print and the thousands Christ has "impressed" with his divine nature. Even the arrangement of the book has a moralizing intent, for, as in so many seventeenth-century Dutch emblem books, the last image is a reminder of mortality; here, the hundredth plate, the final profession, is that of gravedigger *(Doodgraver)*!

The placement of the plate of the *Engraver* constitutes a commentary on the status of the printmaker; it is placed between plates representing the painter and the sculptor, while the plate of the *Copper-Plate Printer (Plaatdrucker; see illus.)* is placed with those of the paper maker, book printer, and bookbinder in another portion of the book. The printmaker is

De Plaatsnyder.   85

'Herstellen alst vervallen, Dat komt van een op allen.

Een Beeld gewerckt in 't kooper stof,
   Geeft duisend Beelden van sich of:
ô Jesus Christus, hoog gepreesen!
   Ghy allerschoonste heemels Beeld,
   Ghy hebt'er duisendē geteeld
Door afdruck van uw heilig weesen.

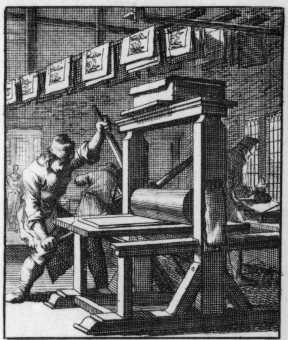

De Plaatdrucker   62

'tGeen 'thert in sich besluit,   Dat druckt het van sich uit.

'tPapier geleegen op de Plaat,
   Mits dat het door de persing gaat,
Ontvangd een Afdruck van zyn weesen:
   De Ziel gedruckt op 't Eeuwich Goed,
   Ontvangd Gods Beeld in zyn Gemoed,
Waar door hy eeuwich werd gepreesen.

210

Jan and Caspar Luyken
The Copper-Plate Printer
Etching
National Gallery of Art, Washington, D.C.

thus by implication an artist – a creator – while the printer is simply a necessary craftsman.

In the plate of the printmaker's workshop we see the engraver grasping the burin, working on a plate that he rotates on a cushion. An even distribution of light for this meticulous work is achieved by means of a screen that diffuses the daylight. In the foreground an assistant pours the acid off a plate that has been etched by erecting a dam of wax around it, so that the plate serves as its own basin to hold the acid. In the plate of the *Copper-Plate Printer* we see the printer operating the rotary press used to print intaglio prints, while, above him, impressions hang drying on the line. At the right, near a window, an assistant daubs ink into the lines of a copper plate.

The Luykens's neat style of etching was inspired by the linear systems of contemporary engraving or by etchers whose style emulated engraving, such as Abraham Bosse, the mid-seventeenth-century French etcher and writer on etching.

211

JAN VAN DER HEYDEN
A House in the Herengracht, burned in the night of 25th – 26th April, 1683 in Jan van der Heyden and Jan van der Heyden the Younger, *Beschryving der Niewlijks uitgevonden en geoctrojeerde Slang-Brand-Spuiten....*
Amsterdam, Jan Rieuwertsz., 1690

Etching
(plate 14)
F.M. 2301, 14; Holl. 14
325 x 235 mm. (platemark); 440 x 265 mm. (page size); vellum
F.M. 2301; Wurz. 1; Holl. 1-19
Museum of Fine Arts, Boston, William A. Sargent Fund. 69.959

The Amsterdam painter of city views Jan van der Heyden (1637-1712) was also a gifted inventor.[1] In 1668 he had introduced a new

1. For the biography of Van der Heyden and the history of his inventions, see Amsterdam, 1971, pp. 9-16.

14.de *Figuur* Pag 32.

Afbeelding van een rang Huizen, op de Heere graft : in welks middelste, tuffen den 25 en 26.den April 1683. Smiddernachts . een zwaaren brandt entfteit't . dool wederom fpoedig door de Slang brand Spuiten. zelfs met behouding van't eerfte entfteeken huis, wierdt geblaft.

Representation d'une rangée de maisons. au milieu de la quelle le feu se prit. avec beaucoup de violence.a minuit le 25.me Avril 1683. et qui fut d'abord eteint par le moyen des Pompes a Boyaux: Si bien même que la maison qui fut la premiere attaquée, fut faurée. comme on le voit, cy deffus.

system of street lighting involving glass lanterns and oil lamps; in 1669 he was made overseer of Amsterdam's street lighting. Van der Heyden's system was soon adopted by other cities such as Berlin. In about 1672 Jan, with the help of his brother Nicolaes, also invented an improved fire engine. Light and easily transported, it involved a double-action pump, which provided a continuous stream of water and a flexible fire hose with couplings rather than a stationary spout. Jan became fire chief of Amsterdam and was later succeeded in this post by his son, Jan the Younger. In 1680 a factory was set up to manufacture the pump, and, in 1690, the first edition appeared of an illustrated book, *Beschryving der Niewlijks...*, by father and son describing the disadvantages of the old firefighting equipment and the advantages of the new. A second edition with additional illustrations was published by the son in 1735.

The illustrations for the book were etched and engraved from Van der Heyden's drawings. In the first edition no name of etcher or engraver appears on the plates, but a variety of styles of execution is discernible. One double-page plate of a conflagration by night (plate no. 7) is either by Romeyn de Hooghe or in his style. Two plates (no. 14, shown here as cat. no. 211, and no. 18) are so distinctive in their meticulous description of the brickwork and the evocation of the color of the fire-blackened brick that they were very likely etched by Van der Heyden himself. The figures, however, may have been drawn by another artist. Figure specialists often painted the figures in Van der Heyden's city views.

Plate 14, as the caption informs us, shows a row of houses on the Herengracht that caught fire at midnight between the 25th and 26th of April 1683. Thanks to the efficiency of the new fire engine, the blaze was extinguished, even the fabric of the house that first caught fire being preserved.

Johannes Teyler
1648 – before 1709

Like Ludwig von Siegen and Prince Ruprecht, who developed the mezzotint medium, Johannes Teyler, who invented a commercially applicable method of printing several colors from a single etched or engraved copper plate, was an ingenious amateur rather than a professional artist.

Born in Nijmegen in 1648, Teyler was the son of an innkeeper. He probably attended Latin School in Nijmegen; at the Kwartierlijke Academie he studed philosophy and, most likely, mathematics. His dissertation in the field of philosophy was accepted in 1668. In the same year he enrolled in Leyden University to study philosophy. In 1670 he was back in Nijmegen and was appointed professor of philosophy and mathematics at the Academie. After a visit to Berlin, he probably settled somewhere in the western Netherlands. In 1668 Teyler applied to the states of Holland and West Friesland for a twenty-five-year patent for his "new method," which may have been his method of color printing but is so vaguely described that it is impossible to know for certain. The text speaks mostly of the new method's military usefulness (printing maps in color?). In 1697 he published in Rotterdam a book on military architecture. He seems to have traveled to Rome and Berlin with his friend Jacob de Heus, the Utrecht painter. In Rome Teyler became a member of the Netherlandish artists' club under the nickname "Speculatie." In Berlin he sought a court appointment but was apparently unsuccessful. The activities of his later years are unknown. When his parents' house was sold in 1709, he, one of the heirs, was not mentioned in the proceedings.

Few, if any, of Teyler's color prints are from his own design. Some are simply the reused plates of other artists. About this time, for example, Teyler or someone in his circle reprinted Esaias van de Velde's square wooded landscape (cat. no. 27) in greens and browns. Many of his prints are details copied from earlier prints, such as engravings of mythological subjects after the French painter Simon Vouet. Some of the topographical views seem to have been designed for him by the Nijmegen artist Jan van Call.

Since the prints are generally unsigned, attributions to Teyler are difficult. His manner of printing color by rubbing several colors into a plate was imitated by contemporary print publishers such as Gerard Valck and Peter Schenk, who also seem to have been friendly with Jan van Call. One may find the same print in different public collections under such diverse names as Teyler, Schenk, and Jan van Call. The best point of departure for attributing color prints to Teyler is provided by the four albums associated with Teyler's name in Berlin, Amsterdam, London, and the Rosenwald Collection of the Library of Congress (dated 1693). The London album, which comes from the Teyler family, bears a calligraphic inscription that suggests that an accumulation of images of this kind (portraits, views, antique sculpture, flowers, and birds) might be of use to artists. Teyler was possibly thinking of putting together a kind of drawing or model book in color. It is currently estimated that he made about 300 to 350 prints.[1]

1. For Teyler's life and career see the exhibition catalogue Nijmegen, 1961, pp. 9–17.

212

303

212

Johannes Teyler
View of the Binnen-Amstel

Etching printed in vermilion, red, blue, blue-green, three browns, two grays and black, hand-colored with watercolor
361 x 494 mm. (sheet)
Coll.: L. Norcross (L. 1751)
Worcester Art Museum, Bequest of Laura
Norcross Marrs. 1926.618

Teyler etched a few very large views that have the scale of paintings and were very likely intended for hanging on the wall. The present large-scale view of the Binnen-Amstel (inner Amstel River) in the center of Amsterdam forms a pair with another large-scale view of the Binnen-Amstel seen from the opposite direction.[1] In a number of Teyler's prints, as here, watercolor passages were added to supplement the passages of color printing, particularly for skies. Here watercolor was used at right on the boat to fill in a passage that was not etched. Whether these watercolor additions were by Teyler's hand or the hand of an assistant such as Jan van Call is impossible to say. Although Teyler's mechanical crisscross of dry, impersonal etched lines is uninspired, the overall feeling of space and of late afternoon light in the print is surprisingly effective.

1. Amsterdam/Toronto, 1977, no. 48, illus. An impression in the Rijksmuseum (34: 613) bears an old inscription at bottom center: "Gezicht van den Binnen-Amstel" ("View of the Binnen-Amstel").

213

Anonymous Artist
Folk or children's print
Published by Jacob Conynenberg,
Amsterdam, active 1711–1723
Magpie on the Stump of a Tree

Woodcut, hand-colored
Amsterdam, *Centsprenten,* 1976, no. 67
Below: *t'Amsterdam Gedrukt / by Jacobus
Conynenberg / Boekverkooper op het water.*
279 x 355 mm. (block)
Rijksmuseum, Amsterdam. OB4632

Popular woodcuts, many of which were intended for children, were originally published in great quantities, but because they were inexpensive, used up by eager young hands, and printed on cheap, coarse paper, they are now excessively rare. The earliest surviving examples in the Netherlands are from the last quarter of the seventeenth century.

Although the woodcut of a magpie on a stump shown here was published in the early eighteenth century by Jacob Conynenberg (active in Amsterdam 1711–1723), its style and the condition of the block suggest that it was originally cut and printed in the seventeenth century. Conynenberg belonged to the third generation of the Lootsman family, which was a leading publisher of folk prints for six generations.

The arbitrary, unnaturalistic application of watercolor in primary colors (red, yellow, and blue) with dauber or stencil in "the Dutch manner" is characteristic of these penny prints. The block is printed on a full sheet of brown-fibered paper, which is close in size to the standard sheet (33 x 41 cm.) commonly used to print these woodcuts.[1]

The typeset verses are addressed to "youths and maidens," advising them not to waste their money on finches and thrushes, for a jaunty magpie is a handsome and clever creature: "and you can teach it to talk, which will increase your pleasure."

1. See Amsterdam, *Centsprenten,* 1976, Introduction, pp. 11ff. and no. 67, p. 104.

Komt nu Vryers en ghy Vrijfters,
Koopt geen Vincken ofte Lijfters,
Maar een Aecxter na de fwier,
't Is een hups en fchrander dier:
Want ghy kund hem Klappen leeren,
Dan kan hy u vreught vermeeren.

t'Amfterdam Gedruckt / by Jacobus Cannenberg / Boekverkooper op het Water.

213

Glossary

Woodcut

In a woodcut the areas around the lines that print the image are excavated and cut away with *knives* or gouges, isolating the lines, which stand up in relief. In a *chiaroscuro woodcut* additional blocks are added to supplement the linear design with tonal passages that provide modeling. A woodcut was printed with vertical pressure in a screw press like that used in the printing of books from type.

Knife

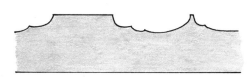

Cross section of wood block

Engraving

In making an engraving, a *burin,* or graver, a faceted steel bar set into a handle, is used to incise the lines into a copper plate. The burin makes a neat V-shaped furrow in the soft copper.

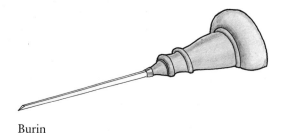

Burin

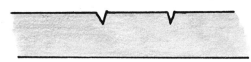

Cross section of an engraved line

Etching

In the etching process the copper plate is coated with a waxy or resinous ground resistant to acid. The *etching needle* scratches away the ground to delineate the image, baring the copper. When the plate is exposed to acid, only the copper exposed by the etching needle is bitten.

Etching needle (after Abraham Bosse, 1645)

Cross section of an etched line

Drypoint

Drypoint lines are created by scratching directly into the copper plate with a sharp point. This action displaces copper, which is thrown up beside the furrow in the form of a rough ridge of metal or *burr*. If the burr is not scraped away it will retain ink and print as a dark, velvety accent. The burr wears down quickly under pressure of printing. Seventeenth-century Dutch artists usually used drypoint without the burr, employing it to achieve very fine lines or to add supplemental detail to an etched plate.

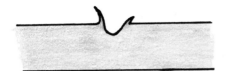

Cross section of a drypoint line with burr

Mezzotint

Mezzotint is a copper-plate process that produces a continuous tone. The *rocker,* a serrated steel blade with a handle, crisscrosses the plate, roughening the entire surface. If the plate were inked and printed at this stage, it would print as a dark, velvety rectangle. The light areas are produced with *scraper* and *burnisher* by scraping and smoothing the roughened surface.

A copper-plate print (engraving, etching, drypoint, mezzotint) is inked by forcing ink into the lines sunk below the surface of the plate. In conventional printing practice the surface of the copper plate was wiped clean of excess ink before printing. Rembrandt sometimes left a film of extra ink on the plate surface, often manipulating it in a painterly fashion before printing. Copper plates were printed by passing the inked plate and dampened paper under a heavy roller on a roller-bed press.

An *impression* is a single printing from a plate. A *state* is any stage in the development of the image on the plate at which impressions are taken. States change only with the addition or subtraction of work on the plate or block.

Mezzotint rocker (after a drawing in a seventeenth-century manuscript by John Evelyn)

Scraper (after a drawing in a seventeenth-century manuscript by John Evelyn)

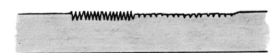

Cross section of a mezzotint plate (before and after scraping and burnishing)

Drawings by Roy Perkinson

307

Abbreviated References Used in the Catalogue

Ackley, 1974
Ackley, Clifford S. Review of *Hercules Segers: The Complete Etchings,* by E. Haverkamp-Begemann. *Print Collector's Newsletter* 5. (Sept.–Oct. 1974), 91–94.

Albertina, cat. drawings, 1928
Stix, Alfred, ed. *Beschreibender Katalog der Handzeichnungen in der Graphischen Sammlung Albertina.* Vienna, 1926–1941. Vol. 2: *Die Zeichnungen der niederländischen Schulen des XV. und XVI. Jahrhunderts,* by Otto Benesch, 1928.

Ambras, Schloss, Inventory, 1596
"Inventari Weiland der fürstlich Durchlaut Erzherzog Ferdinanden zu Österreich etc....," Innsbruck, May 30, 1596. In W. Boheim, ed., "Urkunden und Regesten aus der K.K. Hofbibliothek." *Jahrbuch der kunsthistorischen Sammlungen des allerhöchsten Kaiserhauses* 7 (1888), 226–313.

Ames, 1949
Ames, Winslow. "Some Woodcuts by Hendrick Goltzius and Their Program." *Gazette des Beaux-Arts* 35 (1949), 425–436.

Amsterdam, 1965–1966
Historisch Museum De Waag, Amsterdam. *Arm in de gouden eeuw.* Introduction by Marijke Kok. Amsterdam, 1965.

Amsterdam, 1967
Rijksmuseum, Amsterdam. Prentenkabinet. *Hercules Seghers* [Amsterdam, 1967].

Amsterdam, 1971
Wagner, Helga. *Jan van der Heyden, 1673–1712.* Amsterdam, 1971.

Amsterdam, 1975
Rijksmuseum, Amsterdam. *Leidse Universiteit, 400: Stichting en eerste bloei 1575–ca. 1650.* Amsterdam, 1975.

Amsterdam, 1976
Rijksmuseum, Amsterdam. *Tot lering en vermaak: Betekenissen van Hollandse genrevoorstellingen uit de zeventiende eeuw.* Amsterdam, 1976.

Amsterdam, 1979
Schapelhouman, Marijn. *Tekeningen van Noord- en Zuidnederlandse kunstenaars geboren voor 1600. Oude tekeningen in het bezit van de Gemeentemusea van Amsterdam waaronder de Collectie Fodor,* vol. 2. Amsterdam, 1979.

Amsterdam, cat. drawings, 1978
Boon, K.G. *Netherlandish Drawings of the Fifteenth and Sixteenth Centuries.* Vol. 2: *Catalogue of the Dutch and Flemish Drawings in the Rijksmuseum.* The Hague, 1978.

Amsterdam, Centsprenten, 1976
Veen, C.F. van. *Centsprenten: Nederlandse volks- en kinderprenten* [Catchpennyprints: Dutch Popular and Children's Prints]. Amsterdam, 1976.

Amsterdam/Toledo/Boston, 1980
Nederlands zilver [Dutch silver]. Edited by A.L. den Blaauwen. The Hague, 1979.

Amsterdam/Toronto, 1977
Amsterdams Historisch Museum and Art Gallery of Ontario. *Opkomst en Bloei van het Noordnederlandse Stadsgezicht in de 17de eeuw* [The Dutch Cityscape in the 17th Century and Its Sources]. Amsterdam, 1977.

Andresen
Andresen, Andreas. *Handbuch für Kupferstichsammler....* 2 vols. Leipzig, 1870–1873.

Andrews, 1977
Andrews, Keith. *Adam Elsheimer: Paintings, Drawings, Prints.* Oxford, 1977.

Attwater
Attwater, Donald. *The Penguin Dictionary of Saints.* Harmondsworth, Middlesex, 1965.

B.; Bartsch
Bartsch, Adam. *Le Peintre-graveur.* 21 vols. Vienna, 1803–1821; 2nd ed. Leipzig, 1818–1876.

B.; Bartsch (Rembrandt)
Bartsch, Adam. *Catalogue raisonné de toutes les estampes qui forment l'oeuvre de Rembrandt....* 2 vols. Vienna, 1797.

BB.; Biörklund/Barnard, 1955/1968
Biörklund, George, and Barnard, Osbert H. *Rembrandt's Etchings: True or False.* 2nd ed. Stockholm, 1968.

Baldinucci, 1686
Baldinucci, Filippo. *Cominciamento e progresso dell' arte dell' intagliare in rame, colle vite di molti de' più eccelenti maestri della stessa professione.* Florence, 1686.

Baldinucci, 1686/1808
Baldinucci, Filippo. *Opere di Filippo Baldinucci.* Milan, 1808–1812.

Bauch, 1938
Bauch, Kurt. "Beiträge zum Werk der Vorläufer Rembrandts." *Oud-Holland* 55 (1938), 354–365.

Bauch, 1960
Bauch, Kurt. *Der frühe Rembrandt und seine Zeit.* Berlin [1960].

Beeresteyn, cat., 1695
"Catalogus van uitnemende schoone miniaturen, Italiaanse, Franse, en Nederlantse prentkonst, en teykeningen, van de voornaamste meesters." In *Catalogus variorum exquisitissimorum, raroque occurrentium librorum...viri amplissimi D. Theodori a Beeresteyn.* Sale, Delft, April 18 and following days, 1695.

Benesch
Benesch, Otto. *Drawings of Rembrandt.* 6 vols. London, 1954–1957.

Benesch, 1943
Benesch, Otto. *Artistic and Intellectual Trends from Rubens to Daumier as Shown in Book Illustration.* Cambridge, Mass., 1943.

Bergström, 1956
Bergström, Ingvar. *Dutch Still-Life Painting in the Seventeenth Century.* Trans. by Christian Hedström and Gerald Taylor. New York, 1956.

Bergström, 1970
Bergström, Ingvar. "De Gheyn as a *Vanitas* Painter." *Oud-Holland* 85 (1970), 143–157.

Berlin, 1974
Schulz, Wolfgang. *Die holländische Landschaftszeichnung 1600–1740: Hauptwerke aus dem Berliner Kupferstichkabinett.* Berlin, 1974.

Berlin, 1975
Kupferstichkabinett, West Berlin. *Pieter Bruegel d. Ä. als Zeichner: Herkunft und Nachfolge.* Berlin [1975].

Berlin, 1979
Mielke, Hans. *Manierismus in Holland um 1600. Kupferstiche, Holzschnitte und Zeichnungen aus dem Berliner Kupferstichkabinett.* Berlin, 1979.

Berlin, *Bruegel*
Pieter Bruegel und seine Welt: Ein Colloquium veranstaltet vom Kunsthistorischen Institut der Freien Universität Berlin un dem Kupferstichkabinett der Staatlichen Museen Stiftung Preussischer Kulturbesitz, November 1975. Berlin, 1979.

Berlin, cat. drawings, 1930
Kupferstichkabinett, Berlin. *Die niederländischen Meister.* Berlin, 1930.

Berlin Orn. 1939
Staatliche Museen zu Berlin. *Katalog der Ornamentstichsammlung der Staatlichen Kunstbibliothek Berlin.* Berlin, 1939.

Berliner, 1928
Berliner, Rudolph. "Zur älteren Geschichte der allgemeinen Museumslehre in Deutschland." *Münchner Jahrbuch der bildenden Kunste,* n.s. 5 (1928), 327–352.

Bernt, 1970
Bernt, Walther. *The Netherlandish Painters of the Seventeenth Century.* 3 vols. London, 1970.

Biographisch Woordenboeck, 1852–1878
Aa, Abraham Jacob van der. *Biographisch woordenboeck der Nederlanden....* Haarlem, 1852–1878.

Blankert, 1965
See Utrecht, 1965

Blankert, 1968
Blankert, A. "Over Pieter van Laer als dier- en landschapschilder." *Oud-Holland* 83 (1968), 117–134.

Blankert, 1976
Blankert, Albert. "Ferdinand Bol 1616–1680, een leerling van Rembrandt" [Ferdinand Bol 1616–1680, Rembrandt's Pupil]. Doctoral dissertation, Rijksuniversiteit te Utrecht, 1940.

Bohlin, 1979
Bohlin, Diane DeGrazia. *Prints and Related Drawings by the Carracci Family: A Catalogue Raisonné.* Washington, D.C., 1979.

Bol, 1958
Bol, L.J. "Een Middelburgse Brueghel-groep. VII, VIII: Adriaen Pietersz. van de Venne, schilder en teyckenaer." *Oud-Holland* 73 (1958), 59–79, 128–147.

Bol, 1969
Bol, Laurens Johannes. *Holländische Maler des 17. Jahrhunderts nahe den grossen Meistern: Landschaften und Stilleben.* Braunschweig, 1969.

Bol, 1973
Bol, Laurens Johannes. *Die holländische Marinemalerei des 17. Jahrhunderts.* Braunschweig, 1973.

Bolten, 1979
Bolten, Jacob. "Het Noord- en Zuidnederlandse teken-boek 1600-1750." Doctoral dissertation, Universiteit van Amsterdam, 1979.

Bonacini, 1953
Bonacini, Claudio. *Bibliografia della arti scrittorie e della calligrafia.* Florence, 1953.

Bonger, 1941
Bonger, H. *Dirck Volckertszoon Coornhert: Studie over een nuchter en vroom Nederlander.* Lochem [1941?].

Boon, 1953
Boon, Karel G. "Over vroege staten in het werk van Jan Muller." *Bulletin van het Rijksmuseum,* 1 (1953), 31-33.

Boon, 1964
Boon, Karel G. *Korte geschiedenis van de verzamelingen. Gids voor het Rijksprentenkabinet.* Amsterdam, 1964.

Boon, 1972
Boon, Karel G. "Amor en Venus of het Vroutgen met een Pappotgen." *De Kroniek van het Rembrandthuis* 26 (1972), 27-31.

Bosse, 1645
Bosse, Abraham. *Traicté des manieres de graver en taille douce.* Paris, 1645.

Bosse, 1649
Bosse, Abraham. *Sentimens sur la distinction des diverses manières de peinture, dessein & gravure, & des originaux d'avec leurs copies.* Paris, 1649.

Boston, 1971
Museum of Fine Arts, Boston. *Albrecht Dürer: Master Printmaker.* Boston, 1971.

Boston/New York, 1969
Museum of Fine Arts, Boston, and The Pierpont Morgan Library, New York. *Rembrandt, Experimental Etcher.* Boston, 1969.

Boucot, cat., 1699
"Catalogue des estampes et livres de figures...." In *Catalogue de la bibliothèque du defunt M. Boucot.* Sale, Paris, Nov. 16 and following days, 1699.

Bouvy, 1924
Bouvy, E. *Nanteuil.* Paris, 1924.

Braunschweig, 1978
Herzog Anton Ulrich-Museum. *Die Sprache der Bilder: Realität und Bedeutung in der niederländischen Malerei des 17. Jahrhunderts.* Braunschweig, 1978.

Braunschweig, 1979
Herzog Anton Ulrich-Museum. *Jan Lievens: Ein Maler im Schatten Rembrandts.* Braunschweig, 1979.

Bredius, 1887
Bredius, Abraham. "Een en ander over Caspar Netscher." *Oud-Holland* 5 (1887), 263-274.

Bredius, 1892
Bredius, Abraham. "De Schilder Johannes van de Cappelle." *Oud-Holland* 10 (1892), 26-40, 133-136.

Bredius, *Künstler-Inventare*
Bredius, Abraham. *Künstler-Inventare: Urkunden zur Geschichte der holländischen Kunst des XVIten, XVIIten und XVIIIten Jahrhunderts.* The Hague, 1915-1922.

Bredius/Gerson, 1969
Bredius, Abraham. *The Complete Edition of the Paintings [of] Rembrandt.* 3rd ed., revised by Horst Gerson. London, 1969.

Bremen, 1966
Kunsthalle, Bremen. *Zeichnungen alter Meister aus deutschem Privatbesitz.* Bremen, 1966.

Briquet
Briquet, Charles Moïse. *Les Filigranes: Dictionnaire historique des marques du papier dès leur apparition vers 1282 jusqu'en 1600.* Geneva, 1907.

Brochhagen, 1958
Brochhagen, Ernst. "Karel Dujardin: Ein Beitrag zum Italianismus in Holland im 17. Jahrhundert." Doctoral dissertation, University of Cologne, 1958.

Broos, 1970
Broos, B.P.J. "The O of Rembrandt." *Simiolus* 4 (1970), 150-184.

Brummel, 1949
Visscher, Roemer. *Sinnepoppen.* Amsterdam, 1614. Edited by L. Brummel. The Hague, 1949.

Brunet
Brunet, Jacques Charles. *Manuel du libraire et du l'amateur des livres.* 6 vols. Paris, 1860-1865. Supplement. 2 vols. 1878-1880.

Bruyn, 1959
Bruyn, J. *Rembrandt's keuze van bijbelse onderwerpen.* Utrecht, 1959.

Budapest, cat. drawings, 1971
Szépművészeti Múzeum, Budapest. *Netherlandish Drawings in the Budapest Museum. Sixteenth-century drawings.* Amsterdam, 1971.

Bur.; Burchard, 1917
Burchard, Ludwig. *Die holländischen Radierer vor Rembrandt.* Berlin, 1917.

Burke, 1976
Burke, James D. *Jan Both: Paintings, Drawings and Prints.* [Ph.D. dissertation, Harvard University, 1972.] New York, 1976.

Carosso-Kok, 1975
Carosso-Kok, Marijke. *Amsterdam Historisch.* Bussum, 1975.

Charrington, 1936
Charrington, J. *A Catalogue of the Engraved Portraits in the Library of Samuel Pepys, F.R.S.* Cambridge, 1936.

Chicago, 1969
The Art Institute of Chicago. *Rembrandt after Three Hundred Years: An Exhibition of Rembrandt and His Followers.* Chicago, 1969.

Choulant/Frank, 1920
Choulant, Ludwig. *History and Bibliography of Anatomic Illustration.* Leipzig, 1832. Translated and edited by Mortimer Frank. Chicago, 1920.

Churchill
Churchill, W.A. *Watermarks in Paper.* Amsterdam, 1935.

Clark, 1966
Clark, Kenneth McKenzie. *Rembrandt and the Italian Renaissance.* The Wrightsman Lectures, no. 1. New York, 1966.

Clark, 1976
Clark, Kenneth McKenzie. "Rembrandt's 'Good Samaritan' in the Wallace Collection." *Burlington Magazine* 118 (Dec. 1976), 806-809.

Cleves, 1979
Städtisches Museum Haus Koekkoek. *Soweit der Erdkreis reicht, Johann Moritz von Nassau-Siegen, 1604-1679.* Cleves, 1979.

Croiset van Uchelen, 1976
Croiset van Uchelen, Anthony R.A. "Dutch Writing-Masters and the 'Prix de la Plume Couronné.'" *Quaerendo* 6 (autumn 1976), 319-346.

Davidsohn
Davidsohn, Paul. *Adriaen van Ostade: Verzeichnis seiner original Radierungen.* Leipzig, 1922.

Davies, 1973/1978
Davies, Alice I. *Allart van Everdingen.* [Ph.D. dissertation, Harvard University, 1973.] New York, 1978.

De Bie, 1661
Bie, C. de. *Het Gulden Cabinet vande Edel Vry Schilder Const.* Antwerp, 1661.

De Groot, 1979
Groot, Irene de. *Landscape Etchings by the Dutch Masters of the Seventeenth Century.* Maarssen, 1979.

De Hoop Scheffer, 1976
Hoop Scheffer, Dieuwke de. "Onbeschreven staten in het etswerk van Jan Both." *Bulletin van het Rijksmuseum* 24 (1976), 177-182.

De Jonge, 1938
Jonge, Caroline Henriette de. *Paulus Moreelse, portret- en genreschilder te Utrecht, 1571-1638.* Assen, 1938.

De Jonge, 1942
Jonge, Caroline Henriette de. "Een Familiegroep met zelf-portret van Werner van den Valckert." *Oud-Holland* 59 (1942), 139-143.

De Jongh, 1967
Jongh, E. de. *Zinne- en minnebeelden in de schilderkunst van de zeventiende eeuw.* [N.p., Openbaar Kunstbezit, 1967.]

De la Fontaine Verwey, 1976
Fontaine Verwey, H. de la. *Uit de wereld van het boek.*
Vol. 2: *Drukkers, liefhebbers en piraten in de zeventiende
eeuw.* Amsterdam, 1976.

De Piles, 1699
Piles, Roger de. *Abregé de la vie des peintres....* Paris, 1699.

De Piles, 1706
Piles, Roger de. *The Art of Painting, and the Lives of the
Painters....* London, 1706.

De Roever, 1885
De Roever, N. "Jan Harmensz. Muller." *Oud-Holland* 3
(1885), 266–276.

De Vesme/Massar, 1971
Baudi di Vesme, Alessandro. *Stefano della Bella: Cata-
logue Raisonné.* With introduction and additions by
Phyllis Dearborn Massar. New York, 1971.

De Vries, 1886
Vries, A.D. de. Adrian van de Velde documents in
"Biografische Aanteekeningen." *Oud-Holland* 4 (1886),
143–144.

De Vries, 1899
Vries, Anne Gerard Cristiaan de. *De Nederlandsche
emblemata.* Amsterdam, 1899.

Degenhart and Schmitt, 1968
Degenhart, B., and Schmitt, A. "Exkurs I, Methoden
Vasaris bei der Gestaltung seines 'Libro.'" In *Corpus der
italienischen Zeichnungen 1300–1450*, vol. 2, pp. 628–638.
Berlin, 1968.

Denucé, 1932
Denucé, J. *De Antwerpsche 'Konstkamers': Inventarissen
van kunstverzamelingen te Antwerpen in de 16. en 17.
eeuwen.* Amsterdam, 1932.

Des Moines/Boston, 1975–76
Worthen, Amy N., and Reed, Sue Welsh. *The Etchings of
Jacques Bellange.* Des Moines, 1975.

Drugulin
Drugulin, W. *Allart van Everdingen.* Leipzig, 1873.

Du Gué Trapier, 1952
Trapier, Elizabeth du Gué. *Ribera.* Hispanic Notes and
Monographs, Peninsular Series. New York, 1952.

Dudok van Heel, 1969
Dudok van Heel, S.A.C. "De Rembrandts in de verzamelingen 'Hinloopen.'" *Amstelodamum Maandblad* 59
(1969), 233–237.

Dudok van Heel, 1975
Dudok van Heel, S.A.C. "Honderdvijftig advertenties
van kunstverkopingen uit veertig jaargangen van de
Amsterdamsche Courant, 1672–1711." *Amstelodamum Jaarboek* 67 (1975), 149–173.

Dudok van Heel, 1977
Dudok van Heel, S.A.C. "Jan Pietersz. Zomer (1641–
1724): Makelaar in schilderijen (1690–1724)." *Amstelodamum Jaarboek* 69 (1977), 89–106.

Dudok van Heel, 1978
Dudok van Heel, S.A.C. "Mr. Joannes Wtenbogaert
(1608–1680): Een man Remonstrants milieu en

Rembrandt van Rijn." *Amstelodamum Jaarboek* 70
(1978), 146–169.

Düsseldorf, 1968
Kunstmuseum, Düsseldorf. *Niederländische Handzeich-
nungen 1500–1800 aus dem Kunstmuseum Düsseldorf.*
Düsseldorf, 1968.

Dut.; Dutuit, 1885
Dutuit, Eugène. *Manuel de l'amateur d'estampes.* Vols.
4–6: *Écoles flamande et hollandaise.* Paris, 1881–1885.

El Escorial, cat., 1963–1966
Lasarte, J.A., and Casanovas, A. "Catálogo de la colección
de grabados de la Biblioteca de El Escorial." *Anales y
boletín de los Museos de Arte de Barcelona* 16 (1963–64),
1–397; 17 (1965–66), 1–103.

Emmens, 1964
Emmens, J.A. *Rembrandt en de regels van de kunst.*
Utrecht, 1964.

Erasmus, 1908
Erasmus, Kurt. "Roelant Savery: Sein Leben und seine
Werke." Doctoral dissertation, Friedrichs-Universität,
Halle-Wittenberg, 1908.

Evelyn, 1662
Evelyn, John. *Sculptura: or, the History, and Art of Chal-
cography and Engraving in Copper.* London, 1662. Edited
by C.F. Bell. Oxford, 1906.

F.M.
Muller, F. *De Nederlandsche geschiednis in platen: Beschrijv-
ing van Nederlandsche historieplaten, zinneprenten en his-
torische kaarten.* Amsterdam, 1863–1882.

Fairfax-Murray
Fairfax Murray, Charles. *Catalogue of a Collection of Early
German Books in the Library of C. Fairfax Murray.*
London, 1913.

Filedt Kok, 1972
Filedt Kok, J.P. *Rembrandt Etchings and Drawings in the
Rembrandt House.* Maarssen, 1972.

Florence, 1964
Reznicek, E.K.J. *Mostra di disegni fiamminghi e olandesi.*
Gabinetto designi e stampe degli Uffizi, 18. Florence,
1964.

Fr.-v.d.K.
Franken, Daniel, and Kellen, Johan Philip van der.
*L'Oeuvre de Jan van de Velde, graveur hollandais, 1593–
1641.* Amsterdam, 1968.

Frederiks, 1952
Frederiks, Johan Willem. *Dutch Silver.* 4 vols. The Hague,
1952–1961.

Fuhse, 1895
Fuhse, F. "Zur Dürerforschung im 17. Jahrhundert." *Mit-
teilungen aus dem Germanischen Nationalmuseum,* 1895,
66–75.

G.
Gersaint, Edmé-François. *Catalogue raisonné de toutes les
pièces qui forment l'oeuvre de Rembrandt.* Paris, 1751.

Gerson, 1936
Gerson, Horst. *Philips Koninck: Ein Beitrag zur Erfor-

schung der holländischen Malerei des XVII. Jahrhunderts.*
Berlin, 1936.

Gerson, 1940
Gerson, Horst. "Leven en werken van Claes v. Bere-
steyn." In *Genealogie van het geslacht van Beresteyn*, vol. 2.
The Hague, 1940.

Godefroy
Godefroy, Louis. *L'Oeuvre gravé de Adriaen van Ostade.*
Paris, 1930.

Goossens, 1977
Goossens, Korneel. *David Vinckboons.* Soest, 1977.

Gudlaugsson, 1959
Gudlaugsson, S.J. *Gerhard Ter Borch.* 2 vols. The Hague,
1959–1960.

Guilmard
Guilmard, Désiré. *Les Maîtres ornemanistes....*
Paris, 1880–1881.

Haak, 1969
Haak, Bob. *Rembrandt: His Life, His Work, His Time.*
Translated from the Dutch by Elizabeth Willems-
Treeman. New York, 1969.

The Hague, 1953
Koninklijk Kabinet van Schilderijen, The Hague. *Zo wijd
de wereld strekt* [The Hague], 1953.

The Hague, 1978
Croiset van Uchelen, Anthony R.A. *Nederlandse schrijf-
meesters uit de zeventiende eeuw.* The Hague, 1978.

The Hague, 1979–80
Koninklijk Kabinet van Schilderijen, The Hague. *Maurits
de Braziliaan* [The Hague], 1979.

The Hague, cat. paintings, 1977
Kabinet van Schilderijen, The Hague. *Mauritshuis, the
Royal Cabinet of Paintings.* Illustrated General Catalogue.
The Hague, 1977.

Hajós, 1958
Hajós, E.M. "The Concept of an Engravings Collection
in the Year 1565: Quiccheberg, 'Inscriptiones Vel Tituli
Theatri Amplissimi.'" *Art Bulletin* 40 (1958), 151–156.

Haskell, 1963
Haskell, Francis. *Patrons and Painters: A Study of the
Relations between Italian Art and Society in the Age of the
Baroque.* London, 1963.

Haverkamp-Begemann, 1959
Haverkamp-Begemann, Egbert. *Willem Buytewech.*
Amsterdam, 1959.

Haverkamp-Begemann, 1973
Haverkamp-Begemann, Egbert. *Hercules Segers: The
Complete Etchings.* Amsterdam, 1973.

Haverkamp-Begemann et al., 1962
Yale Art Gallery. *Color in Prints: Catalogue of an Exhibi-
tion of European and American Color Prints from 1500 to the
Present....* New Haven, 1962.

Haverkorn van Rijsewijk, 1904
Haverkorn van Rijsewijk, P. "Een Kijkje op Rotterdam in
1605." *Oud-Holland* 22 (1904), 12–26.

Heawood
Heawood, Edward. *Watermarks, Mainly of the 17th and 18th Century.* Monumenta Chartae Papyraceae Historiam Illustrantia, 1. Hilversum, 1950.

Hees, 1956
Hees, C.A. van. "Nadere gegevens omtrent de Haarlemse vrienden Leendert van der Cooghen en Cornelis Bega." *Oud-Holland* 71 (1956), 243–244.

Held, 1951
Held, Julius S. "Mededelingen van het Rijksbureau voor Kunsthistorische Documentatie; Notes on David Vinckeboons." *Oud-Holland* 66 (1951), 241–246.

Heller, 1831
Heller, J. *Das Leben und die Werke Albrecht Dürers.* Vol. 2. Leipzig, 1831.

Hervey, 1921
Hervey, M.F.S. *The Life, Correspondence and Collections of Thomas Howard, Earl of Arundel.* Cambridge, 1921.

Hind
Hind, Arthur Mayger. *A Catalogue of Rembrandt's Etchings.* 2nd ed. 2 vols. London, 1923.

Hind, 1913
Hind, Arthur Mayger. "Lievens." *The Imprint* 1 (1913), 233–239.

Hind, 1923
Hind, Arthur Mayger. *A History of Engraving and Etching, from the 15th Century to the Year 1914.* 3rd ed. London, 1923.

Hirschmann, 1919
Hirschmann, Otto. *Hendrick Goltzius.* Meister der Graphik, 7. Leipzig, 1919.

Hirschmann, 1921
Hirschmann, Otto. *Verzeichnis des graphischen Werks von Hendrick Goltzius, 1558–1617....* Leipzig, 1921.

Hofstede de Groot, 1906
Hofstede de Groot, Cornelis. *Die Urkunden über Rembrandt (1575–1721).* The Hague, 1906.

Holl.; Hollstein
Hollstein, F.W.H. *Dutch and Flemish Etchings, Engravings, and Woodcuts, ca. 1450–1700.* Amsterdam, 1949–

Holl., German
Hollstein, F.W.H. *German Engravings, Etchings, and Woodcuts, ca. 1400–1700.* Amsterdam, 1954–

Hoogstraten, 1678
Hoogstraten, Samuel van. *Inleyding tot de hooge schoole der schilderkonst; Anders de zichtbaere werelt.* Rotterdam, 1678.

Houbraken, 1718–1721
Houbraken, Arnold. *De Groote schouburgh der Nederlantsche konstschilders en schilderessen....* 3 vols. Amsterdam, 1718–1721.

Hudig, 1937
Hudig, Ferrand Whaley. "Werner van den Valckert, I." *Oud-Holland* 54 (1937), 54–66.

Huygens, *Journalen*
Journaal van Constantijn Huygens, den Zoon, Jan. 1, 1692–Sept. 2, 1696. *Werken uitgegeven door het Historisch Genootschap, gevestigt te Utrecht,* n.s., vol. 25 (1877).

Huygens/Worp
See Worp

IJzerman, 1926
IJzerman, J.W. "Hollandsche prenten als handelsartikel te Patani in 1602." In *Gedenkschrift...van het Koninklijk Instituut voor Taal-, Land- en Volkenkunde van Nederlandsch-Indië.* The Hague, 1926, pp. 84–109.

Innsbruck, 1977
Kunsthistorisches Museum, Innsbruck. *Die Kunstkammer.* Catalogue by E. Scheicher. Innsbruck, 1977.

Ivins, 1953
Ivins, William M. *Prints and Visual Communication.* Cambridge, Mass., 1953.

Janson, 1952
Janson, Horst W. *Apes and Ape Lore in the Middle Ages and the Renaissance.* London, 1952.

Jessen, 1920
Jessen, Peter. *Der Ornamentstich: Geschichte der Vorlagen des Kunsthandwerks seit dem Mittelalter.* Berlin, 1920.

Jessopp, 1887
North, Roger. *The Autobiography of Roger North.* Edited by A. Jessopp. London, 1887.

Judson, 1973
Judson, J. Richard. *The Drawings of Jacob de Gheyn II.* New York, 1973.

Karpinski, 1963
Karpinski, C. "Prints for Sale." *The Metropolitan Museum of Art Bulletin* 22 (1963–1964), 211–220.

Keyes, 1977
Keyes, George S. "Les Eaux-fortes de Ruisdael." *Nouvelles de l'Estampe* 36 (Nov.–Dec. 1977), 7–13.

Knoef, 1920
Knoef, J. "Het Etswerk van Cornelis Bega." *Elsevier's Geillustreerde Maandblad* 60 (1920), 289–295.

Koschatzky, 1963
Koschatzky, W. "Die Gründung der Kunstsammlung des Herzogs Albert von Sachsen-Teschen." *Albertina-Studien* 1 (1963), 5–14.

Kutter, 1926–27
Kutter, P. "Des Mathias Quad von Kinkelbach Nachrichten von Künstlern: Der älteste deutsche Versuch einer Kunstgeschichte gedruckt zu Köln 1609." *Wallraf-Richartz Jahrbuch* 3–4 (1926–1927), 227–233.

Lairesse/Davaco, 1740/1969
Lairesse, Gerard de. *Groot Schilderboek....* Haarlem, 1740. Facsimile ed. [N.p.], 1969.

Landwehr, 1962
Landwehr, John. *Dutch Emblem Books: A Bibliography.* Utrecht, 1962.

Landwehr, 1970
Landwehr, John. *Romeyn de Hooghe (1645–1708) as Book Illustrator: A Bibliography.* Amsterdam, 1970.

Landwehr, 1971
Landwehr, John. *Splendid Ceremonies: State Entries and Royal Funerals in the Low Countries 1515–1791.* Leyden, 1971.

Landwehr, 1973
Landwehr, John. *Romeyn de Hooghe, the Etcher: Contemporary Portrayal of Europe, 1662–1707.* Leyden, 1973.

Lawler, 1898
Lawler, J. *Book Auctions in England in the Seventeenth Century.* London, 1898.

Le Bl.; Le Blanc
Le Blanc, Charles. *Manuel de l'amateur d'estampes....* 4 vols. Paris, 1854–1858; 1887–1890.

Le Comte, 1699
Le Comte, Florent. *Cabinet des singularitez d'architecture, peinture, sculpture, et gravure....* 3 vols. Paris, 1699–1700.

Lehmann-Haupt, 1977
Lehmann-Haupt, Hellmut. *An Introduction to the Woodcut of the Seventeenth Century.* New York, 1977.

Levi d'Ancona
Levi d'Ancona, Mirella. *The Garden of the Renaissance: Botanical Symbolism in Italian Painting.* Florence, 1977.

Levis, 1915
Levis, Howard C. *Extracts from the Diaries and Correspondence of John Evelyn and Samuel Pepys Relating to Engraving.* London, 1915.

Leyden, 1970
Stedelijk Museum "De Lakenhal." *IJdelheid der IJdelheden: Hollandse Vanitas-voorstellingen uit de zeventiende eeuw.* Leyden, 1970.

Lhotsky, 1941–1945
Lhotsky, A. *Die Geschichte der Sammlungen von den Anfängen bis zum Tode Kaiser Karls VI. 1740.* Festschrift des Kunsthistorischen Museums.... Vol. 2. Vienna, 1941–1945.

Lieure, 1924–1929
Lieure, Jules. *Jacques Callot.* Introduction by F. Courboin. 5 vols. Paris, 1924–1929.

London, cat. drawings, 1915–1932
Hind, Arthur Mayger. *Catalogue of Drawings by Dutch and Flemish Artists Preserved in the Department of Prints and Drawings in the British Museum.* 5 vols. London, 1915–1932.

Loriquet, 1886
Loriquet, C. *Robert Nanteuil: Sa vie et son oeuvre.* Reims, 1886.

Loserth, 1911
Loserth, L. *Geschichte des altsteirischen Herren- und Grafenhauses Stubenberg.* Graz and Leipzig, 1911.

Lugt
Lugt, Frits. *Les Marques de collections de dessins et d'estampes.* Amsterdam, 1921. Supplement. The Hague, 1956.

Lugt, 1920
Lugt, Frits. *Mit Rembrandt in Amsterdam.* Berlin, 1920.

Lugt, 1938
Lugt, Frits. *Répertoire des catalogues de ventes....* Vol. 1. The Hague, 1938.

MacLaren
MacLaren, Neil. *The Dutch School.* National Gallery, London, Catalogue. London, 1960.

Maitland, cat., 1688
"A Large Collection of Excellent Prints and Drawings of the Most Eminent Masters of Europe...." In *Catalogus librorum instructissimae bibliothecae nobilis cujusdam Scoto-Britani.* Sale, Benjamin Walford, London, Oct. 30, 1688.

Maitland, cat., 1689
"The Second Part of the Famous Collection of Prints and Drawings, of the Most Eminent Masters of Europe...." In *Catalogus librorum instructissimae bibliothecae doctissimi cujusdam equitis....* Sale, Benjamin Walford, London, Oct. 28, 1689.

Maritieme Encyclopedie, 1970
Maritieme Encyclopedie. 6 vols. Bussum, 1970.

Marolles, 1666
Marolles, Michel de. *Catalogue de livres, d'estampes et de figures en taille-douce....* Paris, 1666.

Marolles, 1672
Marolles, Michel de. *Catalogue de livres d'estampes et de figures en taille douce.* Paris, 1672.

Marolles, 1755
Marolles, Michel de. *Mémoires de Michel de Marolles, Abbé de Villeloin.* Vol. 1. Paris, 1657; Amsterdam, 1755.

Marzoli
Marzoli, Carla, comp. *Calligraphy 1535–1885: A Collection of Seventy-Two Writing Books....* Introduction by Stanley Morison. Milan, 1962.

Mayor, 1971
Mayor, A. Hyatt. *Prints and People: A Social History of Printed Pictures.* New York, 1971.

Meertens, 1943
Meertens, P.J. *Letterkundig leven in Zeeland in de zestiende en de eerste helft der zeventiende eeuw.* Amsterdam, 1943.

Metcalfe, 1912
Metcalfe, L. "A Prince of Print Collectors: Michel de Marolles, Abbé de Villeloin (1600–1681)." *The Print Collector's Quarterly* 2 (Oct. 1912), 316–340.

Middleton, 1878
Middleton, Charles Henry. *A Descriptive Catalogue of the Etched Work of Rembrandt van Rhyn.* London, 1878.

Miedema, 1969
Miedema, Hessel. "Over Hendrick Goltzius' tekeningen naar de antieken." in *Miscellanea I.Q. Van Regteren Altena*, pp. 74ff. Amsterdam, 1969.

Möhle, 1963
Möhle, Hans. "Drawings by Jacques de Gheyn III." *Master Drawings* 1 (summer 1963), 3–12.

Möhle, 1966
Möhle, Hans. *Die Zeichnungen Adam Elsheimers: Das Werk des Meisters und der Problemkreis Elsheimer-Goudt.* Berlin, 1966.

Morse, 1966
Morse, Peter, *Rembrandt's Etching Techniques: An Example.* United States National Museum Bulletin no. 250. Contributions from The Museum of History and Technology, Paper 61. Washington, D.C., 1966.

Mortimer, 1974
Mortimer, Ruth. *Italian 16th Century Books.* 2 vols. Harvard College Library Department of Printing and Graphic Arts Catalogue of Books and Manuscripts, Part 2. Cambridge, Mass., 1974.

Münster, 1974
Westfälisches Landesmuseum. *Gerard Ter Borch: Zwolle 1617–Deventer 1681.* Münster, 1974.

Münz, 1952
Münz, Ludwig. *Rembrandt's Etchings.* 2 vols. London, 1952.

N.N. Biografisch Woordenboek, 1911
Molhuysen, Philip Christian. *Nieuw Nederlandsch Biografisch Woordenboek.* 10 vols. Leyden, 1911–1937.

Nag.; Nagler
Nagler, G.K. *Neues allgemeines Künstler-Lexikon....* 22 vols. Munich, 1835–1852.

Nagler, *Mon.*, 1858–1879
Nagler, Georg Kaspar. *Die Monogrammisten und diejenigen bekannten und unbekannten Künstler aller Schulen....* 5 vols. Munich, 1858–1879.

New York/Paris, 1977–78
Institut néerlandais, Paris. *Rembrandt and His Century: Dutch Drawings of the Seventeenth Century, from the Collection of Frits Lugt, Institut néerlandais, Paris.* New York and Paris, 1977.

Nieuwstraten, 1965
Stechow, Wolfgang. "De Ontwikkeling van Herman Saftlevens kunst tot 1650." *Nederlands Kunsthistorisch Jaarboek* 16 (1965), 81–117.

Nijmegen, 1961
Johannes Teyler: Nederlandse kleurendruk rond 1700. Nijmegen, 1961.

Nissen
Nissen, Claus. *Die botanische Buchillustration: Ihre Geschichte und Bibliographie.* 2 vols. Stuttgart, 1951.

Norman, 1911–12
Norman, Philip, ed. "Nicholas Hilliard's Treatise Concerning 'The Arte of Limning.'" *Volume of the Walpole Society, London* 1 (1912), 1–54.

Oberhuber
See **Vienna, 1967–68**

Oertel, 1936
Oertel, Robert. "Ein Künstler Stammbuch vom Jahre 1616." *Jahrbuch der Preussischen Kunstsammlungen* 57 (1936), 98–108.

Oxford, cat. drawings, 1938
Parker, Karl Theodore. *Catalogue of the Collection of Drawings in the Ashmolean Museum.* Vol. 1: *Netherlandish, German, French, and Spanish Schools.* Oxford, 1938.

Paris, 1968–69
Institut néerlandais, Paris. *Dessins de paysagistes hollandais du XVIIᵉ siècle de la collection particulière conservée à l'Institut néerlandais de Paris.* 2 vols. [Brussels], 1968.

Paris, 1974
Institut néerlandais, Paris. *Dessins flamands et hollandais du dix-septième siècle.* Paris [1974].

Paris, Bibliothèque, 1973
Bibliothèque nationale, Paris. *Les Sorcières.* Paris, 1973.

Paris, cat. drawings, 1931
Lugt, Frits. *École hollandaise.* 3 vols. Inventaire général des Écoles du Nord au Musée de Louvre, vol. 1. Paris, 1929–1933.

Paris/New York, 1979–80
Stampfle, Felice. *Rubens and Rembrandt in Their Century: Flemish and Dutch Drawings of the 17th Century from The Pierpont Morgan Library.* New York, 1979.

Parthey
Parthey, Gustav Friedrich Constantin. *Wenzel Hollar: Beschreibendes Verzeichniss seiner Kupferstiche.* Berlin, 1853.

Pass.; Passavant
Passavant, Johann David. *Le Peintre-graveur.* 6 vols. Leipzig, 1860–1864.

Pelka, 1934
Pelka, Otto. "Matthias Quad von Kinckelbach und seine Abhandlung 'Von den berumpten Kunstlern Teutscher Nation.'" *Gutenberg Jahrbuch* 9 (1934), 187–194.

Pissarro, 1956–1958
Pissarro, Orovida C. "Prince Rupert and the Invention of Mezzotint." *Volume of the Walpole Society* 36 (1956–1958), 1–9.

Praz, 1975
Praz, Mario. *Studies in Seventeenth-Century Imagery.* Sussidi Eruditi, 16. 2nd ed. Rome, 1964. Reprint. 1975.

Princeton/Harvard, 1973–74
Brown, Jonathan. *Jusepe de Ribera: Prints and Drawings.* Princeton, N.J., 1973.

Quadt von Kinckelbach, 1609
Quadt von Kinckelbach, M. *Teutscher Nation Herligkeitt.* Cologne, 1609.

R.-D.
Robert-Dumesnil, A.P.F. *Le Peintre-graveur français....* 11 vols. Paris, 1835–1871.

Rademaker, 1725/1966
Rademaker, Abraham. *Kabinet van Nederlandsche outheden en gezichten.* Amsterdam, 1725. Facsimile ed. Zaltbommel, 1966.

Rave, 1959
Rave, P.O. "Paolo Giovio und die Bildnisvitenbücher des Humanismus." *Jahrbuch der Berliner Museen* 1 (1959), 119–154.

Reitlinger
Reitlinger, Henry, "Hendrick, Count Goudt." *Print Collector's Quarterly* 8 (1921), 231–246.

312

Reznicek, 1956
Reznicek, E.K.J. "Jan Harmensz. Muller als tekenaar." *Nederlands Kunsthistorisch Jaarboek* 7 (1956), 65–120.

Reznicek, 1960
Reznicek, E.K.J. "Het Begin van Goltzius' loopbaan als schilder." *Oud-Holland* 75 (1960), 30–49.

Reznicek, 1961
Reznicek, E.K.J. *Die Zeichnungen von Hendrick Goltzius mit einem beschreibenden Katalog.* Utrecht, 1961.

Reznicek, 1975
Reznicek, E.K.J. "Het Leerdicht van Karel van Mander en de Acribie van Hessel Miedema." *Oud-Holland* 89 (1975), 102–128.

Richter, 1939
Leonardo da Vinci. *The Literary Works of Leonardo da Vinci.* Edited by Jean Paul Richter. 2nd ed. 2 vols. London, 1939.

Rifkin, 1972
Rifkin, Benjamin A. "Problems in Rembrandt's Etchings." *Print Collector's Newsletter* 2 (1972), 123–125.

Riggs, 1971
Riggs, Timothy Allan. "Hieronymus Cock (1510–1570), Printmaker and Publisher at the Sign of the Four Winds." Ph.D. dissertation, Yale University, 1971.

Robbins, 1959
Robbins, Rossel Hope. *The Encyclopedia of Witchcraft and Demonology.* New York, 1959.

Robinson, 1979
Robinson, William R. "Preparatory Drawings by Adriaen van de Velde." *Master Drawings* 17 (1979), 3–23.

Röthlisberger, 1969
Röthlisberger, Marcel. *Bartholomeus Breenbergh.* Disegno: Studien zur Geschichte der europäischen Handzeichnungen, edited by Matthias Winner, vol. 1. Berlin, 1969.

Rosenberg, 1928
Rosenberg, Jakob. *Jacob van Ruisdael.* Berlin, 1928.

Rosenberg, 1944
Rosenberg, Jakob. "Rembrandt and Guercino." *Art Quarterly* 7 (1944), 129–134.

Rosenberg/Slive/Ter Kuile, 1966
Rosenberg, Jakob; Slive, Seymour; and Ter Kuile, E.H. *Dutch Art and Architecture 1600–1800.* Pelican History of Art. Baltimore, 1966.

Rotterdam, 1942–43
Museum Boymans, Rotterdam. *De zwarte-kunst prent 1642–1942.* Rotterdam, 1943.

Rotterdam, 1943–44
Museum Boymans, Rotterdam. *Het Landschap in de Nederlandsche prentkunst.* 4 vols. 1: *De XVI eeuw,* 1943; 2: *1600–1640,* 1943; 3: *1640–1680,* 1944; 4: *De Italianisanten,* 1944.

Rotterdam, 1969
Ihle, B.L.D. *De antike wereld in de prentkunst 1500–1700.* Tentoonstelling Prentenkabinet, Catalogue no. 47. Rotterdam, 1969.

Rotterdam, 1972
Museum Boymans–van Beuningen, Rotterdam. Prentenkabinet. *Goltzius en zijn school.* Rotterdam, 1972.

Rotterdam, 1974
Adèr, Robin. *Denkers, dichters en mannen van de wetenschap, XVe–XVIIe eeuw.* Tentoonstelling Prentenkabinet, Catalogue no. 56. Rotterdam, 1974.

Rotterdam, 1975–76
Museum Boymans–van Beuningen, Rotterdam. *'Dames Gaan Voor': De Vrouw in de prentkunst 1500–1800.* Tentoonstelling Prentenkabinet, Catalogue no. 57. Rotterdam [1975].

Rotterdam, cat. drawings, Rembrandt, 1969
Museum Boymans–van Beuningen, Rotterdam. *Tekeningen van Rembrandt en zijn school.* Edited by H.R. Hoetink. Rotterdam, 1969.

Rotterdam, cat. paintings, 1892
Haverkorn van Rijsewijk, Pieter. *Notice descriptive des tableaux et sculptures du Musée de Rotterdam…* [Rotterdam], 1892.

Rotterdam, *Graveurs,* 1972
Museum Boymans–van Beuningen, Rotterdam. Prentenkabinet. *Hollandse graveurs van de XVIIe eeuw.* Museum Boymans–van Beuningen, Catalogue no. 52 [Rotterdam, 1972].

Rotterdam/Paris, 1975
Willem Buytewech, 1591–1624 [Exhibition]. Rotterdam, Museum Boymans–van Beuningen, Nov. 1974–Jan. 1975; Paris, Institut néerlandais, Jan.–March 1975.

Rov.; Rovinski
Rovinski, Dmitri. *L'Oeuvre gravé de Rembrandt….* Saint Petersburg, 1890.

Rov. El.; Rovinski
Rovinski, Dmitri. *L'Oeuvre gravé des élèves de Rembrandt et des maîtres qui ont gravé dans son goût.* 3 vols. Saint Petersburg, 1894.

Rowlands, 1979
Rowlands, John. *Hercules Segers.* New York, 1979.

Sacramento, 1974
Tümpel, Astrid. *The Pre-Rembrandtists.* Sacramento, 1974.

Sandrart, 1679
Sandrart, Joachim von. "Kunst- und Schatzkammern hoher Potentaten, Chur-Fürsten und Herren." In *Academie der Bau-, Bild- und Mahlerey-Künste von 1675.* Pt. 2, 1679. Edited by A.R. Peltzer. Munich, 1925, pp. 305–334.

Sandrart/Peltzer, 1925
Sandrart, Joachim von. *Academie der Bau-, Bild- und Mahlerey-Künste von 1675.* Edited by A.R. Peltzer. Munich, 1925.

Scheller, 1969
Scheller, R.W. "Rembrandt en de encyclopedische kunstkamer." *Oud-Holland* 84 (1969), 81–147.

Scherer, 1955
Scherer, Margaret Roseman. *Marvels of Ancient Rome.* New York, 1955.

Schneider/Ekkart, 1932/1973
Schneider, Hans. *Jan Lievens: Sein Leben und seine Werke.* 2nd ed. Edited by R.E.O. Ekkart. Amsterdam, 1973.

Schwartz, 1977
[Schwartz, Gary.] *Rembrandt: All the Etchings Reproduced in True Size.* London and Maarssen, 1977.

Sickert, 1911–12
Sickert, Walter. "The Old Ladies of Etching-needle Street." *English Review* 10 (1912), 301–312.

Silver, 1976
Silver, Lawrence A. "Of Beggars – Lucas van Leyden and Sebastian Brant." *Journal of the Warburg and Courtauld Institutes* 39 (1976), 253–257.

Simon
Simon, Maria. "Claes Jansz. Visscher." Dissertation, University of Freiburg, 1958.

Slive, 1953
Slive, Seymour. *Rembrandt and His Critics, 1630–1730.* The Hague, 1953.

Slive, 1965
Slive, Seymour. "An Unpublished *Head of Christ* by Rembrandt." *Art Bulletin* 47 (Dec. 1965), 407–417.

Slive, 1970
Slive, Seymour. *Frans Hals.* London, 1970.

Snoep, 1975
Snoep, D.P. *Praal en propaganda: Triumfalia in de Noordelijke Nederlanden in de 16de en 17de eeuw* [N.p.], 1975.

Springer
Springer, Jaro. *Die Radierungen des Herkules Seghers.* Parts 1–3. Graphische Gesellschaft, *Veröffentlichungen,* 13, 14, 16. Berlin, 1910–1912.
——. *Die Radierungen des Herkules Seghers: Verzeichnis.* Berlin [1913?].

Stechow, 1930
Stechow, Wolfgang. "Bartholomeus Breenbergh, Landschafts- und Historienmaler." *Jahrbuch der Preussischen Kunstsammlungen* 51 (1930), 133–140.

Stechow, 1938
Stechow, Wolfgang. "Ludolph Buesinck." *Print Collector's Quarterly* 25 (1938), 393–419.

Stechow, 1947
Stechow, Wolfgang. "Esajas van de Velde and the Beginnings of Dutch Landscape Painting." *Nederlandsch Kunsthistorisch Jaarboek* 1 (1947), 83–94.

Stechow, 1948
Stechow, Wolfgang. "Jan Baptist Weenix." *Art Quarterly* 11 (1948), 181–198.

Stechow, 1966
Stechow, Wolfgang. *Dutch Landscape Painting of the Seventeenth Century.* London, 1966.

Strauss, 1972
Strauss, Walter L. "The Chronology of H. Goltzius' Chiaroscuro Prints." *Nouvelles de l'Estampe* 5 (Sept.-Oct. 1972), 9-13.

Strauss, 1973
Strauss, Walter L. *Chiaroscuro: The Clair-Obscur Woodcuts by the German and Netherlandish Masters of the XVIth and XVIIth Centuries.* Greenwich, Conn., 1973.

Strauss, 1977
Strauss, Walter L. *Hendrick Goltzius, Master Engraver: A Complete Pictorial Catalogue.* New York, 1977.

Strauss/Van der Meulen, 1979
Strauss, Walter L., and Van Der Meulen, Marjon. *The Rembrandt Documents.* New York, 1979.

Stubbe, 1967
Stubbe, Wolf. *Hundert Meisterzeichnungen aus der Hamburger Kunsthalle, 1500-1800.* Bilderhefte der Hamburger Kunsthalle, 5. Hamburg, 1967.

Sumowski, 1979-
Sumowski, Werner. *Drawings of the Rembrandt School.* New York, 1979-

Sutton, 1979
Sutton, Peter C. *Pieter de Hooch.* Oxford, 1979.

Ter Laan, 1939
Laan, Kornelis ter. *Woordenboek van de Nederlandse geschiedenis* [N.p.], 1939.

Ter Laan, 1963
Laan, E. ter. *Nederlandse spreekwoorden: Spreuken en zegswijzen.* The Hague, 1963.

Thibaudeau, 1857
Thibaudeau, A. "Lettre à l'auteur sur la curiosité." In C. Blanc, *Le Trésor de la curiosité,* vol. 1. Paris, 1857.

Thieme-Becker
Thieme, Ulrich. *Allgemeines Lexikon der bildenden Künstler von der Antike bis zur Gegenwart....* 37 vols. Leipzig, 1907-1950.

Tiele, 1884
Tiele, P.A. *Nederlandsche bibliographie van land- en volkenkunde.* Amsterdam, 1884.

Timm, 1961
Timm, Werner. "Der gestrandete Wal: Eine motivkundliche Studie." Staatliche Museen zu Berlin, *Forschungen und Berichte,* 3-4 (1961), 76-93.

Timmers, 1942
Timmers, J.J.M. *Gérard Lairesse.* Amsterdam, 1942.

Trautscholdt
Trautscholdt, Eduard. *Johannes Ruischer alias Jonge Hercules: Die Radierungen.* Supplement to E. Haverkamp-Begemann, *Hercules Segers: The Complete Etchings,* pp. [113]-136. Amsterdam, 1973.

Trautscholdt, 1961
Trautscholdt, Eduard. "'De Oude Kockebakster': Nachtrag zu Adriaen Brouwer." *Pantheon* 19 (1961), 187-195.

Trautscholdt, 1966
Trautscholdt, E. "Beträge zu Cornelis Dusart." *Nederlandsch Kunsthistorisch Jaarboek* 17 (1966), 171-200.

Tschudin
Tschudin, W. Fr. *The Ancient Paper-Mills of Basle and Their Marks.* Monumenta Chartae Papyraceae Historiam Illustrantia, 7. Hilversum, 1958.

Tsuritani, 1974
Tsuritani, Diane M. "The Etchings of Ferdinand Bol." Master's thesis, Oberlin College, 1974.

Tümpel
Tümpel, Astrid. "Claes Cornelisz. Moeyaert." *Oud-Holland* 88 (1974), 1-163.

Turner
Turner, F. McD. C. *The Pepys Library.* Cambridge [n.d.]

University of Connecticut, 1972
Den Broeder, Frederick. *Hendrick Goltzius and the Printmakers of Haarlem* [Storrs, Conn., 1972].

Utrecht, 1961
Centraal Museum, Utrecht. *Catalogue Raisonné of the Works by Pieter Jansz. Saenredam.* Utrecht [1961[.

Utrecht, 1965
Centraal Museum, Utrecht. *Nederlandse 17e eeuwse Italianiserende landschapschilders* [Utrecht, 1965].

Utrecht, 1980
Jong, Erik de. *De Slapende Mars van Hendrick ter Brugghen. Een Schilderij Centraal.* Utrecht, 1980.

Valentiner, 1930
Valentiner, Elisabeth. *Karel van Mander als Maler.* Zur Kunstgeschichte des Auslandes, no. 132. Strassburg, 1930.

Valentiner, 1939
Valentiner, W.R. "Willem Drost, Pupil of Rembrandt." *Art Quarterly* 2 (1939), 295-325.

Van Bastelaer
Bastelaer, René van. *Les Estampes de Peter Brvegel l'ancien.* Brussels, 1908.

Van Beylen, 1970
Beylen, J. van. *Schepen van de Nederlanden van de late middeleeuwen tot het einde van het 17e eeuw.* Amsterdam, 1970.

Van Dale, 1970
Dale, Johan Hendrick van. *Groot woordenboek der Nederlandse taal.* 9th ed. 2 vols. The Hague, 1970.

Van de Waal, 1940
Waal, Henri van de. "Buytewech en Frisius." *Oud-Holland* 57 (1940), 123-139.

Van de Waal, 1952
Waal, Henri van de. *Drie eeuwen vaderlandsche geschieduitbeelding 1500-1800: Een iconologische studie.* 2 vols. The Hague, 1952.

Van de Waal, 1974
Waal, Henri van de. *Steps towards Rembrandt: Collected Articles 1937-1972.* Amsterdam, 1974.

Van de Waal, Halcyon, 1940
Waal, Henri van de. "De Hollandsche houtsneden der zeventiende eeuw. I: Landschappen van Hendrick Goltzius; II: Werner van den Valckert en Jan Lievens." *Halcyon,* 1940, 1-16.

V.d.K.; Van der Kellen, 1867-1873
Kellen, Johan Philip van der. *Le Peintre-graveur hollandais et flamand....* Utrecht, 1867-1873.

Van der Kellen, 1874, cat. de Ridder
Kellen, Johan Philip van der. *Catalogue raisonné des estampes de l'école hollandaise et flamande formant la collection de feu M. de Ridder.* Rotterdam, 1874.

Van der Tweel, 1977
Tweel, L.H. van der. "An Unrecognised Woodcut by Werner van den Valckert or a Forgery of the Seventeenth Century?" *Burlington Magazine* 119 (Aug. 1977), 567-568.

Van der Willigen, 1870
Willigen, Adriaan van der. *Les Artistes de Harlem.* Haarlem, 1870.

Van Deursen, 1978
Deursen, A. Th. van. *Het Kopergeld van de gouden eeuw.* Vol. 2: *Volkskultur.* Amsterdam, 1978.

Van Dyk, 1790
Dyk, J. van. *Kunst- en historiekundige beschryving van alle schilderijen op het Stadhuis van Amsterdam.* Amsterdam, 1790.

Van Eeghen, 1905
Eeghen, P. van; and Kellen, J. Ph. van der. *Het Werk van Jan en Caspar Luyken.* 2 vols. Amsterdam, 1905.

Van Gelder, 1931
Gelder, Jan Gerrit van. "De Etsen van Willem Buytewech." *Oud-Holland* 48 (1931), 49-72.

Van Gelder, 1933
Gelder, Jan Gerrit van. *Jan van de Velde, 1593-1641, teekenaar-schilder.* The Hague, 1933.

Van Gelder, 1959
Gelder, Jan Gerrit van. *Dutch Drawings and Prints.* London, 1959.

Van Hees, 1956
Hees, C.A. van. "Nadere gegevens omtrent de Haarlemse vrienden Leendert van der Cooghen en Cornelis Bega." *Oud-Holland* 71 (1956), 243-244.

Van Mander/Davaco, 1969
Mander, Carel van. *Het Schilder-boeck....* Haerlem, 1604. Facsimile ed. Utrecht, 1969.

Van Mander/Floerke, 1906
Mander, Carel van. *Das Leben der niederländischen und deutschen Maler.* Edited by H. Floerke. Munich, 1906.

Van Mander/Hoecker, 1916
Mander, Carel van. *Das Lehrgedicht des Karel van Mander.* Edited by R. Hoecker. The Hague, 1916.

Van Regteren Altena, 1936
Regteren Altena, Johan Quirijn van. *The Drawings of Jacques de Gheyn.* Amsterdam, 1936.

Van Regteren Altena, 1954
Regteren Altena, Johan Quirijn van. "Retouches aan ons Rembrandt-beeld. 2: Het Landschap van den Goudweger." *Oud-Holland* 69 (1954), 1-17.

Van Thiel, 1963
Thiel, P.J.J. van. "Een vroeg schilderij van Gerrit Pietersz." *Oud-Holland* 78 (1963), 67–70.

Van Thiel, 1974
Thiel, P.J.J. van. "Andermaal Michiel van Musscher: Zijn zelfportretten." *Bulletin van het Rijksmuseum* [Amsterdam] 22 (1974), 131–149.

Van Thiel, 1978
Thiel, P.J.J. van. "Houtsneden van Werner van den Valckert en Mozes van Uyttenbroeck: De Hollandse houtsnede in het eerste kwart van de zeventiende eeuw." *Oud-Holland* 92 (1978), 7–42.

Vandalle, 1937
Vandalle, M. "Les Frères Vaillant." *Revue belge d'archéologie et d'histoire de l'art* 7 (1937), 341–360.

Vasari/Milanesi, 1878–1885
Vasari, Giorgio. *Le Vite de' più eccellenti pittori, sculptori ed architettori.* Edited by Gaetano Milanesi. Florence, 1878–1885.

Vassar, 1970
Vassar College Art Gallery. *Dutch Mannerism: Apogee and Epilogue.* Poughkeepsie, N.Y., 1970.

Veldman, 1977
Veldman, Ilja M. *Maarten van Heemskerck and Dutch Humanism in the Sixteenth Century.* Translated by Michael Hoyle. Maarssen, 1977.

Verbeek, 1974–75
Verbeek, J. "Vroege staten van etsen van Paul Potter (1625–1654)." *Antiek* 9 (1975), 854–861.

Vermeeren, 1978–79
Vermeeren, Karel. "Constantijn Daniël van Renesse: Zijn leven en zijn werken." 2 parts. *De Kroniek van het Rembrandthuis* 30 (1978), 3–23; 31 (1979), 3–8.

Veth, 1884
Veth, G.H. "Aelbert Cuyp, Jacob Gerritsz en Benjamin Cuyp." *Oud-Holland* 2 (1884), 233–282.

Vienna, 1967–68
Albertina, Vienna. *Zwischen Renaissance und Barock: Das Zeitalter von Bruegel und Bellange.* Die Kunst der Graphik, 5. New York, 1968.

Vis Blokhuyzen, 1870
Vis Blokhuyzen, Dirk. *Description des estampes qui forment l'oeuvre gravé de Dirk de Bray.* Rotterdam, 1870.

Von Moltke, 1938–39
Moltke, Joachim Wolfgang von. "Jan de Bray." *Marburger Jahrbuch für Kunstwissenschaft* 11–12 (1938–39), 421–523.

Vos, 1978
Vos, Rik. *Lucas van Leyden.* Bentveld and Maarssen, 1978.

W.-B.
White, Christopher, and Boon, Karel. *Rembrandt's Etchings.* 2 vols. New York, 1969.

Waddingham, 1960
Waddingham, Malcolm. "Herman van Swanevelt in Rome." *Paragone* 11, no. 121 (1960), 37–50.

Waddingham, 1976–77
Waddingham, Michael R. "Michael Sweerts, *Boy Copying the Head of a Roman Emperor.*" *Minneapolis Institute of Arts Bulletin* 68 (1976–77), 56–65.

Wallace, 1979
Wallace, Richard W. *The Etchings of Salvator Rosa.* Princeton, N.J., 1979.

Waller, 1938
Waller, F.G. *Biographisch woordenboek van Noord Nederlandsche graveurs.* The Hague, 1938.

Walsh, 1974
Walsh, John, Jr. "New Dutch Paintings at the Metropolitan Museum." *Apollo*, n.s. 147 (May 1974), 340–349.

Washington, 1976–77
Rosand, David. *Titian and the Venetian Woodcut: A Loan Exhibition.* Washington, D.C., 1976.

Washington, 1977
Robison, Andrew. *Paper in Prints.* Washington, D.C., 1977.

Weig.; Weigel
Weigel, Rudolph. *Suppléments au Peintre-graveur de Adam Bartsch.* 2 vols. Leipzig, 1843.

Weisner, 1964
Weisner, Ulrich. "Die Gemälde des Moyses van Uyttenbroeck." *Oud-Holland* 64 (1964), 189–228.

Weizsäcker, 1928
Weizsäcker, Heinrich. "Hendrik Goudt." *Oud-Holland* 45 (1929), 110.

Welcker, 1932, etc.
Welcker, A. "Johannes Ruyscher alias Jonge Hercules." *Oud-Holland* 49 (1932), 241–258; 50 (1933), 12–34, 118–131; 51 (1934), 73–96; 53 (1936), 161–181; 54 (1940), 28–39.

Welcker, 1936
Welcker, A. "Simon Wynhoutsz. Frisius Konstryck Plaetsnyder." *Oud-Holland* 53 (1936), 219–240, 241–256.

Wessely, 1877
Wessely, Josef Eduard. "Hans Wilhelm Kress von Kressenstein über Dürer." *Zeitschrift für Bildende Kunst* 13 (1878), 21–23.

Wessely, 1881
Wessely, Josef Eduard. *Wallerant Vaillant: Verzeichniss seiner Kupferstiche und Schabkunstblätter.* Vienna, 1881.

Wessely, 1883
Wessely, Josef Eduard. "Das Manuscript von Paul Behaim's Kupferstichkatalog im Berliner Museum." *Repertorium für Kunstwissenschaft* 6 (1883), 54–63.

Wessely, Verkolje
Wessely, Josef Eduard. "Jan Verkolje: Verzeichniss seiner Schabkunstblätter." *Archiv für die zeichnenden Künste* 14 (1868), 81–115.

Wessely, Waterloo
Wessely, Josef Eduard. *Antonj Waterloo.* Kritische Verzeichnisse von Werken hervorragender Kupferstecher, 7. Hamburg, 1891.

White, 1969
White, Christopher. *Rembrandt as an Etcher: A Study of the Artist at Work.* 2 vols. London, 1969.

White and Boon, 1969
See W.-B.

Wijnman, 1929
Wijnman, H.F. "De van Sichem-puzzle: Een bijdrage tot de geschiedenis van de Nederlandsche grafische kunst." *Oud-Holland* 46 (1929), 233–244.

Wilson, 1974
Wilson, William Harry. "The Art of Romeyn de Hooghe: An Atlas of European Late Baroque Culture." Ph.D. dissertation, Harvard University, 1974.

Woordenboek N.T.
Woordenboek der Nederlandsche Taal. The Hague, 1882–

Worp
Huygens, Constantijn. *De Briefwisseling van Constantijn Huygens.* Edited by J.A. Worp. The Hague, 1911–1917.

Worp, 1891
Worp, J.A. "Constantyn Huygens over de schilders van zijn tijd." *Oud-Holland* 9 (1891), 106–136.

Wurz.; Wurzbach
Wurzbach, Alfred. *Niederländisches Künstlerlexikon….* 3 vols. Vienna and Leipzig, 1906–1911.

Wussin
Wussin, Johann. *Cornel Visscher: Verzeichniss seiner Kupferstiche.* Leipzig, 1865.

Yale University, 1976
Bayard, Jane, and D'Oench, Ellen. *Darkness into Light: The Early Mezzotint.* New Haven, Conn., 1976.

Zomer, cat.
Zomer, J.P. *Catalogus van 't Heerelyk Konst-Kabinet van Tekeningen en Prenten, By een Vergadert door den Konst-Vermaarden Ian Pietersz. Zomer in Amsterdam* [N.p., n.d.]

Zumthor, 1959/1963
Zumthor, Paul. *La Vie quotidienne en Hollande au temps de Rembrandt.* Paris, 1959.
——. *Daily Life in Rembrandt's Holland.* Translated by Simon Watson Taylor. New York, 1963.

Index of Artists

Numbers refer to catalogue entries. The artist's biography precedes the first catalogue entry.